SCHAUM'S OUTLINE OF

THEORY AND PROBLEMS

OF

LAGRANGIAN DYNAMICS

with a treatment of

Euler's Equations of Motion,
Hamilton's Equations
and Hamilton's Principle

•

BY

DARE A. WELLS, Ph.D.
Professor of Physics
University of Cincinnati

•

SCHAUM'S OUTLINE SERIES
McGRAW-HILL BOOK COMPANY
New York, St. Louis, San Francisco, Toronto, Sydney

ISBN 07-069258-0

9 10 11 12 13 14 15 SH SH 8 7 6 5 4 3 2 1

Preface

The Lagrangian method of dynamics is applicable to a very extensive field of particle and rigid body problems, ranging from the simplest to those of great complexity. The advantages of this procedure over conventional methods are, for reasons which follow, of outstanding importance. This is true not only in the broad field of applications but also in a wide area of research and theoretical considerations.

To a large extent the Lagrangian method reduces the entire field of statics, particle dynamics and rigid body dynamics to a single procedure: one involving the same basic steps regardless of the number of masses considered, the type of coordinates employed, the number of constraints on the system and whether or not the constraints and frame of reference are in motion. Hence special methods are replaced by a single general method.

Generalized coordinates of a wide variety may be used. That is, Lagrange's equations are valid in any coordinates (inertial or a combination of inertial and non-inertial) which are suitable for designating the configuration of the system. They give directly the equations of motion in whatever coordinates may be chosen. It is not a matter of first introducing formal vector methods and then translating to desired coordinates.

Forces of constraint, for smooth holonomic constraints, are automatically eliminated and do not appear in the Lagrangian equations. By conventional methods the elimination of these forces may present formidable difficulties.

The Lagrangian procedure is largely based on the scalar quantities: kinetic energy, potential energy, virtual work, and in many cases the power function. Each of these can be expressed, usually without difficulty, in any suitable coordinates. Of course the vector nature of force, velocity, acceleration, etc., must be taken account of in the treatment of dynamical problems. However, Lagrange's equations, based on the above scalar quantities, automatically and without recourse to formal vector methods take full account of these vector quantities. Regardless of how complex a system may be, the terms of a Lagrangian equation of motion consist of proper components of force and acceleration expressed in the selected coordinates.

Fortunately the basic ideas involved in the derivation of Lagrange's equations are simple and easy to understand. When presented without academic trimmings and unfamiliar terminology, the only difficulties encountered by the average student usually arise from deficiencies in background training. The application of Lagrange's equations to actual problems is remarkably simple even for systems which may be quite complex. Except for very elementary problems, the procedure is in general much simpler and less time consuming than the "concise", "elegant" or special methods found in many current texts. Moreover, details of the physics involved are made to stand out in full view.

Finally it should be mentioned that the Lagrangian method is applicable to various fields other than dynamics. It is especially useful, for example, in the treatment of electromechanical sytems.

This book aims to make clear the basic principles of Lagrangian dynamics and to give the reader ample training in the actual techniques, physical and mathematical, of applying Lagrange's equations. The material covered also lays the foundation for a later study of those topics which bridge the gap between classical and quantum mechanics. The method of presentation as well as the examples, problems and suggested experiments has been developed over the years while teaching Lagrangian dynamics to students at the University of Cincinnati.

No attempt has been made to include every phase of this broad subject. Relatively little space is given to the solution of differential equations of motion. Formal vector methods are not stressed; they are mentioned in only a few sections. However, for reasons stated in Chapter 18, the most important vector and tensor quantities which occur in the book are listed there in appropriate formal notation.

The suggested experiments outlined at the ends of various chapters can be of real value. Formal mathematical treatments are of course necessary. But nothing arouses more interest or gives more "reality" to dynamics than an actual experiment in which the results check well with computed values.

The book is directed to seniors and first year graduate students of physics, engineering, chemistry and applied mathematics, and to those practicing scientists and engineers who wish to become familiar with the powerful Lagrangian methods through self-study. It is designed for use either as a textbook for a formal course or as a supplement to all current texts.

The author wishes to express his gratitude to Dr. Solomon Schwebel for valuable suggestions and critical review of parts of the manuscript, to Mr. Chester Carpenter for reviewing Chapter 18, to Mr. Jerome F. Wagner for able assistance in checking examples and problems, to Mr. and Mrs. Lester Sollman for their superb work of typing the manuscript, and to Mr. Daniel Schaum, the publisher, for his continued interest, encouragement and unexcelled cooperation.

D. A. WELLS

October, 1967

CONTENTS

CONTENTS

CONTENTS

CONTENTS

CHAPTER 1 Background Material, I

Basic laws of dynamics. Conditions under which valid. Two principal types of problems and their general treatment.

1.1 Regarding Background Requirements.

The greatest obstacles encountered by the average student in his quest for an understanding of Lagrangian dynamics usually arise, not from intrinsic difficulties of the subject matter itself, but instead from certain deficiencies in a rather broad area of background material. With the hope of removing these obstacles, Chapters 1 and 2 are devoted to detailed treatments of those prerequisites with which students are most frequently unacquainted and which are not readily available in a related unit.

1.2 The Basic Laws of Classical Newtonian Dynamics and Various Ways of Expressing Them.

Newton's three laws (involving, of course, the classical concepts of mass, length, time, force, and the rules of geometry, algebra and calculus) together with the concept of virtual work, may be regarded as the foundation on which all considerations of classical mechanics (that field in which conditions C, D, E of Section 1.6 are fulfilled) rests. However, it is well to realize from the beginning that the basic laws of dynamics can be formulated (expressed mathematically) in several ways other than that given by Newton. The most important of these (each to be treated later) are referred to as

(*a*) D'Alembert's principle
(*b*) Lagrange's equations
(*c*) Hamilton's equations
(*d*) Hamilton's principle .

All are basically equivalent. Starting, for example, with Newton's laws and the principle of virtual work (see Section 2.13, Chapter 2), any one of the above can be derived. Hence any of these five formulations may be taken as the basis for theoretical developments and the solution of problems.

1.3 The Choice of Formulation.

Whether one or another of the above five is employed depends on the job to be done. For example, Newton's equations are convenient for the treatment of many simple problems; Hamilton's principle is of importance in many theoretical considerations. Hamilton's equations have been useful in certain applied fields as well as in the development of quantum mechanics.

However, as a means of treating a wide range of problems (theoretical as well as practical) involving mechanical, electrical, electro-mechanical and other systems, the Lagrangian method is outstandingly powerful and remarkably simple to apply.

1.4 Origin of the Basic Laws.

The "basic laws" of dynamics are merely statements of a wide range of experience. They cannot be obtained by logic or mathematical manipulations alone. In the final analysis the rules of the game are founded on careful experimentation. These rules must be accepted with the belief that, since nature has followed them in the past, she will continue to do so in the future. For example, we cannot "explain" why Newton's laws are valid. We can only say that they represent a compact statement of past experience regarding the behavior of a wide variety of mechanical systems. The formulations of D'Alembert, Lagrange and Hamilton express the same, each in its own particular way.

1.5 Regarding the Basic Quantities and Concepts Employed.

The quantities, length, mass, time, force, etc., continually occur in dynamics. Most of us tend to view them and use them with a feeling of confidence and understanding. However, many searching questions have arisen over the years with regard to the basic concepts involved and the fundamental nature of the quantities employed. A treatment of such matters is out of place here, but the serious student will profit from the discussions of Bridgman and others on this subject.

1.6 Conditions Under Which Newton's Laws are Valid.

Newton's second law as applied to a particle[1] of constant mass m may be written as

$$\mathbf{F} = m\frac{d\mathbf{v}}{dt} \tag{1.1}$$

where the force $\mathbf{F}$ and velocity $\mathbf{v}$ are vector quantities and the mass m and time t are scalars. In component form (*1.1*) becomes,

$$F_x = m\ddot{x}, \quad F_y = m\ddot{y}, \quad F_z = m\ddot{z} \tag{1.2}$$

(Throughout the text we shall use the convenient notation: $\dfrac{dx}{dt} = \dot{x}$, $\dfrac{d^2x}{dt^2} = \ddot{x}$, etc.)

Relations (*1.2*), *in the simple form shown, are by no means true under any and all conditions.* We shall proceed to discuss the conditions under which they are valid.

Condition A.

Equation (*1.1*) implies some "frame of reference" with respect to which $d\mathbf{v}/dt$ is measured. Equations (*1.2*) indicate that the motion is referred to some rectangular axes X, Y, Z.

Now, it is a fact of experience that Newton's second law expressed in the simple form of (*1.2*) gives results in close agreement with experience *when, and only when, the coordinate axes are fixed relative to the average position of the "fixed" stars or moving with uniform linear velocity and without rotation relative to the stars.* In either case the frame of reference (the X, Y, Z axes) is referred to as an INERTIAL FRAME[2] and corresponding coordinates as INERTIAL *COORDINATES.* Stated conversely, a frame which has linear acceleration or is rotating in any manner is NON-INERTIAL[3].

---

[1]The term "particle", a concept of the imagination, may be pictured as a bit of matter so small that its position in space is determined by the three coordinates of its "center". In this case its kinetic energy of rotation about any axis through it may be neglected.

[2]The term "inertial frame" may be defined abstractly, merely as one with respect to which Newton's equations, in the simple form (*1.2*), are valid. But this definition does not tell the engineer or applied scientist where such a frame is to be found or whether certain specific coordinates are inertial. This information is, however, supplied by the fixed-stars definition. Of course it should be recognized that extremely accurate measurements might well prove the "fixed-star" frame to be slightly non-inertial.

[3]Due to annual and daily rotations and other motions of the earth, a coordinate frame attached to its surface is obviously non-inertial. Nevertheless, the acceleration of this frame is so slight that for many (but by no means all) purposes it may be regarded as inertial. A non-rotating frame (axes pointing always toward the same fixed stars) with origin attached to the center of the earth is more nearly inertial. Non-rotating axes with origin fixed to the center of the sun constitutes an excellent (though perhaps not "perfect") inertial frame.

The condition just stated *must be regarded as one of the important foundation stones on which the superstructure of dynamics rests.* Cognizance of this should become automatic in our thinking because, basically, the *treatment of every problem begins with the consideration of an inertial frame.* One must be able to recognize inertial and non-inertial frames by inspection.

The above statements, however, do not imply that non-inertial coordinates cannot be used. On the contrary, as will soon be evident, they are employed perhaps just as frequently as inertial. How Newton's second law equations can be written for non-inertial coordinates will be seen from examples which follow. As shown in Chapters 3 and 4, the Lagrangian equations (after having written kinetic energy in the proper form) give correct equations of motion in inertial, non-inertial or mixed coordinates.

Example 1.1:

As an illustration of condition A consider the behavior of the objects (*a*), (*b*), (*c*), shown in Fig. 1-1, in a railroad car moving with constant acceleration a_x along a straight horizontal track.

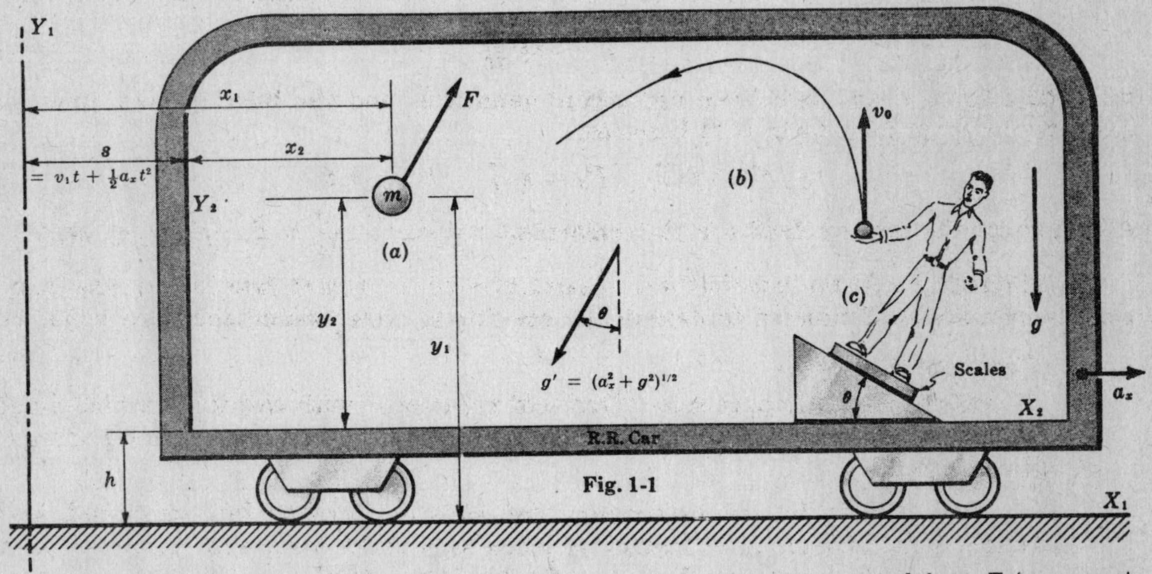

Fig. 1-1

In Fig. 1-1, (*a*) represents a ball of mass m acted upon by some external force F (components F_x, F_y) and the pull of gravity. Assuming X_1, Y_1 to be an inertial frame, considering motion in a plane only and treating the ball as a particle, the equations of motion, *relative to the earth,* are

$$(1)\quad m\ddot{x}_1 = F_x \qquad\qquad (2)\quad m\ddot{y}_1 = F_y - mg$$

Now relations between "earth coordinates" and "car coordinates" of m are seen to be

$$(3)\quad x_1 = x_2 + v_1 t + \tfrac{1}{2}a_x t^2 \qquad\qquad (4)\quad y_1 = y_2 + h$$

Differentiating (*3*) and (*4*) twice with respect to time and substituting into (*1*) and (*2*),

$$(5)\quad m\ddot{x}_2 = F_x - ma_x \qquad\qquad (6)\quad m\ddot{y}_2 = F_y - mg$$

which are the equations of motion of the ball *relative to the car.*

Clearly the y_2 coordinate is inertial since (*2*) and (*6*) have the same form. However, x_2 is non-inertial since (*1*) and (*5*) are different. Equation (*5*) is a simple example of Newton's second law equation in terms of a non-inertial coordinate. (Note how incorrect it would be to write $m\ddot{x}_2 = F_x$.)

Notice that the effect of this non-inertial condition on any mechanical system or on a person in the car is just as if g were increased to $(a_x^2 + g^2)^{1/2}$, acting downward at the angle $\theta = \tan^{-1} a_x/g$ with the vertical, and all coordinates considered as inertial.

If the man pitches a ball, Fig. 1-1(*b*), upward with initial velocity v_0, its path relative to the car is parabolic but it must be computed as if gravity has the magnitude and direction indicated above. If the man has a mass M, what is his "weight" in the car?

As an extension of this example, suppose the car is caused to oscillate along the track about some fixed point such that $s = s_0 + A \sin \omega t$, where s_0, A, ω are constants. Equation (6) remains unchanged, but differentiating $x_1 = x_2 + s_0 + A \sin \omega t$ and inserting in (1) we get

$$m\ddot{x}_2 = mA\omega^2 \sin \omega t + F_x$$

Again it is seen that x_2 is non-inertial.[4]

It is easily seen that the ball in (b) will now move, relative to the car, along a rather complex path determined by a constant downward acceleration g and a horizontal acceleration $A\omega^2 \sin \omega t$.

The man will have difficulty standing on the scales, regardless of where they are placed, because his total "weight" is now changing with time both in magnitude and direction.

Example 1.2:

Consider the motion of the particle of mass m, shown in Fig. 1-2, relative to the X_2, Y_2 axes which are rotating with constant angular velocity ω relative to the inertial X_1, Y_1 frame.

The equations of motion in the inertial coordinates are

$$m\ddot{x}_1 = F_{x_1}, \qquad m\ddot{y}_1 = F_{y_1}$$

where F_{x_1} and F_{y_1} are components of the applied force along the fixed axes. We shall now obtain corresponding equations in the rotating (and as will be seen, non-inertial) coordinates.

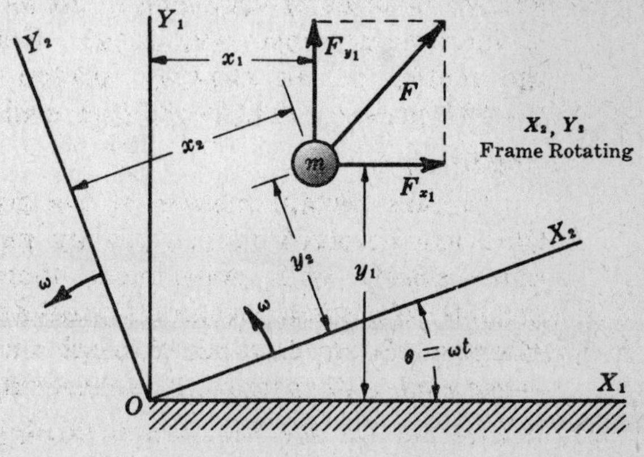

Fig. 1-2

Reference to the figure shows that

$$x_1 = x_2 \cos \omega t - y_2 \sin \omega t$$
$$y_1 = x_2 \sin \omega t + y_2 \cos \omega t$$

Differentiating these equations twice and substituting in the first equations of motion, we obtain

$$F_{x_1} = m[\ddot{x}_2 \cos \omega t - 2\dot{x}_2\omega \sin \omega t - 2\dot{y}_2\omega \cos \omega t - x_2\omega^2 \cos \omega t + y_2\omega^2 \sin \omega t - \ddot{y}_2 \sin \omega t] \quad (9)$$
$$F_{y_1} = m[\ddot{x}_2 \sin \omega t + 2\dot{x}_2\omega \cos \omega t - 2\dot{y}_2\omega \sin \omega t - x_2\omega^2 \sin \omega t - y_2\omega^2 \cos \omega t + \ddot{y}_2 \cos \omega t] \quad (10)$$

Again referring to the figure, it is seen that the components of F in the direction of X_2 and Y_2 are given by $F_{x_2} = F_{x_1} \cos \omega t + F_{y_1} \sin \omega t$ and $F_{y_2} = F_{y_1} \cos \omega t - F_{x_1} \sin \omega t$. Hence multiplying (9) and (10) through by $\cos \omega t$ and $\sin \omega t$ respectively and adding, the result is

$$F_{x_2} = m\ddot{x}_2 - mx_2\omega^2 - 2m\omega\dot{y}_2 \quad (11)$$

Likewise multiplying (9) and (10) through by $\sin \omega t$ and $\cos \omega t$ respectively and subtracting,

$$F_{y_2} = m\ddot{y}_2 - my_2\omega^2 + 2m\omega\dot{x}_2 \quad (12)$$

These are the equations of motion relative to the non-inertial X_2, Y_2 axes. Note that it would indeed be a mistake to write $F_{x_2} = m\ddot{x}_2$ and $F_{y_2} = m\ddot{y}_2$. From this example it should be evident that *any rotating frame is non-inertial.*

Condition B.

Equations (*1.2*) are valid only when m is constant. In case m is variable, equation (*1.1*) must be replaced by

$$\mathbf{F} = \frac{d}{dt}(m\mathbf{v})$$

Various examples can be cited in which the mass of an object varies with coordinates (a snowball rolling down a snow covered hill); with time (a tank car having a hole in one end from which liquid flows or a rocket during the burn-out period); with velocity (any object moving with a velocity approaching that of light). However, we shall not be concerned with variable-mass problems in this text.

---

[4]As a matter of convenience we shall, throughout the book, refer to the product (mass) × (acceleration) as an "inertial force".

Condition C.

In general, the masses of a system must be large compared with the masses of atoms and atomic particles. The dynamics of atomic particles falls within the field of quantum mechanics. But there are "borderline" cases; for example, the deflection of a beam of electrons in a cathode ray tube is usually computed with sufficient accuracy by classical mechanics.

Condition D.

Whether a mass is large or small, its velocity must be low compared with that of light. As is well known from the special theory of relativity, the mass of any object increases with the velocity of the object. For "ordinary" velocities this change in mass is very small, but as the velocity approaches that of light its rate of increase becomes very great. Hence the relation (*1.2*) will not give accurately the motion of an electron, proton or baseball moving with a velocity of say 2×10^{10} cm/sec. (This condition could, of course, be included under *B*.)

Condition E.

In case certain masses of the system are very large and/or long intervals of time are involved (a century or more), the general theory of relativity agrees more closely with experiment than does Newtonian dynamics. For example, general relativistic dynamics predicts that the perihelion of the orbit of the planet Mercury should advance through an angle of 43″ per century, which is in close agreement with astronomical measurements.

In conclusion, we see that when dealing with "ordinary" masses, velocity and time conditions *C*, *D* and *E* are almost always met. Hence in "classical dynamics" the greatest concerns are with *A* and *B*.

It is evident from the above conditions that there exist three more-or-less well defined fields of dynamics: classical, quantum and relativistic. Unfortunately no "unified" theory, applicable to all dynamical problems under any and all conditions, has as yet been developed.

1.7 Two General Types of Dynamical Problems.

Almost every problem in classical dynamics is a special case of one of the following general types:

(*a*) From given forces acting on a system of masses, given constraints, and the known position and velocity of each mass at a stated instant of time, it is required to find the "motion" of the system, that is, *the position, velocity and acceleration of each mass as functions of time.*

(*b*) From *given* motions of a system it is required to find a possible set of forces which will produce such motions. In general some or all of the forces may vary with time.

Of course considerations of work, energy, power, linear momentum and angular momentum may be an important part of either (*a*) or (*b*).

1.8 General Methods of Treating Dynamical Problems.

Most problems in applied dynamics fall under (*a*) above. The general procedure is the same for all of this type. As a matter of convenience it may be divided into the following four steps.

(1) ***Choice of an appropriate coordinate system.***

The ease with which a specific problem may be solved depends largely on the coordinates used. The most advantageous system depends on the problem in hand, and unfortunately no general rules of selection can be given. It is largely a matter of experience and judgment.

(2) *Setting up differential equations of motion.*

Simple examples of equations of motion already have been given. However, to illustrate further the meaning of the term "equations of motion" consider the problem of a small mass m suspended from a coiled spring of negligible mass as shown in Fig. 1-3. Assume that m is free to move in a vertical plane under the action of gravity and the spring. Equations of motion, here expressed in polar coordinates, are

$$\ddot{r} - r\dot{\theta}^2 - g\cos\theta + \frac{k}{m}(r - r_0) = 0$$

$$r\ddot{\theta} + 2\dot{r}\dot{\theta} + g\sin\theta = 0$$

where r_0 is the unstretched length of the spring and k the usual spring constant. Integrals of these second order differential equations give r and θ as functions of time.

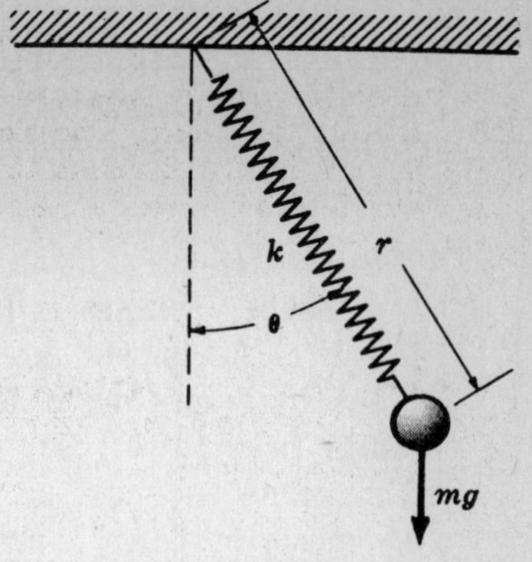

Fig. 1-3

Two points must be emphasized: (*a*) These differential equations can be set up in various ways (see Section 1.2). However, as in most cases, the Lagrangian method is the most advantageous. (*b*) The equations above do not represent the only form in which equations of motion for this pendulum may be expressed. They may, for example, be written out in rectangular or many other types of coordinates (see Chapters 3 and 4). In each case the equations will appear quite different and as a general rule some will be more involved than others. Statements (*a*) and (*b*) are true for dynamical systems in general.

(3) *Solving the differential equations of motion.*

Equations of motion, except in the Hamiltonian form, are of second order. The complexity of the equations depends very largely on the particular problem in hand and the type of coordinates used. Very frequently the equations are nonlinear. *Only in certain relatively few cases,* where for example all differential terms have constant coefficients, *can a general method of solution be given.* It is an important fact that, *although correct differential equations of motion can be written out quite easily for almost any dynamical system, in a great majority of cases the equations are so involved that they cannot be integrated.* Fortunately, however, computers of various types are coming to the rescue and useful solutions to very difficult equations can now be obtained rapidly and with relatively little effort. This means, of course, that differential equations formerly regarded as "hopeless" are presently of great concern to scientists and engineers. Moreover, the more advanced and general techniques of setting up such equations are of increasingly great importance in all fields of research and development.

(4) *Determination of constants of integration.*

The method of determining constants of integration is basically simple. It involves merely the substitution of known values of displacement and velocity at a particular instant of time into the integrated equations. Since the method will be made amply clear with specific examples in the chapters which follow, further details will not be given here.

1.9 A Specific Example Illustrating Sections 1.7 and 1.8.

As a means of illustrating the remarks of the preceding sections and obtaining a general picture of dynamics as a whole, before becoming involved in details of the Lagrangian method, let us consider the following specific example.

The masses m_1 and m_2 are connected to springs (having spring constants k_1 and k_2) and the block B as shown in Fig. 1-4 below. The block is made to move according to the relation $s = A \sin \omega t$ by the force F. p_0, p_1, p_2 are fixed points taken such that $p_0 p_1$ and $p_1 p_2$ are the unstretched lengths of the first and second springs respectively. All motion is along a smooth horizontal line. Masses of the springs are neglected.

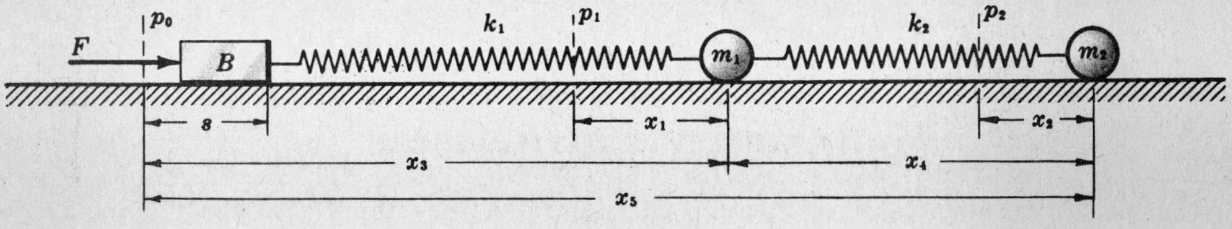

Fig. 1-4

We now set ourselves the task of giving a dynamical analysis of the system. The problem falls under (*a*), Section 1.7. The method of treatment is that of Section 1.8. A broad analysis of the problem would include a determination of:

(*a*) The position of each mass as a function of time.

(*b*) The velocity of each mass at any instant.

(*c*) The energy (kinetic and potential) of the system as functions of time.

(*d*) The acceleration of and force acting on each mass as functions of time.

(*e*) The frequencies of motion of each mass.

(*f*) The force which must be applied to B.

(*g*) The power delivered by B to the system at any instant.

It should be understood that the solutions given below are not for the purpose of showing details but only to illustrate fundamental steps. Hence mathematical manipulations not essential to the picture as a whole are omitted. We shall first determine (*a*), from which (*b*), (*c*), . . . , (*g*) follow without difficulty.

Following the steps listed under Section 1.8, we first select suitable coordinates. Since motion is restricted to the horizontal line, it is evident that only two are necessary, one to determine the position of each mass. Of the coordinates indicated in Fig. 1-4, any one of the following sets may be used, (x_1, x_2), (x_3, x_5), (x_3, x_4), (x_4, x_5), etc. As a matter of convenience (x_1, x_2) have been chosen.

The equations of motion, obtained by a direct application of Newton's laws or Lagrange's equations, are

$$m_1 \ddot{x}_1 + (k_1 + k_2)x_1 - k_2 x_2 = k_1 A \sin \omega t \qquad (1)$$

$$m_2 \ddot{x}_2 + k_2 x_2 - k_2 x_1 = 0 \qquad (2)$$

To make the problem specific, let us set

$$m_1 = 400 \text{ grams}, \quad m_2 = 300 \text{ grams}, \quad A = 5 \text{ cm}$$
$$k_1 = 6 \times 10^4 \text{ dynes/cm}, \quad k_2 = 5 \times 10^4 \text{ dynes/cm}, \quad \omega = 12 \text{ radians/sec}$$

Now, by well-known methods of integration, approximate solutions of (*1*) and (*2*) are

$$x_1 = 6.25A_1 \sin(19.37t + \gamma_1) - 3A_2 \sin(8.16t + \gamma_2) - .95 \sin 12t \qquad (3)$$

$$x_2 = -5A_1 \sin(19.37t + \gamma_1) - 5A_2 \sin(8.16t + \gamma_2) - 7 \sin 12t \qquad (4)$$

which completes the first three steps of Section 1.8.

The arbitrary constants of integration $A_1, A_2, \gamma_1, \gamma_2$ can be determined after assigning specific initial conditions. One could assume for example, as one way of starting the motion, that at $t = 0$,

$$x_1 = 3 \text{ cm}, \quad x_2 = 4 \text{ cm} \qquad (5)$$

$$\dot{x}_1 = 0, \quad \dot{x}_2 = 0 \qquad (6)$$

Putting (*5*) into (*3*) and (*4*), and (*6*) into the first time derivatives of (*3*) and (*4*), there result four algebraic equations from which specific values of the above constants follow at once. The displacements x_1 and x_2 are thus expressed as specific functions of time.

Inspection shows that each of (*b*), (*c*), . . . , (*g*) can be determined almost at once from the final forms of (*3*) and (*4*). Hence further details are left to the reader.

The above simple example presents a rather complete picture of the general procedure followed in treating the wide field of problems mentioned in Section 1.7(*a*). But a word of warning. The equations of motion (*1*) and (*2*) are very simple and hence all steps could be carried out without difficulty. Unfortunately this is by no means the case in general (see Section 1.8, (3)). Moreover, it frequently happens in practice that many details listed under Section 1.9 are not required.

The second general class of problems mentioned in Section 1.7 (*b*) will be treated in Chapter 13.

Summary and Remarks

1. "Classical dynamics" is that branch of dynamics for which Newton's laws are valid under restrictions C, D, E of Section 1.6.

2. The "basic laws" of dynamics are merely compact statements of experimental results. They may be expressed mathematically in a variety of ways, all of which are basically equivalent. Any one form can be derived from any other.

3. A cognizance and understanding of the conditions under which the laws of classical dynamics are valid is of vital importance. The definition of "inertial frame" and a full realization of the part it plays in the treatment of almost every dynamical problem is imperative.

4. There are two principal types of problem in classical dynamics (as discussed in Section 1.7), of which 1.7(*a*) is the most common. Cognizance of this fact and the general order of treatment is of importance.

5. There exist, at the present time, three distinct (from the point of view of treatment) and rather well defined (physically) fields of dynamics: classical, quantum and relativistic. No unified set of laws, applicable to any and all problems, has as yet been developed.

Review Questions and Problems

1.1. State the meaning of the term "classical dynamics". Give specific examples illustrating the remaining two fields.

1.2. What can be said regarding the "origin" of and ways of formulating the basic laws of dynamics?

1.3. Make clear what is meant by the term "inertial frame of reference".

1.4. Prove that any frame of reference moving with constant linear velocity (no rotation) relative to an inertial frame is itself inertial.

1.5. Can one recognize by inspection whether given coordinates are inertial or non-inertial? Is it permissible, for the solution of certain problems, to use a combination of inertial and non-inertial coordinates? (These are important considerations.)

1.6. The cable of an elevator breaks and it falls freely (neglect air resistance). Show that for any mechanical system, the motions of which are referred to the elevator, the earth's gravitational field has, in effect, been reduced to zero.

1.7. A coordinate frame is attached to the inside of an automobile which is moving in the usual manner along a street with curves, bumps, stop lights and traffic cops. Is the frame inertial? Do occupants of the car feel forces other than gravity? Explain.

1.8. If the car, shown in Fig. 1-1, Page 3, were moving with constant speed around a level circular track, which of the coordinates x_2, y_2, z_2 of m_1 (or of any other point referred to the X_2, Y_2, Z_2 frame) would be non-inertial? Explain. (Assume Z_1 taken along the radius of curvature of track.)

1.9. Suppose that the X_2, Y_2 frame, shown in Fig. 1-2, Page 4, has any type of rotation (as for example $\dot{\theta}$ = constant, $\ddot{\theta}$ = constant, or $\theta = \theta_0 \sin \omega t$), show that the x_2, y_2 coordinates are non-inertial. See Example 1.2.

1.10. Suppose that the arrangement of Fig. 1-4, Page 7, be placed in the R.R. car of Fig. 1-1, Page 3, parallel to the X_2 axis and that the car has a constant linear acceleration a_x. Show that the equations of motion, (*1*) and (*2*) of Section 1.9, must now be replaced by

$$m_1 \ddot{x}_1 + (k_1 + k_2)x_1 - k_2 x_2 = k_1 A \sin \omega t - m_1 a_x$$
$$m_2 \ddot{x}_2 + k_2 x_2 - k_2 x_1 = -m_2 a_x$$

1.11. Assuming that the origin of X_2, Y_2, Fig. 1-2, Page 4, has constant acceleration a_x along the X_1 axis while, at the same time, X_2, Y_2 rotate with constant angular velocity ω, show that equations (*11*) and (*12*) of Example 1.2 must now be replaced by

$$F_{x_2} = m\ddot{x}_2 - mx_2\omega^2 - 2m\omega\dot{y}_2 + ma_x \cos \omega t$$
$$F_{y_2} = m\ddot{y}_2 - my_2\omega^2 + 2m\omega\dot{x}_2 - ma_x \sin \omega t$$

1.12. Assuming that the X, Y frame to which the simple pendulum of Fig. 1-5 below is attached has a constant velocity v_x in the X direction and v_y in the Y direction (no rotation of the frame), show that the equation of motion of the pendulum in the θ coordinate is $r\ddot{\theta} = -g \sin \theta$. Is the period of oscillation changed by the motion of its supporting frame?

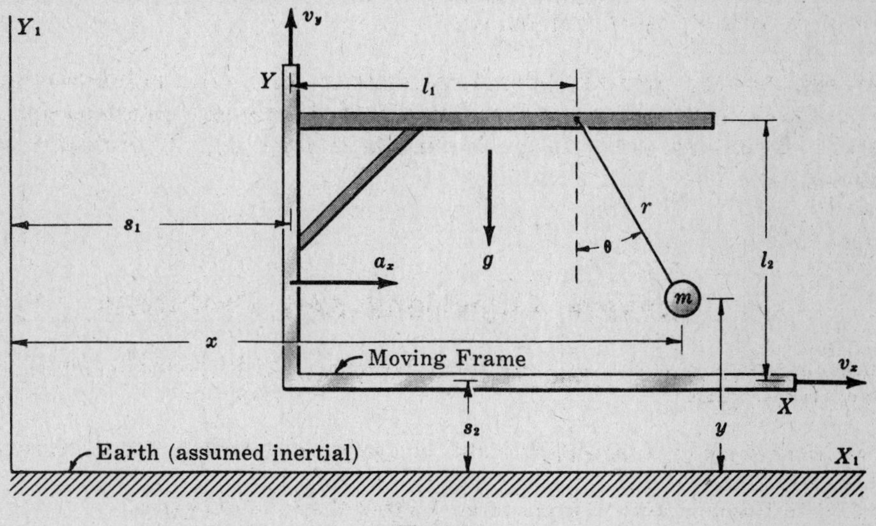

Fig. 1-5

1.13. If the X, Y frame of Fig. 1-5 above has a constant acceleration a_x in the X direction and a constant velocity v_y in the Y direction, show that

$$r\ddot{\theta} = -a_x \cos \theta - g \sin \theta$$

and hence that θ is no longer inertial. Does the pendulum now have the same period as in Problem 1.12?

1.14. State and give examples of the two principal classes of problems encountered in classical dynamics. Outline the general procedure followed in solving problems of the first type.

CHAPTER 2

Background Material, II

Coordinate systems, transformation equations, generalized coordinates. Degrees of freedom, degrees of constraint, equations of constraint. Velocity, kinetic energy, acceleration in generalized coordinates. Virtual displacements and virtual work.

2.1 Introductory Remarks.

Theoretical treatments as well as the solution of applied problems in the field of analytical dynamics involve, in addition to the important matters discussed in Chapter 1, an immediate consideration of generalized coordinates, transformation equations, degrees of freedom, degrees of constraint, equations of constraint, velocity and kinetic energy as expressed in generalized coordinates, general expressions for acceleration, and the meaning and use of virtual displacements and virtual work. *No student is in a position to follow the development of this subject without a clear understanding of each of these topics.*

2.2 Coordinate Systems and Transformation Equations.

The various topics under this heading will be treated, to a large extent, by specific examples.

(1) *Rectangular Systems.*

Consider first the two-dimensional rectangular systems, Fig. 2-1. The lengths x_1, y_1 locate the point p relative to the X_1, Y_1 frame of reference. Likewise x_2, y_2 locate the same point relative to X_2, Y_2. By inspection, the x_1, y_1 coordinates of *any point* in the plane are related to the x_2, y_2 coordinates of the *same point* by the following "transformation equations":

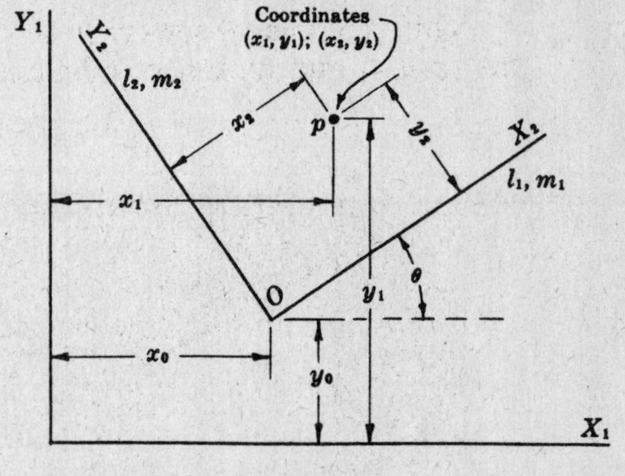

Fig. 2-1

$$\begin{aligned} x_1 &= x_0 + x_2 \cos\theta - y_2 \sin\theta \\ y_1 &= y_0 + x_2 \sin\theta + y_2 \cos\theta \end{aligned} \qquad (2.1)$$

Note that x_1 and y_1 are each functions of both x_2 and y_2.

It is seen that relations (*2.1*) can be written in the more convenient form

$$\begin{aligned} x_1 &= x_0 + l_1 x_2 + l_2 y_2 \\ y_1 &= y_0 + m_1 x_2 + m_2 y_2 \end{aligned} \qquad (2.2)$$

where l_1, m_1 and l_2, m_2 are the direction cosines of the X_2, Y_2 axes respectively relative to the X_1, Y_1 frame.

As a further extension, suppose that the origin of X_2, Y_2 is moving with, say, constant velocity (components v_x, v_y) relative to the X_1, Y_1 frame while, at the same time, the X_2, Y_2 axes rotate with constant angular velocity ω such that $\theta = \omega t$. Equations (*2.1*) or (*2.2*) can be written as

$$\begin{aligned} x_1 &= v_x t + x_2 \cos\omega t - y_2 \sin\omega t \\ y_1 &= v_y t + x_2 \sin\omega t + y_2 \cos\omega t \end{aligned} \qquad (2.3)$$

Note that x_1, y_1 are now each functions of x_2, y_2 and time. Corresponding equations for any assumed motions may, of course, be written out at once.

Transformation equations of the above type are encountered frequently and are often indicated symbolically by

$$x_1 = x_1(x_2, y_2, t), \qquad y_1 = y_1(x_2, y_2, t)$$

Considering three-dimensional rectangular systems, Fig. 2-2, it may be shown, as above, that transformation equations relating the x_1, y_1, z_1 coordinates of a point to the x_2, y_2, z_2 coordinates of the same point are

$$\begin{aligned} x_1 &= x_0 + l_1 x_2 + l_2 y_2 + l_3 z_2 \\ y_1 &= y_0 + m_1 x_2 + m_2 y_2 + m_3 z_2 \\ z_1 &= z_0 + n_1 x_2 + n_2 y_2 + n_3 z_2 \end{aligned} \qquad (2.4)$$

where l_1, m_1, n_1 are direction cosines of the X_2 axis, etc.

Of course the X_2, Y_2, Z_2 frame may be moving, in which case (for known motions) x_0, y_0, z_0 and the direction cosines can be expressed as functions of time, that is, $x_1 = x_1(x_2, y_2, z_2, t)$, etc.

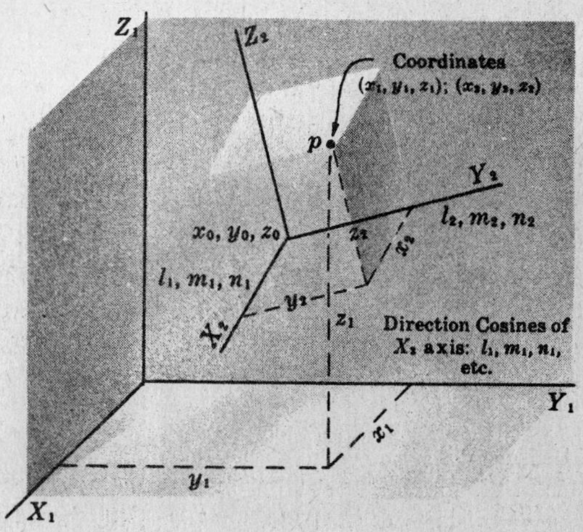

Fig. 2-2

(2) *The Cylindrical System.*

This well-known system is shown in Fig. 2-3. It is seen that equations relating the (x, y, z) and (r, ϕ, z) coordinates are

$$x = \rho \cos\phi, \qquad y = \rho \sin\phi, \qquad z = z \qquad (2.5)$$

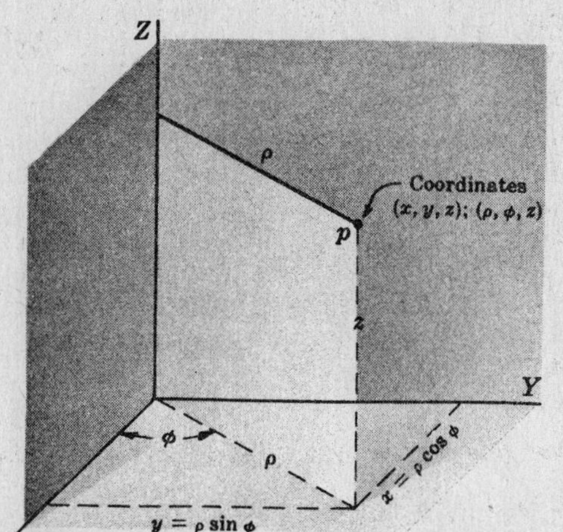

Cylindrical Coordinates ρ, ϕ, z

Fig. 2-3

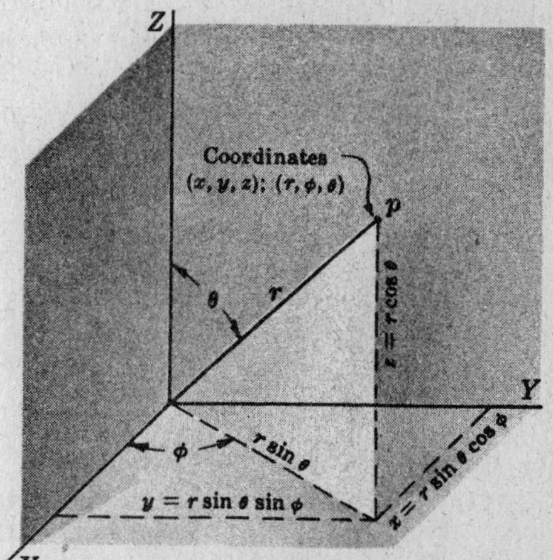

Spherical Coordinates r, θ, ϕ

Fig. 2-4

(3) *The Spherical System.*

Spherical coordinates consisting of two angles ϕ and θ and one length r are usually designated as in Fig. 2-4. Reference to the figure shows that

$$x = r \sin\theta \cos\phi, \qquad y = r \sin\theta \sin\phi, \qquad z = r\cos\theta \qquad (2.6)$$

Note that x and y are each functions of r, ϕ, θ. It happens that z is a function of r and θ only.

(4) *Various Other Coordinate Systems.*

Consider the two sets of axes X, Y and Q_1, Q_2 of Fig. 2-5, where α and β are assumed known. Inspection will show that the point p may be located by several pairs of quantities such as (x, y), (q_1, q_2), (q_1', q_2'), (s_1, s_2), (s_1, x), etc. Each pair constitutes a set of coordinates. Transformation equations relating some of these are

$$\begin{aligned} x &= q_1 \cos\alpha + q_2 \cos\beta \\ y &= q_1 \sin\alpha + q_2 \sin\beta \end{aligned} \qquad (2.7)$$

$$\begin{aligned} q_1' &= q_1 + q_2 \cos(\beta - \alpha) \\ q_2' &= q_2 + q_1 \cos(\beta - \alpha) \end{aligned} \qquad (2.8)$$

$$\begin{aligned} s_2 &= x \sin\beta - y \cos\beta \\ s_1 &= y \cos\alpha - x \sin\alpha \end{aligned} \qquad (2.9)$$

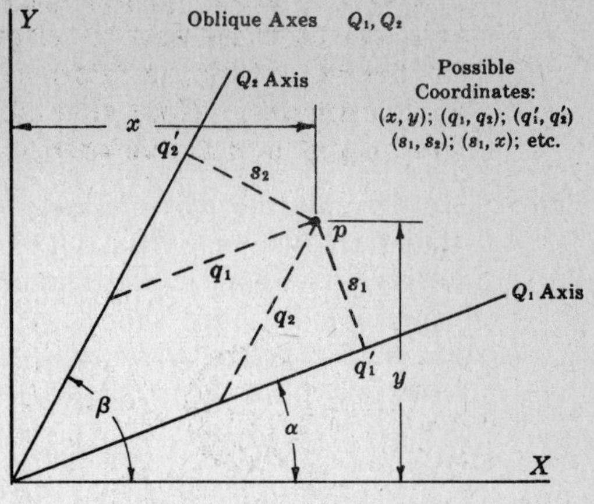

Fig. 2-5

Other interesting possibilities are shown in Fig. 2-6. Measuring r_1 and r_2 from fixed points a and b, it is seen that they determine the position of p anywhere above the X axis (they are not unique throughout the XY plane). Likewise (θ, α) or $(r_1, \sin\theta)$, etc., are suitable coordinates.

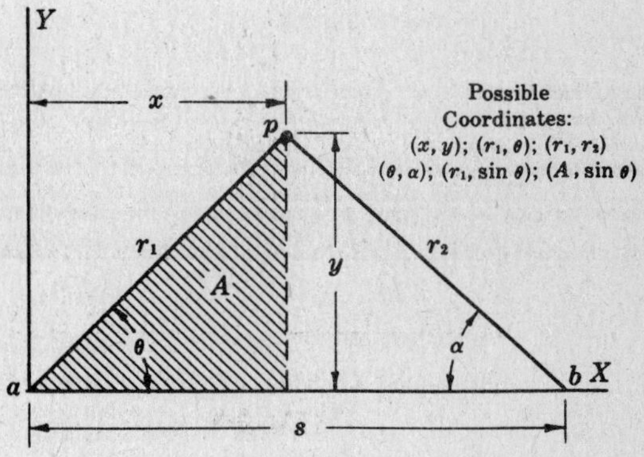

Fig. 2-6

Writing $x = r_1 \cos\theta$, $y = r_1 \sin\theta$ and designating $\sin\theta$ by q, it follows that

$$x = r_1(1 - q^2)^{1/2}, \qquad y = r_1 q \qquad (2.10)$$

which relate the (x, y) and (r_1, q) coordinates.

It is interesting to note that the shaded area A and $\sin\theta$ constitute perfectly good coordinates. Relations between these and x, y are

$$xy = 2A, \qquad y = \left(\frac{q}{\sqrt{1-q^2}}\right)x \qquad (2.11)$$

Coordinate lines corresponding to A and q are shown in Fig. 2-7. The "q-lines" are obtained by holding A constant and plotting the first relation of (*2.11*). Likewise "A-lines" result from the second relation above for q constant.

It is evident from examples given above that a great variety of coordinates (lengths, angles, trigonometric functions, areas, etc.) may be employed.

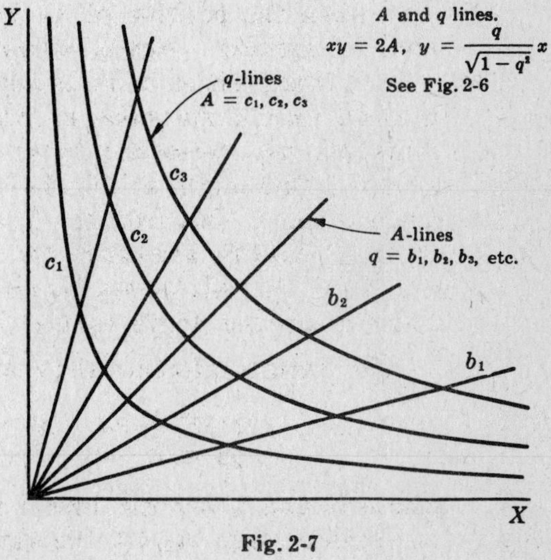

Fig. 2-7

(5) *Coordinates for the Mechanical System of Fig. 2-8 below.*

Assume that the masses m_1 and m_2 are connected by a spring and are free to move along a vertical line only. Since the motion is thus limited, the positions of the masses are determined by specifying only two coordinates as, for example, y_1 and y_2. Also (y_1, y_3), (y_2, y_3), (q_1, y_1), (q_2, y_1), (q_1, y_2), etc., are suitable. When any one of these sets is given, the *configuration of the system* is said to be determined. Obvious relations (transformation equations) exist between these sets of coordinates. Note that since $m_1 q_1 = m_2 q_2$, q_1 and q_2 are not independent. Are q_1 and y_3 suitable coordinates?

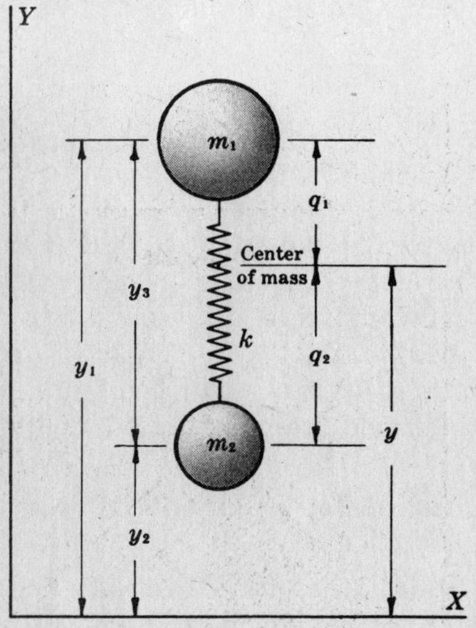

Fig. 2-8

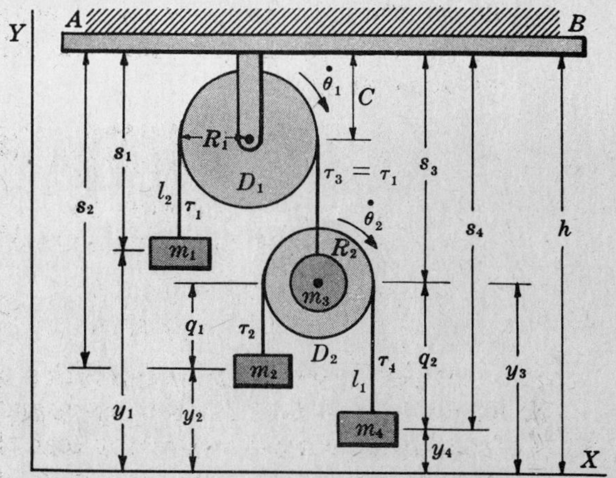

Disc D_1 fixed. D_2 can move vertically. Mass m_3 serves as bearing for D_2 and does not rotate. m_1, m_2, m_3, m_4 have vertical motion only. Tensions in ropes are represented by $\tau_1, \tau_2, \tau_3, \tau_4$. Neglect masses of D_1 and D_2.

Fig. 2-9

(6) *Coordinates for a System of Masses Attached to Pulleys.*

Assuming that the four masses of Fig. 2-9 above move vertically, it is seen that when the position of m_1 is specified by either y_1 or s_1, the position of m_3 is also determined. Again, when the position of m_2 is specified by giving either y_2 or s_2, the position of m_4 is also known. (These statements presuppose, of course, that all fixed dimensions of ropes and pulleys are known.) Hence only two coordinates are necessary to completely determine the configuration of the four masses. One might at first be inclined to say that four coordinates, as y_1, y_2, y_3, y_4, are necessary. But from the figure it is seen that $y_1 + y_3 = C_1$ and $y_2 + y_4 - 2y_3 = C_2$ where C_1 and C_2 are constants. Hence if values of the coordinates in any one of the pairs (y_1, y_2), (y_1, y_4), (y_2, y_3) are given, values of the remaining two can be found from the above equations.

For future reference the reader may show that

$$\begin{aligned} y_1 &= h + s_4 + q_1 - l_1 - l_2 - 2C, \qquad & y_3 &= h - s_4 - q_1 + l_1 \\ y_2 &= h - s_4 - 2q_1 + l_1, & y_4 &= h - s_4 \end{aligned} \tag{2.12}$$

where l_1 and l_2 are the rope lengths shown. Note that for given values of two coordinates only, (s_4, q_1), the vertical positions of *all four masses are known.*

(7) *Possible Coordinates for a Double Pendulum.*

The two masses m_1 and m_2, Fig. 2-10 below, are suspended from a rigid support and are free to swing in the X, Y plane.

(*a*) Assuming that r_1 and r_2 are inextensible strings, two coordinates such as (θ, ϕ), (x_1, x_2), (y_1, y_2), etc., are required.

(*b*) Assuming the masses are suspended from rubber bands or coil springs, four coordinates such as (r_1, r_2, θ, ϕ), (x_1, y_1, x_2, y_2), etc., are necessary. Transformation equations relating the above two sets of coordinates are

$$\begin{aligned} x_1 &= x_0 + r_1 \sin\theta \\ y_1 &= y_0 - r_1 \cos\theta \\ x_2 &= x_0 + r_1 \sin\theta + r_2 \sin\phi \\ y_2 &= y_0 - r_1 \cos\theta - r_2 \cos\phi \end{aligned} \qquad (2.13)$$

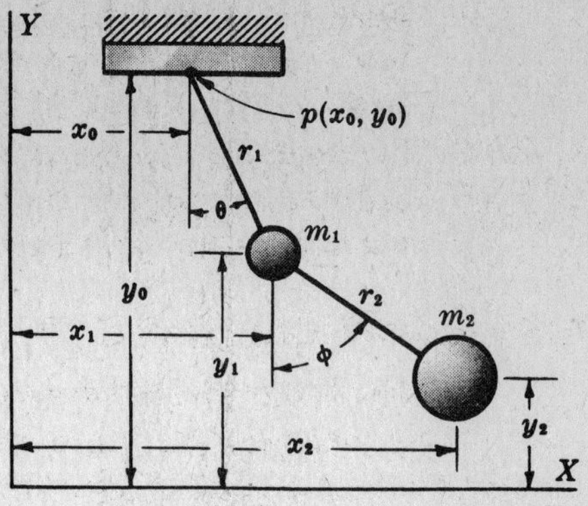

Fig. 2-10

(8) *Moving Frames of Reference and "Moving Coordinates".*

In practice, many problems are encountered for which it is desirable to use moving frames of reference. (As a matter of convenience, coordinates measured relative to such a frame may at times be referred to as "moving coordinates".) General examples are: reference axes attached to the earth for the purpose of determining motion relative to the earth; a reference frame attached to an elevator, a moving train or a rotating platform; a reference frame attached to the inside of an artificial satellite.

One specific example has already been mentioned (see Equation(*2.3*)), but perhaps the following additional ones may be helpful.

(*a*) Suppose that in Fig. 2-1, Page 10, the origin O has initial velocity (v_x, v_y) and constant acceleration (a_x, a_y) while the axes rotate with constant angular velocity ω. Equations (*2.2*) obviously take the form

$$\begin{aligned} x_1 &= v_x t + \tfrac{1}{2}a_x t^2 + x_2 \cos\omega t - y_2 \sin\omega t \\ y_1 &= v_y t + \tfrac{1}{2}a_y t^2 + x_2 \sin\omega t + y_2 \cos\omega t \end{aligned} \qquad (2.14)$$

Again note that $x_1 = x_1(x_2, y_2, t)$, etc.

(*b*) If the support in Fig. 2-10 is made to oscillate along an inclined line such that $x_0 = A_0 + A \sin\omega t$, $y_0 = B_0 + B \sin\omega t$, then relations (*2.13*) have the form

$$\begin{aligned} x_2 &= A_0 + A \sin\omega t + r_1 \sin\theta + r_2 \sin\phi \\ y_2 &= B_0 + B \sin\omega t - r_1 \cos\theta - r_2 \cos\phi \end{aligned} \qquad (2.15)$$

etc., which may be indicated as $x_2 = x_2(r_1, r_2, \theta, \phi, t)$, etc. It is important to understand and develop a feeling for the physical and geometrical meaning associated with symbolic relations of this type.

(*c*) If in Fig. 2-9 the support is given a constant vertical acceleration with initial velocity v_1, $h = v_1 t + \frac{1}{2}at^2$ and relations (*2.12*) must be written as $y_1 = v_1 t + \frac{1}{2}at^2 + s_4 + q_1 + \text{constant}$, etc.

(*d*) Suppose the reference axes Q_1 and Q_2, Fig. 2-5, Page 12, are rotating about the origin with constant angular velocities ω_1 and ω_2 such that $\alpha = \omega_1 t$, $\beta = \omega_2 t$. They still can be used as a "frame of reference" (though for most problems not a very desirable one). Relations (*2.7*) then become

$$\begin{aligned} x &= q_1 \cos\omega_1 t + q_2 \cos\omega_2 t \\ y &= q_1 \sin\omega_1 t + q_2 \sin\omega_2 t \end{aligned} \qquad (2.16)$$

or $x = x(q_1, q_2, t)$, etc.

It is important to note that the moving frame of reference in each of the above examples is non-inertial.

Finally, regarding transformation equations in general:

(i) Each coordinate of one system is as a rule *a function of each and every coordinate of the other and time* (if frames are moving), as illustrated by equations (*2.14*), (*2.15*), (*2.16*).

(ii) In previous examples most transformation equations relate rectangular coordinates to some other type. But when desirable to do so, equations relating various types can usually be written.

2.3 Generalized Coordinates. Degrees of Freedom.

(1) *Generalized Coordinates.*

As seen from previous examples, a great variety of coordinates may be employed. Hence as a matter of convenience the letter q is employed as a symbol for coordinates in general regardless of their nature. Thus q is referred to as a *generalized coordinate.*

For example, eq. (*2.15*) could be written as $x_2 = A_0 + A \sin \omega t + q_1 q_2 + q_3 q_4$ and $y_2 = B_0 + B \sin \omega t - q_1\sqrt{1 - q_2^2} - q_3\sqrt{1 - q_4^2}$, where r_1 is replaced by q_1, $\sin\theta$ by q_2, etc.

In conformity with common practice we shall frequently indicate the n coordinates required to specify the configuration of a system as $q_1, q_2, \ldots, q_n$.

(2) *Degrees of freedom, defined and illustrated.*

One of the first considerations in the solution of a problem is that of determining the number of "degrees of freedom" of the system. This is defined as:

The number of independent coordinates (not including time) required to specify completely the position of each and every particle or component part of the system.

The term "component part" as here used refers to any part of a system such as a lever, disk, gear wheel, platform, etc., which must be treated as a rigid body rather than a particle.

Examples illustrating systems having from one to many degrees of freedom will now be given.

(a) Systems having one degree of freedom.

A particle constrained to move along a straight line (bead on a wire) the equation of which is $y = a + bx$. If either x or y is given the other is known.

A bead free to move on a wire of any known shape: parabolic, helical, etc.

A simple pendulum, motion confined to a plane. Or a pendulum whose string is pulled up through a small hole in a fixed board, at a known rate. (Length of pendulum is a known function of time.) Note that time is never included as a degree of freedom.

The bead, shown in Fig. 2-11 below, free to slide along the rod which rotates about p in any known manner.

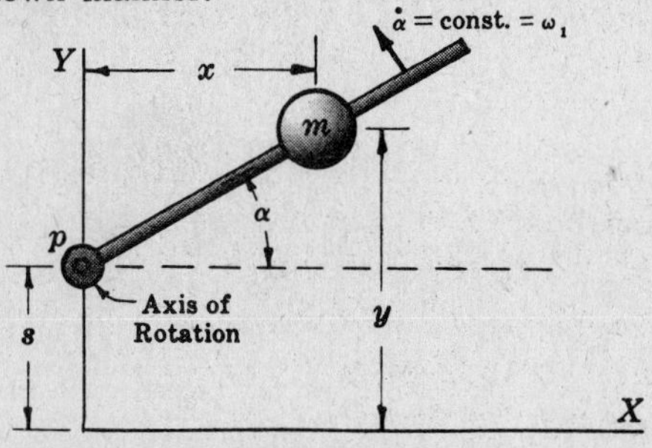

Fig. 2-11

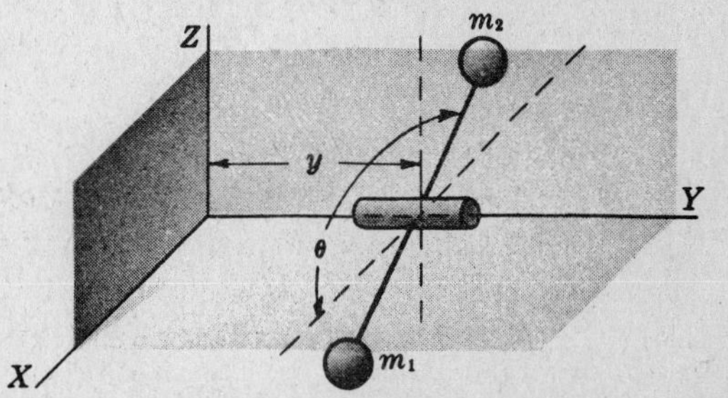

Fig. 2-12

(b) Two degrees of freedom.

A particle free to move in contact with a plane or any known surface: spherical, cylindrical, etc.

The dumbbell, shown in Fig. 2-12 above, free to slide along and at the same time rotate about the Y axis.

The system of masses and pulleys shown in Fig. 2-9, Page 13. Note that by equations (*2.12*), given s_4 and q_1 the complete configuration is known. If support AB is moving, two coordinates and t are required; however, it is still regarded as having two degrees of freedom.

The double pendulum of Fig. 2-10, Page 14, r_1 and r_2 being inextensible strings.

(c) Three degrees of freedom.

A particle free to move in space. Possible coordinates: (x, y, z), (r, ϕ, θ), etc.

A board or any lamina free to slide in contact with a plane. Two coordinates are required for translation and one for rotation.

Double pendulum, as shown in Fig. 2-10, Page 14, assuming that r_1 is a rubber band and r_2 inextensible.

Rigid body free to rotate about any fixed point O, as shown in Fig. 2-13. Orientation is completely determined by θ, ϕ, α. (m is any typical particle of the body.)

The system shown in Fig. 2-8, Page 13, with an additional spring and mass connected to m_2.

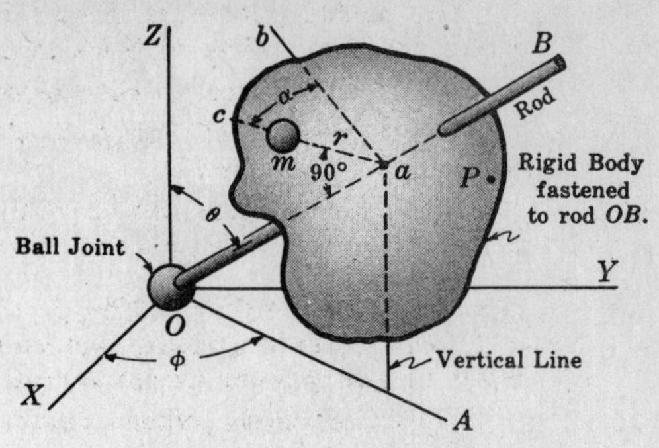

Line ab, normal to rod Oa, and in the AOZ plane. Line ac is normal to rod.

Fig. 2-13

(d) Four degrees of freedom.

The double pendulum, shown in Fig. 2-10, Page 14, with variable lengths r_1 and r_2 (rubber bands or coil springs).

The arrangement shown in Fig. 2-14 below where m_1 is allowed vertical motion only. Particle m_2 is free to move about in any manner under the action of gravity and a rubber band.

The pulley system shown in Fig. 2-15 below, assuming vertical motion only.

The rigid body, shown in Fig. 2-13, with the ball joint free to slide along the X axis.

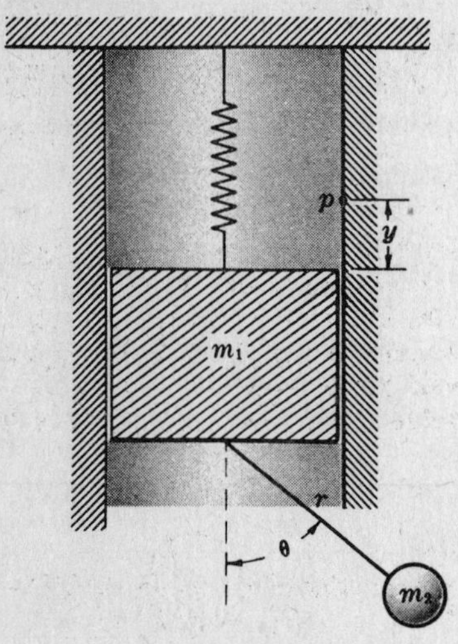

Fig. 2-14

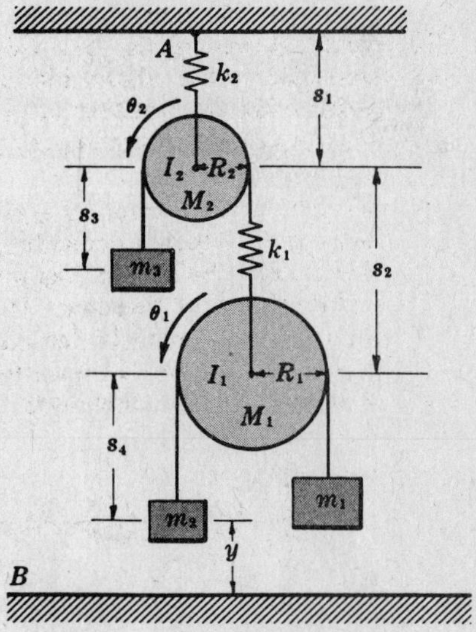

Fig. 2-15

(e) Five degrees of freedom.

The rigid body, Fig. 2-13, with the ball joint free to slide in contact with the XY plane.

A system of five pulleys mounted as indicated in Fig. 2-16 below.

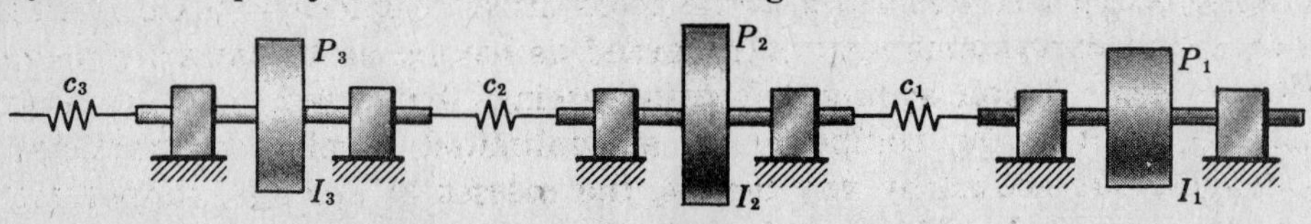

Torsion springs c_1, c_2, c_3, etc., allow disks to move, one relative to the other.

Fig. 2-16

The pulley system shown in Fig. 2-15 above, with a spring inserted in the rope connecting m_1 and m_2.

Five particles connected in line with springs as those shown in Fig. 2-18 below, horizontal motion only (or vertical motion only). Would the degrees of freedom be the same without the springs, that is, with no connection between masses?

(f) Six degrees of freedom.

The double pendulum, shown in Fig. 2-10, Page 14, particles m_1 and m_2 suspended from rubber bands and free to move in space.

A rigid body free to move in space, even though connected in any way to springs.

The rigid body of Fig. 2-13 above with another rigid body connected to it by means of a ball joint, say at point P.

The pulley system, shown in Fig. 2-15 above, with a spring inserted in the rope supporting m_2 and another in the rope supporting m_3.

(g) Many degrees of freedom.

Two boards hinged together so that the angle between them can change but allowed to move freely in any manner except for the constraint of the hinge, has seven degrees of freedom.

A row of seven pulleys as those in Fig. 2-16 above has seven degrees of freedom. A system consisting of three particles suspended from one another so as to form a "triple pendulum" has eight degrees of freedom provided two of the supporting cords are elastic and motion is not confined to a plane. If each of the three cords is elastic, this system has nine degrees of freedom.

Two rigid bodies fastened together with a universal ball joint and allowed to move freely in space has nine degrees of freedom.

The arrangement shown in Fig. 2-17 has ten degrees of freedom. Three coordinates are required to locate the point p, two more to determine the configuration of the bar (we assume that the bar does not rotate about its longitudinal axis), three more to fix the position of m_2, and finally two more to locate m_1 (supporting string assumed to be inextensible).

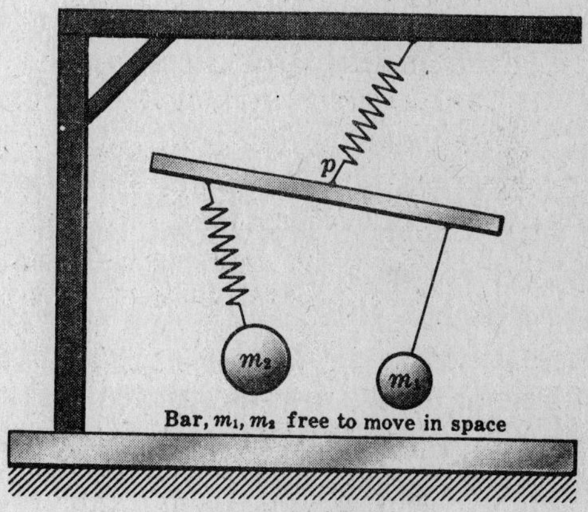

Ten Degrees of Freedom

Fig. 2-17

The arrangement of springs and "particles" in Fig. 2-18 below may have various numbers of degrees of freedom depending on how the masses are allowed to move. If motion is restricted to the Y axis, the system has only four degrees of freedom; if restricted to the XY plane, there are eight degrees of freedom. If m_1 and m_2 are allowed to move along the Y axis only while m_3 and m_4 are free to move in the XY plane, the system is one of six degrees of freedom. If each particle is allowed to move in any manner, the system has twelve degrees of freedom, and if each mass is regarded as a rigid body it has twenty-four.

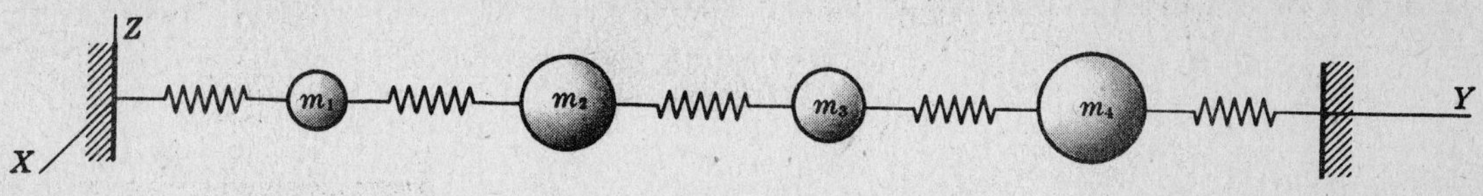

Fig. 2-18

It is thus seen that mechanical systems may have any finite number of degrees of freedom. The actual number in any particular case depends altogether on the number of masses involved and the geometrical restrictions placed on their motions. Indeed certain systems may be regarded as having an unlimited number of degrees of freedom. A coil spring, vibrating string, drumhead, etc., are examples if we imagine each to be composed of an unlimited number of particles. In many problems, but not all by any means, the masses of springs, supporting cords, etc., *may be neglected. This we shall do throughout the text.*

Systems having an "infinite number of degrees of freedom" are treated by methods which are quite distinct.

(3) *Selection of independent coordinates.*

In the mathematical treatment of a system *there is usually a wide range of choice as to which coordinates shall be regarded as independent.*

For a simple pendulum, θ, the angular displacement of the string, is usually selected. However, the x or y coordinate of the bob or many others could be employed.

Referring to Fig. 2-9, Page 13, it is seen that, for given values of the coordinates in either of the following pairs, (y_1, y_2), (s_3, q_2), (y_2, y_4), (s_1, q_1), (s_4, q_1), etc., the position of each mass of the system is determined. Thus either pair may be selected as the *independent coordinates* for treating the system.

It is a well known fact that certain coordinates may be more suitable than others. Hence the quantities chosen in any particular case are those which appear to be most advantageous for the problem in hand. The final choice depends largely on insight and experience.

2.4 Degrees of Constraint, Equations of Constraint, Superfluous Coordinates.

It is evident from the preceding section that the degrees of freedom of a system depend not only on the number of masses involved but also on how the motion of each is restricted physically. A single particle, free to take up any position in space, has three degrees of freedom. Three independent coordinates, (x, y, z), (r, ϕ, θ), etc., are required to determine its position. But if its motion is restricted to a line (bead on a rigid wire), only one coordinate is sufficient. The bead is said to have two *degrees of constraint* and two of the three coordinates required for the free particle are now "superfluous".

Thus it is evident that a system of p particles can have, at most, $3p$ degrees of freedom and that the actual number, n, at any particular instant is given by

$$n = 3p - (\text{degrees of constraint}) \tag{2.17}$$

Now the constraints of a system may be represented by *equations of constraint.* If the bead is constrained to a straight wire in the XY plane, the equation of the wire $y = a + bx$ and $z = 0$ are equations of constraint. If the wire is parabolic in shape, $y = bx^2$ and $z = 0$ are the equations of constraint.

Again consider Fig. 2-9, Page 13. For vertical motion only it is seen that

$$\begin{aligned} &x_1 = C_1,\ z_1 = b_1;\quad x_2 = C_2,\ z_2 = b_2;\quad \text{etc.} \\ &y_1 + y_3 = \text{constant};\quad \tfrac{1}{2}(y_2 + y_4) - y_3 = \text{constant} \end{aligned} \tag{2.18}$$

where x_1, z_1 are the (x, z) coordinates of m_1; C_1, b_1 are constants, etc. Thus, all told, there are ten equations of constraint and the degrees of freedom have been reduced from a maximum of twelve to only two. We may say that ten coordinates are *superfluous.*

2.5 Moving Constraints.

It is frequently the case that some or all constraints of a system are in motion.

A simple example is shown in Fig. 2-11 where the rod is rotating in the XY plane about the axis indicated, with constant angular velocity ω_1. The bead m is free to slide along the rod and since $\alpha = \omega_1 t$, the equation of constraint may be written as $y = s + (\tan \omega_1 t)x$. Note that t *appears explicitly* in this relation.

As an extension of this example, suppose that the X, Y axes above are the X_2, Y_2 translating and rotating axes of Fig. 2-1; then $y_2 = s + (\tan \omega_1 t)x_2$. Therefore transformation equations (*2.14*) written in terms of x_2 and t (they could just as well be expressed in y_2, t) have the form

$$\begin{aligned} x_1 &= v_x t + \tfrac{1}{2}a_x t^2 + x_2 \cos \omega t - (s + x_2 \tan \omega_1 t) \sin \omega t \\ y_1 &= v_y t + \tfrac{1}{2}a_y t^2 + x_2 \sin \omega t + (s + x_2 \tan \omega_1 t) \cos \omega t \end{aligned} \qquad (2.19)$$

where both x_1 and y_1 are now functions of x_2 and t alone.

General remarks: From a purely mathematical point of view, equations of constraint are merely certain relations existing between the possible and otherwise independent $3p$ coordinates. They may be indicated in a general manner as

$$\phi_i(q_1, q_2, \ldots, q_{3p}, t) = 0, \quad \text{where } i = 1, 2, \ldots, 3p-n \qquad (2.20)$$

2.6 "Reduced" Transformation Equations.

Assuming no constraints but possibly moving frames of reference, transformation equations relating the rectangular coordinates of p particles to their $3p$ generalized coordinates may be indicated as $x_i = x_i(q_1, q_2, \ldots, q_{3p}, t)$, etc. However, when there are constraints, stationary or moving, *all superfluous coordinates can be eliminated from the above relations by means of equations of constraint*, giving

$$x_i = x_i(q_1, q_2, \ldots, q_n, t); \quad y_i = y_i(q_1, q_2, \ldots, q_n, t); \quad z_i = z_i(q_1, q_2, \ldots, q_n, t) \qquad (2.21)$$

which now contain only independent coordinates, equal in number to the degrees of freedom of the system. We shall refer to these as "reduced" transformation equations. It should be noted that *t may appear explicitly in (2.21) as a result of moving coordinates and/or moving constraints.* Simple examples of (*2.21*) are equations (*2.12*) in which t does not appear and (*2.19*) in which t appears explicitly.

The great importance of relations (*2.21*) in obtaining expressions for velocity, kinetic energy, potential energy, etc., in just the appropriate number of independent coordinates will soon be evident.

Note. (*a*) In some cases the algebra involved in eliminating superfluous coordinates may be difficult. (*b*) For the relatively rare "non-holonomic" system, equations of constraint must be written in non-integrable differential form. See Section 9.12, Page 193.

2.7 Velocity Expressed in Generalized Coordinates.

Expressions for the velocity of a point or particle may be arrived at by either of the following two procedures. The first brings out the fundamental definition of velocity and the basic physical and geometrical ideas involved. The second is more convenient.

(1) ***Velocity from an element of path length,*** Δs. (Δs regarded as a vector.)

Suppose the point p, shown in Fig. 2-19 below, moves the distance Δs from a to b in time Δt. Its average velocity over the interval is $\Delta s/\Delta t$. When Δt approaches zero, we write

$$\text{velocity} = \lim_{\Delta t \to 0} \frac{\Delta s}{\Delta t} = \dot{s} \qquad (2.22)$$

where $\dot{s}$ is a vector quantity of magnitude $|ds/dt|$, pointing in the direction of the tangent to the path at a. As an aid in appreciating the physics and geometry involved, we may think of a particle as having a velocity "in the direction of its path" at any position in the path.

The above definition of velocity *makes no reference to any particular coordinate system.* But, of course, Δs can be expressed in any coordinates we wish. Hence by so doing and passing to a limit as $\Delta t \to 0$, $\dot{s}$ is expressed in the chosen coordinates. Examples:

In rectangular coordinates, $(\Delta s)^2 = (\Delta x)^2 + (\Delta y)^2 + (\Delta z)^2$. Dividing by $(\Delta t)^2$ and passing to the limit we write,

$$\dot{s}^2 = \dot{x}^2 + \dot{y}^2 + \dot{z}^2 \tag{2.23}$$

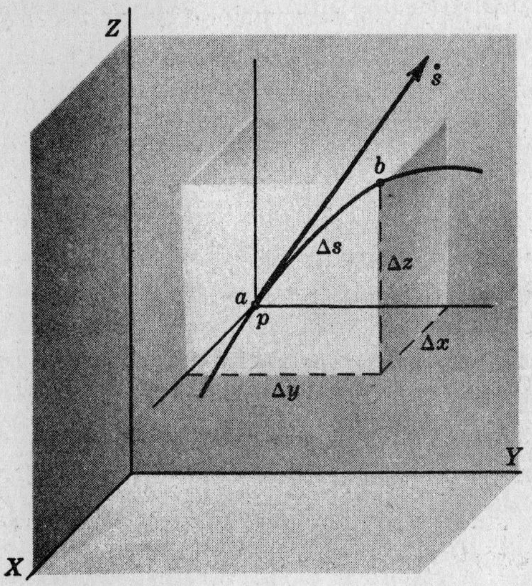

Fig. 2-19

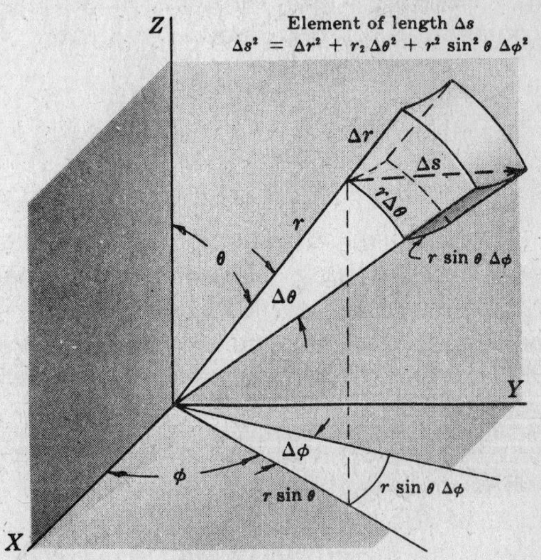

Fig. 2-20

In spherical coordinates (see Fig. 2-20), $(\Delta s)^2 = (\Delta r)^2 + r^2(\Delta\theta)^2 + r^2 \sin^2\theta\,(\Delta\phi)^2$; then

$$\dot{s}^2 = \dot{r}^2 + r^2\dot{\theta}^2 + r^2 \sin^2\theta\,\dot{\phi}^2 \tag{2.24}$$

In the two-dimensional oblique system, Fig. 2-5, Page 12, imagine p given any small general displacement Δs. It is seen, for example, that $(\Delta s)^2 = (\Delta q_1)^2 + (\Delta q_2)^2 + 2(\Delta q_1)(\Delta q_2)\cos(\beta - \alpha)$; then

$$\dot{s}^2 = \dot{q}_1^2 + \dot{q}_2^2 + 2\dot{q}_1\dot{q}_2\cos(\beta - \alpha) \tag{2.25}$$

Let us outline the steps required to find the velocity $\dot{s}_1$ and $\dot{s}_2$ of m_1 and m_2 respectively shown in Fig. 2-10. Basically these are $\Delta s_1/\Delta t$ and $\Delta s_2/\Delta t$. By sketching a small general displacement of the pendulum and indicating Δs_1 and Δs_2 as corresponding general displacements of m_1 and m_2 respectively, one can from the geometry of the drawing (and considerable tedious work) express each in terms of $r_1, \Delta r_1, \theta, \Delta\theta, r_2, \Delta r_2, \phi, \Delta\phi$. Final results, after dividing through by $(\Delta t)^2$ and passing to the limits, are

$$\begin{aligned} \dot{s}_1^2 &= \dot{r}_1^2 + r_1^2\dot{\theta}^2 \\ \dot{s}_2^2 &= \dot{r}_1^2 + r_1^2\dot{\theta}^2 + 2(\dot{r}_1\dot{r}_2 + r_1 r_2\dot{\theta}\dot{\phi})\cos(\phi - \theta) \\ &\quad + \dot{r}_2^2 + r_2^2\dot{\phi}^2 + 2(r_1\dot{r}_2\dot{\theta} - r_2\dot{r}_1\dot{\phi})\sin(\phi - \theta) \end{aligned} \tag{2.26}$$

It should be noted that, *even though the expression for $\dot{s}_2$ appears complicated, basically it is merely an element of length Δs_2 divided by a corresponding element of time Δt.* Also note that, as expressed above, $\dot{s}_2$ is a function of every coordinate as well as their time derivatives, that is, $\dot{s}_2 = \dot{s}_2(r_1, \theta, r_2, \phi, \dot{r}_1, \dot{\theta}, \dot{r}_2, \dot{\phi})$.

(2) *Velocity through the use of transformation equations.*

Given an expression for $\dot{s}$ in one system of coordinates, we can express it in another by means of transformation equations (or reduced transformation equations) relating the two. Examples:

Differentiating equations (*2.6*), Page 11, with respect to time and substituting in (*2.23*), relation (*2.24*) is obtained.

Differentiating relations (*2.13*), Page 14, and inserting in (*2.23*), relations (*2.26*) are obtained with little effort.

It follows at once from relations (*2.12*), Page 13, that velocities of the individual masses, Fig. 2-9, are given by

$$\dot{y}_1 = \dot{s}_4 + \dot{q}_1, \quad \dot{y}_2 = -\dot{s}_4 - 2\dot{q}_1, \quad \dot{y}_3 = -\dot{s}_4 - \dot{q}_1, \quad \dot{y}_4 = -\dot{s}_4 \qquad (2.27)$$

This assumes of course that h is constant. Note that all velocities are expressed in terms of only $\dot{s}_4$ and $\dot{q}_1$.

For use in a later example, consider the vertical velocities $\dot{y}_1$ and $\dot{y}_2$ of m_1 and m_2, shown in Fig. 2-8, Page 13, relative to the fixed X axis. Let us express these in terms of $\dot{y}$ and $\dot{q}_1$. As seen from the diagram, $y_1 = y + q_1$, $y_2 = y - q_2$ and $m_1 q_1 = m_2 q_2$ (center of mass relation). Hence

$$\dot{y}_1 = \dot{y} + \dot{q}_1, \quad \dot{y}_2 = \dot{y} - \frac{m_1}{m_2}\dot{q}_1 \qquad (2.28)$$

(3) *Velocity expressed in terms of moving coordinates.*

One point must be understood: in the Lagrangian treatment one of the first considerations is the velocity of each particle relative to an inertial frame. If a moving frame of reference is used in which some or all of the chosen coordinates are non-inertial (this implies that, eventually, we expect to find the motion of the system relative to the moving frame), the velocity required is *not that relative to the moving frame* but rather equations for velocity *relative to inertial axes, but expressed in terms of the moving coordinates.* (The reason for this will be evident in Chapter 3.) Examples should make clear this statement and how the desired results are obtained.

Assume as a simple case that the X_2, Y_2, Z_2 axes, shown in Fig. 2-2, Page 11, are moving parallel to the fixed X_1, Y_1, Z_1 frame with constant acceleration (a_x, a_y, a_z). Transformation equations are $x_1 = v_x t + \frac{1}{2}a_x t^2 + x_2$, etc. The velocity components of p relative to fixed axes are $\dot{x}_1, \dot{y}_1, \dot{z}_1$ and relative to the moving axes, $\dot{x}_2, \dot{y}_2, \dot{z}_2$. But from the transformation equations,

$$\dot{x}_1 = v_x + a_x t + \dot{x}_2, \text{ etc.} \qquad (2.29)$$

which express the velocity of p relative to the stationary axes but *in terms of velocities relative to the moving axes and time.*

If the X_2, Y_2, Z_2 frame is regarded as moving in any manner (rotation as well as translation), equations corresponding to the above are

$$\dot{x}_1 = \dot{x}_0 + l_1\dot{x}_2 + l_2\dot{y}_2 + l_3\dot{z}_2 + \dot{l}_1 x_2 + \dot{l}_2 y_2 + \dot{l}_3 z_2, \text{ etc.} \qquad (2.30)$$

In this case x_0, y_0, z_0 and all direction cosines are changing with time. Equations (*2.30*) play an important part in the development of rigid body dynamics, Chapter 9.

As a final example consider the following. D_1 and D_2 shown in Fig. 2-21 below are rotating platforms. D_1 is driven by a motor at an angular velocity of $\dot{\theta}_1$ relative to the earth. D_2, mounted on D_1, is driven by another motor at an angular velocity of $\dot{\theta}_2$ relative to D_1. Axes X_1, Y_1 are fixed relative to the earth. Line ab is fixed to the surface of D_1. Axes X_2, Y_2 are fixed to the surface of D_2. A particle of mass m is free to move in contact with D_2. We shall find an expression for its

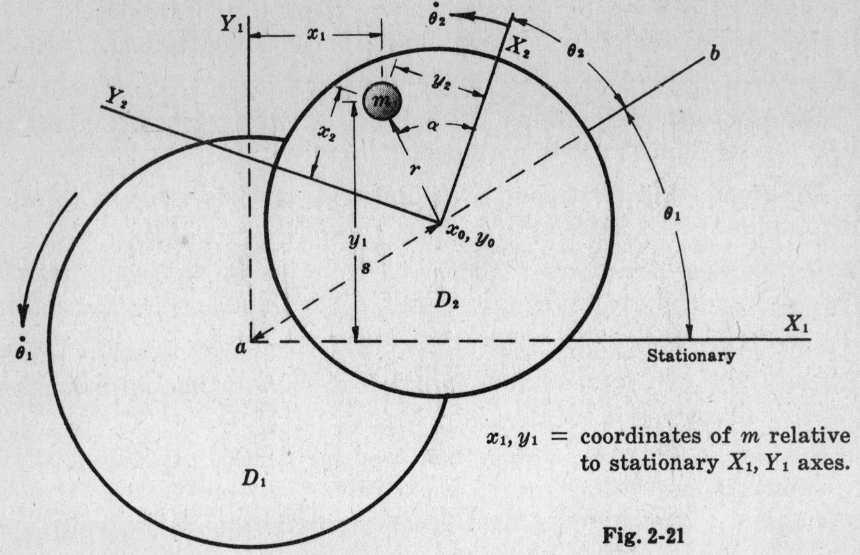

Fig. 2-21

velocity relative to the earth but expressed in terms of the moving polar coordinates r, α and other quantities.

It is easy to see that

$$x_1 = s\cos\theta_1 + r\cos\beta, \qquad y_1 = s\sin\theta_1 + r\sin\beta$$

where $\beta = \theta_1 + \theta_2 + \alpha$. Differentiating and substituting in $v^2 = \dot{x}_1^2 + \dot{y}_1^2$, we get

$$v^2 = s^2\dot{\theta}_1^2 + 2s\dot{\theta}_1\dot{r}\sin(\theta_2 + \alpha) + r^2\dot{\beta}^2 + \dot{r}^2 + 2s\dot{\theta}_1\dot{\beta}r\cos(\theta_2 + \alpha) \qquad (2.31)$$

which is correct regardless of how the motors may cause θ_1 and θ_2 to change with time. If, as a special case, we assume that $\dot{\theta}_1 = \omega_1$ = constant and $\ddot{\theta}_2 = C$ = constant, then v becomes a function of $r, \alpha, \dot{r}, \dot{\alpha}, t$ only.

If desired, v can easily be expressed in terms of the rectangular coordinates x_2, y_2 by differentiating

$$\begin{aligned} x_1 &= s\cos\theta_1 + x_2\cos(\theta_1 + \theta_2) - y_2\sin(\theta_1 + \theta_2) \\ y_1 &= s\sin\theta_1 + x_2\sin(\theta_1 + \theta_2) + y_2\cos(\theta_1 + \theta_2) \end{aligned} \qquad (2.32)$$

and substituting in $v^2 = \dot{x}_1^2 + \dot{y}_1^2$.

2.8 Work and Kinetic Energy.

(1) *Projection of a vector on a line.*

By way of review consider the following form of expressing the projection f of any vector F on the line ob having direction cosines l, m, as shown in Fig. 2-22. Clearly,

$$\begin{aligned} f &= F\cos\theta = F\cos(\alpha - \beta) \\ &= F\cos\alpha\cos\beta + F\sin\alpha\sin\beta \end{aligned}$$

But $F\cos\alpha = F_x$ and $\cos\beta = l$, etc.; hence $f = F_x l + F_y m$. Extended to three dimensions,

$$f = F_x l + F_y m + F_z n \qquad (2.33)$$

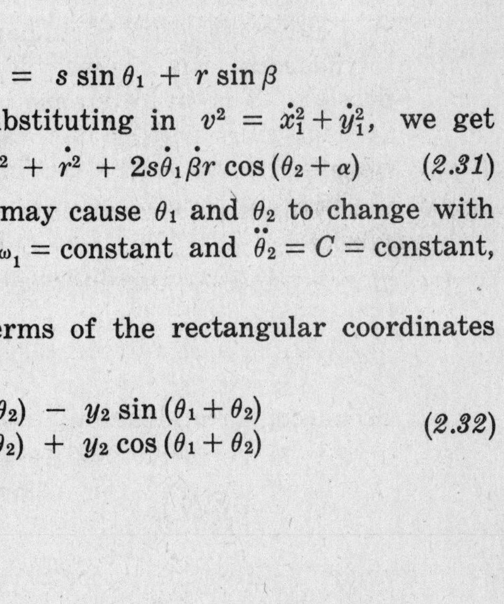

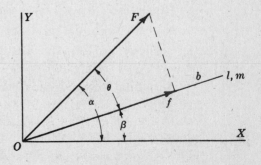

Fig. 2-22

Referring to Fig. 2-23, ds is an element ab of the line AB. τ is tangent to the line at a. Direction cosines of τ are seen to be $dx/ds, dy/ds, dz/ds$. Hence the projection f of any vector F on τ is given by

$$f = F\cos\theta = F_x\frac{dx}{ds} + F_y\frac{dy}{ds} + F_z\frac{dz}{ds} \qquad (2.34)$$

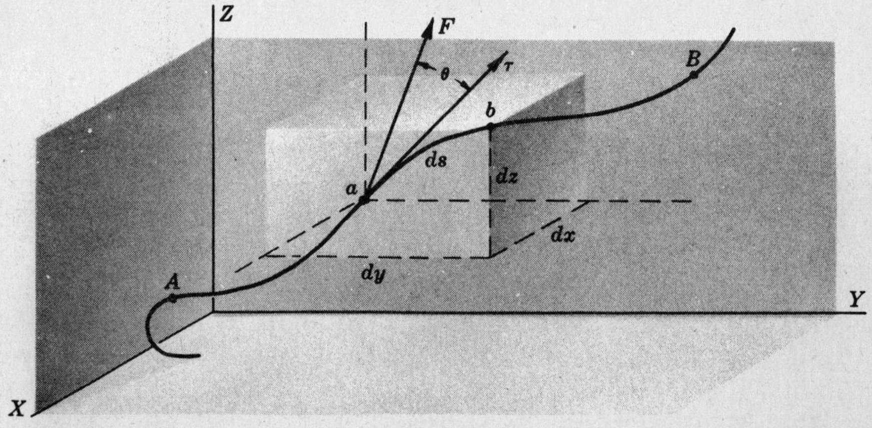

Fig. 2-23

(2) *Definition of work.*

Suppose F is a force acting on a body at point a and that this point of application moves along some general path from a to b. Now, (even though the shift in position may not be entirely due to F; other forces may be acting), the element of work dW done by F is given by $dW = F\,ds\cos\theta$, a scalar quantity. But by (2.34) this may be written as

$$dW = F_x\,dx + F_y\,dy + F_z\,dz \qquad (2.35)$$

Hence the work done over any finite path from A to B is given by

$$W = \int_A^B (F_x\,dx + F_y\,dy + F_z\,dz) \qquad (2.36)$$

This general statement is correct even though F may change in both magnitude and direction along the path (may be a function of x, y, z).

(3) *Definition of kinetic energy.*

Now suppose F is the net force causing a particle of mass m to accelerate as the particle moves along any path AB. The work done on the particle is given by (2.36); *and if X, Y, Z are inertial axes,* $F_x = m\ddot{x}$, etc. Thus writing $\ddot{x}\,dx = \dot{x}\,d\dot{x}$, (2.36) takes the form

$$W = \int_A^B m(\dot{x}\,d\dot{x} + \dot{y}\,d\dot{y} + \dot{z}\,d\dot{z}) = \frac{m}{2}(\dot{x}^2 + \dot{y}^2 + \dot{z}^2)\Big|_A^B = \frac{m}{2}(v_B^2 - v_A^2)$$

which is an expression for the work required to change the velocity of the particle from v_A to v_B. It is a scalar quantity depending only on m and the magnitudes of v_A, v_B.

If the initial velocity $v_A = 0$, then $W = \frac{1}{2}mv_B^2$, which leads us to the following definition of kinetic energy.

The kinetic energy of a particle is the work required to increase its velocity from rest to some value v, relative to an inertial frame of reference.

As shown above, this is $\frac{1}{2}mv^2$; and since it is a scalar quantity, the kinetic energy T of a system of p particles is

$$T = \frac{1}{2}\sum_{i=1}^{p} m_i v_i^2 \tag{2.37}$$

where, of course, the velocities v_i may be expressed in any inertial coordinates and their time derivatives or the *equivalents of these quantities expressed in non-inertial coordinates.*

The kinetic energy of a rigid body rotating with angular velocity $\dot{\theta}$ about a fixed axis follows at once from (*2.37*). The velocity of any typical particle is $r\dot{\theta}$, where r is the perpendicular distance from the axis to the particle. Hence, considering particles of mass dm and replacing the sum with an integral, (*2.37*) may be written as

$$T = \frac{\dot{\theta}^2}{2}\left(\int r^2\,dm\right) = \frac{I\dot{\theta}^2}{2} \tag{2.38}$$

where the "moment of inertia" I, is defined by the integral. We shall assume that the student is familiar with the use of the above relation in simple problems and postpone a general treatment of moments of inertia and kinetic energy of a rigid body until Chapters 7 and 8.

2.9 Examples Illustrating Kinetic Energy.

(1) ***Kinetic energy of a particle.***

$$\begin{aligned} T &= \frac{m}{2}(\dot{x}^2 + \dot{y}^2 + \dot{z}^2), && \text{see equation (2.23)} \\ T &= \frac{m}{2}(\dot{r}^2 + r^2\dot{\theta}^2 + r^2\sin^2\theta\,\dot{\phi}^2), && \text{see equation (2.24)} \\ T &= \frac{m}{2}[\dot{q}_1^2 + \dot{q}_2^2 + 2\dot{q}_1\dot{q}_2\cos(\beta-\alpha)], && \text{see equation (2.25)} \end{aligned} \tag{2.39}$$

Making use of equations (*2.11*), Page 12, and the first equation above (with $\dot{z}=0$), T can for example be expressed in the A, q coordinates and their time derivatives.

(2) ***Kinetic energy of the double pendulum,*** Fig. 2-10, Page 14. In rectangular coordinates,

$$T = \frac{m_1}{2}(\dot{x}_1^2 + \dot{y}_1^2) + \frac{m_2}{2}(\dot{x}_2^2 + \dot{y}_2^2) \tag{2.40}$$

If the masses are suspended from springs or rubber bands, the system has four degrees of freedom and (*2.40*) contains no superfluous coordinates. However, suppose r_1 is an inextensible string, i.e. $x_1^2 + y_1^2 = r_1^2 =$ constant, (an equation of constraint). By means of this we can eliminate say $\dot{y}_1$ from (*2.40*), giving

$$T = \frac{m_1}{2}\left(\frac{\dot{x}_1^2 r_1^2}{r_1^2 - x_1^2}\right) + \frac{m_2}{2}(\dot{x}_2^2 + \dot{y}_2^2) \tag{2.41}$$

In the coordinates r_1, r_2, θ, ϕ (assuming all variable, see equations (*2.26*)),

$$\begin{aligned} T = \frac{m_1}{2}(\dot{r}_1^2 + r_1^2\dot{\theta}^2) + \frac{m_2}{2}[&\dot{r}_1^2 + r_1^2\dot{\theta}^2 + \dot{r}_2^2 + r_2^2\dot{\phi}^2 \\ &+ 2(\dot{r}_1\dot{r}_2 + r_1r_2\dot{\theta}\dot{\phi})\cos(\phi-\theta) + 2(r_1\dot{r}_2\dot{\theta} - r_2\dot{r}_1\dot{\phi})\sin(\phi-\theta)] \end{aligned} \tag{2.42}$$

(3) ***Kinetic energy of the system,*** Fig. 2-9, Page 13, neglecting masses of pulleys and assuming vertical motion only:

$$T = \frac{m_1}{2}\dot{y}_1^2 + \frac{m_2}{2}\dot{y}_2^2 + \frac{m_3}{2}\dot{y}_3^2 + \frac{m_4}{2}\dot{y}_4^2$$

This is correct but, since the system has only two degrees of freedom, the expression contains two superfluous coordinates. However, we see that $y_1 + y_3 = C_1$ and

$(y_3 - y_4) + (y_3 - y_2) = C_2$ (equations of constraint) by means of which two velocities, say $\dot{y}_3$ and $\dot{y}_4$, can be eliminated giving

$$T = \tfrac{1}{2}(m_1 + m_3 + 4m_4)\dot{y}_1^2 + \tfrac{1}{2}(m_2 + m_4)\dot{y}_2^2 + 2m_4\dot{y}_1\dot{y}_2 \qquad (2.43)$$

Applying relations (*2.27*), T can immediately be expressed in terms of $\dot{s}_4$ and $\dot{q}_1$, if so desired.

As noted above, superfluous coordinates may be eliminated from T by means of the equations of constraint. This is an important matter in future developments.

(4) *Kinetic energy expressed in non-inertial coordinates.*

Basically, *kinetic energy is always reckoned relative to an inertial frame* since the velocities v_i in equation (*2.37*) must be measured relative to inertial axes. However, as previously explained, expressions for v_i in inertial coordinates can, by means of proper transformation equations, be written in terms of non-inertial coordinates.

(*a*) Consider the system in Fig. 2-8, Page 13. For vertical motion only, $T = \tfrac{1}{2}m_1\dot{y}_1^2 + \tfrac{1}{2}m_2\dot{y}_2^2$ since y_1 and y_2 are each inertial. Notice that T is *not* equal to $\tfrac{1}{2}m_1\dot{y}_1^2 + \tfrac{1}{2}m_2\dot{y}_3^2$, since y_3 is non-inertial. However, T can be expressed in terms of $\dot{y}_1$ and $\dot{y}_3$ as follows. Since $y_3 = y_1 - y_2$, $\dot{y}_3 = \dot{y}_1 - \dot{y}_2$ and thus

$$T = \tfrac{1}{2}m_1\dot{y}_1^2 + \tfrac{1}{2}m_2(\dot{y}_1 - \dot{y}_3)^2$$

Or again, eliminating $\dot{y}_1$ and $\dot{y}_2$ from our original expression, T in terms of $\dot{y}$ and $\dot{q}_1$ (y is inertial, q_1 is non-inertial) becomes

$$T = \left(\frac{m_1 + m_2}{2}\right)\dot{y}^2 + \frac{m_1}{2}\left(\frac{m_1 + m_2}{m_2}\right)\dot{q}_1^2 \qquad (2.44)$$

In terms of $\dot{y}$ and $\dot{y}_3$, $T = \left(\dfrac{m_1 + m_2}{2}\right)\dot{y}^2 + \dfrac{1}{2}\left(\dfrac{m_1 m_2}{m_1 + m_2}\right)\dot{y}_3^2$.

(*b*) Consider the first example discussed under Section 2.7(3), Page 21. Applying equations (*2.29*) we see that, if p represents a particle, its kinetic energy is

$$T = \tfrac{1}{2}m[(v_x + a_x t + \dot{x}_2)^2 + (v_y + a_y t + \dot{y}_2)^2 + (v_z + a_z t + \dot{z}_2)^2] \qquad (2.45)$$

where v_x, a_x, etc., are constants. Note that this expression contains time explicitly.

(*c*) If the origin O, Fig. 2-1, Page 10, has an initial velocity (v_x, v_y) and constant acceleration (a_x, a_y) while the axes rotate with constant angular velocity ω, from equations (*2.14*) we have

$$\dot{x}_1 = v_x + a_x t + \dot{x}_2\cos\omega t - x_2\omega\sin\omega t - \dot{y}_2\sin\omega t - y_2\omega\cos\omega t$$

Putting this, together with the corresponding expression for $\dot{y}_1$, into $T = \tfrac{1}{2}m(\dot{x}_1^2 + \dot{y}_1^2)$ we have T expressed as a function of $x_2, y_2, \dot{x}_2, \dot{y}_2, t$.

(*d*) Referring to Fig. 2-21, Page 22, and equation (*2.31*) it is seen that the kinetic energy of the particle free to slide in contact with the second rotating table is given by

$$T = \tfrac{1}{2}m[s^2\dot{\theta}_1^2 + 2s\dot{\theta}_1\dot{r}\sin(\theta_2 + \alpha) + r^2\beta^2 + \dot{r}^2 + 2s\dot{\theta}_1\beta r\cos(\theta_2 + \alpha)] \qquad (2.46)$$

It should be noted that (*2.46*) is true regardless of how θ_1 and θ_2 may be assumed to vary with time. For the case of constant angular velocities, we merely replace $\dot{\theta}_1$ and $\dot{\theta}_2$ by the constants ω_1 and ω_2. But if it is assumed, for example, that D_1 and D_2 are made to oscillate such that $\theta_1 = A\sin at$, $\theta_2 = B\sin bt$, then $\dot{\theta}_1$ and $\dot{\theta}_2$ must be replaced by $Aa\cos at$ and $Bb\cos bt$ respectively. In this case T will contain t explicitly.

2.10 "Center of Mass" Theorem for Kinetic Energy.

Consider a system of p particles moving relative to an inertial X, Y, Z frame. Imagine an X', Y', Z' frame whose origin is located at and moves with the center of mass of the particles while X', Y', Z' remain always parallel to X, Y, Z respectively. Transformation equations relating the coordinates of a particle in one system to those of the second are $x = \bar{x} + x'$, $y = \bar{y} + y'$, $z = \bar{z} + z'$ where $\bar{x}, \bar{y}, \bar{z}$ are coordinates of the origin of the moving frame. Hence

$$T = \frac{1}{2}\sum_{i=1}^{p} m_i(\dot{x}_i^2 + \dot{y}_i^2 + \dot{z}_i^2) = \frac{1}{2}\sum_{i=1}^{p} m_i[(\dot{\bar{x}} + \dot{x}_i')^2 + (\dot{\bar{y}} + \dot{y}_i')^2 + (\dot{\bar{z}} + \dot{z}_i')^2]$$

Expanding, writing $M = \Sigma m_i$ and noting from the definition of center of mass $\Sigma m_i x_i = 0$ that $\Sigma m_i \dot{x}_i = 0$, etc., the above reduces to

$$T = \frac{M}{2}(\dot{\bar{x}}^2 + \dot{\bar{y}}^2 + \dot{\bar{z}}^2) + \frac{1}{2}\sum_{i=1}^{p} m_i[(\dot{x}_i')^2 + (\dot{y}_i')^2 + (\dot{z}_i')^2] \tag{2.47}$$

Four important statements should be made regarding (*2.47*):

(*a*) It demonstrates that the kinetic energy of a system of particles is equal to that of a single "particle" of mass $M = \Sigma m_i$ (total mass of system) located at and moving with the center of mass, plus the kinetic energy of each particle figured relative to the X', Y', Z' frame as if these axes were inertial.

(*b*) The above statement is true whether the particles are free or constrained in any manner. Indeed it even applies to a rigid body. In this case, motion relative to the moving frame can only take the form of a rotation.

(*c*) If we think of the particles of the system divided into two or more groups, it is clear that the theorem may be applied to each group individually.

(*d*) Although (*2.47*) is written in rectangular coordinates, one can of course express this form of T in any other convenient coordinates by means of proper transformation equations.

2.11 A General Expression for the Kinetic Energy of p Particles.

We shall now derive a very general expression for the kinetic energy of a system of p particles having n degrees of freedom and $3p - n$ degrees of constraint. It will be assumed that some or all constraints may be moving and that any or all of the generalized coordinates are non-inertial. This expression will be found very useful in the chapters which follow.

(1) As an introductory step let us consider the kinetic energy of a single particle having three degrees of freedom (no constraints). Assuming that any or all of the generalized coordinates q_1, q_2, q_3 are moving, transformation equations may be indicated as

$$x = x(q_1, q_2, q_3, t); \quad y = y(q_1, q_2, q_3, t); \quad z = z(q_1, q_2, q_3, t)$$

By differentiation, $\dot{x} = \frac{\partial x}{\partial q_1}\dot{q}_1 + \frac{\partial x}{\partial q_2}\dot{q}_2 + \frac{\partial x}{\partial q_3}\dot{q}_3 + \frac{\partial x}{\partial t}$, etc.

For convenience we write

$$\dot{x} = a_1\dot{q}_1 + a_2\dot{q}_2 + a_3\dot{q}_3 + \alpha$$

Likewise, $\dot{y} = b_1\dot{q}_1 + b_2\dot{q}_2 + b_3\dot{q}_3 + \beta$, $\quad \dot{z} = c_1\dot{q}_1 + c_2\dot{q}_2 + c_3\dot{q}_3 + \gamma$

where, for example, $b_3 = \partial y/\partial q_3$, etc.

Now squaring these expressions and eliminating $\dot{x}^2, \dot{y}^2, \dot{z}^2$ from $T = \frac{1}{2}m(\dot{x}^2 + \dot{y}^2 + \dot{z}^2)$, we finally get

$$\begin{aligned} T = \tfrac{1}{2}m[&(a_1^2 + b_1^2 + c_1^2)\dot{q}_1^2 + (a_2^2 + b_2^2 + c_2^2)\dot{q}_2^2 + (a_3^2 + b_3^2 + c_3^2)\dot{q}_3^2 \\ &+ 2(a_1a_2 + b_1b_2 + c_1c_2)\dot{q}_1\dot{q}_2 + 2(a_1a_3 + b_1b_3 + c_1c_3)\dot{q}_1\dot{q}_3 \\ &+ 2(a_2a_3 + b_2b_3 + c_2c_3)\dot{q}_2\dot{q}_3 + 2(a_1\alpha + b_1\beta + c_1\gamma)\dot{q}_1 \\ &+ 2(a_2\alpha + b_2\beta + c_2\gamma)\dot{q}_2 + 2(a_3\alpha + b_3\beta + c_3\gamma)\dot{q}_3 + \alpha^2 + \beta^2 + \gamma^2] \end{aligned} \tag{2.48}$$

Note that T contains four types of terms: those containing $\dot{q}_r^2$, $\dot{q}_r\dot{q}_s$ and $\dot{q}_r$ alone as well as those which contain no coordinate velocities. However, each term throughout is dimensionally $|Mv^2|$.

The following example will give more meaning to the above expression. Referring to Fig. 2-5, Page 12, and assuming that the origin of the Q_1, Q_2 axes have a constant linear acceleration a (no rotation), it is seen that

$$\begin{aligned} x &= x_0 + v_x t + \tfrac{1}{2}a_x t^2 + q_1 \cos\alpha + q_2 \cos\beta \\ y &= y_0 + v_y t + \tfrac{1}{2}a_y t^2 + q_1 \sin\alpha + q_2 \sin\beta \end{aligned} \tag{2.49}$$

Differentiating and eliminating $\dot{x}^2$ and $\dot{y}^2$ from $\frac{1}{2}m(\dot{x}^2+\dot{y}^2)$, we have

$$\begin{aligned} T = \tfrac{1}{2}m\{\dot{q}_1^2 &+ \dot{q}_2^2 + 2\dot{q}_1\dot{q}_2\cos(\beta-\alpha) + 2[(v_x+a_x t)\cos\alpha + (v_y+a_y t)\sin\alpha]\dot{q}_1 \\ &+ 2[(v_x+a_x t)\cos\beta + (v_y+a_y t)\sin\beta]\dot{q}_2 + 2(v_x a_x + v_y a_y)t \\ &+ (a_x^2+a_y^2)t^2 + v_x^2 + v_y^2\} \end{aligned} \tag{2.50}$$

Inspection will show that (*2.50*) has just the form of (*2.48*). In fact, of course, all terms in (*2.50*) may be obtained from (*2.48*) by evaluating the a's, b's, c's, etc., from equations (*2.49*).

Relation (*2.50*) presents a good opportunity to emphasize a basic point. In spite of its complexity, the right side of this relation is merely $\frac{m}{2}\left(\frac{\Delta s}{\Delta t}\right)^2$, where Δs is a displacement of p, relative to the inertial X, Y frame.

(2) Now considering the more general case mentioned at the beginning of this section, transformation equations may be written as

$$x_i = x_i(q_1, q_2, \ldots, q_n, t), \quad \text{etc.} \tag{2.51}$$

where i runs from 1 to p and where it *is assumed that superfluous coordinates have been eliminated by equations of constraint.* Differentiating these relations, we have

$$\dot{x}_i = \sum_{k=1}^{n} a_{ik}\dot{q}_k + \alpha_i, \quad \dot{y}_i = \sum_{k=1}^{n} b_{ik}\dot{q}_k + \beta_i, \quad \dot{z}_i = \sum_{k=1}^{n} c_{ik}\dot{q}_k + \gamma_i \tag{2.52}$$

where, for example, $a_{ik} = \partial x_i/\partial q_k$, $\alpha_i = \partial x_i/\partial t$, etc. Note that $a_{ik} \neq a_{ki}$, etc.

By a straightforward process of squaring it may be shown that

$$\dot{x}_i^2 = \sum_{k=1}^{n}\sum_{l=1}^{n} a_{ik}a_{il}\dot{q}_k\dot{q}_l + 2\alpha_i\sum_{k=1}^{n} a_{ik}\dot{q}_k + \alpha_i^2 \tag{2.53}$$

Similar relations are obtained for $\dot{y}_i^2$ and $\dot{z}_i^2$. Eliminating $\dot{x}_i^2$, $\dot{y}_i^2$, $\dot{z}_i^2$ from

$$T = \frac{1}{2}\sum_{i=1}^{p} m_i(\dot{x}_i^2 + \dot{y}_i^2 + \dot{z}_i^2)$$

and collecting terms,

$$\begin{aligned} T = &\sum_{k=1}^{n}\sum_{l=1}^{n}\left[\frac{1}{2}\sum_{i=1}^{p} m_i(a_{ik}a_{il} + b_{ik}b_{il} + c_{ik}c_{il})\right]\dot{q}_k\dot{q}_l \\ &+ \sum_{k=1}^{n}\left[\sum_{i=1}^{p} m_i(\alpha_i a_{ik} + \beta_i b_{ik} + \gamma_i c_{ik})\right]\dot{q}_k + \frac{1}{2}\sum_{i=1}^{p} m_i(\alpha_i^2 + \beta_i^2 + \gamma_i^2) \end{aligned} \tag{2.54}$$

For brevity, the above may be written as

$$T = \sum_{k,l}^{n} A_{kl}\dot{q}_k\dot{q}_l + \sum_{k=1}^{n} B_k\dot{q}_k + C \tag{2.55}$$

where the meanings of A_{kl}, B_k and C are obvious. Note that if t does not enter equations (*2.51*) (no moving constraints or reference frames), $\alpha_i = \beta_i = \gamma_i = 0$. Hence (*2.55*) reduces to

$$T = \sum_{k,l}^{n} A_{kl}\dot{q}_k\dot{q}_l \tag{2.56}$$

It should be understood that (*2.51*), (*2.55*) and (*2.56*) are not mere academic relations which must forever remain in symbolic form. As shown by the example above, relations (*2.51*) (transformation equations with superfluous coordinates removed) can usually be written in explicit form for any particular problem. Hence expressions for a_{ik}, b_{ik}, etc., follow at once by partial differentiation. These quantities are, in general, algebraic relations involving the coordinates and possibly time. Thus we obtain expressions for A_{kl}, B_k and C and finally T. It should be noted that A_{kl}, B_k and C are not, in general, constants but functions of $q_1, q_2, \ldots, q_n$ and t. They are *not* functions of the $\dot{q}$'s. Note that $A_{kl} = A_{lk}$.

An expression for the kinetic energy of a rigid body, more useful than (*2.55*), is derived in Chapter 8. See equation (*8.10*), Page 148.

2.12 Acceleration Defined and Illustrated.

Lagrangian equations, without the necessity of giving any special consideration to the matter, *automatically take complete account of all accelerations.* (See Section 3.9, Page 48, and Section 4.8, Page 69.)

Nevertheless, due to the importance of this quantity in the basic principles and developments of dynamics, a brief review of its definition and the procedures for setting up general expressions will be given here.

(1) *General considerations.*

Imagine a point (or a particle) moving in space along the path AB, as shown in Fig. 2-24 below. At p_1 its velocity is $\boldsymbol{v}_1$. After an interval of time Δt it has arrived at p_2 where the velocity is now $\boldsymbol{v}_2$. In general, $\boldsymbol{v}_2$ has neither the same direction nor magnitude as $\boldsymbol{v}_1$. Thus the change, $\Delta\boldsymbol{v}$, represents a change not only in magnitude but direction as well. With this in mind, the acceleration of the moving point at p_1 is defined by

$$\boldsymbol{a} = \frac{\Delta \boldsymbol{v}_1}{\Delta t} \text{ for } \Delta t \to 0, \qquad \text{or} \qquad \boldsymbol{a} = \frac{d\boldsymbol{v}}{dt} \tag{2.57}$$

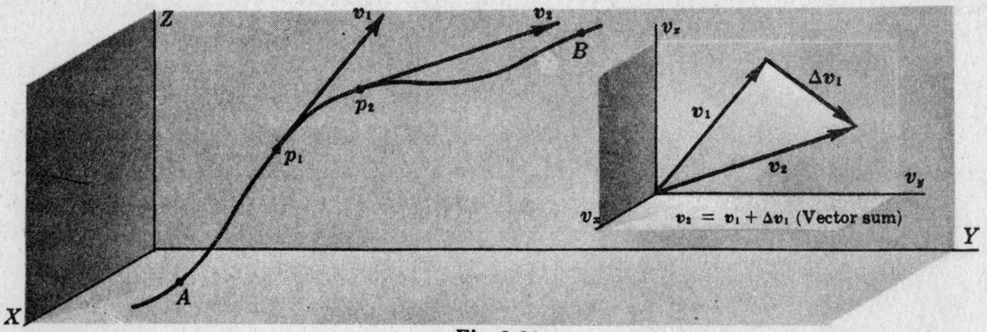

Fig. 2-24

It is clear that $\boldsymbol{a}$ is a vector quantity which has the direction of $\Delta\boldsymbol{v}_1$ for $\Delta t \to 0$. This definition brings out the important fact that the acceleration vector does not in general point in the direction of motion. (Note that the velocity vector $\boldsymbol{v} = ds/dt$, defined in Section 2.7, Page 19, is always in the "direction of the path".)

Acceleration as defined by (*2.57*) is without reference to any particular coordinate system. But since the rectangular components of Δv are $\Delta\dot{x}, \Delta\dot{y}, \Delta\dot{z}$, its magnitude is given by $(\Delta v)^2 = (\Delta\dot{x})^2 + (\Delta\dot{y})^2 + (\Delta\dot{z})^2$. Dividing by $(\Delta t)^2$ and passing to the limit the magnitude of $\boldsymbol{a}$ is given by

$$a^2 = \ddot{x}^2 + \ddot{y}^2 + \ddot{z}^2 \tag{2.58}$$

Clearly its direction is determined by the direction cosines $\ddot{x}/a, \ddot{y}/a, \ddot{z}/a$.

(2) *Acceleration expressed in generalized coordinates.*

The magnitude of a as given by (*2.58*) as well as its direction cosines can be expressed in any other coordinates by means of transformation equations. Examples:

(*a*) Applying relations (*2.6*), Page 11, $\ddot{x}, \ddot{y}, \ddot{z}$ and hence finally (*2.58*) can be written in terms of spherical coordinates.

(*b*) Using the last two equations of (*2.13*), Page 14, and (*2.58*), the acceleration of m_2, Fig. 2-10, can be expressed in terms of r_1, r_2, θ, ϕ and their time derivatives.

(*c*) By means of (*2.32*) and (*2.58*) one can easily obtain a relation for the acceleration of the particle, shown in Fig. 2-21, Page 22, *relative to the stationary axes* X_1Y_1 *but expressed in terms of the moving coordinates* x_2, y_2, *their time derivatives and the time.* (Time enters explicitly when θ_1 and θ_2 are assumed to change in some known manner with time.)

(3) *Components of total acceleration along any line.*

The component a' of acceleration along any line having direction cosines l, m, n is given by (see equation *2.33*)

$$a' = l\ddot{x} + m\ddot{y} + n\ddot{z} \tag{2.59}$$

which can, of course, be expressed in other coordinates.

(*a*) Consider the expressions for (a_r, a_θ, a_ϕ), components of a along coordinate lines in the spherical system; that is, in the directions of line elements indicated by Δr, $r\,\Delta\theta$, $r \sin\theta\,\Delta\phi$ of Fig. 2-20, Page 20. We shall look at a_ϕ in detail. Cosines of the angles which $r \sin\theta\,\Delta\phi$ makes with the X, Y, Z axes are $-\sin\phi$, $\cos\phi$, 0 respectively. Hence $a_\phi = -\ddot{x}\sin\phi + \ddot{y}\cos\phi$. Eliminating $\ddot{x}, \ddot{y}$ by means of (*2.6*), we finally get after considerable tedious work the following expression (and similarly those for a_r and a_θ),

$$\begin{aligned} a_\phi &= r\ddot{\phi}\sin\theta + 2\dot{r}\dot{\phi}\sin\theta + 2r\dot{\phi}\dot{\theta}\cos\theta \\ a_r &= \ddot{r} - r\dot{\theta}^2 - r\dot{\phi}^2\sin^2\theta \\ a_\theta &= r\ddot{\theta} + 2\dot{r}\dot{\theta} - r\dot{\phi}^2\sin\theta\cos\theta \end{aligned} \tag{2.60}$$

(*b*) Referring to Fig. 2-21, Page 22, let us determine the component of the total acceleration of m (relative to the fixed axes X_1, Y_1) along the radius r. Here $a_r = l\ddot{x}_1 + m\ddot{y}_1$ where l, m are direction cosines of r relative to the stationary axes; that is, $l = \cos\beta$, $m = \sin\beta$ (see the last example given under Section 2.7(3)). Applying

$$x_1 = s\cos\theta_1 + r\cos\beta, \qquad y_1 = s\sin\theta_1 + r\sin\beta$$

we obtain

$$a_r = \ddot{r} - r(\dot{\theta}_1 + \dot{\theta}_2 + \alpha)^2 + s\ddot{\theta}_1\sin(\theta_2 + \alpha) - s\dot{\theta}_1^2\cos(\theta_2 + \alpha) \tag{2.61}$$

When the manner in which the tables are made to rotate is specified, a_r contains t explicitly.

As shown in Section 3.9, Chapter 3, these and other expressions for acceleration can easily and quickly be determined from Lagrange's equations.

2.13 "Virtual Displacements" and "Virtual Work."

Virtual displacements and virtual work play a very important part, as a *means to an end,* in the basic developments of analytical dynamics. But after serving a useful purpose they fade from the picture.

(1) *Real and Virtual Displacements; Virtual Work.*

For simplicity consider a particle of mass m constrained to move in contact with a rough surface which is itself in motion. Acted upon by a force F (F = vector sum of an applied force, a frictional force, and a force of constraint*), m moves along some definite path (determined by Newton's laws) in space and at the same time traces a line on the surface. During any given interval of time dt, m undergoes a specific displacement ds (dx, dy, dz) measured say relative to stationary axes. Here ds is referred to as an "actual" or "real" displacement.

Consider now any arbitrary infinitesimal displacement δs $(\delta x, \delta y, \delta z)$ *not necessarily along the above mentioned path.* In this case δs is referred to as a *virtual displacement.* For convenience in what follows, we mention three classes of such displacements: (*a*) δs in any direction in space, completely disregarding the surface (this may require a slight distortion of the constraint); (*b*) δs in any direction on the moving surface and (*c*) in any direction on the surface now regarded as stationary.

For a virtual displacement of any type the "virtual work" done by F is given by

$$\delta W = F\,\delta s \cos(F, \delta s) = F_x\,\delta x + F_y\,\delta y + F_z\,\delta z$$

and considering a system of p particles acted on by forces $F_1, F_2, \ldots, F_p$ and given displacements $\delta s_1, \delta s_2, \ldots, \delta s_p$, the total virtual work is

$$\delta W = \sum_{i=1}^{p} (F_{x_i}\,\delta x_i + F_{y_i}\,\delta y_i + F_{z_i}\,\delta z_i) \qquad (2.62)$$

(2) *Manner in which expressions for δW become useful.*

The surprising importance of (*2.62*) stems eventually from the following considerations.

(*a*) Making use of $x_i = x_i(q_1, q_2, \ldots, q_{3p}, t)$, etc., (in which there is the maximum of $3p$ coordinates), $\delta x_i = \frac{\partial x_i}{\partial q_1}\delta q_1 + \frac{\partial x_i}{\partial q_2}\delta q_2 + \cdots + \frac{\partial x_i}{\partial q_{3p}}\delta q_{3p} + \frac{\partial x_i}{\partial t}\delta t$, etc., for δy_i and δz_i. For these displacements, which are not necessarily in conformity with constraints, δW *clearly contains work done by forces of constraint.*

(*b*) Employing relations (*2.21*), (see Section 2.6, Page 19),

$$\delta x_i = \frac{\partial x_i}{\partial q_1}\delta q_1 + \frac{\partial x_i}{\partial q_2}\delta q_2 + \cdots + \frac{\partial x_i}{\partial q_n}\delta q_n + \frac{\partial x_i}{\partial t}\delta t, \quad \text{etc.}$$

Such displacements *do not violate constraints,* but during the elapsed time δt moving frames and moving constraints have changed position slightly. Hence, as examples will show, δW again contains work done by forces of constraint.

(*c*) However, again determining displacements from (*2.21*) but *holding time fixed,* (that is, including in $\delta x_i, \delta y_i, \delta z_i$ changes in $q_1, q_2, \ldots, q_n$ only and not the terms $\frac{\partial x_i}{\partial t}\delta t$, $\frac{\partial y_i}{\partial t}\delta t$, $\frac{\partial z_i}{\partial t}\delta t$ which represent shifts in the positions of moving frames and constraints),

$$\delta x_i = \frac{\partial x_i}{\partial q_1}\delta q_1 + \frac{\partial x_i}{\partial q_2}\delta q_2 + \cdots + \frac{\partial x_i}{\partial q_n}\delta q_n, \quad \text{etc.} \qquad (2.63)$$

*Tensions in inextensible strings, belts or chain drives; compressions or tensions in connecting rods or supports; reactive forces exerted by smooth wires, rods or guides of any type along which masses may slide; reactive forces between smooth gear teeth, or forces exerted by smooth surfaces with which parts of the system are constrained to move in contact will here be referred to as "forces of constraint". It should be clearly understood that frictional forces are not included in this class. Frictional forces usually depend on forces of constraint and in general they do work (dissipated as heat).

These displacements are in conformity with constraints, and *the work done by the forces of constraint adds up to zero. In effect, forces of constraint have been eliminated from (2.62).*

While the truth of this statement is easily demonstrated with simple examples (Section 2.14), a general proof is usually not attempted. It may be regarded as a basic postulate.

Substituting (*2.63*) into (*2.62*) and collecting terms,

$$\delta W = \sum_{i=1}^{p}\left(F_{x_i}\frac{\partial x_i}{\partial q_1} + F_{y_i}\frac{\partial y_i}{\partial q_1} + F_{z_i}\frac{\partial z_i}{\partial q_1}\right)\delta q_1 + \cdots$$
$$+ \sum_{i=1}^{p}\left(F_{x_i}\frac{\partial x_i}{\partial q_n} + F_{y_i}\frac{\partial y_i}{\partial q_n} + F_{z_i}\frac{\partial z_i}{\partial q_n}\right)\delta q_n \qquad (2.64)$$

Moreover, since the q's are independent, it is permissible to set all δq's equal to zero except one, say δq_r. Hence (*2.64*) becomes

$$\delta W_{q_r} = \sum_{i=1}^{p}\left(F_{x_i}\frac{\partial x_i}{\partial q_r} + F_{y_i}\frac{\partial y_i}{\partial q_r} + F_{z_i}\frac{\partial z_i}{\partial q_r}\right)\delta q_r \qquad (2.65)$$

This likewise contains no forces of constraint even though $\delta s_1, \delta s_2, \ldots, \delta s_p$ are now restricted to values such that q_r only is varied. As illustrated below, in finding an explicit expression for δW_{q_r}, forces of constraint (which originally were assumed to be a part of $F_{x_i}, F_{y_i}, F_{z_i}$) *may be completely ignored.*

This method of eliminating forces of constraint is one of the great achievements of the Lagrangian method.

The above considerations are of vital importance in D'Alembert's principle. The manner in which they become an important part of an actual down-to-earth method of setting up equations of motion for almost any dynamical system, will be made clear in Chapters 3 and 4.

2.14 Examples Illustrating Statements (a), (b), (c) Above.

(i) Consider the simple arrangement shown in Fig. 2-25. The bead of mass m can slide along the smooth rod OA which is made to rotate about O in the XY plane with constant angular velocity ω. A force f_1 due to the spring, the force of constraint f_2 (reactive force of the rod) and applied force f_3 are acting on m. Let us consider three cases:

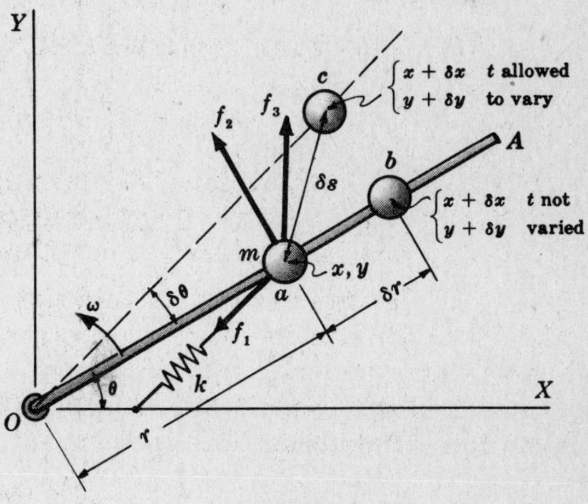

Fig. 2-25

1. Imagine m given a perfectly arbitrary displacement δs as if it were free. (This could involve distorting the rod a bit.) Thus, since in general f_1, f_2, f_3 would each have a component along δs, each force will do work in accord with statement (*a*).

2. Considering m confined to the rod we write $x = r\cos\omega t$, $y = r\sin\omega t$. Hence for an arbitrary displacement in which the bead remains on the rod and time varies (account is taken of the rod's motion),

$$\delta x = \delta r\cos\omega t - r\omega\,\delta t\sin\omega t, \qquad \delta y = \delta r\sin\omega t + r\omega\,\delta t\cos\omega t$$

Here $\delta s = ac$, Fig. 2-25. The constraint is not violated but since each force has a component along ac, each does work in accord with (*b*).

3. Suppose we neglect the rotation of the rod (in effect t is held fixed). δs has components

$\delta x = \delta r \cos \omega t$, $\delta y = \delta r \sin \omega t$. This displacement is along the rod: $\delta s = \delta r = ab$. Clearly f_1 and f_3 do work but f_2 (assumed normal to the rod) does no work, in accord with (*c*).

(ii) Consider the system shown in Fig. 2-9, Page 13. Here τ_1, τ_2, etc., refer to tensions in the inextensible cords. We shall assume that each pulley has mass and thus $\tau_1 \neq \tau_3$, $\tau_2 \neq \tau_4$, $\tau_2 + \tau_4 \neq \tau_3$. Now for a general virtual displacement of each mass vertically (assuming strings always under tension), (*2.62*) becomes

$$\begin{aligned} \delta W \;=\; & (m_1 g - \tau_1)\delta s_1 \;+\; (m_3 g + \tau_2 + \tau_4 - \tau_3)\delta s_3 \\ & + (m_2 g - \tau_2)\delta s_2 \;+\; (m_4 g - \tau_4)\delta s_4 \;+\; (\tau_3 - \tau_1)R_1\,\delta\theta_1 \;+\; (\tau_4 - \tau_2)R_2\,\delta\theta_2 \end{aligned} \tag{2.66}$$

where θ_1 and θ_2 are angular displacements of the upper and lower pulleys respectively and m_3 is regarded as the entire mass of the lower pulley.

Regarding the above displacements as arbitrary (not in conformity with constraints), it is clear that work done by the forces of constraints (tensions) *will not in general be zero.*

Taking account of constraints by the relations

$$\delta s_3 = -\delta s_1, \quad \delta y_4 = 2\,\delta s_1 - \delta y_2, \quad R_1\,\delta\theta_1 = -\delta s_1, \quad R_2\,\delta\theta_2 = \delta y_2 - \delta s_1, \quad \delta y_4 = -\delta s_4, \quad \delta s_2 = -\delta y_2$$

equation (*2.66*) becomes, after eliminating $\delta s_3, \delta s_4, \delta\theta_1, \delta\theta_2$,

$$\begin{aligned} \delta W \;=\; & (m_1 g - \tau_1 - m_3 g - \tau_4 - \tau_2 + \tau_3 + 2\tau_4 - 2m_4 g - \tau_3 + \tau_1 - \tau_4 + \tau_2)\delta s_1 \\ & + (\tau_2 - m_2 g - \tau_4 + m_4 g + \tau_4 - \tau_2)\delta y_2 \end{aligned} \tag{2.67}$$

or

$$\delta W \;=\; (m_1 g - m_3 g - 2m_4 g)\delta s_1 \;+\; (m_4 g - m_2 g)\delta y_2 \tag{2.68}$$

Equations (*2.67*) or (*2.68*) correspond to (*2.64*). It is clear that δs_1 and δy_2 are in conformity with constraints and that the work done by the tensions adds up to zero. Moreover, it is seen that, *for a variation of either* s_1 *or* y_2 *alone, the work of the tensions is zero,* which is in accord with the statement following equation (*2.65*).

It is important to note that we could, for example, just as well have regarded y_3 and q_1 as the independent coordinates of the system. In this case it is again easily shown that, for a variation of either y_3 or q_1 alone, the work done by the tensions is zero.

(iii) Suppose the support AB, shown in Fig. 2-9, is made to move vertically in some known manner with time; for example, $h = h_0 + C \sin \omega t$. Then from relations (*2.12*), $y_1 = C \sin \omega t + s_4 + q_1 + C_1$, $y_2 = C \sin \omega t - s_4 - 2q_1 + C_2$, etc., where C_1 and C_2 are constants. Now the reader can easily show that for a variation of either s_4 or q_1, *holding t fixed,* the work done by the tensions adds up to zero; this is also in accord with the last part of statement (*c*).

Summary and Remarks

1. Coordinate Systems and Transformation Equations (Section 2.2)

One of the first steps in the treatment of any problem is that of selecting appropriate coordinates. Transformation equations play an important part in expressing kinetic energy, acceleration and many other quantities in terms of the chosen coordinates. Many theoretical developments depend on the use of transformation equations.

2. Generalized Coordinates and Degrees of Freedom (Section 2.3)

"Generalized coordinate" is a convenient term for any coordinate whatever. The use of $q_1, q_2, \ldots, q_n$ to designate generalized coordinates is almost universal and has decided advantages.

Before actual work can begin on a problem the number of "degrees of freedom" of the system must be known. This is determined by inspection.

3. Degrees of Constraint, Equations of Constraint, Superfluous Coordinates (Sections 2.4, 2.5, 2.6)

An understanding of the physics and geometry of constraints and how each "degree of constraint" can be expressed by a corresponding "equation of constraint" is imperative.

Through the use of these equations, "superfluous coordinates" can be eliminated from transformation equations, kinetic energy, potential energy and other quantities.

4. Velocity in Generalized Coordinates (Section 2.7)

The velocity of a particle can be expressed in terms of any convenient generalized coordinates and their time derivatives. Frequently t enters. Without a knowledge of how this is done, further steps can not be taken. Hence the importance of Section 2.7.

5. Work and Kinetic Energy (Sections 2.8, 2.9, 2.10, 2.11)

An understanding of the correct definitions of work and kinetic energy is imperative.

It is extremely important to realize that *kinetic energy must be reckoned relative to inertial space.* We always begin by writing T in inertial coordinates. This can then, if so desired, be written in terms of any other coordinates (inertial, non-inertial, or mixed) by means of proper transformation equations.

6. Acceleration (Section 2.12)

The treatment here given is for the purpose of making clear the basic definition of acceleration and demonstrating how its component along any line can be expressed in generalized coordinates. However, in spite of the basic part which acceleration plays in all equations of motion, the above technique is not of vital concern since, as shown in Section 3.10, Page 50, *components of acceleration are automatically taken care of by the Lagrangian equations.*

7. Virtual Displacements and Virtual Work (Sections 2.13, 2.14)

The general methods employed in this book (which, for analytical dynamics, have tremendous advantages over conventional vector methods) depend on the concepts and use of virtual displacements and virtual work. Many important developments which follow make use of the treatment given above.

Final word: As will be evident in Chapters 3 and 4, items **1** to **7** above (excepting **6**) constitute the necessary background material for an understanding of Lagrange's equations and indeed are just the preliminary steps which must be followed in applying these equations.

Problems

Answers to the following problems are given on Page 350.

2.1. Show that the following are transformation equations relating the usual plane polar coordinates r, θ to the q_1, q_2 coordinates shown in Fig. 2-5, Page 12:

$$r \cos\theta = q_1 \cos\alpha + q_2 \cos\beta$$
$$r \sin\theta = q_1 \sin\alpha + q_2 \sin\beta$$

2.2. Write out equations relating the r_2, α coordinates, Fig. 2-6, Page 12, to the A, q coordinates (A is the shaded area and $q = \sin\theta$).

2.3. The family of parabolic lines, shown in Fig. 2-26, is given by $y = bx^2$ where b is constant for any one line. For specific values of x and b, corresponding values of y can be found. Hence in the XY plane, x and b may be regarded as coordinates.

(a) Show that in these coordinates, $T = \frac{1}{2}m[\dot{x}^2 + (\dot{b}x^2 + 2bx\dot{x})^2]$.

(b) Show that T may be expressed in b, θ coordinates, where θ is the usual angle in polar coordinates (r, θ), by eliminating r and $\dot{r}$ from $T = \frac{1}{2}m(\dot{r}^2 + r^2\dot{\theta}^2)$ with the relation $r = (\sin\theta)/(b\cos^2\theta)$.

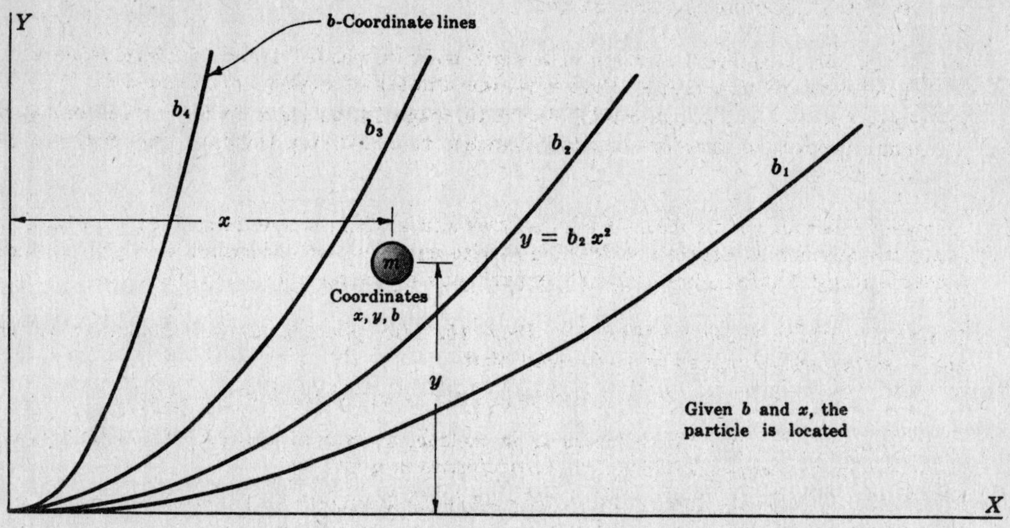

Fig. 2-26

2.4. (a) Write out equations relating coordinates y_1, y_2 to y, q_1, Fig. 2-8, Page 13.

(b) Repeat for y_1, y_2 and y, y_3.

Are q_1 and y_3 inertial?

2.5. The support on which D_1, Fig. 2-21, Page 22, is mounted is moved along the X_1 axis with constant acceleration a_x. Write transformation equations relating x_1, y_1 and x_2, y_2. See relations (2.32).

2.6. Referring to Fig. 2-13, Page 16, show that the rectangular coordinates x, y, z of m are related to the θ, ϕ, α coordinates by

$$x = (R\sin\theta - r\cos\alpha\cos\theta)\cos\phi + r\sin\alpha\sin\phi$$
$$y = (R\sin\theta - r\cos\alpha\cos\theta)\sin\phi - r\sin\alpha\cos\phi$$
$$z = R\cos\theta + r\cos\alpha\sin\theta$$

where $R = Oa$.

2.7. A railroad car is moving around a circular track of radius R with constant tangential acceleration a. Write out transformation equations relating a rectangular system of coordinates attached to the earth (origin at center of circle, Z_1 axis vertical) to a rectangular system attached to the car with Z_2 vertical and Y_2 tangent to the circle, pointing in the direction of motion. X_2 is along a continuation of R. Write the Newtonian equations of motion of a particle relative to X_2, Y_2, Z_2.

2.8. Relating x_1, y_1, z_1 of Problem 2.7 to spherical coordinates r, θ, ϕ attached to the car with origin at the origin of X_2, Y_2, Z_2, show that

$$x_1 = (R + r\sin\theta\cos\phi)\cos\beta - r\sin\theta\sin\phi\sin\beta$$
$$y_1 = (R + r\sin\theta\cos\phi)\sin\beta + r\sin\theta\sin\phi\cos\beta$$
$$z_1 = r\cos\theta$$

2.9. The origin of a set of rectangular axes is attached to the center of the earth, but the directions of the axes are fixed in space. Another rectangular set is fixed to the surface of the earth as shown in Fig. 14-2, Page 286. Write out transformation equations relating the two coordinate systems.

2.10. (a) A rigid wire of any known shape is fastened to disk D_2, Fig. 2-21. A bead is allowed to slide along the wire. Assuming $\theta_2 = \omega_2 t$, $\theta_1 = \omega_1 t$, how many degrees of freedom has the system?

(b) A flat board is fastened to a rigid body by means of a broad door hinge. This arrangement is suspended in any manner by springs. How many degrees of freedom has the system?

2.11. (a) Two rigid bodies, fastened together at one point by means of a ball joint, are free to move in space. How many degrees of freedom has the system?

(b) If one of the above masses is now fastened to a rigid support by another ball joint, how many degrees of freedom has the system?

2.12. (a) A "simple pendulum" consists of a rigid body suspended from an inextensible string. Motion is not confined to a plane. Determine the number of degrees of freedom.

(b) Regarding m_1 and m_2, shown in Fig. 2-10, Page 14, as rigid bodies instead of "particles", how many degrees of freedom has the system? r_1 and r_2 are constant and motion is not confined to a plane.

2.13. A uniform slender rod of mass M and length l slides with its ends in contact with the X and Y axes. State the number of degrees of freedom, write equations of constraint and give an expression for kinetic energy, having eliminated all superfluous coordinates.

2.14. Locating point p, shown in Fig. 2-1, Page 10, with plane polar coordinates (r, α) where $r = Op$ and α is the angle r makes with X_2, show that

$$x_1 = x_0 + r\cos(\alpha+\theta), \qquad y_1 = y_0 + r\sin(\alpha+\theta)$$

Assuming that the X_2, Y_2 frame is in motion, show that the velocity, v, of p relative to the X_1, Y_1 frame but expressed in moving coordinates is given by

$$\begin{aligned} v^2 = {} & \dot{x}_0^2 + \dot{y}_0^2 + \dot{r}^2 + r^2(\dot{\alpha}+\dot{\theta})^2 + 2\dot{r}[\dot{y}_0\sin(\alpha+\theta) + \dot{x}_0\cos(\alpha+\theta)] \\ & + 2r(\dot{\alpha}+\dot{\theta})[\dot{y}_0\cos(\alpha+\theta) - \dot{x}_0\sin(\alpha+\theta)] \end{aligned}$$

2.15. Referring to Problem 2.14, show that acceleration components of p, relative to the X_1, Y_1 frame, in the directions of Δr and $r\,\Delta\alpha$, are respectively

$$\begin{aligned} a_r &= \ddot{x}_0\cos(\alpha+\theta) + \ddot{y}_0\sin(\alpha+\theta) + \ddot{r} - r(\dot{\alpha}+\dot{\theta})^2 \\ a_\alpha &= \ddot{y}_0\cos(\alpha+\theta) - \ddot{x}_0\sin(\alpha+\theta) + 2\dot{r}(\dot{\alpha}+\dot{\theta}) + r(\ddot{\alpha}+\ddot{\theta}) \end{aligned}$$

2.16. Two particles m_1 and m_2 fastened to the ends of a light rigid rod of length l are allowed to move in a plane. Determine the number of degrees of freedom. Write out equations of constraint. Write an expression for the total kinetic energy of the masses in terms of r, θ, ϕ, where r is the distance from the origin to m_1, θ is the angle between the X axis and r, and ϕ the angle between the X axis and the rod, eliminating all but the necessary coordinates. See equations (*2.26*).

Write T for the above using rectangular coordinates of the center of mass and ϕ. See equation (*2.47*).

2.17. The uniform slender rods, Fig. 2-27, having masses M_1, M_2, M_3 and moments of inertia I_1, I_2, I_3 about normal axes through the centers of mass, are hinged as shown. Centers of mass are indicated at points P_1, P_2, P_3. Motion is confined to the XY plane. Write out T in terms of the coordinates indicated. Write out equations by means of which superfluous coordinates may be eliminated from T. How many superfluous coordinates are there? Do springs S_1 and S_2 affect the degrees of freedom of the system?

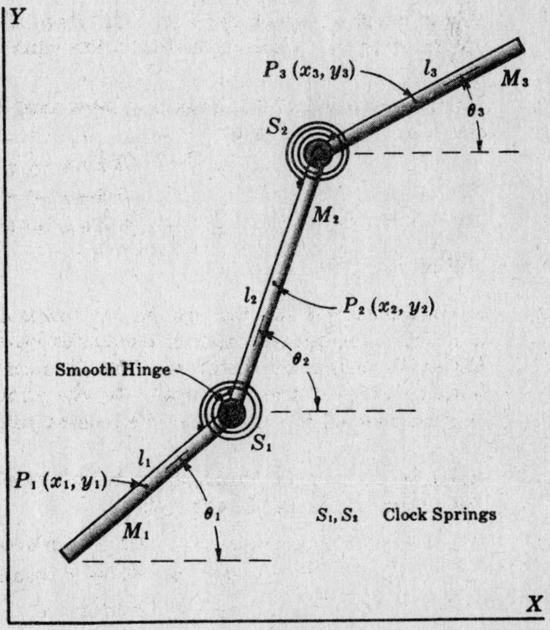

Fig. 2-27

2.18. Particles of mass m_1 and m_3, shown in Fig. 2-28 below, are fastened to the ends of a light rod having a length l. A bead of mass m_2 is free to slide along the rod between m_1 and m_3. Point p is the center of mass of m_1 and m_3, not including m_2. I is the moment of inertia of the m_1, m_3 rod arrangement about an axis perpendicular to the rod and passing through p. All motion is considered in a plane.

(*a*) Write equations giving the position of m_2 in terms of x, y, s, θ.

(*b*) Write out the kinetic energy of the system in coordinates x, y, θ, s.

2.19. Assuming that m_1 and m_2, shown in Fig. 2-9, Page 13, are monkeys climbing up the ropes, determine the degrees of freedom of the system. Write out an expression for T, neglecting masses of monkeys' arms. I_1, I_2 are moments of inertia of D_1, D_2 respectively.

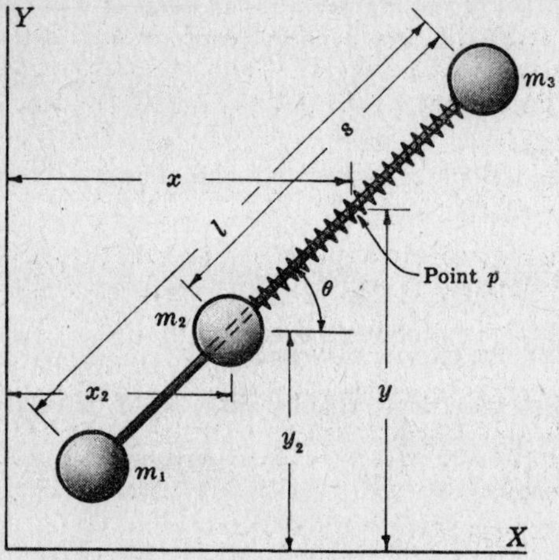

Fig. 2-28

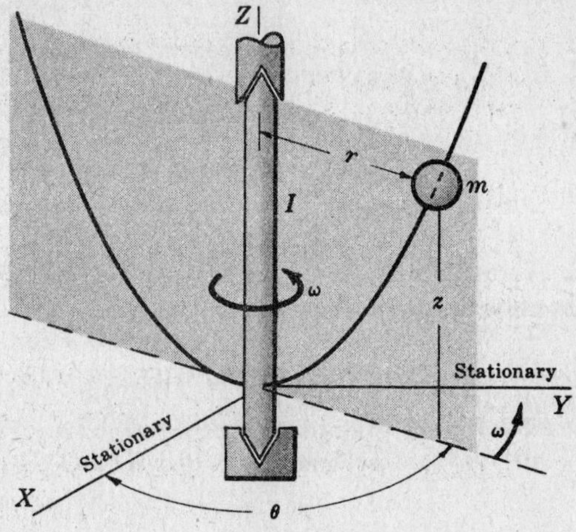

Fig. 2-29

2.20. A rigid parabolic wire having equation $z = ar^2$ is fastened to the vertical shaft of Fig. 2-29 above. A bead of mass m is free to slide along the wire. (*a*) Assuming the vertical shaft, which together with the wire has a moment of inertia I, is free to rotate as indicated, write out an expression for T for the system. (*b*) Now assuming the shaft is driven by a motor at a constant angular velocity $\dot{\theta} = \omega$, write out T.

2.21. Set up an expression for the kinetic energy of the system shown in Fig. 2-15, Page 16, in terms of the s distances. Which of these coordinates are non-inertial?

2.22. Write an expression for the kinetic energy of the three masses, shown in Fig. 2-30 below, using the three coordinates y_1, y_2, y_3 and assuming vertical motion only. Would the expression for T be altered if the springs were removed? y_1 is the distance from the X axis to the center of mass of the system.

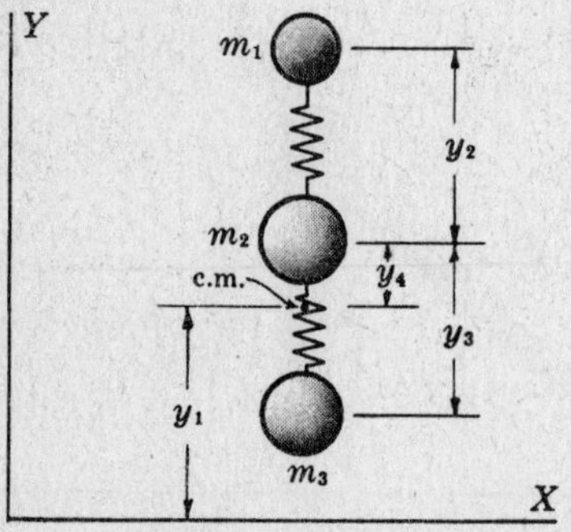

Fig. 2-30

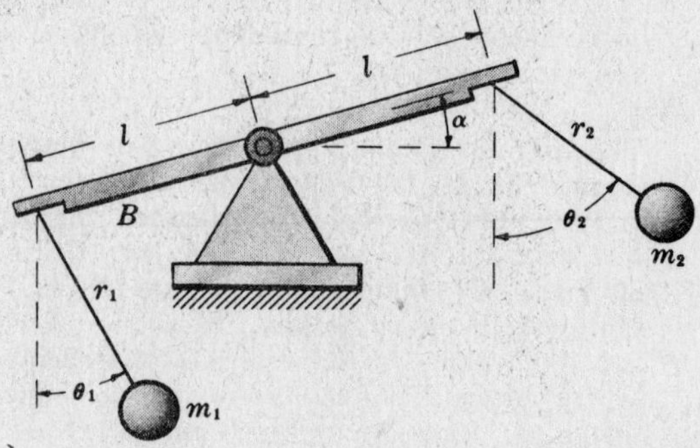

Fig. 2-31

2.23. Masses m_1 and m_2 are suspended by inextensible strings from the ends of the bar B, Fig. 2-31 above. The bar is free to rotate about a horizontal axis as shown. Its moment of inertia about this axis is I. Assuming all motion is confined to the plane of the paper, determine the degrees of freedom of the system and write an expression for T.

2.24. The entire framework in which m_1, shown in Fig. 2-14, Page 16, slides is made to move vertically upward with a constant acceleration a. Assuming that m_2 swings in a plane with r constant, show that

$$T = \tfrac{1}{2}[m_2 r^2 \dot{\theta}^2 + (m_1 + m_2)\dot{y}^2 - 2m_2 r\dot{\theta}\dot{y}\sin\theta + 2m_2 r\dot{\theta}(v_0 + at)\sin\theta - 2(m_1+m_2)\dot{y}(v_0+at) + (m_1+m_2)(v_0+at)^2]$$

where v_0 is the vertical velocity of the framework at $t = 0$. Compare the form of this expression for T with that of equation (*2.48*). Are coordinates y and θ inertial?

2.25. A pendulum bob is suspended by a coil spring from the ceiling of a railway car which is moving with constant angular velocity around a circular track of radius R. The bob is allowed to move in a vertical plane which makes an angle α with R. Show that the kinetic energy of the bob is given by

$$T = \tfrac{1}{2}m(\dot{x}^2 + \dot{y}^2 + \dot{z}^2)$$

where $x = R\cos\omega t + r\sin\theta\cos(\omega t + \alpha)$, $y = R\sin\omega t + r\sin\theta\sin(\omega t + \alpha)$, $z = C - r\cos\theta$.

The origin of the rectangular system is taken at the center of the circle with Z vertical. r is the length of the pendulum, to be regarded as variable, and θ is the angle made by r with a vertical line through the point of support.

2.26. The disk D, shown in Fig. 2-32 below, is free to rotate with angular velocity $\dot{\phi}$ about the horizontal axis op. ϕ is measured from the line ab which remains parallel to the XY plane. The entire system is free to rotate about the vertical axis. A particle of mass m is fastened to the disk as indicated. Show that its kinetic energy is given by

$$T = \tfrac{1}{2}m(R^2\dot{\psi}^2 + r^2\dot{\phi}^2 - 2Rr\dot{\psi}\dot{\phi}\sin\phi + r^2\dot{\psi}^2\cos^2\phi)$$

Show by integration that the kinetic energy of the thin uniform disk is

$$T = \tfrac{1}{2}(MR^2 + I_1)\dot{\psi}^2 + \tfrac{1}{2}I_2\dot{\phi}^2$$

where M is the total mass of the disk, I_1 its moment of inertia about a diametrical line, and I_2 that about the horizontal axis on which it is supported.

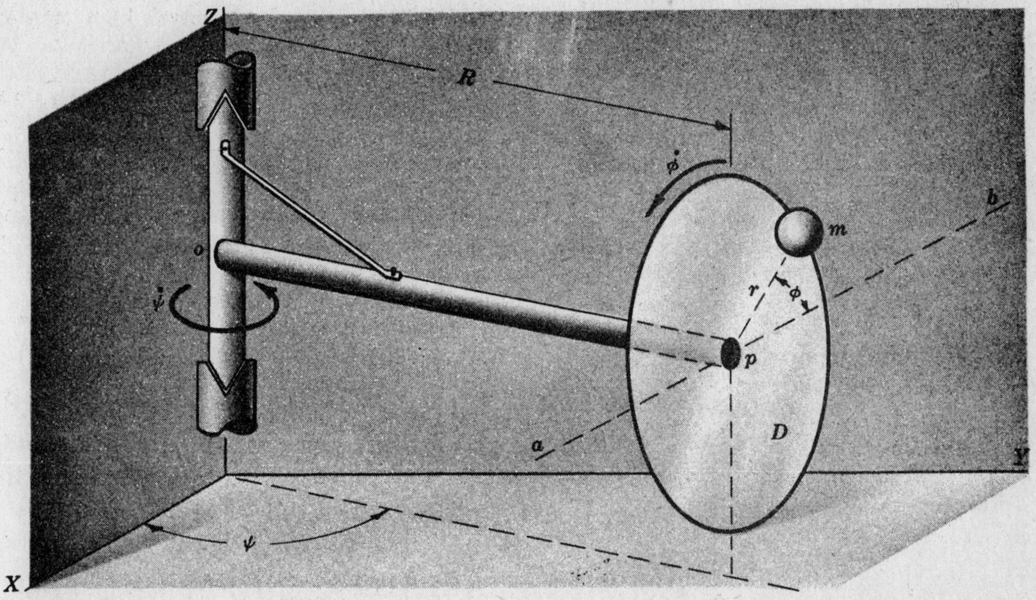

Fig. 2-32

2.27. The following problem is for the purpose of demonstrating that, even in the case of simple systems, expressions for T and equations of constraint may become somewhat involved. As the uniform disk (mass M, radius R), shown in Fig. 2-33 below, rolls with angular velocity $\dot{\theta}_2$ along the X axis, the slender rod (mass m, length $2l$) remains in contact with it without slipping. At the same time the lower end of the rod slides in contact with the X axis.

For the limited range over which the above conditions can hold, write out an expression for T in terms of $\theta_1, \theta_2, x_1, y_1, x_2$ and their time derivatives. How many superfluous coordinates are involved? Show that the equations of constraint are

$$(1) \quad R + R\cos\theta_1 = [L - R(\theta_1 + \theta_2 - {}_0\theta_1)]\sin\theta_1$$

$$(2) \quad x_2 = R\theta_2 + {}_0x_2 \qquad (3) \quad y_1 = l\sin\theta_1$$

$$(4) \quad x_1 + [L - l - R(\theta_1 + \theta_2 - {}_0\theta_1)]\cos\theta_1 + R\sin\theta_1 = x_2$$

where ${}_0\theta_1$ and ${}_0x_2$ are values of θ_1 and x_1 when point p is in contact at b.

Can T be expressed in terms of any one of the above coordinates? Try $x_2, \dot{x}_2$. Write T in terms of $\theta_1, \dot{\theta}_1$.

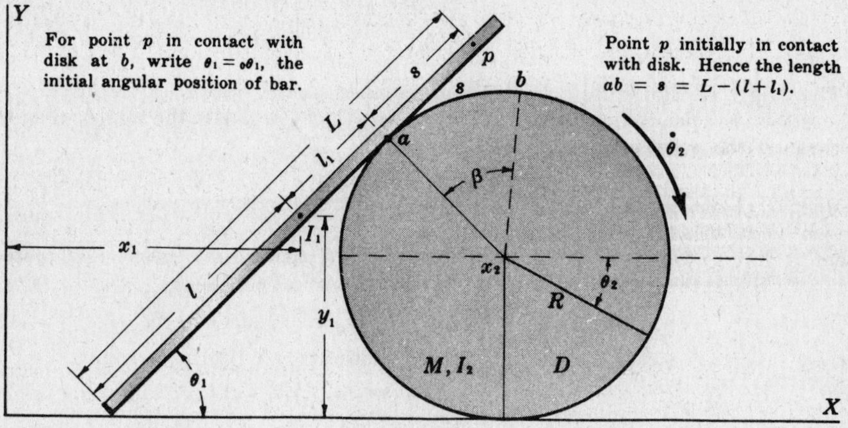
Y
For point p in contact with disk at b, write θ1 = 0θ1, the initial angular position of bar.
Point p initially in contact with disk. Hence the length ab = s = L − (l + l1).
p
s
s
b
L
a
l1
β
θ2
I1
x1
x2
θ2
R
l
y1
θ1
M, I2
D
X

Fig. 2-33

2.28. Referring to Fig. 2-11, Page 15, assume the smooth rod is rotating in a horizontal plane, driven by a motor. Of course, the bead will eventually fly off the end of the rod with considerable kinetic energy.

The reactive force between rod and bead is normal to the rod. Is it correct to conclude that, therefore, the reactive force does no work on m? Explain how the rod imparts energy to m.

2.29. Assume the upper pulley in Fig. 2-9, Page 13, is supported by a coil spring. The system now, of course, has three degrees of freedom. Imagining a general displacement of the entire system, write out an expression for δW regarding (for the moment) each rotation and vertical displacement as independent of every other. Now choosing y_1, q_2, y_4 as the independent coordinates of the system, show (following the steps outlined in Section 14) that in each of the expressions $\delta W_{y_1}, \delta W_{q_2}, \delta W_{y_4}$, the work done by the tensions in the ropes adds up to zero provided displacements are in conformity with constraints.

2.30. Masses m_1 and m_2, shown in Fig. 2-10, Page 14, are given arbitrary displacements. Applying (*2.62*) show that for r_1 and r_2 constants,

$$\begin{aligned}\delta W \;=\;& [(\tau_2\sin\phi - \tau_1\sin\theta)r_1\cos\theta + (\tau_1\cos\theta - \tau_2\cos\phi - m_1g)\,r_1\sin\theta \\ & - \tau_2 r_1\sin\phi\cos\theta + (\tau_2\cos\phi - m_2g)r_1\sin\theta]\delta\theta \\ & + [(\tau_2\cos\phi - m_2g)r_2\sin\phi - \tau_2 r_2\sin\phi\cos\phi]\delta\phi \\ =\;& -(m_1+m_2)\,gr_1\sin\theta\,\delta\theta - m_2gr_2\sin\phi\,\delta\phi\end{aligned}$$

and hence that the tensions τ_1 and τ_2 in the supporting strings (forces of constraint) do no work for a variation of either θ or ϕ alone.

CHAPTER 3

Lagrange's Equations of Motion for a Single Particle

3.1 Preliminary Considerations.

Any one of several formulations of the fundamental laws of dynamics may be taken as the basis for the derivation of the Lagrangian equations. In this text we begin with Newton's laws of motion, establish D'Alembert's equation, and from this finally derive Lagrange's relations. This approach is followed because it leads directly from familiar territory into unknown fields along a path in which it is easy to understand the physical and mathematical significance of each step.

As a further means of eliminating distracting details, we shall here limit ourselves to the derivation and consideration of Lagrange's equations for a single particle. The more general treatment, applicable to a system of many particles, is given in Chapter 4.

3.2 Derivation of Lagrange's equations for a single particle. No moving coordinates or moving constraints.

For the sake of clarity let us be rather specific by assuming that the motion of the particle under consideration is confined to a smooth surface such as a plane or a sphere. Hence it has two degrees of freedom, and there must be one equation of constraint. No frictional force is acting.

Let F, with components F_x, F_y, F_z, represent the vector sum of all forces (externally applied, those due to springs, gravity, the force of constraint, etc.) which may be acting on the particle. Then, assuming constant mass m and that x, y, z are inertial coordinates, we write the "free particle" Newtonian equations of motion:

$$F_x = m\ddot{x}, \qquad F_y = m\ddot{y}, \qquad F_z = m\ddot{z} \tag{3.1}$$

These equations are correct, even though the motion is constrained, because F_x, F_y, F_z are assumed to include whatever force of constraint may be acting.

At this point consider the work δW done by F when it is imagined that the particle undergoes (perhaps under the action of another force not included in F) a *completely arbitrary* infinitesimal displacement δs with components $\delta x, \delta y, \delta z$. (This is referred to as "virtual work" in accord with Section 2.13, Chapter 2.) Thus,

$$\delta W \quad = \quad F\,\delta s \cos(F, \delta s) \quad = \quad F_x\,\delta x \,+\, F_y\,\delta y \,+\, F_z\,\delta z \tag{3.2}$$

Note that, since F includes the force of constraint, (*3.2*) is correct even though δs may not be in conformity with the constraint. (That is, δs could be in a direction such that the surface with which m is in contact is slightly "distorted".) It should also be remembered that the right side of (*3.2*), as shown in Section 2.8, Page 22, takes full account of the fact that F and δs may not be in the same direction.

Now multiplying equations (*3.1*) through by $\delta x, \delta y, \delta z$ respectively and adding*, we get

$$m(\ddot{x}\,\delta x + \ddot{y}\,\delta y + \ddot{z}\,\delta z) \quad = \quad F_x\,\delta x + F_y\,\delta y + F_z\,\delta z \tag{3.3}$$

the right side of which is just the work δW done by F, and the left side may be interpreted as a corresponding slight change in the kinetic energy of m. (See again Section 2.8, Page 22.) We shall refer to this relation as "D'Alembert's equation".

Upon introducing generalized coordinates into (*3.3*) and carrying through a few mathematical manipulations, Lagrange's equations (*3.15*) and (*3.16*) are obtained. Since we assume the motion confined to a surface, two generalized coordinates q_1, q_2 are required. Hence making use of proper transformation equations and one equation of constraint, it is possible to express the x, y, z coordinates of m as functions of q_1 and q_2, indicated as follows (see Section 2.6, Page 19),

$$x = x(q_1, q_2), \quad y = y(q_1, q_2), \quad z = z(q_1, q_2) \tag{3.4}$$

Specific example to show the meaning of (3.4):

Suppose the confining surface is a sphere of constant radius $r = C$. In spherical coordinates, specific relations corresponding to (*3.4*) are then

$$x = C \sin\theta \cos\phi, \qquad y = C \sin\theta \sin\phi, \qquad z = C\cos\theta \tag{3.5}$$

Time does not enter (*3.4*) because we are here assuming stationary X, Y, Z axes and a stationary constraint.

The virtual displacements $\delta x, \delta y, \delta z$, will, for reasons stated below, be determined from (*3.4*). That is,

$$\delta x = \frac{\partial x}{\partial q_1}\delta q_1 + \frac{\partial x}{\partial q_2}\delta q_2, \qquad \delta y = \frac{\partial y}{\partial q_1}\delta q_1 + \frac{\partial y}{\partial q_2}\delta q_2, \qquad \delta z = \frac{\partial z}{\partial q_1}\delta q_1 + \frac{\partial z}{\partial q_2}\delta q_2 \tag{3.6}$$

Substituting (*3.6*) into D'Alembert's equation, (*3.3*), and collecting terms,

$$\begin{aligned} \delta W &= m\left(\ddot{x}\frac{\partial x}{\partial q_1} + \ddot{y}\frac{\partial y}{\partial q_1} + \ddot{z}\frac{\partial z}{\partial q_1}\right)\delta q_1 + m\left(\ddot{x}\frac{\partial x}{\partial q_2} + \ddot{y}\frac{\partial y}{\partial q_2} + \ddot{z}\frac{\partial z}{\partial q_2}\right)\delta q_2 \\ &= \left(F_x\frac{\partial x}{\partial q_1} + F_y\frac{\partial y}{\partial q_1} + F_z\frac{\partial z}{\partial q_1}\right)\delta q_1 + \left(F_x\frac{\partial x}{\partial q_2} + F_y\frac{\partial y}{\partial q_2} + F_z\frac{\partial z}{\partial q_2}\right)\delta q_2 \end{aligned} \tag{3.7}$$

At this point the student should become fully aware of certain basic facts.

(*a*) Since (*3.4*) are the equations of the confining surface, (*3.6*) represent displacements in conformity with the constraint. Hence δW of (*3.7*) is for a displacement δs in conformity with the constraint (along the surface). Considering again the sphere as a special case, $\delta x, \delta y, \delta z$ as determined from (*3.5*) are $\delta x = C\cos\theta\cos\phi\,\delta\theta - C\sin\theta\sin\phi\,\delta\phi$, etc., which clearly represent a displacement *on the sphere.*

(*b*) Coordinates q_1 and q_2 (θ and ϕ in *3.5*) are independently variable; that is, δq_1 and δq_2 may each be given arbitrary small values without violating the constraint.

*Note regarding equation (*3.3*). Multiplying relations (*3.1*) through by a, b, c respectively and adding, we get

$$m(\ddot{x}\,a + \ddot{y}\,b + \ddot{z}\,c) \quad = \quad F_x a + F_y b + F_z c$$

which is a true relation regardless of the quantities a, b, c. (They may represent constants of any value, displacements, velocities, or even functions of variables.) Hence, insofar as (*3.3*) is concerned, $\delta x, \delta y, \delta z$ are *completely arbitrary* quantities. However, for our purpose, we shall regard them as components of δs, the infinitesimal virtual displacement of m. Moreover, in what follows, we shall regard them as in conformity with the constraint. (When so considered (*3.3*) is often referred to as "D'Alembert's Principle".)

(c) As a result of (a) and (b) and the assumption that the constraint is smooth, the work done by the force of constraint when either coordinate alone or both together are varied, is zero. (See Section 2.13, Page 29.) For this reason the force of constraint need no longer be regarded as a part of F_x, F_y, F_z. *In other words, the force of constraint has been eliminated from the picture.* This is a very important fact.

Now since q_1 and q_2 are independently variable, let us fix our attention on δW_{q_1}, the work done when only q_1 is allowed to vary ($\delta q_2 = 0$). (3.7) then reduces to

$$\delta W_{q_1} = m\left(\ddot{x}\frac{\partial x}{\partial q_1} + \ddot{y}\frac{\partial y}{\partial q_1} + \ddot{z}\frac{\partial z}{\partial q_1}\right)\delta q_1 = \left(F_x\frac{\partial x}{\partial q_1} + F_y\frac{\partial y}{\partial q_1} + F_z\frac{\partial z}{\partial q_1}\right)\delta q_1 \qquad (3.8)$$

At this point we shall make use of the following relations, proofs of which are given below*. The reader need not, at the moment, be concerned with the proofs.

$$\ddot{x}\frac{\partial x}{\partial q_1} = \frac{d}{dt}\left(\dot{x}\frac{\partial x}{\partial q_1}\right) - \dot{x}\frac{d}{dt}\left(\frac{\partial x}{\partial q_1}\right) \qquad (3.9)$$

$$\frac{\partial x}{\partial q_1} = \frac{\partial \dot{x}}{\partial \dot{q}_1} \qquad (3.10)$$

$$\frac{d}{dt}\left(\frac{\partial x}{\partial q_1}\right) = \frac{\partial \dot{x}}{\partial q_1} \qquad (3.11)$$

Inserting (3.10) and (3.11) into (3.9), we have

$$\ddot{x}\frac{\partial x}{\partial q_1} = \frac{d}{dt}\left(\dot{x}\frac{\partial \dot{x}}{\partial \dot{q}_1}\right) - \dot{x}\frac{\partial \dot{x}}{\partial q_1} \qquad (3.12)$$

and a little consideration shows that this may be written as

$$\ddot{x}\frac{\partial x}{\partial q_1} = \frac{d}{dt}\left(\frac{\partial(\dot{x}^2/2)}{\partial \dot{q}_1}\right) - \frac{\partial(\dot{x}^2/2)}{\partial q_1} \qquad (3.13)$$

Substituting (3.13) and exactly similar relations involving y and z into (3.8), it follows that

$$\begin{aligned}\delta W_{q_1} &= \left[\frac{d}{dt}\left(\frac{\partial}{\partial \dot{q}_1}\frac{m(\dot{x}^2+\dot{y}^2+\dot{z}^2)}{2}\right) - \frac{\partial}{\partial q_1}\frac{m(\dot{x}^2+\dot{y}^2+\dot{z}^2)}{2}\right]\delta q_1 \\ &= \left(F_x\frac{\partial x}{\partial q_1} + F_y\frac{\partial y}{\partial q_1} + F_z\frac{\partial z}{\partial q_1}\right)\delta q_1\end{aligned} \qquad (3.14)$$

But $\frac{1}{2}m(\dot{x}^2+\dot{y}^2+\dot{z}^2)$ is the kinetic energy T of the particle. Hence we finally write

$$\frac{d}{dt}\left(\frac{\partial T}{\partial \dot{q}_1}\right) - \frac{\partial T}{\partial q_1} = F_x\frac{\partial x}{\partial q_1} + F_y\frac{\partial y}{\partial q_1} + F_z\frac{\partial z}{\partial q_1} \qquad (3.15)$$

---

*To prove relations (3.9), (3.10) and (3.11) we proceed as follows.

$$\frac{d}{dt}\left(\dot{x}\frac{\partial x}{\partial q_1}\right) = \ddot{x}\frac{\partial x}{\partial q_1} + \dot{x}\frac{d}{dt}\left(\frac{\partial x}{\partial q_1}\right)$$

which is (3.9). To obtain (3.10), it is seen that the time derivative of the first equation in (3.4) is $\dot{x} = \frac{\partial x}{\partial q_1}\dot{q}_1 + \frac{\partial x}{\partial q_2}\dot{q}_2$. Now differentiating this partially with respect to $\dot{q}_1$, we see that $\frac{\partial \dot{x}}{\partial \dot{q}_1} = \frac{\partial x}{\partial q_1}$. To prove (3.11) first note that since $x = x(q_1, q_2)$, the partial derivative $\partial x/\partial q_1$ is in general a function of both q_1 and q_2, that is, $\partial x/\partial q_1 = \phi(q_1, q_2)$. Differentiating this with respect to time, we get

$$\frac{d}{dt}\left(\frac{\partial x}{\partial q_1}\right) = \frac{\partial}{\partial q_1}\left(\frac{\partial x}{\partial q_1}\right)\dot{q}_1 + \frac{\partial}{\partial q_2}\left(\frac{\partial x}{\partial q_1}\right)\dot{q}_2$$

But from the above expression for $\dot{x}$ it follows that

$$\frac{\partial \dot{x}}{\partial q_1} = \frac{\partial}{\partial q_1}\left(\frac{\partial x}{\partial q_1}\right)\dot{q}_1 + \frac{\partial}{\partial q_1}\left(\frac{\partial x}{\partial q_2}\right)\dot{q}_2$$

Comparing the last two equations, it is seen that (3.11) is true.

Starting with (*3.7*) and considering the work δW_{q_2} associated with a variation in q_2 alone, it follows in exactly the same manner that

$$\frac{d}{dt}\left(\frac{\partial T}{\partial \dot{q}_2}\right) - \frac{\partial T}{\partial q_2} = F_x\frac{\partial x}{\partial q_2} + F_y\frac{\partial y}{\partial q_2} + F_z\frac{\partial z}{\partial q_2} \qquad (3.16)$$

Equations (*3.15*) and (*3.16*) are the Lagrangian equations which we set out to derive.

As a matter of convenience, write

$$F_x\frac{\partial x}{\partial q_r} + F_y\frac{\partial y}{\partial q_r} + F_z\frac{\partial z}{\partial q_r} = F_{q_r} \qquad (3.17)$$

where q_r is any one of the coordinates appearing in T and F_r is referred to as a "generalized force". Thus the Lagrangian equations take the compact form

$$\frac{d}{dt}\left(\frac{\partial T}{\partial \dot{q}_r}\right) - \frac{\partial T}{\partial q_r} = F_{q_r} \qquad (3.18)$$

As will be seen in the next chapter, Lagrange's equations have exactly the same form for a system of many particles.

For the case just considered (one particle having two degrees of freedom), there are two Lagrangian equations. If we should assume three degrees of freedom (no constraints on the particle), relations (*3.4*) would each contain q_1, q_2, q_3 and finally three Lagrangian equations would be obtained. *In general, there are as many Lagrangian equations of motion as there are degrees of freedom.*

However, (and this is important both from the point of view of basic ideas as well as certain applications) even though, in reality, the particle may have only two degrees of freedom, *three Lagrangian equations can still be written.* Disregarding the constraint, we write $x = x(q_1, q_2, q_3)$, etc. Now pretending that q_1, q_2, q_3 are each independently variable and following exactly the procedure outlined above, a Lagrangian equation corresponding to each of the three coordinates is obtained. There is, however, this important consideration. The displacement δs, corresponding to $\delta q_1, \delta q_2, \delta q_3$, is clearly not in conformity with the constraint. (In the special example we have carried along

$$\delta x = \delta r \sin\theta\cos\phi + r\,\delta\theta\cos\theta\cos\phi - r\,\delta\phi\sin\theta\sin\phi, \qquad \text{etc.}$$

which is not along the surface of the sphere since δr is not assumed to be zero.) Hence δW includes work done by the force of constraint (reaction between bead and surface), and components of this force must be included in F_x, F_y, F_z. *The force of constraint is not eliminated.* With this in mind, the three equations are perfectly correct.

For obvious reasons, therefore, all superfluous coordinates are usually eliminated from transformation equations and T. However, the above procedure of deliberately introducing superfluous coordinates may be made the basis of a powerful method for finding forces of constraint. See Chapter 12.

3.3 Synopsis of Important Details Regarding Lagrange's Equations.

(a) *Differential equations of motion.*

The differential equations of motion for any specific problem are, of course, obtained by performing the operations indicated in (*3.18*). But *for a system of n degrees of freedom, only n coordinates (and their time derivatives) should appear in T.* Superfluous coordinates must be eliminated as per Section 2.6, Page 19.

(b) *The meaning of generalized forces.*

The importance of a clear understanding of the simple physical meaning of generalized forces [relation (*3.17*)] can hardly be overemphasized either from the point of view of basic ideas or applications.

The expression $\delta W = F_x\,\delta x + F_y\,\delta y + F_z\,\delta z$ is a perfectly general equation for the element of work done by a force (components F_x, F_y, F_z) for a completely general displacement δs (components $\delta x, \delta y, \delta z$). But let us consider δW when δs is in conformity with the constraint and such that only q_1 varies ($\delta q_2 = 0$). Such a displacement is assured if $\delta x, \delta y, \delta z$ are obtained from (*3.4*), holding q_2 constant; that is,

$$\delta x = \frac{\partial x}{\partial q_1}\delta q_1, \quad \delta y = \frac{\partial y}{\partial q_1}\delta q_1, \quad \delta z = \frac{\partial z}{\partial q_1}\delta q_1$$

Substituting in the equation above for δW, we have $\delta W_{q_1} = \left(F_x\frac{\partial x}{\partial q_1} + F_y\frac{\partial y}{\partial q_1} + F_z\frac{\partial z}{\partial q_1}\right)\delta q_1$ which is clearly just $F_{q_1}\delta q_1$. Hence a generalized force F_{q_r} is a quantity of such nature that the product $F_{q_r}\delta q_r$ is the work done by driving forces (not including "inertial" forces or forces of constraint) when q_r *alone* is changed to the extent of $+\delta q_r$.

A generalized force is not always a force in the usual sense of the word. For example, if q_r is an angle θ, then F_θ must be a torque in order that $F_\theta\,\delta\theta$ be work. If q_r is the area A, Fig. 2-6, Page 12, $F_A\,\delta A = \delta W$ and clearly F_A must have the dimensions of force divided by length.

(c) *Technique of Obtaining Expressions for Generalized Forces.*

Either of three methods may be followed.

Substituting known expressions for F_x, F_y, F_z together with expressions for $\frac{\partial x}{\partial q_r}, \frac{\partial y}{\partial q_r}, \frac{\partial z}{\partial q_r}$ (obtained by differentiating *3.4*) into (*3.17*) gives F_{q_r}. F_x, F_y, F_z are usually not constant. They may be functions of coordinates, time, velocity, etc. In any case, expressions for these forces must be known from the nature of the problem in hand. This method is straightforward but may be long and tedious.

A second method, and one which in many cases is easier and more appealing from the point of view of what takes place physically, is as follows. Imagine one of the coordinates, q_r, increased to the extent of $+\delta q_r$, *all other coordinates which appear in T held fixed.* Now determine by any convenient manner the work δW_{q_r} done by any and all driving forces (disregard forces of constraint). The following relation is then solved for F_{q_r}:

$$\delta W_{q_r} = F_{q_r}\,\delta q_r \qquad (3.19)$$

In the determination of δW_{q_r}, work is taken positive or negative depending on whether the force or forces involved tend to increase or decrease q_r.

If the particle has two or three degrees of freedom it is sometimes more convenient to assume displacements $\delta q_1, \delta q_2, \delta q_3$ simultaneously and write out the corresponding total work, δW_{total}. It will take the form

$$\delta W_{\text{total}} = [\cdots]\delta q_1 + [\cdots]\delta q_2 + [\cdots]\delta q_3 \qquad (3.20)$$

where the brackets in each case are in the corresponding F_q.

Examples which follow will make clear this technique.

(d) *Regarding inertial forces in Lagrange's equations.*

The expression "inertial force", as here used, refers to (mass) × (acceleration). Terms such as $m\ddot{x}$, $mr\dot{\theta}^2$, $2m\omega\dot{x}$, etc., are examples.

A glance at the left side of (*3.3*) and succeeding equations through (*3.18*) will show that inertial forces appear exclusively in $\frac{d}{dt}\left(\frac{\partial T}{\partial \dot{q}_r}\right) - \frac{\partial T}{\partial q_r}$. Likewise it is clear that only applied forces appear in F_{q_r}. In other words, in writing out the Lagrangian equations of motion for any system, it should be remembered that the *left side of* (*3.18*) *automatically takes full account of all inertial forces while only driving forces are to be considered in finding expressions for* F_{q_r}. (Centrifugal force, Coriolis force, etc., are *never* included in F_{q_r}.)

3.4 Integrating the Differential Equations of Motion.

It is an unfortunate fact, but one which the applied scientist must face, that in a great majority of cases differential equations of motion are so involved that no methods of integration are available. In certain cases justifiable approximations and simplifying assumptions can be made which put the equations in integrable form.

Fortunately, however, computers are coming to the rescue. Through their use, graphical or numerical solutions to otherwise "hopeless" equations can now be obtained. Throughout this text, where possible and advantageous to do so, integrations are carried out in part or in full. But we are primarily concerned with setting up correct equations of motion.

3.5 Illustrative Examples.

The pedagogic value of a few examples may far exceed pages of discussion. It is the ultimate means of "explaining the explanations".

Example 3.1:

Consider the motion of a projectile relative to rectangular axes attached to the earth. Regarding these axes as inertial and treating the projectile as a particle of mass m, we write

$$T = \frac{m}{2}(\dot{x}^2 + \dot{y}^2 + \dot{z}^2) \qquad \text{from which} \qquad \frac{\partial T}{\partial \dot{x}} = m\dot{x}, \quad \frac{d}{dt}\left(\frac{\partial T}{\partial \dot{x}}\right) = m\ddot{x}, \quad \frac{\partial T}{\partial x} = 0$$

Hence $m\ddot{x} = F_x$. Likewise $m\ddot{y} = F_y$, $m\ddot{z} = F_z$. Neglecting air resistance, the only force is the pull of gravity in the negative direction of Z. Hence $\delta W_z = -mg\,\delta z$ and $F_z = -mg$. Clearly, $F_x = F_y = 0$. Thus finally $m\ddot{x} = 0$, $m\ddot{y} = 0$, $m\ddot{z} = -mg$. This simple example does not demonstrate the power of the Lagrangian method. It does show, however, that for a single particle treated in rectangular coordinates, the Lagrangian equations reduce to the Newtonian form.

Example 3.2: *Motion of a bead on a rigid parabolic wire.*

A bead of mass m is free to slide along a smooth parabolic wire the shape of which is given by $y = bx^2$. Since motion is confined to a line, the bead has only one degree of freedom. There are two equations of constraint, $y = bx^2$ and $z = C$. The velocity $\dot{z}$ and either $\dot{y}$ or $\dot{x}$ can be eliminated from $T = \frac{1}{2}m(\dot{x}^2 + \dot{y}^2 + \dot{z}^2)$. Eliminating $\dot{y}$, $T = \frac{1}{2}m\dot{x}^2(1 + 4b^2x^2)$. Applying Lagrange's equation,

$$\frac{\partial T}{\partial \dot{x}} = m\dot{x}(1 + 4b^2x^2), \qquad \frac{d}{dt}\left(\frac{\partial T}{\partial \dot{x}}\right) = m\ddot{x}(1 + 4b^2x^2) + 8m\dot{x}^2xb^2, \qquad \frac{\partial T}{\partial x} = 4m\dot{x}^2xb^2$$

Hence finally

$$m\ddot{x}(1 + 4b^2x^2) + 4m\dot{x}^2xb^2 = F_x$$

Applying (*3.19*) we now find an expression for F_x which, as will be seen, is not merely the x component of a force. Let us assume that the Y axis is vertical and the only force acting (we need not consider the force of constraint) is the pull of gravity. If the bead is given a displacement $+\delta x$ it, of necessity, must move up the wire a corresponding distance $+\delta y$ and the work thus done by gravity is $\delta W = -mg\,\delta y$. But from the equation of constraint, $\delta y = 2bx\,\delta x$. Hence $\delta W = -2mgbx\,\delta x = F_x\,\delta x$, $F_x = -2mgbx$, and the completed equation of motion is

$$m\ddot{x}(1 + 4b^2x^2) + 4m\dot{x}^2xb^2 = -2mgbx$$

As an extension of this, imagine that we pull with constant force f on a string which is attached to the bead. Let us assume that the string is in the plane of the parabola and that its direction, determined by direction cosines α, β, is maintained constant. Thus for a small displacement,

$$\delta W = -mg\,\delta y + \alpha f\,\delta x + \beta f\,\delta y \qquad \text{see equation (2.35)}$$

But again, $\delta y = 2bx\,\delta x$. Hence

$$\delta W = (-2mgbx + \alpha f + 2bx\beta f)\delta x \qquad \text{and} \qquad F_x = 2bx(\beta f - mg) + \alpha f$$

The left hand side of the equation of motion is unchanged.

Note that all of the above results can just as well be expressed in terms of y and $\dot{y}$ instead of x and $\dot{x}$, by first eliminating $\dot{x}$ from T, etc.

Example 3.3: *Motion of a particle on a smooth horizontal table under the action of a spring.*

A string attached to the particle passes through a hole in a smooth horizontal table and is fastened to a light spring as shown in Fig. 3-1. The point to which the lower end of the spring is rigidly attached is so placed that when m is at the hole the spring is unstretched.

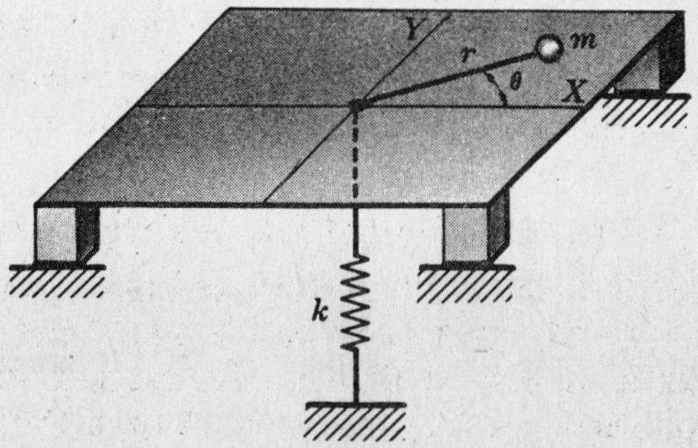

Fig. 3-1

The system has two degrees of freedom and, using polar coordinates, $T = \frac{1}{2}m(\dot{r}^2 + r^2\dot{\theta}^2)$. The only force acting on the mass is that of the spring. Hence for an arbitrary displacement of the particle, $\delta W = -kr\,\delta r$ where k is the usual Hooke's law constant of the spring. No force is acting perpendicular to r. Therefore Lagrange's equations give

$$(1) \quad m\ddot{r} - mr\dot{\theta}^2 = -kr, \qquad (2) \quad \frac{d}{dt}(mr^2\dot{\theta}) = 0$$

From (2) we see that $mr^2\dot{\theta} = p_\theta$ = angular momentum = constant. Eliminating $\dot{\theta}$ from (1), there results an equation involving $\ddot{r}$ and r only, which may be integrated by standard methods.

A treatment of this problem in rectangular coordinates demonstrates how, at times, equations of motion may be considerably simplified by the proper choice of coordinates. Writing

$$T = \tfrac{1}{2}m(\dot{x}^2 + \dot{y}^2) \qquad \text{and} \qquad \delta W = -kr\,\delta r = -k(x\,\delta x + y\,\delta y)$$

it follows that $m\ddot{x} = -kx$, $m\ddot{y} = -ky$. Hence the motion is compounded of two simple harmonic motions at right angles, each having the same period. Thus the path is, in general, that of an ellipse with the origin at its center.

Example 3.4: *The pendulum bob attached to a rubber band,* Fig. 3-2.

For motion in a plane the bob, regarded as a particle, has two degrees of freedom. Using r and θ as coordinates, $T = \frac{1}{2}m(\dot{r}^2 + r^2\dot{\theta}^2)$ from which it follows that $m\ddot{r} - mr\dot{\theta}^2 = F_r$ and $mr^2\ddot{\theta} + 2mr\dot{r}\dot{\theta} = F_\theta$. Let us here illustrate two methods of obtaining generalized forces. Imagine the bob given an arbitrary displacement δs in which θ and r each undergo positive changes. The work done by gravity and the rubber band is given by

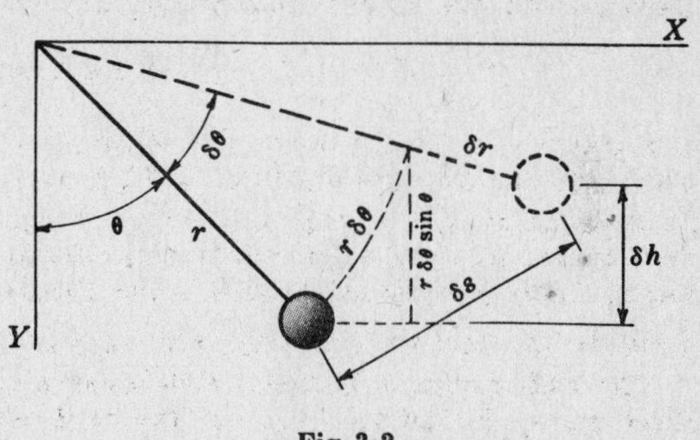

Fig. 3-2

$$\delta W_{\text{total}} = -mg\delta h - k(r - r_0)\delta r$$

where r_0 and k refer to the unstretched length of the band and its Hooke's law constant respectively. Each term on the right is written with a minus sign because work must be done against gravity and against the band in order to make positive displacements of r and θ. But, as can be seen from the figure, $\delta h = r\,\delta\theta \sin\theta - \delta r \cos\theta$ and therefore

$$\delta W_{\text{total}} = -mgr\,\delta\theta \sin\theta - [k(r - r_0) - mg\cos\theta]\delta r$$

Hence the work corresponding to a change in r alone is $\delta W_r = -[k(r - r_0) - mg\cos\theta]\delta r = F_r\,\delta r$ from which

$$F_r = -k(r - r_0) + mg\cos\theta$$

Likewise $F_\theta = -mgr\sin\theta$.

Now let us find F_r and F_θ by a direct application of $F_{q_r} = F_x\dfrac{\partial x}{\partial q_r} + F_y\dfrac{\partial y}{\partial q_r} + F_z\dfrac{\partial z}{\partial q_r}$. Taking account of gravity and the tension in the band, we see that the x and y components of force on the bob are

$$F_x = -k(r - r_0)\sin\theta, \qquad F_y = mg - k(r - r_0)\cos\theta$$

From the relations $x = r\sin\theta$ and $y = r\cos\theta$, $\partial x/\partial r = \sin\theta$ and $\partial y/\partial r = \cos\theta$. Hence

$$F_r = F_x\frac{\partial x}{\partial r} + F_y\frac{\partial y}{\partial r} = -k(r - r_0)\sin^2\theta + [mg - k(r - r_0)\cos\theta]\cos\theta$$

$$= -k(r - r_0) + mg\cos\theta$$

which is the same as previously found for F_r. In the same way F_θ easily follows.

3.6 Lagrange's Equations for a Single Particle, Assuming a Moving Frame of Reference and/or Moving Constraints.

Thus far we have avoided a discussion of systems involving moving frames of reference and/or moving constraints. However, since numerous problems of this type occur in practice, it is important that the derivation and application of Lagrange's equations to such systems be given careful consideration.

Let us again assume that we are dealing with a single particle which is free to move on a smooth surface. Furthermore we shall assume that the surface and/or the frame of reference from which the generalized coordinates q_1 and q_2 are measured are moving in a known manner. Following the exact procedure of Section 3.2, we again write

$$m(\ddot{x}\,\delta x + \ddot{y}\,\delta y + \ddot{z}\,\delta z) \;=\; F_x\,\delta x + F_y\,\delta y + F_z\,\delta z$$

in which $\delta x, \delta y, \delta z$ represent a completely arbitrary displacement and F_x, F_y, F_z are the components of the total force acting on the particle, including the force of constraint. (The XYZ frame is assumed to be inertial.)

Transformation equations relating x, y, z to q_1, q_2, t will now be indicated as

$$x = f_1(q_1, q_2, t), \qquad y = f_2(q_1, q_2, t), \qquad z = f_3(q_1, q_2, t) \tag{3.21}$$

Only two generalized coordinates appear in these equations, and time enters explicitly owing to the assumed motions. From this point on, *equations (3.21) will take account of the constraint and the assumed motions.*

Since $\delta x, \delta y, \delta z$ are each arbitrary we may, if we wish, determine them from equations (*3.21*) allowing t as well as q_1 and q_2 to vary. Hence

$$\delta x \;=\; \frac{\partial x}{\partial q_1}\delta q_1 + \frac{\partial x}{\partial q_2}\delta q_2 + \frac{\partial x}{\partial t}\delta t, \qquad \text{etc.}$$

Substituting in the first equation of this section and collecting terms, we have

$$\begin{aligned} m\left(\ddot{x}\frac{\partial x}{\partial q_1} + \ddot{y}\frac{\partial y}{\partial q_1} + \ddot{z}\frac{\partial z}{\partial q_1}\right)\delta q_1 + m\left(\ddot{x}\frac{\partial x}{\partial q_2} + \ddot{y}\frac{\partial y}{\partial q_2} + \ddot{z}\frac{\partial z}{\partial q_2}\right)\delta q_2 \\ + m\left(\ddot{x}\frac{\partial x}{\partial t} + \ddot{y}\frac{\partial y}{\partial t} + \ddot{z}\frac{\partial z}{\partial t}\right)\delta t \;=\; \left(F_x\frac{\partial x}{\partial q_1} + F_y\frac{\partial y}{\partial q_1} + F_z\frac{\partial z}{\partial q_1}\right)\delta q_1 \\ + \left(F_x\frac{\partial x}{\partial q_2} + F_y\frac{\partial y}{\partial q_2} + F_z\frac{\partial z}{\partial q_2}\right)\delta q_2 + \left(F_x\frac{\partial x}{\partial t} + F_y\frac{\partial y}{\partial t} + F_z\frac{\partial z}{\partial t}\right)\delta t \end{aligned} \tag{3.22}$$

Since $\delta q_1, \delta q_2, \delta t$ are each arbitrary one may set $\delta q_2 = 0$ and $\delta t = 0$. Hence (*3.22*) becomes

$$m\left(\ddot{x}\frac{\partial x}{\partial q_1} + \ddot{y}\frac{\partial y}{\partial q_1} + \ddot{z}\frac{\partial z}{\partial q_1}\right)\delta q_1 \;=\; \left(F_x\frac{\partial x}{\partial q_1} + F_y\frac{\partial y}{\partial q_1} + F_z\frac{\partial z}{\partial q_1}\right)\delta q_1$$

Finally, applying relations (*3.9*), (*3.10*) and (*3.11*) as in Section 3.2 (which are valid even though (*3.21*) contain the time explicitly), a Lagrangian equation having exactly the form of (*3.15*) is obtained. In like manner, setting $\delta q_1, \delta t = 0$, (*3.16*) follows. Hence *moving frames of reference and/or moving constraints make no change in the form of the Lagrangian equations*; (*3.18*) continues to be the general form.

3.7 Regarding Kinetic Energy, Generalized Forces and Other Matters when the Frame of Reference and/or Constraints are Moving.

(*a*) Basically kinetic energy, as emphasized in previous discussions, *must be referred to an inertial frame* (see Sections 2.8 and 2.9, Chapter 2). However, following the procedure described and illustrated in the above reference, T can be expressed in moving coordinates when such are to be used. Also, of course, superfluous coordinates must be eliminated.

(*b*) The following statement regarding generalized forces is very important.

Note that, in the relation $\left(F_x\frac{\partial x}{\partial q_r} + F_y\frac{\partial y}{\partial q_r} + F_z\frac{\partial z}{\partial q_r}\right)\delta q_r = F_{q_r}\,\delta q_r = \delta W_{q_r}$, the derivatives of x, y, z *are with respect to* q_r *only, holding* t *and all other coordinates constant.* Hence it is clear that δW_{q_r} is the work done by the force acting when, under the conditions just mentioned, q_r is given a displacement $+\delta q_r$. In other words, generalized forces are determined by imagining the frame of reference and constraints at rest and then proceeding exactly as explained in Section 3.3(*b*), (*c*) and illustrated in Section 3.5. If it happens that some or all of the applied forces are functions of time, which frequently is the case, the above procedure is still followed. Since any displacement, as determined by equations (*3.21*) with t constant, is in conformity with constraints, the work done by the force of constraint is zero. Hence, as usual, this force is to be disregarded.

(*c*) It will be seen that, by regarding $\delta q_1 = 0$, $\delta q_2 = 0$ and $\delta t \neq 0$, we obtain from (*3.22*) the relation

$$m\left(\ddot{x}\frac{\partial x}{\partial t} + \ddot{y}\frac{\partial y}{\partial t} + \ddot{z}\frac{\partial z}{\partial t}\right)\delta t = \left(F_x\frac{\partial x}{\partial t} + F_y\frac{\partial y}{\partial t} + F_z\frac{\partial z}{\partial t}\right)\delta t \qquad (3.23)$$

As the reader can easily show, the right side of (*3.23*) is just the work done on the particle by the total force (including the force of constraint) when the frame of reference and/or the constraints shift position slightly in time δt. However, since (*3.23*) is redundant insofar as setting up equations of motion is concerned, it will not be given further consideration at this point.

3.8 Illustrative Examples.

Example 3.5:

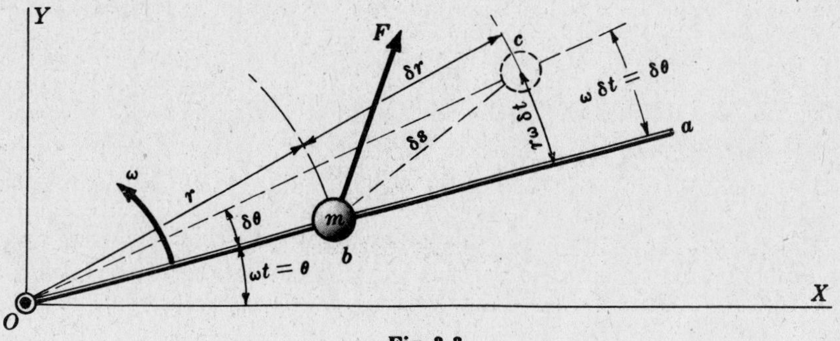

Fig. 3-3

The following simple example should help clarify a number of basic ideas. A smooth rigid rod, shown in Fig. 3-3 above, is made to rotate with constant angular velocity in a plane, about the origin of the X, Y axes. A bead of mass m is free to slide along the rod under the action of a force F, which includes the force of constraint. Let us set up the equation of motion of the bead by a direct application of D'Alembert's equation (*3.3*) which, for this case, is merely

$$m(\ddot{x}\,\delta x + \ddot{y}\,\delta y) = F_x\,\delta x + F_y\,\delta y \qquad (1)$$

The bead has only one degree of freedom. Choosing r as the coordinate, we write

$$x = r\cos\omega t, \qquad y = r\sin\omega t \qquad (2)$$

Hence

$$\delta x = \delta r\cos\omega t - r\omega\,\delta t\sin\omega t, \qquad \delta y = \delta r\sin\omega t + r\omega\,\delta t\cos\omega t \qquad (3)$$

in which both r and t are allowed to vary. Likewise, expressions for $\ddot{x}$ and $\ddot{y}$ are found at once from (*2*). Eliminating $\delta x, \delta y, \ddot{x}, \ddot{y}$ from (*1*), we get

$$m(\ddot{r} - r\omega^2)\delta r + 2mr\dot{r}\omega^2\,\delta t = (F_x\cos\omega t + F_y\sin\omega t)\delta r + (F_y\cos\omega t - F_x\sin\omega t)r\omega\,\delta t \qquad (4)$$

But since δr and δt are arbitrary, it is clear that

$$m(\ddot{r} - r\omega^2)\delta r = (F_x \cos \omega t + F_y \sin \omega t)\delta r \qquad (5)$$

$$(2mr\dot{r}\omega^2)\delta t = (F_y \cos \omega t - F_x \sin \omega t)r\omega\,\delta t \qquad (6)$$

Now inspection of the figure will show that the right side of (5) is just the work done by the total force for a displacement δr along the rod (not for the displacement δs). Moreover, since the displacement is in conformity with the constraint, the work done by the reactive force of the rod on the bead is zero.

Equation (5) is the equation of motion and is just what is obtained by a proper application of Lagrange's equation. (The student should do this.)

Equation (6) corresponds to (3.23). Inspection of Fig. 3-3 shows that the right side of (6) is the work done by F (including the force of constraint) for the displacement $r\omega\,\delta t$.

Example 3.6:

Referring to Fig. 3-4, the rotating table D has an angular velocity $\dot{\alpha}$ determined by the motor M_1. Attached to the table is a driving mechanism M_2 which causes the smooth rod pa to rotate about a horizontal axis at p in some given manner. The rod pa and the vertical lines pb and oc are all in the same plane. A bead of mass m is free to slide along the rod under the action of gravity.

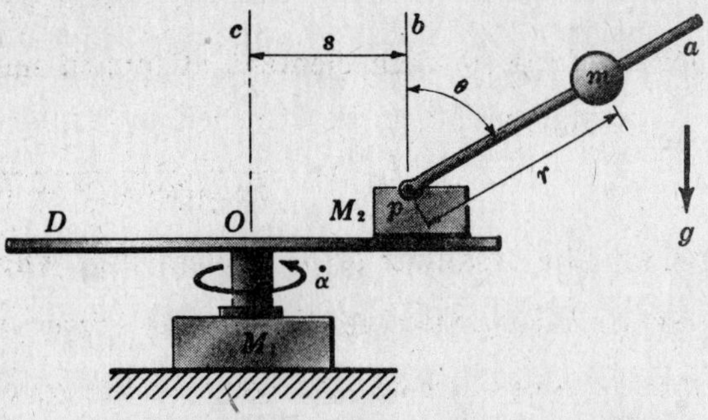

Fig. 3-4

Assuming that α and θ are known functions of time, the system has one degree of freedom. Taking r as the coordinate, let us set up the equation of motion and find F_r.

It easily follows that

$$T = \tfrac{1}{2}m[\dot{r}^2 + r^2\dot{\theta}^2 + \dot{\alpha}^2(s + r\sin\theta)^2] \qquad (1)$$

This is correct regardless of how α and θ may be changing with time. But suppose it is assumed that $\dot{\alpha} = \omega_1 =$ constant and that the rod is forced by mechanism M_2 to oscillate about the vertical line pb according to $\theta = \theta_0 \sin \omega_2 t$. Then

$$T = \tfrac{1}{2}m\{\dot{r}^2 + r^2\theta_0^2\omega_2^2\cos^2\omega_2 t + \omega_1^2[s + r\sin(\theta_0 \sin\omega_2 t)]^2\} \qquad (2)$$

which now contains only r, $\dot{r}$, and t. Applying Lagrange's equation, it follows that

$$m\ddot{r} - m\{r\theta_0^2\omega_2^2\cos^2\omega_2 t + \omega_1^2[s + r\sin(\theta_0\sin\omega_2 t)]\sin(\theta_0\sin\omega_2 t)\} = F_r \qquad (3)$$

In order to find an expression for F_r, *the motions of the table and rod are completely disregarded*; that is, while making a displacement $+\delta r$, t is held fixed (θ and α are held constant). Hence

$$\delta W_r = -mg\cos\theta\,\delta r = -mg\cos(\theta_0\sin\omega_2 t)\,\delta r \quad \text{or} \quad F_r = -mg\cos(\theta_0\sin\omega_2 t)$$

It should be noted that if the rod has no obligatory motion and is thus free to rotate about the axis at p, the system has now two degrees of freedom. Furthermore, neglecting the mass of the rod, (1) is still the correct expression for T. Equations of motion corresponding to r and θ may be written down at once and it is seen that

$$F_r = -mg\cos\theta, \qquad F_\theta = mgr\sin\theta$$

3.9 Determination of Acceleration by Means of Lagrange's Equations.

As previously shown (Section 2.12, Page 28), the component a' of the acceleration vector $\boldsymbol{a}$ along any line having direction cosines l, m, n is given by

$$a' = \ddot{x}\,l + \ddot{y}\,m + \ddot{z}\,n \qquad (1)$$

If a' is to be found in the direction of the tangent to a space curve at some point p, then

$$l = \frac{dx}{ds}, \qquad m = \frac{dy}{ds}, \qquad n = \frac{dz}{ds} \qquad (2)$$

where ds is an element of length of the line at p given by

$$ds^2 = dx^2 + dy^2 + dz^2 \qquad (3)$$

Hence from equations of the space curve l, m, n may be found.

Suppose now that we are to determine a general expression for the component of acceleration along a tangent to the coordinate line of q_1 in which the generalized coordinates q_1, q_2, q_3 are related to rectangular coordinates by

$$x = x(q_1, q_2, q_3, t), \quad y = y(q_1, q_2, q_3, t), \quad z = z(q_1, q_2, q_3, t) \tag{4}$$

The coordinate line of q_1 is determined by holding q_2, q_3, t each constant in (4) and plotting values of x, y, z for varying values of q_1. In like manner coordinate lines of q_2 and q_3 are determined. Hence differentiating (4) holding q_2, q_3, t constant, we get $dx = \dfrac{\partial x}{\partial q_1} dq_1$, etc. Thus (3) becomes

$$ds^2 = \left[\left(\frac{\partial x}{\partial q_1}\right)^2 + \left(\frac{\partial y}{\partial q_1}\right)^2 + \left(\frac{\partial z}{\partial q_1}\right)^2\right] dq_1^2 \tag{5}$$

where ds is now an element of length measured along the q_1 line.

From (2),

$$l_1 = \frac{dx}{dq_1[(\partial x/\partial q_1)^2 + (\partial y/\partial q_1)^2 + (\partial z/\partial q_1)^2]^{1/2}} = \frac{1}{h_1}\frac{\partial x}{\partial q_1} \tag{6}$$

where the meaning of h_1 is clear and where we have written dx/dq_1 as $\partial x/\partial q_1$ since q_2, q_3, t are still regarded as constants. Also $m_1 = \dfrac{1}{h_1}\dfrac{\partial y}{\partial q_1}$, $n_1 = \dfrac{1}{h_1}\dfrac{\partial z}{\partial q_1}$. In like manner the direction cosines of a tangent to the q_2 coordinate line are

$$l_2 = \frac{1}{h_2}\frac{\partial x}{\partial q_2}, \quad m_2 = \frac{1}{h_2}\frac{\partial y}{\partial q_2}, \quad n_2 = \frac{1}{h_2}\frac{\partial z}{\partial q_2} \tag{7}$$

Now denoting a' by a_{q_1}, equation (1) becomes

$$a_{q_1} = \frac{1}{h_1}\left(\ddot{x}\frac{\partial x}{\partial q_1} + \ddot{y}\frac{\partial y}{\partial q_1} + \ddot{z}\frac{\partial z}{\partial q_1}\right) \tag{8}$$

But by the steps followed in arriving at the left side of (3.15), we obviously can write (8) as

$$a_{q_1} = \frac{1}{h_1}\left[\frac{d}{dt}\left(\frac{\partial T'}{\partial \dot{q}_1}\right) - \frac{\partial T'}{\partial q_1}\right] \tag{9}$$

where $T' = \frac{1}{2}(\dot{x}^2 + \dot{y}^2 + \dot{z}^2)$, expressed in generalized coordinates. Or in general,

$$a_{q_r} = \frac{1}{h_r}\left[\frac{d}{dt}\left(\frac{\partial T'}{\partial \dot{q}_r}\right) - \frac{\partial T'}{\partial q_r}\right] \tag{3.24}$$

This is a simple and easy way of arriving at general expressions for components of acceleration along coordinate lines. See the following example.

Example 3.7:

Considering spherical coordinates, let us determine the well-known expression for a_θ, the component of acceleration along a tangent to a θ coordinate line, by an application of (3.24).

For these coordinates (see equation (2.39)), $T' = \frac{1}{2}(\dot{r}^2 + r^2\dot{\theta}^2 + r^2 \sin^2\theta\, \dot{\phi}^2)$ from which

$$\frac{d}{dt}\left(\frac{\partial T'}{\partial \dot{\theta}}\right) - \frac{\partial T'}{\partial \theta} = r^2\ddot{\theta} + 2r\dot{r}\dot{\theta} - r^2\dot{\phi}^2 \sin\theta \cos\theta$$

$$h_\theta = \left[\left(\frac{\partial x}{\partial \theta}\right)^2 + \left(\frac{\partial y}{\partial \theta}\right)^2 + \left(\frac{\partial z}{\partial \theta}\right)^2\right]^{\frac{1}{2}} = [(r\cos\theta\cos\phi)^2 + (r\cos\theta\sin\phi)^2 + r^2\sin^2\theta]^{1/2} = r$$

Hence $a_\theta = r\ddot{\theta} + 2\dot{r}\dot{\theta} - r\dot{\phi}^2 \sin\theta\cos\theta$. Likewise, a_r and a_ϕ can be obtained at once.

If the motion of a point (or particle) is constrained to a moving surface, equations (4), after removing a superfluous coordinate, become

$$x = x(q_1, q_2, t), \quad y = y(q_1, q_2, t), \quad z = z(q_1, q_2, t) \tag{10}$$

which are indeed the equations of the surface at any instant.

Now if we think of holding q_2 and t constant, equations (*10*) represent a q_1 line on the surface. Moreover, it is clear that dx/ds, for example, gives an expression for one of the direction cosines of the tangent to this line at any point. Therefore, if T' is written in terms of $q_1, q_2, \dot{q}_1, \dot{q}_2, t,$ equation (*3.24*) gives components of the acceleration vector along tangents to q_1, q_2 lines on the surface at any given instant.

Again it is important to remember that, basically, accelerations found in this manner are relative to the X, Y, Z frame.

3.10 Another Look at Lagrange's Equations.

For the sake of further clarifying the physical meaning of Lagrange's equations, consider the following.

Writing $T = \frac{1}{2}m(\dot{r}^2 + r^2\dot{\theta}^2 + r^2\dot{\phi}^2 \sin^2\theta)$, it follows from Section 3.9 that

$$\frac{1}{h_\theta}\left[\frac{d}{dt}\left(\frac{\partial T}{\partial \dot{\theta}}\right) - \frac{\partial T}{\partial \theta}\right] = ma_\theta \qquad \text{(see Example 3.7)}$$

Also, the reader may easily show that

$$\frac{1}{h_\theta}\left[F_x\frac{\partial x}{\partial \theta} + F_y\frac{\partial y}{\partial \theta} + F_z\frac{\partial z}{\partial \theta}\right] = \frac{1}{h_\theta}F_\theta = f_\theta \qquad (3.25)$$

where, if f is the force acting on m, f_θ is the component of f in the direction of increasing θ. (Note that f_θ is an actual force and not a torque. Moreover, a_θ is a linear acceleration.) Hence it is clear that the Lagrangian equation gives merely $ma_\theta = f_\theta$ expressed in spherical coordinates. Also, equations corresponding to r and ϕ may be written as $ma_r = f_r$, $ma_\phi = f_\phi$, and likewise for whatever coordinates that may be used.

If there is a constraint on the particle, transformation equations take the form of equations (*10*), Section 3.9. Following the reasoning given at the end of Example 3.7, it follows that the Lagrangian equations corresponding to q_1 and q_2 may be written as $ma_{q_1} = f_{q_1}$, $ma_{q_2} = f_{q_2}$.

Hence, for a one-particle system, the physical interpretation of the Lagrangian equations is very simple. Moreover, we see that in each equation the components of acceleration are automatically taken account of.

This is true for any coordinates and any constraints. Consider, for example, a particle on a rotating platform mounted on an accelerated elevator. Suppose we want the acceleration components of the particle expressed in certain coordinates, the frame of which is attached to the platform where account is taken of the motions of the earth, the elevator and rotation of the platform. Even in this rather complicated case it is easy to write T for the particle, and (*3.24*) gives the desired results at once. The student should compare this with formal vector methods. See Problem 3.34.

3.11 Suggested Experiments:

As previously mentioned, a few experiments which have been found especially worthy of the students' time and efforts are listed at the ends of several chapters. These experiments will contribute greatly to an appreciation of and a down-to-earth feeling for dynamics which pencil and paper alone can never give.

Experiment 3.1:

Determine the period of the pendulum shown in Fig. 3-6 (see Problem 3.7, Page 52). Support the point p by a long light cord fastened directly overhead to a high ceiling. As the pendulum swings, p will move along the arc of a large circle, but for small motion this may be regarded as a horizontal straight line. For carefully determined values of k and m, experimental and computed values of the period check closely.

The experiment may be repeated by adjusting the long string so that p is several centimeters above the horizontal line ab, the springs now forming an inverted V. Of course, the force exerted by the springs must now be approximated, assuming small motion (use Taylor's expansion).

Summary and Remarks

1. **Derivation of Lagrange's Equations: Single particle, no moving coordinates or constraints (Section 3.2).**

   (*a*) D'Alembert's equation is developed from Newton's second law and the concept of virtual work. (It has been seen that virtual work is a simple yet powerful device which is used as a means to an end.)

   (*b*) D'Alembert's equation expressed in generalized coordinates leads directly (with the aid of certain simple mathematical operations) to Lagrange's equations.

2. **Important Details Regarding these Equations (Section 3.3b, c).**

   (*a*) Kinetic energy, T, must be expressed in terms of the chosen generalized coordinates and their time derivatives. All superfluous coordinates should be eliminated from T.

   (*b*) A clear understanding of the physical meaning of generalized forces not only facilitates the use of Lagrange's equations but contributes much to an appreciation of what is taking place.

3. **Derivation of Lagrange's Equations: Moving coordinates and/or moving constraints (Section 3.6).**

   (*a*) Derivation is again based on D'Alembert's equation and the arbitrary character of the virtual displacements $\delta x_i, \delta y_i, \delta z_i$. Equations have same form as before.

   (*b*) T is now a function of the q_r's, $\dot{q}_r$'s and t.

   (*c*) F_{q_r} is found as before, *holding time fixed.* The physical meaning of this (Section 3.7) must be understood for reasons mentioned in 2(*b*) above.

4. **Acceleration Determined by Lagrange's Equations (Section 3.9).**

   As shown in Section 3.9, the component of acceleration of a point or particle along a tangent to a q-line at any point may be obtained at once from equation (*3.24*).

5. **Physical Interpretation of Lagrange's Equations (Section 3.10).**

   For a single-particle system the Lagrangian equations of motion may be reduced to $ma_r = f_r$ where a_r is the component of linear acceleration of m along the tangent to the q_r-line and f_r is the component of the total force on m (disregarding force of constraint) acting along the same tangent. Hence the above equations, regardless of what coordinates may be used, reduce to the simplicity of Newton's second law equations.

Problems

3.1. Assuming that motion is confined to the Q_1Q_2 plane, Fig. 2-5, Page 12, and that gravity acts in the negative direction of the vertical Y axis, set up the equations of motion of a projectile in the q_1, q_2 coordinates. *Ans.* $m[\ddot{q}_1 + \ddot{q}_2 \cos(\beta - \alpha)] = -mg \sin \alpha$, $m[\ddot{q}_2 + \ddot{q}_1 \cos(\beta - \alpha)] = -mg \sin \beta$

3.2. A bead of mass m is constrained to move along a smooth rigid wire having the shape of the hyperbola $xy = C =$ constant. Show that the kinetic energy may be expressed as

$$T = \tfrac{1}{2}m\dot{x}^2\left(1 + \frac{C^2}{x^4}\right)$$

Write out the equation of motion and show that if the Y axis is vertical the generalized force corresponding to x is

$$F_x = mgC/x^2$$

3.3. Note that any point in the XY plane may be located by specifying C and y in the relation $xy = C$. Hence regarding C as a variable, it may be used as a coordinate. Show that for motion in a plane the kinetic energy of a particle may be written as

$$T = \tfrac{1}{2}m\left[\dot{x}^2 + \left(\frac{x\dot{C} - C\dot{x}}{x^2}\right)^2\right]$$

and that, considering gravity acting parallel to and in the negative direction of the Y axis,

$$F_x = +mgC/x^2, \qquad F_C = -mg/x$$

3.4. Instead of the familiar polar r, θ coordinates (plane motion), let us consider r and $\sin\theta$ as coordinates. Writing $x = r\cos\theta$, $y = r\sin\theta$ and denoting $\sin\theta$ by q, we have $x = r\sqrt{1-q^2}$, $y = rq$. Show that the kinetic energy of a particle in r, q coordinates is given by

$$T = \tfrac{1}{2}m\left(\dot{r}^2 + \frac{r^2\dot{q}^2}{1-q^2}\right)$$

3.5. A bead is constrained to move along the smooth conical spiral shown in Fig. 3-5 below. Assuming that $\rho = az$ and $\phi = -bz$, where a and b are constants, show that the equation of motion is

$$\ddot{z}(a^2 + 1 + a^2b^2z^2) + a^2b^2z\dot{z}^2 = -g$$

3.6. Set up the equations (*11*) and (*12*) of Example 1.2, Page 4, by the Lagrangian method.

3.7. The pendulum bob of mass m, shown in Fig. 3-6 below, is suspended by an inextensible string from the point p. This point is free to move along a straight horizontal line under the action of the springs, each having a constant k. Assume that the mass is displaced only slightly from the equilibrium position and released. Neglecting the mass of the springs, show that the pendulum oscillates with a period of

$$P = 2\pi\sqrt{\frac{mg + 2kr}{2kg}}$$

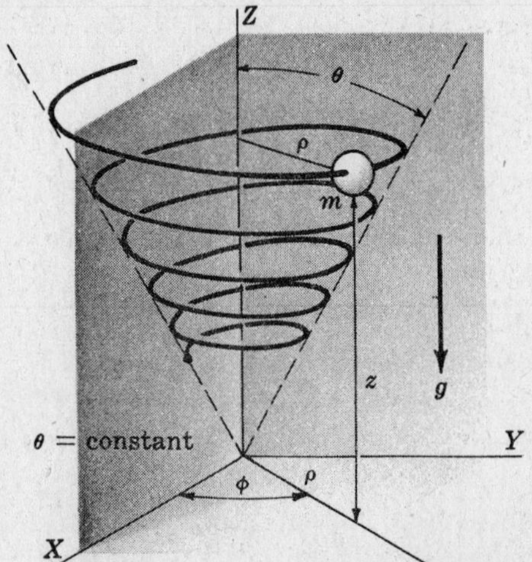

Fig. 3-5

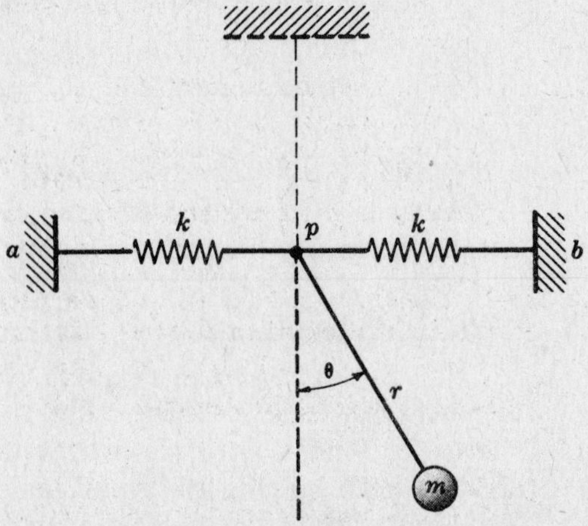

Fig. 3-6

3.8. A solid uniform disk of mass M and radius R has attached to its face a small mass m at a distance r from its center. The disk is free to roll without sliding along a horizontal straight line. Show that

$$T = \tfrac{1}{2}\dot{\theta}^2(MR^2 + I + mR^2 - 2mrR\cos\theta + mr^2)$$

where I is the moment of inertia of the disk about an axis perpendicular to its face through its center and θ is the angular displacement of the disk from its equilibrium position. Show that if the disk is displaced only slightly from its equilibrium position and released it will oscillate with a period

$$P = 2\pi\sqrt{\frac{I + MR^2 + m(R-r)^2}{mgr}}$$

3.9. The particle of mass m, shown in Fig. 3-7 below, is free to move to any position under the action of the two identical springs. When m is in equilibrium at the origin of the coordinate axes, the length S of either spring is greater than the unstretched length l_0. Show that $F_\phi = 0$. Show that, for very small displacements from equilibrium,

$$F_x = -2k(1 - l_0/S)x, \qquad F_y = -2k(1 - l_0/S)y, \qquad F_z = -2kz$$

Set up equations of motion and integrate.

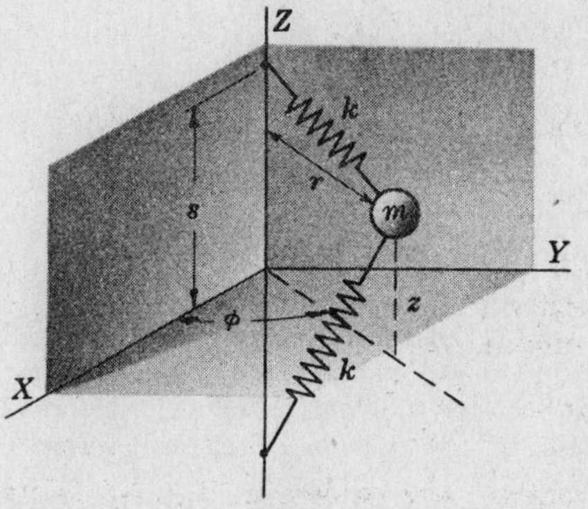

Fig. 3-7

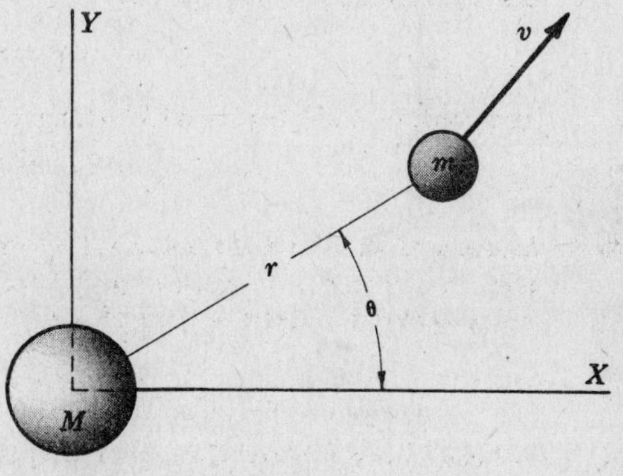

Fig. 3-8

3.10. Mass m, shown in Fig. 3-8 above, is attracted to a stationary mass M by the gravitational force $F = -GmM/r^2$. At an initial distance r_0, m is given an initial velocity v_0 in the XY plane. Set up equations of motion in r, θ coordinates. Show that the angular momentum $p_\theta = mr^2\dot{\theta}$ = constant. With the aid of this, integrate the r equation and show that the path is a conic.

3.11. The rectangular components of force on a charge Q moving through a magnetic and electric field are given by relations (*5.14*), Page 91.

(*a*) An electron gun fires a narrow pencil of electrons, each with the same velocity ($\dot{x}_0, \dot{y}_0, \dot{z}_0$ at origin of axes at $t = 0$) into a uniform magnetic field (no electric field) at some initial angle θ with the lines of flux. Set up equations of motion, integrate and show that the path described by the beam is a cylindrical helix. (Assume B in Z direction.)

(*b*) Set up equations of motion assuming a uniform electric field parallel to the magnetic field. What is now the path?

3.12. A bead of mass m is free to move on a smooth circular wire which is rotating with constant angular velocity ω about a vertical axis perpendicular to the face of the loop and passing through its periphery. Another bead is moving under the action of gravity along an identical loop which is stationary and in a vertical plane. Prove that both beads have exactly the same motion. What quantity in the equation of motion for the first bead corresponds to g in the second equation of motion?

3.13. In Example 3.2, Page 44, consider the location of m with polar coordinates r, θ. Taking θ as the independent coordinate show that

$$x = \frac{\tan\theta}{b}, \qquad y = \frac{\tan^2\theta}{b}$$

Hence T can be written in terms of θ and $\dot{\theta}$. Show that the generalized force is

$$F_\theta = \frac{F_x}{b\cos^2\theta} + \frac{2F_y\tan\theta}{b\cos^2\theta}$$

where F_x and F_y are the force components acting on m. It is clear that θ is not a desirable coordinate for determining the motion of m. Repeat the above procedure for Problem 3.2, Page 52.

3.14. In Fig. 3-9 below the bead of mass m is free to slide along the smooth rod under the action of gravity and the spring. The vertical shaft is made to rotate at constant angular velocity ω. Show that the equation of motion is

$$m\ddot{r} - mr\omega^2 \sin^2\theta = k(l - l_0) - kr - mg\cos\theta$$

and that the mass oscillates with

$$\text{period } P = 2\pi\sqrt{\frac{m}{k - m\omega^2\sin^2\theta}} \quad \text{about the position } r = \frac{k(l-l_0) - mg\cos\theta}{k - m\omega^2\sin^2\theta}$$

where $l = r + s$ and l_0 is the unstretched length of the spring.

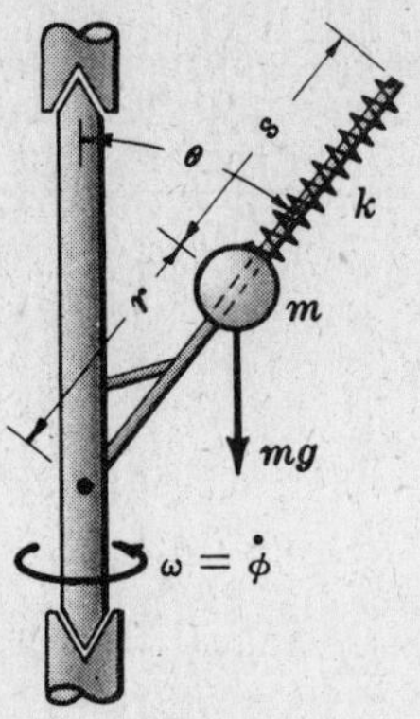

Fig. 3-9

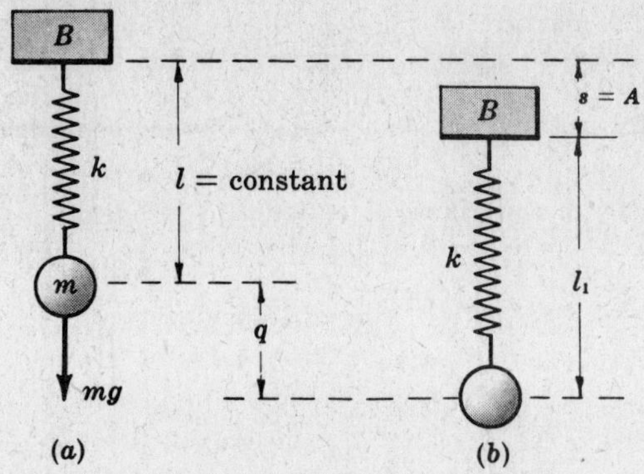

Fig. 3-10

3.15. Assume that block B, shown in Fig. 3-10 above, to which the spring is attached is forced to oscillate vertically according to the relation $s = A\sin\omega t$. Let (*a*) represent the position of the system with no motion applied to B and m in equilibrium under the action of gravity and the spring. Let (*b*) represent any general position of the system. Show that in effect the motion of B applies a force of $kA\sin\omega t$ to m. Also show that the motion of m is given by

$$q = C\sin(\sqrt{k/m}\,t + \delta) + \frac{Ak}{m(k/m - \omega^2)}\sin\omega t$$

3.16. A massive uniform disk of radius R rolls down an inclined plane without slipping. X and Y axes are attached to the face of the disk with origin at its center. A particle of mass m is free to move in the plane of the disk under the action of gravity and springs, the specific arrangement of which need not be given. From elementary considerations it is known that, neglecting the small mass of the particle, the center of the disk moves with linear acceleration $a = \frac{2}{3}g\sin\alpha$, where α is the angle of the incline. Show that the kinetic energy of the particle in polar coordinates r, θ (θ measured from the X axis attached to the disk) is given by (measure β between X and a fixed line normal to the inclined plane)

$$T = \tfrac{1}{2}m[a^2t^2 + \dot{r}^2 + r^2(\dot{\beta} - \dot{\theta})^2 + 2at\dot{r}\sin(\beta - \theta) + 2atr(\dot{\beta} - \dot{\theta})\cos(\beta - \theta)]$$

where $\dot{\beta} = (a/R)t$. Compare T here with the general form (*2.55*), Page 27.

3.17. The string supporting the pendulum bob, Fig. 3.11, passes through a small hole in the board B which is forced to oscillate vertically along the Y axis such that $s = A\sin\omega t$. Show that

$$\begin{aligned} T = \tfrac{1}{2}m[&2A^2\omega^2\cos^2\omega t + (l - A\sin\omega t)^2\dot{\theta}^2 \\ &- 2A^2\omega^2\cos^2\omega t\cos\theta \\ &- 2(l - A\sin\omega t)A\omega\dot{\theta}\cos\omega t\sin\theta] \end{aligned}$$

where $l = r + s =$ constant.

Write out the equation of motion. Show that

$$F_\theta = -mgr\sin\theta = -mg(l - A\sin\omega t)\sin\theta$$

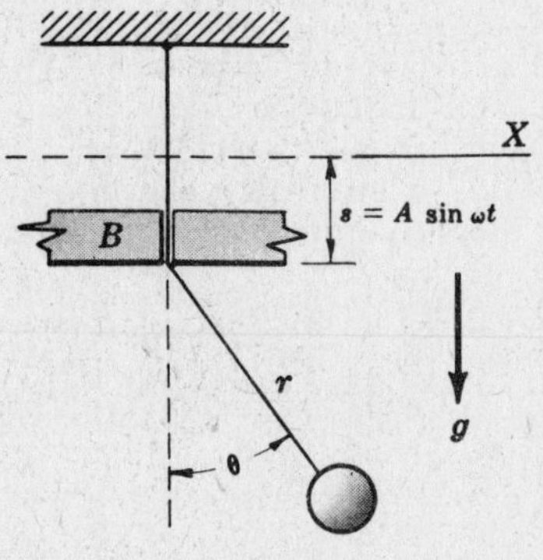

Fig. 3-11

3.18. Referring to Example 3.6 and Fig. 3-4, Page 48, assume that $\dot{\alpha} = \omega =$ constant, that the mass of the rod pa is negligible, and that the driving arrangement M_2 is replaced with springs which tend to keep pa in a vertical position by a torque of $-C\theta$. Set up equations of motion corresponding to r and θ. Note that the expression for T [equation (*1*), Example 3.6] still holds.

3.19. Show that if the spiral, Problem 3.5, Fig. 3-5, is rotating about its own axis with constant angular velocity ω,

$$T = \tfrac{1}{2}m[\dot{z}^2(a^2+1) + a^2z^2(\omega - b\dot{z})^2]$$

Also show that if the spiral has a rotation given by $\omega t + \frac{1}{2}\alpha t^2$,

$$T = \tfrac{1}{2}m[a^2\dot{z}^2 + a^2z^2(\omega + \alpha t - b\dot{z})^2 + \dot{z}^2]$$

Note that in each case the generalized force corresponding to z is $-mg$.

3.20. Let us suppose that the disk, shown in Fig. 3-12, can be given any desired rotational motion by a motor (not shown) attached to its axis. The string to which m is attached is wrapped around and fastened to the disk. The angular position of the disk is given by α, measured from the fixed X axis to a line drawn on the face of the disk. Angular position of the string (assumed always to be tangent to the pulley) is given by θ. r_0 is the initial length of the string as indicated. Show that for mass m,

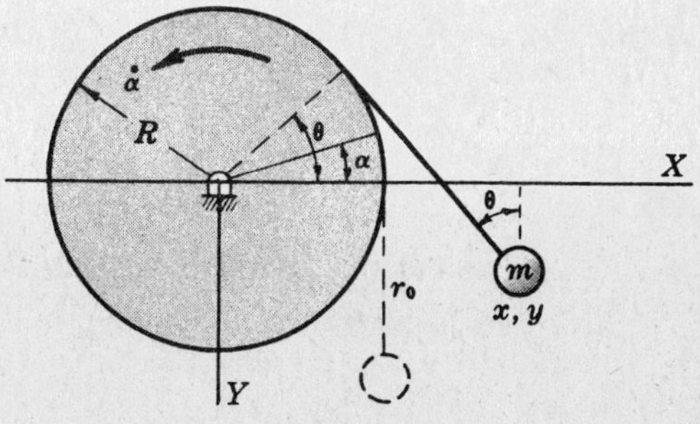

Fig. 3-12

$$T = \tfrac{1}{2}m[R^2\dot{\alpha}^2 + (r_0 + R\theta - R\alpha)^2\dot{\theta}^2]$$

$$F_\theta = -mg(r_0 + R\theta - R\alpha)\sin\theta$$

and that the equation of motion is

$$m(r_0 + R\theta - R\alpha)\ddot{\theta} - 2mR\dot{\theta}\dot{\alpha} + mR\dot{\theta}^2 = -mg\sin\theta$$

where α is assumed to be some known function of time.

3.21. In Fig. 3-13 below the rigid parabolic wire rotates in some known manner about the Z_2 axis while the platform to which X_2, Y_2, Z_2 are attached moves with constant acceleration a parallel to the Y_1 axis. The bead of mass m is free to slide along the smooth wire under the force of gravity. (a) Show that

$$T = \tfrac{1}{2}m[\dot{r}^2 + r^2\dot{\phi}^2 + a^2t^2 + 2\dot{r}at\sin\phi + 2r\dot{\phi}at\cos\phi + 4b^2r^2\dot{r}^2]$$

Assuming $\dot{\phi} = \omega =$ constant, set up the equation of motion corresponding to r and show that

$$F_r = -2mgbr$$

3.22. As the wire in the above problem rotates it generates a parabolic cup. Suppose that m is confined to move in contact with the inside surface of a stationary cup having this shape. The expression for its kinetic energy is just as written in Problem 3.21, except that ϕ must now be regarded as an independent coordinate. Write out equations of motion for this case. Show that F_r is the same as above and $F_\phi = 0$.

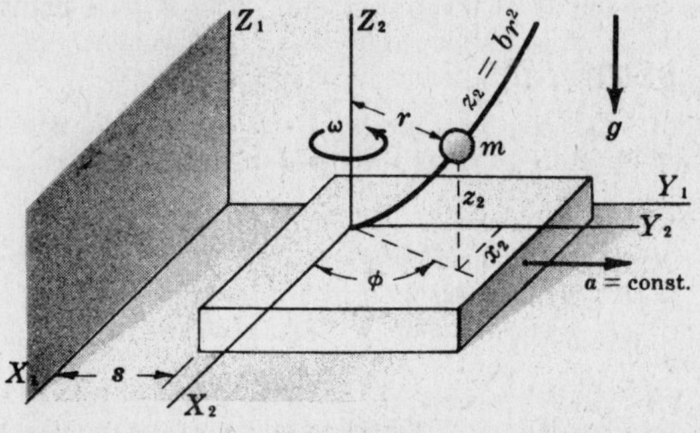

Fig. 3-13

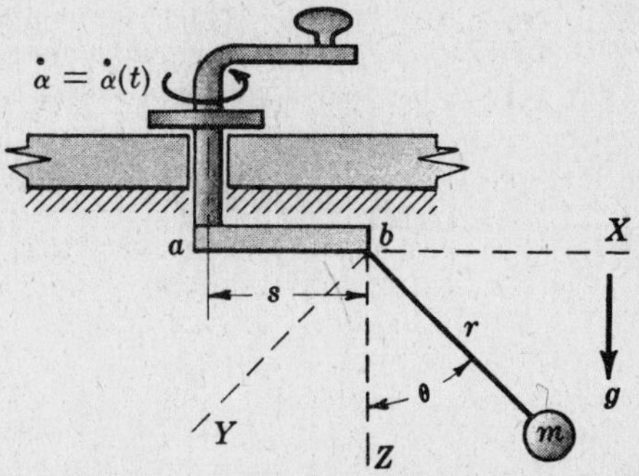

Fig. 3-14

3.23. By means of the crank handle the support of the pendulum, shown in Fig. 3-14 above, can be given any desired rotation. Show that T for the pendulum is

$$T = \tfrac{1}{2}m[s^2\dot{\alpha}^2 + r^2\dot{\theta}^2 + r^2(\dot{\alpha} - \dot{\phi})^2\sin^2\theta - 2sr\dot{\alpha}\dot{\theta}\cos\theta\sin\phi + 2sr\dot{\alpha}(\dot{\alpha} - \dot{\phi})\sin\theta\cos\phi]$$

where r, θ, ϕ are spherical coordinates measured relative to the X, Y, Z axes attached to and rotating with the horizontal bar ab. In this problem r is taken constant.

Assuming r variable (rubber band) repeat above. Write T as the sum of three terms corresponding to those in equation (*2.55*), Page 27.

3.24. Assuming $\dot\theta_1 = \omega_1 =$ constant, $\dot\theta_2 = \omega_2 =$ constant, show that the kinetic energy of the particle in Fig. 2-21, Page 22, with motion confined to the X_2Y_2 plane, is given by

$$T = \tfrac{1}{2}m\{\dot r^2 + r^2\dot\alpha^2 + [2s\omega_1 \sin(\omega_2 t + \alpha)]\dot r + [2r^2(\omega_1+\omega_2) + 2s\omega_1 r\cos(\omega_2 t+\alpha)]\dot\alpha + [r^2(\omega_1+\omega_2)^2 + 2s\omega_1(\omega_1+\omega_2)r\cos(\omega_2 t+\alpha) + s^2\omega_1^2]\}$$

Note that this has just the form of relation (*2.55*) where quantities corresponding to A, B, C are evident.

3.25. A rotating platform P_2, shown in Fig. 3-15 below, is mounted on a second rotating platform P_1 which is in turn mounted on an elevator. P_1 is driven by a motor at a constant speed ω_1. In like manner P_2 rotates with constant speed ω_2 relative to P_1. The simple pendulum of length l attached to P_2 is allowed to swing in a plane containing the vertical axis of rotation of P_2 and its point of suspension. The elevator has a constant upward acceleration a. Find the equation of motion of the pendulum.

$$m[l^2\ddot\theta + l\cos\theta\,(s_1 - l\sin\theta)(\omega_1+\omega_2)^2 + s_2\omega_1^2 l\cos\theta\cos\omega_2 t + al\sin\theta] = -mgl\sin\theta$$

Note that the left of this is merely $(ml)a_\theta$, where a_θ is the linear acceleration of m relative to an inertial frame, in the direction of increasing θ. [See equation (*3.24*).]

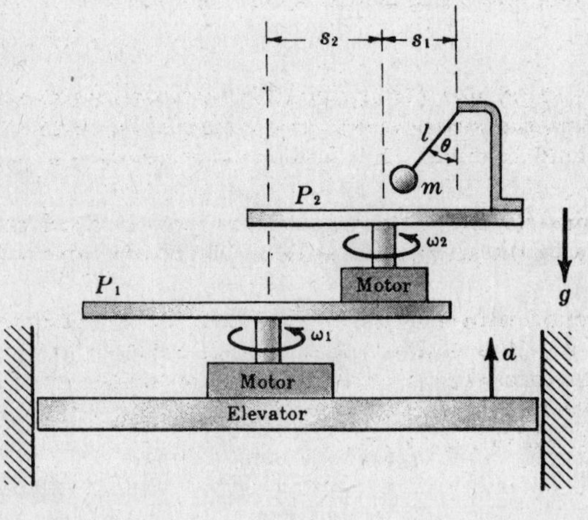

Fig. 3-15

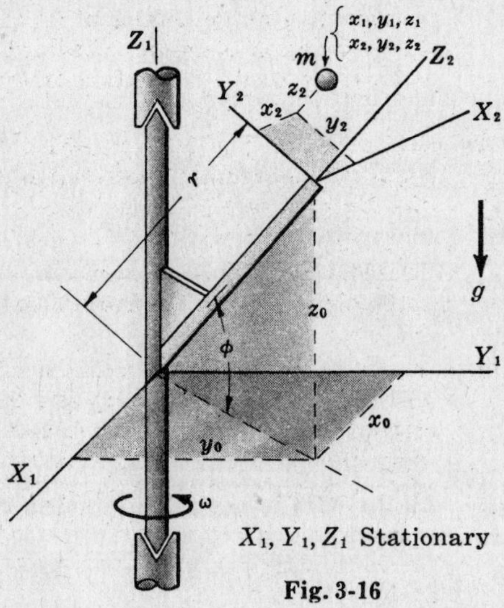

Fig. 3-16

3.26. An X, Y, Z frame of reference is attached to the inside of an automobile. The Y axis points directly forward, the Z axis vertically upward, and the X axis to the right side. The position of a particle is to be located in spherical coordinates r, θ, ϕ measured relative to this frame.

Assuming that the car is moving along a level circular road of radius R with constant tangential acceleration a, write out T and set up equations of motion for the free particle, gravity alone acting.

3.27. The vertical shaft with an arm of length r rigidly attached as shown in Fig. 3-16 above is made to rotate with constant angular velocity ω. Write an expression for T and the equations of motion of the particle relative to the rotating X_2, Y_2, Z_2 system. For a hint and the answers, refer to equations (*14.15*), Page 287.

3.28. Considering cylindrical coordinates r, ϕ, z, the relation $z = br^2$ represents a parabolic "cup" for b constant. The x and y coordinates of any particular point on the cup may be written as $x = r\cos\phi$ and $y = r\sin\phi$. Now, just as an aid in becoming accustomed to all sorts of coordinates, suppose b is regarded as a variable. Then b, r, ϕ may be regarded as coordinates locating any point in space. Hence the above three relations are the transformation equations relating the rectangular and the b, r, ϕ coordinates.

Show that in these coordinates the kinetic energy of a particle is given by

$$T = \tfrac{1}{2}m[\dot r^2(1 + 4b^2r^2) + r^2\dot\phi^2 + \dot b^2 r^4 + 4br^3\dot b\dot r]$$

For gravity acting in the negative direction of Z, show that

$$F_r = -2mgbr, \qquad F_b = -mgr^2, \qquad F_\phi = 0$$

3.29. Determine an expression for the acceleration of m, shown in Fig. 3-9, Page 54, in the direction of increasing r. Assume that the vertical axis is given constant angular acceleration $\ddot{\phi} = c$. See Problem 3.14.

Show that under these same conditions

$$a_r = \ddot{r} - rc^2t^2 \sin^2 \theta, \qquad a_\theta = -rc^2t^2 \sin \theta \cos \theta, \qquad a_\phi = 2\dot{r}ct \sin \theta + rc \sin \theta$$

are a_r, a_θ, a_ϕ relative to an inertial frame.

What are the components of the reactive force in the directions of increasing θ and ϕ? Note that, to get the above results, we in reality introduce θ and ϕ as superfluous coordinates. See remarks at end of Section 3.2.

3.30. Referring to Fig. 2-5, Page 12, it is clear that for motion in the XY plane the general acceleration vector of point p has a component along the Q_1 axis given by $a_{q_1} = \ddot{x}\,l + \ddot{y}\,m$ where l, m are direction cosines of this axis. Show that this expression reduces to $a_{q_1} = \ddot{q}_1 + \ddot{q}_2 \cos(\beta - \alpha)$ and that the latter may be obtained directly from equation (*3.24*).

3.31. Referring to Problem 3.22 and applying the methods of Section 3.9, find the component of the acceleration along a tangent to a line (on the cup) for which $r = \text{constant}$. Compare results with the ϕ equation of motion obtained in Problem 3.22. Repeat for a line for which $\phi = \text{constant}$ and compare with the r equation of motion.

3.32. Referring to Fig. 2-21, Page 22, equations (*2.32*) and (*3.24*), determine general expressions for the x_2, y_2 components of acceleration of m. Are the accelerations thus obtained in reality relative to the X_1, Y_1 frame? What forces F_{x_2}, F_{y_2} would be required to hold m fixed relative to X_2, Y_2?

3.33. Referring to Fig. 3-16, write out expressions for the components of the general acceleration vector of m along the X_2, Y_2, Z_2 axes, but relative to the inertial axes X_1, Y_1, Z_1. See Problem 3.27.

3.34. A rotating platform is mounted on the ground with axis of rotation vertical. A rectangular frame of reference is attached to the platform, and the position of a particle relative to this frame is determined by spherical coordinates. Find expressions in the spherical coordinates for the acceleration components a_r, a_θ, a_ϕ relative to an inertial frame, taking account of the earth's rotation as well as that of the platform. See Section 14.7(*b*), Page 290.

CHAPTER 4

Lagrange's Equations of Motion for a System of Particles

4.1 Introductory Remarks.

For pedagogic reasons, the treatment of Lagrange's equations given in Chapter 3 is restricted to systems involving a single particle only. We shall now derive these equations (they finally take the same form as equation (*3.18*)) for a very general type of dynamical system consisting of many particles having any finite number of degrees of freedom and in which there may be moving constraints, moving frames of reference or both. Following this, the remainder of the chapter is concerned with the techniques of applying Lagrange's equations to many and varied types of systems and to *the important matter of understanding the physical significance of the mathematical relations employed.*

4.2 Derivation of Lagrange's Equations for a System of Particles.

We shall first set up the general form of D'Alembert's equation. Consider a system of p particles having masses $m_1, m_2, \ldots, m_p$ acted upon by forces $F_1, F_2, \ldots, F_p$ respectively. Let it be understood that F_1, for example, represents the vector sum of all forces of whatever nature (*including forces of constraint*) acting on m_1, etc. Thus, assuming constant mass and an inertial frame of reference, the "free particle" equations for the individual particles are

$$\begin{array}{l} F_{x_1} = m_1\ddot{x}_1, \quad F_{y_1} = m_1\ddot{y}_1, \quad F_{z_1} = m_1\ddot{z}_1 \\ \cdots\cdots\cdots\cdots\cdots\cdots\cdots\cdots \\ F_{x_p} = m_p\ddot{x}_p, \quad F_{y_p} = m_p\ddot{y}_p, \quad F_{z_p} = m_p\ddot{z}_p \end{array} \tag{4.1}$$

where $F_{x_1}, F_{y_1}, F_{z_1}$ are the rectangular components of F_1, etc. It is important to note that, since F_1, F_2, etc., are assumed to include forces of constraint, relations (*4.1*) are true even though the particles may be constrained in any manner.

Now imagining that each particle of the system undergoes a linear virtual displacement, components of which are $\delta_{x_1}, \delta_{y_1}, \delta_{z_1}$, etc., let us carry through the following simple mathematical operations. Multiplying $F_{x_1} = m\ddot{x}_1$ through by δ_{x_1}, $F_{y_1} = m_1\ddot{y}_1$ by δy_1, etc., for all relations in (*4.1*) and adding the entire group, we obtain

$$\sum_{i=1}^{p} m_i(\ddot{x}_i\,\delta x_i + \ddot{y}_i\,\delta y_i + \ddot{z}_i\,\delta z_i) \quad = \quad \sum_{i=1}^{p} (F_{x_i}\,\delta x_i + F_{y_i}\,\delta y_i + F_{z_i}\,\delta z_i) \tag{4.2}$$

which, when properly interpreted, leads to far reaching results. (See equation (*3.3*).) We shall refer to (*4.2*) as D'Alembert's equation.

At this point several important statements, similar to those following equation (*3.7*), must be made regarding (*4.2*).

(*a*) In so far as the validity of (*4.2*) is concerned, $\delta x_i, \delta y_i, \delta z_i$ need not represent displacements nor do they have to be infinitesimal quantities. Indeed they could be replaced by completely arbitrary quantities a_i, b_i, c_i.

(b) However, assuming that they do represent infinitesimal displacements of the particles, it is clear that the right side of (*4.2*) is just a general expression for the total work δW done by the forces $F_1, F_2, \ldots$ in the displacements $\delta x_1, \delta y_1, \delta z_1, \ldots$ of each and every particle. That is,

$$\delta W = \sum_{i=1}^{p} (F_{x_i}\,\delta x_i + F_{y_i}\,\delta y_i + F_{z_i}\,\delta z_i) \tag{4.3}$$

(c) The above is true even though the imagined (virtual) displacements are not in conformity with the constraints; that is, we may regard the constraints slightly "distorted". In this case δW, of course, includes work done by the forces of constraint.

(d) *But now considering displacements which are in conformity with constraints,* the work done by forces of constraint adds up to zero. (See Sections 2.13 and 2.14, Chapter 2.) In other words, forces of constraint are in effect eliminated from (*4.2*) and (*4.3*).

(e) Under conditions stated in (*d*), relation (*4.2*) is referred to as D'Alembert's principle or equation.

Though on first acquaintance rather unimpressive, *D'Alembert's equation is perhaps the most all-inclusive principle in the entire field of classical mechanics. It includes statics as a special case of dynamics. The equations of motion of any system having a finite number of degrees of freedom, can be obtained directly from (4.2) in any coordinates upon applying proper transformation equations and equations of constraint. Lagrange's equations are merely a more convenient form of (4.2).* All other formulations such as Hamilton's equations, Hamilton's principle, Gauss' principle of least constraint, etc., can be obtained from D'Alembert's equations.

To continue with the derivation, suppose now that the system has n degrees of freedom, where $n \leq 3p$, and that the $3p - n$ equations of constraint are of such a form that all superfluous coordinates can be eliminated from the transformation equations,

$$\begin{aligned} x_i &= x_i(q_1, q_2, \ldots, q_n, t) \\ y_i &= y_i(q_1, q_2, \ldots, q_n, t) \\ z_i &= z_i(q_1, q_2, \ldots, q_n, t) \end{aligned} \tag{4.4}$$

With regard to these equations, we must keep in mind the following facts.

(a) Relations (*4.4*), as indicated above, are transformation equations from which superfluous coordinates have been eliminated and previously referred to as "reduced" equations. Only holonomic systems are considered here. See Section 9.12, Page 193.

(b) Due to constraints the number of generalized coordinates occurring in (*4.4*) is $3p - n$ less than the number of rectangular coordinates.

(c) The appearance of t indicates moving constraints, a moving frame of reference or both.

(d) These equations take full account of constraints in the sense that displacements $\delta x_i, \delta y_i, \delta z_i$ obtained by applying the relations

$$\delta x_i = \frac{\partial x_i}{\partial q_1}\delta q_1 + \frac{\partial x_i}{\partial q_2}\delta q_2 + \cdots + \frac{\partial x_i}{\partial q_n}\delta q_n, \quad \text{etc.} \tag{4.5}$$

(*with t held constant*) to (*4.4*), are in conformity with constraints.

(e) Hence, if $\delta x_i, \delta y_i, \delta z_i$ in (*4.2*) are thus determined, we can be assured that the work done by the forces of constraint adds up to zero. *Therefore forces of constraint may be disregarded.* See Section 2.14, Page 31.

Substituting relations (*4.5*) into (*4.2*) we get, after collecting terms,

$$\sum_{i=1}^{p} m_i\left(\ddot{x}_i\frac{\partial x_i}{\partial q_1} + \ddot{y}_i\frac{\partial y_i}{\partial q_1} + \ddot{z}_i\frac{\partial z_i}{\partial q_1}\right)\delta q_1 + \cdots + \sum_{i=1}^{p} m_i\left(\ddot{x}_i\frac{\partial x_i}{\partial q_n} + \ddot{y}_i\frac{\partial y_i}{\partial q_n} + \ddot{z}_i\frac{\partial z_i}{\partial q_n}\right)\delta q_n$$
$$= \sum_{i=1}^{p}\left(F_{x_i}\frac{\partial x_i}{\partial q_1} + F_{y_i}\frac{\partial y_i}{\partial q_1} + F_{z_i}\frac{\partial z_i}{\partial q_1}\right)\delta q_1 + \cdots + \sum_{i=1}^{p}\left(F_{x_i}\frac{\partial x_i}{\partial q_n} + F_{y_i}\frac{\partial y_i}{\partial q_n} + F_{z_i}\frac{\partial z_i}{\partial q_n}\right)\delta q_n \tag{4.6}$$

But since $q_1, q_2, \ldots, q_n$ are each independently variable (physically, this means that the particles of the system are free to shift positions in such a way that, without violating constraints, any one of the q's may take on any value irrespective of what values the others may have) we can regard each δq as arbitrary. Hence let us suppose that all are zero except, for example, δq_1. Equation (*4.6*) then reduces to

$$\delta W_{q_1} = \sum_{i=1}^{p} m_i\left(\ddot{x}_i\frac{\partial x_i}{\partial q_1} + \ddot{y}_i\frac{\partial y_i}{\partial q_1} + \ddot{z}_i\frac{\partial z_i}{\partial q_1}\right)\delta q_1 = \sum_{i=1}^{p}\left(F_{x_i}\frac{\partial x_i}{\partial q_1} + F_{y_i}\frac{\partial y_i}{\partial q_1} + F_{z_i}\frac{\partial z_i}{\partial q_1}\right)\delta q_1 \tag{4.7}$$

Here, employing relations corresponding to (*3.9*), (*3.10*), (*3.11*) and following the same procedure outlined in Chapter 3, (*4.7*) may be written as

$$\delta W_{q_1} = \left\{\frac{d}{dt}\left[\frac{\partial}{\partial \dot{q}_1}\sum_{i=1}^{p}\frac{m_i}{2}(\dot{x}_i^2 + \dot{y}_i^2 + \dot{z}_i^2)\right] - \frac{\partial}{\partial q_1}\sum_{i=1}^{p}\frac{m_i}{2}(\dot{x}_i^2 + \dot{y}_i^2 + \dot{z}_i^2)\right\}\delta q_1$$
$$= \sum_{i=1}^{p}\left(F_{x_i}\frac{\partial x_i}{\partial q_1} + F_{y_i}\frac{\partial y_i}{\partial q_1} + F_{z_i}\frac{\partial z_i}{\partial q_1}\right)\delta q_1 \tag{4.8}$$

Exactly similar equations follow in the same way involving $q_2, q_3, \ldots, q_n$. That is,

$$\frac{d}{dt}\left(\frac{\partial T}{\partial \dot{q}_r}\right) - \frac{\partial T}{\partial q_r} = F_{q_r} \tag{4.9}$$

where $r = 1, 2, \ldots, n$ and generalized forces F_{q_r} are

$$F_{q_r} = \sum_{i=1}^{p}\left(F_{x_i}\frac{\partial x_i}{\partial q_r} + F_{y_i}\frac{\partial y_i}{\partial q_r} + F_{z_i}\frac{\partial z_i}{\partial q_r}\right) \tag{4.10}$$

Note that (*4.9*) has just the same form as (*3.18*), Page 42.

4.3 Expressing T in Proper Form.

Although $T = \frac{1}{2}\sum_{i=1}^{p} m_i(\dot{x}_i^2 + \dot{y}_i^2 + \dot{z}_i^2)$, where the frame of reference is inertial and there are $3p$ rectangular coordinates, may be regarded as a basic expression for kinetic energy, its final form to which the Lagrangian equations are applied should be expressed in terms of $q_1, q_2, \ldots, q_n$ generalized coordinates, their time derivatives and possibly t. The steps required for this are explained and illustrated in Section 2.7, Page 19. As shown there and in examples which follow, *it is frequently advantageous first to write T in any number of any convenient coordinates.* Then, by means of transformation equations and equations of constraint, it may be put in final form containing no superfluous coordinates.

4.4 Physical Meaning of Generalized Forces.

Again, as in Chapter 3, a generalized force F_{q_r} corresponding to coordinate q_r is a quantity (not always a force in the simple sense of the word) such that $F_{q_r}\delta q_r$ is the work done by all applied forces when q_r alone (time and all other coordinates held fixed) is increased to the extent of $+\delta q_r$. However, in this more general case, it is important to realize that, for a system of p particles having various constraints, *an increase in q_r alone may require a shift in the positions of several or even all the particles. Therefore δW_{q_r} must include the work done by the applied forces acting on all particles, which as a result of $+\delta q_r$ must shift position.*

As proof of the above statements, note that (*4.3*) is a general expression for the work when every particle is given an *arbitrary* infinitesimal displacement. But assuming that q_r only varies, (*4.5*) reduces to

$$\delta x_i = \frac{\partial x_i}{\partial q_r}\delta q_r, \qquad \delta y_i = \frac{\partial y_i}{\partial q_r}\delta q_r, \qquad \delta z_i = \frac{\partial z_i}{\partial q_r}\delta q_r$$

and hence (*4.3*) becomes

$$\delta W_{q_r} = \sum_{i=1}^{p}\left(F_{x_i}\frac{\partial x_i}{\partial q_r} + F_{y_i}\frac{\partial y_i}{\partial q_r} + F_{z_i}\frac{\partial z_i}{\partial q_r}\right)\delta q_r$$

which by (*4.10*) is just $F_{q_r}\delta q_r$. (See Example 4.1, Page 62.)

Inertial forces (see Section 3.3(d), Page 43) are taken complete account of by the left side of (4.9). For reasons discussed and illustrated in the last part of Chapter 2, forces of constraint (for "smooth" constraints) cancel out in (*4.10*). Hence in the discussion of techniques and examples which follow, these forces are disregarded.

4.5 Finding Expressions for Generalized Forces.

Expressions for F_{q_r} may be found by either of the following techniques. They are applicable to any and all types of *applied forces* and are basically the same as those given in Section 3.3(*c*), Page 43. (Inertial forces are *never included*.)

(*a*) Relation (*4.10*) may be applied directly. $F_{x_i}, F_{y_i}, F_{z_i}$, the rectangular components of the force F_i acting on m_i, must be determined from known forces on the system. Explicit expressions for $\partial x_i/\partial q_r$, $\partial y_i/\partial q_r$, $\partial z_i/\partial q_r$ may be obtained from (*4.4*). Frequently this method is tedious.

(*b*) Assuming that all moving constraints and/or moving frames of reference are stationary and that all coordinates except q_r are constant, imagine q_r increased to the extent $+\delta q_r$.

Now by inspection of the particular problem in hand, write out an expression for the work, δW_{q_r}, done by all applied forces on the particles which must shift in position as a result of $+\delta q_r$. This can usually be done directly without the use of rectangular components of force. Then from the relation

$$\delta W_{q_r} = F_{q_r}\delta q_r \qquad (4.11)$$

F_{q_r} follows at once.

In applying this method it is frequently advantageous first to write δW_{q_r} in terms of any number of any coordinates and later express it in terms of $q_1, q_2, \ldots, q_n$.

(*c*) Following the procedure outlined above in (*b*), it is possible and in many cases distinctly advantageous to write an expression for the total work δW_{total} when all coordinates are varied simultaneously. As can be seen from (*4.6*) and from examples to follow, this can be written in the form

$$\delta W_{\text{total}} = [\cdots\cdot]_1\delta q_1 + [\cdots\cdot]_2\delta q_2 + \cdots + [\cdots\cdot]_n\delta q_n \qquad (4.12)$$

where the brackets may be constants but are usually functions of coordinates, velocity, time, etc. It is clear that the bracket $[\ldots.]_r$ is just F_{q_r}. Hence all generalized forces may be read directly from (*4.12*).

An additional note: For a system having, say, four degrees of freedom, let $F_{q_1}, F_{q_2}, F_{q_3}, F_{q_4}$ indicate the generalized forces corresponding to q_1, q_2, q_3, q_4. Now suppose we start the problem over, replacing q_3 and q_4 by different coordinates q_3' and q_4'. Generalized forces are now $F_{q_1}, F_{q_2}, F_{q_3'}, F_{q_4'}$; but F_{q_1} and F_{q_2} of the second instance *are in general not equal to* F_{q_1}, F_{q_2} *of the first,* even though they do correspond to the same coordinates. (See Example 4.1.)

(It should be stated here that: When forces are conservative, it is usually more convenient to determine F_{q_r} from a potential energy function; see Chapter 5. For many dissipative forces the "power function" method offers advantages; see Chapter 6. However, *regardless of the type of applied forces, either (a), (b) or (c) is applicable.*)

4.6 Examples Illustrating the Application of Lagrange's Equations to Systems Involving Several Particles.

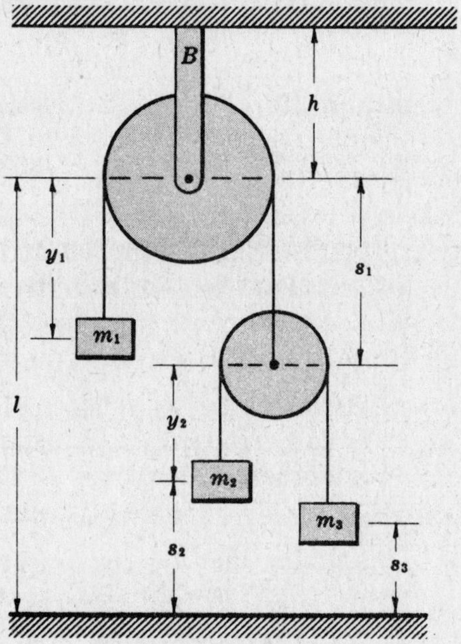

Fig. 4-1

Example 4.1. *A system of three particles.*

Consider the arrangement shown in Fig. 4-1. Assuming vertical motion only, the system has two degrees of freedom. Of the various coordinates which could be used, we shall choose y_1 and y_2. Disregarding masses of the pulleys,

$$T = \tfrac{1}{2}m_1\dot{y}_1^2 + \tfrac{1}{2}m_2\dot{s}_2^2 + \tfrac{1}{2}m_3\dot{s}_3^2$$

But as is easily seen, $\dot{s}_2 = \dot{y}_1 - \dot{y}_2$ and $\dot{s}_3 = \dot{y}_1 + \dot{y}_2$. Hence

$$T = \tfrac{1}{2}m_1\dot{y}_1^2 + \tfrac{1}{2}m_2(\dot{y}_1 - \dot{y}_2)^2 + \tfrac{1}{2}m_3(\dot{y}_1 + \dot{y}_2)^2$$

which now involves $\dot{y}_1$ and $\dot{y}_2$ only. (Note that y_2 is a non-inertial coordinate.)

The equation of motion corresponding to y_1 is obtained as follows:

$$\frac{\partial T}{\partial \dot{y}_1} = m_1\dot{y}_1 + m_2(\dot{y}_1 - \dot{y}_2) + m_3(\dot{y}_1 + \dot{y}_2)$$

and

$$\frac{d}{dt}\left(\frac{\partial T}{\partial \dot{y}_1}\right) = (m_1 + m_2 + m_3)\ddot{y}_1 + (m_3 - m_2)\ddot{y}_2, \qquad \frac{\partial T}{\partial y_1} = 0$$

Hence $\quad (m_1 + m_2 + m_3)\ddot{y}_1 + (m_3 - m_2)\ddot{y}_2 = F_{y_1}$

To obtain an expression for F_{y_1} we shall apply equation (*4.11*). Hence we determine the work done by driving forces (gravity), neglecting forces of constraint (tensions in the cords), when y_1 is increased to the extent of $+\delta y_1$ (m_1 moved down a bit) with y_2 kept constant. This is $\delta W_{y_1} = +m_1 g\,\delta y_1 - (m_2 + m_3)g\,\delta y_1$. The second term in this expression comes from the fact that, since y_2 remains constant, m_2 and m_3 must be lifted up the same distance that m_1 moves down. Therefore $F_{y_1} = (m_1 - m_2 - m_3)g$ and the complete equation of motion corresponding to y_1 is

$$(m_1 + m_2 + m_3)\ddot{y}_1 + (m_3 - m_2)\ddot{y}_2 = (m_1 - m_2 - m_3)g \qquad (1)$$

To obtain the y_2 equation of motion, it is seen that

$$\frac{d}{dt}\left(\frac{\partial T}{\partial \dot{y}_2}\right) = (m_2 + m_3)\ddot{y}_2 + (m_3 - m_2)\ddot{y}_1 \qquad \text{and} \qquad \frac{\partial T}{\partial y_2} = 0$$

An expression for F_{y_2} is obtained by letting y_2 increase to the extent of $+\delta y_2$, with y_1 constant. Clearly the work done by gravity is $\delta W_{y_2} = (m_2 - m_3)g\,\delta y_2 = F_{y_2}\,\delta y_2$. Hence, finally, the y_2 equation of motion has the form

$$(m_2 + m_3)\ddot{y}_2 + (m_3 - m_2)\ddot{y}_1 = (m_2 - m_3)g \qquad (2)$$

Relations (*1*) and (*2*) can be solved simultaneously for $\ddot{y}_1$ and $\ddot{y}_2$, and the resulting equations integrated at once.

As a simple example of (*4.12*), note that

$$\delta W_{\text{total}} = (m_1\,\delta y_1 - m_2\,\delta s_2 - m_3\,\delta s_3)g \qquad (3)$$

But $\delta s_2 = \delta y_1 - \delta y_2$ and $\delta s_3 = \delta y_1 + \delta y_2$. Hence, eliminating δs_2 and δs_3,

$$\delta W_{\text{total}} = (m_1 - m_2 - m_3)g\,\delta y_1 + (m_2 - m_3)g\,\delta y_2$$

from which F_{y_1} and F_{y_2} may be read off directly.

As an extension of this example, let us use y_1 and s_2 as coordinates. Since $s_2 + s_3 - 2y_1 =$ constant, $\dot{s}_3 = 2\dot{y}_1 - \dot{s}_2$. Hence

$$T = \tfrac{1}{2}m_1\dot{y}_1^2 + \tfrac{1}{2}m_2\dot{s}_2^2 + \tfrac{1}{2}m_3(2\dot{y}_1 - \dot{s}_2)^2$$

from which

$$(m_1 + 4m_3)\,\ddot{y}_1 - 2m_3\,\ddot{s}_2 = F_{y_1} \qquad (4)$$

$$(m_2 + m_3)\,\ddot{s}_2 - 2m_3\,\ddot{y}_1 = F_{s_2} \qquad (5)$$

To find F_{y_1}, hold s_2 fixed (m_2 not allowed to shift position) and imagine y_1 increased to $y_1 + \delta y_1$ (m_1 is moved down a bit). But, as seen by inspection, this requires an upward shift of m_3 to the extent of $2\,\delta y_1$. Hence

$$\delta W_{y_1} = +m_1 g\,\delta y_1 - 2m_3 g\,\delta y_1 \qquad \text{or} \qquad F_{y_1} = (m_1 - 2m_3)g$$

(Note that expressions for F_{y_1} in (*1*) and (*4*) are not the same.) In a similar manner it follows that $F_{s_2} = (m_3 - m_2)g$.

Applying (*4.12*), we can again use (*3*). Eliminating δs_3 by $\delta s_3 = 2\,\delta y_1 - \delta s_2$,

$$\delta W_{\text{total}} = (m_1 - 2m_3)g\,\delta y_1 + (m_3 - m_2)g\,\delta s_2$$

giving again the same expressions for F_{y_1} and F_{s_2}.

It should be noted that, when varying one of the n coordinates, holding the others fixed, other coordinates not used in treating the problem may, of course, vary. For example, F_{y_1} (see first part of above example) was found by holding y_2 fixed and varying y_1. In so doing, each of s_1, s_2, s_3 varied.

Example 4.2. *Further emphasis on generalized forces.*

In Fig. 4-2, neglect masses of pulleys and assume vertical motion only with gravity and external forces $f_1, \ldots, f_5$ acting. For example, note that, for a displacement $+\delta q_1$ (all other coordinates held fixed), m_1 moves down a distance δq_1 and m_5 must move up a distance $4\,\delta q_1$. Following this reasoning,

$$F_{q_1} = (m_1 g + f_1) - 4(m_5 g + f_5)$$
$$F_{q_2} = m_2 g + f_2 - (m_3 g + f_3)$$
$$F_{q_3} = -(m_2 + m_3)g - f_2 - f_3 + 2(m_5 g + f_5)$$
$$F_{q_4} = m_5 g + f_5 - (m_4 g + f_4)$$

Now using q_1, q_2, s, q_4 as coordinates, show that

$$F_{q_1} = m_1 g + f_1 - (m_2 g + m_3 g + f_2 + f_3) - 2(m_5 g + f_5)$$
$$F_s = (m_2 + m_3)g + f_2 + f_3 - 2(m_5 g + f_5)$$

F_{q_2} *and* F_{q_4} are the same as above. Note the difference in F_{q_1} in the two cases.

In general the expression for F_{q_r} depends on what other coordinates are employed.

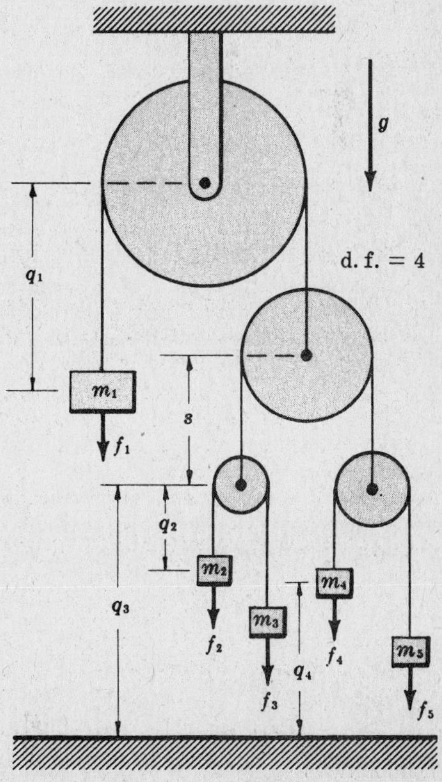

Fig. 4-2

Example 4.3. *Motion of a dumbbell in a vertical plane.*

The particles having masses m_1 and m_2, shown in Fig. 4-3, are rigidly fastened to a light rod and are free to move in the vertical XY plane under the action of gravity. Assuming no rotation about the rod as an axis and applying the center-of-mass theorem, we write

$$T \quad = \quad \frac{m_1 + m_2}{2}(\dot{x}^2 + \dot{y}^2) \; + \; \frac{I}{2}\dot{\theta}^2$$

where (x, y) locate the center of mass, I is the moment of inertia of the dumbbell about an axis through its center of mass and perpendicular to the rod, and θ is the angle indicated. Since the system has three degrees of freedom and x, y, θ are convenient coordinates, T is already in appropriate form.

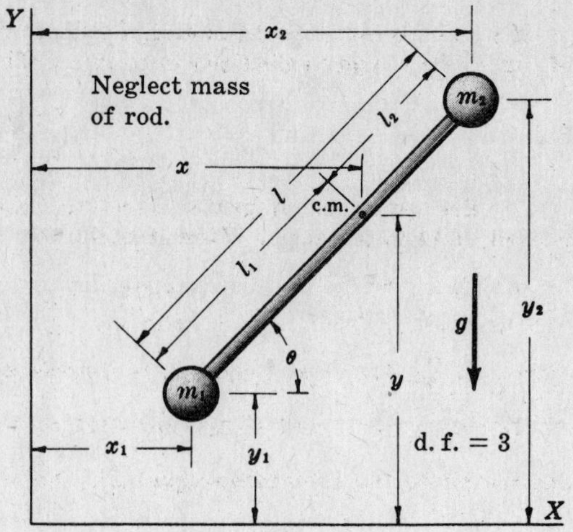

Fig. 4-3

Applying Lagrange's equations, it follows at once that

$$(m_1 + m_2)\,\ddot{x} \;=\; F_x, \qquad (m_1 + m_2)\,\ddot{y} \;=\; F_y, \qquad I\,\ddot{\theta} = F_\theta$$

Holding y and θ fixed and increasing x to $x + \delta x$, it is clear that the work done by gravity $\delta W_x = 0$. Hence $F_x = 0$. Likewise $F_y = -(m_1 + m_2)g$ and $F_\theta = 0$. Therefore the equations of motion in final form are

$$\ddot{x} = 0, \qquad \ddot{y} = -g, \qquad \ddot{\theta} = 0$$

This means that the center of mass has the simple motion of a projectile (neglecting air resistance) and the dumbbell rotates with constant angular velocity $\dot{\theta}$.

Example 4.3A. *Extension of Example 4.3.*

Let us set up the equations of motion of the dumbbell using coordinates x_1, y_1, θ. T may be written as $T = \frac{1}{2}m_1(\dot{x}_1^2 + \dot{y}_1^2) + \frac{1}{2}m_2(\dot{x}_2^2 + \dot{y}_2^2)$. But it is seen that $x_2 = x_1 + l\cos\theta$, $y_2 = y_1 + l\sin\theta$. Differentiating these relations and eliminating $\dot{x}_2, \dot{y}_2$ from the above, we get

$$T \quad = \quad \frac{m_1 + m_2}{2}(\dot{x}_1^2 + \dot{y}_1^2) \; + \; \frac{m_2}{2}(l^2\dot{\theta}^2 - 2l\dot{x}_1\dot{\theta}\sin\theta + 2l\dot{y}_1\dot{\theta}\cos\theta)$$

Applying Lagrange's equations, the following results are obtained:

$$(m_1 + m_2)\,\ddot{x}_1 \;-\; m_2 l\,\ddot{\theta}\sin\theta \;-\; m_2 l\,\dot{\theta}^2\cos\theta \;=\; F_{x_1}$$

$$(m_1 + m_2)\,\ddot{y}_1 \;+\; m_2 l\,\ddot{\theta}\cos\theta \;-\; m_2 l\,\dot{\theta}^2\sin\theta \;=\; F_{y_1}$$

$$m_2(l^2\,\ddot{\theta} \;-\; l\,\ddot{x}_1\sin\theta \;+\; l\,\ddot{y}_1\cos\theta) \;=\; F_\theta$$

It easily follows that $F_{x_1} = 0$, $F_{y_1} = -(m_1 + m_2)g$ and $F_\theta = -m_2 gl\cos\theta$.

It is important to note that when coordinates are changed the form of the equations of motion may change greatly. Also, even when some of the original coordinates are retained (θ in this case), the corresponding generalized forces change as shown in Example 4.2.

Example 4.4. *Pendulum with a sliding support.*

The pendulum of Fig. 4.4 is attached to a block of mass m_1 which is free to slide without friction along the horizontal X axis. Assuming r constant and all motion confined to the XY plane, the system has two degrees of freedom. We shall use coordinates x_1 and θ. Starting with coordinates x_1, x_2, y_2 it is seen that

$$T \quad = \quad \tfrac{1}{2}m_1\dot{x}_1^2 \; + \; \tfrac{1}{2}m_2(\dot{x}_2^2 + \dot{y}_2^2)$$

But $x_2 = x_1 + r\sin\theta$ and $y_2 = r\cos\theta$. Eliminating $\dot{x}_2$ and $\dot{y}_2$ from T, we finally get

$$T \quad = \quad \tfrac{1}{2}m_1\dot{x}_1^2 + \tfrac{1}{2}m_2(\dot{x}_1^2 \; + \; 2r\dot{x}_1\dot{\theta}\cos\theta \; + \; r^2\dot{\theta}^2)$$

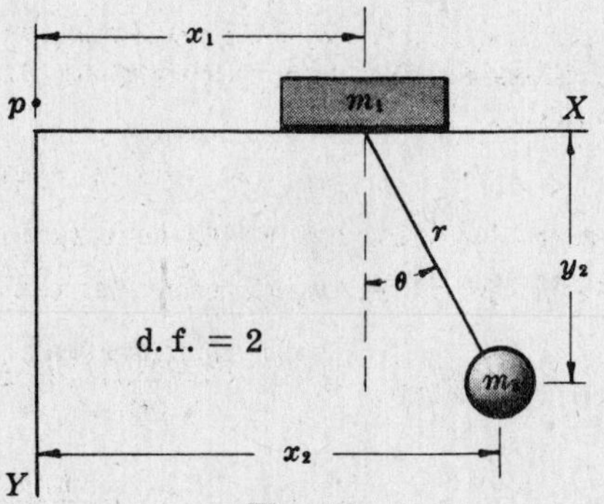

Fig. 4-4

from which $(m_1 + m_2)\,\ddot{x}_1 + m_2 r\,\ddot{\theta}\cos\theta - m_2 r\dot{\theta}^2\sin\theta \;=\; F_{x_1}$ and $m_2 r\,\ddot{x}_1\cos\theta + m_2 r^2\,\ddot{\theta} \;=\; F_\theta$. In the usual way we find $F_x = 0$ and $F_\theta = -m_2 gr\sin\theta$, and thus the equations of motions are complete.

If it is assumed that the motion is such that θ is always quite small, we can replace $\cos\theta$ in T by unity, $\sin\theta$ in F_θ by θ, and neglect the term in $\dot{\theta}^2$. The equations of motion then become

$$(m_1 + m_2)\ddot{x}_1 + m_2 r\ddot{\theta} = 0$$
$$m_2 r\ddot{x}_1 + m_2 r^2\ddot{\theta} = -m_2 g r\theta$$

The first equation integrates directly. Eliminating $\ddot{x}_1$ from the second equation by the first, we obtain an easily integrated form. Final results are

$$x_1 + \frac{m_2 r\theta}{m_1 + m_2} = C_1 t + C_2, \qquad \theta = A\sin(\omega t + \delta)$$

where C_1, C_2, A, δ are arbitrary constants to be determined by specific initial conditions and $\omega = \sqrt{\dfrac{(m_1+m_2)g}{rm_1}}$. Let us assume that at $t = 0$, $x_1 = x_0$, $\dot{x}_1 = \dot{x}_0$, $\theta = \theta_0$ and $\dot{\theta} = \dot{\theta}_0$. Substituting these conditions into the integrated equations, we obtain four equations from which it follows that

$$C_1 = \dot{x}_0 + \frac{m_2 r}{m_1 + m_2}\dot{\theta}_0, \qquad C_2 = x_0 + \frac{m_2 r}{m_1 + m_2}\theta_0, \qquad A = \sqrt{\theta_0^2 + \frac{\dot{\theta}_0^2}{\omega^2}}, \qquad \tan\delta = \frac{\theta_0\omega}{\dot{\theta}_0}$$

which illustrates the general method of determining constants of integration from given initial conditions.

Example 4.5. *The masses of Fig. 4-5 move vertically under the action of gravity and the springs.*

Applying the theorem of Section 2.10, Page 26, it is seen that

$$T = \left(\frac{m_1 + m_2 + m_3}{2}\right)\dot{y}^2 + \frac{m_1}{2}\dot{q}_1^2 + \frac{m_2}{2}\dot{q}_2^2 + \frac{m_3}{2}\dot{q}_3^2$$

But from the definition of center-of-mass, $m_1 q_1 = m_2 q_2 + m_3 q_3$. Differentiating this and eliminating $\dot{q}_1$ from T, we have

$$T = \frac{M}{2}\dot{y}^2 + \frac{m_1}{2}\left(\frac{m_2}{m_1}\dot{q}_2 + \frac{m_3}{m_1}\dot{q}_3\right)^2 + \frac{m_2}{2}\dot{q}_2^2 + \frac{m_3}{2}\dot{q}_3^2$$

where $M = m_1 + m_2 + m_3$. Since the system has three degrees of freedom and y, q_2, q_3 are suitable coordinates, it is seen that the second form of T contains no superfluous coordinates.

Applying Lagrange's equations, the following equations of motion are easily obtained:

$$\frac{m_2}{m_1}(m_1 + m_2)\ddot{q}_2 + \frac{m_2 m_3}{m_1}\ddot{q}_3 = F_{q_2},$$

$$\frac{m_2 m_3}{m_1}\ddot{q}_2 + \frac{m_3(m_1 + m_3)}{m_1}\ddot{q}_3 = F_{q_3}, \qquad M\ddot{y} = F_y$$

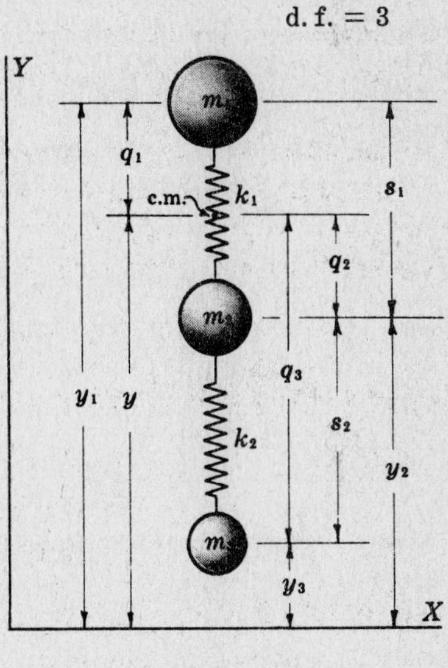

Fig. 4-5

The following is a clear demonstration of the nature of generalized forces and the technique of finding expressions for same. Inspection will show that for a general displacement of the entire system (see equation (*4.12*)),

$$\delta W_{\text{total}} = -k_1(q_1 + q_2 - l_1)(\delta q_1 + \delta q_2) - k_2(q_3 - q_2 - l_2)(\delta q_3 - \delta q_2) - Mg\,\delta y$$

where k_1, k_2 are the spring constants and l_1, l_2 are the unstretched lengths of the upper and lower springs respectively. But again using the center of mass relation, $\delta q_1 = \dfrac{m_2}{m_1}\delta q_2 + \dfrac{m_3}{m_1}\delta q_3$. Eliminating q_1 and δq_1,

$$\delta W_{\text{total}} = \left[\frac{-k_1(m_1+m_2)}{m_1}\left(\frac{m_1+m_2}{m_1}q_2 + \frac{m_3}{m_1}q_3 - l_1\right) + k_2(q_3 - q_2 - l_2)\right]\delta q_2$$
$$+ \left[\frac{-k_1 m_3}{m_1}\left(\frac{m_1+m_2}{m_1}q_2 + \frac{m_3}{m_1}q_3 - l_1\right) - k_2(q_3 - q_2 - l_2)\right]\delta q_3 - Mg\,\delta y$$

This has the form of (*4.12*) and it is clear that the coefficients of $\delta q_2, \delta q_3, \delta y$ are the generalized forces F_{q_2}, F_{q_3}, F_y respectively. Hence the equations of motion are complete. See Problem 4.5, Page 74.

As an extension of the example, let us determine the generalized forces by a direct application of (*4.10*) which, for this system, takes the form

$$F_{q_r} = F_{y_1}\frac{\partial y_1}{\partial q_r} + F_{y_2}\frac{\partial y_2}{\partial q_r} + F_{y_3}\frac{\partial y_3}{\partial q_r}$$

where q_r may represent y, q_2 or q_3. F_{y_1} is the total vertical force on m_1, etc. Inspection of the figure shows that (since $q_1 = \frac{m_2}{m_1}q_2 + \frac{m_3}{m_1}q_3$)

$$F_{y_1} = -m_1 g - k_1\left(\frac{m_2}{m_1}q_2 + \frac{m_3}{m_1}q_3 + q_2 - l_1\right)$$

$$F_{y_2} = -m_2 g + k_1\left(\frac{m_2}{m_1}q_2 + \frac{m_3}{m_1}q_3 + q_2 - l_1\right) - k_2(q_3 - q_2 - l_2)$$

$$F_{y_3} = -m_3 g + k_2(q_3 - q_2 - l_2)$$

Also $$y_1 = y + \frac{m_2}{m_1}q_2 + \frac{m_3}{m_1}q_3, \qquad y_2 = y - q_2, \qquad y_3 = y - q_3$$

Hence F_{q_2}, for example, is given by

$$F_{q_2} = F_{y_1}\frac{\partial y_1}{\partial q_2} + F_{y_2}\frac{\partial y_2}{\partial q_2} + F_{y_3}\frac{\partial y_3}{\partial q_2}$$

But $\frac{\partial y_1}{\partial q_2} = \frac{m_2}{m_1}$, $\frac{\partial y_2}{\partial q_2} = -1$, $\frac{\partial y_3}{\partial q_2} = 0$. Thus the above relation easily reduces to the previously found expression for F_{q_2}. In like manner, F_{q_3} and F_y follow at once.

The equation of motion corresponding to y shows that the center of mass falls with constant acceleration g. The remaining two easily integrated equations may be put in the form

$$a_{11}\ddot{q}_2 + b_{11}q_2 + a_{12}\ddot{q}_3 + b_{12}q_3 = A$$
$$a_{21}\ddot{q}_2 + b_{21}q_2 + a_{22}\ddot{q}_3 + b_{22}q_3 = B$$

where the a's, b's and A, B are constants. We shall not consider these equations further at this point since methods for integrating this type are treated in detail in Chapter 10.

Example 4.6. *The double pendulum of Fig. 2-10, Page 14.*

Let us assume that the strings supporting the masses are inextensible and that motion is confined to a plane. Expression (*2.42*), Page 24, reduces to

$$T = \frac{m_1}{2}r_1^2\dot{\theta}^2 + \frac{m_2}{2}[r_1^2\dot{\theta}^2 + r_2^2\dot{\phi}^2 + 2r_1r_2\dot{\theta}\dot{\phi}\cos(\phi - \theta)]$$

Thus $$\frac{\partial T}{\partial\dot{\theta}} = m_1r_1^2\dot{\theta} + m_2r_1^2\dot{\theta} + m_2r_1r_2\dot{\phi}\cos(\phi-\theta)$$

$$\frac{d}{dt}\left(\frac{\partial T}{\partial\dot{\theta}}\right) = (m_1+m_2)r_1^2\ddot{\theta} + m_2r_1r_2\ddot{\phi}\cos(\phi-\theta) - m_2r_1r_2\dot{\phi}(\dot{\phi}-\dot{\theta})\sin(\phi-\theta)$$

Hence $$\frac{\partial T}{\partial\theta} = m_2r_1r_2\dot{\theta}\dot{\phi}\sin(\phi-\theta)$$

$$(m_1+m_2)r_1^2\ddot{\theta} + m_2r_1r_2\ddot{\phi}\cos(\phi-\theta) - m_2r_1r_2\dot{\phi}^2\sin(\phi-\theta) = F_\theta$$

Similarly, the equation corresponding to ϕ is

$$m_2r_2^2\ddot{\phi} + m_2r_1r_2\ddot{\theta}\cos(\phi-\theta) + m_2r_1r_2\dot{\theta}^2\sin(\phi-\theta) = F_\phi$$

To find F_θ, imagine that θ is increased to the extent of $+\delta\theta$ with ϕ held fixed. This means that *both masses* must be lifted up slightly. Thus

$$\delta W_\theta = -(m_1+m_2)gr_1\sin\theta\,\delta\theta \qquad \text{and} \qquad F_\theta = -(m_1+m_2)gr_1\sin\theta$$

With θ fixed, m_1 does not move and $\delta W_\phi = -m_2gr_2\sin\phi\,\delta\phi$, from which $F_\phi = -m_2gr_2\sin\phi$. Therefore the equations of motion are complete. For small motion (θ and ϕ always small) these equations of motion reduce to the same form as those of Example 4.5 and can, therefore, be integrated. See Chapter 10.

Example 4.7. *A system moving with constant linear acceleration.* (Fig. 4-1.)

The support of the pulley system, shown in Fig. 4-1, Page 62, is moving upward with constant acceleration a. In this case,

$$T = \tfrac{1}{2}m_1(\dot{l}-\dot{y}_1)^2 + \tfrac{1}{2}m_2\dot{s}_2^2 + \tfrac{1}{2}m_3\dot{s}_3^2$$

where $\dot{l} = at$, $\dot{y}_2 + \dot{s}_2 - \dot{y}_1 = at$, $\dot{s}_3 = 2\dot{y}_2 + \dot{s}_2$. Thus

$$T = \tfrac{1}{2}m_1(at-\dot{y}_1)^2 + \tfrac{1}{2}m_2(at+\dot{y}_1-\dot{y}_2)^2 + \tfrac{1}{2}m_3(at+\dot{y}_1+\dot{y}_2)^2$$

from which the equations of motion are

$$(m_1+m_2+m_3)\ddot{y}_1 + (m_3-m_2)\ddot{y}_2 + (m_2+m_3-m_1)a = F_{y_1}$$

$$(m_3-m_2)\ddot{y}_1 + (m_2+m_3)\ddot{y}_2 + (m_3-m_2)a = F_{y_2}$$

Since in the determination of generalized forces time is held fixed, $F_{y_1} = (m_1-m_2-m_3)g$, $F_{y_2} = (m_2-m_3)g$ exactly as in Example 4.1. Indeed, for this simple case of constant linear acceleration, the equations of motion are just the same except that, in effect, g is increased to $g+a$.

As an extension of this the student can easily write out equations of motion assuming that h varies in any known manner with time. (See Problem 4.16, Page 77.)

Example 4.8. *A system moving with rotation and linear acceleration.*

Consider the system shown in Fig. 4-6. A smooth tube containing masses m_1 and m_2 connected with springs is mounted on a rotating table at an angle α. A vertical plane passing through the center of the tube also passes through the axis of rotation of the table. The table is mounted on an elevator which moves up with an acceleration a. We shall obtain the equations of motion of m_1 and m_2 in terms of the coordinates q_1 and q_2.

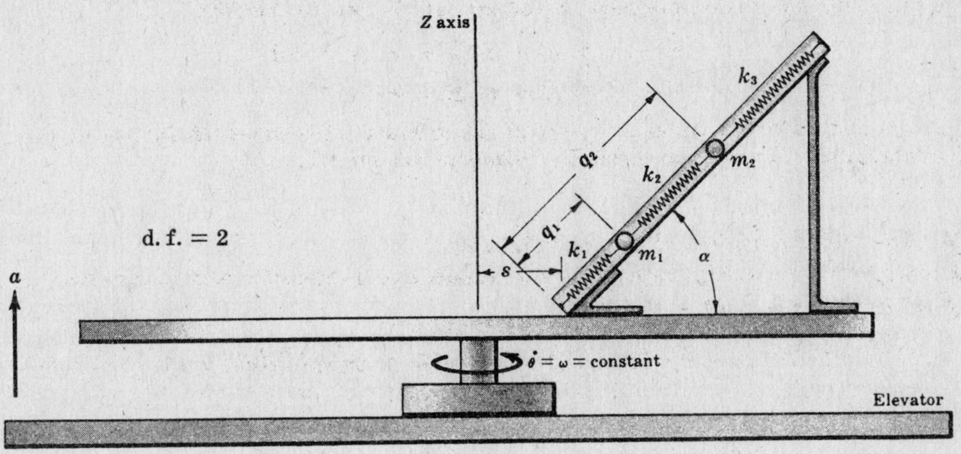

Fig. 4-6

In cylindrical coordinates fixed relative to the earth and assumed inertial,

$$T = \tfrac{1}{2}m_1(\dot{r}_1^2 + r_1^2\dot{\theta}_1^2 + \dot{z}_1^2) + \tfrac{1}{2}m_2(\dot{r}_2^2 + r_2^2\dot{\theta}^2 + \dot{z}_2^2)$$

Taking the origin of these coordinates at the center of rotation of the disk, it is seen that

$$r_1 = s + q_1\cos\alpha, \quad \theta_1 = \omega t, \quad z_1 = q_1\sin\alpha + \tfrac{1}{2}at^2$$

$$r_2 = s + q_2\cos\alpha, \quad \theta_2 = \omega t, \quad z_2 = q_2\sin\alpha + \tfrac{1}{2}at^2$$

By means of these relations T is easily expressed as

$$T = \tfrac{1}{2}m_1[\dot{q}_1^2 + 2\dot{q}_1 at\sin\alpha + (s+q_1\cos\alpha)^2\omega^2 + a^2t^2] + \tfrac{1}{2}m_2[\dot{q}_2^2 + 2\dot{q}_2 at\sin\alpha + (s+q_2\cos\alpha)^2\omega^2 + a^2t^2]$$

The only coordinates now occurring in T are q_1 and q_2, and it should be noted that time appears explicitly.

An application of Lagrange's equations gives

$$m_1(\ddot{q}_1 + a \sin\alpha) - m_1\omega^2(s + q_1 \cos\alpha)\cos\alpha = F_{q_1}$$

$$m_2(\ddot{q}_2 + a \sin\alpha) - m_2\omega^2(s + q_2 \cos\alpha)\cos\alpha = F_{q_2}$$

Disregarding the motion of the system, the work done by gravity and the springs when q_1 alone is increased slightly is

$$\delta W_{q_1} = -m_1 g \sin\alpha\, \delta q_1 - k_1(q_1 - l_1)\,\delta q_1 + k_2(q_2 - q_1 - l_2)\,\delta q_1$$

where l_1 and l_2 represent the unstretched lengths of the first and second springs respectively. Thus

$$F_{q_1} = -m_1 g \sin\alpha - (k_1 + k_2)q_1 + k_2 q_2 + k_1 l_1 - k_2 l_2$$

Similarly,

$$F_{q_2} = -m_2 g \sin\alpha - (k_2 + k_3)q_2 + k_2 q_1 + k_2 l_2 + k_3(l_1 + l_2)$$

This completes the equations of motion. Inspection will show that the acceleration of the elevator has the effect of increasing g to the extent of a.

Example 4.9. *Equations of motion where parts of a system are forced to move in a known manner.*

A type of problem sometimes encountered in practice may be illustrated by the following.

Assuming that a mechanism attached to the ground, Fig. 4-1, exerts a variable force on m_2 such that s_2 varies in a known manner with time, we shall determine the equation of motion for the remainder of the system. Neglect masses of pulleys.

Due to this forced motion (that is, since s_2 is a known function of time) the system now has, assuming vertical motions only, one degree of freedom. Either y_1 or y_2 is a suitable coordinate and, assuming the cords are always tight, $s_1 + y_2 + s_2 = C_1$ and $s_1 + y_1 = C_2$. Thus $\dot{y}_2 = \dot{y}_1 - \dot{s}_2$. Hence we write

$$T = \tfrac{1}{2}m_1\dot{y}_1^2 + \tfrac{1}{2}m_2\dot{s}_2^2 + \tfrac{1}{2}m_3(2\dot{y}_1 - \dot{s}_2)^2$$

To be more specific, suppose the force applied to m_2 is such that $s_2 = s_0 + A \sin\omega t$, where s_0 is a constant; then

$$T = \tfrac{1}{2}m_1\dot{y}_1^2 + \tfrac{1}{2}m_2 A^2\omega^2\cos^2\omega t + \tfrac{1}{2}m_3(2\dot{y}_1 - A\omega\cos\omega t)^2$$

and the equation of motion is

$$(m_1 + 4m_3)\,\ddot{y}_1 + 2m_3 A\omega^2 \sin\omega t = F_{y_1}$$

(Note that the second term in T, which is a function of t alone, need not be retained.) Applying $\delta W_{y_1} = F_{y_1}\,\delta y_1$, holding t constant, we find $F_{y_1} = (m_1 - 2m_3)g$. This completes the equation of motion. It is seen that F_{y_1} here is not the same as in Example 4.1.

As a further example consider the system shown in Fig. 2-15, Page 16, which has four degrees of freedom. But suppose that an external vertical force acting on the shaft of the upper pulley causes s_1 to vary in a known manner and another acting on m_2 gives it a known motion. The system now has only two degrees of freedom and, assuming the cords always tight, T can be written in terms of, say, $\dot{s}_2, \dot{s}_3, t$. (See Problem 4.19, Page 78.)

4.7 Forces on and Motion of Charged Particles in an Electromagnetic Field.

The treatment of the motion of charged particles and masses through electric and magnetic fields is an important branch of dynamics. However, except for the special case of inertial coordinate systems and relatively low velocities (which we shall assume below), the problem must be treated by relativistic methods. This topic could constitute a sizeable chapter in itself.

On the above assumptions the rectangular components of force on a particle carrying a charge Q and moving with velocity $(\dot{x}, \dot{y}, \dot{z})$ through a space in which there exists an electric field E, components (E_x, E_y, E_z), and magnetic field $B(B_x, B_y, B_z)$ are given by

$$F_x = QE_x + Q(\dot{y}B_z - \dot{z}B_y), \quad F_y = QE_y + Q(\dot{z}B_x - \dot{x}B_z), \quad F_z = QE_z + Q(\dot{x}B_y - \dot{y}B_x) \qquad (4.13)$$

where E and B may be functions of coordinates and time.

Using these expressions for F_x, F_y, F_z in (*4.10*), Page 60, the procedure for setting up equations of motion is just the same as in previous examples.

Example 4.10. *Equations of Motion of a charged dumbbell in an electric and magnetic field.*

The small spheres, Fig. 4-3, Page 64, carry uniformly distributed charges $-Q_1$ and $+Q_2$ respectively. Assume a magnetic field in the direction of the Z axis and an electric field E in the direction of X, each being uniform throughout the XY plane. Let us consider motion in the XY plane only.

As the dumbbell moves, m_1 experiences a force

$$F_{x_1} = -Q_1E - Q_1B\dot{y}_1, \qquad F_{y_1} = Q_1B\dot{x}_1$$

and similarly for m_2. Hence for a general virtual displacement,

$$\delta W_{\text{total}} = -(Q_1E + Q_1B\dot{y}_1)\,\delta x_1 + Q_1B\dot{x}_1\,\delta y_1 + (Q_2E + Q_2B\dot{y}_2)\,\delta x_2 - Q_2B\dot{x}_2\,\delta y_2$$

Choosing x, y, θ as generalized coordinates (see Example 4.3), it follows from the relations $x_1 = x - l_1\cos\theta$, $y_1 = y - l_1\sin\theta$, etc., that $\dot{x}_1 = \dot{x} + l_1\dot{\theta}\sin\theta$, $\delta x_1 = \delta x + l_1\sin\theta\,\delta\theta$, etc. Hence the above can finally be written as

$$\begin{aligned}\delta W_{\text{total}} = {} & [(Q_2 - Q_1)E + B(Q_2 - Q_1)\dot{y} + B(Q_2l_2 + Q_1l_1)\dot{\theta}\cos\theta]\,\delta x \\ & + [B(Q_1 - Q_2)\dot{x} + B(Q_1l_1 + Q_2l_2)\dot{\theta}\sin\theta]\,\delta y \\ & - (Q_1l_1 + Q_2l_2)[E\sin\theta + B(\dot{x}\cos\theta + \dot{y}\sin\theta)]\,\delta\theta\end{aligned}$$

from which expressions for the generalized forces are read off directly. (This has the form of (*4.12*).) T and hence the left side of the equations of motion are exactly as in Example 4.3. (See Problem 4.20.)

4.8 Regarding the Physical Meaning of Lagrange's Equations.

The remarks of Section 3.10, Page 50, having to do with a single particle, will now be extended to a system of p particles.

Suppose that t and all coordinates except q_r in equations (*4.4*) are held constant. These equations then, in effect, become

$$x_i = x_i(q_r), \qquad y_i = y_i(q_r), \qquad z_i = z_i(q_r) \tag{4.14}$$

Since x_i, y_i, z_i are the rectangular coordinates of the individual particle m_i, there is a set of these equations for each of the p particles. That is, (*4.14*) represents p sets of equations.

Now allowing q_r to vary and plotting the x_i, y_i, z_i coordinates, (*4.14*), of any one particle m_i, a curve (in general a three-dimensional space curve) is obtained which represents a possible path of m_i in conformity with constraints. We shall refer to this as a q_r-line for m_i. Clearly the location and shape of this curve depends on the constant values assigned to t and the remaining coordinates as well as the nature of the constraints. In this sense there can be an unlimited number of q_r-lines for any one particle. But at any given instant and for given values of the other coordinates a specific q_r-line can be plotted relative to X, Y, Z axes. In the same way q_r-lines can be plotted for each of the particles.

The above ideas are not difficult to follow since they concern familiar three-dimensional lines and surfaces. As a simple example consider the double pendulum of Fig. 2-10, Page 14. Equations (*2.13*) correspond to (*4.4*), Page 59. For various constant values of ϕ, θ-lines for m_1 as well as m_2 can be traced on the XY plane. Likewise ϕ-lines can be drawn for m_2. (There are no ϕ-lines for m_1.) See also Example 4.11.

The above meaning of q_r-lines serves a useful purpose in what follows.

Writing δs_{ir} as the linear displacement of m_i along a q_r-line, it is seen that its components $\delta x_i, \delta y_i, \delta z_i$ are just the virtual displacements considered in equations (*4.2*), (*4.3*), etc. Direction cosines l_{ir}, m_{ir}, n_{ir} of the tangent to a q_r-line at any point are given by

$$l_{ir} = \frac{\delta x_i}{\delta s_{ir}}, \qquad m_{ir} = \frac{\delta y_i}{\delta s_{ir}}, \qquad n_{ir} = \frac{\delta z_i}{\delta s_{ir}} \tag{4.15}$$

where the element of path length $\delta s_{ir} = (\delta x_i^2 + \delta y_i^2 + \delta z_i^2)^{1/2}$. (Note that δs_{ir} is exactly the displacement (linear) which we imagine given to m_i for purposes of determining δW_{q_r} in equation (*4.11*).) But from (*4.4*), with t and all q's except q_r held fixed, $\delta x_i = \dfrac{\partial x_i}{\partial q_r}\delta q_r$, etc. Thus

$$\delta s_{ir} = \left[\left(\frac{\partial x_i}{\partial q_r}\right)^2 + \left(\frac{\partial y_i}{\partial q_r}\right)^2 + \left(\frac{\partial z_i}{\partial q_r}\right)^2\right]^{1/2} \delta q_r = h_{ir}\,\delta q_r \tag{4.16}$$

Finally,

$$l_{ir} = \frac{1}{h_{ir}}\frac{\partial x_i}{\partial q_r}, \qquad m_{ir} = \frac{1}{h_{ir}}\frac{\partial y_i}{\partial q_r}, \qquad n_{ir} = \frac{1}{h_{ir}}\frac{\partial z_i}{\partial q_r} \tag{4.17}$$

Since the component v' of any vector v along a line having direction cosines l, m, n is given by $v' = lv_x + mv_y + nv_z$, it follows that f_{ir}, the component of the applied force F_i acting on m_i projected on the tangent to its q_r-line, is

$$f_{ir} = \frac{1}{h_{ir}}\left(F_{x_i}\frac{\partial x_i}{\partial q_r} + F_{y_i}\frac{\partial y_i}{\partial q_r} + F_{z_i}\frac{\partial z_i}{\partial q_r}\right) \tag{4.18}$$

Likewise, the component a_{ir} of the acceleration vector a_i of particle m_i along the same tangent is

$$a_{ir} = \frac{1}{h_{ir}}\left(\ddot{x}_i\frac{\partial x_i}{\partial q_r} + \ddot{y}_i\frac{\partial y_i}{\partial q_r} + \ddot{z}_i\frac{\partial z_i}{\partial q_r}\right) \tag{4.19}$$

Now multiplying and dividing each side of (*4.7*), (with δq_1 replaced by δq_r), by h_{ir} and using the relation $\delta s_{ir} = h_{ir}\,\delta q_r$, it is seen that the Lagrangian equations may be written as

$$\sum_{i=1}^{p} m_i a_{ir}\,\delta s_{ir} = \sum_{i=1}^{p} f_{ir}\,\delta s_{ir} = F_{q_r}\,\delta q_r \tag{4.20}$$

Keeping in mind the simple meaning of a_{ir}, f_{ir}, and δs_{ir}, the correspondingly simple physical and geometrical interpretation of Lagrange's equations is made clear by (*4.20*).

Furthermore notice that, as can be seen from (*4.19*), an expression for a_{ir}, the linear acceleration of m_i along its q_r-line, may be obtained at once from

$$m_i a_{ir} = \frac{1}{h_{ir}}\left[\frac{d}{dt}\left(\frac{\partial T_i}{\partial \dot{q}_r}\right) - \frac{\partial T_i}{\partial q_r}\right] \tag{4.21}$$

where $T_i = \frac{1}{2}m_i(\dot{x}_i^2 + \dot{y}_i^2 + \dot{z}_i^2)$ is expressed in generalized coordinates by means of equations (*4.4*).

Example 4.11.

Consider the system shown in Fig. 4-7 below. Particles of mass m_1 and m_2 are suspended from the ends of a string which passes through small smooth rings at a and b. m_1 is free to move in contact with the cone C. m_2 is constrained (by means of two plane, parallel and smooth surfaces, not shown) to move in contact with the vertical plane P. The cone is stationary, but P is made to oscillate about the vertical axis B according to $\alpha = A \sin \omega t$, where α is measured from the X axis.

Since $r_1 + r_2 = c =$ constant and $\theta_1 =$ constant, the system has three degrees of freedom. In keeping with the general notation let us write $q_1 = r_1$, $q_2 = \phi$, $q_3 = \theta_2$. In these coordinates equations (*4.4*), as can easily be seen from the figure, have the form: for m_1,

$$x_1 = q_1 \cos q_2 \sin \theta_1, \qquad y_1 = q_1 \sin q_2 \sin \theta_1, \qquad z_1 = h - q_1 \cos \theta_1 \tag{1}$$

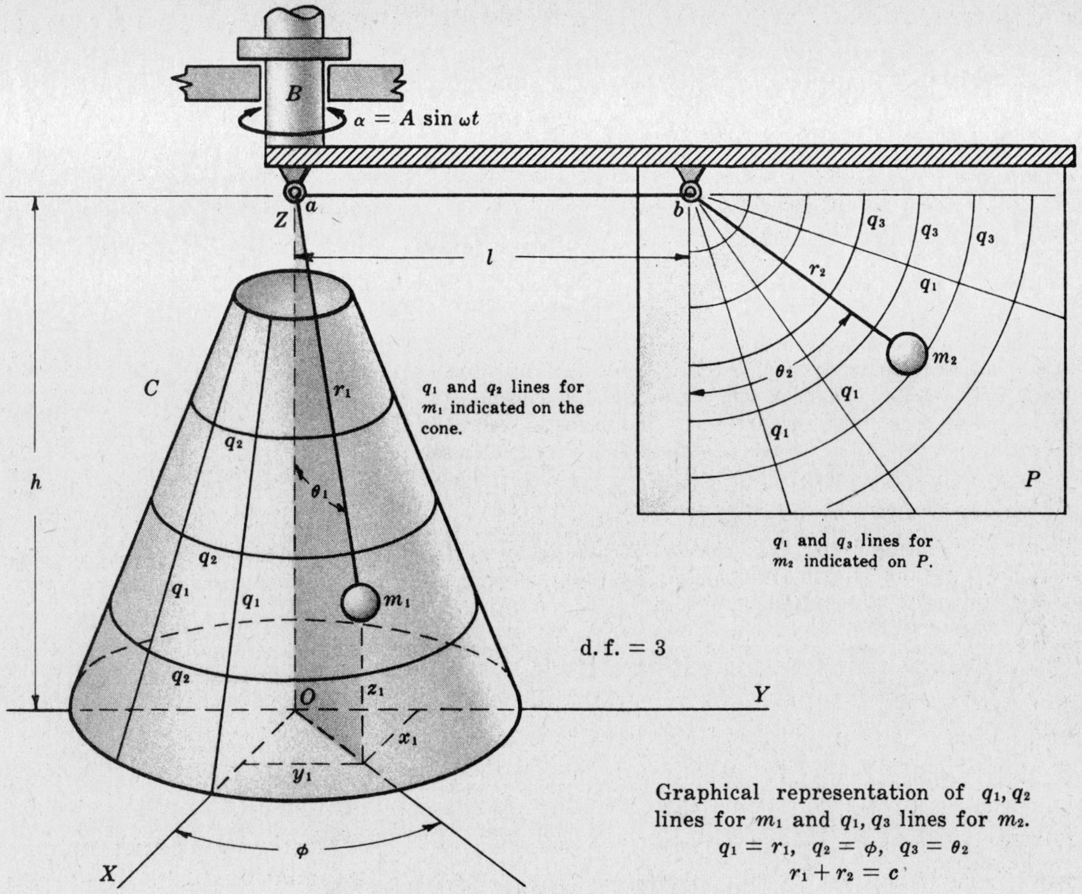

Fig. 4-7

and for m_2,

$$
\begin{aligned}
x_2 &= [l + (c - q_1)\sin q_3]\cos(A\sin\omega t),\\
y_2 &= [l + (c - q_1)\sin q_3]\sin(A\sin\omega t), \qquad (2)\\
z_2 &= h - (c - q_1)\cos q_3
\end{aligned}
$$

Note that in this particular example not all of the coordinates appear in every equation of (*1*) and (*2*).

Allowing q_1 to vary and plotting relations (*1*) and likewise (*2*) for various constant values of q_2, q_3, t, q_1-lines of m_1 (straight lines on the cone) and q_1-lines of m_2 (radial lines on P) are obtained. In like manner q_2-lines of m_1 and q_3-lines of m_2 are obtained. Since q_3 does not appear in (*1*), there are no q_3-lines for m_1. It is also clear that there are no q_2-lines for m_2. Note that a_{11} is the component of linear acceleration of m_1 along one of its q_1-lines on the cone. a_{21} is the acceleration of m_2 along its q_1 line on P. Also a_{23}, for example, is the acceleration of m_2 along a q_3-line on the P plane. Expressions for these accelerations may be found by applying (*4.21*) to

$$T = \tfrac{1}{2}m_1(\dot{q}_1^2 + q_1^2\dot{q}_2^2\sin^2\theta_1) + \tfrac{1}{2}m_2[\dot{q}_1^2 + (c-q_1)^2\dot{q}_3^2 + (l + (c-q_1)\sin q_3)^2 A^2\omega^2\cos^2\omega t]$$

4.9 Suggested Experiment.

A determination of the frequencies of motion of the "two-particle" system shown in Fig. 4-8 below.

The required equipment is simple and the results obtained are interesting and instructive. Nothing is very critical about the values of masses and spring constants required. Those shown in the diagram are only suggestive.

Assuming vertical motion only and using as coordinates q_1 and q_2, the vertical displacements of m_1 and m_2 from their positions of equilibrium, set up the equations of motion. These second order equations with constant coefficients can easily be integrated by standard methods. Solutions will show that, when the system is started moving in an arbitrary manner, the motion of each mass is compounded of two simple harmonic oscillations having distinct frequencies f_1 and f_2. (Each mass oscillates with the same two frequencies but with different amplitudes.)

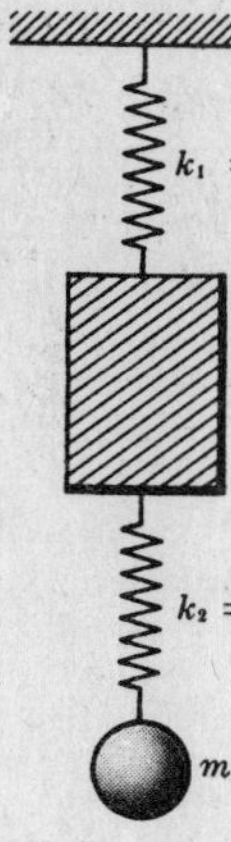

Fig. 4-8

To obtain an experimental check on the computed frequencies, we may proceed as follows. Applying an oscillatory motion to m_1 (or m_2) with the hand, one can after a little practice excite either f_1 or f_2 alone. Immediate success is assured if we keep in mind the fact that, when the applied frequency is approximately equal to either f_1 or f_2, very little effort is required to establish large oscillations. On removing the hand the system continues to oscillate with one of its natural modes. The time of fifty oscillations determined with a reliable stop-watch gives a good experimental value of the frequency. For reasonable accuracy in the measurements of m_1, m_2, k_1, k_2, experimental and computed values of f_1 and f_2 will agree closely.

A qualitative check on the relative amplitudes of motion of m_1 and m_2, for either f_1 or f_2 excited, can easily be made by direct observation.

Considerable insight into the behavior of oscillating systems may be obtained from an inspection of the motions of m_1 and m_2 when the system has been set in motion in some arbitrary manner so that both frequencies are excited simultaneously.

Summary and Remarks

1. Derivation of Lagrange's Equations, General Form (Section 4.2)

The equations are here derived for a system of p particles having n degrees of freedom and $3p - n$ degrees of constraint. Coordinates and constraints may be moving or stationary.

The derivation, again based on D'Alembert's equation and the assumption that forces of constraint do no work for displacements in conformity with constraints, follows the same pattern as in Chapter 3.

2. Proper Form for Kinetic Energy (Section 4.3)

T is now the sum of the kinetic energy of p particles. It is expressed in terms of $q_1, q_2, \ldots, q_n$, $\dot{q}_1, \dot{q}_2, \ldots, \dot{q}_n$ and t, having eliminated $3p - n$ superfluous coordinates.

3. Physical Meaning of Generalized Forces (Section 4.4)

The physical meaning of the now extended definition of F_{q_r} is, as pointed out in Section 4.4, still quite simple. A clear understanding of this is important because it greatly facilitates the application of Lagrange's equations.

4. Finding Expressions for F_{q_r} (Section 4.5)

Three techniques are described. All are essentially the same, but in certain circumstances one may be more convenient than another.

5. Physical Interpretation of Lagrange's Equations (Section 4.8)

Since each of the quantities δs_{ir}, f_{ir} and a_{ir} has a very elementary meaning, it follows that $\frac{d}{dt}\left(\frac{\partial T}{\partial \dot{q}_r}\right) - \frac{\partial T}{\partial q_r} = F_{q_r}$ (which in terms of the above quantities may be written as $\sum_{i=1}^{p} m_i a_{ir}\,\delta s_{ir} = \sum_{i=1}^{p} f_{ir}\,\delta s_{ir}$) has a simple physical interpretation.

Problems

4.1. Referring to Fig. 4-1, Page 62, assume that the upper pulley is suspended from a coil spring of constant k, in place of the bar B. Neglecting masses of the pulleys, show that

$$T = \tfrac{1}{2}m_1(\dot{l}-\dot{y}_1)^2 + \tfrac{1}{2}m_2(\dot{l}+\dot{y}_1-\dot{y}_2)^2 + \tfrac{1}{2}m_3(\dot{l}+\dot{y}_1+\dot{y}_2)^2$$

Write out equations of motion and show that

$$F_{y_1} = (m_1-m_2-m_3)g, \qquad F_{y_2} = (m_2-m_3)g, \qquad F_l = k(C-l-h_0) - (m_1+m_2+m_3)g$$

where $h+l = C =$ constant and h_0 is the value of h when the spring is unstretched.

4.2. Show that for the mass, pulley system of Fig. 4-9,

$$T = \tfrac{1}{2}m_1(\dot{y}+\dot{y}_1)^2 + \tfrac{1}{2}m_2(\dot{y}-\dot{y}_1)^2 + \tfrac{1}{2}M\dot{y}^2 + \tfrac{1}{2}(I/R^2)\dot{y}_1^2$$

Write out equations of motion corresponding to y and y_1 in the usual way and then show that

$$\ddot{y} = -k\left(\frac{B}{AB-C^2}\right)(y-y_0) + g, \qquad B\ddot{y}_1 + C\ddot{y} = Cg$$

where $A = m_1+m_2+M$, $B = m_1+m_2+I/R^2$, $C = m_1-m_2$ and y_0 is the value of y when the spring is unstretched. Integrate these equations and describe briefly the motion.

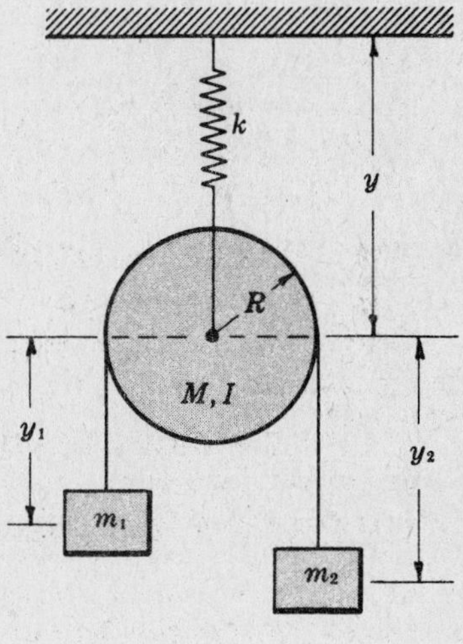

Fig. 4-9

4.3. As an extension of Example 4.4, Page 64, write out equations of motion when:

(a) m_1 is compelled by some external force to move according to the relation $x_1 = B_1 \sin\omega_1 t$.

(b) A horizontal periodic force, $F = B_2 \sin\omega_2 t$, is applied to m_1.

(c) A coil spring, in a horizontal position, connects m_1 to the point p.

4.4. Referring to Fig. 4-5, Page 65, show that when coordinates y, s_1, s_2 are used, $q_1M = s_1(m_2+m_3) + s_2m_3$, $q_2M = s_1m_1 - s_2m_3$, and thus since

$$T = \tfrac{1}{2}M\dot{y}^2 + \tfrac{1}{2}m_1\dot{q}_1^2 + \tfrac{1}{2}m_2\dot{q}_2^2 + \tfrac{1}{2}m_3\left(\frac{m_1}{m_3}\dot{q}_1 - \frac{m_2}{m_3}\dot{q}_2\right)^2$$

it can easily be expressed in terms of $\dot{y}, \dot{s}_1, \dot{s}_2$. Show that generalized forces corresponding y, s_1, s_2 are $F_y = -Mg$, $F_{s_1} = -k_1(s_1-l_1)$, $F_{s_2} = -k_2(s_2-l_2)$ where $M = m_1+m_2+m_3$ and l_1, l_2 are the unstretched lengths of the springs respectively.

In applying (4.11) to a determination of F_{s_1}, for example, show with the aid of a diagram what virtual displacements must be given each mass.

Here generalized forces are quite simple, but see Problem 4.5.

4.5. Show that when coordinates y, y_1 and y_2 are used to represent the configuration of the system in Fig. 4-5, the corresponding generalized forces are

$$F_y = -Mg + k_2\frac{M}{m_3}\left[\left(\frac{m_2+m_3}{m_3}\right)y_2 + \frac{m_1}{m_3}y_1 - \frac{M}{m_3}y - l_2\right]$$

$$F_{y_1} = -k_1(y_1 - y_2 - l_1) - k_2\frac{m_1}{m_3}\left[\left(\frac{m_2+m_3}{m_3}\right)y_2 + \frac{m_1}{m_3}y_1 - \frac{M}{m_3}y - l_2\right]$$

$$F_{y_2} = +k_1(y_1 - y_2 - l_1) - k_2\left(\frac{m_2+m_3}{m_3}\right)\left[\left(\frac{m_2+m_3}{m_3}\right)y_2 + \frac{m_1}{m_3}y_1 - \frac{M}{m_3}y - l_2\right]$$

4.6. In Fig. 4-10 below, the XY plane is horizontal. A fixed shaft S extends along the Z axis. Smooth bearings support rods A and B, one just above the other, on the shaft. A clock spring with torsional constant k connects A to B as shown. Moments of inertia of the rods are I_1 and I_2 as indicated. The rods are free to rotate about the shaft under the action of the spring. Using θ_1 and α as coordinates, show that

$$\frac{I_1 I_2}{I_1 + I_2}\ddot{\alpha} = -k\alpha, \qquad (I_1 + I_2)\dot{\theta}_1 - I_2\dot{\alpha} = P_{\theta_1} = \text{constant}$$

Integrate these equations and describe briefly the motion.

Show that if θ_1 and θ_2 are regarded as coordinates of the system, the generalized forces $F_{\theta_1} = F_{\theta_2} = -k(\theta_1 + \theta_2)$. Assume spring undistorted when A and B are collinear.

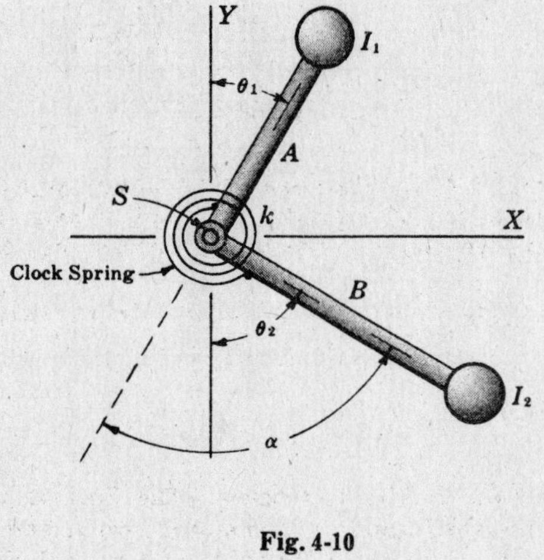

Fig. 4-10

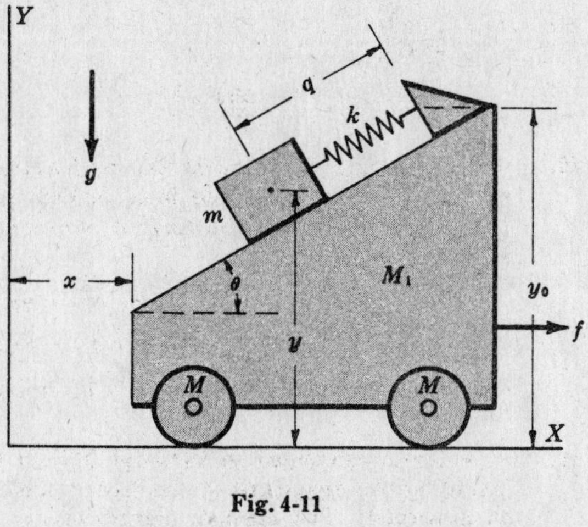

Fig. 4-11

4.7. (a) The block of mass m, shown in Fig. 4-11 above, is free to slide along the inclined plane on the cart under the action of gravity and the spring. The body of the cart has mass M_1. Each wheel has mass M, radius r and moment of inertia I about its axle. A constant force f is exerted on the cart. Neglecting bearing friction, show that

$$\left(M_1 + 4M + \frac{4I}{r^2} + m\right)\ddot{x} + \frac{m}{\tan\theta}\ddot{y} = f, \qquad \frac{m}{\sin^2\theta}\ddot{y} + \frac{m}{\tan\theta}\ddot{x} = -mg + \frac{k}{\sin\theta}\left(\frac{y_0 - y}{\sin\theta} - q_0\right)$$

where q_0 is the value of q when the spring is unstretched.

(b) Set up the equations of motion in the x,q coordinates. Show that $F_x = f$ and $F_q = + mg\sin\theta - k(q - q_0)$.

4.8. If a light driving mechanism (a piston operated by compressed air for example) forces the block, Fig. 4-11, to oscillate along the inclined plane so that displacements relative to the plane are given by $A\sin\omega t$, show that

$$T = \tfrac{1}{2}(M_1 + 4M + 4I/r^2 + m)\dot{x}^2 + \tfrac{1}{2}m(-2\dot{x}A\omega\cos\omega t\cos\theta + A^2\omega^2\cos^2\omega t)$$

and that, assuming f not acting, the motion of the cart is determined by

$$(M_1 + 4M + 4I/r^2 + m)\dot{x} - mA\omega\cos\theta\cos\omega t = \text{constant}$$

4.9. Particles having masses m_1 and m_2 are connected with a cord in which a spring is located, as shown in Fig. 4-12 below. The cord passes over a light pulley and the particles are free to slide in the smooth horizontal tubes. The tubes together with the shaft have a moment of inertia I about the vertical axis.

(*a*) Using θ, r_1, r_2 as coordinates and assuming no torque applied to the vertical shaft, show that

$$(I + m_1 r_1^2 + m_2 r_2^2)\dot{\theta} = P_\theta = \text{constant}$$
$$m_1 \ddot{r}_1 - m_1 r_1 \dot{\theta}^2 = -k(r_1 + r_2 - c)$$
$$m_2 \ddot{r}_2 - m_2 r_2 \dot{\theta}^2 = -k(r_1 + r_2 - c)$$

(*b*) Assuming that the shaft is driven by a motor at constant speed $\dot{\theta} = \omega$, write out the equations of motion for m_1 and m_2.

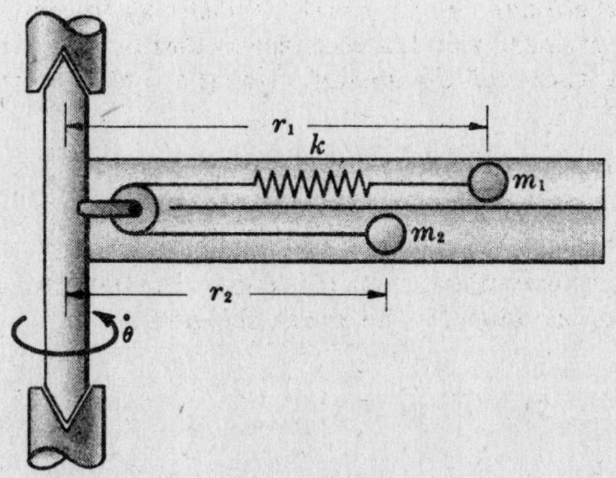

Fig. 4-12

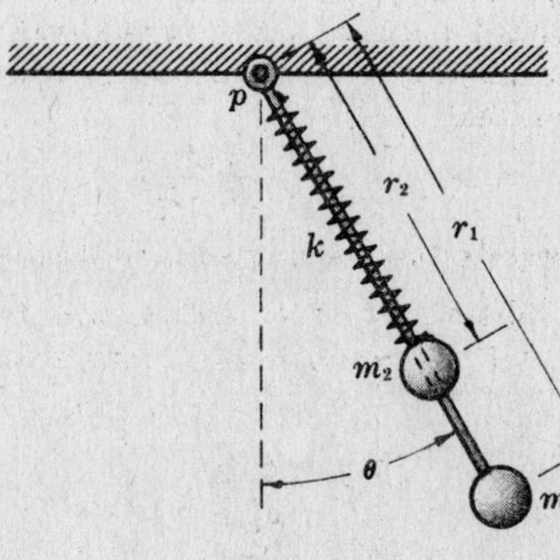

Fig. 4-13

4.10. The *light* rigid rod supporting the "particle" of mass m_1, shown in Fig. 4-13 above, is pivoted at p so that it is free to rotate in a vertical plane under the action of gravity. The bead of mass m_2 is free to slide along the smooth rod under the action of gravity and the spring. Show that the equations of motion are

$$(m_1 r_1^2 + m_2 r_2^2)\ddot{\theta} + 2m_2 r_2 \dot{r}_2 \dot{\theta} + (m_1 r_1 + m_2 r_2) g \sin\theta = 0$$
$$m_2 \ddot{r}_2 - m_2 r_2 \dot{\theta}^2 - m_2 g \cos\theta + k(r_2 - l_0) = 0$$

where l_0 is the unstretched length of the spring.

4.11. A motor is connected to three pulleys in the manner shown in Fig. 4-14 below. The first pulley, including the armature of the motor, has a moment of inertia I_1, and the remaining two I_2 and I_3 as indicated. The springs (equivalent to elastic shafts coupling the pulleys) have torsional constants k_1 and k_2.

(*a*) Neglecting bearing friction, set up equations of motion assuming the motor exerts a torque $\tau(t)$ which is a known function of time.

(*b*) Set up equations of motion assuming that regardless of the motions of the second and third disk the motor has constant speed.

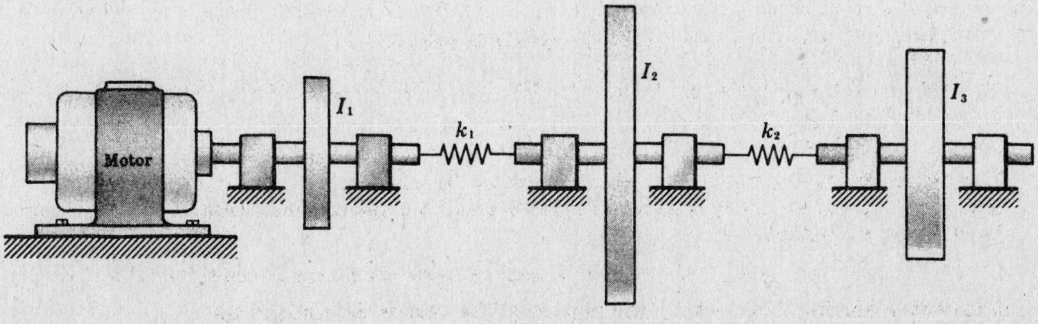

Fig. 4-14

4.12. Disk D_1, shown in Fig. 4-15 below, is fastened to the vertical shaft of a motor which exerts on it a torque τ_1. On the face of D_1 is mounted another motor the vertical shaft of which forms the axis of disk D_2. This motor exerts a torque τ_2. Show that,

$$T = \tfrac{1}{2}I_1\dot{\theta}_1^2 + \tfrac{1}{2}I_2(\dot{\theta}_1 + \dot{\theta}_2)^2 + \tfrac{1}{2}M_2r^2\dot{\theta}_1^2$$

$$I_2\ddot{\theta}_2 + \ddot{\theta}_1(I_1 + M_2r^2 + I_2) = F_{\theta_1} = \tau_1$$

$$I_2(\ddot{\theta}_1 + \ddot{\theta}_2) = F_{\theta_2} = \tau_2$$

where I_1 includes the combined moment of inertia of D_1, armature of first motor and stator of second. I_2 includes D_2 and armature of second motor. M_2 is the mass of D_2 plus that of second armature.

Show that if we were using θ_1 and α as coordinates, then $F_{\theta_1} = \tau_1 - \tau_2$, $F_\alpha = \tau_2$. Note that above relations are true even though τ_1 and τ_2 may vary with time.

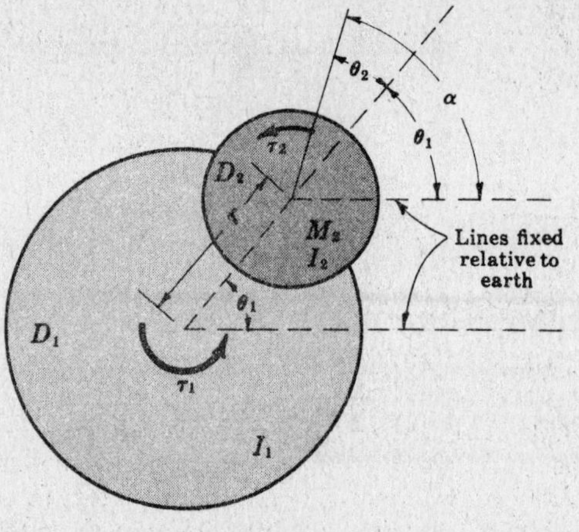

Fig. 4-15

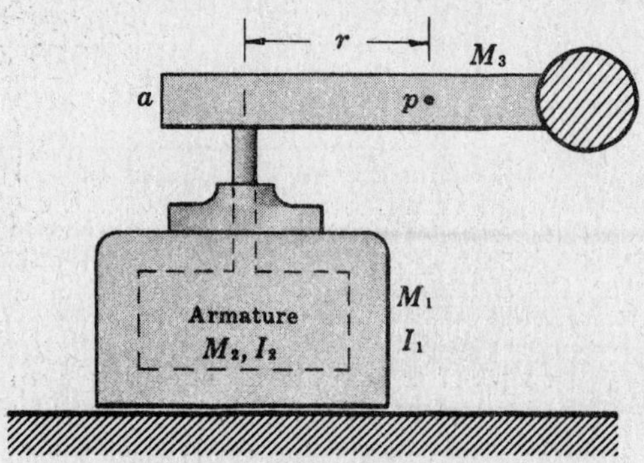

Fig. 4-16

4.13. The electric motor, shown in Fig. 4-16 above, is free to slide to any position on a smooth horizontal plane. The center of mass of the frame and armature are each on the axis of rotation of the shaft. The frame, armature plus shaft and arm ab have masses M_1, M_2, M_3 respectively. The frame and armature have moments of inertia I_1 and I_2 respectively about the axis of the shaft. The arm has a moment of inertia I_3 about a vertical axis through its center of mass at p. Show that

$$T = \tfrac{1}{2}(M_1 + M_2 + M_3)(\dot{x}^2 + \dot{y}^2) + \tfrac{1}{2}I_1\dot{\theta}_1^2 + \tfrac{1}{2}(I_2 + I_3 + M_3r^2)\dot{\theta}_2^2 + M_3r\dot{\theta}_2(\dot{y}\cos\theta_2 - \dot{x}\sin\theta_2)$$

where x, y are the rectangular coordinates of the center of the motor (X, Y taken in the plane on which the motor slides) and θ_1, θ_2 are the angular displacements of the frame and armature respectively relative to the X axis.

Show that, neglecting friction, $F_x = 0$, $F_y = 0$, $F_{\theta_1} = -\tau$, $F_{\theta_2} = \tau$ where τ, the torque of the motor, may be regarded as a known function of time.

4.14. In the system of gear wheels shown in Fig. 4-17 below, the shafts $S_1, \ldots, S_4$ are supported in fixed bearings $b_1, \ldots, b_4$. Gears A, D, E, F are keyed to their respective shafts. An extension of shaft S_3 forms a crank as shown. Gear C is free to rotate on the crank handle. B is a "pie pan" (shown cut away) with gear teeth g on its outer rim and similar teeth g' on the inner rim. B is free to rotate on S_1. It is seen that if, for example D is held fixed and A turned, C and the crank (thus E and F) each revolves.

Moments of inertia of the gears, including that of the shaft to which they are keyed, are as indicated in the figure. Radii of the gear wheels are r_1, r_2, etc. Springs, having torsional constants k_1 and k_2, are fastened to S_2 and S_4 as indicated. Measuring θ_3 relative to the crank C and all other angles relative to fixed vertical lines, show that

$$T = \tfrac{1}{2}I_1\dot{\theta}_1^2 + \frac{1}{2}\left[I_2 + I_4\left(\frac{r_2}{r_4}\right)^2\right]\dot{\theta}_2^2 + \frac{1}{2}\left(\frac{I_3}{4r_3^2}\right)[(R + r_3)\dot{\theta}_2 - r_1\dot{\theta}_1]^2$$

$$+ \frac{1}{2}\left[\frac{I_5 + MR^2}{4R^2} + \frac{I_6}{4R^2}\left(\frac{r_5}{r_6}\right)^2\right](r_1\dot{\theta}_1 + R\dot{\theta}_2 + r_3\dot{\theta}_2)^2$$

Write out the equations of motion and find expressions for F_{θ_1} and F_{θ_2} assuming each spring exerts a torque proportional to the angular displacement of the shaft to which it is fastened.

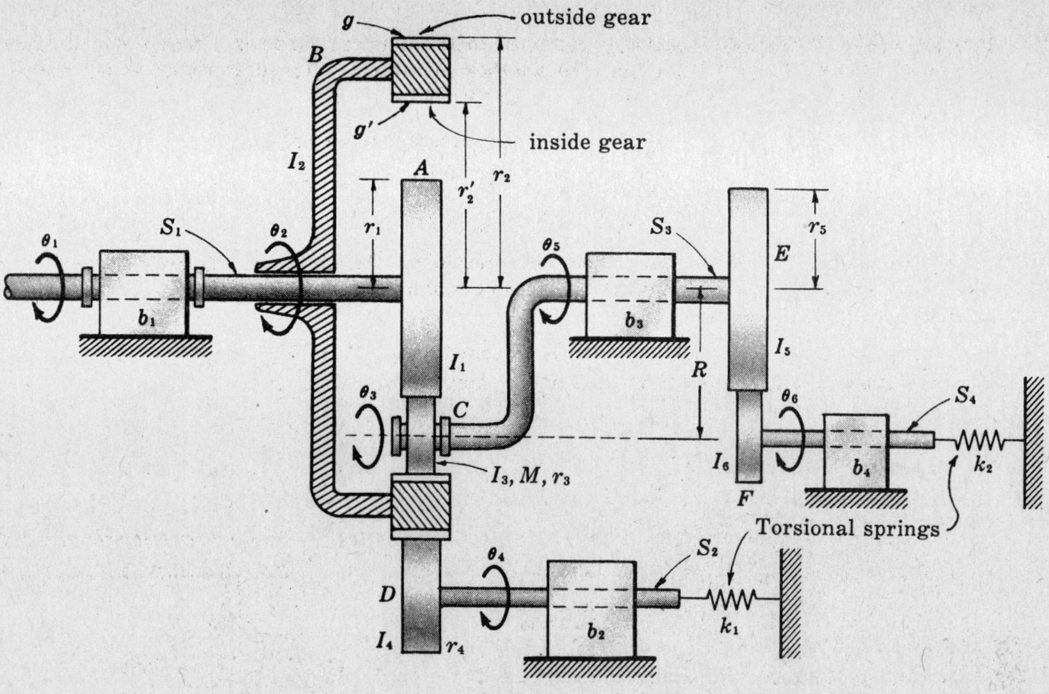

Fig. 4-17

4.15. Assume that masses m_1 and m_2, shown in Fig. 4-3, Page 64, are attracted to the origin (perhaps by a large spherical mass, not shown) with forces $f_1 = cm_1/r_1^2$, $f_2 = cm_2/r_2^2$ respectively where c is a constant and r_1, r_2 are radial distances from m_1 and m_2 to the origin. By inspection it is seen that for a general displacement of the dumbbell, $\delta W_{\text{total}} = -(cm_1/r_1^2)\,\delta r_1 - (cm_2/r_2^2)\,\delta r_2$. Using coordinates x, y, θ as in Example 4.3, show that

$$\begin{aligned}\delta W_{\text{total}} \;=\; & -c\left[\frac{m_1}{r_1^3}(x - l_1\cos\theta) + \frac{m_2}{r_2^3}(x + l_2\cos\theta)\right]\delta x \\ & -c\left[\frac{m_1}{r_1^3}(y - l_1\sin\theta) + \frac{m_2}{r_2^3}(y + l_2\sin\theta)\right]\delta y \\ & -c\left[\frac{m_1}{r_1^3}(xl_1\sin\theta - yl_1\cos\theta) + \frac{m_2}{r_2^3}(yl_2\cos\theta - xl_2\sin\theta)\right]\delta\theta\end{aligned}$$

where l_1 and l_2 are distances measured along the rod from m_1 and m_2 respectively to the center of mass. Note that δW_{total} has the form of equation (*4.12*). Coefficients of $\delta x, \delta y, \delta\theta$ are the generalized forces F_x, F_y, F_θ respectively, after expressing r_1 and r_2 in terms of x, y, θ.

Write δW_{total} again, using coordinates r_1, α, θ where α is the angle between r_1 and the x axis. Also write out T in these coordinates.

4.16. Referring to Fig. 4-1, Page 62, suppose that, with the supporting bar B removed, the shaft of the large pulley is made to oscillate vertically according to $h = h_0 + A\sin\omega t$ by a force $f(t)$ applied to the shaft. Set up equations of motion for the system. Does f appear in the generalized forces? Explain. (Assume strings are always under tension.)

4.17. Assuming the rotating table, shown in Fig. 4-6, Page 67, is on a cart (instead of the elevator) which is moving horizontally with constant acceleration a, show that

$$\begin{aligned}T \;=\; & \tfrac{1}{2}m_1[a^2t^2 + (s + q_1\cos\alpha)^2\omega^2 + \dot{q}_1^2 - 2at\omega(s + q_1\cos\alpha)\sin\omega t + 2at\dot{q}_1\cos\alpha\cos\omega t] \\ & + \tfrac{1}{2}m_2[a^2t^2 + (s + q_2\cos\alpha)^2\omega^2 + \dot{q}_2^2 - 2at\omega(s + q_2\cos\alpha)\sin\omega t + 2at\dot{q}_2\cos\alpha\cos\omega t]\end{aligned}$$

where the line from which θ is measured is taken in the direction of a. The distance moved by the center of the disk, from some fixed point on this line, is given by $s = \frac{1}{2}at^2$. Set up equations of motion and show that F_{q_1} and F_{q_2} are the same as in Example 4.8, Page 67.

4.18. A dumbbell is free to move in the X_2Y_2 plane of the rotating frame, shown in Fig. 3-16, Page 56. Known forces (f_{x_1}, f_{y_1}) and (f_{x_2}, f_{y_2}) act on m_1 and m_2 respectively. Using coordinates corresponding to (x, y, θ) of Fig. 4-3, Page 64, set up equations of motion assuming constant angular velocity ω for the vertical shaft. See Section 14.6, Page 286.

4.19. A mechanism attached to A, shown in Fig. 2-15, Page 16, exerts a vertical force f_1 on the axis of the upper pulley. Another fastened to B exerts a force f_2 on m_2. Let us assume these forces are such that s_1 and y each varies in a known manner with time. (For example $s_1 = s_0 + A_1 \sin(\omega t + \delta)$ and $y = \dot{y}_0 t + \frac{1}{2}at^2$.) Assuming that each rope is always under tension, show that differential equations corresponding to s_3 and s_4 are

$$(I_2/R_2^2 + m_3)\ddot{s}_3 + m_3\ddot{s}_1 + k_1(C - y - s_1 - s_4) - m_3 g = 0$$

$$(M_1 + I_1/R_1^2 + 4m_1)\ddot{s}_4 + (M_1 + 2m_1)\ddot{y} - k_1(C - y - s_1 - s_4) + (M_1 + 2m_1)g = 0$$

where C is a constant and $s_1, \ddot{s}_1, y, \ddot{y}$ are to be written in as known functions of time determined by the types of motion assumed.

4.20. The masses of the double pendulum, shown in Fig. 2-10, Page 14, carry electrical charges Q_1 and Q_2 respectively. A magnetic field is established normal to the XY plane. Consider all coordinates variable.

(a) Find the generalized forces $F_{r_1}, F_{r_2}, F_\theta, F_\phi$, taking account of the forces due to the motion of the charges in the field. Neglect gravitational forces. See Example 4.10, Page 69.

(b) Determine the generalized forces when r_1 and r_2 are constant; r_1 variable and r_2 constant; r_2 variable and r_1 constant.

4.21. The dumbbell, Fig. 4-18, with equal charges $+Q$ and $-Q$ uniformly distributed over the small spheres is free to move in space. By means of a large parallel plate condenser (plates parallel to the XY plane) connected to an alternating source of potential, a uniform alternating electric field $E_z = E_0 \sin \omega_1 t$ is established. Likewise large plane pole-pieces furnish a uniform magnetic field such that $B_y = B_0 \sin \omega_2 t$.

Write out proper expressions for the rectangular components of force on each charge and determine generalized forces corresponding to x, y, z, θ, ϕ (see Example 4.10, Page 69).

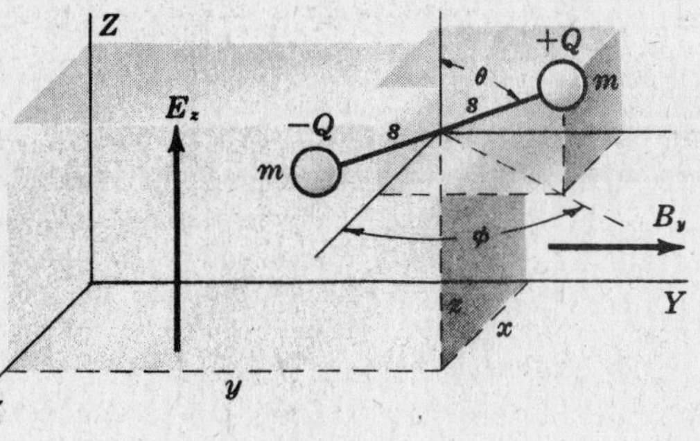

Fig. 4-18

4.22. (a) In Fig. 4-9, Page 73, consider any particle m_i (coordinates x_i, y_i) in the pulley and show using D'Alembert's equation that

$$\sum_i (\ddot{x}_i\,\delta x_i + \ddot{y}_i\,\delta y_i) = M\ddot{y}\,\delta y + I\ddot{\theta}\,\delta\theta$$

(b) By a direct application of D'Alembert's equation, (4.2), set up the equations of motion corresponding to y and y_1 for the system referred to in part (a). Compare results with those previously obtained.

4.23. Assuming that the vertical shaft, Fig. 4-12, Page 75, is forced to rotate according to the relation $\theta = \omega_0 t + \frac{1}{2}at^2$, set up equations of motion corresponding to r_1 and r_2 by a direct application of D'Alembert's equation. See Problem 4.9.

4.24. Obtain the equations of motion given in Problem 4.10 by a direct application of D'Alembert's equation.

4.25. Consider the dumbbell of Fig. 4-3, treated in Example 4.3, Page 64. Show that, using coordinates x, y, θ: for m_1, $h_{1x} = h_{1y} = 1$ and $h_{1\theta} = l_1$; and for m_2, $h_{2x} = h_{2y} = 1$ and $h_{2\theta} = l_2$.

Now applying relation (4.21), Page 70, to

$$T_1 = \tfrac{1}{2}m_1[\dot{x}^2 + \dot{y}^2 + l_1^2\dot{\theta}^2 + 2l_1\dot{\theta}(\dot{x}\sin\theta - \dot{y}\cos\theta)]$$

and a similar expression for T_2, find $a_{1x}, a_{1y}, a_{1\theta}$ and $a_{2x}, a_{2y}, a_{2\theta}$. State the geometrical meaning of each. Applying (4.20), write out the equations of motion of the system corresponding to x, y, θ.

4.26. Show that, for the double pendulum of Example 4.6, Page 66,

$$h_{1\theta} = r_1,\ \ h_{2\theta} = r_1;\quad h_{1\phi} = 0,\ \ h_{2\phi} = r_2$$

$$a_{1\theta} = r_1\ddot{\theta}, \qquad a_{2\theta} = r_1\ddot{\theta} + r_2\ddot{\phi}\cos(\phi-\theta) - r_2\dot{\phi}^2\sin(\phi-\theta)$$

$$f_{1\theta} = -m_1 g\sin\theta, \qquad f_{2\theta} = -m_2 g\sin\theta, \qquad \delta s_{1\theta} = \delta s_{2\theta} = r_1\,\delta\theta$$

Hence show that (4.20) corresponding to θ

$$m_1 a_{1\theta}\,\delta s_{1\theta} + m_2 a_{2\theta}\,\delta s_{2\theta} = f_{1\theta}\,\delta s_{1\theta} + f_{2\theta}\,\delta s_{2\theta}$$

is just the equation of motion corresponding to θ obtained in Example 4.6. Interpret results physically.

Set up the equation of motion corresponding to ϕ in the same way.

4.27. Referring to Fig. 2-15, Page 16, show that generalized forces corresponding to s_1, s_2, s_3, s_4 are

$$F_{s_1} = (M_1 + M_2 + m_1 + m_2 + m_3)g - k_2(s_1 - {}_0s_1) \qquad F_{s_3} = m_3 g - k_1(s_2 - {}_0s_2)$$

$$F_{s_2} = (M_1 + m_1 + m_2)g - k_1(s_2 - {}_0s_2) \qquad F_{s_4} = (m_2 - m_1)g$$

4.28. *Supplementary exercise in the determination of generalized forces.*

For the student who still feels a need, the following examples should contribute greatly to a clear understanding of generalized forces and the techniques involved in finding expressions for same.

Various sets of coordinates, any one of which is suitable for a determination of the motion of the system, are listed in Figures 4-19 and 4-20. Find generalized forces corresponding to the coordinates of each set. Repeat this for the systems for which certain specified motions are indicated.

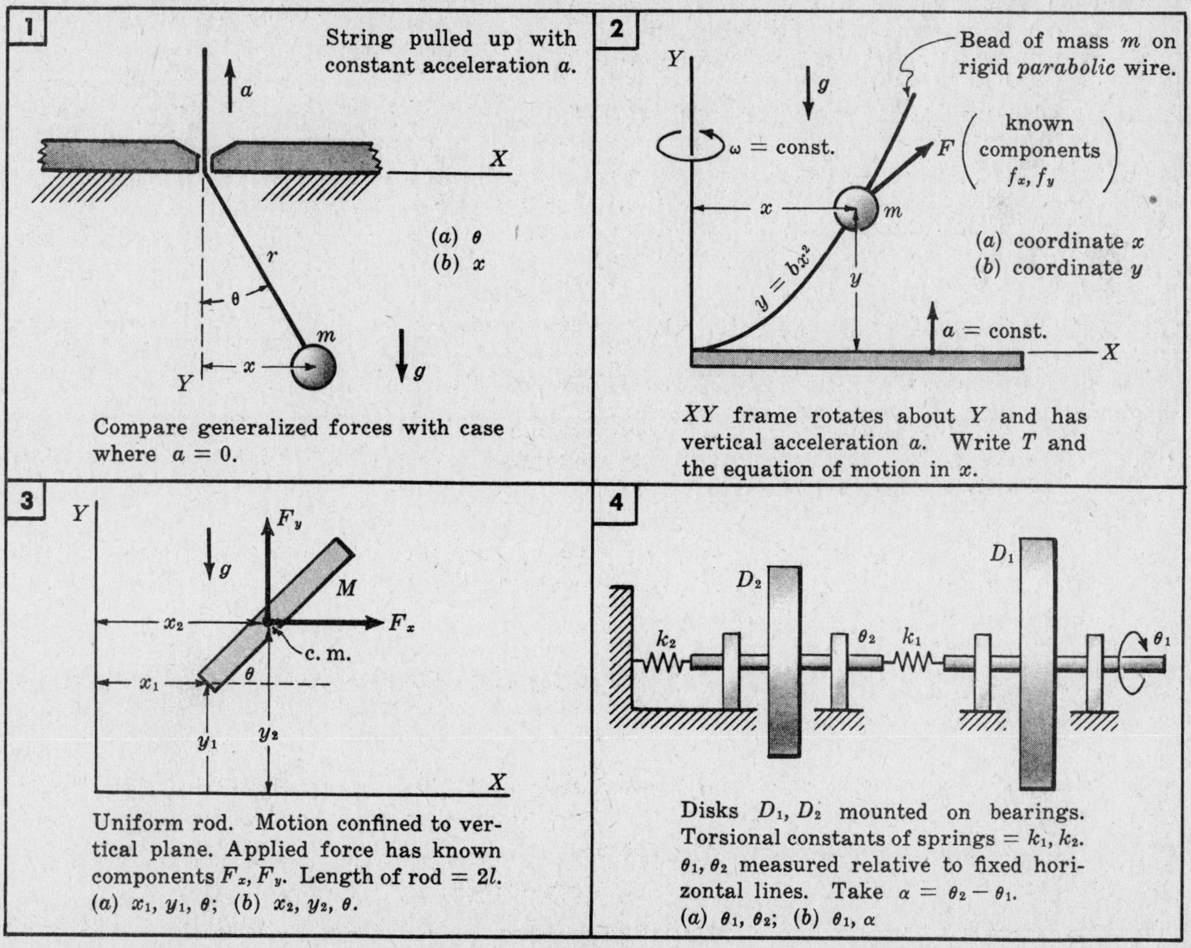

Fig. 4-19

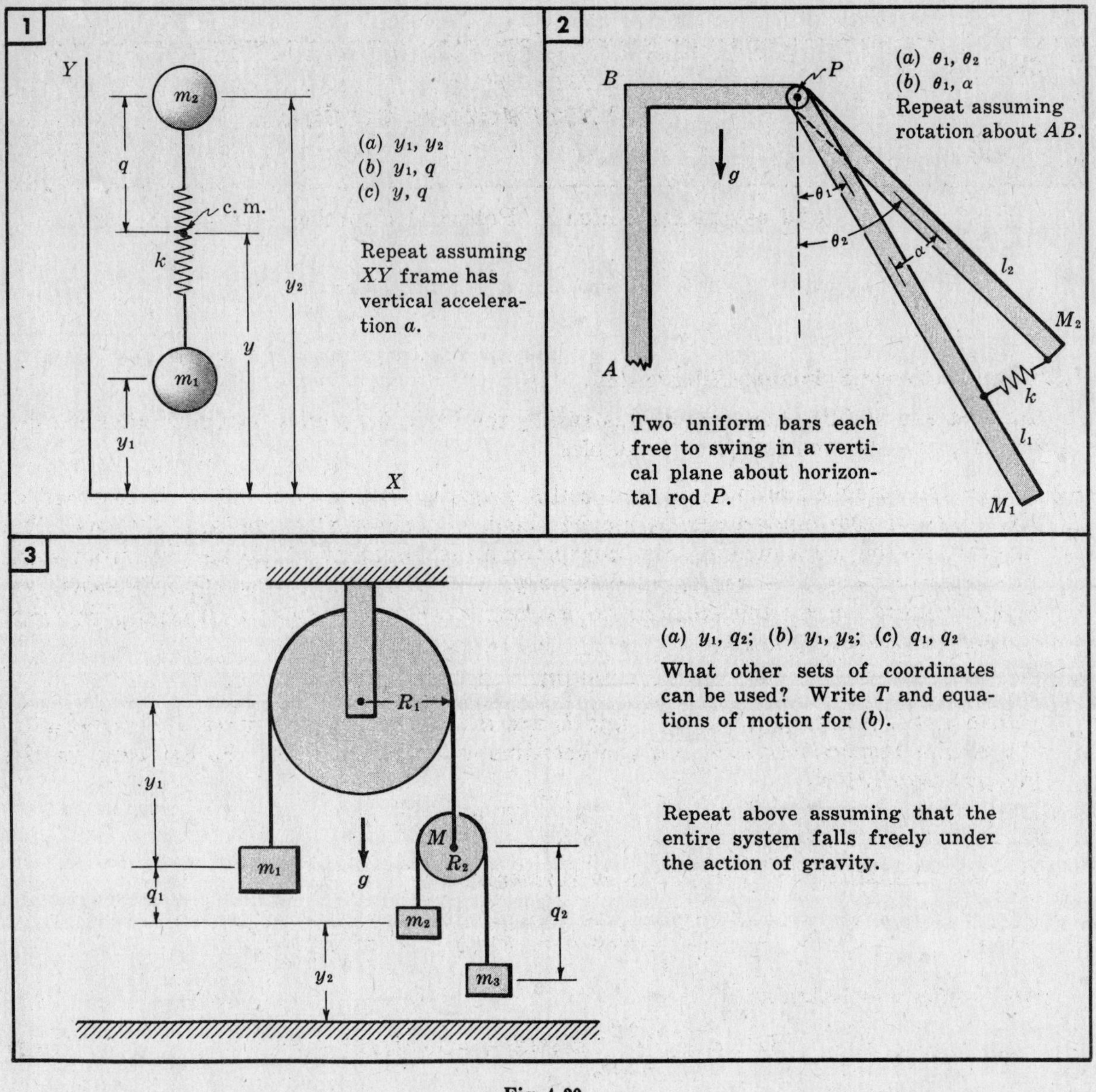
1
Y
X
m₂
m₁
q
c. m.
k
y₂
y
y₁
(a) y₁, y₂
(b) y₁, q
(c) y, q
Repeat assuming XY frame has vertical acceleration a.
2
B
A
P
g
θ₁
θ₂
α
l₂
l₁
k
M₂
M₁
(a) θ₁, θ₂
(b) θ₁, α
Repeat assuming rotation about AB.
Two uniform bars each free to swing in a vertical plane about horizontal rod P.
3
R₁
R₂
M
g
m₁
m₂
m₃
y₁
q₁
y₂
q₂
(a) y₁, q₂; (b) y₁, y₂; (c) q₁, q₂
What other sets of coordinates can be used? Write T and equations of motion for (b).
Repeat above assuming that the entire system falls freely under the action of gravity.

Fig. 4-20

CHAPTER

5 Conservative Systems

and others for which a "Potential Function" may be written

5.1 Certain Basic Principles Illustrated.

As a means of introducing and illustrating the basic principles on which this chapter is founded, consider the following examples.

(*a*) A particle, attached to one end of a coil spring the other end of which is fastened at the origin of coordinates, can be moved about on a smooth horizontal XY plane. Let us compute the work done *by the spring* for a displacement of the particle from some reference point x_0, y_0 to a general point x, y. Assuming the spring obeys Hooke's law and exerts no force perpendicular to its length, the rectangular components of force on the particle are given by

$$F_x = -k(l - l_0)(x/l), \qquad F_y = -k(l - l_0)(y/l)$$

where k is the spring constant, l and l_0 are the stretched and unstretched lengths of the spring respectively, and x, y the coordinates of the particle. Substituting in the general expression

$$W = \int_{x_0, y_0}^{x, y} (F_x\,dx + F_y\,dy)$$

and noting that $l^2 = x^2 + y^2$, it easily follows that

$$W = \int_{x_0, y_0}^{x, y} \left[-kx\,dx - ky\,dy + kl_0 \frac{(x\,dx + y\,dy)}{\sqrt{x^2 + y^2}}\right]$$

which may be written as

$$W = -\int_{x_0, y_0}^{x, y} d[\tfrac{1}{2}k(x^2 + y^2 - 2l_0\sqrt{x^2 + y^2})] \tag{5.1}$$

Hence
$$W = -\tfrac{1}{2}k(x^2 + y^2 - 2l_0\sqrt{x^2 + y^2}) + \tfrac{1}{2}k(x_0^2 + y_0^2 - 2l_0\sqrt{x_0^2 + y_0^2}) \tag{5.2}$$

Here the following points should be noted. First, as is evident from (*5.2*), W is a function of x_0, y_0 and x, y only (depends only on *end points of path*). Or, regarding x_0, y_0 as a fixed reference point, W, except for an additive constant, is a function of x, y only. *Hence the work done by the spring does not depend on the length or shape of the path taken by the particle from* x_0, y_0 *to* x, y. It is also clear that for any closed path $W = 0$. Secondly, F_x and F_y are of such a nature (they depend on x and y in such a way) that dW [see (*5.1*)] is an exact differential. Hence writing $dW = \frac{\partial W}{\partial x}dx + \frac{\partial W}{\partial y}dy$ and comparing with $dW = F_x\,dx + F_y\,dy$, it is evident that $F_x = \partial W/\partial x$, $F_y = \partial W/\partial y$. That these relations are correct can be verified by differentiating (*5.2*).

As another example of this type let us suppose that $F_x = 3Bx^2y^2$, $F_y = 2Bx^3y$, where B is constant. Hence $dW = F_x\,dx + F_y\,dy = d(Bx^3y^2)$ or $W = +Bx^3y^2 - Bx_0^3y_0^2$ a quantity independent of path and for which $F_x = \partial W/\partial x$, $F_y = \partial W/\partial y$.

(*b*) Now consider the work done by a frictional force F exerted by a rough plane on a particle, for a displacement from x_0, y_0 to x, y. Assuming only gravity acting normal to the plane, $F = \mu mg$ (μ = coefficient of friction) in a direction opposite to the element of displacement $ds = (dx^2 + dy^2)^{1/2}$. Hence $F_x = -\mu mg(dx/ds)$ and $F_y = -\mu mg(dy/ds)$. Thus from $dW = F_x\,dx + F_y\,dy$,

$$W = -\mu mg \int_{x_0}^{x} [1 + (dy/dx)^2]^{1/2}\,dx \tag{5.3}$$

The quantity under the integral is not an exact differential. Hence the path, $y = y(x)$, must be specified before the integration can be performed. *W depends on the path* and (*5.3*) does not yield a function of x, y such that $F_x = \partial W/\partial x$, $F_y = \partial W/\partial y$.

As a final example suppose $F_x = axy$, $F_y = bxy$ where a and b are constants. Then $dW = axy\,dx + bxy\,dy$ which is not exact. Therefore W again depends on the path.

Examples under (*a*) and (*b*) above illustrate simple "Conservative" and "Non-conservative" forces respectively.

5.2 Important Definitions.

(a) ***Conservative Forces; Conservative System.***

If the forces are of such a nature (depend on coordinates in such a way) that when the system is displaced from one configuration to another the work done by the forces depends only on the initial and final coordinates of the particles, the forces are said to be *conservative* and the system is referred to as a *conservative system.*

(b) ***Potential Energy.***

The work done by conservative forces in a transfer of the system *from a general configuration A* (where coordinates of the particles are x_1, y_1, z_1, x_2, y_2, z_2, etc.) *to a reference configuration B* (coordinates now ${}_0x_1, {}_0y_1, {}_0z_1$, ${}_0x_2, {}_0y_2, {}_0z_2$, etc.) *is defined as the potential energy V* (x_i, y_i, z_i) *which the system at A has with respect to B.* Note that V is here defined as the work *from the general to the reference configuration* and not the other way around.

Familiar examples of conservative forces are: gravitational forces between masses, forces due to all types of springs and elastic bodies (assuming "perfectly elastic" material), and forces between stationary electric charges. Non-conservative forces include those of friction, the drag on an object moving through a fluid, and various types which depend on time and velocity.

5.3 General Expression for V and a Test for Conservative Forces.

Consider a system of p particles on which conservative forces $F_1, F_2, \ldots, F_p$ are acting. From the above definition it is clear that

$$\begin{aligned} V &= \int_{x_i, y_i, z_i}^{{}_0x_i, {}_0y_i, {}_0z_i} \sum_{i=1}^{p} (F_{x_i}\,dx_i + F_{y_i}\,dy_i + F_{z_i}\,dz_i) \\ &= -\int_{{}_0x_i, {}_0y_i, {}_0z_i}^{x_i, y_i, z_i} \sum_{i=1}^{p} (F_{x_i}\,dx_i + F_{y_i}\,dy_i + F_{z_i}\,dz_i) \end{aligned} \tag{5.4}$$

The integral (*5.4*) is in reality a general expression for work (regardless of the nature of the forces). But in order that the result be independent of the path, the quantity under the integral must be an exact differential. That is, it must be that

$$F_{x_i} = -\frac{\partial V}{\partial x_i}, \quad F_{y_i} = -\frac{\partial V}{\partial y_i}, \quad F_{z_i} = -\frac{\partial V}{\partial z_i} \tag{5.5}$$

Now if, for example, we differentiate F_{x_3} partially with respect to y_4, and F_{y_4} with respect to x_3, we have

$$\frac{\partial F_{x_3}}{\partial y_4} = -\frac{\partial^2 V}{\partial y_4\,\partial x_3}, \quad \frac{\partial F_{y_4}}{\partial x_3} = -\frac{\partial^2 V}{\partial x_3\,\partial y_4} \quad \text{or} \quad \frac{\partial F_{x_3}}{\partial y_4} = \frac{\partial F_{y_4}}{\partial x_3}$$

Thus in general,

$$\frac{\partial F_{x_i}}{\partial y_r} = \frac{\partial F_{y_r}}{\partial x_i}, \quad \frac{\partial F_{x_i}}{\partial z_r} = \frac{\partial F_{z_r}}{\partial x_i}, \quad \text{etc.} \tag{5.6}$$

It can be shown that these relations constitute necessary and sufficient conditions that the quantity under integral (*5.4*) be exact. Also, of course, *relations* (*5.6*) *may be used as a test to determine whether or not given forces are conservative.*

The greatest usefulness of the potential energy function stems from the fact (see Section 5.6) that, when V is expressed in generalized coordinates, generalized forces are given by $F_{q_r} = -\partial V/\partial q_r$. (*Note.* In order to integrate (*5.4*) expressions for $F_{x_i}, F_{y_i}, F_{z_i}$ must be known. But since we already know them, why bother to find V and determine them again from $F_{x_i} = -\partial V/\partial x_i$, etc? This seems absurd. But there is a payoff, not the least of which derives from the fact that, for conservative forces, $F_{q_r} = -\partial V/\partial q_r$.)

5.4 Determination of Expressions for V.

Basically all expressions for V are obtained by evaluating integral (*5.4*). However, the following points are of importance.

(*a*) This integral may be evaluated in any convenient coordinates (rectangular or otherwise) and then, when so desired, expressed in other coordinates by means of transformation equations. Care must be taken to give force components their proper algebraic signs.

(*b*) Potential energy is a relative quantity and the value of $\partial V/\partial q_r$ is not affected by an additive constant. Hence such constants may be dropped.

(*c*) It frequently happens that when the potential energy of a system is due to springs, gravity, electrical charges, etc., V can be written down at once, *using any number of any convenient coordinates,* making use of already well known simple expressions for the potential energy of individual springs, etc. See Section 5.5(4). The final form of V, containing just the proper number n of any desired coordinates, can then be obtained by means of transformation equations.

(*d*) In applying (*c*) there may be a question as to the algebraic sign of certain potential energy terms. In this case it is well to remember that if work must be done by some outside agency in order to transfer a particle from a general position x, y, z to a reference point x_0, y_0, z_0, *its potential energy relative to* x_0, y_0, z_0 *is negative*; *otherwise, positive.*

5.5 Simple Examples Illustrating the Above Statements.

(1) The potential energy of the pendulum, Fig. 5-1, may be referred to lines a_1b_1, a_2b_2, a_3b_3, etc., in which case $V = +mgh, -mgs, -mg(l+s)$ respectively. If θ is to be used as coordinate, h and s may be eliminated, giving

$$V = mgr(1-\cos\theta), \quad mg(l - r\cos\theta), \quad -mgr\cos\theta$$

which are all equal except for a constant term. (Constant additive terms may always be dropped.)

Since $y = r\cos\theta$, the potential energy expressed in y is merely $V = -mgy$.

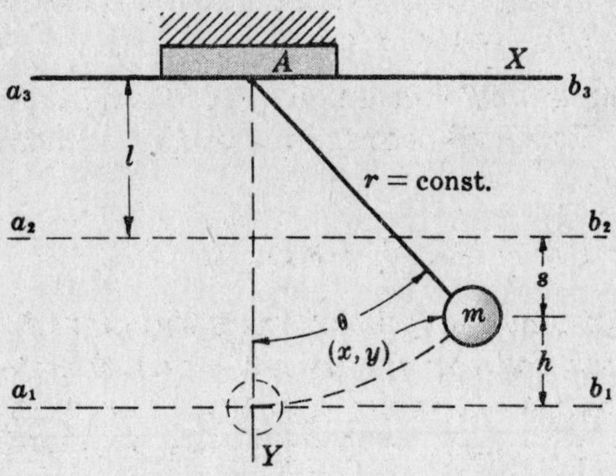

Fig. 5-1

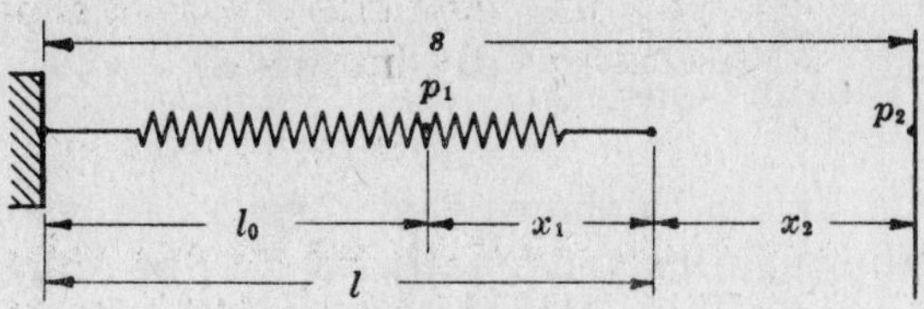

Fig. 5-2

(2) The familiar expression for the potential energy of a stretched spring is $V = \frac{1}{2}k(l - l_0)^2$ where k is the spring constant and l and l_0 are the stretched and unstretched lengths of the spring. Hence in Fig. 5-2, referring V to p_1, $V = +\frac{1}{2}kx_1^2$. However, referred to the fixed point p_2, recalling that V is the work done by the spring from the general point x_1 to p_2, it follows that $V = -[\frac{1}{2}k(s - l_0)^2 - \frac{1}{2}kx_1^2]$. Again, both expressions are the same except for a constant term in the second.

If so desired, V may be expressed in terms of x_2 by the relation $s = x_1 + x_2 + l_0$. Hence $V = +\frac{1}{2}k(s - l_0 - x_2)^2$ or, dropping a constant term, $V = -k(s - l_0)x_2 + \frac{1}{2}kx_2^2$.

(3) Consider the uniformly charged spheres A and B, Fig. 5-3. Regarding A as fixed at the origin and assuming empty space, it follows at once by integration that the potential energy of B with respect to infinity is $V = +Q_1Q_2/r$. But referred to point p, $V = -[Q_1Q_2/s - Q_1Q_2/r]$ which, dropping the constant term, leaves the same expression.

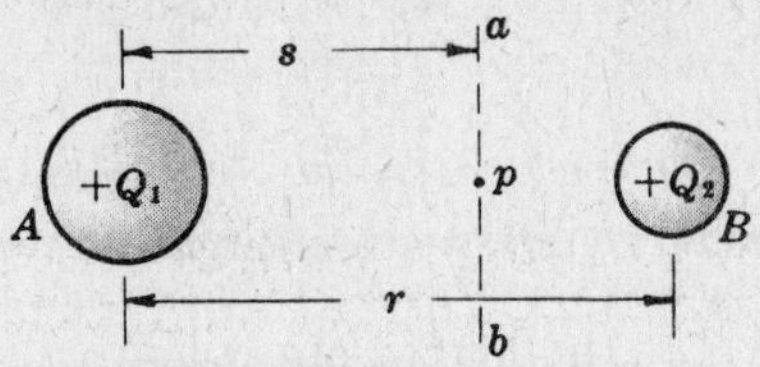

Fig. 5-3

(4) A more complex system: Referring to Fig. 5-4, a sphere of mass m carrying a uniformly distributed charge $+Q_1$ is attached to the springs as indicated. Another similar charge $+Q_2$ is located on the X axis.

Assuming that the upper sphere is free to move in the vertical XY plane (two degrees

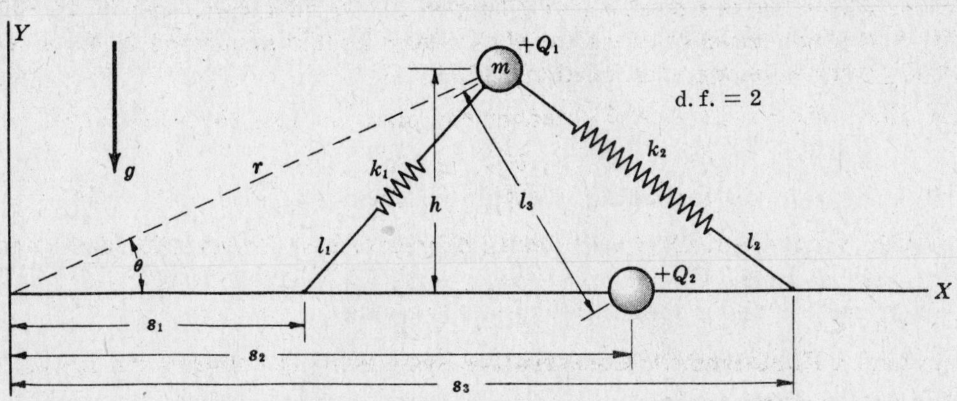

For demonstrating a useful technique in finding V.

Fig. 5-4

of freedom) under the action of gravity, the springs and the electrical repulsion, we shall finally express V for the system in terms of r and θ.

First we write V as per Section 5.4(*c*) using any convenient coordinates, paying no attention to how many may be superfluous. Later all coordinates except r and θ can be eliminated. By inspection,

$$V = \tfrac{1}{2}k_1(l_1 - {}_0l_1)^2 + \tfrac{1}{2}k_2(l_2 - {}_0l_2)^2 + Q_1Q_2/l_3 + mgh$$

where l_1, l_2 and ${}_0l_1, {}_0l_2$ are the stretched and unstretched lengths of the springs, and k_1, k_2 the spring constants. (It has been assumed that the springs do not affect the electric fields about the charges.) Note that V contains the variables l_1, l_2, l_3, h: too many coordinates and not the ones desired. However, by means of the relation $l_1 = [r^2 + s_1^2 - 2rs_1 \cos\theta]^{1/2}$ and similar relations for l_2 and l_3, V may be written in terms of r and θ only. Further details need not be given. This technique of determining V is simple and frequently very convenient.

5.6 Generalized Forces as Derivatives of V.

As explained in Chapter 4, any generalized force, whether individual forces are conservative or non-conservative, may be expressed as

$$F_{q_r} = +\sum_{i=1}^{p}\left(F_{x_i}\frac{\partial x_i}{\partial q_r} + F_{y_i}\frac{\partial y_i}{\partial q_r} + F_{z_i}\frac{\partial z_i}{\partial q_r}\right)$$

Assuming the forces are conservative using equations (*5.5*), this may be written as

$$F_{q_r} = -\sum_{i=1}^{p}\left(\frac{\partial V}{\partial x_i}\frac{\partial x_i}{\partial q_r} + \frac{\partial V}{\partial y_i}\frac{\partial y_i}{\partial q_r} + \frac{\partial V}{\partial z_i}\frac{\partial z_i}{\partial q_r}\right)$$

But by well known rules of differentiation the right side of this equation is just $-\partial V/\partial q_r$. Hence

$$F_{q_r} = -\frac{\partial V}{\partial q_r} \tag{5.7}$$

For example, applying (*5.7*) to $V = -mgr\cos\theta$, the potential energy of the simple pendulum, we obtain $F_\theta = -\partial V/\partial\theta = -mgr\sin\theta$. Or again, generalized forces corresponding to r and θ, Fig. 5-4, are given by $F_r = -\partial V/\partial r$, $F_\theta = -\partial V/\partial\theta$ where V is the final form of potential energy discussed in the latter part of Section 5.5.

It should be clear, however, that *any generalized force which can be found by* (*5.7*) *can also be found by the methods of Chapter 4.* Nevertheless, as will be evident from examples and other considerations to follow, considerable advantage is to be gained from the use of potential energy and relations (*5.7*).

Also, since $F_{q_r} = -\partial V/\partial q_r$ the student can show at once that, for conservative forces,

$$\frac{\partial F_{q_r}}{\partial q_s} = \frac{\partial F_{q_s}}{\partial q_r} \tag{5.8}$$

which is just a statement of (*5.6*) in terms of generalized forces and coordinates.

5.7 Lagrange's Equations for Conservative Systems (only conservative forces acting).

Using (*5.7*), we may write

$$\frac{d}{dt}\left(\frac{\partial T}{\partial \dot{q}_r}\right) - \frac{\partial T}{\partial q_r} = -\frac{\partial V}{\partial q_r} \quad \text{or} \quad \frac{d}{dt}\left(\frac{\partial T}{\partial \dot{q}_r}\right) - \frac{\partial}{\partial q_r}(T - V) = 0$$

Introducing the so-called "Lagrangian function" L, defined by $L = T - V$, the above becomes

$$\frac{d}{dt}\left(\frac{\partial L}{\partial \dot{q}_r}\right) - \frac{\partial L}{\partial q_r} = 0 \tag{5.9}$$

It is permissible to replace T by L in $\partial T/\partial \dot{q}_r$ because, in the usual mechanical problem, V is not a function of $\dot{q}_r$. The usefulness of (*5.9*) will become evident from examples which follow and from the applications made of it in the remaining chapters.

5.8 Partly Conservative and Partly Non-Conservative Systems.

It should here be stated that, if some of the forces acting on the system are non-conservative, Lagrange's equations obviously may be written as

$$\frac{d}{dt}\left(\frac{\partial L}{\partial \dot{q}_r}\right) - \frac{\partial L}{\partial q_r} = F_{q_r} \tag{5.10}$$

where F_{q_r} is found in the usual way, (Section 4.5, Page 61), taking account of non-conservative forces only.

5.9 Examples Illustrating the Application of Lagrange's Equations to Conservative Systems.

Example 5.1. *A pendulum bob suspended from a rubber band.*

Assuming motion in a vertical plane only and using r and θ as coordinates, $T = \frac{1}{2}m(\dot{r}^2 + r^2\dot{\theta}^2)$ and $V = \frac{1}{2}k(r - r_0)^2 - mgr\cos\theta$ where the first term is based on the assumption that the rubber band obeys Hooke's law. Hence $L = \frac{1}{2}m(\dot{r}^2 + r^2\dot{\theta}^2) - \frac{1}{2}k(r - r_0)^2 + mgr\cos\theta$, from which it follows that

$$m\ddot{r} - mr\dot{\theta}^2 + k(r - r_0) - mg\cos\theta = 0 \qquad \text{and} \qquad mr^2\ddot{\theta} + 2mr\dot{r}\dot{\theta} + mgr\sin\theta = 0$$

These are just the equations of motion obtained in Example 3.4, Page 45.

Example 5.2. *A particle of mass m attached to a light rod pivoted at p,* Fig. 5-5.

The kinetic energy for this arrangement is merely $T = \frac{1}{2}mr^2\dot{\theta}^2$. For small angular motion from the horizontal position, an approximate expression for V may be written as

$$V = \tfrac{1}{2}k_1(l + s_1\theta - l_1)^2 + \tfrac{1}{2}k_2(l + s_2\theta - l_2)^2 + mgr\theta$$

where l_1 and l_2 are the unstretched lengths of the first and second springs respectively. Thus

$$L = \tfrac{1}{2}mr^2\dot{\theta}^2 - \tfrac{1}{2}k_1(l + s_1\theta - l_1)^2 - \tfrac{1}{2}k_2(l + s_2\theta - l_2)^2 - mgr\theta$$

from which the equation of motion is found to be

$$mr^2\ddot{\theta} + k_1s_1(l + s_1\theta - l_1) + k_2s_2(l + s_2\theta - l_2) + mgr = 0$$

Let us assume that the springs have been so adjusted that the rod is in static equilibrium for $\theta = 0$. This means that $k_1s_1(l - l_1) + k_2s_2(l - l_2) + mgr = 0$. Hence the equation of motion reduces to $mr^2\ddot{\theta} + (k_1s_1^2 + k_2s_2^2)\theta = 0$. This simple equation integrates at once giving simple harmonic motion with a period of $2\pi\left(\dfrac{mr^2}{k_1s_1^2 + k_2s_2^2}\right)^{1/2}$.

Example 5.3. *The system of springs and pulleys shown in Fig. 5-6.*

Assuming vertical motion only, it follows without difficulty that

$$T = \frac{1}{2}\left(\frac{I_2}{R_2^2} + m_1\right)\dot{y}_1^2 + \frac{1}{2}\left(\frac{I_1}{R_1^2} + \frac{I_2}{R_2^2} + m_2\right)\dot{y}_2^2 - \frac{I_2}{R_2^2}\dot{y}_1\dot{y}_2$$

where the meaning of each symbol is clear from the figure.

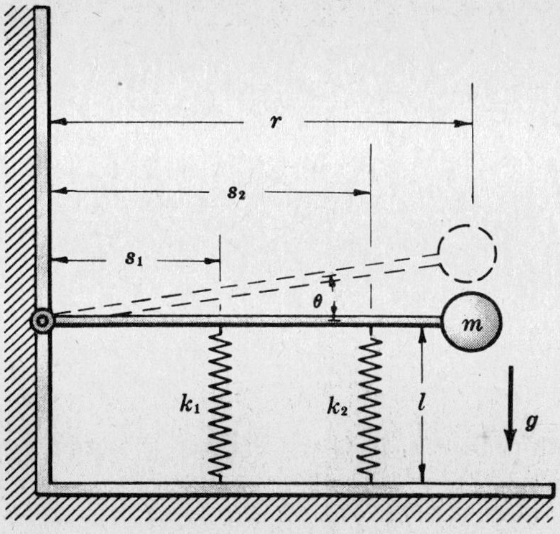

Fig. 5-5

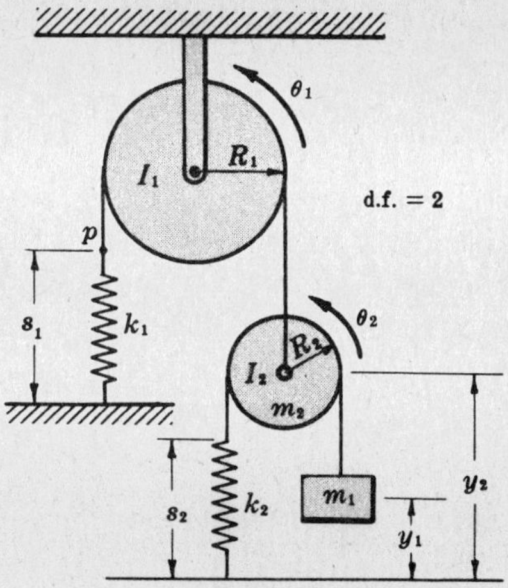

Fig. 5-6

Referring gravitational potential energy to the lower horizontal line from which y_1 and y_2 are measured and writing potential energy for the springs in the usual way,

$$V = m_1 g y_1 + m_2 g y_2 + \tfrac{1}{2}k_1(s_1 - l_1)^2 + \tfrac{1}{2}k_2(s_2 - l_2)^2$$

where l_1 and l_2 are unstretched lengths. But $s_1 + y_2 = C_1$ and $(y_2 - s_2) + (y_2 - y_1) = C_2$ where C_1 and C_2 are constants. Eliminating s_1 and s_2 with these relations, we get

$$V = m_1 g y_1 + m_2 g y_2 + \tfrac{1}{2}k_1(C_1 - y_2 - l_1)^2 + \tfrac{1}{2}k_2(2y_2 - y_1 - C_2 - l_2)^2$$

which contains no superfluous coordinates. This completes the task of finding L. The equations of motion follow at once. If y_1 and y_2 are measured from equilibrium positions of m_1 and m_2 respectively, equations of motion simplify somewhat and can easily be integrated.

As an extension of this example, the reader may show that, using the angular displacements of the disks, θ_1 and θ_2, as coordinates:

$$\begin{aligned} L \;=\; & \tfrac{1}{2}[(m_1 + m_2)R_1^2 + I_1]\dot{\theta}_1^2 + \tfrac{1}{2}(m_1 R_2^2 + I_2)\dot{\theta}_2^2 + m_1 R_1 R_2 \dot{\theta}_1 \dot{\theta}_2 \\ & - m_1 g(C_3 - R_1\theta_1 - R_2\theta_2) - m_2 g(C_3 - R_1\theta_1) \\ & - \tfrac{1}{2}k_1[(C_1 - C_3 + R_1\theta_1) - l_1]^2 - \tfrac{1}{2}k_2[(C_3 - C_2 - R_1\theta_1 + R_2\theta_2) - l_2]^2 \end{aligned}$$

where it is assumed that when the system is in equilibrium, $\theta_1 = \theta_2 = 0$.

Example 5.4. *Potential energy and generalized forces for the double pendulum,* Fig. 2-10, Page 14.

Referring potential energy to a horizontal line through $p(x_0, y_0)$,

$$V = -m_1 g r_1 \cos\theta - m_2 g(r_1 \cos\theta + r_2 \cos\phi)$$

from which $F_\theta = -\partial V/\partial\theta = -(m_1 + m_2) g r_1 \sin\theta$, $\quad F_\phi = -\partial V/\partial\phi = -m_2 g r_2 \sin\phi$

These are the same as previously found.

As an extension of this example the reader should show that, assuming m_1 and m_2 suspended from light coil springs of constants k_1, k_2,

$$V = -m_1 g r_1 \cos\theta - m_2 g(r_1\cos\theta + r_2\cos\phi) + \tfrac{1}{2}k_1(r_1 - {}_0r_1)^2 + \tfrac{1}{2}k_2(r_2 - {}_0r_2)^2$$

and write out generalized forces corresponding to r_1, r_2, θ, ϕ.

Example 5.5. *Potential energy of a number of masses connected "in line" with springs,* Fig. 5-7.

Let us assume (*a*) that the masses are on a smooth horizontal plane, (*b*) that the motion of each mass is "small" and is confined to a line perpendicular to ab, (*c*) that when the masses are in their equilibrium positions along ab the springs are unstretched. The potential energy of the first spring is clearly

$$V_1 = \tfrac{1}{2}k_1\left(\sqrt{s_1^2 + y_1^2} - s_1\right)^2 = \tfrac{1}{2}k_1\left(y_1^2 + 2s_1^2 - 2s_1^2\sqrt{1 + y_1^2/s_1^2}\right)$$

Now assuming that y_1 is less than s_1, we write

$$V_1 = \tfrac{1}{2}k_1\left[y_1^2 + 2s_1^2 - 2s_1^2\left(1 + \frac{1}{2}\frac{y_1^2}{s_1^2} - \frac{1}{8}\frac{y_1^4}{s_1^4} + \frac{3}{48}\frac{y_1^6}{s_1^6} - \cdots\right)\right]$$

Retaining only the first three terms of the expansion the above reduces to $V_1 = (k_1/8s_1^2)y_1^4$. In like manner the potential energy of the second spring is given by $V_2 = (k_2/8s_2^2)(y_1 - y_2)^4$, etc. Finally the approximate expression for the total potential energy becomes

$$V = \frac{k_1}{8s_1^2}y_1^4 + \frac{k_2}{8s_2^2}(y_1 - y_2)^4 + \frac{k_3}{8s_3^2}(y_2 - y_3)^4 + \frac{k_4}{8s_4^2}y_3^4$$

Hence $$F_{y_1} = -\frac{\partial V}{\partial y_1} = -\frac{k_1}{2s_1^2}y_1^3 - \frac{k_2}{2s_2^2}(y_1 - y_2)^3, \quad \text{etc.}$$

If the masses are free to move in a plane, then V will, of course, involve the x and y coordinates of each mass.

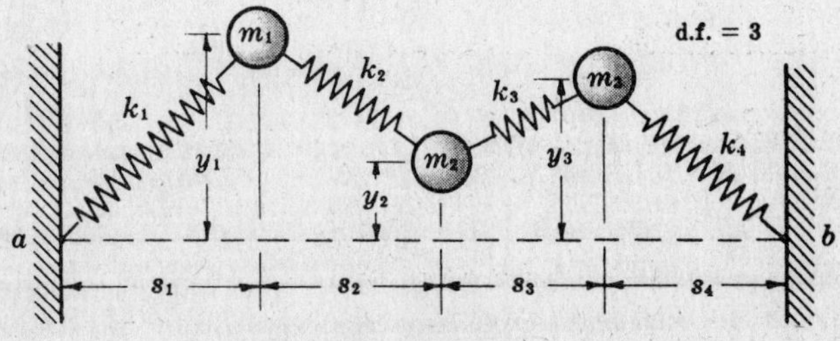

Fig. 5-7

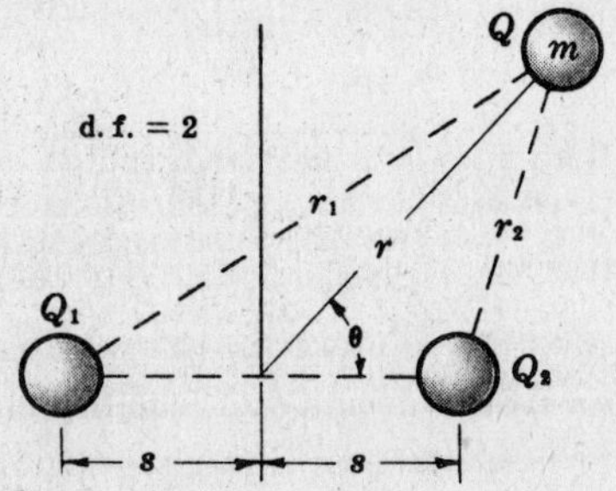

Fig. 5-8

Example 5.6. *The spheres of Fig. 5-8 carry uniformly distributed charges Q, Q_1, Q_2.*

Q_1 and Q_2 are fixed while Q is free to move in a plane. Considering only electrostatic forces, we write (see Section 5.5(4), Page 84) $V = +QQ_1/r_1 + QQ_2/r_2$. Introducing r and θ, this becomes

$$V = \frac{QQ_1}{(r^2 + s^2 + 2rs\cos\theta)^{1/2}} + \frac{QQ_2}{(r^2 + s^2 - 2rs\cos\theta)^{1/2}}$$

It follows from the binomial expansion that for $Q_1 = -Q_2$ and $r \gg s$, $V = -(2QQ_1s\cos\theta)/r^2$; and for $Q_1 = Q_2$ and r very large, $V = 2QQ_1/r$.

Example 5.7. *The "two body" central force system.*

Imagine two homogeneous spheres, Fig. 5-9, having masses m_1, m_2 moving through space under the influence of *no force except their mutual gravitational attraction.*

Axes X, Y, Z, with origin at the center of m_1, remain parallel to the inertial X_1, Y_1, Z_1 axes. Coordinates of c.m. relative to X_1, Y_1, Z_1 are $\bar{x}, \bar{y}, \bar{z}$. A simple integration shows that, referring the potential energy of the system to $r = \infty$, $V = -Gm_1m_2/r$ where G is the gravitational constant. Applying the "center of mass" theorem, Page 26, the reader can show without too much effort that

$$L = \tfrac{1}{2}M(\dot{\bar{x}}^2 + \dot{\bar{y}}^2 + \dot{\bar{z}}^2) + \tfrac{1}{2}\mu(\dot{r}^2 + r^2\dot{\theta}^2 + r^2\sin^2\theta\,\dot{\phi}^2) + Gm_1m_2/r$$

where $M = m_1 + m_2$ and the "reduced mass" $\mu = m_1m_2/(m_1 + m_2)$.

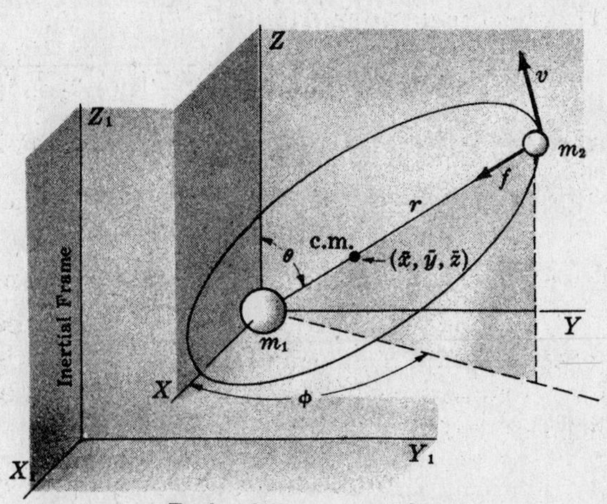

Path of m_2 as seen from m_1.

Two-body Central Force Problem

Fig. 5-9

Many interesting facts may be obtained from a solution of the equations of motion. For example, c.m. moves through space along a straight line with constant velocity. The path of m_2, as seen from m_1, is an ellipse, parabola or hyperbola depending on whether $\mathcal{E} = T + V$ is less than, equal to, or greater than zero. Assuming that initial motion starts in such a way that $\dot{\phi}_0 = 0$, it is seen that since $\partial L/\partial\dot{\phi} = \mu r^2 \sin\theta\dot{\phi} = p_\phi =$ constant, ϕ remains constant for all time. Hence for the general case motion is in a plane and we can write (neglecting motion of c.m.)

$$L = \tfrac{1}{2}\mu(\dot{r}^2 + r^2\dot{\theta}^2) + Gm_1m_2/r$$

5.10 Approximate Expression for the Potential Energy of the System of Springs, Fig. 5-10.

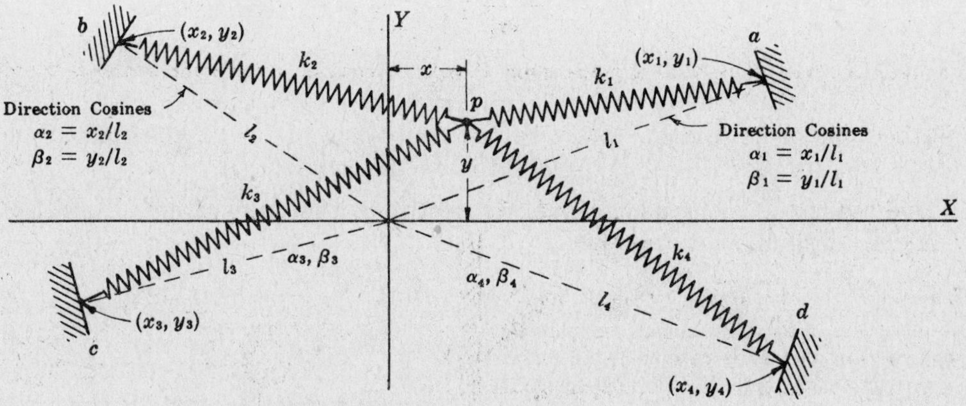

Potential Energy of a Group of Springs

Fig. 5-10

The springs are flexibly fastened at points a, b, c, d with opposite ends flexibly connected together at p. This junction is free to move in the XY plane. We shall determine an approximate expression for V assuming x and y always small.

An exact expression for the potential energy of the first spring is simply $V_1 = \frac{1}{2}k_1(L_1 - l_1')^2$ where L_1 is the length pa and l_1' the unstretched length of the spring. But $L_1^2 = (l_1\alpha_1 - x)^2 + (l_1\beta_1 - y)^2$ where l_1 and the direction cosines α_1, β_1 are shown on the diagram.

Now applying Taylor's expansion for n variables (see Page 206) and retaining first and second order terms (the $(V)_{00}$ term is constant and may be dropped), it follows after a bit of tedious work that

$$V_{1\,(\text{approx.})} = -k_1(l_1 - l_1')(x\alpha_1 + y\beta_1) + \frac{k_1}{2}(x^2 + y^2) - \frac{k_1 l_1'}{2l_1}(x\beta_1 - y\alpha_1)^2 \qquad (1)$$

Hence for a group of S springs arranged as in Fig. 5-10,

$$V_{(\text{approx.})} = \sum_{i=1}^{S}\left[-k_i(l_i - l_i')(x\alpha_i + y\beta_i) + \frac{k_i}{2}(x^2 + y^2) - \frac{k_i l_i'}{2l_i}(x\beta_i - y\alpha_i)^2\right] \qquad (2)$$

In use, proper algebraic signs must be given to the direction cosines.

If the junction p is in equilibrium at the origin (which was not assumed in the above derivation), the first order terms in Taylor's expansion will be zero even though some or all springs may still be stretched. This is because at the origin $F_x = -(\partial V/\partial x)_0 = 0$, etc. Hence (2) reduces to

$$V_{(\text{approx.})} = \frac{1}{2}\sum_{i=1}^{S}\left[k_i(x^2 + y^2) - \frac{k_i l_i'}{l_i}(x\beta_i - y\alpha_i)^2\right] \qquad (5.11)$$

For any particular problem in hand the constants l_i, α_i, β_i can be measured with good accuracy. (Given the spring constants, unstretched lengths and locations $a, b, c, d,$ the task of computing the equilibrium position of p and thus l_i, α_i, β_i is more involved than might be expected. This is a good job for a computer.)

Note that since $\alpha_i = x_i/l_i$, $\beta_i = y_i/l_i$, equation (*5.11*) can be written as

$$V_{(\text{approx.})} \quad = \quad \frac{1}{2}\sum_{i=1}^{S}\left[k_i(x^2+y^2) \;-\; \frac{k_i l_i'}{l_i^3}(xy_i - yx_i)^2\right] \qquad (5.12)$$

Denoting the ends of several coil springs by a_1, b_1, a_2, b_2, etc., let the a ends be fastened at various random points to the inside walls of a rigid box and the b ends fastened together at a common junction which can be moved about in the box.

If the origin of an XYZ frame is taken at the equilibrium position of this junction, it is easily shown (see Problem 5.16, Page 96) that

$$V_{(\text{approx.})} \quad = \quad \frac{1}{2}\sum_{i=1}^{S}\left[\frac{k_i l_i'}{l_i}(x\alpha_i + y\beta_i + z\gamma_i)^2 \;+\; k_i\left(\frac{l_i - l_i'}{l_i}\right)(x^2+y^2+z^2)\right] \qquad (5.13)$$

where S is the number of springs, k_i the spring constants and $\alpha_i, \beta_i, \gamma_i$ are direction cosines of the axes of the springs when the junction is at the origin.

The above approximations are frequently useful in the field of small oscillations and will be referred to again in Chapter 10.

Example 5.8.

The mass m, Fig. 5-11, connected to springs by means of a string as shown, is free to move about on the smooth horizontal plane ab under the central force determined by the springs. Each spring has a constant k. Then $V = k(l_1 - l_0)^2$ where l_1 and l_0 are the stretched and unstretched lengths of either spring. Let y represent the displacement of the junction from its position p when the springs are unstretched as shown in the figure. Then $l_1 = [s_1^2 + (s_0 + y)^2]^{1/2}$. Thus, dropping constant terms, $V = kl_1^2 - 2kl_0 l_1$ or

$$V \quad = \quad ky^2 + 2ks_0 y - 2kl_0[s_1^2 + (s_0+y)^2]^{1/2}$$

Now applying either equation (*10.6*), Page 207, to the above expression for V or (*5.11*) directly, we find that

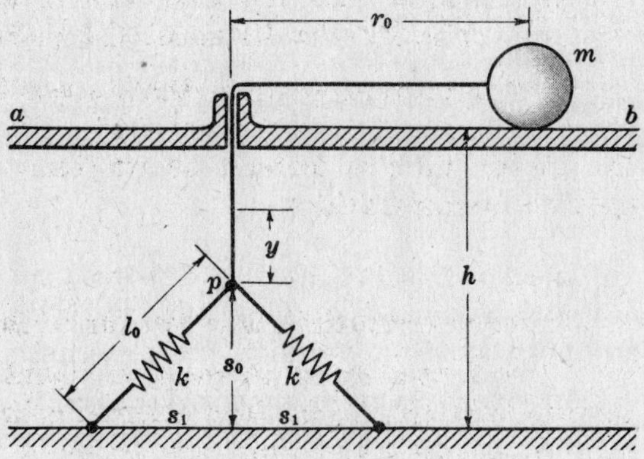

Fig. 5-11

$$V_{(\text{approx.})} \quad = \quad k(s_0^2/l_0^2)y^2 \quad = \quad k(s_0^2/l_0^2)(r - r_0)^2$$

since $y = r - r_0$. By inspection, for r equal to or less than r_0, the tension in the string drops to zero; but for small displacements in which $r > r_0$,

$$L \quad = \quad \tfrac{1}{2}m(\dot{r}^2 + r^2\dot{\theta}^2) \;-\; k(s_0^2/l_0^2)(r - r_0)^2$$

5.11 Systems in which Potential Energy Varies with Time. Examples.

It frequently happens that the forces acting on a system are functions of time as well as coordinates. Moreover, these forces may be of such a nature that relations (*5.6*) hold true. When this is the case it is clear that an integration of (*5.4*), *holding t constant*, will give a quantity V (a potential energy which changes with time) such that $F_{q_r} = -\partial V/\partial q_r$. Hence relations (*5.7*) are directly applicable. Two simple examples are given below.

Example 5.9.

Suppose that the string to which a pendulum bob is attached passes through a small hole in the support. Imagine the string pulled up through the hole with constant speed v. The length r of the pendulum is given by $r = r_0 - vt$. Hence, referring potential energy to a horizontal line passing through the support, $V = -mg(r_0 - vt)\cos\theta$ from which $-\partial V/\partial\theta = -mg(r_0 - vt)\sin\theta = F_\theta$. That this expression for F_θ is correct can easily be checked by the methods of Chapter 4.

Example 5.10.

One end of a light coil spring is made to oscillate about the origin of coordinates along the X axis according to the relation $s = A \sin \omega t$, on a smooth horizontal plane. To the other end of the spring is attached a particle of mass m. The particle is free to move about on the plane under the action of the spring. We shall assume that the axis of the spring remains straight and that no force is exerted normal to this axis (no bending moment exists).

By inspection F_x, the x component of the force on m, is given by

$$F_x = -k(l-l_0)\cos(l,x) = -k\{[(x-A\sin\omega t)^2+y^2]^{1/2}-l_0\}\frac{(x-A\sin\omega t)}{[(x-A\sin\omega t)^2+y^2]^{1/2}}$$

where l is the stretched and l_0 the unstretched length of the spring. F_y is given by a similar expression. Note that F_x and F_y are each functions of t as well as x and y.

An application of the test (*5.6*) shows that $\partial F_x/\partial y = \partial F_y/\partial x$. Hence a potential energy function may be determined from (*5.4*), holding t constant. Writing $V = \frac{1}{2}k(l-l_0)^2$ and replacing l by $[(x-A\sin\omega t)^2+y^2]^{1/2}$ gives $V = \frac{1}{2}k\{[(x-A\sin\omega t)^2+y^2]^{1/2}-l_0\}^2$. Now an application of $F_x = -\partial V/\partial x$, $F_y = -\partial V/\partial y$ leads to the same expressions as those obtained above.

Note that if it were desirable to use polar coordinates, V may easily be expressed in terms of r and θ, eliminating x and y by $x = r\cos\theta$, $y = r\sin\theta$. Generalized forces corresponding to r and θ then follow at once from $F_r = -\partial V/\partial r$, $F_\theta = -\partial V/\partial\theta$.

Many examples similar to (*5.9*) and (*5.10*) could be given. Imagine: the support A, Fig. 5-1, made to oscillate or rotate in a circle; the point p, Fig. 2-10, Page 14, made to oscillate vertically; the distances s, Fig. 5-8, to vary in some known manner with time; etc.

It is important to note that, since the quantities we have written as V contain t, $T+V \neq$ constant (see Section 5.13). In other words, if the forces depend explicitly on t the energy integral cannot be written. The reason for this may be seen at once from physical considerations.

5.12 Vector Potential Function for a Charge Moving in an Electromagnetic Field.

The components of force on a "point" charge $+Q$ moving with velocity $(\dot{x}, \dot{y}, \dot{z})$ in an electric field (E_x, E_y, E_z) and magnetic induction (B_x, B_y, B_z), each of which may be functions of position and time, are given by

$$\begin{aligned} f_x &= QE_x + Q(\dot{y}B_z - \dot{z}B_y) \\ f_y &= QE_y + Q(\dot{z}B_x - \dot{x}B_z) \\ f_z &= QE_z + Q(\dot{x}B_y - \dot{y}B_x) \end{aligned} \tag{5.14}$$

For a mechanical system on which such forces are acting, an application of either (*4.10*), (*4.11*) or (*4.12*), Page 61, gives corresponding generalized forces.

However, the above forces are of such nature that neither a scalar potential V nor a power function P (see Chapter 6) can be written such that $F_{q_r} = -\partial V/\partial q_r$ or $F_{q_r} = \partial P/\partial \dot{q}_r$. But it is possible to write a "vector potential" function leading to a new form of L such that (*5.9*) takes complete account of these electromagnetic forces. We mention this possibility here for the sake of completeness. A treatment of the matter will not be given.

See for example: Roald K. Wangsness *Introduction to Theoretical Physics*, John Wiley & Sons, Inc., 1963, Pages 397-400.

5.13 The "Energy Integral".

Under certain rather special conditions it may be shown that the total energy of a system is constant.

Consider a system for which L *does not contain time explicitly and on which only conservative forces are acting.* (It should be evident to the student that the first assumption means no moving coordinates or constraints and V is not of the form discussed in Section 5.11.)

Hence, since $L = L(q_r, \dot{q}_r)$, its total time derivative is

$$\frac{dL}{dt} = \sum_{r=1}^{n} \frac{\partial L}{\partial \dot{q}_r} \ddot{q}_r + \sum_{r=1}^{n} \frac{\partial L}{\partial q_r} \dot{q}_r$$

Introducing (*5.9*), this can be written as

$$\frac{dL}{dt} = \sum_{r=1}^{n} \frac{\partial L}{\partial \dot{q}_r} \ddot{q}_r + \sum_{r=1}^{n} \dot{q}_r \frac{d}{dt}\left(\frac{\partial L}{\partial \dot{q}_r}\right) \qquad \text{which is just} \qquad \frac{dL}{dt} = \frac{d}{dt}\left(\sum_{r=1}^{n} \dot{q}_r \frac{\partial L}{\partial \dot{q}_r}\right)$$

Integrating this once,

$$\sum_{r=1}^{n} \dot{q}_r \frac{\partial L}{\partial \dot{q}_r} = L + \mathcal{E} \tag{5.15}$$

where $\mathcal{E}$ is a constant of integration. Now writing $T = \sum_{kr}^{n} A_{kr}\dot{q}_k\dot{q}_r$ [see equation (*2.56*), Page 27],

$$\frac{\partial T}{\partial \dot{q}_r} = 2\sum_{k=1}^{n} A_{kr}\dot{q}_k = \frac{\partial L}{\partial \dot{q}_r}$$

since V does not contain $\dot{q}$. Substituting this into (*5.15*), we have $2\sum_{kr}^{n} A_{kr}\dot{q}_k\dot{q}_r = L + \mathcal{E}$. The sum is just $2T$. Hence $2T = T - V + \mathcal{E}$ or

$$T + V = \mathcal{E} = \text{constant} \tag{5.16}$$

This "energy integral" or "first integral" of the system plays an important part in the solution of many problems.

5.14 Suggested Experiments.

(1) Determine the period of oscillation of the system shown in Fig. 5-14, for small vertical motion. See Problem 5.7, Page 93.

(2) Determine the period of oscillation of the rod of Fig. 5-13 for small motion. See Problem 5.6.

(3) Determine the two periods of oscillation of the system of Fig. 5-20 for small values of θ and ϕ. See Problem 5.14, Page 95.

Equipment for these experiments is easily and quickly assembled. The results obtained are gratifying and well worth the small effort required.

Problems

Note. Drop constant additive terms in V.

5.1. Determine which of the following forces are conservative. Find V for those that are conservative.

(*a*) $F_x = 0,\ F_y = -mg$ (*b*) $F_x = -kx,\ F_y = -ky$ (*c*) $F_x = -ky,\ F_y = +kx$

(*d*) $F_x = Axy,\ F_y = Bxy$ (*e*) $F_x = Ayz,\ F_y = Axz,\ F_z = Axy$

(*f*) $F_r = 3Br^2 \sin\theta\cos\phi,\ F_\theta = Br^3\cos\theta\cos\phi,\ F_\phi = -Br^3\sin\theta\sin\phi$

(*g*) $F_r = f_1(r),\ F_\theta = f_2(\theta),\ F_\phi = f_3(\phi)$ (*h*) $F_x = -kx\sin\omega t,\ F_y = kty$

5.2. Show that the work done by the forces of Problem 5.1(*c*) in passing around a rectangle having sides $x_2 - x_1$ and $y_2 - y_1$ is $2k(x_2 - x_1)(y_2 - y_1)$. Show that the work done by forces $F_x = 3Bx^2y^2$, $F_y = 2Bx^3y$ in traversing the same rectangle is zero.

5.3. Determine V for the system described in Problem 4.5, Page 74. Show that $F_{q_r} = -\partial V/\partial q_r$ gives the same expressions for generalized forces as were obtained from $\delta W = F_{q_r}\,\delta q_r$.

5.4. Write V in terms of θ_1, θ_2, Fig. 4-10, Page 74. Show that $F_{\theta_1} = -\partial V/\partial\theta_1$ and $F_{\theta_2} = -\partial V/\partial\theta_2$ check with previously found values of the generalized forces.

5.5. The mass m, Fig. 5-12, is free to move along a smooth horizontal rod under the action of the spring. When the mass is in its equilibrium position the spring is still stretched. Show that for small displacements from equilibrium the potential energy is closely approximated by

$$V = \frac{k(s - l_0)}{2s}x^2 + \frac{kl_0}{8s^3}x^4$$

where l_0 is the unstretched length of the spring.

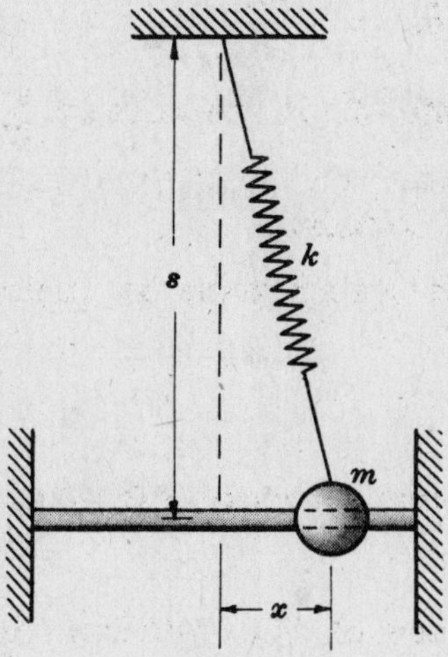

Fig. 5-12

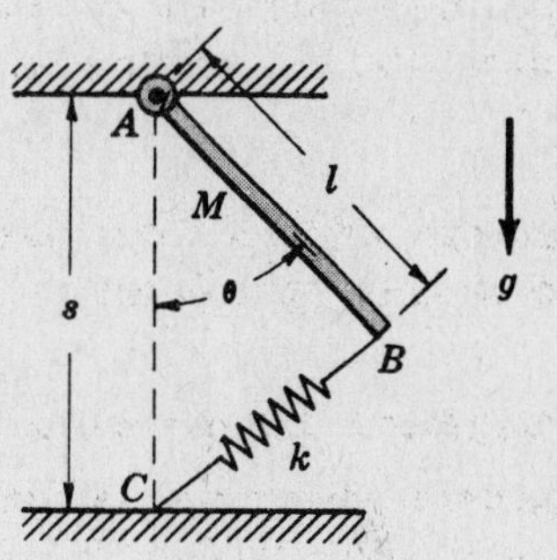

Fig. 5-13

5.6. The uniform bar AB of mass M and length l, Fig. 5-13, is supported by a smooth bearing at A. The end B is attached to the spring BC as shown. For $\theta = 0$ the spring is still stretched. Neglecting the mass of the spring show that V for the system is

$$V = -\tfrac{1}{2}Mgl\cos\theta + \tfrac{1}{2}k[(s^2 + l^2 - 2sl\cos\theta)^{1/2} - l_0]^2$$

Assuming θ small, approximate V by Taylor's expansion and determine the period of oscillation of the rod.

5.7. The bar plus block, Fig. 5-14, have a mass M. The two springs are identical.

(*a*) Write an exact expression for V. Does this lead to a "linear" force on M?

(*b*) s_0 = distance ab when system is in equilibrium ($s = 0$). Given k, s_1, M and the unstretched length l_0 (same for each spring), show that to find s_0 it is necessary to solve the following fourth degree equation:

$$4k^2s_0^4 - 4Mgks_0^3 + (M^2g^2 + 4k^2s_1^2 - 4k^2l_0^2)s_0^2 - 4Mgks_1^2s_0 + M^2g^2s_1^2 = 0$$

(*c*) Assuming the equilibrium length l of each spring is known, approximate the potential energy (see equation (*2*), Page 89) and find an expression for the period of oscillation about the position of equilibrium.

(*d*) Assuming s_0 known, show that $l = 2kl_0s_0/(2ks_0 - Mg)$.

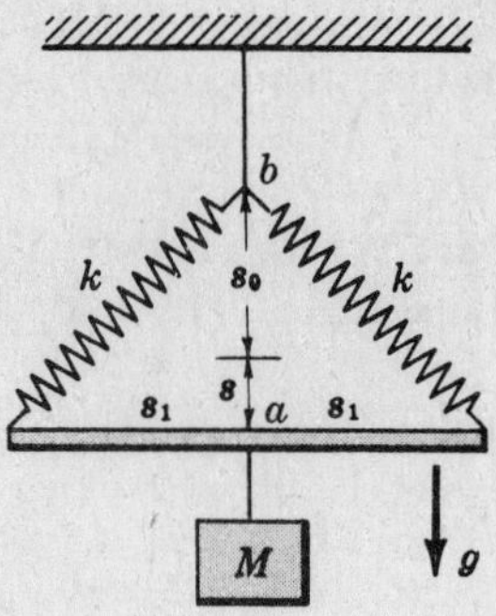

Fig. 5-14

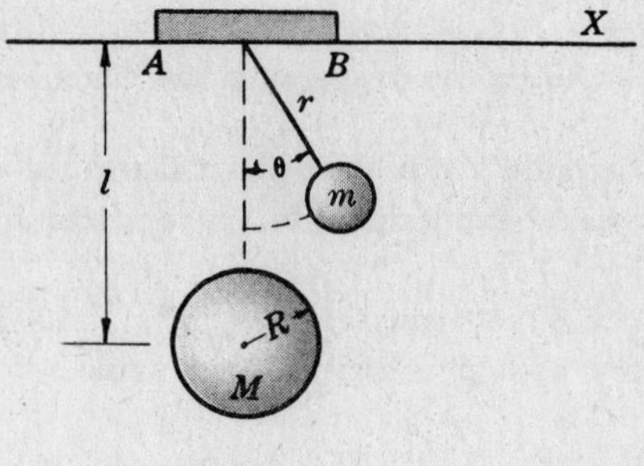

Fig. 5-15

5.8. The simple pendulum is supported near a large uniform sphere of mass M, Fig. 5-15. Write V in terms of θ, taking account of the gravitational attraction between M and m. Approximate this for small θ and l only slightly greater than $R+r$. Determine the period of oscillation for small motion. Neglect earth's gravitational field.

5.9. Three spheres carrying uniformly distributed charges $+Q, -2Q, +Q$ are fixed on the X axis as shown in Fig. 5-16. Another sphere having mass m and charge $+Q_1$ is free to move in the XY plane under the action of the electrical forces. Assuming empty space, write an exact expression for V. Show that for $r \gg s$ this may be written as

$$V_{(\text{approx.})} = \frac{2QQ_1 s^2 \cos^2\theta}{r^3} - \frac{QQ_1 s^2 \sin^2\theta}{r^3}$$

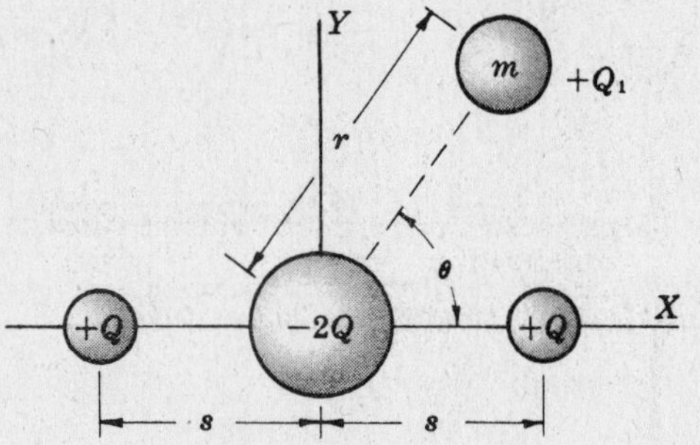

Fig. 5-16

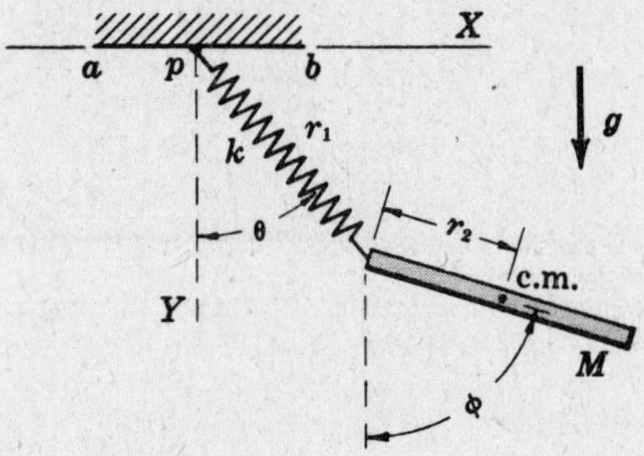

Fig. 5-17

5.10. Determine the generalized forces F_{y_1} and F_{y_2}, Example 5.3, Page 86, Fig. 5-6, by the method of Chapter 4 and compare with $-\partial V/\partial y_1$, $-\partial V/\partial y_2$ respectively.

5.11. A uniform bar of length $2r_2$ and mass M is attached to the end of a coil spring as shown in Fig. 5-17. Assuming motion in a plane show that

$$L = \tfrac{1}{2}M\left(\dot{r}_1^2 + r_1^2\dot{\theta}^2 + r_2^2\dot{\phi}^2 + 2\cos(\phi-\theta)\, r_1 r_2 \dot{\theta}\dot{\phi} - 2\sin(\phi-\theta)\, r_2 \dot{r}_1 \dot{\phi}\right)$$
$$+ \tfrac{1}{2}I\dot{\phi}^2 - \tfrac{1}{2}k(r_1 - r_0)^2 + Mg(r_1\cos\theta + r_2\cos\phi)$$

where I is the moment of inertia of the bar about an axis through c.m. and perpendicular to its length, k is the spring constant, and r_0 the unstretched length of the spring.

5.12. The tightly stretched string of Fig. 5-18 is loaded with equally spaced beads. Assuming they are displaced in the directions of y_1, y_2, etc., only and that the displacements are so slight that the tension τ remains constant, show that the potential energy of the system (neglecting gravity) is given by

$$V = \frac{\tau}{a}[y_1^2 + y_2^2 + y_3^2 + y_4^2 + y_5^2 - y_1 y_2 - y_2 y_3 - y_3 y_4 - y_4 y_5]$$

and that for n beads we may write $V = \dfrac{1}{2}\displaystyle\sum_{r=0}^{n} \frac{\tau}{a}(y_{r+1} - y_r)^2$ where $y_0 = y_{n+1} = 0$.

Show that the potential energy of a uniform, tightly stretched flexible string, having any slight distortion $y = y(x)$, is given by $V = \frac{1}{2}\tau \int_0^l (\partial y/\partial x)^2\,dx$.

Show that for the distortion $Y = A \sin \pi x/l$, $V = A^2\pi^2\tau/4l$.

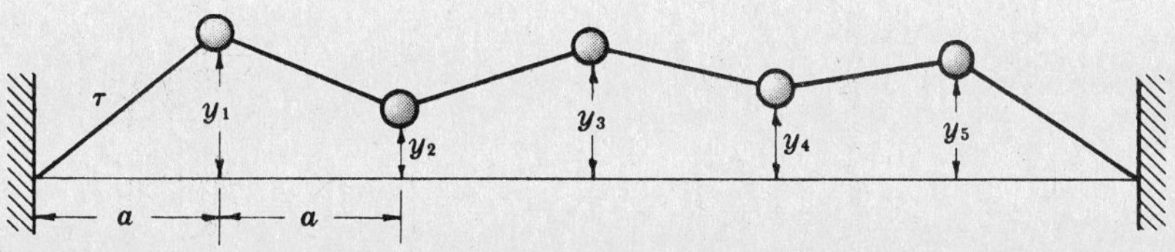

Fig. 5-18

5.13. Three meshed gears G_1, G_2, G_3 are coupled through torsional springs to disks D_1, D_2, D_3 as shown in Fig. 5-19. Show that the Lagrangian function for the system is

$$L = \frac{I_1}{2}\dot{\theta}_1^2 + \frac{d_2^2}{2}\left(\frac{I_3}{d_1^2} + \frac{I_4}{d_2^2} + \frac{I_5}{d_3^2}\right)\dot{\theta}_4^2 + \frac{I_6}{2}\dot{\theta}_6^2 + \frac{I_7}{2}\dot{\theta}_7^2$$
$$- \frac{k_1}{2}(\theta_4 - \theta_1)^2 - \frac{k_2 d_2^2}{2}\left(\frac{\theta_4}{d_1} - \frac{\theta_6}{d_2}\right)^2 - \frac{k_3 d_2^2}{2}\left(\frac{\theta_4}{d_3} - \frac{\theta_7}{d_2}\right)^2$$

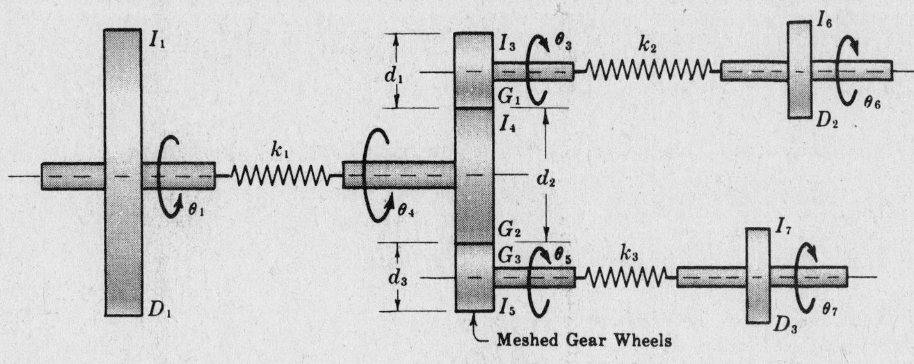

Fig. 5-19

5.14. Springs having constants k_1 and k_2 are attached to m_1 of the double pendulum as indicated in Fig. 5-20. When the system is at rest m_1 is at p and the springs are still under tension. Lower ends of the springs are attached to points a and b (known coordinates (x_1, y_1) and (x_2, y_2) respectively).

(a) Show that for the springs (not including gravity),

$$V_{(\text{exact})} = \tfrac{1}{2}k_1(s_1 - l_1')^2 + \tfrac{1}{2}k_2(s_2 - l_2')^2$$

where
$$s_1^2 = (x_1 - x)^2 + (y_1 + y)^2$$
$$s_2^2 = (x_2 + x)^2 + (y_2 + y)^2$$

How may V_{exact} be written in terms of θ?

(b) Applying equation (2), Page 89, show that for θ small,

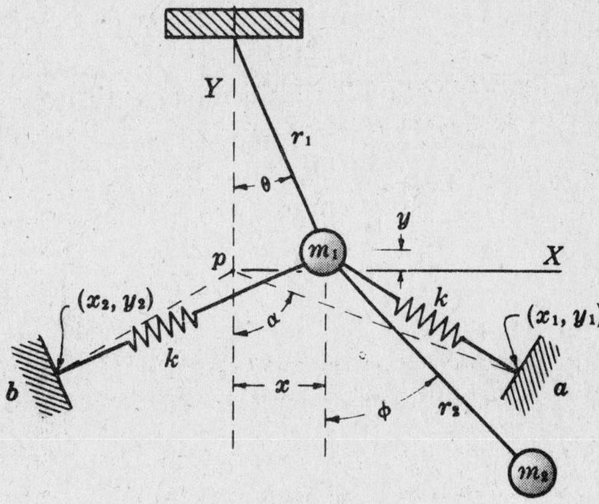

Fig. 5-20

$$V_{(\text{approx.})} = \frac{1}{2}(k_1 + k_2)r_1^2\theta^2 + \frac{1}{2}\left[k_1 y_1\left(\frac{l_1 - l_1'}{l_1}\right) + k_2 y_2\left(\frac{l_2 - l_2'}{l_2}\right)\right]r_1\theta^2$$
$$- \frac{1}{2}\left[\frac{k_1 l_1'}{l_1^3}y_1^2 + \frac{k_2 l_2'}{l_2^3}y_2^2\right]r_1^2\theta^2$$

5.15. Referring to Fig. 5-21, assume ab is the equilibrium position of the rod. Let l_1 and l_2 (with components l_x, l_y, s_x, s_y) represent equilibrium lengths of the springs.

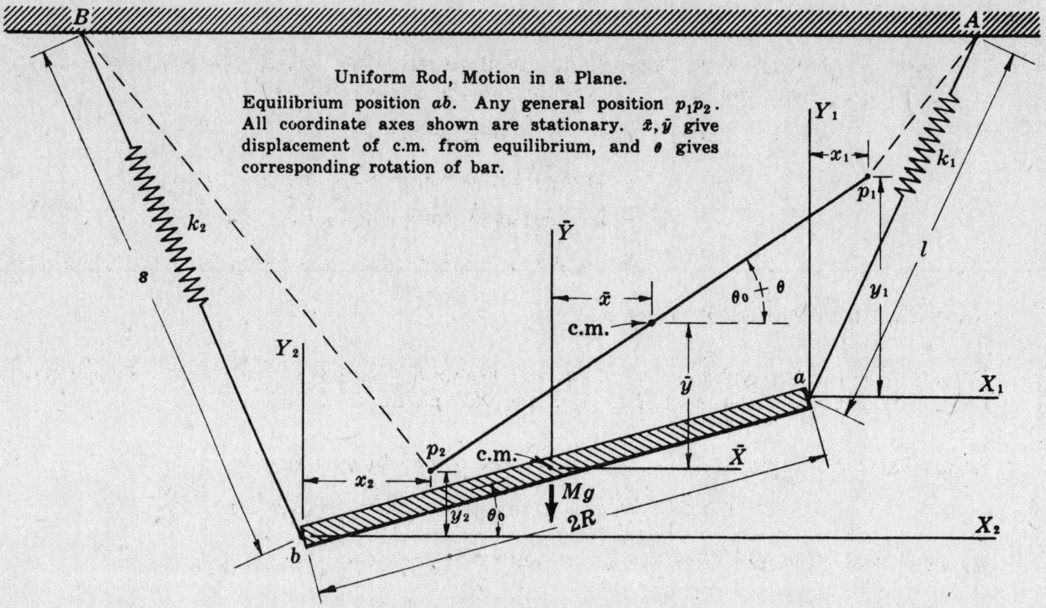

Uniform Rod, Motion in a Plane.
Equilibrium position ab. Any general position p₁p₂. All coordinate axes shown are stationary. x̄, ȳ give displacement of c.m. from equilibrium, and θ gives corresponding rotation of bar.
B
A
k₁
k₂
s
l
Y₁
Y₂
Ȳ
X̄
X₁
X₂
x₁
x₂
y₁
y₂
x̄
ȳ
θ₀ + θ
θ₀
c.m.
p₁
p₂
a
b
Mg
2R

Fig. 5-21

(a) Show that an exact expression for the potential energy of the system may be written as

$$V_{(\text{exact})} = \tfrac{1}{2}k_1\{[(l_x - x_1)^2 + (l_y - y_1)^2]^{1/2} - l_0\} + \tfrac{1}{2}k_2\{[(s_x + x_2)^2 + (s_y - y_2)^2]^{1/2} - s_0\} + Mg\bar{y}$$

where l_0 and s_0 are unstretched lengths of the springs.

(b) Show that relations relating x_1, y_1, x_2, y_2 and $\bar{x}, \bar{y}, \theta$ are

$$2R\cos(\theta_0 + \theta) + x_2 = 2R\cos\theta_0 + x_1 \qquad 2R\sin(\theta_0 + \theta) + y_2 = 2R\sin\theta_0 + y_1$$

$$R\cos(\theta_0 + \theta) + \bar{x} = R\cos\theta_0 + x_1 \qquad R\sin(\theta_0 + \theta) + \bar{y} = R\sin\theta_0 + y_1$$

Note that by means of these equations V_{exact} may be expressed in terms of $\bar{x}, \bar{y}, \theta$.

(c) Applying equation (*2*), Page 89, and making use of the above show that, for small motion about the equilibrium position,

$$\begin{aligned}V_{(\text{approx.})} = {} & \tfrac{1}{2}[k_1 + k_2 - Al_y^2 - Bs_y^2]\bar{x}^2 + \tfrac{1}{2}[k_1 + k_2 - Al_x^2 - Bs_x^2]\bar{y}^2 \\ & + \tfrac{1}{2}[k_1R(1 - l_0/l)(l_x\cos\theta_0 + l_y\sin\theta_0) + k_2R(1 - s_0/s)(s_x\cos\theta_0 - s_y\sin\theta_0) \\ & \quad + (k_1 + k_2)R^2 - (Al_xl_y - Bs_xs_y)R^2\sin\theta_0\cos\theta_0 \\ & \quad - (Al_y^2 + Bs_y^2)R^2\sin^2\theta_0 - (Al_x^2 + Bs_x^2)R^2\cos^2\theta_0]\theta^2 \\ & + [Al_xl_y - Bs_xs_y]\bar{x}\bar{y} \\ & + [(k_2 - k_1)R\sin\theta_0 + (Al_xl_y + Bs_xs_y)R\cos\theta_0 + (Al_y^2 - Bs_y^2)R\sin\theta_0]\bar{x}\theta \\ & - [(k_2 - k_1)R\cos\theta_0 + (Al_xl_y + Bs_xs_y)R\sin\theta_0 + (Al_x^2 - Bs_x^2)R\cos\theta_0]\bar{y}\theta\end{aligned}$$

where $A = k_1l_0/l^3$ and $B = k_2s_0/s^3$, and that

$$L = \tfrac{1}{2}I\dot{\theta}^2 + \tfrac{1}{2}M(\dot{\bar{x}}^2 + \dot{\bar{y}}^2) - V_{(\text{approx.})}$$

where I is the moment of inertia of the rod about a normal axis through c.m.

5.16. Give a detailed proof of relation (*5.13*), Page 90.

5.17. Suppose the entire framework supporting the double pendulum and springs in Fig. 5-20 is made to move vertically upward with constant acceleration a. Will this change the potential energy of the springs? To what extent may we regard the gravitational potential energy as having increased? Write out the new expression for T.

5.18. The support ab, Fig. 5-17, is made to oscillate vertically about the position now shown, with $y = A \sin \omega t$. Show that the Lagrangian for the system is

$$\begin{aligned} L \;=\; & \tfrac{1}{2}M[\dot{r}_1^2 + r_1^2\dot{\theta}^2 + r_2^2\dot{\phi}^2 + A^2\omega^2\cos^2\omega t \\ & + 2r_1r_2\dot{\theta}\dot{\phi}\cos(\phi-\theta) - 2\dot{r}_1r_2\dot{\phi}\sin(\phi-\theta) \\ & + 2A\omega\cos\omega t\,(\dot{r}_1\cos\theta - r_1\dot{\theta}\sin\theta - r_2\dot{\phi}\sin\phi)] \\ & + \tfrac{1}{2}I\dot{\phi}^2 - \tfrac{1}{2}k(r_1 - r_0)^2 + Mg(r_1\cos\theta + r_2\cos\phi + A\sin\omega t) \end{aligned}$$

Compare this with L in Problem 5.11.

5.19. Determine L for the system of Problem 5.11 assuming point p is made to move with constant linear speed v in a small circle of radius a in the XY plane.

5.20. Referring to Example 5.7, Page 88, show that L may be written as

$$L = \frac{M}{2}(\dot{x}^2 + \dot{y}^2 + \dot{z}^2) + \frac{m_1M}{2m_2}(\dot{\rho}_1^2 + \rho_1^2\dot{\theta}^2) + \frac{G\mu m_2}{\rho_1}$$

where ρ_1 is the distance from m_1 to c.m. and $r = \rho_1 + \rho_2$, $m_1\rho_1 = m_2\rho_2$.

5.21. Referring to Fig. 5-22, the vertical shaft is made to rotate in some known manner. The X, Y axes are attached to and rotate with the system. The "particle" of mass m is free to move in the XY plane under the action of the springs and gravity. Show that

$$L = \tfrac{1}{2}m[(R+x)^2\dot{\theta}^2 + \dot{x}^2 + \dot{y}^2] - mgy - \tfrac{1}{2}k_1\{[x^2 + (s-y)^2]^{1/2} - l_1'\}^2 - \tfrac{1}{2}k_2[(x^2+y^2)^{1/2} - l_2']^2$$

Assuming $\dot{\theta} = \omega =$ constant, show that conditions to be met for "steady motion" ($x =$ constant, $y =$ constant, $\dot{x} = \dot{y} = 0$) are

$$m(R + x_0)\omega^2 - (k_1 + k_2)x_0 + \frac{k_1x_0l_1'}{\sqrt{x_0^2 + (s-y_0)^2}} + \frac{k_2x_0l_2'}{\sqrt{x_0^2 + y_0^2}} = 0$$

$$mg + (k_1 + k_2)y_0 - k_1s + \frac{k_1(s-y_0)l_1'}{\sqrt{x_0^2 + (s-y_0)^2}} - \frac{k_2y_0l_2'}{\sqrt{x_0^2 + y_0^2}} = 0$$

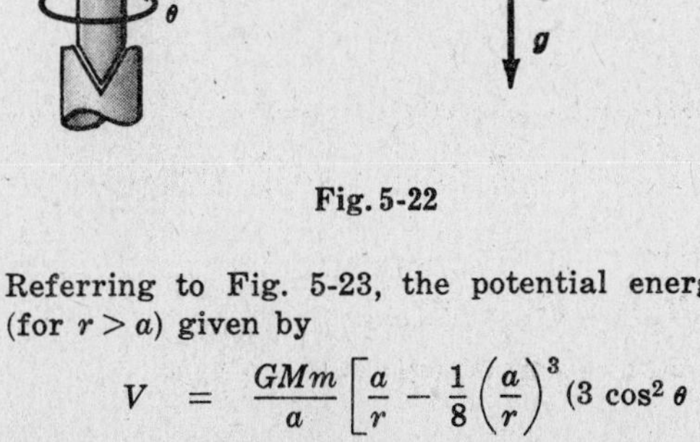

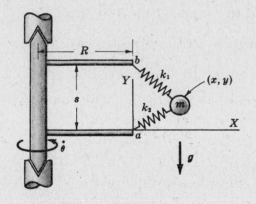

Fig. 5-22

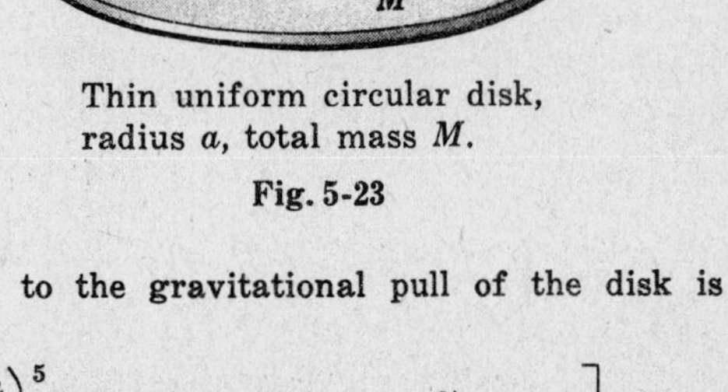

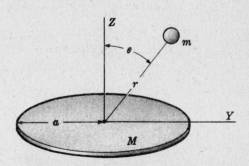

Thin uniform circular disk, radius a, total mass M.

Fig. 5-23

5.22. Referring to Fig. 5-23, the potential energy of m due to the gravitational pull of the disk is (for $r > a$) given by

$$V = \frac{GMm}{a}\left[\frac{a}{r} - \frac{1}{8}\left(\frac{a}{r}\right)^3(3\cos^2\theta - 1) + \frac{1}{64}\left(\frac{a}{r}\right)^5(35\cos^4\theta - 30\cos\theta - 3) - \cdots\right]$$

Write L and the equations of motion of m.

5.23. Referring to Example 5.7, Page 88, prove that the motions of m_1 and m_2 are confined to a plane whose orientation does not change relative to an inertial frame.

Show that, in plane polar coordinates measured in this plane,

$$L = \frac{\mu}{2}(\dot{r}^2 + r^2\dot{\theta}^2) + \frac{Gm_1m_2}{r^2}$$

where the term due to the motion of c.m. has been dropped. Also show that

$$L = \frac{m_2^2}{\mu}(\dot{r}_2^2 + r_2^2\dot{\theta}^2) + \frac{Gm_1^2m_2}{Mr_2}$$

where $r_1 + r_2 = r$ and $m_1r_1 = m_2r_2$; r_1 and r_2 are measured from c.m. to m_1 and m_2 respectively.

5.24. Show, for any system in which L does not contain time explicitly (see Section 5.8) but on which non-conservative forces are acting, that the time rate of change of the total energy of the system is given by

$$\frac{d}{dt}(T + V) = \sum_{r=1}^{n} F_{q_r}\dot{q}_r$$

where the generalized forces, F_{q_r}, include only the non-conservative forces.

5.25. Suppose the supports a, b, c, d, Fig. 5-10, Page 89, fastened to a rigid movable structure such as a picture frame. The frame is now forced to move, rotate and translate, in any given manner in its own plane. Assuming X, Y fastened to the frame and x, y measured as indicated, is expression (*2*) in any way changed?

Assuming the frame oscillates parallel to X about some point, fixed relative to inertial space, with motion given by $s = A \sin \omega t$, and assuming a particle m fastened to p (junction of springs) write out L for the particle.

Note. As a good example of V, see Problem 13.15, Page 279.

CHAPTER

6

Determination of F_{q_r} for Dissipative Forces

(a) **Usual Procedure**
(b) **Use of "Power Function"**

6.1 Definition and Classification.

Dissipative forces include any and all types of such a nature that energy is dissipated from the system when motion takes place. The "lost" energy is usually accounted for by the formation of heat.

It frequently happens in practice that the magnitude of the force, f, on a particle (or on an element of area) may be closely represented, over certain ranges of velocity at least, by

$$f = av^n \tag{6.1}$$

where v is the velocity of the particle, n is some number and a may be a constant or a function of coordinates and/or time. As will be seen, this is an important and rather general (but not the only) type of dissipative force.

(*a*) *Frictional forces.* The frictional force required to slide one surface over another is assumed to be proportional to the normal force between surfaces, independent of the area in contact and independent of speed, once motion has started. (We shall not discuss "static" friction.) Hence for $n = 0$ and a equal to the coefficient of friction times the normal force, (*6.1*) represents a frictional force. If the coefficient of friction changes from point to point and if, perhaps, the normal force holding one surface against the other changes with time, we have an example in which a is a function of coordinates and time.

If both surfaces are moving, the frictional force on either one is opposite in direction to the velocity of that surface relative to the other.

(*b*) *Viscous forces.* When the force on an object varies as the first power of its speed and is opposite in direction to its motion, it is said to be "viscous". The drag on an object moving slowly through a fluid of any kind or the drag on a magnetic pole which is moving near a conducting sheet are examples of viscous forces. For $n = 1$, (*6.1*) represents such a force.

(*c*) *Forces proportional to higher powers of speed.* Except at low velocities the drag on an object moving in a fluid is not a simple viscous force. However, it may be possible to represent it, at least over a limited range, by (*6.1*). In certain cases n may be considerably greater than one. (Also, see Section 6.6, Page 103.)

6.2 General Procedure for Determination of F_{q_r}.

Two methods will be employed. The first, treated and illustrated in the following sections, is based on the general relations (*4.10*) and (*4.12*), Page 61. The second, in which the F_{q_r} are obtained from a "power function", is given in Section 6.8.

Assuming f expressed by (*6.1*) and directed opposite to v, it follows that, since $\dot{x}/v =$ cosine of the angle between v and X, $f_x = -av^n(\dot{x}/v) = -a\dot{x}v^{n-1}$. Likewise $f_y = -a\dot{y}v^{n-1}$, $f_z = -a\dot{z}v^{n-1}$. Hence, assuming p particles and n the same for each, δW_{total} and generalized forces are determined as summarized below.

$$\delta W_{\text{total}} = -\sum_{i=1}^{p} a_i(\dot{x}_i\,\delta x_i + \dot{y}_i\,\delta y_i + \dot{z}_i\,\delta z_i)v_i^{n-1} \tag{6.2}$$

General expression for δW_{total}. Eliminating $\dot{x}_i, \delta x_i$, etc., in favor of $q_1, \dot{q}_1, \delta q_1$, etc., this becomes

$$\delta W_{\text{total}} = [\cdots]\,\delta q_1 + [\cdots]\,\delta q_2 + \cdots + [\cdots]\,\delta q_n \tag{6.3}$$

Thus the coefficients of $\delta q_1, \delta q_2, \ldots, \delta q_n$ in (6.3) are the generalized forces.

6.3 Examples: Generalized Frictional Forces.

In the following examples the dissipative forces are assumed to be dry friction for which $n = 0$.

Example 6.1. *Motion of a particle on a rough inclined plane.*

A particle of mass m is projected upward along the rough inclined plane as in Fig. 6-1. The total frictional force $f = \mu mg\cos\alpha$ is assumed to be constant in magnitude and opposite in direction to the motion. Since $\dot{x}/\sqrt{\dot{x}^2+\dot{y}^2}$, for example, is the cosine of the angle between the velocity of m and the X axis, it is clear that the components of frictional force are

$$(1)\quad f_x = -f\dot{x}/\sqrt{\dot{x}^2+\dot{y}^2}, \qquad (2)\quad f_y = -f\dot{y}/\sqrt{\dot{x}^2+\dot{y}^2}$$

which, in this simple example are the generalized frictional forces. Thus, taking account of gravity also, the equations of motion are

$$m\ddot{x} = -\mu mg\cos\alpha\,\frac{\dot{x}}{(\dot{x}^2+\dot{y}^2)^{1/2}}, \qquad m\ddot{y} = -\mu mg\cos\alpha\,\frac{\dot{y}}{(\dot{x}^2+\dot{y}^2)^{1/2}} - mg\sin\alpha$$

Important note. If the particle were projected upward along a line x = constant, with initial velocity $\dot{y}_0$ ($\dot{x} = \ddot{x} = 0$ for all time), the second equation would become $m\ddot{y} = -\mu mg\cos\alpha - mg\sin\alpha$. It will evidently reach a certain height and (possibly) start back down the incline. One might infer from the above equation that $\mu mg\cos\alpha$ is always in the negative direction of Y. However, we know that on starting back the frictional force reverses direction and $\mu mg\cos\alpha$ must now be regarded as positive. The force is discontinuous and one must be alert to this possibility in dealing with frictional forces. See Problem 6.12, Page 113.

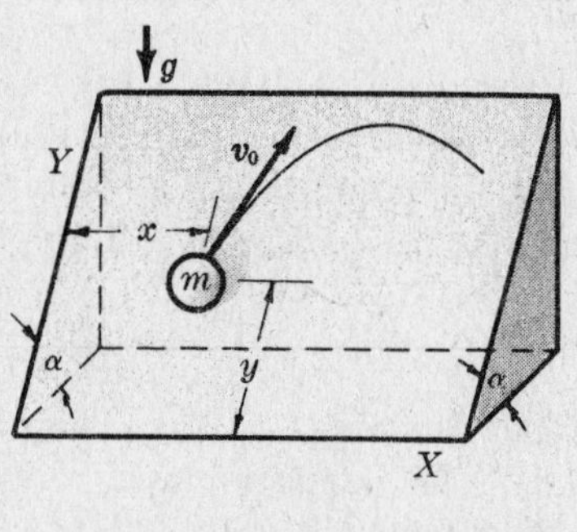

Particle Moving on Rough Inclined Plane
Fig. 6-1

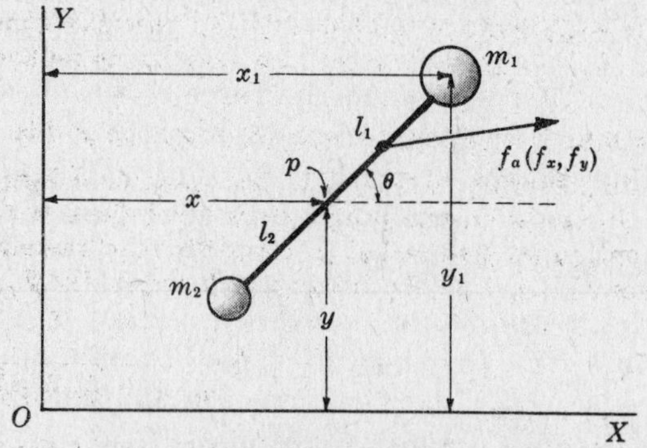

Dumbbell Sliding on the Rough Horizontal XY Plane
Fig. 6-2

Example 6.2. *Two particles connected with a light rod are moving on a rough horizontal plane,* Fig. 6-2.

Let us find the generalized frictional forces. (Other forces which may be acting will not be considered.) The dumbbell has three degrees of freedom and we shall use the coordinates x, y, θ shown on the drawing. The magnitudes of the frictional forces on m_1 and m_2 are $f_1 = \mu m_1 g$ and $f_2 = \mu m_2 g$ respectively. Assuming the connecting rod is not in contact with the plane and applying relation (6.2) for $n = 0$,

$$\delta W_{\text{total}} = -\frac{f_1\dot{x}_1\,\delta x_1}{\sqrt{\dot{x}_1^2+\dot{y}_1^2}} - \frac{f_1\dot{y}_1\,\delta y_1}{\sqrt{\dot{x}_1^2+\dot{y}_1^2}} - \frac{f_2\dot{x}_2\,\delta x_2}{\sqrt{\dot{x}_2^2+\dot{y}_2^2}} - \frac{f_2\dot{y}_2\,\delta y_2}{\sqrt{\dot{x}_2^2+\dot{y}_2^2}} \tag{1}$$

where x_1, y_1 and x_2, y_2 are the rectangular coordinates of m_1 and m_2 respectively and $-f_1\dot{x}_1/\sqrt{\dot{x}_1^2 + \dot{y}_1^2}$, for example, is the component of the frictional force on m_1 in the direction of x_1. But from the figure it is seen that

$$x_1 = x + l_1 \cos\theta, \qquad y_1 = y + l_1 \sin\theta, \qquad \text{etc.} \tag{2}$$

Thus $x_1, y_1, \delta x_1$, etc. can easily be eliminated from (1), giving

$$\begin{aligned} -\delta W &= f_2 \frac{(\dot{x} + l_2\dot{\theta}\sin\theta)\,\delta x + (\dot{y} - l_2\dot{\theta}\cos\theta)\,\delta y + [l_2(\dot{x}\sin\theta - \dot{y}\cos\theta) + l_2^2\dot{\theta}]\,\delta\theta}{\sqrt{(\dot{x} + l_2\dot{\theta}\sin\theta)^2 + (\dot{y} - l_2\dot{\theta}\cos\theta)^2}} \\ &\quad + f_1 \frac{(\dot{x} - l_1\dot{\theta}\sin\theta)\,\delta x + (\dot{y} + l_1\dot{\theta}\cos\theta)\,\delta y + [l_1(\dot{y}\cos\theta - \dot{x}\sin\theta) + l_1^2\dot{\theta}]\,\delta\theta}{\sqrt{(\dot{x} - l_1\dot{\theta}\sin\theta)^2 + (\dot{y} + l_1\dot{\theta}\cos\theta)^2}} \end{aligned} \tag{3}$$

Expressions for the generalized frictional forces F_x, F_y and F_θ may now be read directly from (3). For example,

$$F_x = -\frac{f_2(\dot{x} + l_2\dot{\theta}\sin\theta)}{\sqrt{(\dot{x} + l_2\dot{\theta}\sin\theta)^2 + (\dot{y} - l_2\dot{\theta}\cos\theta)^2}} - \frac{f_1(\dot{x} - l_1\dot{\theta}\sin\theta)}{\sqrt{(\dot{x} - l_1\dot{\theta}\sin\theta)^2 + (\dot{y} + l_1\dot{\theta}\cos\theta)^2}} \tag{4}$$

For special cases such as $\dot{x} = \dot{y} = 0$ and $\dot{\theta} \neq 0$ or $\dot{y} = \dot{\theta} = 0$ and $\dot{x} \neq 0$, the reader may easily show that F_x, F_y, F_θ reduce to simple expressions which may be verified by elementary considerations.

It is clear from this relatively simple example that frictional forces may become frightfully involved. Thus, resulting differential equations may be difficult or impossible to solve except by computer methods.

Example 6.3. *A more general case of the above.*

Suppose that instead of the two shown in Fig. 6-2, there are p particles arranged in any pattern on the XY plane and connected together with a rigid framework of rods. The system has only three degrees of freedom and x, y, θ are still suitable coordinates. Relation (6.2) becomes

$$\delta W_{\text{total}} = -\sum_{i=1}^{p} \frac{f_i(\dot{x}_i\,\delta x_i + \dot{y}_i\,\delta y_i)}{(\dot{x}_i^2 + \dot{y}_i^2)^{1/2}} \tag{6.4}$$

Eliminating $\dot{x}_i$, δx_i, etc., in favor of $\dot{x}, \delta x, \dot{y}, \delta y, \theta, \delta\theta$, (6.4) may be written as

$$\delta W_{\text{total}} = [\cdots]\,\delta x + [\cdots]\,\delta y + [\cdots]\,\delta\theta \tag{6.5}$$

which is just a special case of (6.3).

Thus coefficients of $\delta x, \delta y, \delta\theta$ in (6.5) are the generalized forces F_x, F_y, F_θ. It is important to realize that the $f_i = \mu_i$ (normal force) are assumed to be known.

Example 6.4. *Generalized frictional forces on a thin rod sliding in contact with a rough plane.*

Again referring to Fig. 6-2, first imagine a large number, p, of particles distributed along the rod, each in contact with the rough plane. Relations (6.4) and (6.5) lead to the generalized frictional forces. For a continuous thin rod it is clear that the summation in (6.4) must be replaced by an integral. The reader may show that the integral expression for F_x, for example, is

$$F_x = \int_{-l_2}^{l_1} \frac{f(\dot{x} - l\dot{\theta}\sin\theta)\,dl}{[\dot{x}^2 + \dot{y}^2 + l^2\dot{\theta}^2 + 2l\dot{\theta}(\dot{y}\cos\theta - \dot{x}\sin\theta)]^{1/2}} \tag{6.6}$$

where f is the frictional force per unit length of the rod (assumed known) and dl is an element of length of the rod. l is measured from point p to dl. l_1 and l_2 are lengths above and below p. All quantities, except l, are here regarded as constants.

Integral expressions for F_y and F_θ follow in the same way.

Example 6.5. *Generalized frictional forces on a board sliding in contact with a rough plane.*

Referring to Fig. 6-3 below it is seen that this is merely an extension of the problem discussed in Example 6.4. Using the relations

$$x_1 = x + x_2\cos\theta - y_2\sin\theta, \qquad y_1 = y + x_2\sin\theta + y_2\cos\theta$$

and remembering that, so far as the motion of the board is concerned x_2, y_2 are constant, the student may show that an integral expression for F_θ, for example, is given by

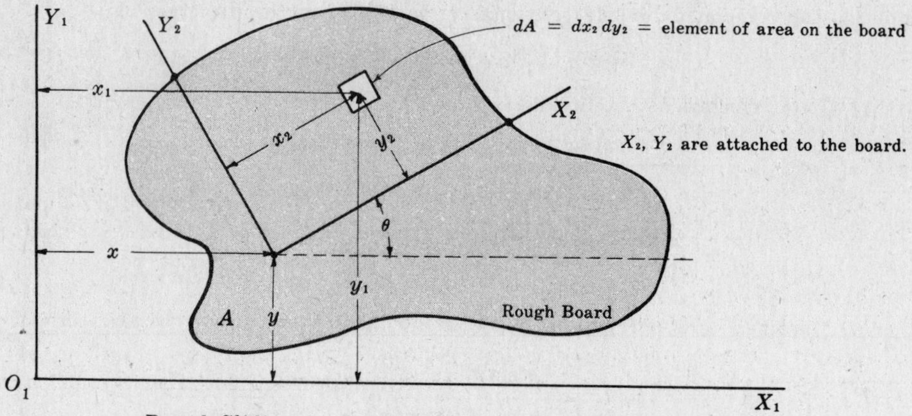

Board Sliding in Contact with Rough X_1Y_1 Plane

Fig. 6-3

$$F_\theta = -\int \frac{f[(x_2^2 + y_2^2)\dot{\theta} + (\dot{y}x_2 - \dot{x}y_2)\cos\theta - (\dot{x}x_2 + \dot{y}y_2)\sin\theta]\,dx_2\,dy_2}{[\dot{x}^2 + \dot{y}^2 + (x_2^2 + y_2^2)\dot{\theta}^2 + 2\dot{\theta}\cos\theta(\dot{y}x_2 - \dot{x}y_2) - 2\dot{\theta}\sin\theta(\dot{x}x_2 + \dot{y}y_2)]^{1/2}} \tag{6.7}$$

where all quantities, except x_2, y_2, are held constant and the integral is taken over the entire surface of the board in contact with the X_1Y_1 plane. $f\,dx_2\,dy_2$ is the magnitude of frictional force on the element of area $dx_2\,dy_2$. f is here assumed to be a known constant. Similar expressions follow for F_x, F_y.

The evaluation of these integrals is not simple. A somewhat more tractable form for finding generalized forces of this and other types is given in Section 6.8.

6.4 Examples: Generalized Viscous Forces.

Setting $n = 1$ in (*6.2*), that relation is applicable and reduces to

$$\delta W_{\text{total}} = -\sum_{i=1}^{p} a_i(\dot{x}_i\,\delta x_i + \dot{y}_i\,\delta y_i + \dot{z}_i\,\delta z_i)$$

Example 6.6. *Viscous forces on a dumbbell.*

Let us assume that forces acting on m_1 and m_2, Fig. 6-2, are viscous rather than frictional. Then

$$\delta W_{\text{total}} = -a_1\dot{x}_1\,\delta x_1 - a_1\dot{y}_1\,\delta y_1 - a_2\dot{x}_2\,\delta x_2 - a_2\dot{y}_2\,\delta y_2$$

Eliminating $\dot{x}_1, \delta x_1$, etc., by the relations $x_1 = x + l_1\cos\theta$, $y_1 = y + l_1\sin\theta$, etc.,

$$\begin{aligned}\delta W_{\text{total}} = &-[(a_1 + a_2)\dot{x} + (a_2l_2 - a_1l_1)\dot{\theta}\sin\theta]\,\delta x - [(a_1 + a_2)\dot{y} - (a_2l_2 - a_1l_1)\dot{\theta}\cos\theta]\,\delta y \\ &-[(a_2l_2^2 + a_1l_1^2)\dot{\theta} + (a_2l_2 - a_1l_1)(\dot{x}\sin\theta - \dot{y}\cos\theta)]\,\delta\theta\end{aligned}$$

from which F_x, F_y, F_θ may be read off directly.

Example 6.7. *Viscous forces on a moving plane surface.*

Imagine that the board, Fig. 6-3, is now moving near and parallel to the stationary X_1Y_1 plane. Suppose that a viscous liquid fills the space between. We shall *assume* that the drag on each element $dx_2\,dy_2$ of the moving surface is viscous and that force components on the element are given by $df_x = -\alpha\dot{x}_1\,dx_2\,dy_2$, $df_y = -\alpha\dot{y}_1\,dx_2\,dy_2$, where α is the viscous drag per unit area per unit velocity.

Hence, for a general virtual displacement of the entire surface,

$$\delta W_{\text{total}} = -\alpha\int[\dot{x}_1\,\delta x_1 + \dot{y}_1\,\delta y_1]\,dx_2\,dy_2$$

where the integration extends over the entire moving surface. Again employing relations $x_1 = x + x_2\cos\theta - y_2\sin\theta$, etc., the above may be expressed as

$$\delta W_{\text{total}} = -\alpha \int \{(\dot{x} - x_2\dot{\theta}\sin\theta - y_2\dot{\theta}\cos\theta)\,\delta x + (\dot{y} + x_2\dot{\theta}\cos\theta - y_2\dot{\theta}\sin\theta)\,\delta y$$
$$+ [(x_2^2 + y_2^2)\dot{\theta} + (\dot{y}x_2 - \dot{x}y_2)\cos\theta - (\dot{x}x_2 + \dot{y}y_2)\sin\theta]\,\delta\theta\}\,dx_2\,dy_2 \tag{6.8}$$

Integrating over the moving surface, holding all quantities except x_2, y_2 constant, the coefficients of $\delta x, \delta y, \delta\theta$ are the desired expressions for F_x, F_y, F_θ.

Example 6.8.

Suppose the surface above is a rectangle of area $A = 2a \times 2b$ with axes X_2, Y_2 parallel to its sides and origin at its center. Evaluating the above integral for the limits $x = -a$ to a and $y = -b$ to b, we get

$$-\delta W_{\text{total}} = A\alpha\dot{x}\,\delta x + A\alpha\dot{y}\,\delta y + \tfrac{1}{3}A\alpha(a^2+b^2)\dot{\theta}\,\delta\theta$$

Hence $\quad F_x = -A\alpha\dot{x}, \quad F_y = -A\alpha\dot{y}, \quad F_\theta = -\tfrac{1}{3}A\alpha(a^2+b^2)\dot{\theta}$

These simple results depend, of course, on the validity of the assumption regarding the drag on each element of area. Note that the generalized viscous forces are very simple compared with those of dry friction.

6.5 Example: Forces Proportional to nth Power of Speed, $n > 1$.

Relations (*6.2*) and (*6.3*) apply directly.

Example 6.9.

As a means of illustrating the method of finding generalized forces for any values of n, consider again the dumbbell, Fig. 6-2. Let us assume that forces on m_1 and m_2 are given in magnitude by $f_1 = a_1 v_1^{n_1}$, $f_2 = a_2 v_2^{n_2}$ respectively, and that each is opposite in direction to the motion of the corresponding particle. Applying (*6.2*), we have

$$\delta W_{\text{total}} = -[a_1 v_1^{n_1-1}(\dot{x}_1\,\delta x_1 + \dot{y}_1\,\delta y_1) + a_2 v_2^{n_2-1}(\dot{x}_2\,\delta x_2 + \dot{y}_2\,\delta y_2)]$$

Writing $v^{n_1-1} = (\dot{x}_1^2 + \dot{y}_1^2)^{(n_1-1)/2}$, etc., and eliminating $\dot{x}_1, \delta x_1$ by $x_1 = x + l_1\cos\theta$, etc., an expression is obtained from which F_x, F_y, F_θ can be read directly. For example,

$$F_\theta = -a_1 v_1^{n_1-1} l_1(\dot{y}\cos\theta - \dot{x}\sin\theta + l_1\dot{\theta}) - a_2 v_2^{n_2-1} l_2(\dot{x}\sin\theta - \dot{y}\cos\theta + l_2\dot{\theta})$$

Note. Assuming that the drag df on an element of area dA, Fig. 6-3, is given by $df = av^n\,dx_2\,dy_2 = a(\dot{x}_1^2 + \dot{y}_1^2)^{n/2}\,dx_2\,dy_2$, an extension of the method employed above leads directly to integral expressions for the generalized forces F_x, F_y, F_θ on the board.

6.6 Forces Expressed by a Power Series.

Assume that the magnitude of the force on a particle (or element of area) may better be represented by a series of terms as

$$f = a_0 + a_1 v + a_2 v^2 + a_3 v^3 + \cdots \tag{6.9}$$

where v is the velocity of the particle and $a_0, a_1, a_2, \ldots$ are constants or perhaps functions of coordinates and/or time. If f is opposite in direction to v,

$$f_x = -(a_0 + a_1 v + a_2 v^2 + a_3 v^3 + \cdots)(\dot{x}/v)$$

Hence with this and corresponding relations for f_y, f_z, expressions for generalized forces follow in the usual way.

6.7 Certain Interesting Consequences of Friction and Other Forces.

Consider the following questions:

(*a*) In removing a tightly fitting cylinder from inside another, why do we always twist one with respect to the other as they are pulled apart, and likewise in removing a cork from a bottle?

(*b*) Why is it that a block of wood, held in contact with a moving belt, can be slid sideways with very little force; or when dragging a long, heavy object (such as a tank of compressed gas) along a concrete floor, the "free end" in contact with the floor swings sideways so easily?

(c) A penny is placed on a rough inclined plane. The tilt of the plane is not sufficient for the coin to slide down under the action of gravity, even when started. Yet if given a flick in the horizontal direction, its path is curved downward. Explain.

Answers to these and other questions may be obtained from the following considerations.

The block B of mass M, Fig. 6-4, rests on a cylinder of radius r which is made to rotate with angular velocity $\dot{\theta}$. The block is prevented from rotating by smooth guides not shown.

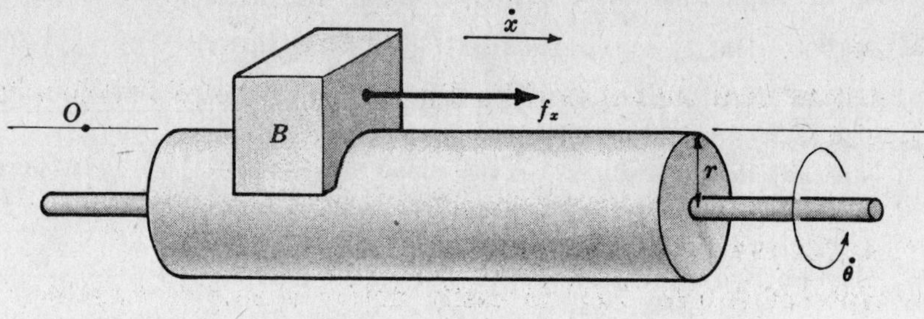

Block B Sliding on Rotating Cylinder

Fig. 6-4

Reference to Sections 6.3, 6.4 and 6.5 will show that the force f_x required to pull the block along the cylinder with velocity $\dot{x}$ ($\dot{x}$ measured relative to the fixed line OX), is given by

$$(1)\ f_x = \frac{A\dot{x}}{(\dot{x}^2 + r^2\dot{\theta}^2)^{1/2}}, \qquad (2)\ f_x = B\dot{x}, \qquad (3)\ f_x = C\dot{x}(\dot{x}^2 + r^2\dot{\theta}^2)^{1/2}$$

assuming in (1) that the basic force is dry friction, in (2) that it is a viscous drag and in (3) that it is proportional to the square of the velocity of the block relative to the cylindrical surface. (A, B, C are constants.)

Considering (1), it is seen that for $r\dot{\theta} \gg \dot{x}$, f is small and in effect is viscous in nature. In (2), f is independent of the rotational speed of the cylinder. Under conditions stated for (3) (or for any power of relative velocity greater than one), f increases with $r\dot{\theta}$.

The above facts are of importance in many applications.

6.8 A "Power Function", P, for the Determination of Generalized Forces.

There exists a wide range of forces, including conservative as well as many forms of dissipative, for which it is possible to write a function P such that generalized forces are given by

$$F_{q_r} = \frac{\partial P}{\partial \dot{q}_r} \tag{6.10}$$

P is analogous to the potential function V but considerably broader in scope.

For a system of p particles, each acted upon by forces $(f_{x_i}, f_{y_i}, f_{z_i})$, let us consider the following integral which, as will be seen, defines P:

$$P = \int \sum_{i=1}^{p} (f_{x_i}\,d\dot{x}_i + f_{y_i}\,d\dot{y}_i + f_{z_i}\,d\dot{z}_i) \tag{6.11}$$

Now if the forces are of such a nature (depend on coordinates, velocity and time in such a way) that

$$\frac{\partial f_{x_i}}{\partial \dot{y}_k} = \frac{\partial f_{y_k}}{\partial \dot{x}_i} \tag{6.12}$$

for all combinations, the quantity under the integral is *exact.* Hence when the integral is evaluated, *holding all coordinates and time constant,* we have a quantity P such that, $f_{x_i} = \partial P/\partial \dot{x}_i$, etc. Moreover, as shown below, (*6.10*) is true.

Substituting $f_{x_i} = \partial P/\partial \dot{x}_i$, etc., into the general expression (*4.10*), Page 60, for F_{q_r} and remembering that $\partial x_i/\partial q_r = \partial \dot{x}_i/\partial \dot{q}_r$, etc., we get

$$F_{q_r} = \sum_{i=1}^{p} \left(\frac{\partial P}{\partial \dot{x}_i} \frac{\partial \dot{x}_i}{\partial \dot{q}_r} + \frac{\partial P}{\partial \dot{y}_i} \frac{\partial \dot{y}_i}{\partial \dot{q}_r} + \frac{\partial P}{\partial \dot{z}_i} \frac{\partial \dot{z}_i}{\partial \dot{q}_r} \right)$$

which is just $\partial P/\partial \dot{q}_r$.

From (*6.11*) it is evident that P has the dimensions of power. Hence it is referred to as a "power function".

6.9 Special Forms for the Power Function.

For certain types of forces (*6.11*) is easily put in a simple, directly applicable form.

Consider the case (quite wide in scope) for which f_i, the force on m_i, is given by $f_i = \phi_i(x_i, y_i, z_i, v_i, t)$ where, as indicated, ϕ_i is an arbitrary function of the coordinates of the particle, its velocity v_i and time t. We will assume that f_i has the direction (or opposite) of v_i. Hence $f_{x_i} = \dot{x}_i \phi_i / v_i$, $f_{y_i} = \dot{y}_i \phi_i / v_i$, etc. Thus

$$\frac{\partial f_{x_i}}{\partial \dot{y}_i} = \dot{x}_i \frac{\partial}{\partial v_i}\left(\frac{\phi_i}{v_i}\right) \frac{\dot{y}_i}{v_i} = \frac{\partial f_{y_i}}{\partial \dot{x}_i}, \quad \text{etc.}$$

Also, $\dfrac{\partial f_{x_i}}{\partial \dot{y}_k} = \dfrac{\partial f_{y_k}}{\partial \dot{x}_i} = 0$ for $i \neq k$. Hence (*6.12*) is satisfied. Relation (*6.11*) then becomes

$$P = \int \sum_{i=1}^{p} \frac{\phi_i}{v_i}(\dot{x}_i \, d\dot{x}_i + \dot{y}_i \, d\dot{y}_i + \dot{z}_i \, d\dot{z}_i) = \int \sum_{i=1}^{p} \phi_i \, dv_i \tag{6.13}$$

A summary of certain useful forms taken by (*6.13*) is given below.

Special Forms of the Power Function		
For $f_i = a_i v_i^n$,	$P = \sum_{i=1}^{p} \dfrac{a_i v_i^{n+1}}{n+1}$	(*6.14*)
For dry friction, $n = 0$	$P = \sum_{i=1}^{p} a_i v_i$	(*6.15*)
For viscous drag, $n = 1$	$P = \frac{1}{2} \sum_{i=1}^{p} a_i v_i^2$	(*6.16*)
Surface moving in contact with another. $df = av^n \, dA$, where df = force on element of area dA.	$P = \int \dfrac{av^{n+1}}{n+1} \, dA$	(*6.17*)
For f_i a function of coordinates and t alone; f_i conservative, for example.	$P = \sum_{i=1}^{p} (f_{x_i}\dot{x}_i + f_{y_i}\dot{y}_i + f_{z_i}\dot{z}_i)$	(*6.18*)

Important note. If the system is acted upon by a combination of forces, say dry friction and conservative, a total P taking account of both types is merely the sum of (*6.15*) and (*6.18*). Relation (*6.16*) is the *Rayleigh dissipation function.*

6.10 Examples Illustrating the Use of P.

The following examples are for the most part taken from those already given above. Hence the two methods of determining the F_{q_r} may be *compared directly*.

Example 6.10.

A pendulum consisting of a small sphere suspended from a light coil spring (constant $= k$) is free to swing in space under gravity, the spring and a dissipative force proportional to the nth power of its speed. Applying (*6.14*) and (*6.18*), the total P expressed in spherical coordinates is

$$P \quad = \quad \frac{-a}{n+1}(\dot{r}^2 + r^2\dot{\theta}^2 + r^2 \sin^2\theta\, \dot{\phi}^2)^{(n+1)/2} \;-\; k(r - r_0)\dot{r} \;+\; mg(\dot{r}\cos\theta - r\dot{\theta}\sin\theta)$$

from which generalized forces follow at once.

Example 6.11.

Consider again the problem treated in Example 6.9. Assuming the plane is inclined at an angle α, it follows from (*6.14*) and (*6.18*) that

$$P \quad = \quad -\frac{a_1(\dot{x}_1^2 + \dot{y}_1^2)^{(n_1+1)/2}}{n_1+1} - \frac{a_2(\dot{x}_2^2 + \dot{y}_2^2)^{(n_2+1)/2}}{n_2+1} - m_1 g \sin\alpha\, \dot{y}_1 - m_2 g \sin\alpha\, \dot{y}_2$$

Transforming this to x, y, θ coordinates,

$$\begin{aligned} P \quad = \quad & -\frac{a_1}{n_1+1}[(\dot{x} - l_1\dot{\theta}\sin\theta)^2 + (\dot{y} + l_1\dot{\theta}\cos\theta)^2]^{(n_1+1)/2} - \frac{a_2}{n_2+1}[(\dot{x} + l_2\dot{\theta}\sin\theta)^2 + (\dot{y} - l_2\dot{\theta}\cos\theta)^2]^{(n_2+1)/2} \\ & - m_1 g \sin\alpha\,(\dot{y} + l_1\dot{\theta}\cos\theta) - m_2 g \sin\alpha\,(\dot{y} - l_2\dot{\theta}\cos\theta) \end{aligned} \tag{6.19}$$

Thus generalized forces corresponding to x, y, θ follow at once from $F_x = \partial P/\partial\dot{x}$, etc.

Note that putting $n_1 = n_2 = 0$, the above applies to frictional forces; or for $n_1 = n_2 = 1$ it is the proper P-function for viscous forces.

Example 6.12.

Referring to Example 6.7 and Fig. 6-3, we will determine a P-function for the board of any shape.

For this problem (*6.16*) takes the integral form (viscous forces assumed)

$$P \quad = \quad -\frac{1}{2}\int a v^2\, dx_2\, dy_2 \tag{6.20}$$

where $v^2 = \dot{x}_1^2 + \dot{y}_1^2$. Eliminating $\dot{x}_1, \dot{y}_1$ as in Example 6.7 and integrating over the area A (holding all quantities constant except x_2, y_2), we obtain

$$P \quad = \quad -[\tfrac{1}{2}aA(\dot{x}^2 + \dot{y}^2) + \tfrac{1}{2}I\dot{\theta}^2 - aA\dot{\theta}\dot{x}(\bar{x}_2\sin\theta + \bar{y}_2\cos\theta) + aA\dot{\theta}\dot{y}(\bar{x}_2\cos\theta - \bar{y}_2\sin\theta)]$$

where $I = \int a(x_2^2 + y_2^2)\,dA$, $\int x_2\,dA = \bar{x}_2 A$, etc., and $\bar{x}_2, \bar{y}_2$ locate the "center of gravity" of A.

As seen from (*6.20*), P is just the negative of the "kinetic energy" of a lamina of any shape moving in any manner in the X_1Y_1 plane, where a replaces mass per unit area.

Example 6.13.

Referring to Example 6.4, Page 101, let us determine a P-function for the rod assuming here that the force df on an element of length dl is given by $df = av^n\,dl$.

Applying (*6.17*), we write $P = -\int_{-l_2}^{+l_1}\frac{av^{n+1}}{n+1}\,dl$ which when expressed in terms of x, y, θ by the relations $x_1 = x + l\cos\theta$, etc., becomes

$$P \quad = \quad -\int_{-l_2}^{+l_1}\frac{a}{n+1}[(\dot{x} - l\dot{\theta}\sin\theta)^2 + (y + l\dot{\theta}\cos\theta)^2]^{(n+1)/2}\,dl \tag{6.21}$$

An evaluation of this integral, holding all quantities constant except l, gives a quantity from which all three generalized forces may be determined by $F_{q_r} = \partial P/\partial\dot{q}_r$.

Important note. If the force on an element of area $dA = dx_2\,dy_2$, Fig. 6-3, is given by $df = av^n\,dx_2\,dy_2$, the method employed above may be extended without difficulty to a determination of P for any surface. (For $n \neq 1$, integrals are usually quite involved.)

6.11 Forces Which Depend on Relative Velocity.

Forces of this type may be illustrated by the following example.

Example 6.14.

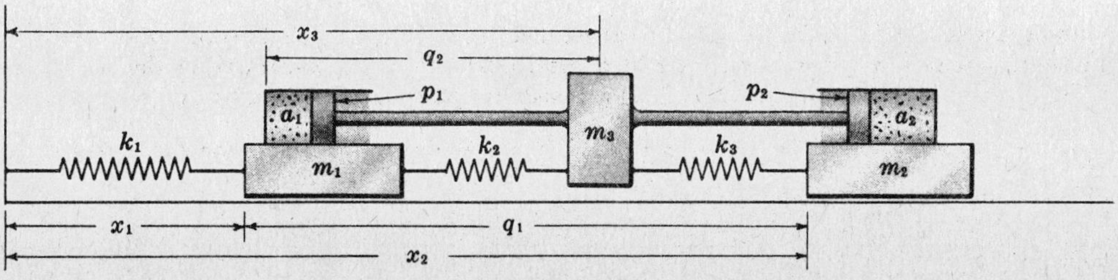

Fig. 6-5

The motions of m_1 and m_2, Fig. 6-5, are confined to a smooth horizontal line. Dashpots in which pistons p_1, p_2 can move are rigidly fastened to m_1 and m_2. The pistons and m_3 are rigidly fastened to the horizontal rod. Springs are connected to m_1, m_3 and m_3, m_2 as indicated. We shall assume that the equal and opposite force on a cylinder and its piston is in each case proportional to the nth power of the velocity of the piston relative to the cylinder ($n > 1$), proportionality constants being a_1 and a_2. Hence the magnitude of the force on m_1 due to its dashpot is given by

$$f_1 = a_1(\dot{x}_3 - \dot{x}_1)^n$$

Now f_1 may act in either the positive or negative direction of x_1 depending on whether $\dot{x}_3 - \dot{x}_1$ is positive or negative. But if, for example, n is an even integer, $(\dot{x}_3 - \dot{x}_1)^n$ is always positive. To indicate this condition we write

$$f_1 = a_1 |\dot{x}_3 - \dot{x}_1|^{n-1} (\dot{x}_3 - \dot{x}_1)$$

where the absolute value $|\dot{x}_3 - \dot{x}_1|^{n-1}$ is always to be taken positive.

Expressing forces on m_2 and m_3 in a similar manner, it follows that δW_{total}, neglecting the springs since their contribution to generalized forces can most easily be taken account of by a potential energy function, is given by

$$\begin{aligned}\delta W_{\text{total}} &= a_1 |\dot{x}_3 - \dot{x}_1|^{n-1} (\dot{x}_3 - \dot{x}_1)\, \delta x_1 - a_2 |\dot{x}_2 - \dot{x}_3|^{n-1} (\dot{x}_2 - \dot{x}_3)\, \delta x_2 \\ &\quad - a_1 |\dot{x}_3 - \dot{x}_1|^{n-1} (\dot{x}_3 - \dot{x}_1)\, \delta x_3 + a_2 |\dot{x}_2 - \dot{x}_3|^{n-1} (\dot{x}_2 - \dot{x}_3)\, \delta x_3\end{aligned}$$

But if, for example, we wish to use coordinates x_1, q_1, q_2, then $\dot{x}_2, \dot{x}_3, \delta x_2, \delta x_3$ can easily be eliminated from the above relation, and finally

$$F_{x_1} = 0, \qquad F_{q_1} = -a_2 |\dot{q}_1 - \dot{q}_2|^{n-1} (\dot{q}_1 - \dot{q}_2), \qquad F_{q_2} = a_2 |\dot{q}_1 - \dot{q}_2|^{n-1} (\dot{q}_1 - \dot{q}_2) - a_1 |\dot{q}_2|^{n-1} \dot{q}_2$$

The above example demonstrates the principles involved in the treatment of many problems of this general type. Solutions to such problems may be obtained with the help of a computer.

6.12 Forces Not Opposite in Direction to the Motion.

The assumption made thus far that the dissipative force acting on a particle or an element of area is always opposite in direction to its motion is by no means true in all cases. Consider the arrangement shown in Fig. 6-6 below.

A magnetic pole moves with velocity v, parallel to the XY plane, near a grill of electrically conducting wires. As a result of the motion, currents are established in the wires; thus there is a force on the magnet in the negative direction of y given by $f_y = -Cv \sin \phi$ where C is a factor which depends on the strength of the magnet, its distance from the grill, and the resistance and spacing of the grill wires. The force on the pole in the x direction will be regarded as zero. Hence, regardless of the motion, the force on the pole is always perpendicular to the wires and opposite in direction, not to v, but to the component of v normal to the wires.

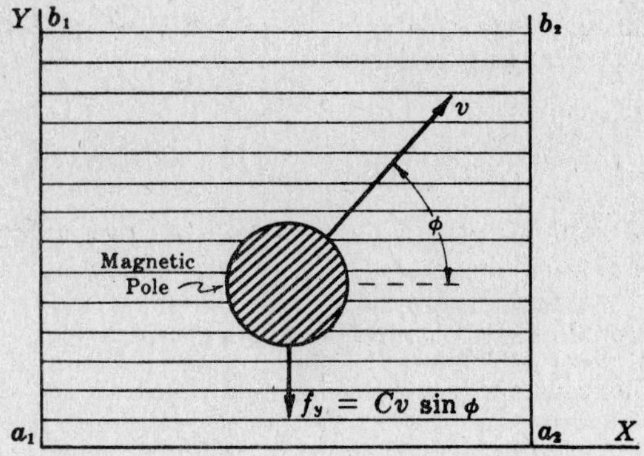

Magnetic pole is moving in XY plane near grill of electrically conducting wires. Ends of each wire are connected to conducting bars a_1b_1, a_2b_2.

Fig. 6-6

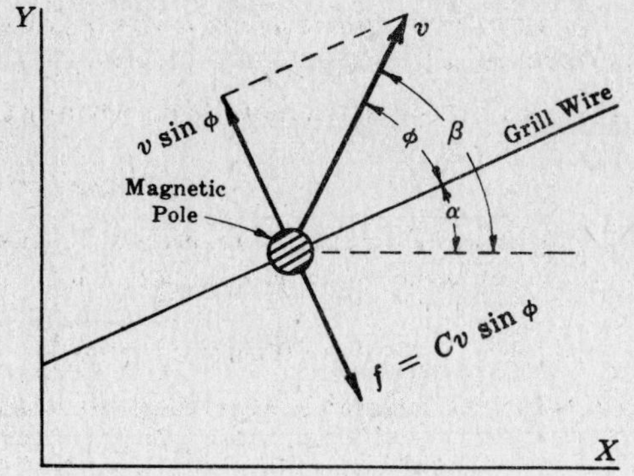

Fig. 6-7

If the grill is placed so that its wires make an angle α, Fig. 6-7, with the X axis, it is seen that $f_x = (Cv \sin\phi)\sin\alpha$ and $f_y = (-Cv\sin\phi)\cos\alpha$ where ϕ is still measured relative to the wires. Using the relations $\phi = \beta - \alpha$, $\dot{x} = v\cos\beta$, $\dot{y} = v\sin\beta$, the above expressions can be written as

$$\begin{aligned} f_x &= C\sin\alpha\,(\dot{y}\cos\alpha - \dot{x}\sin\alpha) \\ f_y &= C\cos\alpha\,(\dot{x}\sin\alpha - \dot{y}\cos\alpha) \end{aligned} \tag{6.22}$$

It should be pointed out that, if the grill is made up of wires which are not uniformly spaced or which vary in resistance from one to the next, the value of C in (*6.22*) becomes a function of x and y. If the grill is moved in some known manner, C may be a function of coordinates and time as well. (*Note.* v must be measured relative to grill.)

Example 6.15.

Imagine an "isolated" pole suspended from a rubber band so that it can swing in a vertical plane as a pendulum of variable length near a vertical grill, the wires of which make an angle α with the horizontal X axis. We shall find the generalized forces which arise as a result of the reaction between grill and magnet (not bothering here to include forces due to gravity and the rubber band) for the usual pendulum coordinates θ and r. To this end we merely apply the relation $\delta W_{\text{total}} = f_x\,\delta x + f_y\,\delta y$. Eliminating $\dot{x}, \dot{y}, \delta x, \delta y$ by the relations $x = r\sin\theta$, $y = y_0 - r\cos\theta$, it follows that

$$\begin{aligned} F_\theta &= Cr\dot{r}\cos(\theta-\alpha)\sin(\theta-\alpha) - Cr^2\dot{\theta}\sin^2(\theta-\alpha) \\ F_r &= Cr\dot{\theta}\sin(\theta-\alpha)\cos(\theta-\alpha) - C\dot{r}\cos^2(\theta-\alpha) \end{aligned}$$

The reader may show that the following P-function can be written for this problem:

$$\begin{aligned} P &= C(\dot{x}\dot{y}\sin\alpha\cos\alpha - \tfrac{1}{2}\dot{x}^2\sin^2\alpha - \tfrac{1}{2}\dot{y}^2\cos^2\alpha) \\ &= -\tfrac{1}{2}C(\dot{x}\sin\alpha - \dot{y}\cos\alpha)^2 \end{aligned}$$

As an example similar to the above type, consider the motion of an object in contact with a grooved surface (a small block of wood in contact with a phonograph record). The force required to move it along the grooves may be considerably less than in a direction normal to them.

Example 6.16.

Referring to Fig. 6-8 below, p_1p_2 represents the *extended pole face* of a wide thin bar magnet which is free to move so that p_1p_2 remains in the XY plane (with body of the magnet always normal to this plane). Just below the XY plane is a grill as shown in Fig. 6-6, with the wires parallel to the X axis. Assuming that p_1p_2 is uniformly magnetized, let us determine generalized forces corresponding to x_1, y_1, θ.

The force df on an element dl of the pole face is given by $df = a\,dl\,v\sin\phi$ where $v^2 = \dot{x}^2 + \dot{y}^2$ and a is a constant. Since df is in the negative direction of y and $v\sin\phi = \dot{y}$, we write $df_y = -a\,dl\,\dot{y}$ and, of course, $df_x = 0$.

Now for a general virtual displacement of the entire pole face,

$$\delta W_{\text{total}} = \int_0^{l_1} (df_x\,\delta x + df_y\,\delta y)$$

where the integral must be employed to take care of the distributed force along the entire length $p_1p_2 = l_1$. But from $y = y_1 + l\sin\theta$, $\dot{y} = \dot{y}_1 + l\dot{\theta}\cos\theta$ and $\delta y = \delta y_1 + l\,\delta\theta\cos\theta$. Hence

$$\delta W_{\text{total}} = -a\int_0^{l_1} (\dot{y}_1 + l\dot{\theta}\cos\theta)(\delta y_1 + l\,\delta\theta\cos\theta)\,dl$$

Integrating with respect to l, holding all other quantities constant, we get

$$\delta W_{\text{total}} = -a(\dot{y}_1 l_1 + \tfrac{1}{2}l_1^2\dot{\theta}\cos\theta)\,\delta y_1 - a(\tfrac{1}{2}\dot{y}_1 l_1^2\cos\theta + \tfrac{1}{3}l_1^3\dot{\theta}\cos^2\theta)\,\delta\theta$$

Thus expressions for the generalized forces F_{y_1} and F_θ are read off directly.

The reader may show that, for this problem,

$$P = -\tfrac{1}{2}a[\dot{y}_1^2 l_1 + \dot{y}_1 l_1^2\dot{\theta}\cos\theta + \tfrac{1}{3}l_1^3\dot{\theta}^2\cos^2\theta]$$

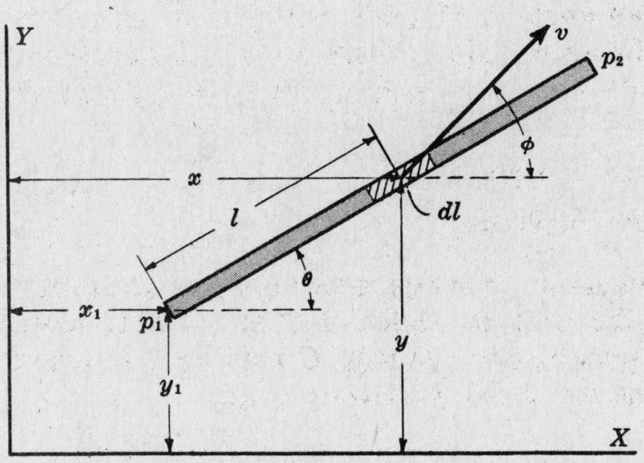

Extended pole face of magnet p_1, p_2 free to move in XY plane near grill wires located exactly as in Fig. 6-6.

Fig. 6-8

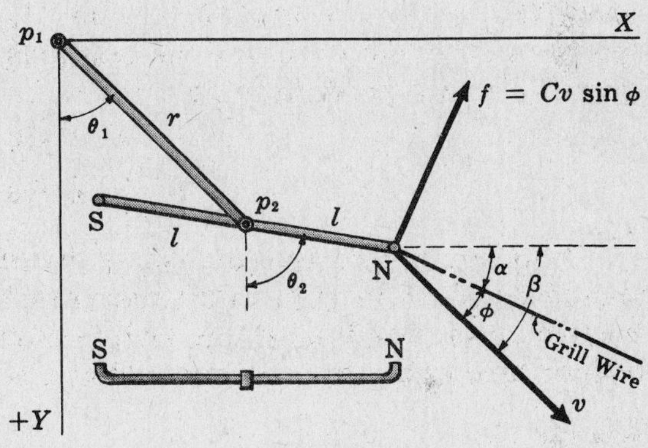

Fig. 6-9

Example 6.17.

A rigid rod of length r is pivoted at p_1, Fig. 6-9. On the other end of this a bar magnet (shaped as shown at the lower left) is supported in a smooth bearing at p_2. All motion is confined to the vertical XY plane. Due to a grill of parallel wires (one wire indicated on the diagram) located just back of the pole pieces, forces of the type given by (*6.22*) act on each pole. We shall write a P-function in terms of coordinates θ_1 and θ_2 for this system (gravity not considered).

Inserting relations (*6.22*) into (*6.11*) and integrating for the single pole of Fig. 6-7, $P = -\frac{1}{2}C(\dot{x}\sin\alpha - \dot{y}\cos\alpha)^2$. Hence for the problem in hand,

$$P = -\tfrac{1}{2}C[(\dot{x}_1\sin\alpha - \dot{y}_1\cos\alpha)^2 + (\dot{x}_2\sin\alpha - \dot{y}_2\cos\alpha)^2]$$

where x_1, y_1 and x_2, y_2 are coordinates of N and S respectively. But $x_1 = r\sin\theta_1 + l\sin\theta_2$, $x_2 = r\sin\theta_1 - l\sin\theta_2$, etc. Thus P finally reduces to

$$P = -C[r^2\dot{\theta}_1^2\sin^2(\theta_1 + \alpha) + l^2\dot{\theta}_2^2\sin^2(\theta_2 + \alpha)]$$

A Word of Caution. Much remains to be said about the basic expressions for f_x, f_y, f_z on a particle (or an element of area) due to the various dissipative forces. For example, the magnitudes of frictional forces depend somewhat on velocity. Usually, so-called viscous forces are not "viscous" except at very low velocities, etc. Hence it is not to be expected that the simple expressions which have here been assumed in order to illustrate general techniques are strictly valid in all cases. However, given more exact expressions for f_x, f_y, f_z for any particular problem, the methods illustrated lead to correct expressions for the generalized forces.

6.13 Suggested Experiment.

Various interesting and instructive experiments can be performed with the arrangement shown in Fig. 6-10. The block may be of wood or metal and the cylinders of any convenient size. For relatively large values of $\dot{\theta}$, it is an intriguing surprise to see what little force is required to move the block along the cylinders. Indeed the cylinders must be leveled very carefully to prevent the free block from drifting under the slightest component of gravity.

With cord and weight arrangement shown, it should be possible to make quantitative measurements of f_x (see Fig. 6-4) for various values of $\dot{\theta}, \dot{x}$ and with cylinders either dry or lubricated.

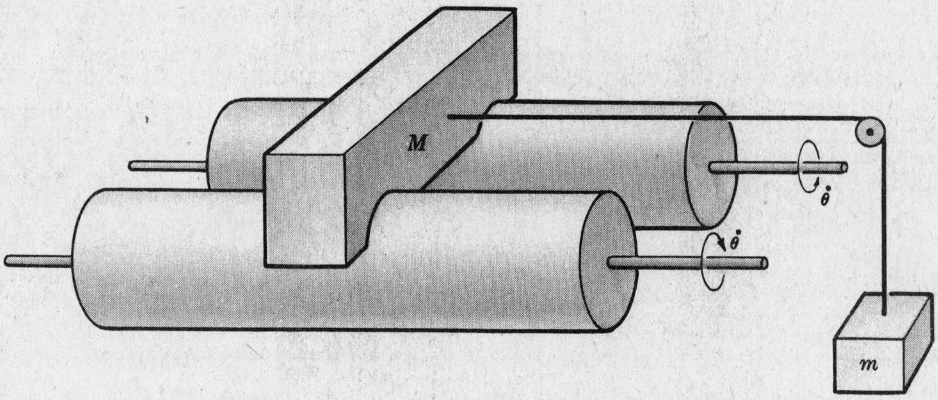

Parallel Cylinders Rotating in Opposite Directions
Fig. 6-10

Problems

A. Use of standard methods [relations (4.10), (6.2), (6.3)] for the determination of generalized forces.

6.1. A small sphere is suspended from a rubber band in a viscous liquid. Assuming a simple viscous force acting on the sphere and no drag on the band, show that generalized viscous forces corresponding to the spherical coordinates r, θ, ϕ are

$$F_r = -a\dot{r}, \qquad F_\theta = -ar^2\dot{\theta}, \qquad F_\phi = -ar^2 \sin^2\theta\,\dot{\phi}$$

where a is the viscous force per unit velocity on the sphere.

6.2. Referring to Example 6.6, Page 102, and Fig. 6-2, show that generalized viscous forces corresponding to coordinates x_1, y_1, θ are

$$F_{x_1} = -(a_1 + a_2)\dot{x}_1 - a_2 l\dot{\theta}\sin\theta, \qquad F_{y_1} = -(a_1 + a_2)\dot{y}_1 + a_2 l\dot{\theta}\cos\theta,$$

$$F_\theta = -a_2 l^2\dot{\theta} - a_2 l(\dot{x}_1 \sin\theta - \dot{y}_1\cos\theta)$$

where $l = l_1 + l_2$.

6.3. Spheres m_1, m_2, Fig. 6-11, are submerged in a viscous liquid. Show that generalized viscous forces corresponding to coordinates y and y_3 are

$$F_y = -a_1(\dot{y}_3 + \dot{y}) + a_2(\dot{y}_3 - \dot{y})$$

$$F_{y_3} = -a_1(\dot{y}_3 + \dot{y}) - a_2(\dot{y}_3 - \dot{y})$$

where a_1 and a_2 represent the viscous force per unit velocity on m_1 and m_2 respectively.

Repeat above using coordinates y_1 and y_3.

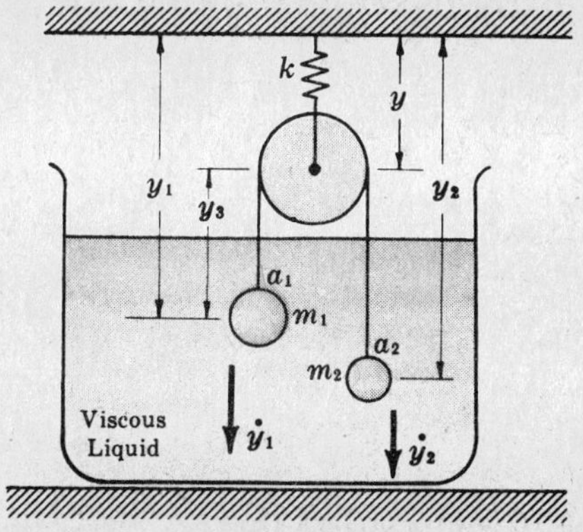

Fig. 6-11

6.4. The masses m_1, m_2, m_3, Fig. 6-12, are free to slide along a straight line on a horizontal plane. Coefficients of viscous drag between blocks and the plane are a_1, a_2, a_3 respectively. Each of the magnets A and B exerts a viscous drag on m_2, and the force in either case is determined by the velocity of the magnet relative to m_2. Coefficients of viscous drag are a_4, a_5.

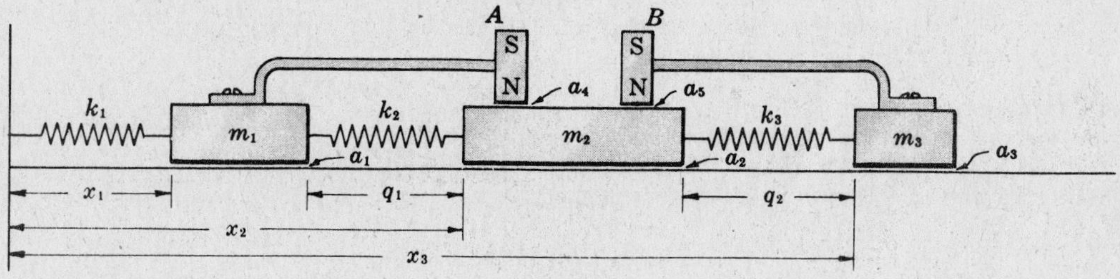

Fig. 6-12

Show that the generalized forces (not including forces exerted by the springs) corresponding to coordinates x_1, x_2, x_3 are

$$F_{x_1} = -a_1\dot{x}_1 + a_4(\dot{x}_2 - \dot{x}_1)$$

$$F_{x_2} = -a_2\dot{x}_2 + a_4(\dot{x}_1 - \dot{x}_2) + a_5(\dot{x}_3 - \dot{x}_2)$$

$$F_{x_3} = -a_3\dot{x}_3 + a_5(\dot{x}_2 - \dot{x}_3)$$

and that for x_1, q_1, q_2,

$$F_{x_1} = -a_1\dot{x}_1 - a_2(\dot{x}_1 + \dot{q}_1) - a_3(\dot{x}_1 + \dot{q}_1 + \dot{q}_2)$$

$$F_{q_1} = -a_4\dot{q}_1 - a_2(\dot{x}_1 + \dot{q}_1) - a_3(\dot{x}_1 + \dot{q}_1 + \dot{q}_2)$$

$$F_{q_2} = -a_5\dot{q}_2 - a_3(\dot{x}_1 + \dot{q}_1 + \dot{q}_2)$$

6.5. Referring to Fig. 6-13, the horseshoe magnet and copper disk are supported by three lengths of piano wire, forming a double torsional pendulum. Torsional constants of the wires are C_1, C_2, C_3 respectively. There is a viscous drag a_1 per unit velocity between the disk and brake blocks B_1, B_2, and a similar drag a_2 between the magnetic poles and the disk. Show that the equations of motion for the system are (assuming a_1 and a_2 acting at radial distances r_1, r_2)

$$I_1\ddot{\theta}_1 + C_3\theta_1 + C_2(\theta_1 - \theta_2) + 2a_1r_1^2\dot{\theta}_1 + 2a_2r_2^2(\dot{\theta}_1 - \dot{\theta}_2) = 0$$

$$I_2\ddot{\theta}_2 - C_2(\theta_1 - \theta_2) + C_1\theta_2 - 2a_2r_2^2(\dot{\theta}_1 - \dot{\theta}_2) = 0$$

where I_1, I_2 are moments of inertia of the disk and magnet respectively and θ_1, θ_2 corresponding angular displacements.

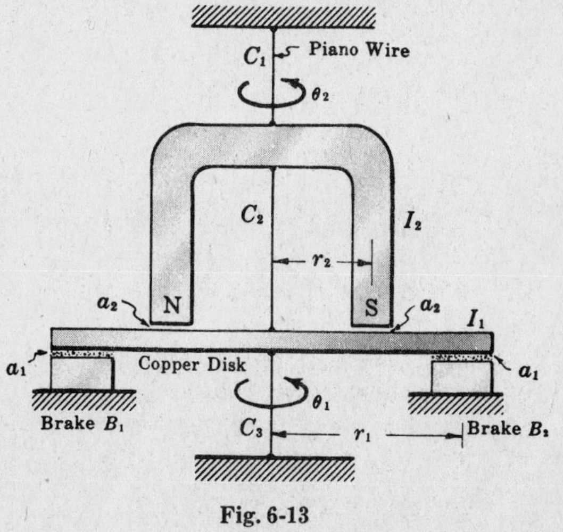

Fig. 6-13

6.6. A flat circular disk of radius r is in contact with a plane surface coated with oil. Assuming the oil exerts a uniform viscous drag on every element of area of the disk, show that the generalized forces corresponding to x, y, θ are

$$F_x = -Aa\dot{x}, \qquad F_y = -Aa\dot{y}, \qquad F_\theta = -\tfrac{1}{2}Aar^2\dot{\theta}$$

where x, y locate the center of the disk and θ its angular position. $A = \pi r^2$ and a is the viscous force per unit area per unit velocity. Note that each force depends only on the corresponding velocity.

6.7. The bar magnet and "isolated" poles, Fig. 6-14, each exerts a viscous force on the conducting sheet. Show that the generalized dissipative forces corresponding to coordinates y_1 and y_2 are

$$F_{y_1} = -4(a_1 + a_2 + a_3)\dot{y}_1 + 2(a_2 - a_3)\dot{y}_2$$

$$F_{y_2} = 2(a_2 - a_3)\dot{y}_1 - (a_2 + a_3)\dot{y}_2$$

where a_1, a_2, a_3 represent the viscous forces per unit relative velocity exerted by the three magnets respectively on the conducting sheet. Assume vertical motion only for the sheet, bar and poles.

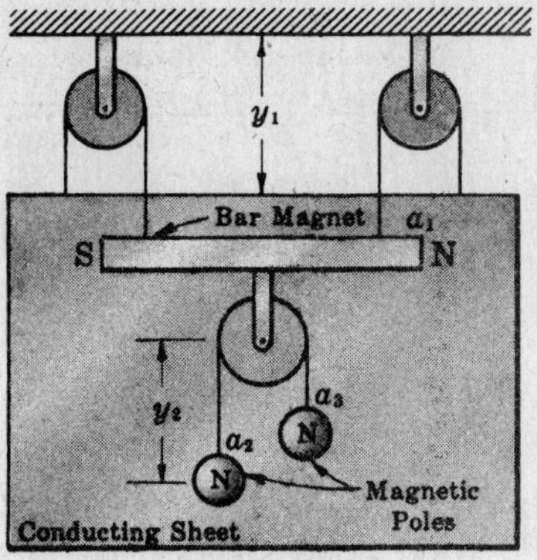

Fig. 6-14

6.8. Assuming the force of dry friction is independent of velocity, show how an almost "frictionless" bearing can be constructed. Sketch possible arrangement.

6.9. A small mass m_1 attached to a light spring of length r, unstretched length r_0 and spring constant k, can swing as a pendulum on the rough inclined plane, Fig. 6-1. Using polar coordinates show that for a general virtual displacement (assuming kinetic friction in action),

$$\delta W_{\text{total}} = \left[-k(r - r_0) + mg \sin\alpha \cos\theta - \frac{f\dot{r}}{(\dot{r}^2 + r^2\dot{\theta}^2)^{1/2}}\right]\delta r$$

$$- \left[mgr \sin\alpha \sin\theta + \frac{fr^2\dot{\theta}}{(\dot{r}^2 + r^2\dot{\theta}^2)^{1/2}}\right]\delta\theta = F_r\,\delta r + F_\theta\,\delta\theta$$

where $f = \mu mg \cos\alpha$. Under what conditions may the frictional forces be discontinuous?

6.10. A particle is free to move in contact with the face of a disk rotating with angular velocity ω (constant or varying with time) about a vertical axis. Polar coordinates (r, θ) of the particle are referred to inertial X, Y axes with origin at the center of the disk.

(a) Assuming dry friction between particle and disk, show that

$$F_r = -\frac{\mu mg\dot{r}}{[\dot{r}^2 + r^2(\dot{\theta} - \omega)^2]^{1/2}}, \qquad F_\theta = -\frac{\mu mgr^2(\dot{\theta} - \omega)}{[\dot{r}^2 + r^2(\dot{\theta} - \omega)^2]^{1/2}}$$

(b) Assuming a viscous drag, show that

$$F_r = -a\dot{r}, \qquad F_\theta = -ar^2(\dot{\theta} - \omega)$$

Note that if the disk is made to oscillate so that its angular displacement α is given by $\alpha = \alpha_0 \sin\beta t$, for example, then $\omega = \dot{\alpha} = \alpha_0\beta \cos\beta t$ and thus time enters explicitly into all forces above except F_r in the second case.

6.11. A particle moves in contact with a rough horizontal board. Assuming the coefficient of friction for motion in the X direction is μ_x and in the Y direction μ_y, show that the generalized frictional forces corresponding to polar coordinates are

$$F_r = -f(\mu_x \cos\theta + \mu_y \sin\theta), \qquad F_\theta = -fr(\mu_y \cos\theta - \mu_x \sin\theta)$$

where f is the normal force between particle and board.

6.12. Blocks a and b, Fig. 6-15, fastened rigidly together with a light rod of length l, slide in contact with blocks c and d. Block e slides without friction along the smooth rod. Block c slides along the X axis and d is fixed. Coefficients of friction between surfaces in contact, are μ_1, μ_2, μ_3 as indicated. Note that each of the normal forces between surfaces in contact depends on the position of m_4.

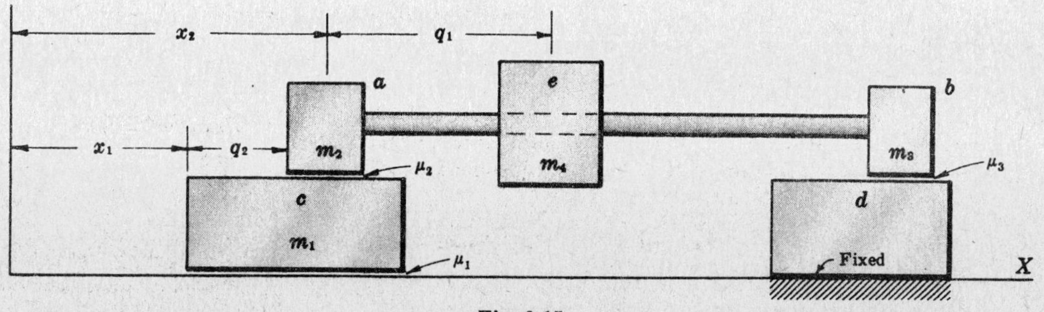

Fig. 6-15

Assuming the system is in motion such that $\dot{x}_2$ and $\dot{x}_1$ are positive and $\dot{x}_2 > \dot{x}_1$, show that generalized forces corresponding to x_1, q_1, q_2 are

$$F_{x_1} = -[\mu_1(m_1 + m_2 + m_4 - m_4 q_1/l) + \mu_3(m_3 + m_4 q_1/l)]g$$

$$F_{q_2} = -[\mu_2(m_2 + m_4 - m_4 q_1/l) + \mu_3(m_3 + m_4 q_1/l)]g, \qquad F_{q_1} = 0$$

Are the above expressions valid if, for example, $\dot{x}_1 > \dot{x}_2$? Obviously, forces of this type must be treated with caution.

6.13. A rectangle of dimensions $2a \times 2b$ is drawn on a flat board. Four tacks having small round heads are driven in, one at each corner of the rectangle. The board is then placed, heads down, on a rough plane. Using x, y, θ as coordinates (x, y measured to the center of the rectangle and θ taken as the angle between the $2a$ side and X) and assuming dry friction, show that δW_{total} is given by

$$\begin{aligned} -\delta W_{\text{total}} = \; & f_1\{[\dot{x} + r\dot{\theta}\sin(\theta+\beta)][\delta x + r\,\delta\theta\sin(\theta+\beta)] \\ & \quad + [\dot{y} - r\dot{\theta}\cos(\theta+\beta)][\delta y - r\,\delta\theta\cos(\theta+\beta)]\}\frac{1}{v_1} \\ & + f_2\{[\dot{x} - r\dot{\theta}\sin(\theta-\beta)][\delta x - r\,\delta\theta\sin(\theta-\beta)] \\ & \quad + [\dot{y} + r\dot{\theta}\cos(\theta-\beta)][\delta y + r\,\delta\theta\cos(\theta-\beta)]\}\frac{1}{v_2} \\ & + f_3\{[\dot{x} - r\dot{\theta}\sin(\theta+\beta)][\delta x - r\,\delta\theta\sin(\theta+\beta)] \\ & \quad + [\dot{y} + r\dot{\theta}\cos(\theta+\beta)][\delta y + r\,\delta\theta\cos(\theta+\beta)]\}\frac{1}{v_3} \\ & + f_4\{[\dot{x} + r\dot{\theta}\sin(\theta-\beta)][\delta x + r\,\delta\theta\sin(\theta-\beta)] \\ & \quad + [\dot{y} - r\dot{\theta}\cos(\theta-\beta)][\delta y - r\,\delta\theta\cos(\theta-\beta)]\}\frac{1}{v_4} \end{aligned}$$

where

$$r^2 = a^2 + b^2, \qquad \tan\beta = b/a, \qquad v_1 = \{\dot{x}^2 + \dot{y}^2 + r^2\dot{\theta}^2 + 2r\dot{\theta}[\dot{x}\sin(\theta+\beta) - \dot{y}\cos(\theta+\beta)]\}^{1/2}$$

with similar expressions for v_2, v_3, v_4. $f_1 = \mu$(normal force on first tack head), etc. f_1, f_2, f_3, f_4 are assumed to be known.

Note that generalized forces can be read off from δW_{total}.

6.14. A circle of radius R is drawn on a flat board. n tacks having small round heads are driven in at equal spacings on the circle, as in Fig. 6-16. (Angular spacing between each is α.) The board is then placed, heads down, on a rough plane. Measuring x and y to the center of the circle, denoting angular displacement of the board by θ, and assuming frictional forces, show that an expression for δW_{total} from which F_x, F_y, F_θ may be obtained is

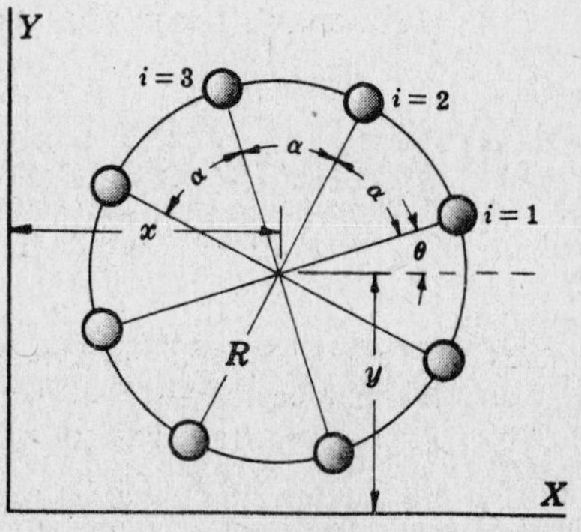

Fig. 6-16

$$\delta W_{\text{total}} = -f\sum_{i=1}^{n}\frac{1}{v_i}[\dot{x} - R\dot{\theta}\sin(\beta_i+\theta)][\delta x - R\,\delta\theta\sin(\beta_i+\theta)]$$
$$- f\sum_{i=1}^{n}\frac{1}{v_i}[\dot{y} + R\dot{\theta}\cos(\beta_i+\theta)][\delta y + R\,\delta\theta\cos(\beta_i+\theta)]$$

where f is the magnitude of the frictional force on each sphere (all assumed equal), $\beta_i = (i-1)\alpha$, and

$$v_i^2 = [\dot{x} - R\dot{\theta}\sin(\beta_i+\theta)]^2 + [\dot{y}_i + R\dot{\theta}\cos(\beta_i+\theta)]^2$$

6.15. A thin circular ring of radius R is placed in contact with a rough plane. Using coordinates x, y, θ where x, y locate the center of the ring and θ its angular displacement relative to the X axis, show that the generalized frictional force corresponding to x is given by

$$F_x = -f\int_0^{2\pi}\frac{[\dot{x} - R\dot{\theta}\sin(\theta+\alpha)]\,R\,d\alpha}{\{[\dot{x} - R\dot{\theta}\sin(\theta+\alpha)]^2 + [\dot{y} + R\dot{\theta}\cos(\theta+\alpha)]^2\}^{1/2}}$$

where $R\,d\alpha$ is an element of length of the ring and f is the frictional force per unit length of ring. Compare above result with that of Problem 6.14.

6.16. Show that if the drag exerted by each magnet in Problem 6.7 is assumed to be proportional to the square of its speed relative to the sheet, the generalized forces are

$$F_{y_1} = -8a_1'|\dot{y}_1|\dot{y}_1 - 2a_2'|2\dot{y}_1 - \dot{y}_2|(2\dot{y}_1 - \dot{y}_2) - 2a_3'|2\dot{y}_1 + \dot{y}_2|(2\dot{y}_1 + \dot{y}_2)$$
$$F_{y_2} = +a_2'|2\dot{y}_1 - \dot{y}_2|(2\dot{y}_1 - \dot{y}_2) - a_3'|2\dot{y}_1 + \dot{y}_2|(2\dot{y}_1 + \dot{y}_2)$$

B. Use of power function for determination of generalized forces.

6.17. Show that P for the sphere in Problem 6.1, Page 110, is

$$P = -\tfrac{1}{2}a(\dot{r}^2 + r^2\dot{\theta}^2 + r^2\sin^2\theta\,\dot{\phi}^2)$$

Apply (*6.10*), Page 104, and compare results with previously found expressions for generalized forces.

6.18. Show that for Problem 6.3, Page 111,

$$P = -\tfrac{1}{2}a_1\dot{y}_1^2 - \tfrac{1}{2}a_2\dot{y}_2^2 = -\tfrac{1}{2}a_1(\dot{y} + \dot{y}_3)^2 - \tfrac{1}{2}a_2(\dot{y} - \dot{y}_3)^2$$

Determine F_y, F_{y_3} and check with previous results.

6.19. A dumbbell consisting of two small equal spheres fastened rigidly to the ends of a thin, smooth rod is free to move in space through a viscous fluid. Neglecting drag on the rod and assuming no rotation of the spheres about the rod as an axis, show that

$$P = -\tfrac{1}{2}a(\dot{x}^2 + \dot{y}^2 + \dot{z}^2) - a(l^2\dot{\theta}^2 + l^2\dot{\phi}^2\sin^2\theta)$$

where x, y, z locate c.m. of the dumbbell, l is the length from c.m. to the center of a sphere and θ, ϕ are usual spherical coordinates.

6.20. A flat circular disk of radius r is in contact with a plane surface coated with oil. Assuming the oil exerts a viscous drag (coefficient per unit area $= a$), show that the proper P-function is

$$P = -\tfrac{1}{2}\pi r^2 a(\dot{x}^2 + \dot{y}^2) - \tfrac{1}{4}\pi r^4 a\dot{\theta}^2$$

where $\dot{x}$ and $\dot{y}$ are the velocity components of the center of the disk. Likewise show that for a rectangle of area $A = 2b \times 2c$,

$$P = -\tfrac{1}{2}aA(\dot{x}^2 + \dot{y}^2) - \tfrac{1}{6}aA(b^2 + c^2)\dot{\theta}^2$$

Coordinates x and y are measured to the center of the surface in each case above. (See Example 6.8, Page 103.)

6.21. Show that for the particle in Example 6.1, Page 100,

$$P = -\mu mg \cos\alpha\,(\dot{x}^2 + \dot{y}^2)^{1/2} - mg\dot{y}\sin\alpha$$

6.22. Show that P for Problem 6.9, Page 112, is

$$P = -a(\dot{r}^2 + r^2\dot{\theta}^2)^{1/2} - k(r - r_0)\dot{r} + mg\sin\alpha\,(\dot{r}\cos\theta - r\dot{\theta}\sin\theta)$$

Compare generalized forces obtained from (*6.10*), Page 104, and those read from δW_{total}.

6.23. Referring to Problem 6.15, Page 114, show that the corresponding P-function is given by

$$P = -f\int_0^{2\pi} \{[\dot{x} - R\dot{\theta}\sin(\theta+\alpha)]^2 + [\dot{y} + R\dot{\theta}\cos(\theta+\alpha)]^2\}^{1/2} R\,d\alpha$$

where f is the frictional force per unit length of the ring.

6.24. Show that the integral expression for the P-function for a flat disk of radius R in contact with a rough plane using the same coordinates as in Problem 6.23 is

$$P = -f\int_0^R\int_0^{2\pi} \{[\dot{x} - r\dot{\theta}\sin(\theta+\alpha)]^2 + [\dot{y} + r\dot{\theta}\cos(\theta+\alpha)]^2\}^{1/2} r\,dr\,d\alpha$$

where f is now the dry frictional force per unit area in contact. Write the integral for viscous drag.

6.25. A thin rod of length l is in contact with a rough plane. Assuming a frictional drag, show that (x and y measured to end of rod)

$$P = -f\int_0^l [\dot{x}^2 + \dot{y}^2 + r^2\dot{\theta}^2 + 2r\dot{\theta}(\dot{y}\cos\theta - \dot{x}\sin\theta)]^{1/2}\,dr$$

This integral clearly takes the form

$$\int_0^l (ar^2 + br + c)^{1/2}\,dr$$

where $a = \dot{\theta}^2$, $b = 2\dot{\theta}(\dot{y}\cos\theta - \dot{x}\sin\theta)$, $c = \dot{x}^2 + \dot{y}^2$.

6.26. Assuming that the force introduced by the dashpot, Fig. 6-17, is proportional to the cube of the velocity with which the piston moves in or out of the cylinder (proportionality factor $= b$) and that there is a viscous drag between each pair of flat surfaces (corresponding constants involved, a_1, a_2, a_3), show that

$$P = -\tfrac{1}{2}[a_1\dot{x}_1^2 + a_2(\dot{x}_2 - \dot{x}_1)^2 + a_3(\dot{x}_3 - \dot{x}_1)^2] - \tfrac{1}{4}b(\dot{x}_3 - \dot{x}_2)^4$$
$$+ k_1(l_1 - x_1)\dot{x}_1 + k_2(l_2 + x_1 - x_2)(\dot{x}_2 - \dot{x}_1) + k_3(l_3 + x_2 - x_3)(\dot{x}_3 - \dot{x}_2)$$

where k_1, k_2, k_3 are spring constants and l_1, l_2, l_3 are unstretched lengths of the springs respectively.

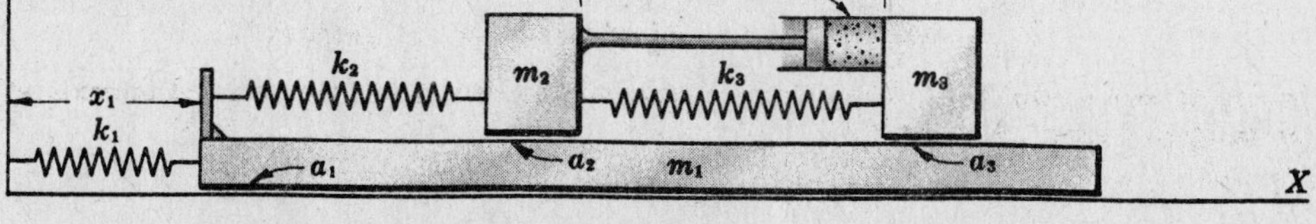

Fig. 6-17

6.27. If the grill, Fig. 6-6, Page 108, is rotating with angular velocity $\dot{\alpha}$ about an axis perpendicular to the XY plane and passing through the origin, show that equations (*6.22*), Page 108, must be replaced by

$$f_x = C[\dot{y} \cos\alpha - \dot{x} \sin\alpha - (x\cos\alpha + y\sin\alpha)\dot{\alpha}] \sin\alpha$$

$$f_y = -C[\dot{y} \cos\alpha - \dot{x} \sin\alpha - (x\cos\alpha + y\sin\alpha)\dot{\alpha}] \cos\alpha$$

Show that $P = -\frac{1}{2}C[\dot{y}\cos\alpha - \dot{x}\sin\alpha - \dot{\alpha}(x\cos\alpha + y\sin\alpha)]$.

6.28. A grill of conducting wires such as shown in Fig. 6-6, Page 108, is fastened to a flat board which is free to slide about to any position on a smooth stationary XY plane. Coordinates x_1, y_1 locate its center of mass and θ its angular position. A magnetic pole, located by coordinates (x, y), is free to move parallel to (but not quite in contact with) the grill surface. Assuming a force on the magnet and an equal and opposite force on the grill due to relative motion of the two, find generalized forces corresponding to x, y, x_1, y_1, θ.

$$f_x = C\{[\dot{y} - \dot{y}_1 - (x - x_1)\dot{\theta}] \cos\theta - [\dot{x} - \dot{x}_1 + (y - y_1)\dot{\theta}] \sin\theta\} \sin\theta$$

$$f_y = -C\{[\dot{y} - \dot{y}_1 - (x - x_1)\dot{\theta}] \cos\theta - [\dot{x} - x_1 + (y - y_1)\dot{\theta}] \sin\theta\} \cos\theta$$

$$f_{x_1} = -f_x, \qquad f_{y_1} = -f_y, \qquad f_\theta = f_{y_1}(x - x_1) - f_{x_1}(y - y_1)$$

Show that all forces above may be obtained from

$$P = -\tfrac{1}{2}C\{[\dot{y} - \dot{y}_1 - (x - x_1)\dot{\theta}] \cos\theta - [\dot{x} - \dot{x}_1 + (y - y_1)\dot{\theta}] \sin\theta\}^2$$

6.29. Referring to Example 6.2, Fig. 6-2, Page 100, let us assume that the rough plane on which the X, Y axes are drawn is in motion. Origin O has a velocity $v = (\dot{x}_0^2 + \dot{y}_0^2)^{1/2}$ and X, Y rotate in the plane of the paper with angular velocity $\dot{\alpha}$. x_0, y_0 are measured relative to some inertial frame, say X', Y', and α is the angle between X' and X.

Note that expressions for F_x, F_y, F_θ (see top of Page 101) are unchanged by the motion. However, in writing T in terms of $x, y, \theta, \dot{x}, \dot{y}, \dot{\theta}$ the translation and rotation of X, Y must of course, be taken account of.

The above illustrates a rather general procedure which can be applied to Example 6.5, Example 6.12, and many other problems where the "dissipative surface" is in motion.

6.30. Suppose the force on an element of area $dx_2\,dy_2$ is given by $f = av^n\,dx_2\,dy_2$. (See Fig. 6-3, Page 102.) Then by (*6.17*), Page 105, $P = -a\iint \frac{v^n\,dx_2\,dy_2}{n+1}$ which can be written as

$$P = -a\iint \frac{1}{n+1}[(\dot{x} - x_2\dot{\theta}\sin\theta - y_2\dot{\theta}\cos\theta)^2 + (\dot{y} + x_2\dot{\theta}\cos\theta - y_2\dot{\theta}\sin\theta)^2]^{n/2}\,dx_2\,dy_2$$

But, at any instant considered, let us regard X_1, Y_1 as inertial and superimposed on X_2, Y_2. Then $\theta = 0$ $(\dot{\theta} \neq 0)$ and

$$P = -a\iint \frac{1}{n+1}[(\dot{x} - y_2\dot{\theta})^2 + (\dot{y} + x_2\dot{\theta})^2]^{n/2}\,dx_2\,dy_2$$

which is considerably simpler than the original expression.

CHAPTER

7

General Treatment of Moments and Products of Inertia

Rigid Body Dynamics: Part I

A clear and comprehensive understanding of moments and products of inertia and the many important details associated with them *is essential to a study of the motions of rigid bodies.* Hence the subject is here treated in a separate chapter before attempting a discussion of rigid body dynamics. It is assumed that the reader is familiar with the definition of moment of inertia and its use in the solution of elementary problems.

7.1 General Expression for the Moment of Inertia of a Rigid Body About Any Axis.

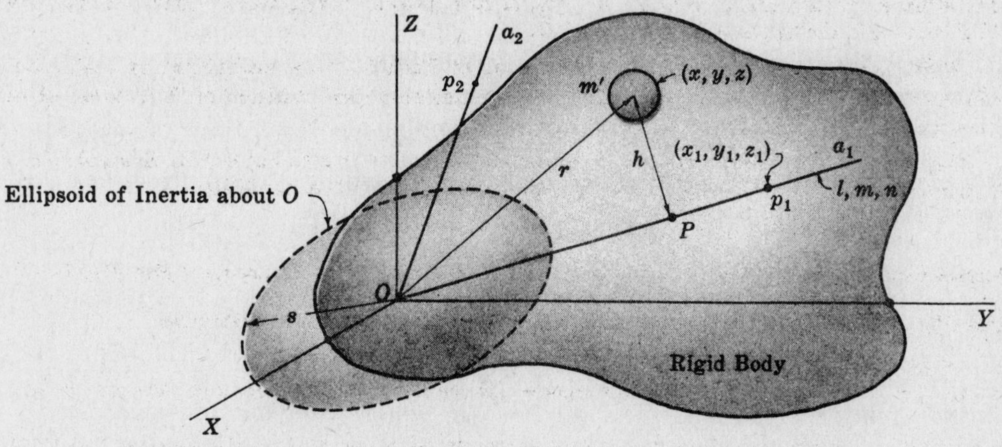

Fig. 7-1

Referring to Fig. 7-1, it is seen that the moment of inertia I_{Oa_1} of the rigid body about line Oa_1 is merely $I_{Oa_1} = \sum m'h^2$ where m' is the mass of a typical particle, h the normal distance from Oa_1 to m', and the summation includes all particles of the body. But $h^2 = r^2 - \overline{OP}^2$, $r^2 = x^2+y^2+z^2$, $\overline{OP} = lx+my+nz$ and $l^2+m^2+n^2 = 1$, where l,m,n are direction cosines of Oa_1. Hence we write

$$I_{Oa_1} = \sum m'(r^2 - \overline{OP}^2) = \sum m'[(x^2+y^2+z^2)(l^2+m^2+n^2) - (lx+my+nz)^2]$$

from which

$$I_{Oa_1} = l^2 \sum m'(y^2+z^2) + m^2 \sum m'(x^2+z^2) + n^2 \sum m'(x^2+y^2) - 2lm \sum m'xy - 2ln \sum m'xz - 2mn \sum m'yz \qquad (7.1)$$

Clearly $\sum m'(y^2+z^2) = I_x$ is the moment of inertia about the X axis, etc. $\sum m'xy = I_{xy}$ is called a product of inertia. Thus

$$I_{Oa_1} = I_x l^2 + I_y m^2 + I_z n^2 - 2I_{xy}lm - 2I_{xz}ln - 2I_{yz}mn \tag{7.2}$$

where, for convenience, we have written I_x instead of I_{xx}, etc. As a matter of clarity, summation rather than integral signs have been used in (*7.1*). For a continuous distribution of mass,

$$I_x = \int (y^2+z^2)\,dm, \quad \text{etc.}$$

Relation (*7.2*) is very important in that it constitutes the basis for all further treatments of moments and products of inertia.

Notice that I_x, I_{xy}, etc., are fixed quantities for a given body-fixed frame X, Y, Z. However, they will in general have different values for different locations and/or orientations of the frame.

It is important to realize that for known values of I_x, I_{xy}, etc., the moment of inertia of the body *about any line of given direction through* O, can be computed at once by (*7.2*).

7.2 The Ellipsoid of Inertia.

Selecting any point $p_1(x_1, y_1, z_1)$ on Oa_1, Fig. 7-1, at a distance s_1 from O, it is seen that $x_1 = s_1 l$, $y_1 = s_1 m$, $z_1 = s_1 n$. Eliminating l, m, n, (*7.2*) may be written as

$$I_{Oa_1}s_1^2 = I_x x_1^2 + I_y y_1^2 + I_z z_1^2 - 2I_{xy}x_1y_1 - 2I_{xz}x_1z_1 - 2I_{yz}y_1z_1 \tag{7.3}$$

Considering any other line, say Oa_2, an exactly similar expression holds for $I_{Oa_2}s_2^2$ where again s_2 is an arbitrary distance along Oa_2, measured from the origin to any point $p_2(x_2, y_2, z_2)$ on the line. Hence the form (*7.3*) is applicable to all lines passing through O.

Now imagining a large number of straight lines drawn in various directions through O, let us select s for each line such that

$$I_{Oa}\,s^2 = 1 \tag{7.4}$$

Therefore we can write the general relation

$$I_x x^2 + I_y y^2 + I_z z^2 - 2I_{xy}xy - 2I_{xz}xz - 2I_{yz}yz = 1 \tag{7.5}$$

which is the equation of an ellipsoidal surface (in general *not* one of revolution) oriented in some, as yet undetermined, manner with respect to X, Y, Z as indicated in the figure. It is referred to as the *ellipsoid of inertia* about O.

The above results apply to an object of any shape: a stone, a chair, a steel girder, etc. But it must not be supposed that there is only one ellipsoid per body. Indeed ellipsoids in general, each of different size and orientation, can be drawn for all points in and throughout space around every object.

The fact that there is an unlimited number of ellipsoids for any object is not as frightful as it may appear since, as will soon be shown, when the ellipsoid about the center of mass is known all other moments and products of inertia and ellipsoids can be computed.

It should be clear that *the moment of inertia about any line drawn through O is given by $I_{Oa} = 1/s^2$* where s is now the distance from O to where the line pierces the ellipsoid. Also note that we could just as well have written (*7.4*) as $I_{Oa}s^2 = C =$ any constant, thereby giving the ellipsoid any convenient size.

7.3 Principal Moments of Inertia. Principal Axes and their Directions.

With axes X, Y, Z taken along the principal diameters $2a, 2b, 2c$ of any ellipsoid, the equation of its surface has the form

$$\frac{x^2}{a^2} + \frac{y^2}{b^2} + \frac{z^2}{c^2} = 1 \tag{7.6}$$

Likewise, if X, Y, Z are taken along the principal diameters of the ellipsoid of inertia, the products of inertia are zero and thus

$$I_x^p x^2 + I_y^p y^2 + I_z^p z^2 = 1 \quad \text{or} \quad I_{Oa} = I_x^p l^2 + I_y^p m^2 + I_z^p n^2 \tag{7.7}$$

where I_x^p, I_y^p, I_z^p are referred to as "principal moments of inertia". Corresponding axes X^p, Y^p, Z^p are called "principal axes of inertia".

From known values of I_x, I_{xy}, etc., in (*7.5*), *the directions of the principal axes as well as values of* I_x^p, I_y^p, I_z^p *can be found as follows.* It can be shown that the direction cosines l, m, n of a line drawn normal to the surface $\phi(x, y, z) = C$ are proportional to $\partial\phi/\partial x$, $\partial\phi/\partial y$, $\partial\phi/\partial z$ respectively, that is,

$$\frac{\partial\phi}{\partial x} = kl, \quad \frac{\partial\phi}{\partial y} = km, \quad \frac{\partial\phi}{\partial z} = kn \tag{7.8}$$

where k is a constant. Applying these relations to the ellipsoidal surface (*7.5*), we have

$$\begin{aligned} I_x x - I_{xy} y - I_{xz} z &= kl \\ I_y y - I_{xy} x - I_{yz} z &= km \\ I_z z - I_{xz} x - I_{yz} y &= kn \end{aligned} \tag{7.9}$$

But a principal axis is normal to the surface where it pierces the ellipsoid and at this point (distant r from the origin and having coordinates x, y, z) $l = x/r$, $m = y/r$, $n = z/r$. Note carefully that r is the length of a principal radius and l, m, n are here direction cosines of a principal axis of inertia.

Now eliminating x, y, z from (*7.9*), multiplying through by l, m, n respectively and adding the group, there results

$$k/r = I_x l^2 + I_y m^2 + I_z n^2 - 2I_{xy} lm - 2I_{xz} ln - 2I_{yz} mn$$

Comparing with (*7.2*), $k = I^p r$ where, clearly, I^p is a principal moment of inertia. Relations (*7.9*) can now be written as

$$\begin{aligned} (I^p - I_x)l + I_{xy} m + I_{xz} n &= 0 \\ I_{xy} l + (I^p - I_y)m + I_{yz} n &= 0 \\ I_{xz} l + I_{yz} m + (I^p - I_z)n &= 0 \end{aligned} \tag{7.10}$$

from which the three principal moments of inertia and their directions will now be obtained.

In order that these equations have other than trivial solutions, it is necessary that

$$\begin{vmatrix} I^p - I_x & I_{xy} & I_{xz} \\ I_{xy} & I^p - I_y & I_{yz} \\ I_{xz} & I_{yz} & I^p - I_z \end{vmatrix} = 0 \tag{7.11}$$

An expansion of this determinant gives a cubic equation in I^p. Inserting known values of I_x, I_{xy}, etc., (found by computation or by experiment) and solving for the three roots, we have I_1^p, I_2^p, I_3^p, the three principal moments of inertia. (Roots of the above equation are easily found by the "Graeffe Root Squaring Method". See *Mathematics of Modern Engineering*, by R. E. Doherty and E. G. Keller, John Wiley, 1936, pp. 98-130. This powerful method, which is applicable to equations of any degree, has many practical applications.)

Inserting I_1^p into (*7.10*), these relations may be solved for relative values (only) of l_1, m_1, n_1, direction cosines of the principal axis corresponding to I_1^p. Writing expressions thus obtained as $c_1 l_1, c_1 m_1, c_1 n_1$ (c_1 is some constant) we have $l_1 = c_1 l_1/(c_1^2 l_1^2 + c_1^2 m_1^2 + c_1^2 n_1^2)^{1/2}$, etc. Likewise direction cosines of the remaining two principal axes follow.

Note. As seen from (*7.10*) the relative values of l_1, m_1, n_1 are just the cofactors of the first, second and third elements respectively of the first row (or any row) of (*7.11*) with I_1^p inserted; etc. (For definition of "cofactor" see Page 210, directly above (*10.11*).)

7.4 Given Moments and Products of Inertia Relative to Any Rectangular Axes with Origin at the Center of Mass, to Find:

(*a*) Corresponding quantities referred to any parallel system of axes.

(*b*) The moment of inertia about any given line.

(*c*) The ellipsoid of inertia about any point.

Developments of this and coming chapters may be simplified by the following easy-to-remember notation. Plain symbols such as X, Y, Z indicate any frame (origin *not* at c.m.), and I_x, I_{xy}, etc., indicate corresponding moments and products of inertia. A bar over a symbol indicates a center-of-mass quantity. $\bar{X}, \bar{Y}, \bar{Z}$ represents a frame with origin at c.m., and $\bar{I}_x$, $\bar{I}_{xy}$, etc., refer to corresponding moments and products of inertia. A superscript p indicates a "principal" quantity. X^p, Y^p, Z^p are principal axes (origin not at c.m.), and I_x^p, I_y^p, I_z^p are corresponding principal moments of inertia. $\bar{X}^p, \bar{Y}^p, \bar{Z}^p$ are principal axes through c.m., and $\bar{I}_x^p, \bar{I}_y^p, \bar{I}_z^p$ are corresponding principal moments of inertia.

(*a*) In Fig. 7-2 the origin of $\bar{X}, \bar{Y}, \bar{Z}$ is at c.m., and that of the parallel frame X, Y, Z is at any point O. Both frames are regarded as attached to the body.

The moment of inertia I_z about OZ, for example, is given by

$$I_z = \sum m'(x^2 + y^2)$$

But $x = x_1 + \bar{x}$, etc. Hence

$$\begin{aligned} I_z &= \sum m'[(x_1 + \bar{x})^2 + (y_1 + \bar{y})^2] \\ &= \sum m'(x_1^2 + y_1^2) \\ &\quad + (\bar{x}^2 + \bar{y}^2) \sum m' \\ &\quad + 2\bar{x} \sum m'x_1 + 2\bar{y} \sum m'y_1 \end{aligned}$$

Since O_1 is at c.m. the last two terms are zero. Hence

$$I_z = \bar{I}_z + M(\bar{x}^2 + \bar{y}^2)$$

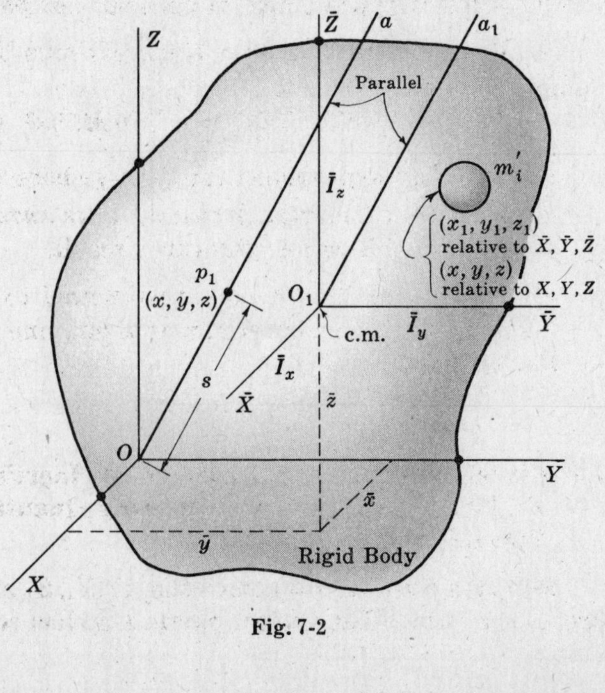

Fig. 7-2

where M is the total mass of the body and $(\bar{x}^2+\bar{y}^2)^{1/2}$ is the normal distance between Z and $\bar{Z}$. (Obviously this relation applies to any two axes, one of which passes through c.m. Thus, for example, $I_{Oa} = I_{O_1a_1} + Md^2$ where d is the normal distance between Oa and O_1a_1.)

The product of inertia $I_{xy} = \sum m'(xy)$, by the same steps as above, is given by $I_{xy} = \bar{I}_{x_1y_1} + M\bar{x}\bar{y}$. Thus in general,

$$I_x = \bar{I}_x + M(\bar{y}^2+\bar{z}^2), \qquad I_y = \bar{I}_y + M(\bar{x}^2+\bar{z}^2), \qquad I_z = \bar{I}_z + M(\bar{x}^2+\bar{y}^2) \tag{7.12}$$

$$I_{xy} = \bar{I}_{xy} + M\bar{x}\bar{y}, \qquad I_{xz} = \bar{I}_{xz} + M\bar{x}\bar{z}, \qquad I_{yz} = \bar{I}_{yz} + M\bar{y}\bar{z} \tag{7.13}$$

Moments and products of inertia relative to X, Y, Z, Fig. 7-2, in terms of c.m. quantities.

(*b*) From relations (*7.2*), (*7.12*) and (*7.13*) it follows that the moment of inertia about any axis Oa, Fig. 7-2, through O is given by

$$\begin{aligned} I_{Oa} \;=\; & [\bar{I}_x + M(\bar{y}^2+\bar{z}^2)]l^2 + [\bar{I}_y + M(\bar{x}^2+\bar{z}^2)]m^2 + [\bar{I}_z + M(\bar{x}^2+\bar{y}^2)]n^2 \\ & - 2(\bar{I}_{xy} + M\bar{x}\bar{y})lm - 2(\bar{I}_{xz} + M\bar{x}\bar{z})ln - 2(\bar{I}_{yz} + M\bar{y}\bar{z})mn \end{aligned} \tag{7.14}$$

Moment of inertia of body about any line Oa, Fig. 7-2, in terms of c.m. quantities.

Thus *given moments and products of inertia relative to any frame with origin at c.m., we can write at once an expression for the moment of inertia about any desired line.*

(*c*) From (*7.14*) it is clear that we can write

$$\begin{aligned} & [\bar{I}_x + M(\bar{y}^2+\bar{z}^2)]x^2 + [\bar{I}_y + M(\bar{x}^2+\bar{z}^2)]y^2 + [\bar{I}_z + M(\bar{x}^2+\bar{y}^2)]z^2 \\ & - 2(\bar{I}_{xy} + M\bar{x}\bar{y})xy - 2(\bar{I}_{xz} + M\bar{x}\bar{z})xz - 2(\bar{I}_{yz} + M\bar{y}\bar{z})yz = 1 \end{aligned} \tag{7.15}$$

The ellipsoid of inertia about O in terms of c.m. quantities.

If $\bar{X}, \bar{Y}, \bar{Z}$ are principal axes, $\bar{I}_{xy} = \bar{I}_{xz} = \bar{I}_{yz} = 0$ and the above simplifies somewhat. But since (*7.15*) still contains products of inertia, $I_{xy} = M\bar{x}\bar{y}$, etc., it is evident that X, Y, Z are in general not principal axes through O. Thus principal axes through any arbitrary point are, in general, *not parallel to those through c.m.*

However, if O is on a principal axis through c.m., $\bar{Z}^p$, for example, $\bar{x} = \bar{y} = 0$ and (*7.15*) reduces to

$$1 = (\bar{I}_x^p + M\bar{z}^2)x^2 + (\bar{I}_y^p + M\bar{z}^2)y^2 + \bar{I}_z^p z^2 \tag{7.16}$$

with similar expressions for O anywhere on $\bar{X}^p$ or $\bar{Y}^p$. Since these relations contain no products of inertia, *principal axes through any point on $\bar{X}^p$, $\bar{Y}^p$, $\bar{Z}^p$ are parallel to these axes*; this is an important result.

The planes $\bar{X}^p$, $\bar{Y}^p$, etc. are referred to as "principal planes" and it may be shown that for any point on either of them, one principal axis is normal to the plane. See Problem 7.19.

7.5 Given Moments and Products of Inertia (I_{x_1}, $I_{x_1y_1}$, etc.) Relative to Any Frame X_1, Y_1, Z_1, to Find Corresponding Quantities (I_{x_2}, $I_{x_2y_2}$, etc.) Relative to Any Other Parallel Frame X_2, Y_2, Z_2.

Referring to Fig. 7-3 below, the X_1, Y_1, Z_1 and X_2, Y_2, Z_2 frames are parallel, but neither origin is at c.m. The typical particle m' has coordinates x_1, y_1, z_1 and x_2, y_2, z_2.

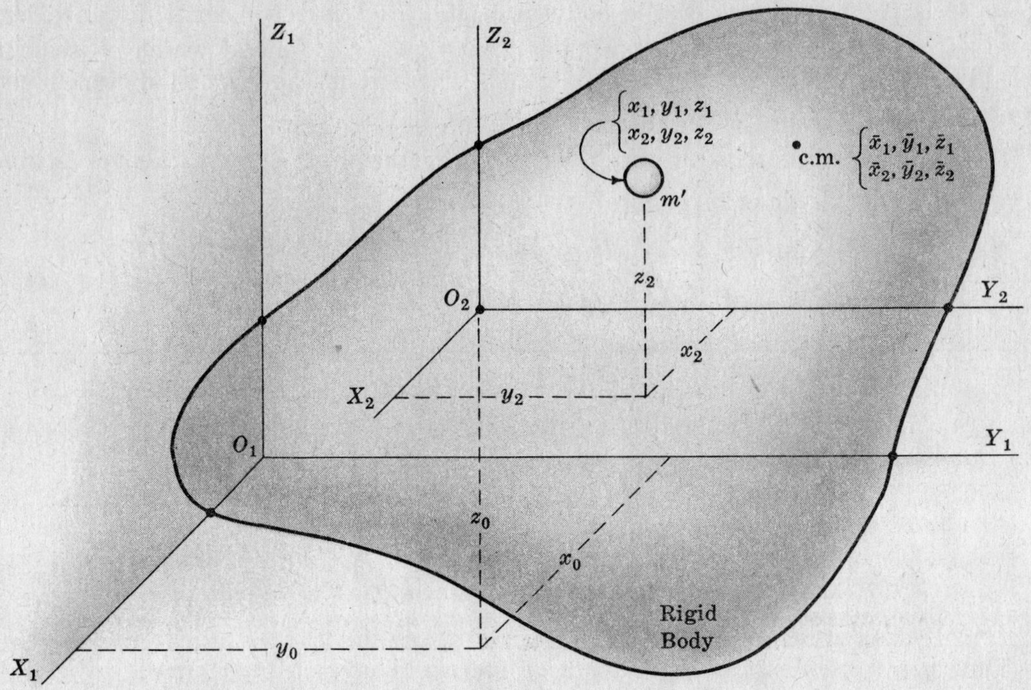

Fig. 7-3

Writing $I_{x_1} = \sum m'(y_1^2 + z_1^2)$, $I_{x_1y_1} = \sum m'x_1y_1$ and employing the relations $x_1 = x_0 + x_2$, etc., it follows at once that

$$\begin{aligned} I_{x_1} &= I_{x_2} + M(y_0^2 + z_0^2) + 2M(y_0\bar{y}_2 + z_0\bar{z}_2) \\ I_{x_1y_1} &= I_{x_2y_2} + Mx_0y_0 + M(x_0\bar{y}_2 + y_0\bar{x}_2) \end{aligned} \qquad (7.17)$$

where $\bar{x}_2, \bar{y}_2, \bar{z}_2$ are coordinates of c.m. relative to X_2, Y_2, Z_2. Similar relations follow for $I_{y_1}, I_{x_1y_1}$, etc. (For a slightly different form of (*7.17*), see Problem 7.25.)

7.6 Given I_{x_1}, $I_{x_1y_1}$, etc., Relative to X_1, Y_1, Z_1, Fig. 7-4, to Find I_x, I_{xy}, etc., Relative to the Rotated X, Y, Z Frame.

Let $\alpha_{11}, \alpha_{12}, \alpha_{13}$ be direction cosines of OX, etc., as indicated in Fig. 7-4. Then applying (*7.2*), it is clear that

$$I_x = I_{x_1}\alpha_{11}^2 + I_{y_1}\alpha_{12}^2 + I_{z_1}\alpha_{13}^2 - 2I_{x_1y_1}\alpha_{11}\alpha_{12} - 2I_{x_1z_1}\alpha_{11}\alpha_{13} - 2I_{y_1z_1}\alpha_{12}\alpha_{13} \qquad (7.18)$$

Moment of inertia I_x about axis X in terms of moments and products relative to the rotated X_1, Y_1, Z_1 frame. I_y and I_z are given by exactly similar relations.

In order to determine products of inertia, I_{xy} for example, we return to the definition $I_{xy} = \sum m'xy$. Eliminating x, y with the transformation equations

$$x = \alpha_{11}x_1 + \alpha_{12}y_1 + \alpha_{13}z_1, \quad y = \alpha_{21}x_1 + \alpha_{22}y_1 + \alpha_{23}z_1$$

we obtain

$$I_{xy} = \sum m'(\alpha_{11}x_1 + \alpha_{12}y_1 + \alpha_{13}z_1)(\alpha_{21}x_1 + \alpha_{22}y_1 + \alpha_{23}z_1)$$

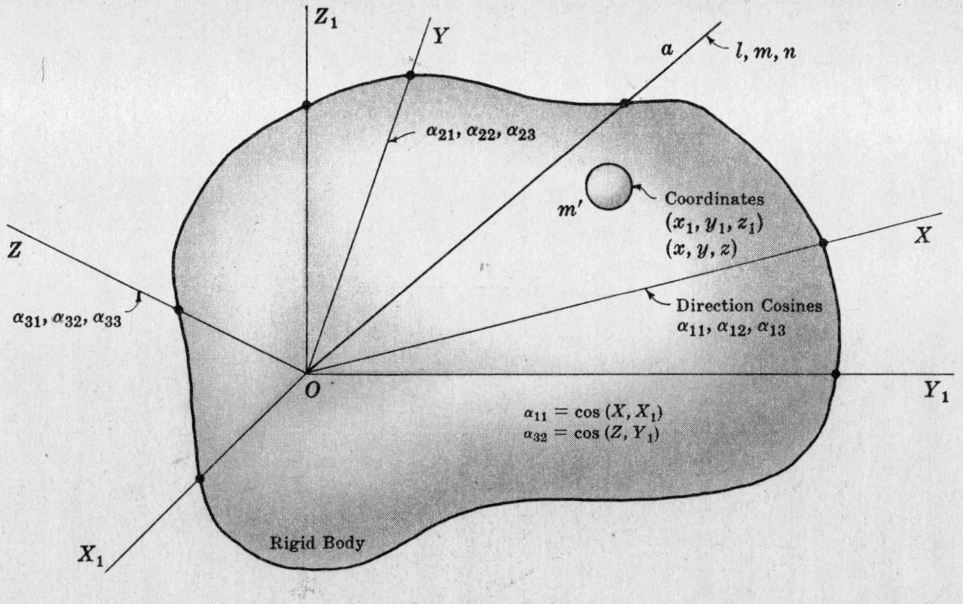

Fig. 7-4

The reader may easily show that this reduces to the first relation in (*7.19*) below. (*Note.* In order to show, in this reduction, that

$$\sum m'(\alpha_{11}\alpha_{21}x_1^2 + \alpha_{12}\alpha_{22}y_1^2 + \alpha_{13}\alpha_{23}z_1^2) \quad = \quad -(\alpha_{11}\alpha_{21}I_{x_1} + \alpha_{12}\alpha_{22}I_{y_1} + \alpha_{13}\alpha_{23}I_{z_1})$$

we subtract from the sum the zero quantity

$$(\alpha_{11}\alpha_{21} + \alpha_{12}\alpha_{22} + \alpha_{13}\alpha_{23})(x_1^2 + y_1^2 + z_1^2)$$

and collect terms.)

$$\begin{aligned}
I_{xy} &= (\alpha_{11}\alpha_{22} + \alpha_{12}\alpha_{21})I_{x_1y_1} + (\alpha_{11}\alpha_{23} + \alpha_{13}\alpha_{21})I_{x_1z_1} + (\alpha_{12}\alpha_{23} + \alpha_{13}\alpha_{22})I_{y_1z_1} \\
&\quad - (\alpha_{11}\alpha_{21}I_{x_1} + \alpha_{12}\alpha_{22}I_{y_1} + \alpha_{13}\alpha_{23}I_{z_1}) \\
I_{xz} &= (\alpha_{11}\alpha_{32} + \alpha_{12}\alpha_{31})I_{x_1y_1} + (\alpha_{11}\alpha_{33} + \alpha_{13}\alpha_{31})I_{x_1z_1} + (\alpha_{12}\alpha_{33} + \alpha_{32}\alpha_{13})I_{y_1z_1} \\
&\quad - (\alpha_{11}\alpha_{31}I_{x_1} + \alpha_{12}\alpha_{32}I_{y_1} + \alpha_{13}\alpha_{33}I_{z_1}) \\
I_{yz} &= (\alpha_{21}\alpha_{32} + \alpha_{22}\alpha_{31})I_{x_1y_1} + (\alpha_{21}\alpha_{33} + \alpha_{31}\alpha_{23})I_{x_1z_1} + (\alpha_{22}\alpha_{33} + \alpha_{23}\alpha_{32})I_{y_1z_1} \\
&\quad - (\alpha_{21}\alpha_{31}I_{x_1} + \alpha_{22}\alpha_{32}I_{y_1} + \alpha_{23}\alpha_{33}I_{z_1})
\end{aligned} \tag{7.19}$$

Products of inertia relative to the rotated X, Y, Z frame.

Hence the moment of inertia about any line Oa having direction cosines l, m, n relative to X, Y, Z can be found in terms of $I_{x_1}, I_{x_1y_1}$, etc., from

$$I_{Oa} \quad = \quad I_x l^2 + I_y m^2 + I_z n^2 - 2lmI_{xy} - 2lnI_{xz} - 2mnI_{yz}$$

and relations (*7.18*) and (*7.19*).

If it is assumed that I_x, I_{xy}, etc. are given, to find I_{x_1}, I_{y_1}, etc., the reader may show, following just the procedure outlined above, that

$$\begin{aligned}
I_{x_1} &= I_x\alpha_{11}^2 + I_y\alpha_{21}^2 + I_z\alpha_{31}^2 - 2I_{xy}\alpha_{11}\alpha_{21} - 2I_{xz}\alpha_{11}\alpha_{31} - 2I_{yz}\alpha_{21}\alpha_{31} \\
I_{x_1y_1} &= (\alpha_{11}\alpha_{22} + \alpha_{12}\alpha_{21})I_{xy} + (\alpha_{11}\alpha_{32} + \alpha_{12}\alpha_{31})I_{xz} \\
&\quad + (\alpha_{21}\alpha_{32} + \alpha_{22}\alpha_{31})I_{yz} - (\alpha_{11}\alpha_{12}I_x + \alpha_{21}\alpha_{22}I_y + \alpha_{31}\alpha_{32}I_z)
\end{aligned} \tag{7.20}$$

Similar relations follow for $I_{y_1}, I_{z_1}, I_{x_1z_1}, I_{y_1z_1}$.

Important note. *Given moments and products of inertia relative to any rectangular frame, we can now, applying (7.17), (7.18), (7.19), determine corresponding quantities relative to any other such frame located and orientated in any manner with respect to the first.* Indeed the second frame might be moving in some known manner relative to the first.

7.7 Examples of Moments, Products and Ellipsoids of Inertia.

Example 7.1.

The basic physical and geometrical ideas of the past sections can be made clear by a consideration of the simple "rigid body" shown in Fig. 7-5 which, as will be seen, has all the dynamical properties of any ordinary body such as a wheel, beam, chair, etc.

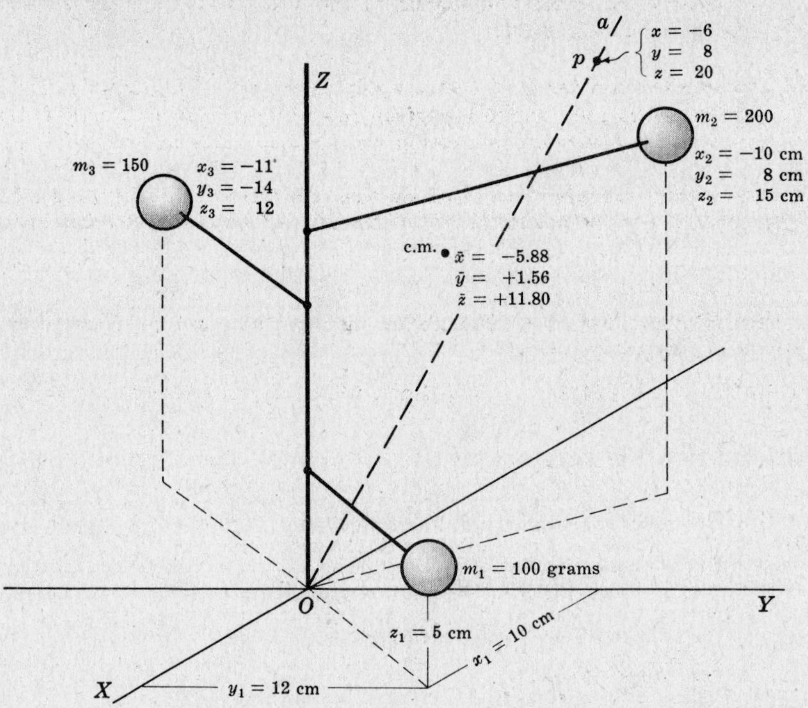

Fig. 7-5

The arrangement consists of three particles rigidly connected to the Z axis by thin "massless" rods. The X, Y, Z frame and the particles form a rigid unit. The mass and coordinates of each particle are indicated on the figure.

(*a*) Let us first determine the moments and products of inertia relative to X, Y, Z.

$$I_x = \sum m_i(y_i^2 + z_i^2) = m_1(y_1^2 + z_1^2) + m_2(y_2^2 + z_2^2) + m_3(y_3^2 + z_3^2)$$
$$= 100(144 + 25) + 200(64 + 225) + 150(144 + 196) = 125{,}700 \text{ g-cm}^2$$

Likewise, $I_y = 117{,}250$, $I_z = 104{,}750$.

$$I_{xy} = \sum m_i(x_iy_i) = 100(12 \times 10) - 200(10 \times 8) + 150(11 \times 14) = 19{,}100 \text{ g-cm}^2$$

Similarly, $I_{xz} = -44{,}800$, $I_{yz} = 4800$.

(*b*) From the above values we can immediately write the following expression for the ellipsoid of inertia about the origin O.

$$125{,}700x^2 + 117{,}250y^2 + 104{,}750z^2 - 2(19{,}100)xy + 2(44{,}800)xz - 2(4800)yz = 1$$

(c) The moment of inertia of the "body" about any line through O, as Oa, may be found as follows. A point p on Oa has coordinates shown. Hence direction cosines of this line are $-6/s$, $8/s$, $20/s$ where $s = \sqrt{6^2 + 8^2 + 20^2}$. That is, $l = -.268$, $m = .358$, $n = .895$. Hence by (7.2),

$$I_{Op} = (.268)^2(125{,}700) + (.358)^2(117{,}250) + (.895)^2(104{,}750)$$
$$+ 2(.268)(.358)(19{,}100) - 2(.268)(.895)(44{,}800) - 2(.358)(.895)(4800)$$

(d) Consider moments and products of inertia relative to axes $\bar{X}, \bar{Y}, \bar{Z}$ (not shown on the diagram) parallel to X, Y, Z and with origin at c.m. By equation (7.12),

$$\bar{I}_z = I_z - M(\bar{x}^2 + \bar{y}^2) = 104{,}750 - 450(5.88^2 + 1.56^2), \qquad \text{etc.}$$

By (7.13)

$$\bar{I}_{xy} = I_{xy} - M\bar{x}\bar{y} = 19{,}100 - 450(-5.88 \times 1.56), \qquad \text{etc.}$$

Hence we can find at once the moment of inertia of the body about any line through c.m., as well as the ellipsoid of inertia about this point.

(e) Since we have numerical values for $\bar{I}_x$, $\bar{I}_{xy}$, etc., applying results of Section 7.4, *a numerical value for the moment of inertia of the body about any given line in space can be found at once. Likewise, an expression for the ellipsoid of inertia about any given point in space can immediately be written down.*

(f) Finally, note that on applying the results of Section 7.3 the principal moments of inertia and the directions of corresponding principal axes at O, at c.m., or indeed at any point in space, could be found.

Example 7.2.

Consider the thin triangle, Fig. 7-6. The following moments and products of inertia relative to X, Y, Z are easily obtained by integration.

$$I_x = \tfrac{1}{6}Mb^2, \quad I_y = \tfrac{1}{6}Ma^2, \quad I_z = \tfrac{1}{6}M(a^2 + b^2), \quad I_{xy} = \tfrac{1}{12}Mab, \quad I_{xz} = I_{yz} = 0$$

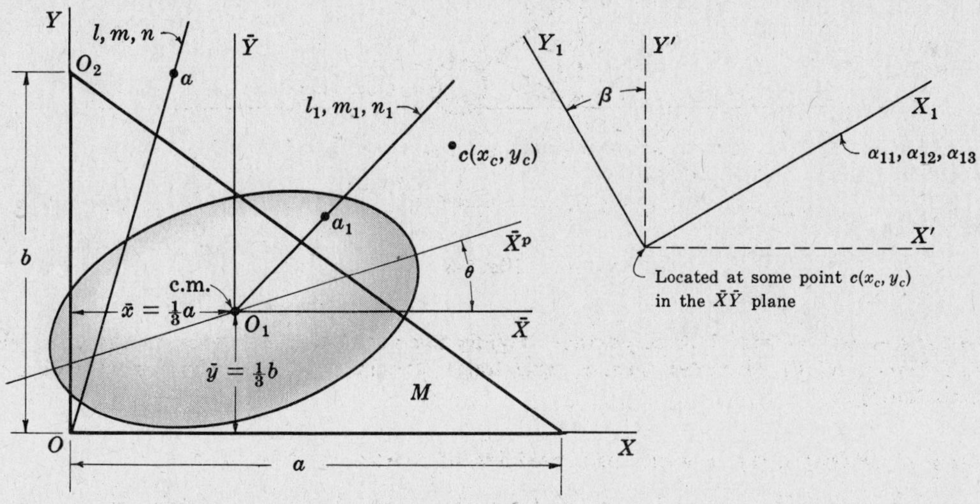

Fig. 7-6

(a) The ellipsoid of inertia about the corner O is

$$\tfrac{1}{6}M[b^2x^2 + a^2y^2 + (a^2 + b^2)z^2 - abxy] = 1$$

(b) The moment of inertia about any line Oa, not necessarily in the XY plane, is given by

$$I_{Oa} = \tfrac{1}{6}M[b^2l^2 + a^2m^2 + (a^2 + b^2)n^2 - ablm]$$

where l, m, n are the direction cosines of Oa relative to X, Y, Z.

(c) From (7.12) and (7.13), we find

$$\bar{I}_x = \tfrac{1}{18}Mb^2, \quad \bar{I}_y = \tfrac{1}{18}Ma^2, \quad \bar{I}_z = \tfrac{1}{18}M(a^2+b^2), \quad \bar{I}_{xy} = -\tfrac{1}{36}Mab, \quad \bar{I}_{xz} = \bar{I}_{yz} = 0$$

Thus the ellipsoid about c.m. is

$$\tfrac{1}{18}M[b^2x_1^2 + a^2y_1^2 + (a^2+b^2)z_1^2 + abx_1y_1] = 1$$

(d) The moment of inertia of the triangle about any line O_1a_1, not necessarily in the plane of the triangle, is

$$I_{O_1a_1} = \tfrac{1}{18}M[b^2l_1^2 + a^2m_1^2 + (a^2+b^2)n_1^2 + abl_1m_1]$$

(e) Following Section 7.3, the principal moments of inertia about axes through c.m. are

$$\bar{I}^p_{1,2} = \tfrac{1}{36}M(a^2 + b^2 \pm \sqrt{a^4+b^4-a^2b^2}), \qquad \bar{I}^p_3 = \bar{I}^p_1 + \bar{I}^p_2 = \tfrac{1}{18}M(a^2+b^2)$$

Writing (l_1, m_1, n_1), (l_2, m_2, n_2) and (l_3, m_3, n_3) as the direction cosines of the principal axes, it is seen from (7.10) that $n_1 = n_2 = 0$, $n_3 = 1$, $l_3 = m_3 = 0$, and l_1, l_2, m_1, m_2 are determined from

$$l = -\bar{I}_{xy}[\bar{I}^2_{xy} + (\bar{I}^p - \bar{I}_x)^2]^{-1/2}, \qquad m = (\bar{I}^p - \bar{I}_x)[\bar{I}^2_{xy} + (\bar{I}^p - \bar{I}_x)^2]^{-1/2}$$

Thus, for given values of $a, b, M,$ the angle θ (see figure) can be determined.

(f) The origin of X_1, Y_1 (see upper right hand sketch in Fig. 7-6) is located at $c(x_c, y_c)$ in the $\bar{X}\bar{Y}$ plane. Y_1 makes an angle β with $\bar{Y}$. Z_1 and $\bar{Z}$ are parallel. x_c, y_c are measured relative to $\bar{X}, \bar{Y}$. Let us determine moments and products of inertia of the triangle relative to X_1, Y_1, Z_1. It is seen that

$$I'_x = \tfrac{1}{18}Mb^2 + My_c^2, \quad I'_y = \tfrac{1}{18}Ma^2 + Mx_c^2, \quad I'_{xy} = Mx_cy_c - \tfrac{1}{36}Mab,$$
$$I'_{xz} = I'_{yz} = 0, \quad I'_z = \tfrac{1}{18}M(a^2+b^2) + M(x_c^2 + y_c^2)$$

Direction cosines of the X_1, Y_1, Z_1 are

$$\alpha_{11} = \cos\beta, \quad \alpha_{12} = \sin\beta, \quad \alpha_{13} = 0, \quad \alpha_{21} = -\sin\beta, \quad \alpha_{22} = \cos\beta, \quad \alpha_{23} = 0, \quad \alpha_{31} = \alpha_{32} = 0, \quad \alpha_{33} = 1$$

Thus from relations (7.18) and (7.19) it follows that

$$I_{x_1} = M(\tfrac{1}{18}b^2 + y_c^2)\cos^2\beta + M(\tfrac{1}{18}a^2 + x_c^2)\sin^2\beta - 2M(x_cy_c - \tfrac{1}{36}ab)\sin\beta\cos\beta$$
$$I_{y_1} = M(\tfrac{1}{18}b^2 + y_c^2)\sin^2\beta + M(\tfrac{1}{18}a^2 + x_c^2)\cos^2\beta + 2M(x_cy_c - \tfrac{1}{36}ab)\sin\beta\cos\beta$$
$$I_{x_1y_1} = M(x_cy_c - \tfrac{1}{36}ab)\cos 2\beta + M(\tfrac{1}{18}b^2 + y_c^2)\sin\beta\cos\beta - M(\tfrac{1}{18}a^2 + x_c^2)\sin\beta\cos\beta$$
$$I_{z_1} = I'_z = \tfrac{1}{18}M(a^2+b^2) + M(x_c^2 + y_c^2), \qquad I_{x_1z_1} = I_{y_1z_1} = 0$$

(g) Suppose that the X_1Y_1 axes rotate in some known manner about the fixed position of Z_1. β then varies with time and the above quantities become known functions of t.

Example 7-3.

Fig. 7-7 represents a *thin* lamina such as can be cut from sheet metal or thin plywood.

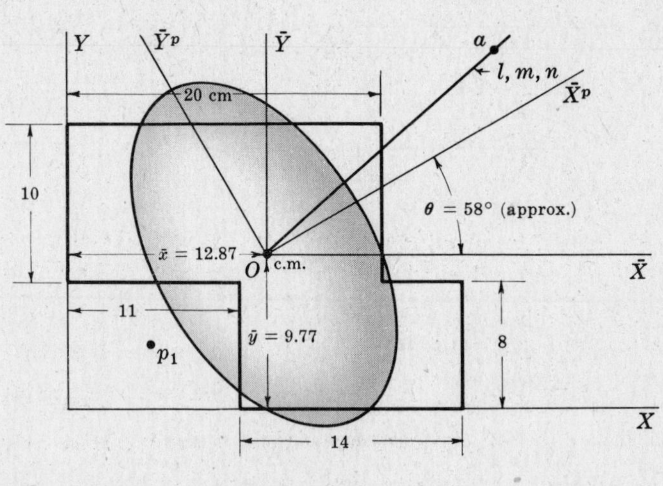

Fig. 7-7

Assuming an area density $\rho = 2$ grams/cm^2, the following values relative to $\bar{X}, \bar{Y}, \bar{Z}$ have been computed:

$$\bar{I}_x = 1.61 \times 10^4 \text{ g-cm}^2, \quad \bar{I}_y = 2.62 \times 10^4, \quad \bar{I}_z = 4.23 \times 10^4, \quad \bar{I}_{xy} = -1.036 \times 10^4, \quad \bar{I}_{xz} = \bar{I}_{yz} = 0 \qquad (1)$$

(*a*) Principal moments of inertia and angle θ are found to be (see Section 7.3)

$$\bar{I}^p_x = 3.26 \times 10^4, \quad \bar{I}^p_y = .97 \times 10^4, \quad \bar{I}^p_z = 4.23 \times 10^4 \qquad (2)$$

$\theta = 58^\circ$ approximately.

(*b*) The ellipsoid about c.m. can be written in terms of either set of values, (*1*) or (*2*); that is,

$$(1.61x_1^2 + 2.62y_1^2 + 4.23z_1^2 + 2 \times 1.036x_1y_1)10^4 = 1 \qquad (3)$$

$$(3.26x_2^2 + .97y_2^2 + 4.23z_2^2)10^4 = 1 \qquad (4)$$

where x_1, y_1, z_1 are relative to $\bar{X}, \bar{Y}, \bar{Z}$, and x_2, y_2, z_2 to $\bar{X}^p, \bar{Y}^p, \bar{Z}^p$.

(*c*) Note that

$$I_{Oa} = (3.26l_2^2 + .97m_2^2 + 4.23n_2^2)10^4 \qquad (5)$$

or again,

$$I_{Oa} = (1.61l_1^2 + 2.62m_1^2 + 4.23n_1^2 + 2 \times 1.036l_1m_1)10^4 \qquad (6)$$

where l_1, m_1, n_1 correspond to x_1, y_1, z_1, etc. (*5*) and (*6*), of course, give the same value for any particular line Oa.

Example 7.4.

Consider the rectangular block, Fig. 7-8. Here

$$\bar{I}_x = \tfrac{1}{3}M(b^2 + c^2)$$

$$\bar{I}_y = \tfrac{1}{3}M(a^2 + c^2)$$

$$\bar{I}_z = \tfrac{1}{3}M(a^2 + b^2)$$

$$\bar{I}_{xy} = \bar{I}_{xz} = \bar{I}_{yz} = 0$$

(*a*) Then $\bar{X}, \bar{Y}, \bar{Z}$ are principal axes, $\bar{I}_x = \bar{I}^p_x$, etc., and the ellipsoid of inertia about c.m. is $\bar{I}^p_x x^2 + \bar{I}^p_y y^2 + \bar{I}^p_z z^2 = 1$.

(*b*) Moments and products of inertia relative to X, Y, Z are easily shown to be

$$I_x = \tfrac{4}{3}M(b^2 + c^2)$$

$$I_y = \tfrac{4}{3}M(a^2 + c^2)$$

$$I_z = \tfrac{4}{3}M(a^2 + b^2)$$

$$I_{xy} = Mab \qquad I_{xz} = Mac \qquad I_{yz} = Mbc$$

The ellipsoid about O follows at once.

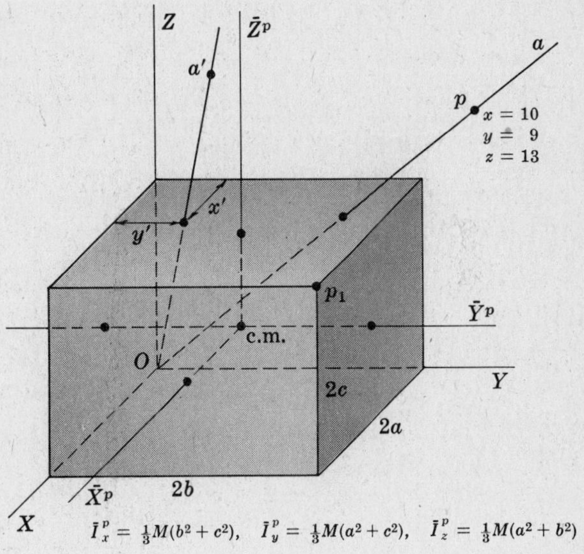

Fig. 7-8

(*c*) Let us determine the moment of inertia about any line Oa. The direction of Oa is determined by the fact that at some point p the coordinates have, for example, the values shown. Hence direction cosines of Oa are

$$l = 10/(10^2 + 9^2 + 13^2)^{1/2} = 10/18.7, \quad m = 9/18.7, \quad n = 13/18.7$$

Thus applying (*7.2*),

$$I_{Oa} = \tfrac{1}{350}[\tfrac{4}{3}M(b^2 + c^2)\,10^2 + \tfrac{4}{3}M(a^2 + c^2)\,9^2 + \tfrac{4}{3}M(a^2 + b^2)\,13^2$$

$$- 2Mab \times 90 - 2Mac \times 130 - 2Mab \times 117]$$

Note that (*7.3*) may be used directly, perhaps with some advantage because here no thought need be given to direction cosines.

Example 7.5.

Consider the uniform solid cone of Fig. 7-9. As determined by integration,

$$\bar{I}_x^p = \bar{I}_y^p = \tfrac{3}{80}M(4r^2+h^2), \quad \bar{I}_z^p = \tfrac{3}{10}Mr^2,$$

$$\bar{I}_{xy} = \bar{I}_{xz} = \bar{I}_{yz} = 0$$

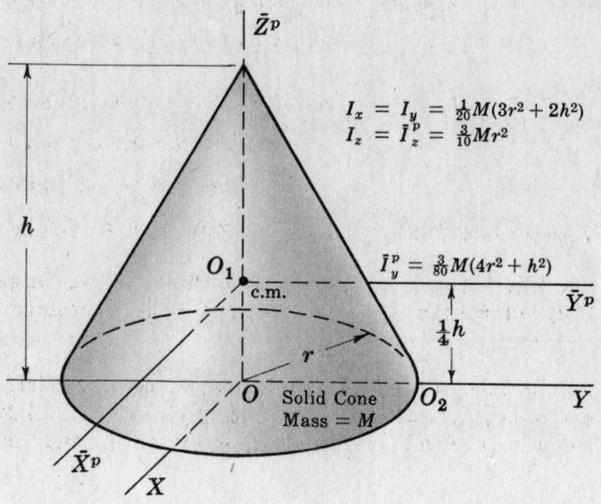

Fig. 7-9

(*a*) Applying the results of Section 7.4, we can find I_x, I_{xy}, etc., relative to any parallel frame, the moment of inertia of the cone about any line of given direction and, of course, the ellipsoid of inertia about any point. Relative to the X, Y, Z axes shown,

$$I_x = \tfrac{3}{80}M(4r^2+h^2) + \tfrac{1}{16}Mh^2; \qquad I_{xy} = 0, \quad \text{etc.}$$

(*b*) Taking X, Y, Z parallel to $\bar{X}^p, \bar{Y}^p, \bar{Z}^p$ but with origin at O_2,

$$I_x = \tfrac{3}{80}M(4r^2+h^2) + M(r^2 + \tfrac{1}{16}h^2); \qquad I_{xy} = 0$$

$$I_y = \tfrac{3}{80}M(4r^2+h^2) + \tfrac{1}{16}Mh^2; \qquad I_{yz} = -\tfrac{1}{4}Mrh, \quad \text{etc.}$$

(*c*) Applying the results of Section 7.6, I_x, I_{xy}, etc., can be found relative to any frame with origin located at any point in space and axes rotated in any manner with respect to, say, $\bar{X}^p, \bar{Y}^p, \bar{Z}^p$. (See the following example.)

Example 7.6.

The block of Fig. 7-10 (same as the one in Example 7.4) is shown in a rotated position. Axes X_1, Y_1, Z_1 indicate the original location. To make clear the position now occupied, imagine the block first rotated about OZ_1 through an angle ψ, keeping OX in the X_1Y_1 plane. Then rotate it about OX, making an angle θ between OZ_1 and OZ.

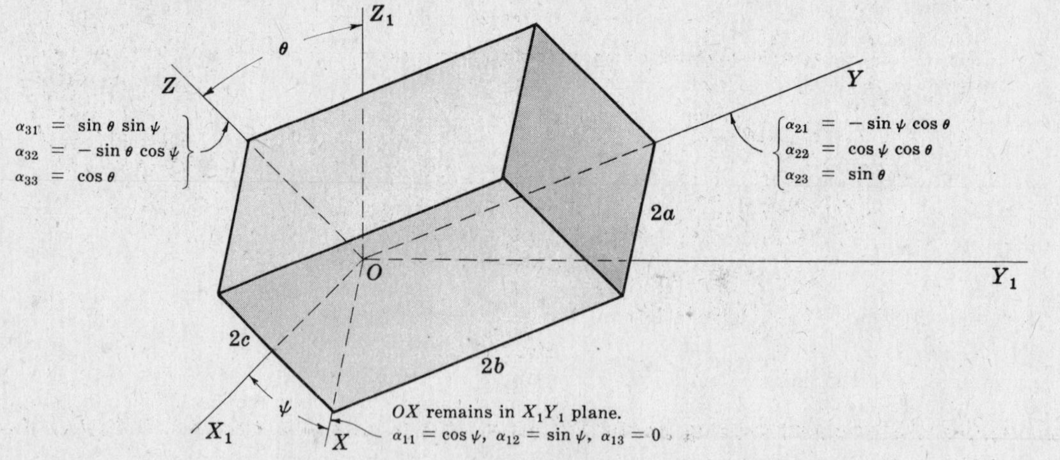

Fig. 7-10

Let us determine moments and products of inertia of the block relative to the X_1, Y_1, Z_1 frame.

With a box in hand as a model, the reader can readily show that direction cosines of X, Y, Z are as given on the diagram.

Applying (7.20) and using values of I_x, I_{xy}, etc., from Example 7.4, it follows that

$$I_{x_1} = \tfrac{4}{3}M[(b^2+c^2)\cos^2\psi + (a^2+c^2)\sin^2\psi\cos^2\theta + (a^2+b^2)\sin^2\psi\sin^2\theta + \tfrac{3}{2}ab\sin\psi\cos\psi\cos\theta - \tfrac{3}{2}ac\sin\psi\cos\psi\sin\theta + \tfrac{3}{2}bc\sin^2\psi\sin\theta\cos\theta]$$

$$I_{x_1y_1} = Mab(\cos^2\psi - \sin^2\psi)\cos\theta + Mac(\sin^2\psi - \cos^2\psi)\sin\theta + 2Mbc\sin\psi\cos\psi\sin\theta\cos\theta - \tfrac{4}{3}M(b^2+c^2)\sin\psi\cos\psi + \tfrac{4}{3}M(a^2+c^2)\sin\psi\cos\psi\cos^2\theta + \tfrac{4}{3}M(a^2+b^2)\sin\psi\cos\psi\sin^2\theta$$

Expressions for I_{y_1}, $I_{x_1z_1}$, etc., follow in the same way.

Note. Imagine that either or both of the angles θ, ψ are changing in some known manner with time. Then, of course, I_{x_1}, $I_{x_1y_1}$, etc., may be expressed as functions of time. The results of this example are very important in Chapter 8.

In this example it was assumed for simplicity that the OX axis remains in the X_1Y_1 plane. When this is not the case, the orientation of the X, Y, Z frame may be determined by three "Euler angles" θ, ϕ, ψ, the use of which is explained in detail in the following chapter.

7.8 "Foci" and "Spherical" Points of Inertia.

The following results are interesting and of practical importance. Let $\bar{X}^p, \bar{Y}^p, \bar{Z}^p$, Fig. 7-11, be principal axes through c.m. As previously shown, principal axes through any point on either $\bar{X}^p, \bar{Y}^p$, or $\bar{Z}^p$ are parallel to these axes. For the discussion which follows let it be assumed that $\bar{I}^p_x > \bar{I}^p_y > \bar{I}^p_z$.

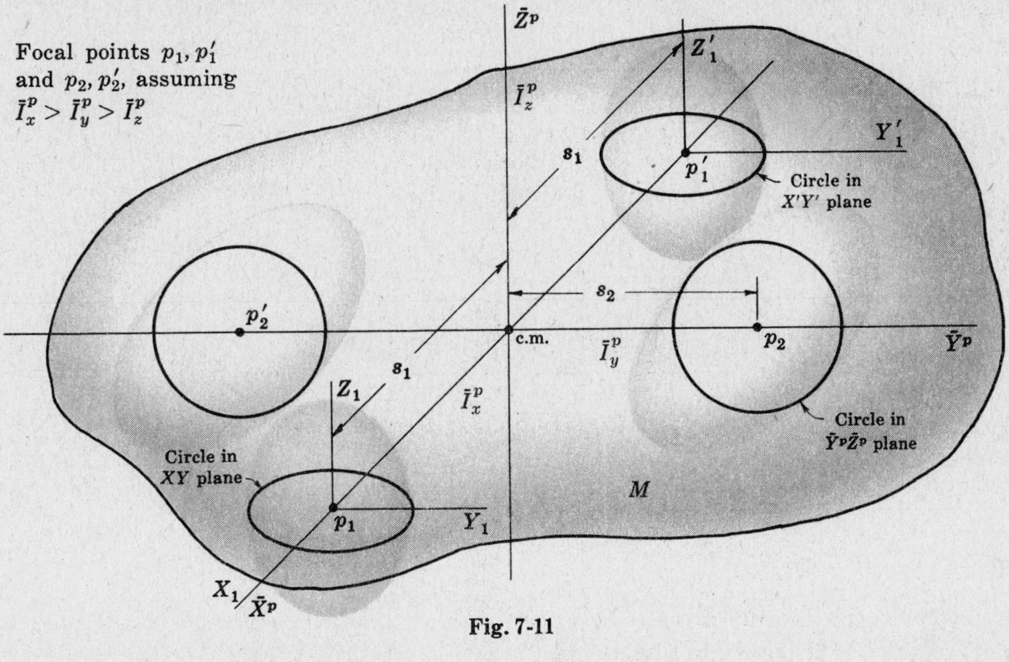

Fig. 7-11

(a) Consider ellipsoids of inertia about points p_1 and p'_1 at distances $s_1 = \pm[(\bar{I}^p_x - \bar{I}^p_y)/M]^{1/2}$ from the origin.

$$I_{x_1} = \bar{I}^p_x, \qquad I_{y_1} = \bar{I}^p_y + Ms_1^2 = \bar{I}^p_y + \bar{I}^p_x - \bar{I}^p_y = \bar{I}^p_x$$

Thus $I_{x_1} = I_{y_1}$; and since X_1, Y_1, Z_1 are principal axes through p_1, the ellipsoid about this point is one of revolution about Z_1. Thus a section of the ellipsoid in the X_1Y_1 plane is a circle. A similar statement holds for p'_1. p_1 and p'_1 are referred to as "foci of inertia". Show that another pair of focal points exist on $\bar{X}^p$. Determine focal points on $\bar{Y}^p$. Are there focal points on $\bar{Z}^p$?

(b) If $\bar{I}_y^p = \bar{I}_z^p$ and $\bar{I}_x^p > \bar{I}_y^p$, then at points p_1, p_1' on $\bar{X}^p$ at distances $s = \pm[(\bar{I}_x^p - \bar{I}_y^p)/M]^{1/2}$, $I_x = I_y = I_z = \bar{I}_x^p$. Hence the ellipsoid about either of these points is a sphere. p_1 and p_1' are here called "spherical points". If the ellipsoid about c.m. is one of revolution, do spherical points always exist? (Find spherical points near a thin uniform disk.)

Example 7.7.

Referring to Fig. 7-8 (see Example 7.4), assume for example that $a > b > c$. Thus $\bar{I}_z^p > \bar{I}_y^p > \bar{I}_x^p$.

(a) Selecting points p, p' on the $\bar{Z}^p$ axis at distances $s = \pm[(\bar{I}_z^p - \bar{I}_y^p)/M]^{1/2}$,

$$I_z = \bar{I}_z^p, \qquad I_y = \bar{I}_y^p + Ms^2 = \bar{I}_y^p + \bar{I}_z^p - \bar{I}_y^p = \bar{I}_z^p$$

Hence a section of the ellipsoid about p or p' in the YZ plane is a circle. Thus p and p' are focal points. The reader may find other such points.

(b) Suppose now that $b = c$ and $a < b$, that is, $\bar{I}_y^p = \bar{I}_z^p$, $\bar{I}_x^p > \bar{I}_y^p$. Selecting points on the $\bar{X}^p$ axis at distances $s = \pm[(\bar{I}_x^p - \bar{I}_y^p)/M]^{1/2}$,

$$I_x = \bar{I}_x^p, \qquad I_y = \bar{I}_y^p + \bar{I}_x^p - \bar{I}_y^p = \bar{I}_x^p, \qquad I_z = \bar{I}_z^p + \bar{I}_x^p - \bar{I}_y^p = \bar{I}_x^p$$

Hence $I_x = I_y = I_z = \bar{I}_x^p$ in this case, $s = \pm[\frac{1}{3}(b^2 - a^2)]^{1/2}$ and $I_x = \frac{2}{3}Mb^2$. Thus the moment of inertia of the block about *any line* through either point $= \frac{2}{3}Mb^2$.

7.9 Physical Significance of Products of Inertia.

Imagine the thin lamina, Fig. 7-12, rotating with constant angular velocity ω about the axis shown, in fixed bearings B_1 and B_2. Each particle of the lamina, as m', exerts a centrifugal force $f = m'\omega^2 r$ on the surrounding material. (Neglect gravity.)

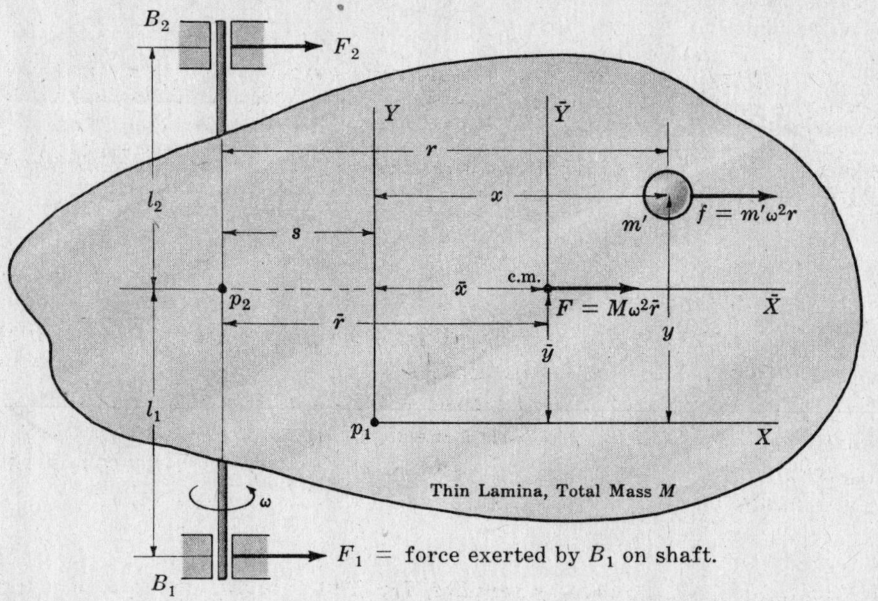

Fig. 7-12

An appreciation of the physical significance and importance of products of inertia may be obtained from a determination of the total moment τ_z of all centrifugal forces about the Z axis with origin of X, Y, Z at p_1. As can be seen from the diagram,

$$\tau_z = \sum m'\omega^2 ry = \sum m'\omega^2(x+s)y = \omega^2 \sum m'xy + \omega^2 s \sum m'y \qquad (1)$$

which for convenience we take as positive in a clockwise direction. Thus it is seen that

$$\tau_z = \omega^2 I_{xy} + \omega^2 sM\bar{y} \qquad (2)$$

But $I_{xy} = \bar{I}_{xy} + M\bar{x}\bar{y}$ ($\bar{I}_{xy}$ determined relative to $\bar{X}, \bar{Y}$), from which

$$\tau_z = \omega^2 \bar{I}_{xy} + (\omega^2 M\bar{r})\bar{y} \tag{3}$$

Now the total centrifugal force F due to all particles is $F = \sum m'\omega^2 r = M\omega^2\bar{r}$. Hence the second term of (3) is just $F\bar{y}$, with F regarded as acting at c.m.

Hence τ_z, the total clockwise moments of the centrifugal forces about Z, may be regarded as due to a couple $\omega^2 \bar{I}_{xy}$ acting in the plane of the lamina plus the moment $F\bar{y}$, F acting at c.m. Note that the location of p_1, the origin of X, Y, Z, does not affect the value of the couple. Thus the moment about *any axis normal to the lamina* can be written down at once. For example, about one through p_2, $\tau_2 = \omega^2 \bar{I}_{xy}$; through the center of B_1, $\tau_{B_1} = \omega^2 \bar{I}_{xy} + \omega^2 M\bar{r}l_1$, etc.

To find F_1, F_2, the forces exerted by the bearings on the shaft, we write, taking moments about the center of B_2,

$$F_1(l_1 + l_2) + M\omega^2\bar{r}l_2 - \bar{I}_{xy}\omega^2 = 0 \quad \text{or} \quad F_1 = \frac{\omega^2}{l_1 + l_2}(\bar{I}_{xy} - M\bar{r}l_2)$$

Likewise, $$F_2 = -\frac{\omega^2}{l_1 + l_2}(\bar{I}_{xy} + M\bar{r}l_1)$$

(Of course F_1 and F_2 can be found by writing $F_1 + F_2 + M\bar{r}\omega^2 = 0$ and taking moments about p_2.) If $\bar{X}, \bar{Y}$ are principal axes, $\bar{I}_{xy} = 0$ and F_1, F_2 are due only to the centrifugal force $M\omega^2\bar{r}$ acting at c.m. If, in addition to this, c.m. is on the axis of rotation, $F_1 = F_2 = 0$.

The above discussion will later be extended to a rigid body of any shape rotating in any manner. (See Example 9.7, Page 187; also Problem 9.17, Page 200.)

Example 7.8.

Suppose the triangle, Fig. 7-6, Page 125, is rotating with constant angular velocity ω about the Y axis in fixed bearings located at O and O_2, (distance between bearings $= b$). Find the bearing forces (gravity not considered).

From Example 7.2, $\bar{I}_{xy} = -\frac{1}{36}Mab$. Hence bearing force at O is $F_1 = (\omega^2/b)(\frac{2}{9}Mab + \frac{1}{36}Mab) = \frac{1}{4}\omega^2 Ma$ and at O_2 it is $F_2 = \frac{1}{12}\omega^2 Ma$.

7.10 Dynamically Equivalent Bodies.

Two or more bodies which are entirely different in appearance and in mass distributions may behave exactly the same dynamically when acted upon by equal forces applied in the same manner. This is clearly the case when their total masses are equal and the principal moments of inertia through their centers of mass are the same. Such bodies are said to be "equimomental". The general method of finding such bodies is illustrated by the following examples.

Example 7.9.

(*a*) Suppose that the pairs of equally massive particles, Fig. 7-13(1) below, are fastened to a rigid massless frame as indicated. X, Y, Z are obviously principal axes through c.m., and the ellipsoid of inertia about c.m. is seen to be

$$(2m_2b^2 + 2m_3c^2)x^2 + (2m_1a^2 + 2m_3c^2)y^2 + (2m_1a^2 + 2m_2b^2)z^2 = 1$$

Values of m_1, m_2, m_3 and the lengths a, b, c can be so chosen by the following procedure that the arrangement is equimomental to any given body.

Consider *any object* having principal moments of inertia $\bar{I}^p_x, \bar{I}^p_y, \bar{I}^p_z$ at c.m. and a total mass M. It is clear that if values of m_1, m_2, m_3 and a, b, c satisfy the relations $2(m_1 + m_2 + m_3) = M$, $\bar{I}^p_x = 2(m_2b^2 + m_3c^2)$, etc., the arrangement shown in the figure is dynamically equivalent to the body.

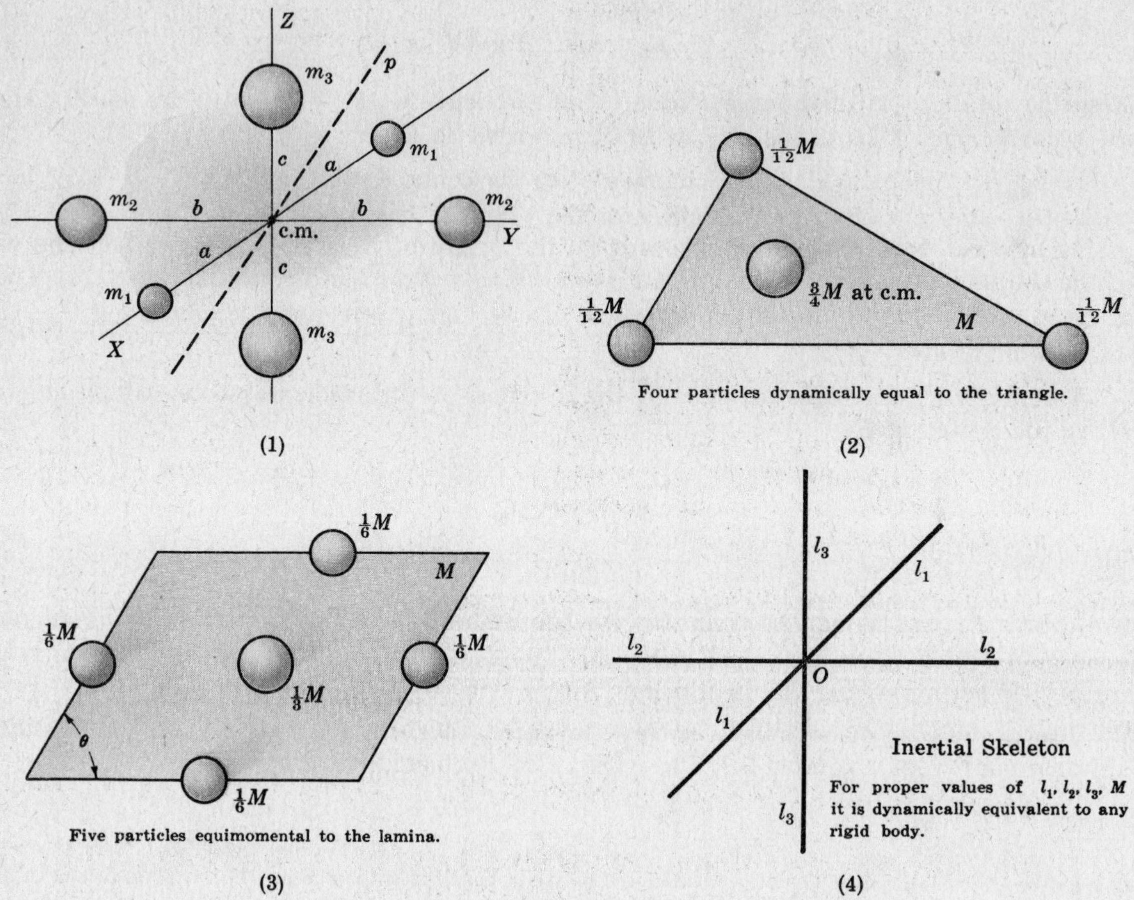

Fig. 7-13

An easy solution is obtained by setting $m_1 = m_2 = m_3 = M/6$ and solving for a, b, c. Here $a = [(3/2M)(\bar{I}_y^p + \bar{I}_z^p - \bar{I}_x^p)]^{1/2}$, etc.

(*b*) It may be shown that the four particles, Fig. 7-13(2), are equimomental to the thin uniform triangle. Also, the five particles of Fig. 7-13(3) are dynamically equal to the rectangle.

(*c*) An "inertial skeleton", Fig. 7-13(4), consisting of three mutually perpendicular slender rods rigidly fastened together at O, can always be found which is dynamically equivalent to any rigid body.

7.11 Experimental Determination of Moments and Products of Inertia.

The experimental determination of moments and products of inertia is easy, and with reasonable care results are quite accurate. For bodies of irregular shape this is the only practical way of finding these quantities.

If moments and products of inertia relative to axes with origin at c.m. are known, corresponding quantities relative to any other axes may readily be computed. Hence we outline briefly an experimental method of determining these center-of-mass values.

(*a*) Select any two or more points on the body. Suspend it by a cord, first from one and then from another of these points. Thus c.m. is, of course, located at the intersection of the lines of suspension. Hence three mutually perpendicular axes, $\bar{X}, \bar{Y}, \bar{Z}$, with origin at c.m. can then be chosen.

(b) Having done this, fasten the body in a supporting frame F of a torsion pendulum, Fig. 7-14, so that, say the $\bar{Z}$ axis, coincides with the axis of oscillation of the pendulum. With the aid of a good stop watch determine the period of oscillation P. As can easily be shown, $P = 2\pi\sqrt{(\bar{I}_z + I_f)/c}$ where $\bar{I}_z$ and I_f are moments of inertia of the body and frame respectively about the axis of oscillation and c the torsional constant due to the upper and lower piano wires. (Values of I_f and c can be determined using, in place of the body shown, say uniform rods the moments of inertia of which are known from dimensions and mass.) Thus $\bar{I}_z = P^2c/4\pi^2 - I_f$. In like manner $\bar{I}_x$ and $\bar{I}_y$ are found.

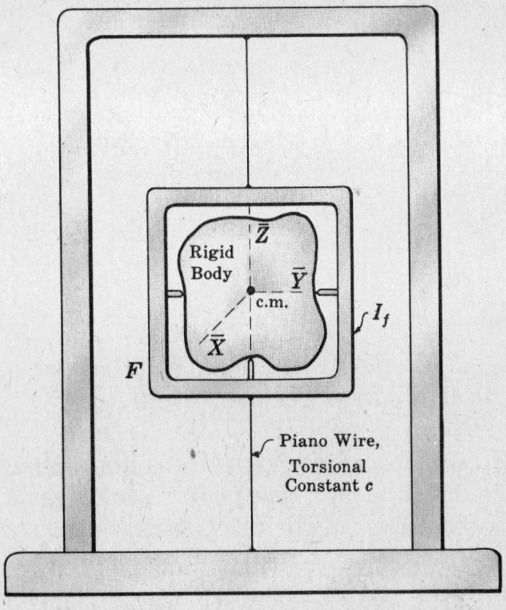

Fig. 7-14

(c) Now having selected three other axes Op_1, Op_2, Op_3 (passing through c.m.) whose direction cosines (l_1, m_1, n_1, etc.) are known, determine as before $I_{Op_1}, I_{Op_2}, I_{Op_3}$. But

$$I_{Op_1} = \bar{I}_x l_1^2 + \bar{I}_y m_1^2 + \bar{I}_z n_1^2 - 2\bar{I}_{xy} l_1 m_1 - 2\bar{I}_{xz} l_1 n_1 - 2\bar{I}_{yz} n_1 m_1 \quad \text{etc.}$$

Hence with previously determined values of $\bar{I}_x, \bar{I}_y, \bar{I}_z$ these equations can be solved for $\bar{I}_{xy}, \bar{I}_{xz}, \bar{I}_{yz}$.

If, as a matter of convenience, Op_1 is taken in the $\bar{X}\bar{Y}$ plane at 45° from either axis, $l_1 = m_1 = .707$, $n_1 = 0$. Hence $I_{Op_1} = .5(\bar{I}_x + \bar{I}_y) - \bar{I}_{xy}$ or finally $\bar{I}_{xy} = .5(\bar{I}_x + \bar{I}_y) - I_{Op_1}$. In like manner $\bar{I}_{xz}$ and $\bar{I}_{yz}$ are found.

7.12 Suggested Project on the Ellipsoid of Inertia.

This project and the following suggested experiment will give the reader confidence in the theory and a down-to-earth feeling of familiarity with the material covered in this chapter.

Two thin rectangular plyboards, of any convenient dimensions, are cut and rigidly glued together at right angles as indicated in Fig. 7-15. Assuming an area density of say 10 grams/cm², compute I_x, I_y, I_z for the "thin board" combination. Show that $I_{xy} = I_{xz} = I_{yz} = 0$ and hence that $\bar{X}, \bar{Y}, \bar{Z}$ are principal axes. Write an equation for the ellipsoid about c.m. In the relation $Is^2 = c$, choose c some convenient constant and draw to scale sections of the ellipsoid about c.m. in the XY and YZ planes and (on a cardboard insert) in the XZ plane. Measure the distance s from c.m. to any point on the ellipsoid and

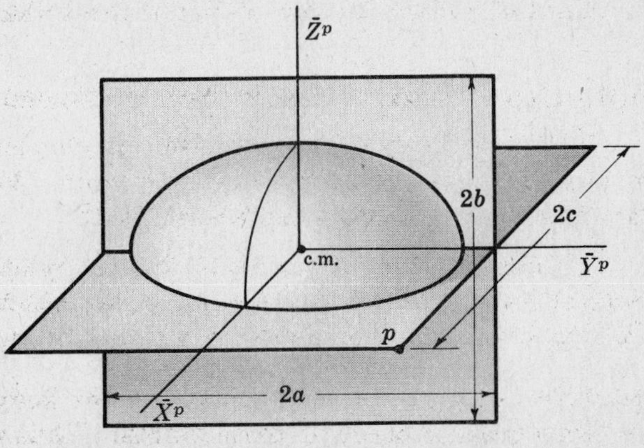

Fig. 7-15

compare c/s^2 with the computed value of I about this line of known direction.

What changes would be made in the ellipsoid if a particle of mass m were glued to the model at, say, point p? Sketch a section of the ellipsoid for this case.

7.13 Suggested Experiment.

Determination of the ellipsoid of inertia of a thin lamina.

The frame ab of the torsion pendulum, Fig. 7-16, consists of two flat metal strips separated by only a fraction of an inch. A thin lamina of any shape, cut from plyboard, is clamped between the strips with a bolt B passing horizontally through the strips and board at point p_1. The lamina can be set at any angular position relative to the axis of rotation by turning it around B.

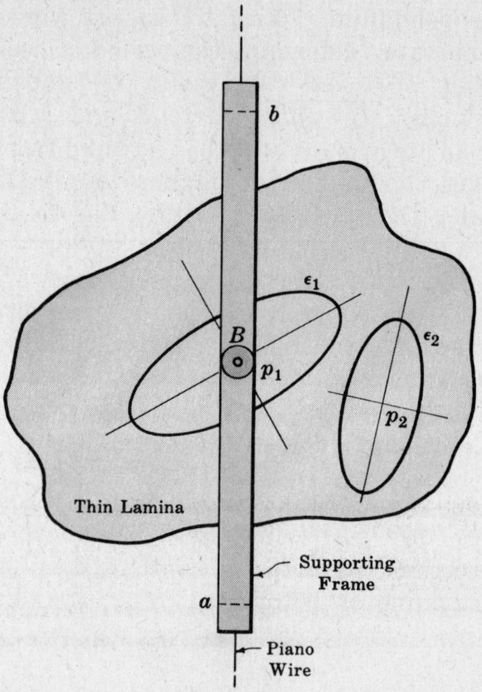

Fig. 7-16

Following the method outlined in Section 7.11, moments of inertia about several lines, all passing through the center of the bolt and spaced say 15° apart from 0 to 180°, are determined. With this data and the relation $Is^2 = c$, a section of the ellipsoid of inertia ϵ_1 can be plotted on the lamina. With reasonable care a surprisingly good ellipse is obtained.

Using the above data, compute and plot an ellipse ϵ_2 about some other point p_2. (This will be a bit less tedious if the first ellipse is about c.m.) Repeating the first experimental procedure with B passing through p_2, compare computed and experimental results.

This interesting and instructive experiment gives real meaning to "ellipsoid of inertia", "principal axes", etc. It never fails to make a lasting impression on the student who performs it.

Problems

7.1. (a) The line Oa, Fig. 7-17 below, makes an angle $\theta = 30°$ with $\bar{Z}$. Show that $I_{Oa} = \frac{7}{16}MR^2$.

(b) The coordinates of a point on a line Oa' (not shown) are $x = 5$, $y = 4$, $z = 6$ cm. Show that $I_{Oa'} = \frac{113}{308}MR^2$.

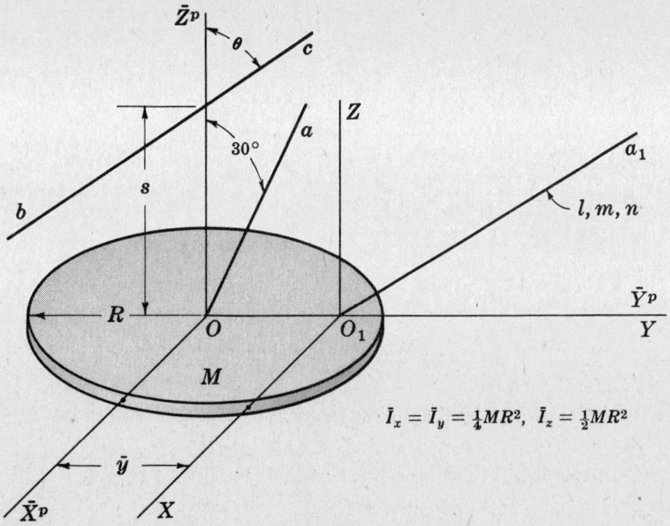

Fig. 7-17

7.2. (a) Obtain by integration expressions for I_x, I_y, I_z, I_{xy}, Fig. 7-6, Page 125.

(b) The coordinates of a point on line Oa are $x = 4,\ y = 5,\ z = 7$ cm. Show that

$$I_{Oa} = \frac{M}{6 \times 90}[16b^2 + 25a^2 + 49(a^2 + b^2) - 20ab]$$

7.3. Show that the moment of inertia of a body about any line Oa through the origin of coordinates is given by

$$I_{Oa} = (I_x x^2 + I_y y^2 + I_z z^2 - 2I_{xy}xy - 2I_{xz}xz - I_{yz}yz)(x^2 + y^2 + z^2)^{-1}$$

where x, y, z are coordinates of *any point* on Oa.

7.4. Show that the moment of inertia of the block, Fig. 7-8, Page 127, about the line Oa' is given by

$$I_{Oa'} = M[\tfrac{4}{3}(b^2 + c^2)x'^2 + \tfrac{4}{3}(a^2 + c^2)y'^2 + \tfrac{4}{3}(a^2 + b^2)(4c^2) - 2abx'y' - 4ac^2x' - 4bc^2y'][x'^2 + y'^2 + 4c^2]^{-1}$$

7.5. (a) A line Oa (not shown) passes through O, Fig. 7-9, making an angle θ with OZ. Show that

$$I_{Oa} = [\tfrac{1}{16}Mh^2 + \tfrac{3}{80}M(4r^2 + h^2)]\sin^2\theta + \tfrac{3}{10}Mr^2\cos^2\theta$$

(b) A line parallel to Oa passes through c.m. Show that the moment of inertia about this line is $\frac{3}{80}M(4r^2 + h^2)\sin^2\theta + \frac{3}{10}Mr^2\cos^2\theta$.

7.6. (a) A line bc, Fig. 7-17, makes an angle θ with $\bar{Z}^p$. Show that

$$I_{bc} = \tfrac{1}{2}Mr^2\cos\theta + (\tfrac{1}{4}MR^2 + Ms^2)\sin^2\theta$$

(b) Show that the moment of inertia about O_1a_1 is

$$I_{O_1a_1} = (\tfrac{1}{4}MR^2 + M\bar{y}^2)l^2 + (\tfrac{1}{4}MR^2)m^2 + (\tfrac{1}{2}MR^2 + M\bar{y}^2)n^2$$

7.7. Write an expression for the moment of inertia of the block, Fig. 7-8, Page 127, about a line having direction cosines l, m, n which passes through the point x_0, y_0, z_0. (l, m, n and x_0, y_0, z_0 are measured relative to $\bar{X}^p, \bar{Y}^p, \bar{Z}^p$.) The line does not necessarily pass through c.m.

7.8. Show that for any rigid body, the moment of inertia about any line passing through two points x_1, y_1, z_1 and x_2, y_2, z_2 measured relative to $\bar{X}, \bar{Y}, \bar{Z}$ (not necessarily principal axes) is

$$I = [\bar{I}_x + M(y_1^2 + z_1^2)]\left(\frac{x_2 - x_1}{s}\right)^2 + [\bar{I}_y + M(x_1^2 + z_1^2)]\left(\frac{y_2 - y_1}{s}\right)^2 + [\bar{I}_z + M(x_1^2 + y_1^2)]\left(\frac{z_2 - z_1}{s}\right)^2$$
$$- 2(\bar{I}_{xy} + Mx_1y_1)\frac{(x_2 - x_1)(y_2 - y_1)}{s^2} - 2(\bar{I}_{xz} + Mx_1z_1)\frac{(x_2 - x_1)(z_2 - z_1)}{s^2}$$
$$- 2(\bar{I}_{yz} + My_1z_1)\frac{(y_2 - y_1)(z_2 - z_1)}{s^2}$$

where $s^2 = (x_2 - x_1)^2 + (y_2 - y_1)^2 + (z_2 - z_1)^2$.

7.9. Write an expression for the ellipsoid of inertia about a point on the periphery of the disk, Fig. 7-17.

7.10. Write an expression for the ellipsoid of inertia about the point $p_1(x_0, y_0, z_0)$, Fig. 7-18.

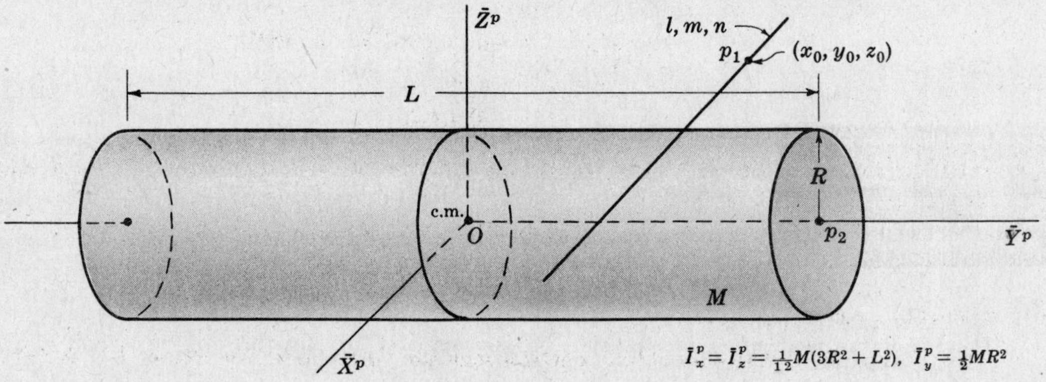

Fig. 7-18

7.11. Referring to Fig. 7-7, Page 126, show that the angle $\theta = 58°$.

7.12. For the block, Fig. 7-8, $M = 1000$ grams, $a = 3$ cm, $b = 5$ cm, $c = 5$ cm. Determine numerical values for the principal moments of inertia about the corner p_1. From equations (*7.10*), Page 119, determine two sets of direction cosines of the principal axes of the ellipsoid of inertia about p_1. Show that these sets are equivalent.

7.13. Considering a thin lamina of any shape, take reference axes X, Y, Z, with X, Y in its plane and the origin at any point p. I_x, I_y, I_z, I_{xy} are relative to these axes. Prove that the principal moments of inertia I_1^p, I_2^p, I_3^p about principal axes X^p, Y^p, Z^p respectively are given by

$$I_{1,2}^p = \tfrac{1}{2}[I_z \pm \sqrt{I_z^2 - 4(I_xI_y - I_{xy}^2)}], \qquad I_3^p = I_x + I_y$$

Show that Z^p (corresponding to I_3^p) is normal to the lamina and that the angle θ which X^p makes with X is given by

$$\tan\theta = \frac{I_{xy}}{I_y - I_1^p} \qquad \text{or} \qquad \tan\theta = \frac{I_x - I_1^p}{I_{xy}}$$

7.14. Refer to Fig. 7-5, Page 124. At a point p_1 where $x = 5$ cm, $y = 4$, $z = 0$ measured relative to X, Y, Z, compute the principal moments of inertia and find directions of principal axes.

7.15. Show that the ellipsoid of inertia about p_2, Fig. 7-18, is given by

$$1 = [\tfrac{1}{12}M(3R^2 + L^2) + \tfrac{1}{4}ML^2](x^2 + z^2) + (\tfrac{1}{2}MR^2)y^2$$

and that principal axes at p_2 are parallel to $\bar{X}^p, \bar{Y}^p, \bar{Z}^p$.

7.16. Show that the moment of inertia is the same about all axes passing through either O or p_1, Fig. 7-19; that is, p_1 and O are spherical points. Check this by the methods of Section 7.8.

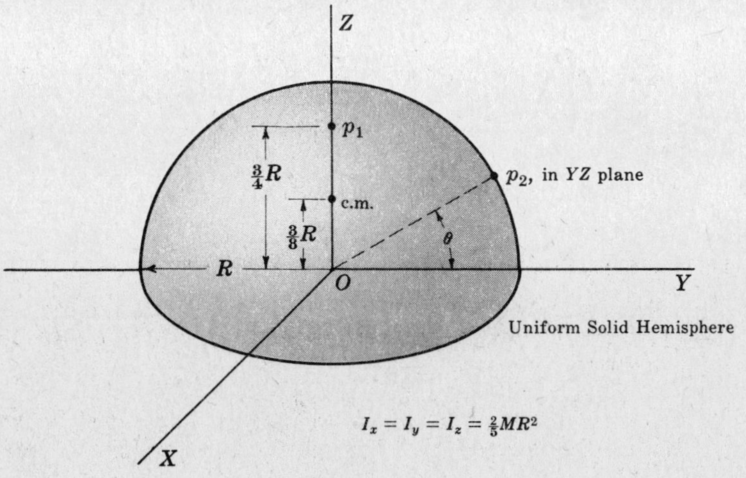

Fig. 7-19

7.17. Show that the moment of inertia about any line having direction cosines l, m, n and passing through p_2, Fig. 7-19, is given by

$$I = \tfrac{1}{20}MR^2[(24 - 15\sin\theta)l^2 + (4 + 20\sin^2\theta - 15\sin\theta)m^2 + (4 + 20\cos^2\theta)n^2 - 10(\sin\theta\cos\theta - \tfrac{3}{8}\cos\theta)mn]$$

7.18. Referring to Fig. 7-18, show that:

(a) for $L = R\sqrt{3}$, the ellipsoid of inertia about c.m. is a sphere for which $I = \frac{1}{2}MR^2$.

(b) for $R = L$ there are spherical points on the $\bar{Y}^p$ axis at points distant $\pm R/\sqrt{6}$ from the origin. Here $I = \frac{1}{2}MR^2$ about every axis through these points.

(c) for $L > R\sqrt{3}$, focal points exist on the $\bar{X}^p$ and $\bar{Z}^p$ axes at $s = \pm\sqrt{(\bar{I}_x - \bar{I}_y)/M}$.

(d) for L very small, spherical points exist on $\bar{Y}^p$ at distances $\pm\frac{1}{2}R$ from the origin. Do spherical or focal points exist on $\bar{Z}^p$?

7.19. Consider any line parallel to the principal axis $\bar{Z}^p$ through c.m. of any rigid body. Prove that it is a principal axis of an ellipsoid drawn about the point where it pierces the "principal plane" $\bar{X}^p\,\bar{Y}^p$. Show that, where ϕ = angle between X^p and $\bar{X}^p$,

$$\tan 2\phi = \frac{2M\bar{x}\bar{y}}{(\bar{I}_y^p + M\bar{x}^2) - (\bar{I}_x^p + M\bar{y}^2)}$$

The same general results are true, of course, for lines normal to the $\bar{X}^p\,\bar{Z}^p$ and $\bar{Y}^p\,\bar{Z}^p$ planes.

7.20. Consider a rectangular lamina, dimensions $2a \times 2b$, mass M. Draw $\bar{X}^p, \bar{Y}^p, \bar{Z}^p$ axes through c.m. with $\bar{X}^p$ parallel to a and $\bar{Z}^p$ perpendicular to the surface.

Consider another frame $\bar{X}_1, \bar{Y}_1, \bar{Z}_1$ through c.m. with $\bar{Z}^p$ and $\bar{Z}_1$ collinear but $\bar{X}_1$ along a diagonal of the rectangle. $\bar{I}_x^p = \frac{1}{3}Mb^2$, $\bar{I}_y^p = \frac{1}{3}Ma^2$. Show that

$$\bar{I}_{x_1} = \tfrac{2}{3}M\left(\frac{a^2b^2}{a^2+b^2}\right), \quad \bar{I}_{y_1} = \tfrac{1}{3}M\left(\frac{a^4+b^4}{a^2+b^2}\right), \quad \bar{I}_{z_1} = \tfrac{1}{3}M(a^2+b^2), \quad \bar{I}_{x_1y_1} = \tfrac{1}{3}Mab\left(\frac{b^2-a^2}{a^2+b^2}\right)$$

7.21. For the triangular lamina, Fig. 7-20 below, values of $\bar{I}_{x_1}$, etc., are as given on the drawing. Prove that:

$$\bar{I}_{x_2} = \bar{I}_{x_1}\cos^2\theta + \bar{I}_{y_1}\sin^2\theta - 2\bar{I}_{x_1y_1}\sin\theta\cos\theta$$

$$\bar{I}_{y_2} = \bar{I}_{x_1}\sin^2\theta + \bar{I}_{y_1}\cos^2\theta + 2\bar{I}_{x_1y_1}\sin\theta\cos\theta$$

$$\bar{I}_{x_2y_2} = \bar{I}_{x_1y_1}(\cos^2\theta - \sin^2\theta) + (\bar{I}_{x_1} - \bar{I}_{y_1})\sin\theta\cos\theta$$

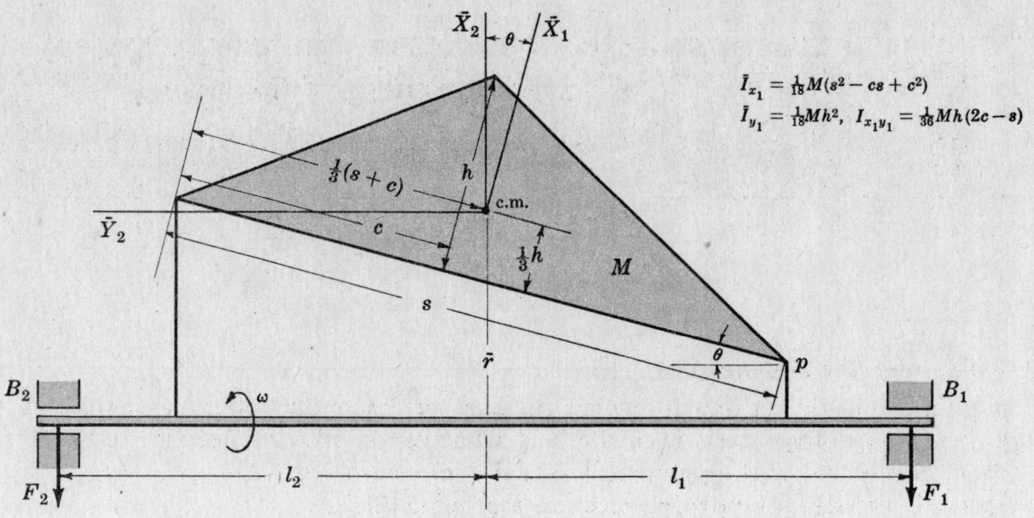

Fig. 7-20

7.22. The triangular lamina, Fig. 7-20, is rotating with constant angular velocity ω about the axis shown, in fixed bearings B_1 and B_2. Show that the couple due to centrifugal forces is

$$C = \omega^2[\tfrac{1}{36}Mh(2c - s)\cos 2\theta + \tfrac{1}{18}M(s^2 - cs + c^2 - h^2)\sin\theta\cos\theta]$$

Determine the bearing forces F_1 and F_2, neglecting gravity.

7.23. (*a*) Prove that the four particles, Fig. 7-13(2), are equimomental to the uniform triangle.

(*b*) Design a skeleton of inertia which is equimomental to the hemisphere, Fig. 7-19.

7.24. Imagine the rigid body of Fig. 8-16, Page 156, replaced by the cone, Fig. 7-9, Page 128. The apex is fixed at the origin O, otherwise the cone can move in any manner about this point. X, Y, Z are fixed to the cone with Z along its axis. Show that I_{x_1}, the moment of inertia of the cone about the fixed X_1 axis, is given by

$$I_{x_1} = \tfrac{3}{20}M[r^2 + h^2 - (4h^2 - r^2)\sin^2\theta\sin^2\psi]$$

Test this for $\theta = 0$, $\psi = 0$, and for $\theta = \psi = 90°$. Write an expression for $I_{x_1y_1}$. (See Section 8.8, Page 157. Note that direction cosines of X, Y, Z relative to X_1, Y_1, Z_1 in terms of Euler angles, are listed in Table 8.2, Page 158.)

The student should realize that, regardless of how the cone may be spinning and swinging about O, the above expressions are true for any position. If the motion were known, I_{x_1}, $I_{x_1y_1}$, etc., could then be written as functions of time.

7.25. For a more general case than the above, suppose the X, Y, Z axes, Fig. 8-16, Page 156, are principal axes through O for a body of any general shape similar to the one shown. Corresponding moments of inertia are I_x^p, I_y^p, I_z^p.

Show that moments and products of inertia relative to the fixed X_1, Y_1, Z_1 axes are given by $I_{x_1} = I_x^p(\cos\phi\cos\psi - \sin\phi\sin\psi\cos\theta)^2 + I_y^p(\sin\phi\cos\psi + \cos\phi\sin\psi\cos\theta)^2 + I_z^p\sin^2\theta\sin^2\psi$, etc.

CHAPTER

8

Lagrangian Treatment of Rigid Body Dynamics

Rigid Body Dynamics: Part II

8.1 Preliminary Remarks.

A "rigid body" is one in which no part of its mass undergoes a change in position relative to any other part, regardless of what forces may be acting. Strictly speaking no such object exists, but in practice there is of course an extensive field of dynamics for which this greatly simplifying assumption is justifiable.

Basically no difference exists between rigid-body and particle dynamics since any rigid body may be regarded as a very large number of particles constrained to remain at fixed distances one with respect to the other. The primary reason for treating rigid-body dynamics as a separate phase of the general subject is that certain special techniques are required for writing appropriate expressions for T.

In setting up equations of motion, one of the following two methods is usually employed.

(*a*) *The Lagrangian Method* (treated in this chapter) in which, after writing a suitable expression for T, Lagrange's equations are applied in the usual way.

(*b*) *The Euler Method* (treated in the next chapter) in which the *Euler equations* for translation and rotation of the body are applied directly without considering T.

Whether one method is more suitable than the other depends somewhat on the problem in hand but, in general, the Lagrangian has many advantages: simplicity, ease of writing equations of motion, elimination of forces of constraint, readily applicable in any suitable coordinates and for any number of rigid bodies.

A mastery of the basic principles and techniques of rigid-body dynamics requires a clear understanding of (*a*) the background material covered in Section 8.2, (*b*) the derivation of T given in Section 8.3 and (*c*) the many examples given throughout. (*a*), (*b*), (*c*) are by no means independent units. A full appreciation of (*a*) requires an understanding of (*b*) and (*c*), etc. Hence considerable rereading, with close attention to detail, is required.

8.2 Necessary Background Material.

A. *Angular velocity as a vector quantity.*

Referring to Fig. 8-1 let us assume that the body, fixed at O, is free to turn in any manner about this point. All quantities here considered will be regarded as measured relative to X, Y, Z. Hence whether this frame is inertial or not is of no concern at the moment. Let it be assumed that, at some given instant, the body has an angular velocity ω about some line Oa. As a result of this the particle m has a linear velocity $\mathbf{v}$ normal to the Oam' plane and of magnitude $v = \omega h$ where h is the normal distance from m' to the axis of rotation Oa.

We shall now show that angular velocity may be regarded as a vector $\boldsymbol{\omega}$ directed along Oa and of magnitude equal to its absolute value. That is, $\boldsymbol{\omega}$ can be replaced by X, Y, Z components $\omega_x, \omega_y, \omega_z$ and treated in all respects as a vector. As will soon be evident, this is of paramount importance in the treatment of rigid-body dynamics.

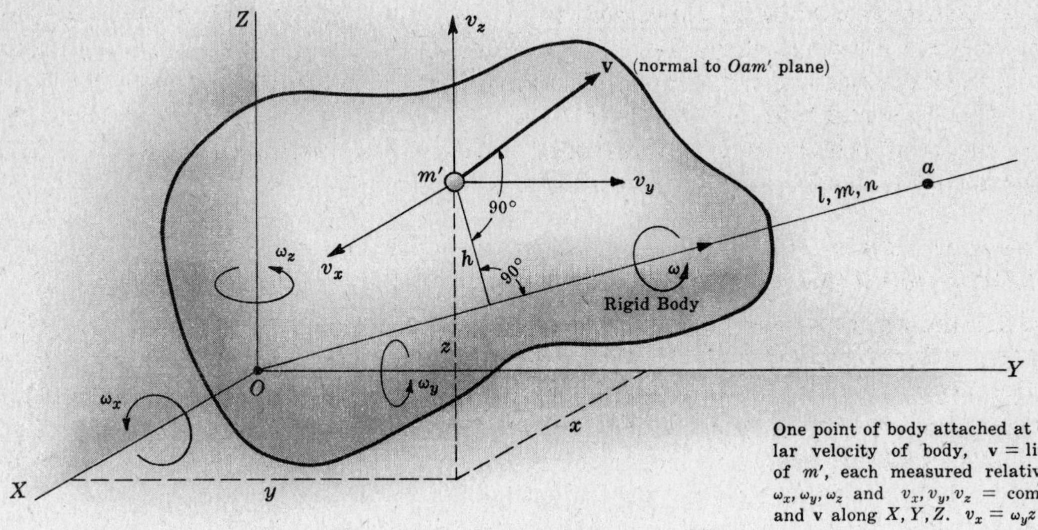

One point of body attached at O. ω = angular velocity of body, v = linear velocity of m', each measured relative to X, Y, Z. $\omega_x, \omega_y, \omega_z$ and v_x, v_y, v_z = components of ω and v along X, Y, Z. $v_x = \omega_y z - \omega_z y$, etc.

Fig. 8-1

X, Y, Z components of **v** may be written as follows,

$$v_x = v\alpha_1 = \omega h\alpha_1, \quad v_y = \omega h\alpha_2, \quad v_z = \omega h\alpha_3 \tag{1}$$

where $\alpha_1, \alpha_2, \alpha_3$ are direction cosines of **v** (direction cosines of a line normal to the Oam' plane) which, as the reader can show (see Problem 8.1), are

$$\alpha_1 = (mz - ny)/h, \quad \alpha_2 = (nx - lz)/h, \quad \alpha_3 = (ly - mx)/h \tag{8.0}$$

where x, y, z are coordinates of m', and l, m, n are direction cosines of Oa. Thus from (*1*),

$$v_x = m\omega z - n\omega y, \quad \text{etc.} \tag{2}$$

Hence, regarding ω as a vector along Oa, $n\omega$ is its component ω_y on Y. Likewise $n\omega = \omega_z$, etc., and so we write

$$v_x = \omega_y z - \omega_z y, \quad v_y = \omega_z x - \omega_x z, \quad v_z = \omega_x y - \omega_y x \tag{8.1}$$

Correct expressions v_x, v_y, v_z (and thus **v**) are therefore obtained by treating angular velocity as a vector $\boldsymbol{\omega}$ along Oa, the sense of which is determined by the right-hand screw rule. (In vector notation relations (*8.1*) are equivalent to $\mathbf{v} = \boldsymbol{\omega} \times \mathbf{r}$. See Chapter 18.)

Relations (*8.1*) may be given a clear physical and geometrical interpretation as follows. As can be seen from the figure, a rotational speed of ω_x about X gives m' a linear velocity $\omega_x z$ in the negative direction of Y. Likewise $\omega_z x$ is a velocity in the positive direction. Hence $v_y = \omega_z x - \omega_x z$, etc.

As a result of the above it follows that:

(*a*) Any number of angular velocities as $\boldsymbol{\omega}_1, \boldsymbol{\omega}_2, \boldsymbol{\omega}_3$ about axes through O can be added vectorially to give a resultant $\boldsymbol{\omega} = \boldsymbol{\omega}_1 + \boldsymbol{\omega}_2 + \boldsymbol{\omega}_3$ having magnitude $\omega = (\omega_x^2 + \omega_y^2 + \omega_z^2)^{1/2}$ and direction determined by the cosines ω_x/ω, etc., where $\omega_x = \omega_{1x} + \omega_{2x} + \omega_{3x}$, etc. (For another proof of this see Problem 8.2, Page 167.)

(*b*) The component of $\boldsymbol{\omega}$ along any line Ob (not shown) is given by

$$\omega_{Ob} = \omega_x l + \omega_y m + \omega_z n \tag{8.2}$$

where, in this case, l, m, n are direction cosines of Ob.

Note that velocities cannot be expressed as $\omega_x = \dot{\theta}_1$, $\omega_y = \dot{\theta}_2$, $\omega_z = \dot{\theta}_3$ where $\theta_1, \theta_2, \theta_3$ represent finite angular rotations about X, Y, Z respectively. The final orientation of a body, as a result of such rotations, is not unique. It depends on the order in which the rotations are made. (The reader should try this with a box.) Nevertheless, $\omega_x, \omega_y, \omega_z$ can easily be expressed in terms of suitable "true coordinates" as, for example, Euler angles and their time derivatives. Various examples illustrating this will soon be given.

B. *Inertial-space velocity of m', Fig. 8-2. Body translating and rotating. X, Y, Z frame rotating about O relative to body.*

In Fig. 8-2 the body is assumed to be rotating and translating through space. The X, Y, Z frame, with origin attached to the body at O, may be rotating in any manner relative to the body. The X', Y', Z' axes with origin also fastened to O, remain parallel to the inertial X_1, Y_1, Z_1 axes. x, y, z and x', y', z' are coordinates of m' with respect to X, Y, Z and X', Y', Z' respectively.

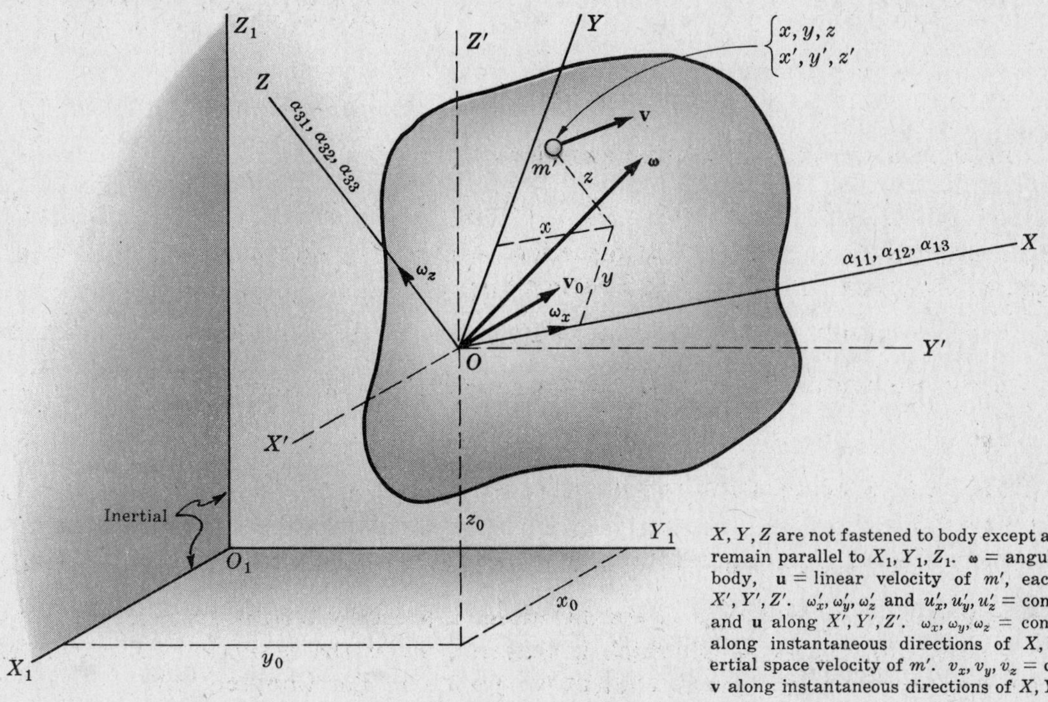

X, Y, Z are not fastened to body except at O. X', Y', Z' remain parallel to X_1, Y_1, Z_1. **ω** = angular velocity of body, **u** = linear velocity of m', each relative to X', Y', Z'. $\omega'_x, \omega'_y, \omega'_z$ and u'_x, u'_y, u'_z = components of **ω** and **u** along X', Y', Z'. $\omega_x, \omega_y, \omega_z$ = components of **ω** along instantaneous directions of X, Y, Z. **v** = inertial space velocity of m'. v_x, v_y, v_z = components of **v** along instantaneous directions of X, Y, Z.

Fig. 8-2

Let **ω** be the angular velocity of the body and **u** the linear velocity of m', *each measured relative to X', Y', Z'*. Components of **ω** and **u** along these axes are indicated by $\omega'_x, \omega'_y, \omega'_z$ and u'_x, u'_y, u'_z respectively. Then following (*8.1*) above, we have $u'_x = \omega'_y z' - \omega'_z y'$, etc. Letting u_x, u_y, u_z be components of **u** along instantaneous positions of X, Y, Z, we can write $u_x = u'_x\alpha_{11} + u'_y\alpha_{12} + u'_z\alpha_{13}$, etc., where $\alpha_{11}, \alpha_{12}, \alpha_{13}$ are direction cosines of X relative to X', Y', Z' (the same as with respect to X_1, Y_1, Z_1). Thus

$$u_x = (\omega'_y z' - \omega'_z y')\alpha_{11} + (\omega'_z x' - \omega'_x z')\alpha_{12} + (\omega'_x y' - \omega'_y x')\alpha_{13}$$

Eliminating x', y', z' by $x' = x\alpha_{11} + y\alpha_{21} + z\alpha_{31}$, etc., it follows at once (details left to reader; see Appendix) that

$$u_x = \omega_y z - \omega_z y \qquad \text{where} \quad \omega_y = \omega'_x\alpha_{21} + \omega'_y\alpha_{22} + \omega'_z\alpha_{23}$$

But this is just the component of **ω** along Y. Likewise ω_z is the component of **ω** along Z, etc.

Now assuming that O has an inertial-space velocity $\mathbf{v}_0$ with components v_{0x}, v_{0y}, v_{0z} along the instantaneous directions of X, Y, Z, components v_x, v_y, v_z of the inertial space velocity of m' along these same axes can be expressed as

$$v_x = v_{0x} + \omega_y z - \omega_z y, \qquad v_y = v_{0y} + \omega_z x - \omega_x z, \qquad v_z = v_{0z} + \omega_x y - \omega_y x \tag{8.3}$$

C. *Summary of important points regarding (8.3).*

The full meaning and importance of these relations can be made clear by a consideration of the following statements together with a study of examples to follow.

(*a*) As assumed in the derivation of (*8.3*), the origin O must be attached to some point (any point) of the body.

(*b*) As is evident from the derivation, relations (*8.3*) are valid even though the X, Y, Z frame (origin fixed at O) may rotate relative to the body. Of course this frame may be "body-fixed" (rigidly attached so that it has all motions of the body). In the first case x, y, z are variable and in the second they are constant. In practice, body-fixed axes are almost always employed.

(*c*) v_{0x}, v_{0y}, v_{0z} must be so expressed (examples will demonstrate how this may be done) as to give components of $\mathbf{v}_0$, the inertial-space velocity of O, Fig. 8-2, *along instantaneous directions of X, Y, Z.*

(*d*) For a given location of O, v_{0x}, v_{0y}, v_{0z} are the same regardless of what particle may be considered (regardless of the values of x, y, z). Hence $\mathbf{v}_0$ *represents a linear velocity of the body as a whole.*

(*e*) The magnitude and direction of $\mathbf{v}_0$ will, in general, depend on the location of O. For example, imagine a body fixed in space at one point p. With O taken at p, $v_{0x} = v_{0y} = v_{0z} = 0$. But this is not true for any other location of O.

(*f*) Keeping in mind dynamical problems to follow, $\boldsymbol{\omega}$ the total angular velocity of the body *is always measured relative to an inertial frame,* or what is the same thing, relative to non-rotating axes as X', Y', Z', Fig. 8-2.

(*g*) $\omega_x, \omega_y, \omega_z$ must be so expressed as to give components of $\boldsymbol{\omega}$ *along the instantaneous directions of X, Y, Z.* (See Examples.)

(*h*) Regardless of the location of O in the body, $\boldsymbol{\omega}$ has the same magnitude and direction. But as is evident from the derivation of (*8.3*), whatever the location of O, $\boldsymbol{\omega}$ *is always regarded as directed* along some line Oa passing through O. This means that this vector can be shifted, without change in magnitude or direction, from any origin to any other origin in the body. See Problem 8.3, Page 168.)

(*i*) As the body moves through space under the action of forces, $\boldsymbol{\omega}$ and $\mathbf{v}_0$ will in general change in magnitude and direction. Moreover, their directions are not fixed relative to the body.

(*j*) Equations (*8.3*) form the basis for writing a general expression for the kinetic energy of a rigid body. See Section 8.3.

D. *Components of the inertial space velocity of a free particle along instantaneous directions of moving axes.*

Relations (*8.4*) below, though quite useful in certain particle problems, are not required for our immediate purpose. However, this is the most suitable place for their derivation.

Referring to Fig. 8-3 below, regard X_1, Y_1, Z_1 as inertial. Assume that the X, Y, Z frame is translating and rotating in any manner (fastened to the deck of a boat which is rolling, pitching, yawing and moving forward, for example). Let $\boldsymbol{\Omega}$ indicate the angular

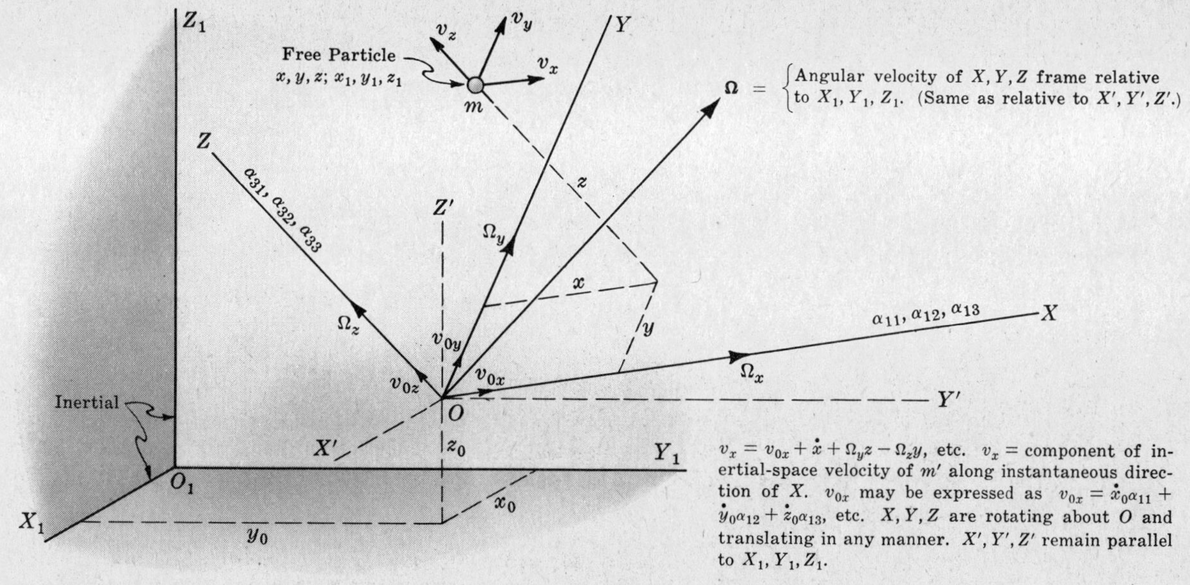

Fig. 8-3

velocity of the X, Y, Z frame, measured relative to X_1, Y_1, Z_1 (or to X', Y', Z') and having components $\Omega_x, \Omega_y, \Omega_z$ along *instantaneous directions* of X, Y, Z. Take $\mathbf{v}_0$ as the inertial space velocity of O with components v_{0x}, v_{0y}, v_{0z} along X, Y, Z. The free particle (not one of a rigid body) has coordinates x_1, y_1, z_1 and x, y, z relative to X_1, Y_1, Z_1 and X, Y, Z respectively. Let $\mathbf{v}$ indicate the inertial-space velocity of m' with components v_x, v_y, v_z *along instantaneous positions of* X, Y, Z. We shall now obtain, in a descriptive yet meaningful manner, expressions for v_x, v_y, v_z.

First suppose that m' is fixed to the X, Y, Z frame at some point $p(x, y, z)$. Then by equations (*8.3*), $v_x = v_{0x} + \Omega_y z - \Omega_z y$, etc. But now regarding m' as free with velocity components $\dot{x}, \dot{y}, \dot{z}$ *relative to* X, Y, Z ($\dot{x}, \dot{y}, \dot{z}$ are measured by an observer riding the X, Y, Z frame), the above expression for v_x and corresponding ones for v_y and v_z may be written as

$$v_x = v_{0x} + \dot{x} + \Omega_y z - \Omega_z y, \qquad v_y = v_{0y} + \dot{y} + \Omega_z x - \Omega_x z, \qquad v_z = v_{0z} + \dot{z} + \Omega_x y - \Omega_y x \qquad (8.4)$$

A straightforward but somewhat tedious derivation of (*8.4*) may be given as suggested in Problem 8.9, Page 169. See Examples 8.2, Page 145.

E. *Examples illustrating the treatment of angular velocity of a body and linear velocity of a typical particle.*

Example 8.1.

The frame supporting the rigid body, Fig. 8-4 below, can rotate about a vertical shaft AO_1 with angular velocity $\dot{\psi}$. At the same time the body can rotate about a shaft, supported in bearings B_1, B_2, with an angular velocity $\dot{\phi}$. This axis makes a constant angle θ with the vertical. ψ is measured as shown and ϕ is measured from line ab (see auxiliary drawing) which remains horizontal and in the plane of the section shown.

The total angular velocity $\boldsymbol{\omega}$ of the body is obviously the vector sum of $\dot{\boldsymbol{\psi}}$ and $\dot{\boldsymbol{\phi}}$ regardless of where reference axes X, Y, Z may be taken. We shall now consider components of $\boldsymbol{\omega}$ and the linear velocity of a typical particle for various locations of the X, Y, Z frame.

(*a*) Let us take body-fixed axes X, Y, Z as shown, with origin O at the intersection of the vertical AO_1 line and the B_1B_2 axis. $\dot{\boldsymbol{\phi}}$ as a vector is drawn along Z, and $\dot{\boldsymbol{\psi}}$ along the vertical line AO. X, Y, Z components of $\boldsymbol{\omega}$ (which for this position of X, Y, Z we label $\omega_{ax}, \omega_{ay}, \omega_{az}$) are obtained by taking components of $\dot{\boldsymbol{\psi}}$ and $\dot{\boldsymbol{\phi}}$ along X, Y, Z. Thus

$$\omega_{ax} = \dot{\psi} \sin\theta \sin\phi, \qquad \omega_{ay} = \dot{\psi} \sin\theta \cos\phi, \qquad \omega_{az} = \dot{\phi} + \dot{\psi}\cos\theta \qquad (1)$$

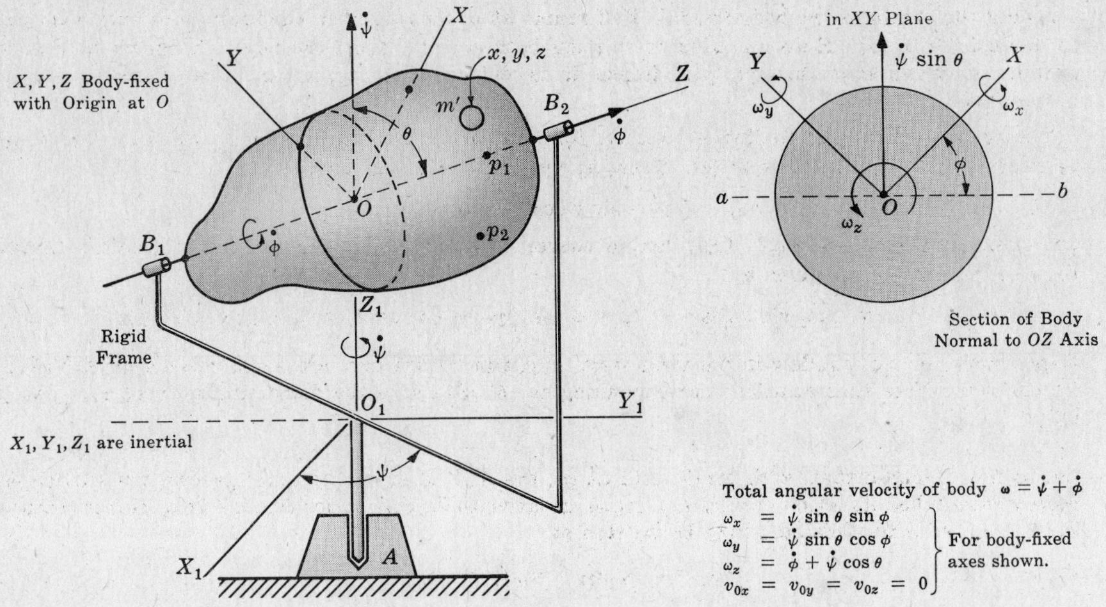

Fig. 8-4

Note that these components are along the "instantaneous" positions of X, Y, Z. That is, relations (*1*) are so expressed as to give $\omega_{ax}, \omega_{ay}, \omega_{az}$ for any position X, Y, Z (assumed body-fixed as mentioned above) can have relative to the X_1, Y_1, Z_1 frame.

With O located as stated above, $\mathbf{v}_0$, the inertial space velocity of O, is zero. Then $v_{0x} = v_{0y} = v_{0z} = 0$. Hence components of the inertial-space velocity of m' *along instantaneous directions of* X, Y, Z *are* [see expressions (*8.3*)]

$$\begin{aligned} v_x &= \dot{\psi}z \sin\theta \cos\phi - (\dot{\phi} + \dot{\psi} \cos\theta)y \\ v_y &= (\dot{\phi} + \dot{\psi}\cos\theta)x - \dot{\psi}z \sin\theta \sin\phi \\ v_z &= \dot{\psi}y \sin\theta \sin\phi - \dot{\psi}x \sin\theta \cos\phi \end{aligned} \qquad (2)$$

where x, y, z are coordinates of m'.

(*b*) Now suppose that the origin of X, Y, Z is taken at p_1, each axis remaining parallel to its first position. The total angular velocity is of course unchanged. Shifting $\dot{\psi}$ to a vertical line through p_1 and taking components of $\dot{\psi}$ and $\dot{\phi}$, we obtain (since the frame is parallel to its original position) exactly expressions (*1*) again.

But in this case $v_0 = \dot{\psi}l \sin\theta$ (l = distance Op_1), which is directed along line Ob in the auxiliary drawing. Hence components of the inertial-space velocity of p_1 (the new origin) along instantaneous directions of X, Y, Z are

$$v_{0x} = \dot{\psi}l \sin\theta \cos\phi, \qquad v_{0y} = -\dot{\psi}l \sin\theta \sin\phi, \qquad v_{0z} = 0 \qquad (3)$$

(Note that (*3*) can be obtained directly from (*2*) by setting $z = l$, $x = y = 0$. This technique is important in many problems.) Hence components of the inertial-space velocity of m' along axes in the new position are

$$\begin{aligned} v_x &= \dot{\psi}l \sin\theta \cos\phi + [\dot{\psi}z \sin\theta \cos\phi - (\dot{\phi} + \dot{\psi}\cos\theta)y] \\ v_y &= -\dot{\phi}l \sin\theta \sin\phi + [(\dot{\phi} + \dot{\psi}\cos\theta)x - \dot{\psi}z \sin\theta \sin\phi] \\ v_z &= \dot{\psi}y \sin\theta \sin\phi - \dot{\psi}x \sin\theta \cos\phi \end{aligned} \qquad (4)$$

where x, y, z are measured relative to X, Y, Z in the new position. The reader can show at once that (*2*) and (*4*) give just the same values.

It is important to realize the full meaning of v_x, v_y, v_z. Imagine that an observer located on the base A measures the velocity $\mathbf{v}$ of m' relative to X_1, Y_1, Z_1. Then v_x, v_y, v_z as given by (*4*) are components of $\mathbf{v}$ along the body-fixed axes X, Y, Z respectively in the position they occupy at the instant the observer takes the measurement.

(c) Consider the origin of the body-fixed X, Y, Z frame at p_2 (any point in the body) with each axis parallel to its position in (a). Here we think of shifting both $\dot{\psi}$ and $\dot{\phi}$ from the positions shown in Fig. 8-4 to parallel lines passing through p_2. Hence it is evident that $\omega_{cx}, \omega_{cy}, \omega_{cz}$ are equal to $\omega_{ax}, \omega_{ay}, \omega_{az}$ respectively.

A convenient way of finding v_{0x}, v_{0y}, v_{0z} for this case is as follows. Let x_2, y_2, z_2 be coordinates of p_2 relative to X, Y, Z in position (a). Then, applying (2), v_{0x} is given by

$$v_{0x} = \dot{\psi} z_2 \sin\theta \cos\phi - (\dot{\phi} + \dot{\psi}\cos\theta) y_2$$

and similarly for v_{0y} and v_{0z}. (They can, of course, be obtained from proper transformation equations.) Hence v_x for case (c) is given by

$$v_x = \dot{\psi} z_2 \sin\theta \cos\phi - (\dot{\phi} + \dot{\psi}\cos\theta) y_2 + [\dot{\psi} z \sin\theta\cos\phi - (\dot{\phi} + \dot{\psi}\cos\theta) y] \tag{5}$$

Expressions for v_y, v_z follow in the same way. x, y, z in (5) are here measured relative to X, Y, Z in the (c) position. Note that relations corresponding to (5) also give the same values of v_x, v_y, v_z as given by (2).

(d) Let us now suppose that, with origin still at p_2, the X, Y, Z frame has any general orientation in the body where X has direction cosines $\alpha_{11}, \alpha_{12}, \alpha_{13}$ relative to X, Y, Z in position (a), etc. Hence components $\omega_{dx}, \omega_{dy}, \omega_{dz}$ of $\boldsymbol{\omega}$ for this case may be written as

$$\omega_{dx} = \omega_{ax}\alpha_{11} + \omega_{ay}\alpha_{12} + \omega_{az}\alpha_{13}, \quad \text{etc.} \tag{6}$$

Letting u_{0x}, u_{0y}, u_{0z} be components of the inertial-space velocity of p_2 along instantaneous positions of X, Y, Z, u_{0x} may be expressed as

$$u_{0x} = v_{0x}\alpha_{11} + v_{0y}\alpha_{12} + v_{0z}\alpha_{13}, \quad \text{etc.} \tag{7}$$

From (6) and (7), X, Y, Z components u_x, u_y, u_z of the inertial-space velocity of m' may be written out at once. Note that for any specific orientation of the frame in (d) relative to X, Y, Z in (a), values of $\alpha_{11}, \alpha_{12}, \alpha_{13}$, etc., are known. The above is well worth careful study.

(e) Consider stationary axes X', Y', Z' parallel to X_1, Y_1, Z_1 respectively with origin at O. Components of $\boldsymbol{\omega}$ along these axes are seen to be

$$\omega'_x = \dot{\phi}\sin\theta\cos\psi, \quad \omega'_y = \dot{\phi}\sin\theta\sin\phi, \quad \omega'_z = \dot{\psi} + \dot{\phi}\cos\theta \tag{8}$$

Here $\mathbf{v}_0 = 0$. Hence components of the inertial-space velocity of m' along these fixed axes are $v'_x = \dot{\phi} z' \sin\theta\sin\phi - (\dot{\psi} + \dot{\phi}\cos\theta) y'$, etc., where x', y', z' are the X', Y', Z' coordinates of m'. As the body moves, x', y', z' change in value.

Note. Considering the inertial X_1, Y_1, Z_1 axes shown, components of $\boldsymbol{\omega}$ along these are just those given by (8) and O_1 is at rest. Are the X_1, Y_1, Z_1 components of the inertial-space velocity of m' given by $v_{1x} = \dot{\phi} x_1 \sin\theta\sin\phi - (\dot{\psi} + \dot{\phi}\cos\theta) y_1$, etc., where x_1, y_1, z_1 are the X_1, Y_1, Z_1 coordinates of m'? See Section 8.2C(a), Page 142.

Example 8.2.

The disk D, Fig. 8-5 below, is free to rotate about the shaft bc with angular velocity $\dot{\phi}$ where ϕ is measured relative to the shaft as indicated by pointer p_2. At the same time ab can rotate with angular velocity $\dot{\psi}$ where ψ is taken as the angle between the fixed X_1Z_1 plane and the rotating abc plane.

The total angular velocity $\boldsymbol{\omega}$ of D is the vector sum of $\dot{\boldsymbol{\phi}}$ and $\dot{\boldsymbol{\psi}}$. Shifting $\dot{\boldsymbol{\psi}}$ to O and taking components along the body-fixed X, Y, Z axes, it is seen that, just as in Example 8.1,

$$\omega_x = \dot{\psi}\sin\theta\sin\phi, \quad \omega_y = \dot{\psi}\sin\theta\cos\phi, \quad \omega_z = \dot{\phi} + \dot{\psi}\cos\theta \tag{1}$$

Similarly, components $\omega_{1x}, \omega_{1y}, \omega_{1z}$ along the fixed axes are

$$\omega_{1x} = \dot{\phi}\sin\theta\cos\psi, \quad \omega_{1y} = \dot{\phi}\sin\theta\sin\psi, \quad \omega_{1z} = \dot{\psi} + \dot{\phi}\cos\theta \tag{2}$$

The magnitude of the total angular velocity of D is given by

$$\omega = (\omega_x^2 + \omega_y^2 + \omega_z^2)^{1/2} = (\omega_{1x}^2 + \omega_{1y}^2 + \omega_{1z}^2)^{1/2} = (\dot{\phi}^2 + \dot{\psi}^2 + 2\dot{\phi}\dot{\psi}\cos\theta)^{1/2} \tag{3}$$

The direction of $\boldsymbol{\omega}$ relative to the moving X, Y, Z axes is determined by the direction cosines l, m, n where

$$l = \frac{\dot{\psi}\sin\theta\sin\phi}{(\dot{\phi}^2 + \dot{\psi}^2 + 2\dot{\phi}\dot{\psi}\cos\theta)^{1/2}}, \quad \text{etc.} \tag{8.5}$$

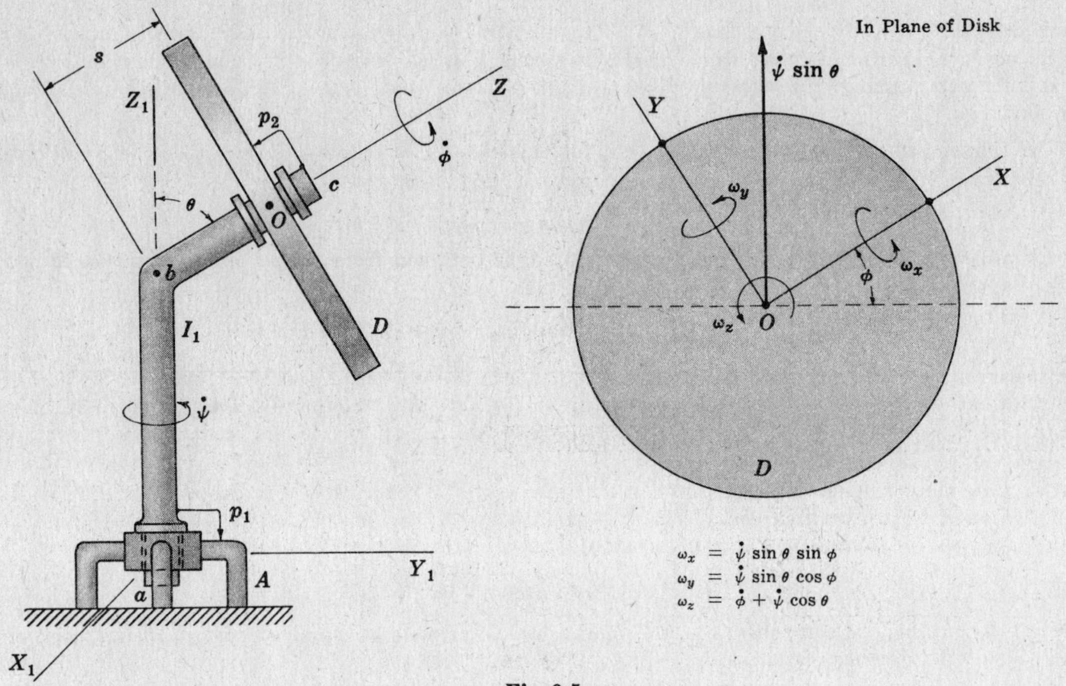

Fig. 8-5

Likewise, direction cosines l_1, m_1, n_1 of $\boldsymbol{\omega}$ relative to $X_1 Y_1 Z_1$ are

$$l_1 = \frac{\dot\phi \sin\theta \cos\psi}{(\dot\phi^2 + \dot\psi^2 + 2\dot\phi\dot\psi \cos\theta)^{1/2}}, \quad \text{etc.}$$

X, Y, Z components of the linear inertial-space velocity of a typical particle in D are found exactly as in Example 8.1(*b*).

As an illustration of the use of equations (*8.4*), Page 143, suppose that the motion of a free particle (not a part of D) of mass m and acted on by an external force $\mathbf{f}$ is to be found relative to the X, Y, Z axes in Fig. 8-5. Applying (*8.4*) it is seen that (see expressions (*4*), Example 8.1) the component v_x of the inertial-space velocity of m in the direction of X is given by

$$v_x = \dot x + \dot\psi s \sin\theta \cos\phi + [\dot\psi z \sin\theta \cos\phi - y(\dot\phi + \dot\psi \cos\theta)]$$

with similar expressions for v_y and v_z. Then applying Lagrange's equations to $T = \frac{1}{2}m(v_x^2 + v_y^2 + v_z^2)$ gives the desired equations of motion.

Example 8.3.

Referring to Fig. 8-6, the disks D_1, D_2, D_3 are mounted, one on the other, as shown. Angles $\theta_1, \theta_2, \theta_3$ are measured relative to A, B, C respectively as indicated by pointers p_1, p_2, p_3. $\dot{\boldsymbol\theta}_1, \dot{\boldsymbol\theta}_2, \dot{\boldsymbol\theta}_3$ regarded as vector quantities are indicated by appropriate arrows. Let us fix attention on D_3. Shifting $\dot{\boldsymbol\theta}_1$ and $\dot{\boldsymbol\theta}_2$ to the origin O as shown, the total angular velocity $\boldsymbol\omega$ of D_3 is the vector sum $\boldsymbol\omega = \dot{\boldsymbol\theta}_1 + \dot{\boldsymbol\theta}_2 + \dot{\boldsymbol\theta}_3$, and the reader can show at once that components of $\boldsymbol\omega$ along the body-fixed X, Y, Z axes (see auxiliary drawing to the right) are

$$\omega_x = (\dot\theta_1 \cos\alpha + \dot\theta_2 \cos\beta) \sin\theta_3, \quad \omega_y = (\dot\theta_1 \cos\alpha + \dot\theta_2 \cos\beta) \cos\theta_3, \quad \omega_z = \dot\theta_3 + \dot\theta_1 \sin\alpha + \dot\theta_2 \sin\beta \qquad (1)$$

Considering a typical particle m' in D with coordinates x, y, z relative to X, Y, Z, components of the inertial-space velocity of m' along these axes are $v_x = v_{0x} + \omega_y z - \omega_z y$, etc., where v_{0x}, v_{0y}, v_{0z} are of course the X, Y, Z components of the inertial-space velocity of O. Expressions for v_{0x}, etc., are in this case somewhat involved but can be found without great difficulty. See Problem 8.12(*c*), Page 169.

Components of $\boldsymbol\omega$ along the space-fixed X_1, Y_1, Z_1 axes are seen to be

$$\omega_{1x} = [\dot\theta_2 \sin(\beta - \alpha) + \dot\theta_3 \cos\alpha] \cos\theta_1, \quad \omega_{1y} = [\dot\theta_2 \sin(\beta - \alpha) + \dot\theta_3 \cos\alpha] \sin\theta_1,$$
$$\omega_{1z} = \dot\theta_1 + \dot\theta_2 \cos(\beta - \alpha) + \dot\theta_3 \sin\alpha \qquad (2)$$

The magnitude and direction of $\boldsymbol\omega$ can be found exactly as in Example 8.2.

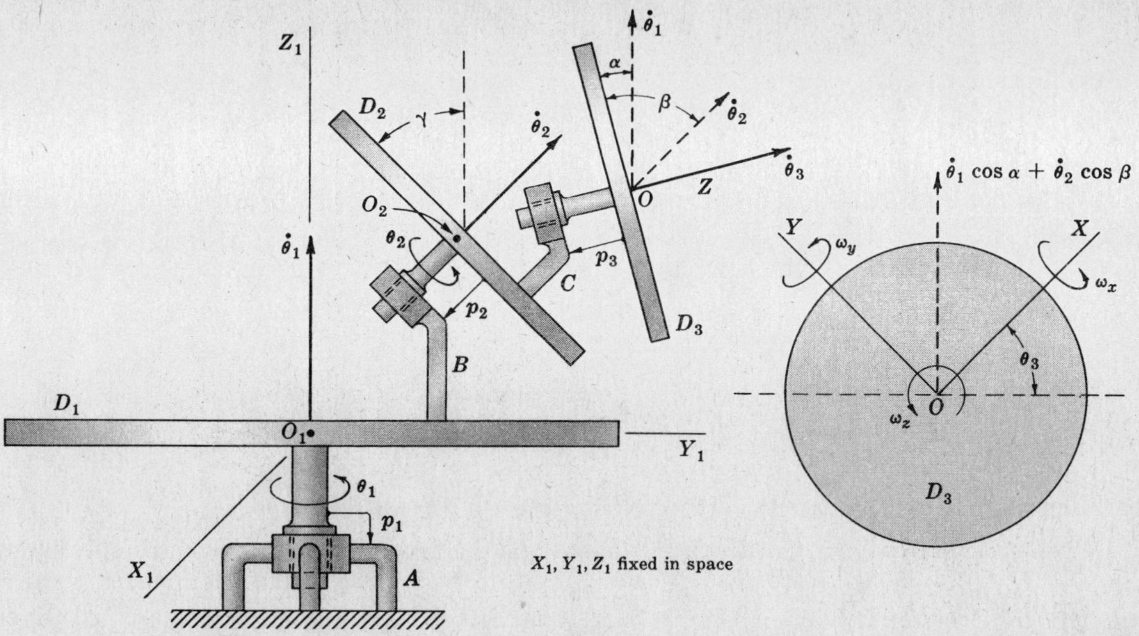

Fig. 8-6

As further exercises in the treatment of angular velocity, the reader may check expressions for $\omega_x, \omega_y, \omega_z$ given in Example 8.13, Page 155, or equations (*8.11*), Page 157.

F. *Torque as a vector quantity.*

To show the vector nature of torque we may proceed as follows. Suppose a force $\mathbf{F}(f_x, f_y, f_z)$ is acting on the body, Fig. 8-7, at the point $p(x, y, z)$. The torque τ exerted by this force about any line Oa having direction cosines l, m, n and which we assume passes through the origin, is defined as $\tau = F'h$ where h is the normal distance from p to the Oa line and F' is the component of $\mathbf{F}$ normal to the Oap plane. But $F' = f_x\alpha_1 + f_y\alpha_2 + f_z\alpha_3$ where $\alpha_1, \alpha_2, \alpha_3$ are direction cosines of the above mentioned normal and are given by (*8.0*), Page 140. Eliminating F', introducing expressions for the α's and summing over all forces acting on the body, we get for the total torque about Oa,

$$\tau_{Oa} = l\sum(f_z y - f_y z) + m\sum(f_x z - f_z x) + n\sum(f_y x - f_x y) \tag{8.6}$$

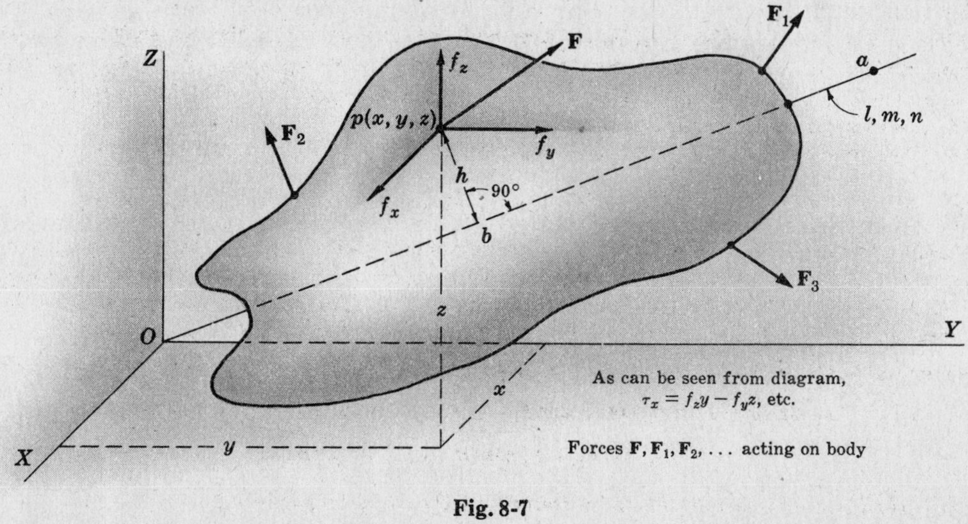

Fig. 8-7

But from the original definition of torque (or by a direct inspection of Fig. 8-7) it is seen that $\sum(f_z y - f_y z)$ is the torque exerted by all forces about X, etc. That is,

$$\tau_x = \sum(f_z y - f_y z), \quad \tau_y = \sum(f_x z - f_z x), \quad \tau_z = \sum(f_y x - f_x y) \tag{8.7}$$

Hence we can write
$$\tau_{Oa} = \tau_x l + \tau_y m + \tau_z n \tag{8.8}$$

from which it is seen that τ_{Oa} is the component of a vector $\boldsymbol{\tau}$ having components τ_x, τ_y, τ_z expressed as in (8.7). The magnitude of $\boldsymbol{\tau}$ is given by $\tau = (\tau_x^2 + \tau_y^2 + \tau_z^2)^{1/2}$ and its direction by τ_x/τ, etc. It must be remembered that in (8.7) x, y, z are coordinates of the points of application of the forces. Note that the above treatment of torque is in vector notation equivalent to

$$\boldsymbol{\tau} = \sum \mathbf{r}\times\mathbf{F} = \mathbf{i}\sum(f_z y - f_y z) + \mathbf{j}\sum(f_x z - f_z x) + \mathbf{k}\sum(f_y x - f_x y)$$

See Chapter 18.

8.3 General Expression for the Kinetic Energy of a Free Rigid Body.

When interpreted as in Section 8.2C, equations (8.3) express the X, Y, Z components of the inertial space velocity of any particle in a rigid body, Fig. 8-2. Hence a general expression for T is obtained by inserting these relations in $T = \frac{1}{2}\sum m'(v_x^2 + v_y^2 + v_z^2)$. On collecting terms,

$$\begin{aligned} T = {} & \tfrac{1}{2}M(v_{0x}^2 + v_{0y}^2 + v_{0z}^2) + \tfrac{1}{2}\omega_x^2 \sum m'(y^2 + z^2) + \tfrac{1}{2}\omega_y^2 \sum m'(x^2 + y^2) \\ & + \tfrac{1}{2}\omega_z^2 \sum m'(x^2 + y^2) - \omega_x\omega_y \sum m'xy - \omega_x\omega_z \sum m'xz - \omega_y\omega_z \sum m'yz \\ & + v_{0x}\left(\omega_y \sum m'z - \omega_z \sum m'y\right) + v_{0y}\left(\omega_z \sum m'x - \omega_x \sum m'z\right) \\ & + v_{0z}\left(\omega_x \sum m'y - \omega_y \sum m'x\right) \end{aligned} \tag{8.9}$$

which obviously takes the following form,

$$\begin{aligned} T = {} & \tfrac{1}{2}Mv_0^2 + \tfrac{1}{2}[I_x\omega_x^2 + I_y\omega_y^2 + I_z\omega_z^2 - 2I_{xy}\omega_x\omega_y - 2I_{xz}\omega_x\omega_z - 2I_{yz}\omega_y\omega_z] \\ & + M[v_{0x}(\omega_y\bar{z} - \omega_z\bar{y}) + v_{0y}(\omega_z\bar{x} - \omega_x\bar{z}) + v_{0z}(\omega_x\bar{y} - \omega_y\bar{x})] \end{aligned} \tag{8.10}$$

General Expression for Kinetic Energy of Rigid Body.

8.4 Summary of Important Considerations Regarding T.

(a) As previously stated, $\boldsymbol{\omega}$ is the angular velocity of the body *relative to inertial space* and $\mathbf{v}_0$ the linear inertial-space velocity of O. $\omega_x, \omega_y, \omega_z$ and v_{0x}, v_{0y}, v_{0z} are components of $\boldsymbol{\omega}$ and $\mathbf{v}_0$ respectively *along instantaneous directions of* X, Y, Z. They must be written in terms of specific coordinates. As examples will show, it is not difficult to express these quantities so as to meet the above requirements regardless of the orientation of X, Y, Z. I_x, I_{xy}, etc., and $\bar{x}, \bar{y}, \bar{z}$ must be determined with respect to X, Y, Z. (Fig. 8-2, Page 141.)

(b) With ω_x, I_x, v_{0x}, etc., determined as stated above, expression (8.10) is valid for X, Y, Z *either body-fixed or rotating about O in any manner relative to the body.* This includes the case for which X, Y, Z may be fixed in direction. But remember that O is assumed attached to the body.

(c) For the case in which the X, Y, Z frame may rotate relative to the body, x, y, z in (8.9) are of course variable. Hence I_x, I_{xy}, etc., as well as $\bar{x}, \bar{y}, \bar{z}$ vary with the motion. As would be expected, this introduces complexities. However, if we wish to use such a frame (which is rarely the case) the difficulties are not insurmountable. See Section 8.9, Example 8.19, Page 162.

(*d*) Regarding X, Y, Z as body-fixed, I_x, I_{xy}, etc., and $\bar{x}, \bar{y}, \bar{z}$ are constant. Hence body-fixed axes are almost always employed. But in any case statements made under (*a*) must be kept in mind. See Problems 7.24 and 7.25, Page 138.

(*e*) Under certain conditions, which are frequently but not always convenient to meet, (*8.10*) can be greatly simplified. For O at center of mass, $\bar{x} = \bar{y} = \bar{z} = 0$ and the last term of T becomes zero. Note that this is true even though X, Y, Z are not rigidly fastened (except at O) to the body. If *any point* in the body is fixed relative to an inertial frame and O is located at this point, $v_{0x} = v_{0y} = v_{0z} = 0$ and both the first and last terms are zero. If, for example O is at center of mass and body-fixed X, Y, Z axes are taken along principal axes of inertia,

$$T = \tfrac{1}{2}Mv^2_{\text{c.m.}} + \tfrac{1}{2}(\bar{I}^p_x\omega^2_x + \bar{I}^p_y\omega^2_y + \bar{I}^p_z\omega^2_z)$$

where $\bar{I}^p_x$, $\bar{I}^p_y$ and $\bar{I}^p_z$ are constants.

(*f*) It may seem to the reader that the simple basic principle of kinetic energy is completely lost sight of in the formidable relation (*8.10*). However, it is evident from the derivation of (*8.9*) that basically T as given by (*8.10*) is just $\frac{1}{2}\sum m'v'^2$.

8.5 Setting Up Equations of Motion.

As previously stated, once T [relation (*8.10*)] has been expressed in the proper number of suitable coordinates, *equations of motion of a rigid body are obtained in the usual way by an application of Lagrange's equations.* The same may be said for a system of bodies.

Of course, there may be constraints. When this is the case superfluous coordinates must be eliminated from T exactly as in previous chapters. (We are here assuming holonomic systems. See Section 9.12, Page 193.) A free rigid body has six degrees of freedom. Hence for b bodies, $n = 6b -$ (degrees of constraint). See Section 2.4, Page 18.

Generalized forces present no difficulties. They have the same meaning as in particle dynamics, and the basic procedure for obtaining expressions for F_{q_r} are exactly those described in Section 4.5, Page 61.

The following examples of degrees of freedom (d.f.) should be of help.

Single body completely free, d.f. = 6; one point constrained to move on a plane, d.f. = 5; two points confined to a plane, d.f. = 4; one point fixed in space, d.f. = 3; any three non-collinear points confined to a plane, d.f. = 3; the gyroscope, Fig. 8-18, d.f. = 3; Fig. 8-12, assuming disk free to slide along ab, d.f. = 3; disk, Fig. 8-12, fixed to shaft, d.f. = 2; disk, Fig. 8-13, rolls without slipping on rough X_1Y_1 plane, ball joint at p, d.f. = 1; any two points in rigid body fixed in space, d.f. = 1; rigid body pendulum, Fig. 8-19, r const., d.f. = 5; entire system, Fig. 8-14, block B free to slide on X_1Y_1 plane, d.f. = 5; entire system, Fig. 8-15, block A free to slide on X_1Y_1 plane, d.f. = 6; masses of Fig. 8-20, d.f. = 9; two bodies connected with springs in any manner and free to move in space, d.f. = 12. It should be remembered that forces of any type, other than those of constraint, do not change the number of degrees of freedom.

Note. In the treatment of rigid bodies, one may encounter difficulties in visualizing all angles and motion in space. The solution to this problem is a simple model.

8.6 Examples Illustrating Kinetic Energy and Equations of Motion.

In the following group of examples *body-fixed axes have been employed throughout.* This is in general the most convenient procedure. The use of "direction-fixed" axes will be illustrated in Section 8.9, Page 161.

Example 8.4.

Three views of a physical pendulum, consisting of a lamina pivoted at p and free to swing in a vertical plane through angle θ, are shown in Fig. 8-8. A consideration of expressions for T, choosing axes fixed to the lamina at the three locations shown, will help in understanding (*8.10*).

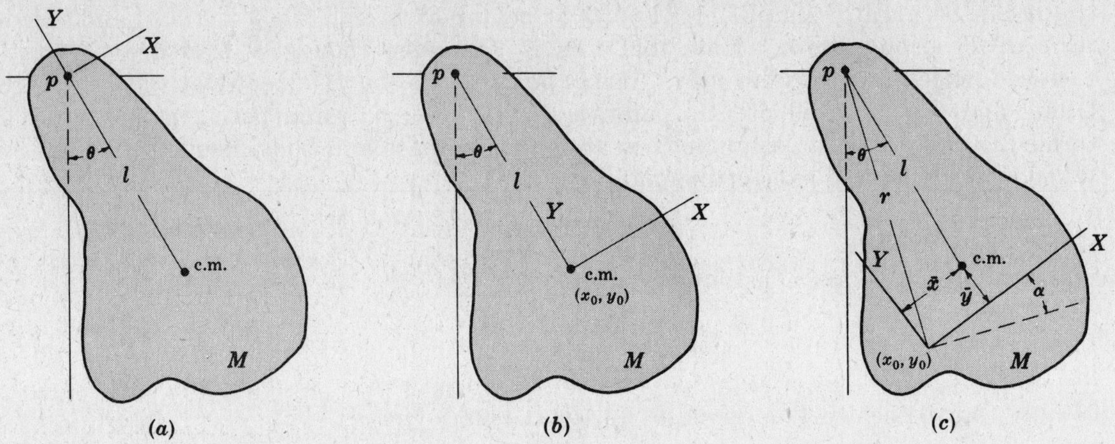

Fig. 8-8

(1) Assuming axes X, Y, Z located as in (*a*), where Z is normal to the paper, it is seen that $\omega_x = \omega_y = 0$, $\omega_z = \dot{\theta}$. Since the origin is stationary, $v_{0x} = v_{0y} = v_{0z} = 0$. Hence (*8.10*) reduces to $T = \frac{1}{2}I_z\dot{\theta}^2$ as is to be expected from elementary considerations.

(2) In (*b*) the origin is at c.m. Again $\omega_x = \omega_y = 0$, $\omega_z = \dot{\theta}$. Here $v_{0x} = l\dot{\theta}$, $v_{0y} = v_{0z} = 0$, $\bar{x} = \bar{y} = \bar{z} = 0$. Hence $T = \frac{1}{2}Ml^2\dot{\theta}^2 + \frac{1}{2}\bar{I}_z\dot{\theta}^2$.

(3) In (*c*) the axes are oriented in a more general way. As above, $\omega_x = \omega_y = 0$, $\omega_z = \dot{\theta}$. But $v_{0x} = r\dot{\theta}\cos\alpha$, $v_{0y} = -r\dot{\theta}\sin\alpha$, $v_{0z} = 0$ and $\bar{x}, \bar{y}$ have the values indicated. Hence

$$T = \tfrac{1}{2}Mr^2\dot{\theta}^2 + \tfrac{1}{2}I_z\dot{\theta}^2 - Mr\dot{\theta}^2(\bar{x}\sin\alpha + \bar{y}\cos\alpha)$$

where I_z is now about Z in the position here considered.

The reader should show that expressions for T in (2) and (3) reduce to the expression in (1). Note that I_z appearing in (1), (2), (3) is different in each case.

The equation of motion is found by applying the Lagrangian equation to either of the above forms of T. In each case $F_\theta = -Mgl\sin\theta$.

Example 8.5.

The lamina, Fig. 8-9, is free to move in the X_1Y_1 plane under known forces F_1, F_2.

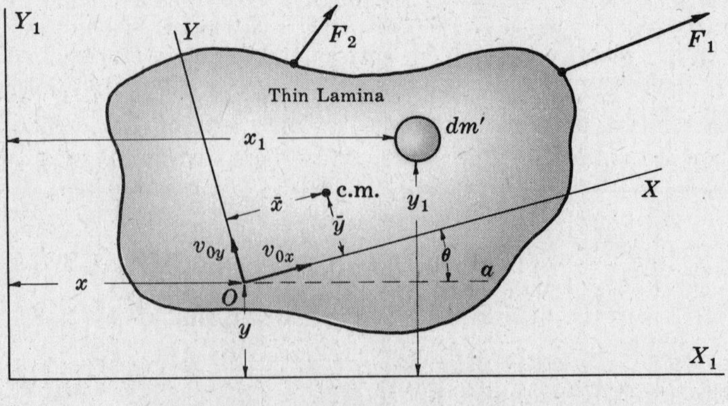

Fig. 8-9

(*a*) Axes X, Y, Z are attached to the lamina with origin O at any arbitrary point. D.f. = 3, and x, y, θ are suitable coordinates. $\omega_x = \omega_y = 0$, $\omega_z = \dot{\theta}$. It is seen that $v_{0x} = \dot{x}\cos\theta + \dot{y}\sin\theta$, $v_{0y} = \dot{y}\cos\theta - \dot{x}\sin\theta$, $v_{0z} = 0$. (Note that v_{0x}, v_{0y} are components of the velocity of O taken along the instantaneous positions of X and Y.) Hence (*8.10*) gives

$$T = \tfrac{1}{2}M(\dot{x}^2 + \dot{y}^2) + \tfrac{1}{2}I_z\dot{\theta}^2 + M\dot{\theta}[(\dot{y}\bar{x} - \dot{x}\bar{y})\cos\theta - (\dot{x}\bar{x} + \dot{y}\bar{y})\sin\theta] \qquad (1)$$

from which equations of motion corresponding to x, y, θ follow at once. For example, the θ equation is

$$I_z\ddot{\theta} + M[(\ddot{y}\,\bar{x} - \ddot{x}\,\bar{y})\cos\theta - (\ddot{x}\,\bar{x} + \ddot{y}\,\bar{y})\sin\theta] = F_\theta$$

Writing x_1', y_1' and x_2', y_2' as coordinates of the points of application of the forces F_1 and F_2 relative to X, Y,

$$F_\theta = \tau_\theta = f_{1y}x_1' - f_{1x}y_1' + f_{2y}x_2' - f_{2x}y_2'$$

where f_{1x}, f_{1y} are X, Y components of F_1, etc.

Note that the generalized forces corresponding to x and y are $F_x = f_{1x} + f_{2x}$ and $F_y = f_{1y} + f_{2y}$.

(*b*) It is interesting and instructive to determine T directly by evaluating the integral

$$T = \frac{1}{2}\int (\dot{x}_1^2 + \dot{y}_1^2)\,dm' \qquad (2)$$

where dm' is an element of mass having coordinates x_1, y_1 relative to the X_1, Y_1 frame. Here

$$x_1 = x + x_m\cos\theta - y_m\sin\theta, \qquad y_1 = y + x_m\sin\theta + y_m\cos\theta \qquad (3)$$

where x_m, y_m are X, Y coordinates of dm'. Differentiating (*3*), inserting in (*2*) and integrating, we obtain (*1*). (Take $dm' = \rho\,dx_m\,dy_m$; ρ = uniform area density.)

(*c*) Expression (*1*) above for T and the corresponding equations of motion are somewhat involved. However, locating O at c.m., $\bar{x} = \bar{y} = \bar{z} = 0$ and

$$T = \tfrac{1}{2}M(\dot{x}^2 + \dot{y}^2) + \tfrac{1}{2}\bar{I}_z\dot{\theta}^2$$

Hence equations of motion are greatly simplified. Generalized forces follow as in (*a*).

Example 8.6.

The lamina, Fig. 8-10(1) is suspended by a string of constant length r and can swing as a "double pendulum" in a vertical plane.

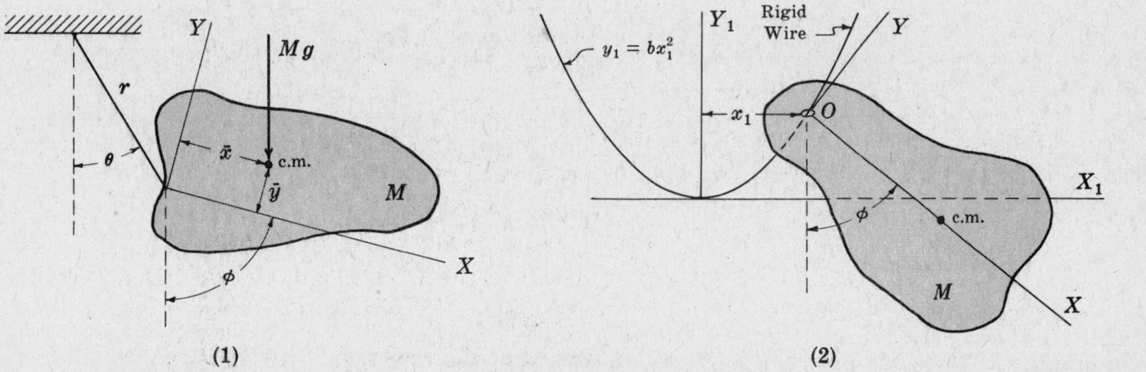

Fig. 8-10

(*a*) Choosing body-fixed axes X, Y, Z as shown, θ and ϕ are suitable coordinates. It is seen that $\omega_x = \omega_y = 0$, $\omega_z = \dot{\phi}$, $(\omega_z \neq \dot{\theta} + \dot{\phi})$ and $v_0 = r\dot{\theta}$. Now v_{0x}, v_{0y} components of $\bar{v}_0$ must be taken along X and Y. Hence $v_{0x} = r\dot{\theta}\sin(\phi - \theta)$, $v_{0y} = r\dot{\theta}\cos(\phi - \theta)$. Thus

$$T = \tfrac{1}{2}Mr^2\dot{\theta}^2 + \tfrac{1}{2}I_z\dot{\phi}^2 + Mr\dot{\theta}\dot{\phi}[\bar{x}\cos(\phi - \theta) - \bar{y}\sin(\phi - \theta)]$$

from which equations of motion follow at once. Expressions for F_θ and F_ϕ are obtained in the usual way, regarding Mg as acting at c.m.

(b) As a variation of the above problem, suppose point O on the lamina is free to slide along the smooth parabolic line $y_1 = bx_1^2$ as shown in Fig. 8-10(2). It is seen that

$$v_0^2 = (\dot{x}_1^2 + \dot{y}_1^2), \qquad v_{0x} = \dot{x}_1 \sin\phi - \dot{y}_1 \cos\phi, \qquad v_{0y} = \dot{x}_1 \cos\phi + \dot{y}_1 \sin\phi$$

and
$$T = \tfrac{1}{2}M(\dot{x}_1^2 + \dot{y}_1^2) + \tfrac{1}{2}I_z\dot{\phi}^2 + M\dot{\phi}[\bar{x}(\dot{x}_1 \cos\phi + \dot{y}_1 \sin\phi) - \bar{y}(\dot{x}_1 \sin\phi - \dot{y}_1 \cos\phi)]$$

$\dot{y}_1$, for example, can be eliminated by $\dot{y}_1 = 2bx_1\dot{x}_1$, and equations of motion corresponding to x_1, ϕ can be determined at once.

Example 8.7.

A slender rod of mass ρ per unit length and total length L, Fig. 8-11, is free to rotate through angle θ_2 about a horizontal axis in the bearing at O. This bearing is fixed to the horizontal arm AB. Let us determine directly, by integration, the kinetic energy of the rod and compare results with those obtained by applying relation (8.10).

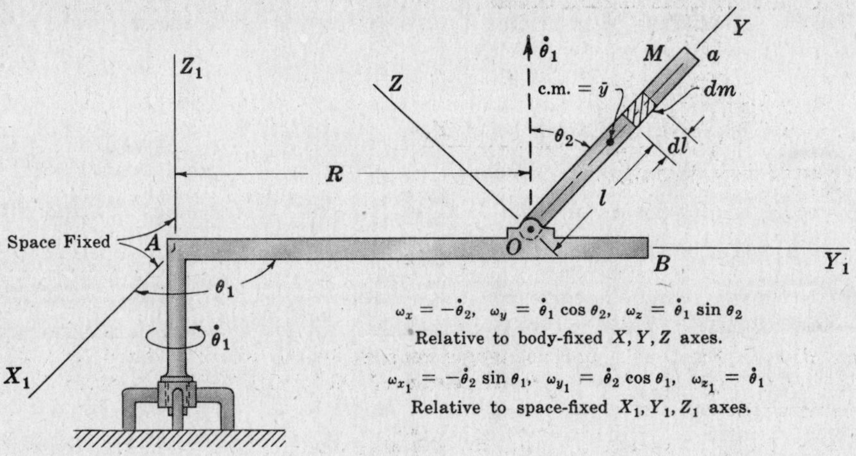

Fig. 8-11

As easily seen, the defining equation $T = \dfrac{1}{2}\displaystyle\int v^2\,dm$ can be written as

$$T = \frac{1}{2}\int_0^L [(R + l\sin\theta_2)^2\dot{\theta}_1^2 + l^2\dot{\theta}_2^2]\rho\,dl$$

or
$$T = \tfrac{1}{2}R^2\dot{\theta}_1^2 \int_0^L \rho\,dl + \tfrac{1}{2}\dot{\theta}_1^2 \sin^2\theta_2 \int_0^L \rho l^2\,dl + R\dot{\theta}_1^2 \sin\theta_2 \int_0^L \rho l\,dl + \tfrac{1}{2}\dot{\theta}_2^2 \int_0^L \rho l^2\,dl$$

which, by inspection, can be put in the form

$$T = \tfrac{1}{2}MR^2\dot{\theta}_1^2 + \tfrac{1}{2}I_z\dot{\theta}_1^2 \sin^2\theta_2 + M\bar{y}R\dot{\theta}_1^2 \sin\theta_2 + \tfrac{1}{2}I_x\dot{\theta}_2^2$$

The reader may show that a proper application of (8.10) gives exactly the same expression for T.

Example 8.8.

In Fig. 8-12, the uniform disk D can rotate with angular velocity $\dot{\phi}$ relative to the supporting frame. At the same time the frame rotates with angular velocity $\dot{\psi}$ about the vertical axis, ψ measured between Y_1 and the cOa plane. To find T for the disk, take body-fixed axes X, Y, Z with origin O at c.m. Thus $\bar{x} = \bar{y} = \bar{z} = 0$. Since c.m. is at rest, $v_{0x} = v_{0y} = v_{0z} = 0$. From the two figures it is seen that

$$\omega_x = \dot{\psi}\sin\theta\sin\phi, \qquad \omega_y = \dot{\psi}\sin\theta\cos\phi, \qquad \omega_z = \dot{\phi} + \dot{\psi}\cos\theta$$

Note that $\bar{I}_x = \bar{I}_y$, $I_{xy} = I_{xz} = I_{yz} = 0$. Hence

$$T = \tfrac{1}{2}\bar{I}_x\dot{\psi}^2 \sin^2\theta + \tfrac{1}{2}\bar{I}_z(\dot{\phi} + \dot{\psi}\cos\theta)^2$$

If the frame (moment of inertia $= I_f$) is to be taken account of, we merely add $\tfrac{1}{2}I_f\dot{\psi}^2$.

For any known forces acting, the complete equations of motion can now be written.

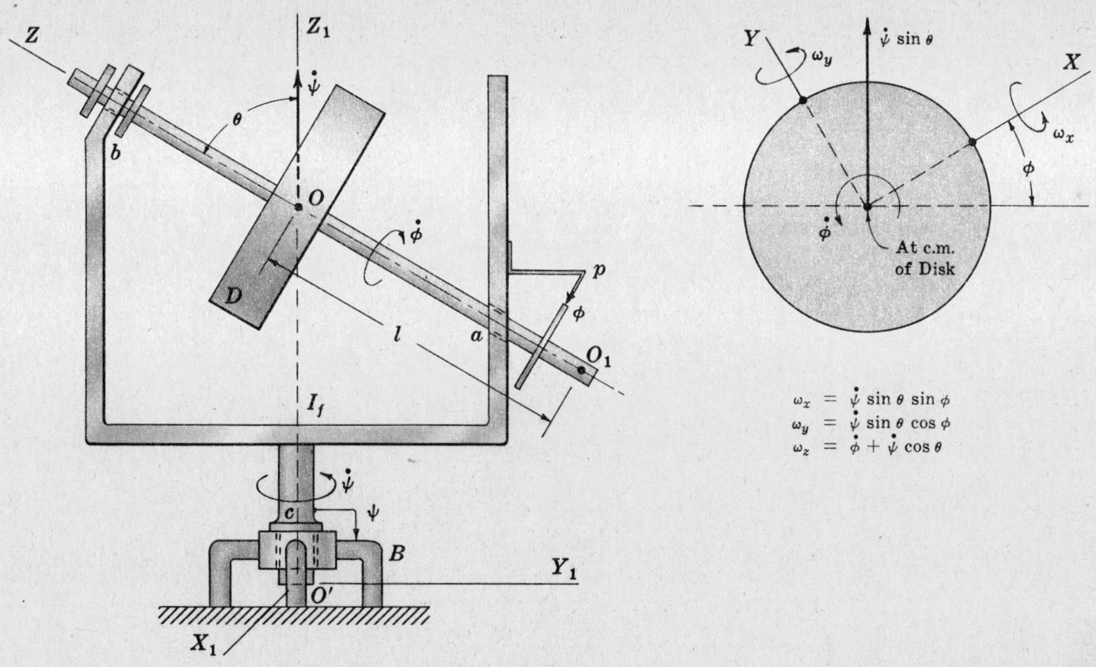

Fig. 8-12

Example 8.9.

Consider again disk D, Fig. 8-12. For pedagogic reasons let us take body-fixed axes X, Y, Z parallel to those shown but with origin at O_1. (O_1 is at center of shaft and distance l from O.) In this case $\omega_x, \omega_y, \omega_z$ are the same as above,

$$\bar{x} = \bar{y} = 0, \qquad \bar{z} = +l, \qquad v_{0x} = -l\dot\psi \sin\theta \cos\phi, \qquad v_{0y} = l\dot\psi \sin\theta \sin\phi$$

$$I_{xy} = I_{xz} = I_{yz} = 0, \qquad I_x = I_y, \qquad I_z = \bar{I}_z$$

Hence

$$T = \tfrac{1}{2}Ml^2\dot\psi^2 \sin^2\theta + \tfrac{1}{2}I_x\dot\psi^2 \sin^2\theta + \tfrac{1}{2}\bar{I}_z(\dot\phi + \dot\psi\cos\theta)^2 - Ml^2\dot\psi^2\sin^2\theta$$

where I_x is about X in its new position. The reader can show that this reduces at once to the expression for T in Example 8.8. Equations of motion follow at once.

The origin of body-fixed axes may of course be located at any point in the body, and the axes may have any orientation. However, it is clear that certain locations and orientations are much more advantageous than others.

Example 8.10.

Suppose the disk, Fig. 8-12, is replaced by a rigid body of any shape. Let us take body-fixed axes X, Y, Z exactly as shown on the figure. Assume that c.m. is not located at the origin and that X, Y, Z are not principal axes.

(*a*) Since $\mathbf{v}_0 = 0$, the first and last terms of (*8.10*) are zero even though c.m. is not at O. Hence

$$T = \tfrac{1}{2}[I_x\dot\psi^2\sin^2\theta\sin^2\phi + I_y\dot\psi^2\sin^2\theta\cos^2\phi + I_z(\dot\phi + \dot\psi\cos\theta)^2]$$
$$- [I_{xy}\dot\psi^2\sin^2\theta\sin\phi\cos\phi + I_{xz}(\dot\psi\sin\theta\sin\phi)(\dot\phi + \dot\psi\cos\theta) + I_{yz}(\dot\psi\sin\theta\cos\phi)(\dot\phi + \dot\psi\cos\theta)]$$

(*b*) As an extension of this example, let us take body-fixed axes X_p, Y_p, Z_p (origin still at O) along the principal axes of inertia of the body. Let $\alpha_{11}, \alpha_{12}, \alpha_{13}$ be direction cosines of X_p relative to X, Y, Z, etc. Products of inertia vanish but components of $\boldsymbol{\omega}$ $(\omega_1, \omega_2, \omega_3)$ along X_p, Y_p, Z_p are required; that is,

$$\omega_1 = (\dot\psi\sin\theta\sin\phi)\alpha_{11} + (\dot\psi\sin\theta\cos\phi)\alpha_{12} + (\dot\phi + \dot\psi\cos\theta)\alpha_{13}, \qquad \text{etc.}$$

Thus we can finally write $\qquad T = \tfrac{1}{2}[I_x^p\omega_1^2 + I_y^p\omega_2^2 + I_z^p\omega_3^2]$

(c) As a further demonstration of basic principles, consider body-fixed axes X', Y', Z' orientated in any manner with origin O' at any point in the body. Let x, y, z be coordinates of O' relative to the X, Y, Z axes shown. Let $\beta_{11}, \beta_{12}, \beta_{13}$ represent direction cosines of X' relative to X, Y, Z, etc.

Components of $v_{O'}$, the velocity of O' relative to X_1, Y_1, Z_1, along X, Y, Z are

$$v_x = \omega_y z - \omega_z y, \qquad v_y = \omega_z x - \omega_x z, \qquad v_z = \omega_x y - \omega_y x$$

Hence
$$v_{O'}^2 = v_x^2 + v_y^2 + v_z^2 \tag{1}$$

Components of $v_{O'}$, along X', Y', Z' are given by

$$v_{O'x} = v_x\beta_{11} + v_y\beta_{12} + v_z\beta_{13}, \qquad \text{etc.} \tag{2}$$

Components of ω along these same axes are

$$\omega'_x = \omega_x\beta_{11} + \omega_y\beta_{12} + \omega_z\beta_{13}, \qquad \text{etc.} \tag{3}$$

Thus inserting (1), (2), (3) together with given values of $\bar{x}, \bar{y}, \bar{z}$ and I'_x, I'_{xy}, etc., into (8.10) gives T.

Example 8.11.

The heavy disk, Fig. 8-13, can roll, without slipping, in contact with the rough X_1Y_1 plane. Taking body-fixed X, Y, Z axes with origin at O and Z along the axis of the shaft Oc (X, Y not shown), it is seen that

$$\omega_x = \dot\psi \sin\theta \sin\phi, \qquad \omega_y = \dot\psi \sin\theta\cos\phi, \qquad \omega_z = \dot\phi + \dot\psi\cos\theta$$

exactly as in Fig. 8-5, Page 146. But here $\theta = \text{constant}$, $\sin\theta = r_1/r_3$, $\cos\theta = r_2/r_3$ and $r_3\psi = -r_2\phi$. Hence

$$\omega_x = \dot\psi\frac{r_1}{r_3}\sin\phi, \qquad \omega_y = \dot\psi\frac{r_1}{r_3}\cos\phi, \qquad \omega_z = -\dot\psi\frac{r_1^2}{r_2r_3}$$

Thus, since $I_x = I_y$ and $I_{xy} = I_{xz} = I_{yz} = 0$, ($\psi$ measured from Y_1 to projection of OZ on X_1Y_1 plane)

$$T = \tfrac{1}{2}[I_x(\omega_x^2 + \omega_y^2) + I_z\omega_z^2]$$

from which the following equation of motion is obtained

$$\frac{r_1}{r_3}\left(I_x + I_z\frac{r_1^2}{r_2^2}\right)\ddot\psi = -Mgl\sin\epsilon\sin\psi$$

where we have assumed the X_1Y_1 plane tilted at an angle ϵ, with Y_1 down the incline and ψ measured from Y_1 to the projection of Z on the X_1Y_1 plane. See suggested experiment, Page 167. Also see the Euler treatment of this problem, Example 9.6, Page 185. See Example 12.5, Page 261.

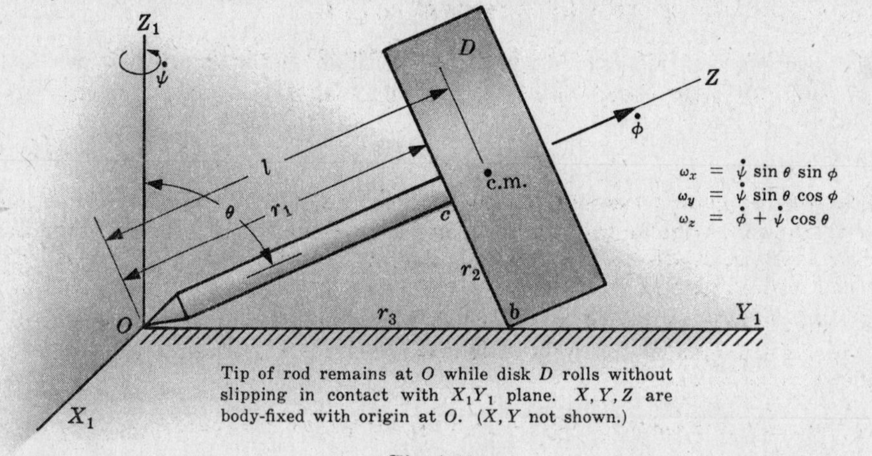

Tip of rod remains at O while disk D rolls without slipping in contact with X_1Y_1 plane. X, Y, Z are body-fixed with origin at O. (X, Y not shown.)

Fig. 8-13

Example 8.12.

Referring to Fig. 8-14, the mass M_1 is free to slide along and rotate about the rod ab which is rigidly attached to block B. This block can slide freely in contact with the X_1Y_1 plane. We shall outline steps for finding T of the system in terms of coordinates $x_1, y_1, r, \theta_1, \theta_2$.

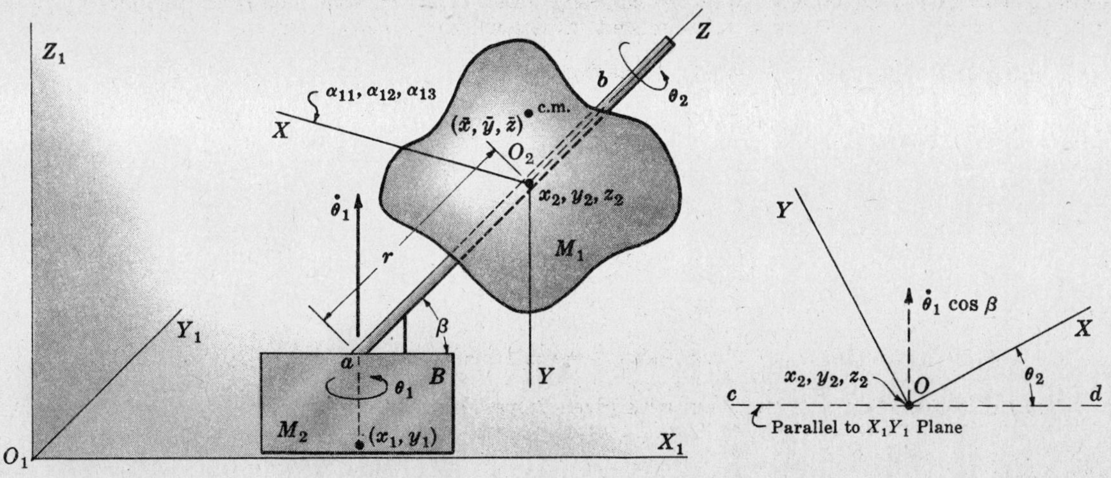

Fig. 8-14

Take X, Y, Z as body-fixed axes for M_1. Let $\alpha_{11}, \alpha_{12}, \alpha_{13}$ represent direction cosines of X relative to the inertial X_1, Y_1, Z_1 axes, etc. From the figure,

$$\omega_x = \dot{\theta}_1 \cos\beta \sin\theta_2, \qquad \omega_y = \dot{\theta}_1 \cos\beta \cos\theta_2, \qquad \omega_z = \dot{\theta}_1 \sin\beta + \dot{\theta}_2$$

where θ_1 is the angular position of B relative to X_1 and θ_2 is measured relative to the rod. Letting x_2, y_2, z_2 be the X_1, Y_1, Z_1 coordinates of O,

$$x_2 = x_1 + r\cos\beta\cos\theta_1, \qquad y_2 = y_1 + r\cos\beta\sin\theta_1, \qquad z_2 = r\sin\beta + \text{constant}$$

$v_0 = (\dot{x}_2^2 + \dot{y}_2^2 + \dot{z}_2^2)^{1/2}$ can be obtained. Components of $\mathbf{v}_0$ along X, Y, Z are given by $v_{0x} = \dot{x}_2\alpha_{11} + \dot{y}_2\alpha_{12} + \dot{z}_2\alpha_{13}$, etc. Hence, with known values of $\bar{x}, \bar{y}, \bar{z}, I_x, I_{xy}$, etc., relative to the body-fixed axes, T_1 of M_1 follows at once from (*8.10*).

The kinetic energy of M_2 (assuming for simplicity that the vertical dotted line through (x_1, y_1) passes through c.m. of B) is merely $T_2 = \frac{1}{2}M_2(\dot{x}_1^2 + \dot{y}_1^2) + \frac{1}{2}I\dot{\theta}_1^2$ where I is the moment of inertia of the block about the dotted line. Thus, for the system, $T = T_1 + T_2$.

For any known forces acting, equations of motion follow at once by an application of Lagrange's equations in the usual way. Forces of constraint, as between the rod and M_1, will not appear in these equations. Note that $\alpha_{11}, \alpha_{12}, \alpha_{13}$, etc., can be expressed in terms of $\theta_1, \theta_2, \beta$.

For example,
$$\alpha_{11} = -(\sin\theta_1\cos\theta_2 + \cos\theta_1\sin\theta_2\sin\beta),$$
$$\alpha_{12} = \cos\theta_1\cos\theta_2 - \sin\theta_1\sin\theta_2\sin\beta, \qquad \alpha_{13} = \sin\theta_2\cos\beta, \qquad \text{etc.}$$

Example 8.13.

In Fig. 8-15 below, support A can move to any position on the X_1Y_1 plane. The shaft ab, on which the rigid body can rotate with angular velocity $\dot{\beta}$, is hinged at O and can swing in a vertical plane. θ_1 is measured relative to X_1, θ_2 relative to A, θ_3 as indicated, and β relative to the shaft ab. The following is an outline of steps for finding T of the system.

Let us assume body-fixed axes X, Y, Z with origin at O, and Z along ba. $\dot{\theta}_3$ is horizontal and always normal to the abc plane. Angular velocity of table B is $\dot{\theta}_1 + \dot{\theta}_2$. Hence with the aid of the upper right hand sketch the reader may show that

$$\omega_x = (\dot{\theta}_1 + \dot{\theta}_2)\cos\theta_3\sin\beta - \dot{\theta}_3\cos\beta, \quad \omega_y = (\dot{\theta}_1 + \dot{\theta}_2)\cos\theta_3\cos\beta + \dot{\theta}_3\sin\beta, \quad \omega_z = \dot{\beta} + (\dot{\theta}_1 + \dot{\theta}_2)\sin\theta_3$$

$\mathbf{v}_0$, the velocity of O, and its components along X, Y, Z [see Problem 8.12(*d*)] may be found by the method outlined in Example 8.12. Thus for known values of $\bar{x}, \bar{y}, \bar{z}$ and I_x, I_{xy}, etc., T_1, the kinetic energy of M_1 can be obtained. For known masses, moments of inertia, etc., of rod ab, table B and support A, corresponding kinetic energies T_2, T_3, T_4 can be written out at once. Hence T for the system is just $T = T_1 + T_2 + T_3 + T_4$ from which equations of motion corresponding to $x_1, y_1, \theta_1, \theta_2, \theta_3, \beta$ follow in the usual way. It is important to note that, assuming smooth bearings, all forces of constraint are automatically eliminated from equations of motion. This illustrates one of the great advantages of the Lagrangian over the Euler method. See Chapter 9.

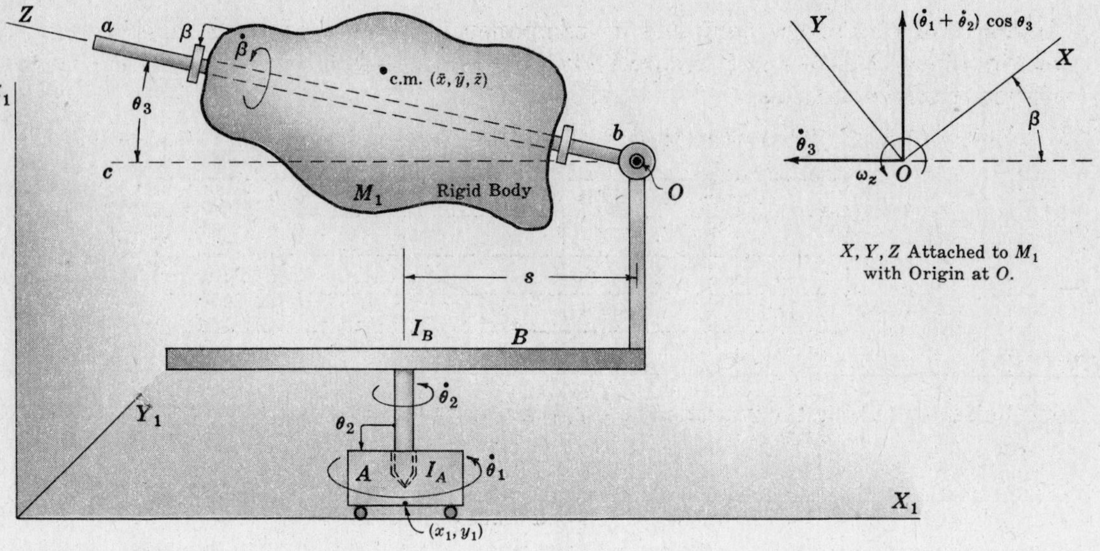

Fig. 8-15

8.7 EULER ANGLES DEFINED. EXPRESSING ω AND ITS COMPONENTS IN THESE ANGLES.

(*a*) Euler angles θ, ψ, ϕ shown in Fig. 8-16 are widely used in rigid body dynamics. The manner in which they are measured is quite simple. In view of applications which immediately follow, we shall assume X_1, Y_1, Z_1 fixed in space. The rigid body, one point of which is fixed at O, is free to turn in any manner about O. Axes X, Y, Z are attached to the body. θ is the angle between Z_1 and Z. Line ON is determined by the intersection of the moving XY and stationary X_1Y_1 planes. Angle ψ is measured between X_1 and ON, and ϕ between ON and X. (A simple model is very helpful in understanding and working with these angles.)

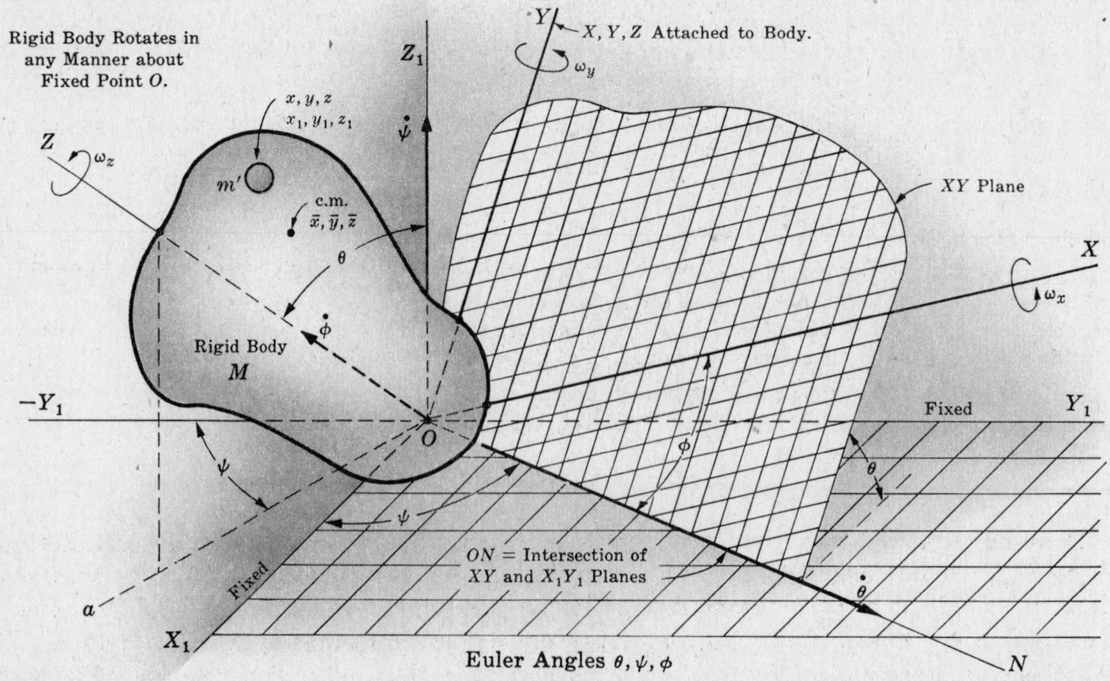

Euler Angles θ, ψ, ϕ

Fig. 8-16

(b) Angular velocity of the body and its components. Note that $\dot{\theta}, \dot{\psi}, \dot{\phi}$ may be regarded as vectors along ON, Z_1 and Z respectively. The total angular velocity $\boldsymbol{\omega}$ is the vector sum of these three quantities.

Making use of the following direction cosines (the reader may verify same),

Cosines of Angles between X, Y, Z and Z_1, ON			
	X	Y	Z
Z_1	$\sin\theta \sin\phi$	$\sin\theta \cos\phi$	$\cos\theta$
ON	$\cos\phi$	$-\sin\phi$	0

Table 8.1

it follows, by taking components of $\dot{\theta}, \dot{\psi}, \dot{\phi}$ along the body-fixed X, Y, Z axes, that

$$\begin{aligned} \omega_x &= \dot{\psi}\sin\theta\sin\phi + \dot{\theta}\cos\phi \\ \omega_y &= \dot{\psi}\sin\theta\cos\phi - \dot{\theta}\sin\phi \\ \omega_z &= \dot{\phi} + \dot{\psi}\cos\theta \end{aligned} \tag{8.11}$$

Hence, for example, components of $\mathbf{v}$ (the inertial space velocity of any typical particle m') along instantaneous directions of X, Y, Z are given by

$$v_x = (\dot{\psi}\sin\theta\cos\phi - \dot{\theta}\sin\phi)z - (\dot{\phi} + \dot{\psi}\cos\theta)y, \qquad \text{etc.}$$

where x, y, z are the X, Y, Z coordinates of m'.

8.8 Use of Euler Angles: Body Moving in Any Manner.

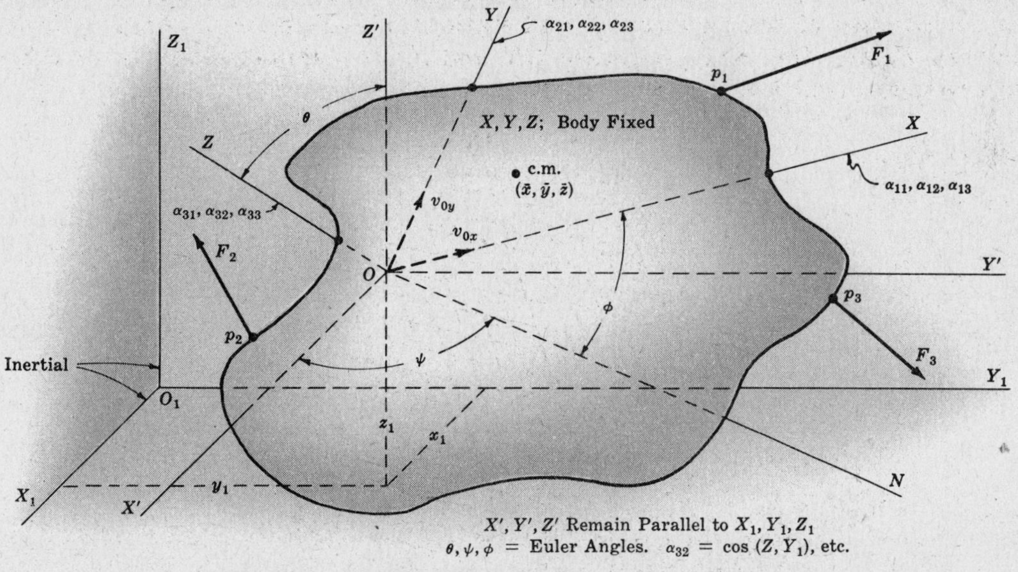

Fig. 8-17

Assume that the body, Fig. 8-17, is free to move in any manner under the action of forces F_1, F_2, etc. Regard X, Y, Z as body-fixed and assume that X', Y', Z', with origin attached to the body at O, remain parallel to inertial axes X_1, Y_1, Z_1. Euler angles are measured as indicated. Let $\alpha_{11}, \alpha_{12}, \alpha_{13}$ represent direction cosines of X relative to X', Y', Z' (or, of course, relative to X_1, Y_1, Z_1), etc., a complete table of which follows. The reader should verify these expressions.

Cosines of Angles between X, Y, Z and X_1, Y_1, Z_1. Refer to Fig. 8-16 or 8-17.			
	X	Y	Z
X_1	$\alpha_{11} = \cos\phi\cos\psi - \sin\phi\sin\psi\cos\theta$	$\alpha_{21} = -\sin\phi\cos\psi - \cos\phi\sin\psi\cos\theta$	$\alpha_{31} = \sin\theta\sin\psi$
Y_1	$\alpha_{12} = \cos\phi\sin\psi + \sin\phi\cos\psi\cos\theta$	$\alpha_{22} = -\sin\phi\sin\psi + \cos\phi\cos\psi\cos\theta$	$\alpha_{32} = -\sin\theta\cos\psi$
Z_1	$\alpha_{13} = \sin\theta\sin\phi$	$\alpha_{23} = \sin\theta\cos\phi$	$\alpha_{33} = \cos\theta$

Table 8.2

Components of the total angular velocity $\boldsymbol{\omega}$ relative to inertial space, taken along X, Y, Z are given directly by (*8.11*).

The velocity $\mathbf{v}_0$ of O relative to inertial space is just $v_0 = (\dot{x}_1^2 + \dot{y}_1^2 + \dot{z}_1^2)^{1/2}$ where x_1, y_1, z_1 are X_1, Y_1, Z_1 coordinates of O. $\dot{x}_1, \dot{y}_1, \dot{z}_1$ can of course be expressed in other coordinates such as cylindrical or spherical, if so desired.

Finally v_{0x}, v_{0y}, v_{0z}, components of $\mathbf{v}_0$ in the instantaneous directions of X, Y, Z, are given by $v_{0x} = \dot{x}_1\alpha_{11} + \dot{y}_1\alpha_{12} + \dot{z}_1\alpha_{13}$, etc.

Hence, applying (*8.10*), T may be expressed in terms of the six coordinates $x_1, y_1, z_1, \theta, \psi, \phi$ and their time derivatives. An application of Lagrange's equations gives six equations of motion. If there are constraints, such that equations of constraint can be written out in algebraic form (the type dealt with in all previous chapters), a corresponding number of coordinates can be eliminated from T in the usual way.

Suppose, for example, that components $f'_{x_i}, f'_{y_i}, f'_{z_i}$ of F_i, parallel to X_1, Y_1, Z_1, and coordinates x_i, y_i, z_i of points of application p_i relative to X, Y, Z, are known. Then generalized forces corresponding to x_1, y_1, z_1 are merely

$$F_{x_1} = \sum f'_{x_i}, \qquad F_{y_1} = \sum f'_{y_i}, \qquad F_{z_1} = \sum f'_{z_i}$$

In order to find F_θ we may proceed as follows. The component of τ, the total torque vector, about X for example, is given by $\tau_x = \sum (f_{z_i} y_i - f_{y_i} z_i)$ where f_{x_i} is the component of F_i in the direction of the body-fixed X axis, etc. But $f_{x_i} = f'_{x_i}\alpha_{11} + f'_{y_i}\alpha_{12} + f'_{z_i}\alpha_{13}$, etc. for f_{y_i} and f_{z_i}. Having determined τ_x, τ_y, τ_z, $\tau_\theta = \tau_x\cos\phi - \tau_y\sin\phi = F_\theta$, with similar expressions for τ_ψ and τ_ϕ. That is,

$$\begin{aligned} F_\theta &= \tau_x\cos\phi - \tau_y\sin\phi, \qquad F_\phi = \tau_z \\ F_\psi &= \tau_x\sin\theta\sin\phi + \tau_y\sin\theta\cos\phi + \tau_z\cos\theta \end{aligned} \tag{8.12}$$

If all forces are conservative, a potential energy function $v(x_1, y_1, z_1, \theta, \psi, \phi)$ may be written and all generalized forces found at once from $F_{q_r} = -\partial V/\partial q_r$. Or, of course, a Lagrangian function L may be applied in the usual way.

As previously shown, T and consequently equations of motion can usually be greatly simplified by properly choosing the location of O and the orientation of the body-fixed axes. The reader should determine expressions for generalized forces assuming $f_{x_i}, f_{y_i}, f_{z_i}$ given instead of $f'_{x_i}, f'_{y_i}, f'_{z_i}$.

Example 8.14. *Equations of motion of a top.*

Imagine the body, Fig. 8-16, replaced by a top with the tip stationary at O and its axis of symmetry along Z. Take X, Y, Z axes shown as body-fixed.

Since $I_x = I_y$ and O is at rest, T simplifies and L may be written as

$$L = \tfrac{1}{2}[I_x(\dot{\theta}^2 + \dot{\psi}^2 \sin^2\theta) + I_z(\dot{\phi} + \dot{\psi}\cos\theta)^2] - Mgr\cos\theta$$

where M is the total mass and r the distance along the axis of symmetry from O to c.m. Applying Lagrange's equation, the following equations of motion are obtained.

$$I_x\ddot{\theta} + [(I_z - I_x)\dot{\psi}\cos\theta + I_z\dot{\phi}]\dot{\psi}\sin\theta = Mgr\sin\theta$$

$$I_z(\dot{\psi}\cos\theta + \dot{\phi}) = P_\phi = \text{constant} \tag{8.13}$$

$$I_x\dot{\psi}\sin^2\theta + P_\phi\cos\theta = P_\psi = \text{constant}$$

Detailed treatments of these equations, which may be found in many books, will not be repeated here. See, for example: *Gyrodynamics and its Engineering Applications* by R. N. Arnold and L. Maunder, Chapter 7, Academic Press, 1961; or *A Treatise on Gyrostatics and Rotational Motion* by Andrew Gray, Chapter V, The Macmillan Co., 1918. The latter book gives extensive treatments of tops, gyroscopes, etc.

Example 8.15. *Kinetic energy of top with tip free to slide on the smooth X_1Y_1 plane.*

Assuming body-fixed axes as in Example 8.14 and locating O (the tip) by (x_1, y_1), the first term of (*8.10*) is merely $\tfrac{1}{2}M(\dot{x}_1^2 + \dot{y}_1^2)$. Expressions for $\omega_x, \omega_y, \omega_z$ are as before. Hence the second term is $\tfrac{1}{2}[I_x(\dot{\theta}^2 + \dot{\psi}^2\sin^2\theta) + I_z(\dot{\phi} + \dot{\psi}\cos\theta)^2]$. Since $\bar{x} = \bar{y} = 0$, $\bar{z} = r$, the third term of T reduces to $Mr[v_{0x}\omega_y - v_{0y}\omega_x]$ in which v_{0x}, v_{0y} must be components of $\mathbf{v}_0$ along the instantaneous directions of X, Y respectively. That is, $v_{0x} = \dot{x}_1\alpha_{11} + \dot{y}_1\alpha_{12}$, $v_{0y} = \dot{x}_1\alpha_{21} + \dot{y}_1\alpha_{22}$. Note that v_{0z} is not required. Introducing these and expressions for ω_y, ω_x completes the third term.

Equations of motion corresponding to $x_1, y_1, \theta, \psi, \phi$ can be obtained at once. Note that, assuming the X_1Y_1 plane smooth, the reactive force on the tip will not appear in the generalized forces.

An alternative method of obtaining T, requiring perhaps less tedious work, is the following. Imagine body-fixed axes taken as above but with origin at c.m. Since $\bar{x} = \bar{y} = \bar{z} = 0$, the third term of (*8.10*) drops out. $\mathbf{v}_0$, not so simple as before, may be obtained from the following relations. Coordinates x, y, z of the origin of body-fixed axes relative to the X_1, Y_1, Z_1 frame are $x = x_1 + r\alpha_{31}$, $y = y_1 + r\alpha_{32}$, $z = r\alpha_{33}$. Differentiating and substituting into $v_0^2 = \dot{x}^2 + \dot{y}^2 + \dot{z}^2$, we have an appropriate expression for v_0^2. Hence

$$T = \tfrac{1}{2}Mv_0^2 + \tfrac{1}{2}[\bar{I}_x^p(\omega_x^2 + \omega_y^2) + \bar{I}_z^p\omega_z^2]$$

where $\omega_x, \omega_y, \omega_z$ are the same as in the first part of the example and $\bar{I}_x^p, \bar{I}_z^p$ are principal moments of inertia through c.m. (As a third method we can write $v_0^2 = \dot{x}^2 + \dot{y}^2 + r^2\dot{\theta}^2\sin^2\theta$.)

Example 8.16. *Kinetic energy and equations of motion of the gyroscope.*

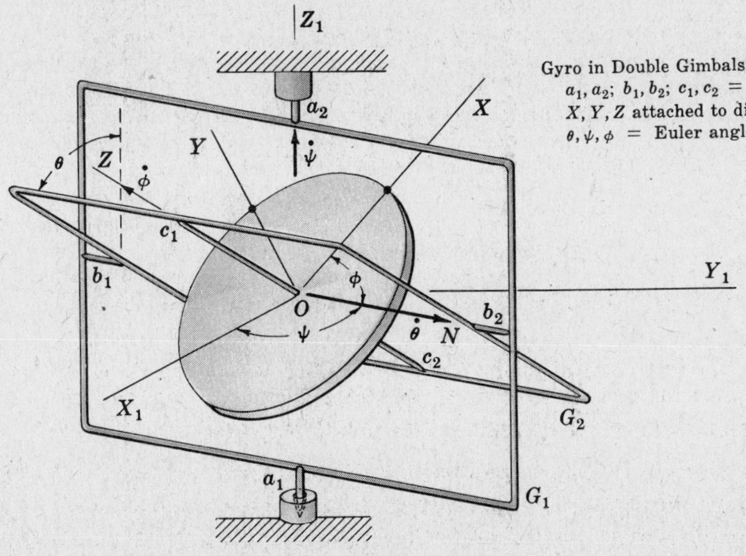

Gyro in Double Gimbals:
a_1, a_2; b_1, b_2; c_1, c_2 = bearings
X, Y, Z attached to disk
θ, ψ, ϕ = Euler angles

Fig. 8-18

A gyroscope in a two-gimbal mounting is shown in Fig. 8-18 above. With X_1, Y_1, Z_1 regarded as fixed, it is seen that Euler angles θ, ψ, ϕ measured as follows are suitable coordinates. ψ is determined by the rotation of the outer gimbal G_1 about axis a_1a_2; θ by a rotation of G_2 about b_1b_2 and ϕ is a rotation of the disk about c_1c_2. Line ON as indicated here has the same significance as in Fig. 8-16.

Thus, neglecting moments of inertia of the gimbals and assuming the origin of body-fixed axes X, Y, Z located at the center of the disk, T is just

$$T = \tfrac{1}{2}\bar{I}^p_x(\dot{\psi}^2 \sin^2\theta + \dot{\theta}^2) + \tfrac{1}{2}\bar{I}^p_z(\dot{\psi}\cos\theta + \dot{\phi})^2$$

from which equations of motion follow at once. Neglecting bearing friction and assuming c.m. at O, each generalized force is zero.

If so desired, the kinetic energy of the gimbal rings can easily be included.

For an extensive treatment of gyroscopes see, besides the references given in Example 8.14, *The Gyroscope* by James Scarborough, Interscience Publishers, 1958, and *Theory of the Gyroscopic Compass* by A. L. Rawlings, The Macmillan Co., 1944. For interesting reading, see *Spinning Tops and Gyroscopic Motions* by John Perry, Dover Publications.

Example 8.17.

The rigid body, Fig. 8-19, is suspended by a string of constant length r_1. Except for this one constraint it is free to move about in any manner under the action of gravity. Hence the system has five degrees of freedom. We shall outline steps for finding T.

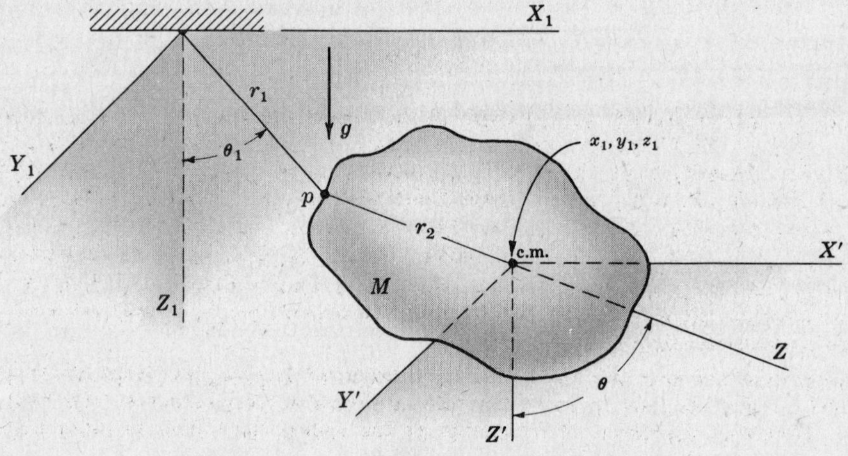

Fig. 8-19

Let r_1, θ_1, ϕ_1, the usual spherical coordinates (ϕ_1 not shown), determine the position of p. Assume that axes X', Y', Z' with origin attached to the body at c.m. remain parallel to the inertial axes X_1, Y_1, Z_1. Taking body-fixed axes X, Y, Z with origin at c.m., we shall measure Euler angles between these and X', Y', Z'. (Neither X, Y, nor ψ, ϕ are shown on the diagram.) Angular velocities $\omega_x, \omega_y, \omega_z$ are given by relations (*8.11*). Since $\bar{x} = \bar{y} = \bar{z} = 0$, the last term of (*8.10*) drops out. $\mathbf{v}_0$, the velocity of c.m. relative to X_1, Y_1, Z_1, is given by $v_0^2 = \dot{x}_1^2 + \dot{y}_1^2 + \dot{z}_1^2$ where x_1, y_1, z_1, the X_1, Y_1, Z_1 coordinates of c.m., can be expressed in terms of the constants r_1, r_2 and the angles $\theta_1, \phi_1, \theta, \psi$. [See (2.26) Page 20.] Hence v_0^2 can be expressed in terms of these coordinates and their time derivatives. If X, Y, Z are chosen along the principal axes of inertia,

$$T = \tfrac{1}{2}Mv_0^2 + \tfrac{1}{2}[\bar{I}^p_x\omega_x^2 + \bar{I}^p_y\omega_y^2 + \bar{I}^p_z\omega_z^2]$$

Here $V = -Mg(r_1\cos\theta_1 + r_2\cos\theta)$. Thus equations of motion follow at once.

The reader should find an explicit expression for T and write out equations of motion.

Example 8.18. *The two masses M_a and M_b, Fig. 8-20 below, are fastened together by means of a ball joint at O.*

Otherwise they are perfectly free to move in space, perhaps under the action of springs, gravity, etc. Clearly the system has nine degrees of freedom. An outline of the procedure for finding T and the nine equations of motion follows.

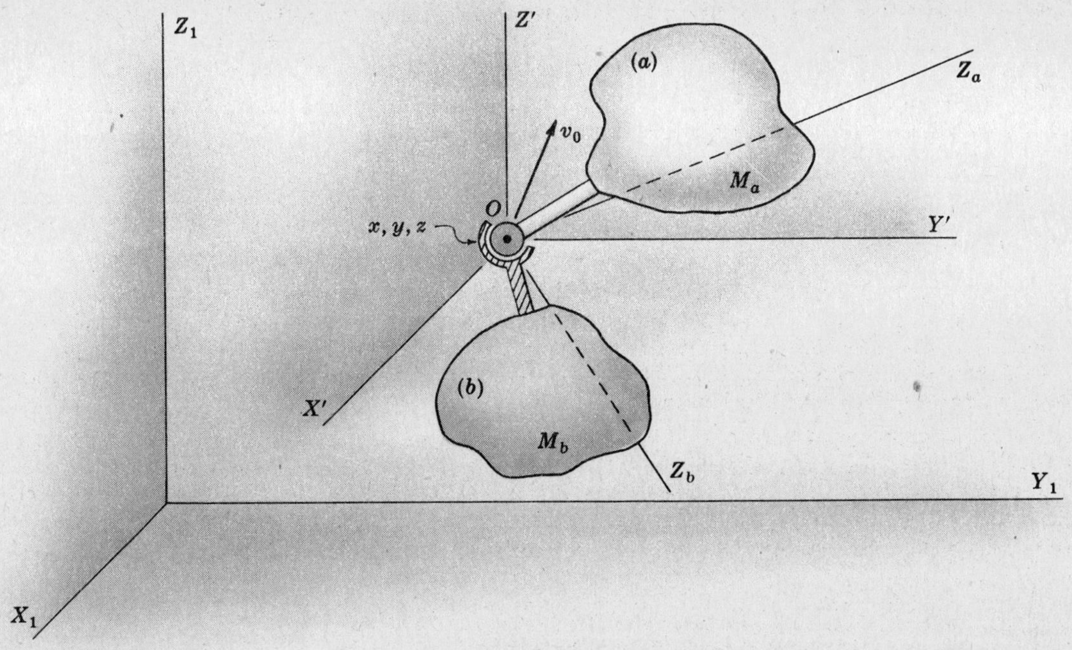

Fig. 8-20

Let coordinates x, y, z represent the position of the center of the ball (point O) relative to inertial axes X_1, Y_1, Z_1. The X', Y', Z' frame, with origin attached to O, moves with O but remains always parallel to X_1, Y_1, Z_1. Axes X_a, Y_a, Z_a and X_b, Y_b, Z_b, with common origin at O are attached to M_a and M_b respectively (X_a, Y_a and X_b, Y_b not shown). Hence Euler angles θ_1, ψ_1, ϕ_1 of M_a and θ_2, ψ_2, ϕ_2 of M_b can, for each mass, be measured relative to X', Y', Z' just as in Fig. 8-17. Thus T_a, the kinetic energy of M_a, can be written in terms of $x, y, z, \theta_1, \psi_1, \phi_1$ and their time derivatives by a direct application of (*8.10*). Likewise, T_b may be expressed in terms of $x, y, z, \theta_2, \psi_2, \phi_2$; and finally the total T is just $T_a + T_b$ which involves nine coordinates. Note that $\mathbf{v}_0$ is the same for each mass but expressions for v_{0x}, v_{0y}, v_{0z} for M_a are not the same as corresponding quantities for M_b.

Equations of motion are now obtained by an application of Lagrange's equation. If springs, gravity, externally applied forces, etc., are acting, generalized forces corresponding to the various coordinates give no trouble. Note that the force of constraint at the smooth ball joint is automatically eliminated.

8.9 Kinetic Energy Making Use of Direction-fixed Axes. [See Section 8.4(*c*).]

In all previous examples of this chapter, body-fixed axes have been employed. However, as previously pointed out direction-fixed axes can also be used. In this case moments and products of inertia (variable quantities), components of $\boldsymbol{\omega}$ (angular velocity of the body relative to inertial space), coordinates of c.m. and components of $\mathbf{v}_0$ *must all be expressed relative to the direction-fixed axes.*

To illustrate this, consider again the body shown in Fig. 8-17. Components of $\boldsymbol{\omega}$ along the direction-fixed X', Y', Z' axes are given by

$$\omega_x' = \omega_x \alpha_{11} + \omega_y \alpha_{21} + \omega_z \alpha_{31}, \qquad \text{etc.}$$

where $\omega_x = \dot{\psi} \sin\theta \sin\phi + \dot{\theta}\cos\phi$, etc. See equations (*8.11*). Moments and products of inertia I_x', I_{xy}', etc., relative to X', Y', Z' may be expressed in terms of I_x, I_{xy}, etc., relative to the body-fixed X, Y, Z axes by means of equations (*7.20*), Page 123. Coordinates of c.m. in terms of $\bar{x}, \bar{y}, \bar{z}$ relative to body-fixed axes may be written as $\bar{x}' = \bar{x}\alpha_{11} + \bar{y}\alpha_{21} + \bar{z}\alpha_{31}$, etc. $\mathbf{v}_0$ has the same meaning as before, but its components must be taken along the fixed directions of X', Y', Z'.

On substituting the above "direction-fixed" values into (*8.10*), a valid expression for T is obtained. Note that this expression will finally reduce to exactly the same as obtained by the use of body-fixed axes.

The above procedure is usually far less convenient than the body-fixed method. However, for the sake of illustrating basic principles, we give the following specific example.

Example 8.19.

Referring to Fig. 8-16, suppose M a spinning top with body-fixed axis Z along its axis of symmetry and the tip fixed at O. We shall find T using quantities relative to the fixed X_1, Y_1, Z_1 frame.

$$\omega_{x_1} = \dot{\theta}\cos\psi + \dot{\phi}\sin\theta\sin\psi, \qquad \omega_{y_1} = \dot{\theta}\sin\psi - \dot{\phi}\sin\theta\cos\psi, \qquad \omega_{z_1} = \dot{\psi} + \dot{\phi}\cos\theta$$

From relations (*7.20*), Page 123,

$$I_{x_1} = I_x(\cos^2\psi + \cos^2\theta\sin^2\psi) + I_z\sin^2\theta\sin^2\psi$$
$$I_{y_1} = I_x(\sin^2\psi + \cos^2\theta\cos^2\psi) + I_z\sin^2\theta\cos^2\psi$$
$$I_{z_1} = I_x\sin^2\theta + I_z\cos^2\theta$$

$$I_{x_1y_1} = -I_x\sin^2\theta\sin\psi\cos\psi + I_z\sin^2\theta\sin\psi\cos\psi$$
$$I_{x_1z_1} = I_x\sin\theta\cos\theta\sin\psi - I_z\sin\theta\cos\theta\sin\psi$$
$$I_{y_1z_1} = -I_x\sin\theta\cos\theta\cos\psi + I_z\sin\theta\cos\theta\cos\psi$$

Since the tip is fixed, $v_0 = 0$ and thus

$$T = \tfrac{1}{2}[I_{x_1}\omega_{x_1}^2 + I_{y_1}\omega_{y_1}^2 + I_{z_1}\omega_{z_1}^2 - 2(I_{x_1y_1}\omega_{x_1}\omega_{y_1} + I_{x_1z_1}\omega_{x_1}\omega_{z_1} + I_{y_1z_1}\omega_{y_1}\omega_{z_1})]$$

On substituting from above, T becomes, after some long tedious reductions,

$$T = \tfrac{1}{2}I_x(\dot{\theta}^2 + \dot{\psi}^2\sin^2\theta) + \tfrac{1}{2}I_z(\dot{\phi} + \dot{\psi}\cos\theta)^2$$

which is just what was obtained in Example 8.14 making use of body-fixed axes.

8.10 Motion of a Rigid Body Relative to a Translating and Rotating Frame of Reference.

The general type of problem to be considered may be stated and illustrated as follows. Let X_2, Y_2, Z_2, Fig. 8-21 below, be regarded as inertial. Imagine, for example, X_1, Y_1, Z_1 attached to the cabin of a ship which is moving (translating, rolling, yawing, pitching) in any *known* or assumed manner relative to X_2, Y_2, Z_2. The motion of a rigid body, acted upon by given forces $\mathbf{F}_1, \mathbf{F}_2$, etc., is to be determined *relative to the cabin*.

It is evident that, basically, the required procedure is the same as that followed in all previous examples because, *under any and all conditions, relation (8.10), Page 148, is valid without change in form provided* $\omega_x, \omega_y, \omega_z$ *and* v_{0x}, v_{0y}, v_{0z} *are so expressed that they represent components of* $\boldsymbol{\omega}$ (total angular velocity of the body relative to inertial space) and $\mathbf{v}_0$ (the linear inertial-space velocity of O) *respectively, along the instantaneous directions of the body-fixed X, Y, Z axes*. Details of how these quantities can properly be expressed for this problem are given below.

Let $\boldsymbol{\Omega}_1$ represent the angular velocity of the X_1, Y_1, Z_1 frame (the boat) relative to X_2, Y_2, Z_2. Write components of $\boldsymbol{\Omega}_1$ along X_1, Y_1, Z_1 as $\Omega_{1x}, \Omega_{1y}, \Omega_{1z}$. Take $\boldsymbol{\Omega}$ as the angular velocity of the body relative to X_1, Y_1, Z_1 with components $\Omega_x, \Omega_y, \Omega_z$ *along the body-fixed X, Y, Z axes*. Let the orientation of the X_1, Y_1, Z_1 frame *relative to inertial space* (X_2, Y_2, Z_2) be determined by Euler angles θ_1, ψ_1, ϕ_1 as shown in the figure, and that of the body *relative to the cabin* by θ, ψ, ϕ (not shown but measured in the usual way with respect to X_1, Y_1, Z_1). Hence we write [see (*8.11*), Page 157],

$$\Omega_{1x} = \dot{\psi}_1\sin\theta_1\sin\phi_1 + \dot{\theta}_1\cos\phi_1, \qquad \text{etc.} \tag{1}$$

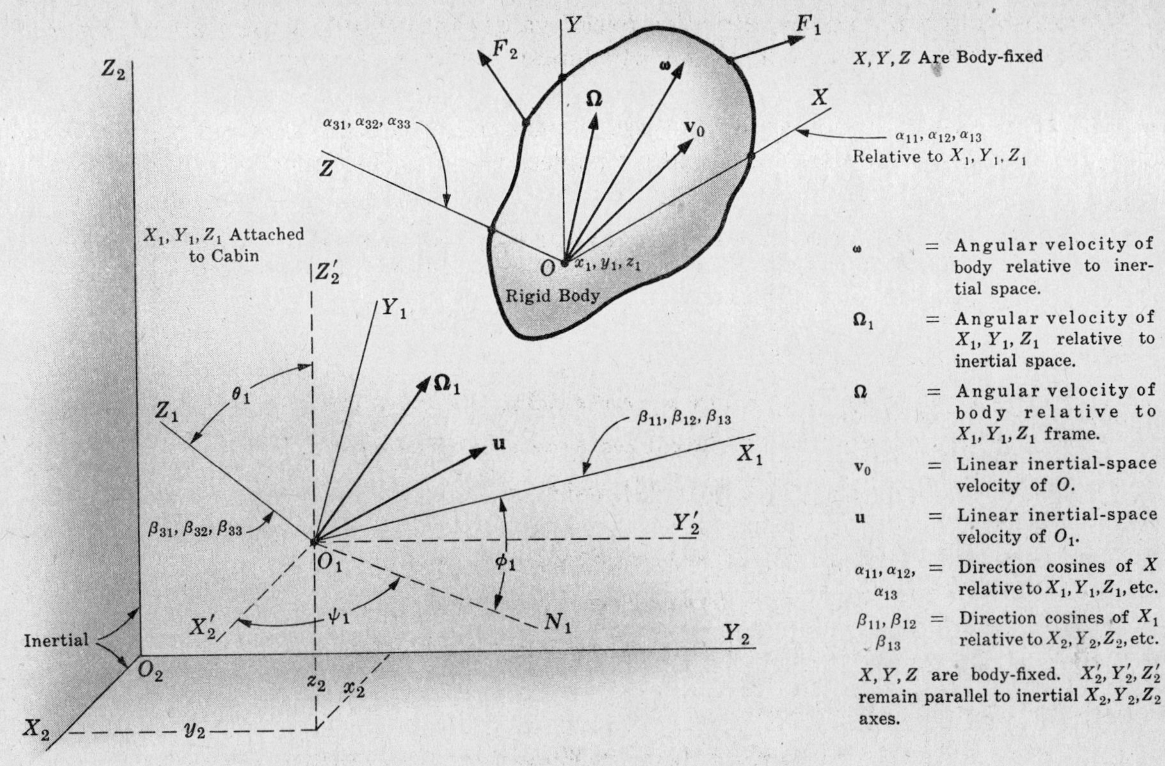

Fig. 8-21

and likewise
$$\Omega_x = \dot{\psi}\sin\theta\sin\phi + \dot{\theta}\cos\phi, \quad \text{etc.} \tag{2}$$

Therefore $\omega_x, \omega_y, \omega_z$, as defined above, are given by

$$\begin{aligned}
\omega_x &= \Omega_x + \Omega_{1x}\alpha_{11} + \Omega_{1y}\alpha_{12} + \Omega_{1z}\alpha_{13} \\
\omega_y &= \Omega_y + \Omega_{1x}\alpha_{21} + \Omega_{1y}\alpha_{22} + \Omega_{1z}\alpha_{23} \\
\omega_z &= \Omega_z + \Omega_{1x}\alpha_{31} + \Omega_{1y}\alpha_{32} + \Omega_{1z}\alpha_{33}
\end{aligned} \tag{8.14}$$

where $\alpha_{11}, \alpha_{12}, \alpha_{13}$, etc., are given in Table 8.2, Page 158. These are the expressions for $\omega_x, \omega_y, \omega_z$ required in (*8.10*), Page 148.

Indicating the linear velocity of O_1 relative to X_2, Y_2, Z_2 by **u**, with components u_x, u_y, u_z along X_1, Y_1, Z_1, we write
$$u_x = \dot{x}_2\beta_{11} + \dot{y}_2\beta_{12} + \dot{z}_2\beta_{13}, \quad \text{etc.} \tag{3}$$
where the meanings of x_2, β_{11}, etc., are indicated on the figure. Of course, **u** may be expressed in terms of spherical or other coordinates, if so desired.

Now writing v_1, v_2, v_3 as components of $\mathbf{v}_0$ ($\mathbf{v}_0$ = inertial space velocity of the origin O of X, Y, Z) along instantaneous directions of X_1, Y_1, Z_1, it follows from (*8.4*), Page 143, that

$$\begin{aligned}
v_1 &= \dot{x}_2\beta_{11} + \dot{y}_2\beta_{12} + \dot{z}_2\beta_{13} + \dot{x}_1 + \Omega_{1y}z_1 - \Omega_{1z}y_1 \\
v_2 &= \dot{x}_2\beta_{21} + \dot{y}_2\beta_{22} + \dot{z}_2\beta_{23} + \dot{y}_1 + \Omega_{1z}x_1 - \Omega_{1x}z_1 \\
v_3 &= \dot{x}_2\beta_{31} + \dot{y}_2\beta_{32} + \dot{z}_2\beta_{33} + \dot{z}_1 + \Omega_{1x}y_1 - \Omega_{1y}x_1
\end{aligned} \tag{8.15}$$

where x_1, y_1, z_1 are the X_1, Y_1, Z_1 coordinates of O and the β's are obtained from Table 8.2, Page 158, replacing θ by θ_1, etc. Thus v_0^2 which appears in (*8.10*) is given by

$$v_0^2 = v_1^2 + v_2^2 + v_3^2 \tag{4}$$

Also v_{0x}, v_{0y}, v_{0z}, as defined above, are

$$v_{0x} = v_1\alpha_{11} + v_2\alpha_{12} + v_3\alpha_{13}, \quad v_{0y} = v_1\alpha_{21} + v_2\alpha_{22} + v_3\alpha_{23}, \quad v_{0z} = v_1\alpha_{31} + v_2\alpha_{32} + v_3\alpha_{33} \tag{5}$$

Now inserting (4) in the first term of (8.10) and the results of (8.14) and (5) into the second and third terms, we have

$$T = T\begin{pmatrix} x_1, y_1, z_1;\ x_2, y_2, z_2;\ \theta_1, \psi_1, \phi_1;\ \theta, \psi, \phi \\ \text{and their time derivatives} \end{pmatrix} \tag{8.16}$$

But assuming that the motion of the ship (the X_1, Y_1, Z_1 frame) is known, x_2, y_2, z_2 and θ_1, ψ_1, ϕ_1 are known functions of time. Hence T can finally be put in the form

$$T = T(x_1, y_1, z_1;\ \dot{x}_1, \dot{y}_1, \dot{z}_1;\ \theta, \psi, \phi;\ \dot{\theta}, \dot{\psi}, \dot{\phi};\ t) \tag{8.17}$$

which contains no coordinates other than those which locate the body relative to the cabin. Thus equations of motion of the body *relative to the cabin* follow at once by an application of Lagrange's equations. Expressions for generalized forces are obtained in the usual way.

Note that if O is taken at the center of mass, the third term of (8.10) drops out and relations (5), which may be quite messy, are not necessary.

Results of the above section are illustrated by the following specific examples. As further illustrations see Problems 14.30, 14.31 and 14.32, Pages 299-301.

Example 8.20.

Referring to Fig. 8-22, the horizontal arm AB is made to rotate with angular velocity $\dot{\psi}_1$ about a vertical axis as shown. Disk D rotates with angular velocity $\dot{\phi}_1$, measured relative to the support C. Axes X_2, Y_2, Z_2 are assumed inertial. X_1, Y_1, Z_1 are attached to D. Z_1 extended backward intersects the vertical line about which AB rotates. We shall regard ψ_1 and ϕ_1 as known functions of time.

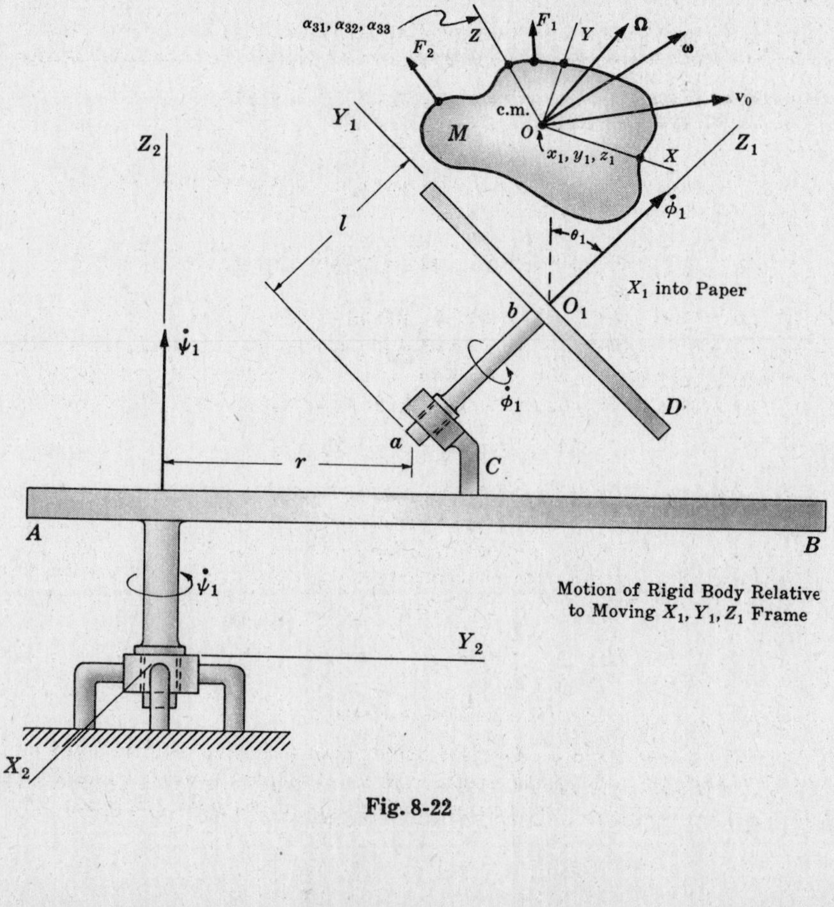

Fig. 8-22

A rigid body of mass M is acted upon by forces F_1, F_2, etc., (magnitude, direction and point of application of each assumed known). Following the same general notation and method outlined above in Section 8.10, let us determine the equations of motion of the body relative to the X_1, Y_1, Z_1 *frame.*

It may be seen from the figure that

$$\Omega_{1x} = \dot{\psi}_1 \sin\theta_1 \sin\phi_1, \qquad \Omega_{1y} = \dot{\psi}_1 \sin\theta_1 \cos\phi_1, \qquad \Omega_{1z} = \dot{\phi}_1 + \dot{\psi}_1 \cos\theta_1$$

Also, $\Omega_x = \dot{\psi}\sin\theta\sin\phi + \dot{\theta}\cos\phi$, etc. ($\theta, \psi, \phi$ are, of course, the Euler angles which determine the orientation of the body relative to X_1, Y_1, Z_1). Hence, just as in (*8.14*), Section 8.10,

$$\omega_x = \Omega_x + \Omega_{1x}\alpha_{11} + \Omega_{1y}\alpha_{12} + \Omega_{1z}\alpha_{13}, \qquad \text{etc.}$$

O_1 has a linear velocity $\mathbf{u}$ relative to inertial space of magnitude $(r + l\sin\theta_1)\dot{\psi}$. Components along X_1, Y_1, Z_1 are

$$u_x = (r + l\sin\theta_1)\dot{\psi}_1 \cos\phi_1, \qquad u_y = -(r + l\sin\theta_1)\dot{\psi}_1 \sin\phi_1, \qquad u_z = 0$$

Hence it is seen [following (*8.15*), Section 8.10] that

$$v_1 = (r + l\sin\theta_1)\dot{\psi}_1\cos\phi_1 + \dot{x}_1 + (\dot{\psi}_1 \sin\theta_1\cos\phi_1)z_1 - (\dot{\phi}_1 + \dot{\psi}_1\cos\theta_1)y_1$$

and corresponding expressions for v_2, v_3. Assuming that O is at c.m., expressions for v_{0x}, v_{0y}, v_{0z} are not required. And if X, Y, Z are taken along principal axes of inertia, T reduces to

$$T = \tfrac{1}{2}M(v_1^2 + v_2^2 + v_3^2) + \bar{I}_x^p\omega_x^2 + \bar{I}_y^p\omega_y^2 + \bar{I}_z^p\omega_z^2$$

which, assuming ψ_1 and ϕ_1 are known functions of time, is expressed as a function of $x_1, y_1, z_1, \theta, \psi, \phi$, their time derivatives and t. For the special case of $\dot{\psi}_1 = \text{constant}$ and $\dot{\phi}_1 = \text{constant}$, the expression for T is relatively simple.

Equations of motion are obtained at once by an application of Lagrange's equations. No further details need be given.

Example 8.21. *Regarding AB, D and M, Fig. 8-22, as a system of rigid bodies; to determine equations of motion of the system.*

We shall assume that known forces are applied to each component part, to find all motions of the entire system. A brief outline of steps required for the determination of the total kinetic energy follows.

Assuming X_2, Y_2, Z_2 as inertial, T_1, the kinetic energy of AB, is just

$$T_1 = \tfrac{1}{2}I_1\dot{\psi}_1^2$$

where I_1 is the moment of inertia of the arm AB, the vertical shaft and block C about Z_2. It easily follows that T_2, the kinetic energy of D *alone*, is

$$T_2 = \tfrac{1}{2}M_1(r + l\sin\theta_1)^2\dot{\psi}_1^2 + \tfrac{1}{2}\bar{I}_{x_1}^p\dot{\psi}_1^2\sin^2\theta_1 + \tfrac{1}{2}\bar{I}_{z_1}^p(\dot{\phi}_1 + \dot{\psi}_1\cos\theta_1)^2$$

where M_1 = mass of the uniform disk and $\bar{I}_{x_1}^p$ and $\bar{I}_{z_1}^p$ are moments of inertia of D about X_1 and Z_1 respectively. The expression for T_3, the kinetic energy of the rigid body, is exactly the one for T obtained in Example 8.20 above where, for this problem, ψ_1 and ϕ_1 are *not* assumed to be known functions of time. T_4, kinetic energy of rod ab (mass M_2, radius r, length l), is left to reader. Hence finally,

$$T_{\text{total}} = T_1 + T_2 + T_3 + T_4$$

Note the following: (*a*) The system has eight degrees of freedom. (*b*) T_{total} is expressed in terms of the eight coordinates $\psi_1, \phi_1; x_1, y_1, z_1; \theta, \psi, \phi$ and their time derivatives. (*c*) An application of Lagrange's equations gives the eight equations of motion. Generalized forces are obtained in the usual way. *Bearing forces* (bearings assumed smooth) *do not enter.* (*d*) Solutions to these equations give the rotational motion of AB relative to the X_2, Y_2, Z_2 frame, the rotation of D relative to C, and the motion of the rigid body relative to the X_1, Y_1, Z_1 frame.

Example 8.22. *Motion of a space ship and rigid body inside ship.*

Referring to Fig. 8-23 below, suppose the rigid body inside the space ship is acted on by forces F_1, F_2, etc., as well as the gravitational pull of the earth. Let us consider the problem of finding the motion of the ship relative to X_2, Y_2, Z_2 (assumed inertial) and the motion of the body relative to the ship (X_1, Y_1, Z_1).

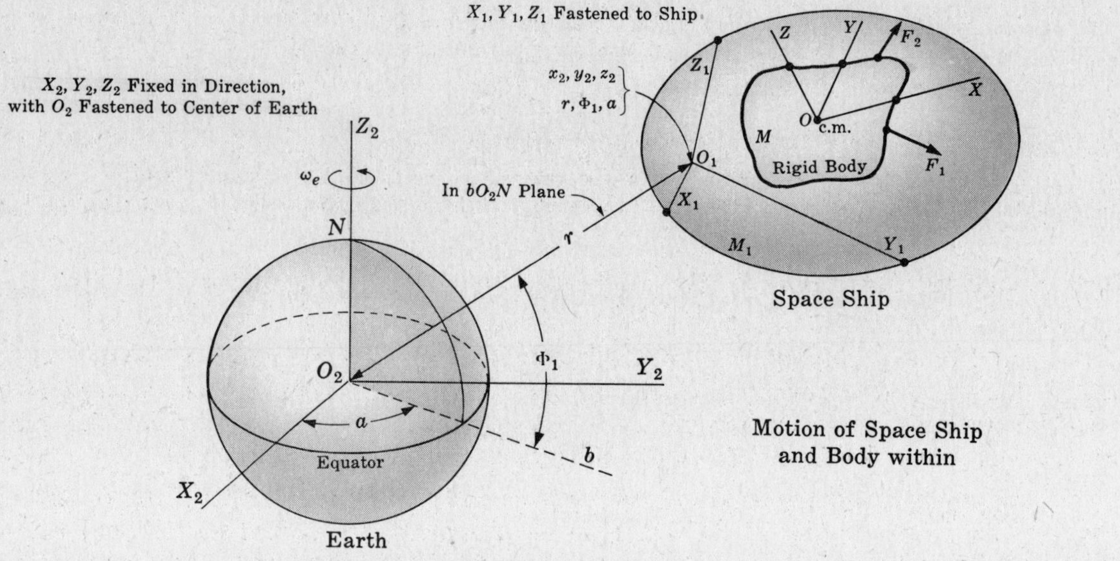

Fig. 8-23

T_1, the kinetic energy of the space ship, may be written in the usual way in terms of x_2, y_2, z_2 (or r, Φ_1, a, see below) and Euler angles θ_1, ψ_1, ϕ_1 (not shown) and their time derivatives. An expression for T_2, the kinetic energy of the rigid body, may be written in exactly the form of (*8.16*), Page 164. Thus

$$T_{\text{total}} = T_1 + T_2$$

and for given forces (including gravity) the equations of motion follow at once.

It is important to note that: (*a*) The system has twelve degrees of freedom, assuming the rigid body not constrained. (*b*) For this problem it is better to replace x_2, y_2, z_2 by r, Φ_1 and angle a. If desired, a can be written as $a = \omega_e t + \lambda$ where $\omega_e =$ angular velocity of earth and λ is the longitude of the meridian through which r passes. (See Fig. 14-4, Page 144.) (*c*) Generalized forces are found in the usual way. However, it must be remembered that for every force exerted on the body by, say, a light mechanism attached to the ship, there is an equal and opposite force on the ship itself.

Example 8.23. *Illustrating the meaning of equations (8.4), Page 143.*

In Fig. 8-24 axes X, Y, Z are attached to the rotating table. Base B, resting on an elevator, has a constant acceleration, a, upward. X_1, Y_1, Z_1 are attached to the earth and regarded as inertial. Line Oc is drawn on the table. Angle $\beta =$ constant. Assume θ, a and v_0 (the initial upward velocity of the elevator) as known quantities.

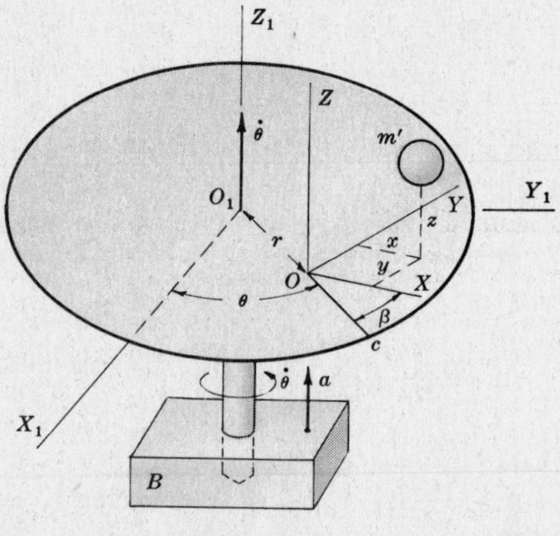

Fig. 8-24

Applying (*8.2*) it follows that for the particle m',

$$v_x = r\dot{\theta}\sin\beta + \dot{x} - \dot{\theta}y$$

$$v_y = r\dot{\theta}\cos\beta + \dot{y} + \dot{\theta}x$$

$$v_z = v_0 + at + \dot{z}$$

where v_x, v_y, v_z are components of the inertial-space velocity of m' along X, Y, Z. Hence

$$T = \tfrac{1}{2}m'[\dot{x}^2 + \dot{y}^2 + r^2\dot{\theta}^2 + (x^2+y^2)\dot{\theta}^2 + 2r\dot{\theta}^2(x\cos\beta - y\sin\beta)$$
$$+ 2r\dot{\theta}(\dot{y}\cos\beta + \dot{x}\sin\beta) + 2\dot{\theta}(x\dot{y} - y\dot{x}) + (v_0 + at + \dot{z})^2]$$

Show that transformation equations relating the inertial-space coordinates x_1, y_1, z_1 of m' with x, y, z are

$$x_1 = r\cos\theta + x\cos(\theta+\beta) - y\sin(\theta+\beta)$$

$$y_1 = r\sin\theta + x\sin(\theta+\beta) + y\cos(\theta+\beta)$$

$$z_1 = z + v_0 t + \tfrac{1}{2}at^2$$

and check the above results by an application of these relations.

Let **A** represent the linear acceleration of m' relative to inertial space. Find expressions for its components A_x, A_y, A_z along the instantaneous directions of X, Y, Z. Apply the method of Chapter 3, Page 48.

8.11 Suggested Experiment: Determination of the period of oscillation of disk D, Fig. 8-13, Page 154.

A metal disk of any convenient thickness and radius, mounted on a slender rod with end p sharpened as a pencil, is placed on an inclined plane consisting of a sheet of plate glass (glass greatly reduces damping). If the angle of incline is not too great, the disk will oscillate for some time about its equilibrium position without sliding down.

Find the period experimentally and compare with the computed value. With reasonable care in the determination of moments of inertia, mass, etc., experimental and computed values of the period will agree closely. For best results the mass, etc., of the supporting rod (length r_1 along Z) should be taken account of. This introduces no difficulties.

The theory involved in computing the period includes many of the basic principles of rigid body dynamics. Moreover, the experiment is quite interesting and inspires confidence in the general methods employed.

Problems

A. Angular velocities and their components.

8.1. Prove expressions (*8.0*), Page 140.

8.2. Assume that the rigid body, Fig. 8-1, Page 140, is rotating about lines Oa_1 and Oa_2 (not shown) with angular velocities ω_1 and ω_2 respectively. Corresponding linear velocities of m' are $v_1 = \omega_1 h_1$ and $v_2 = \omega_2 h_2$. Hence the magnitude of the total velocity **v** is given by

$$v^2 = \omega_1^2 h_1^2 + \omega_2^2 h_2^2 + 2\omega_1\omega_2 h_1 h_2 \cos\beta \qquad (a)$$

where β is the angle between v_1 and v_2.

But assuming that ω_1 and ω_2 can be combined as vectors, the resultant ω is given by $\omega^2 = \omega_1^2 + \omega_2^2 + 2\omega_1\omega_2\cos\theta$ where θ is the angle between ω_1 and ω_2. Hence it should be that

$$v^2 = \omega^2 h^2 \qquad (b)$$

where h is the normal distance from the line indicating ω to m'. Show that the two expressions (*a*) and (*b*) are equal. To simplify the work take Oa_1 along X and Oa_2 somewhere in the XY plane but m at some general point x, y, z.

8.3. Referring to Fig. 8-25, assume that the body, with one point fixed at O_1, has an angular velocity $\boldsymbol{\omega}(\omega_{1x}, \omega_{1y}, \omega_{1z})$ relative to X_1, Y_1, Z_1. As a result, m' has a linear velocity with components along X_1, Y_1, Z_1 given by $v_x = \omega_{1y}z_1 - \omega_{1z}y_1$, etc., where x_1, y_1, z_1 are the X_1, Y_1, Z_1 coordinates of m'.

Now consider the X, Y, Z frame with origin attached to the body at O. Assuming that these axes remain parallel to X_1, Y_1, Z_1, it is seen that $x_1 = x_0 + x$, etc. Extending the above, prove the statement made in Section 8.2C(h), Page 142.

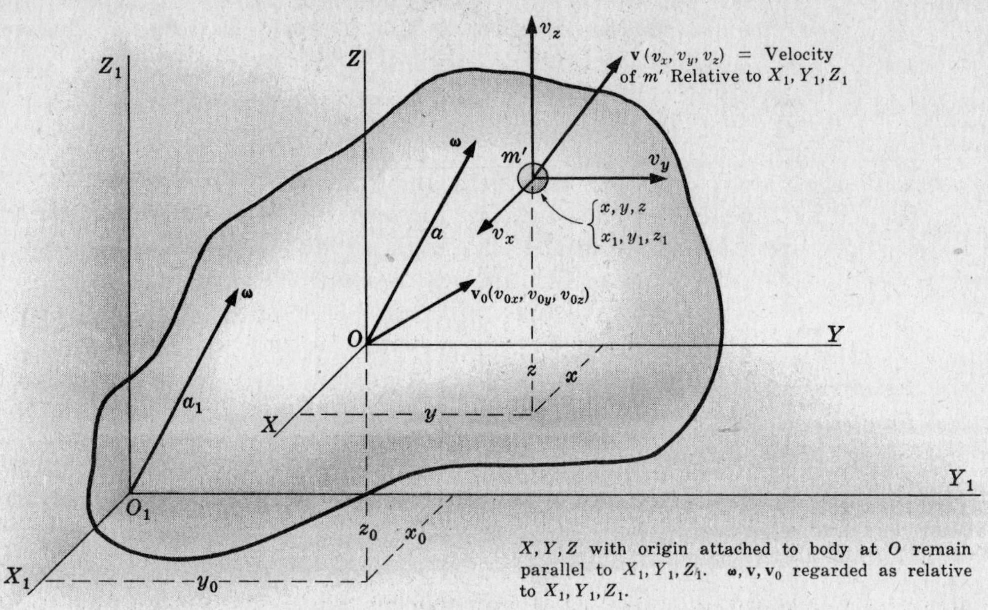

Fig. 8-25

8.4. Prove relations (1) and (2), Example 8.3, Page 146. Indicating direction cosines of the total angular velocity vector $\boldsymbol{\omega}$ by l, m, n relative to X, Y, Z, and l_1, m_1, n_1 relative to $X_1Y_1Z_1$, show that,

$$l = (\dot{\theta}_1 \cos\alpha + \dot{\theta}_2 \cos\beta)(\sin\theta_3)/\omega, \quad \text{etc.}$$

and

$$l_1 = (\dot{\theta}_2 \sin(\beta - \alpha) + \dot{\theta}_3 \cos\alpha)(\cos\theta_1)/\omega, \quad \text{etc.}$$

8.5. Referring to Fig. 8-11, Example 8.7, Page 152, show that the direction of the angular velocity vector of the rod relative to instantaneous positions of the body-fixed axes is given by

$$l = -\dot{\theta}_2/\omega, \quad m = (\dot{\theta}_1 \cos\theta_2)/\omega, \quad n = (\dot{\theta}_1 \sin\theta_2)/\omega$$

where $\omega^2 = \dot{\theta}_1^2 + \dot{\theta}_2^2$; and that relative to the space-fixed X_1, Y_1, Z_1 axes,

$$l_1 = -(\dot{\theta}_2 \sin\theta_1)/\omega, \quad m_1 = (\dot{\theta}_2 \cos\theta_1)/\omega, \quad n_1 = \dot{\theta}_1/\omega$$

8.6. Referring to Fig. 8-12, Example 8.8, Page 153, verify expressions given for $\omega_x, \omega_y, \omega_z$.

8.7. In Fig. 8-26 the disk D rotates through angle θ_3 measured by pointer p from a horizontal line parallel to the face and passing through the center of D. Shaft bd can rotate in a vertical plane through angle θ_2, about a horizontal bearing at b. The vertical shaft rotates through angle θ_1 measured from the fixed X_1 axis.

With body-fixed axes attached to D as in Fig. 8-5, Page 146, show that components of the angular velocity $\boldsymbol{\omega}$ along these axes are

$$\omega_x = \dot{\theta}_1 \cos\theta_2 \sin\theta_3 - \dot{\theta}_2 \cos\theta_3, \quad \omega_y = \dot{\theta}_1 \cos\theta_2 \cos\theta_3 + \dot{\theta}_2 \sin\theta_3, \quad \omega_z = \dot{\theta}_3 + \dot{\theta}_1 \sin\theta_2$$

Show that components of $\boldsymbol{\omega}$ along the inertial X_1, Y_1, Z_1 axes are

$$\omega_{x_1} = \dot{\theta}_3 \cos\theta_2 \cos\theta_1 + \dot{\theta}_2 \sin\theta_1, \quad \omega_{y_1} = \dot{\theta}_3 \cos\theta_2 \sin\theta_1 - \dot{\theta}_2 \cos\theta_1, \quad \omega_{z_1} = \dot{\theta}_1 + \dot{\theta}_3 \sin\theta_2$$

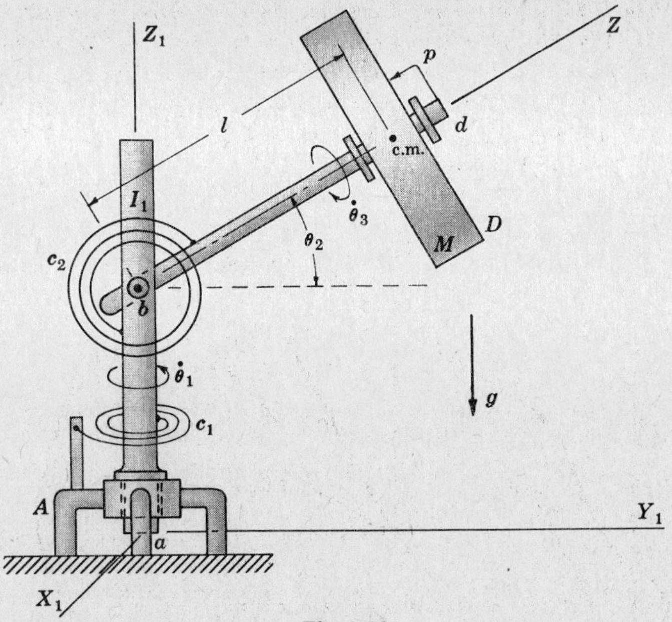

Fig. 8-26

8.8. Verify the important relations (*8.11*), Page 157. Also verify expressions for the direction cosines given in Table 8.2, Page 158. *Note.* A simple model is very helpful.

8.9. Referring to Fig. 8-3 and regarding m as a free particle, write $x_1 = x_0 + x\alpha_{11} + y\alpha_{21} + z\alpha_{31}$, etc. for y_1 and z_1. Differentiate these relations, regarding all quantities as variables. Making use of relations (*8.11*), Page 157, show that the expression for v_x (the component of the inertial space velocity of m along the instantaneous direction of X), $v_x = \dot{x}_1\alpha_{11} + \dot{y}_1\alpha_{12} + \dot{z}_1\alpha_{13}$, finally reduces to the first of (*8.4*), Page 143. The above requires patience but is a valuable exercise.

8.10. Referring to Example 8.20, Page 164, write out in full expressions for $\omega_x, \omega_y, \omega_z$.

B. Kinetic energy and equations of motion.

8.11. (*a*) In Fig. 8-5, Page 146, A is at rest. The origin O of body-fixed axes is at c.m. of the disk. Show that T for the entire system is

$$T = \tfrac{1}{2}(Ms^2 + \bar{I}_x^p)\dot{\psi}^2 \sin^2\theta + \tfrac{1}{2}\bar{I}_z^p(\dot{\psi}\cos\theta + \dot{\phi})^2 + \tfrac{1}{2}I_1\dot{\psi}^2$$

(*b*) Taking body-fixed axes as before but with origin at b, write an expression for T and show that it reduces to the one above. Can we regard b as attached to D?

8.12. (*a*) With the aid of relations (*8.3*), Page 142, determine T for the thin disk, Fig. 8-5, Page 146, by evaluating the integral $T = \frac{1}{2}\int v^2\,dm$ and compare with the expression for T found in Problem 8.11(*a*).

(*b*) The disk in Fig. 8-5 is replaced by a rigid body of any shape. Assuming the X, Y, Z axes to be the same as in part (*a*) (principal axes with origin at c.m.), show by integration that the expression for T is the same as in (*a*).

(*c*) Referring to Fig. 8-6 and Example 8.3, Page 146, show that v_{0x} is given by

$$v_{0x} = -(s\dot{\theta}_1\cos\theta_2 + \dot{\theta}_1 z_2\cos\theta_2\cos\gamma)\sin\theta_3\sin(\gamma-\alpha)$$
$$+ [-s\dot{\theta}_1\sin\theta_2 + (\dot{\theta}_2 + \dot{\theta}_1\sin\gamma)x_2 - \dot{\theta}_1 z_2\sin\theta_2\cos\gamma]\cos\theta_3 - \dot{\theta}_1 x_2\cos\theta_2\cos\gamma\sin\theta_3\cos(\gamma-\alpha)$$

(*d*) Referring to Fig. 8-15, Page 156, find expressions for v_{0x}, v_{0y}, v_{0z} employing equations (*8.3*), Page 142.

8.13. Taking body-fixed axes as indicated in Fig. 8-10(1), Example 8.6, Page 151, and assuming that r is a coil spring with constant k, show that

$$T = \tfrac{1}{2}M(\dot{r}^2 + r^2\dot{\theta}^2) + \tfrac{1}{2}I_z\dot{\phi}^2 - M\dot{r}\dot{\phi}[\bar{x}\sin(\phi-\theta) + \bar{y}\cos(\phi-\theta)]$$
$$- Mr\dot{\phi}\dot{\theta}[\bar{x}\cos(\phi-\theta) - \bar{y}\sin(\phi-\theta)]$$

Show that the r equation of motion is

$$m(\ddot{r} - r\dot{\theta}^2) - M\ddot{\phi}[\bar{x}\sin(\phi-\theta) + \bar{y}\cos(\phi-\theta)]$$
$$- M\dot{\phi}^2[\bar{x}\cos(\phi-\theta) - \bar{y}\sin(\phi-\theta)] = Mg\cos\theta - k(r - r_0)$$

Write the θ and ϕ equations.

8.14. Disks D_1 and D_2, Fig. 8-27, mounted in smooth bearings on a light bar ab, are free to rotate relative to the bar of length l with velocities $\dot{\theta}_1$ and $\dot{\theta}_2$. It is assumed the rims are in contact and rotate without slipping. The combination is free to slide about in any manner on the smooth inertial X_1Y_1 plane. How many degrees of freedom has the system? Show that

$$T = \tfrac{1}{2}(M_1 + M_2)(\dot{x}^2 + \dot{y}^2) + \tfrac{1}{2}M_2 l\dot{\theta}(l\dot{\theta} + 2\dot{y}\cos\theta - 2\dot{x}\sin\theta)$$
$$+ \tfrac{1}{2}I_1(\dot{\theta}_1 + \dot{\theta}_2)^2 + \tfrac{1}{2}I_2(R_1\dot{\theta}_1/R_2 + \dot{\theta})^2$$

A force F is applied to the rim of D_1 at p as indicated. As motion takes place, F remains in the same direction (α = constant). Show that generalized forces corresponding to x, y, θ_1, θ are

$$F_x = F\cos\alpha, \quad F_y = -F\sin\alpha, \quad F_{\theta_1} = -FR_1\sin(\theta_1 + \theta_2 + \alpha), \quad F_\theta = -FR_1\sin(\theta_1 + \theta + \alpha)$$

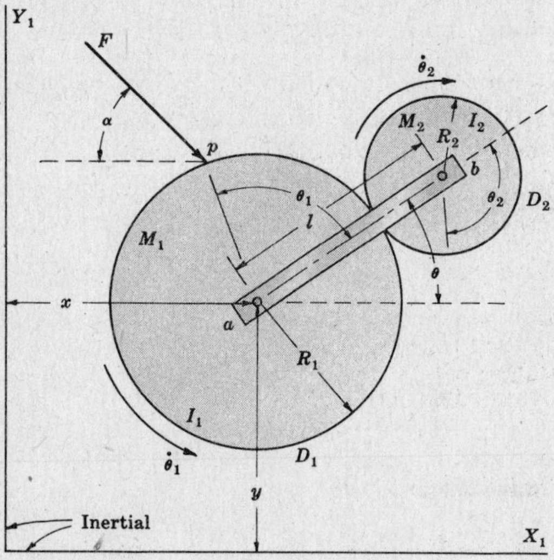

Fig. 8-27

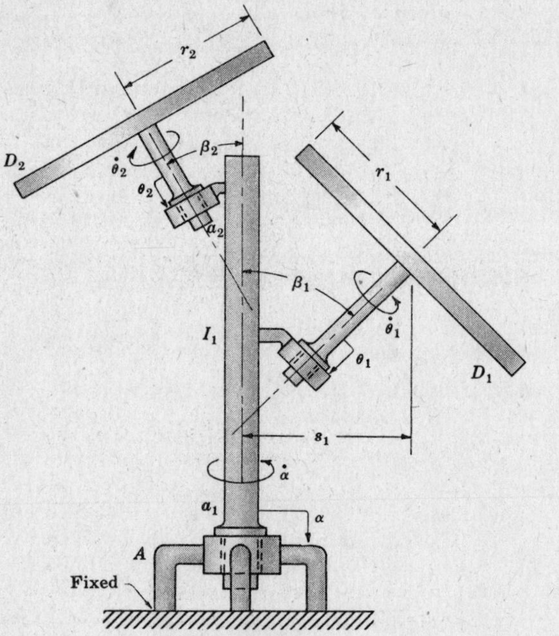

Fig. 8-28

8.15. The uniform disks D_1 and D_2, Fig. 8-28, are mounted on the vertical shaft as shown. Angles $\alpha, \theta_1, \theta_2$ are measured by pointers as indicated. Neglecting masses of the shafts which support the disks, show that T for the system is

$$T = \tfrac{1}{2}[M_1 s_1^2 + M_2 s_2^2 + \bar{I}_{x_1}\sin^2\beta_1 + \bar{I}_{x_2}\sin^2\beta_2]\dot{\alpha}^2$$
$$+ \tfrac{1}{2}\bar{I}_{z_1}(\dot{\theta}_1 + \dot{\alpha}\sin\beta_1)^2 + \tfrac{1}{2}\bar{I}_{z_2}(\dot{\alpha}\sin\beta_2 - \dot{\theta}_2)^2$$

8.16. Referring to Fig. 8-5, Page 146, a free particle m has coordinates x, y, z in the X, Y, Z frame. Making use of relations (*8.4*), Page 143, write T for the particle. Show by the method outlined in Chapter 3, Page 48, that the X component of the inertial space acceleration of m is given by

$$a_x = \ddot{x} + [(s+z)\ddot{\psi} + 2\dot{z}\dot{\psi} - (x\cos\phi - y\sin\phi)\dot{\psi}^2\sin\theta]\sin\theta\cos\phi$$
$$- y(\ddot{\phi} + \ddot{\psi}\cos\theta) - 2\dot{y}(\dot{\phi} + \dot{\psi}\cos\theta) - x(\dot{\phi} + \dot{\psi}\cos\theta)^2 + (s+z)\dot{\psi}^2\sin\theta\cos\theta\sin\phi$$

Check the above by means of equation (*9.6a*), Page 179. a_y and a_z follow in the same way.

8.17. Using the results of Problem 8.7 and neglecting the mass of rod bd but including I_1, show that

$$T = \tfrac{1}{2}Ml^2\dot{\theta}_1^2\cos^2\theta_2 + \tfrac{1}{2}\bar{I}_x(\dot{\theta}_2^2 + \dot{\theta}_1^2\cos^2\theta_2) + \tfrac{1}{2}\bar{I}_z(\dot{\theta}_3 + \dot{\theta}_1\sin\theta_2)^2 + \tfrac{1}{2}I_1\dot{\theta}_1^2$$

Taking account of the torsional springs and gravity, show that generalized forces corresponding to $\theta_1, \theta_2, \theta_3$ are

$$F_{\theta_1} = c_1\theta_1, \quad F_{\theta_2} = -c_2\theta_2 - Mgl\cos\theta_2, \quad F_{\theta_3} = 0$$

where c_1, c_2 are torsional constants and the springs are assumed undistorted for $\theta_1 = 0$, $\theta_2 = 0$.

8.18. Rigid body B, Fig. 8-29, is mounted on A by a shaft S. The two, thus attached, are free to move in space under the action of known forces. Origin O_1 of X_1', Y_1', Z_1' is fastened to c.m. of A. These axes, not otherwise attached to the body, remain parallel to an inertial frame (not shown). The same is true of O_2 and X_2', Y_2', Z_2'. Take X_a, Y_a, Z_a and X_b, Y_b, Z_b as body-fixed X_1, Y_1, Z_1 axes of A and B respectively. Z_b is, for convenience, taken as an extension of Z_a. B can rotate with angular velocity $\dot{\alpha}$ relative to A. Euler angles for the masses are measured as indicated.

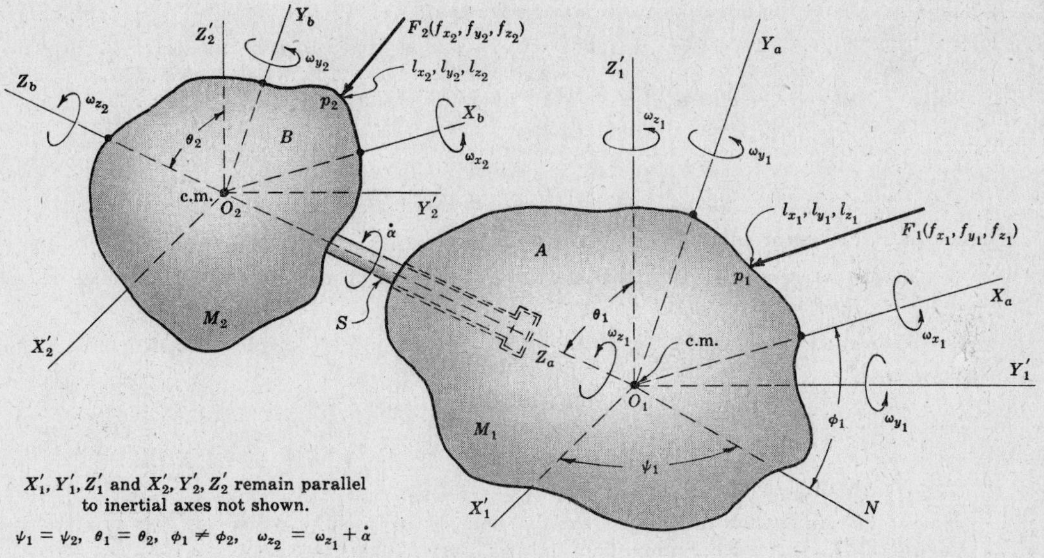

Fig. 8-29

Show that the system has seven degrees of freedom and that x_1, y_1, z_1 (coordinates of O_1 relative to some inertial frame), θ_1, ψ_1, ϕ_1 (Euler angles for A), and the Euler angle ϕ_2 for B are suitable coordinates. Prove the following relations:

$$\theta_1 = \theta_2, \quad \psi_1 = \psi_2, \quad x_2 = x_1 + l\sin\theta_1\sin\psi_1, \quad y_2 = y_1 - l\sin\theta_1\cos\psi_1, \quad z_2 = z_1 + l\cos\theta_1$$

where x_2, y_2, z_2 are coordinates of O_2 relative to the inertial frame and l is the constant distance between O_1 and O_2. Note that angular velocities are given by relations (*8.11*), Page 157, and that $\omega_{z_2} = \omega_{z_1} + \dot{\alpha}$. Write out expressions for all angular velocities and eliminate superfluous coordinates.

Assuming that body-fixed axes are principal axes of inertia, show that

$$T = \tfrac{1}{2}(M_1 + M_2)(\dot{x}_1^2 + \dot{y}_1^2 + \dot{z}_1^2) + \tfrac{1}{2}M_2[l^2\dot{\theta}_1^2 + l^2\dot{\psi}_1^2\sin^2\theta_1 + 2l\dot{\theta}_1\cos\theta_1(\dot{x}_1\sin\psi_1 - \dot{y}_1\cos\psi)$$
$$+ 2l\dot{\psi}_1\sin\theta_1(\dot{x}_1\cos\psi_1 + \dot{y}_1\sin\psi_1) - 2l\dot{z}_1\dot{\theta}_1\sin\theta_1]$$
$$+ \tfrac{1}{2}(\bar{I}^p_{x_1}\omega^2_{x_1} + \bar{I}^p_{y_1}\omega^2_{y_1} + \bar{I}^p_{z_1}\omega^2_{z_1}) + \tfrac{1}{2}(\bar{I}^p_{x_2}\omega^2_{x_2} + \bar{I}^p_{y_2}\omega^2_{y_2} + \bar{I}^p_{z_2}\omega^2_{z_2})$$

where $\omega_{x_1} = \dot{\psi}_1\sin\theta_1\sin\phi_1 + \dot{\theta}_1\cos\phi_1$, etc.; $\omega_{x_2} = \dot{\psi}_1\sin\theta_1\sin\phi_2 + \dot{\theta}_1\cos\phi_2$, etc.

Suppose that a known force F_1 (components $f_{x_1}, f_{y_1}, f_{z_1}$ along X_a, Y_a, Z_a) is acting on A at a point p_1, coordinates of which in the X_a, Y_a, Z_a system are $l_{x_1}, l_{y_1}, l_{z_1}$. Likewise, F_2 (components $f_{x_2}, f_{y_2}, f_{z_2}$) acts on B at p_2. Show that the generalized force corresponding to x_1 is

$$\begin{aligned} F_{x_1} \;=\; & f_{x_1}(\cos\phi_1\cos\psi_1 - \sin\phi_1\cos\theta_1\sin\psi_1) - f_{y_1}(\sin\phi_1\cos\psi_1 + \cos\phi_1\cos\theta_1\sin\psi_1) \\ & + f_{z_1}\sin\theta_1\sin\psi_1 + f_{x_2}(\cos\phi_2\cos\psi_1 - \sin\phi_2\cos\theta_1\sin\psi_1) \\ & - f_{y_2}(\sin\phi_2\cos\psi_1 + \cos\phi_2\cos\theta_1\sin\psi_1) + f_{z_2}\sin\theta_1\sin\psi_1 \end{aligned}$$

Write corresponding expressions for F_{y_1}, F_{z_1}. Show, for example, that

$$\begin{aligned} F_{\psi_1} \;=\; & (l_{y_1}f_{z_1} - l_{z_1}f_{y_1})\sin\theta_1\sin\phi_1 + (l_{z_1}f_{x_1} - l_{x_1}f_{z_1})\sin\theta_1\cos\phi_1 \\ & + (l_{x_1}f_{y_1} - l_{y_1}f_{x_1})\cos\theta_1 + (l_{y_2}f_{z_2} - l_{z_2}f_{y_2})\sin\theta_1\sin\phi_2 \\ & + (l_{z_2}f_{x_2} - l_{x_2}f_{z_2})\sin\theta_1\cos\phi_2 + (l_{x_2}f_{y_2} - l_{y_2}f_{x_2})\cos\theta_1 \end{aligned}$$

Find expressions for $F_{\phi_1}, F_{\phi_2}, F_{\theta_1}$.

8.19. See Section 8.4(*f*), Page 149. Consider a body, free to move in any manner. Take body-fixed axes along the principal axes of inertia with origin O at c.m. At any given moment the body may be regarded as having an angular velocity $\boldsymbol{\omega}$ about some instantaneous axis through O. Direction cosines of this line are ω_x/ω, etc. Indicating the variable moment of inertia of the body about this line by I, prove that $T = \frac{1}{2}Mv^2_{\text{c.m.}} + \frac{1}{2}I\omega^2$, which is just the "center of mass" theorem (Page 26) as applied to a rigid body.

C. *T* and equations of motion relative to moving frames.

8.20. In Fig. 8-30, X_2, Y_2 are fixed in space. X_1, Y_1 are attached to a horizontal rotating table which has an angular velocity $\dot{\alpha}$ about a vertical axis through O_2. X, Y, Z are fastened to a lamina of mass M which is free to slide on the X_1Y_1 plane under the action of forces f_1, f_2, etc. The lamina is located relative to X_1, Y_1 by coordinates x_1, y_1, θ as shown.

Show that $\omega_x = \omega_y = 0$, $\omega_z = \dot{\theta} + \dot{\alpha}$ and that

$$\dot{x}_2 \;=\; (\dot{x}_1 - y_1\dot{\alpha})\cos\alpha - [\dot{y}_1 + \dot{\alpha}(r + x_1)]\sin\alpha$$

with a similar expression for $\dot{y}_2$.

Show that components of the inertial space velocity of O along instantaneous positions of X and Y are given by

$$v_{0x} \;=\; \dot{x}_2\cos(\theta+\alpha) + \dot{y}_2\sin(\theta+\alpha), \qquad v_{0y} \;=\; -\dot{x}_2\sin(\theta+\alpha) + \dot{y}_2\cos(\theta+\alpha)$$

Show that for the lamina,

$$\begin{aligned} T \;=\; & \tfrac{1}{2}M[(\dot{x}_1 - y\dot{\alpha})^2 + (\dot{y}_1 + \dot{\alpha}(r+x_1))^2] + \tfrac{1}{2}I_z(\dot{\theta}+\dot{\alpha})^2 \\ & + M(\dot{\theta}+\dot{\alpha})\{[\dot{y}_1 + (r+x_1)\dot{\alpha}](\bar{x}\cos\theta - \bar{y}\sin\theta - (\dot{x}_1 - y_1\dot{\alpha})(\bar{x}\sin\theta + \bar{y}\cos\theta)\} \end{aligned}$$

Assuming α to vary in any known manner with time, $T = T(x_1, y_1, \theta; \dot{x}_1, \dot{y}_1, \dot{\theta}; t)$. Hence equations of motion (which are easily written out) determine the motion of the lamina relative to the moving X_1, Y_1 axes. Note simplification of T for O taken at c.m.

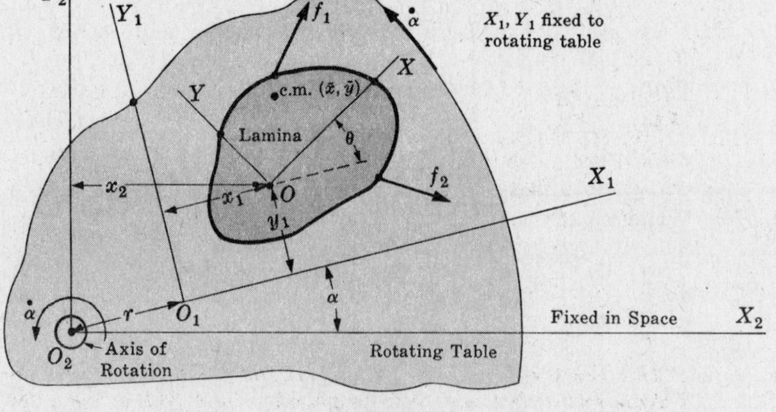

Fig. 8-30

8.21. Suppose that base B, Fig. 8-12, Page 153, is fastened at a distance R from the center of a horizontal table which rotates with known angular velocity $\dot{\alpha}$ about a vertical shaft through its center. Let X_1 be an extension of R. Taking body-fixed axes as shown for the disk, show that

$$\omega_x = (\dot{\alpha}+\dot{\psi})\sin\theta\sin\phi, \qquad \omega_y = (\dot{\alpha}+\dot{\psi})\sin\theta\cos\phi, \qquad \omega_z = \dot{\phi}+(\dot{\alpha}+\dot{\psi})\cos\theta$$

$$v_{0x} = R\dot{\alpha}(\cos\phi\sin\psi+\sin\phi\cos\theta\cos\psi), \qquad v_{0y} = -R\dot{\alpha}(\sin\phi\sin\psi-\cos\phi\cos\theta\cos\psi)$$

$$v_{0z} = -R\dot{\alpha}\sin\theta\cos\psi, \qquad v_0^2 = R^2\dot{\alpha}^2$$

where v_{0x}, v_{0y}, v_{0z} = components of $\mathbf{v}_0$, the inertial-space velocity of O, taken along instantaneous directions of the body-fixed axes X, Y, Z. Write out T. Compare with T given in Example 8.8, Page 152.

8.22. In Fig. 8-31, the X_1, Y_1, Z_1 frame is attached to the earth with Y_1 tangent to a great circle and pointing northward, Z_1 normal to the earth's surface and X_1 pointing to the east. Bearings supporting the a_1a_2 axis of the gyro are fixed relative to the earth. The gyro can rotate about a_1a_2 and b_1b_2. Show that, taking account of the earth's rotation,

$$\omega_x = (\dot{\theta}_1+\omega_e\sin\Phi)\sin\theta_2 + \omega_e\cos\Phi\cos\theta_1\cos\theta_2$$

$$\omega_y = (\dot{\theta}_1+\omega_e\sin\Phi)\cos\theta_2 - \omega_e\cos\Phi\cos\theta_1\sin\theta_2$$

$$\omega_z = \dot{\theta}_2 + \omega_e\cos\Phi\sin\theta_1$$

and that

$$T = \tfrac{1}{2}\bar{I}_x^p[(\dot{\theta}_1+\omega_e\sin\Phi)^2+\omega_e^2\cos^2\Phi\cos^2\theta_1] + \tfrac{1}{2}\bar{I}_z^p[\dot{\theta}_2+\omega_e\cos\Phi\sin\theta_1]^2 + \text{constant}$$

where ω_e is the angular velocity of the earth and Φ the latitude. The origin O of body-fixed axes X, Y, Z is taken at c.m.

Write equations of motion and show that, neglecting a term with ω_e^2 ($\omega_e = 7.29\times10^{-5}$ rad/sec),

$$\bar{I}_x^p\ddot{\alpha} + c\omega_e\cos\Phi\sin\alpha = 0$$

where $\theta_1+\alpha = 90°$ and $\partial T/\partial\dot{\theta}_2 = c$ = constant.

For α small, show that $2\pi(\bar{I}_x^p/c\omega_e\cos\Phi)^{1/2}$ is the period of oscillation of the b_1b_2 axis about the Y_1 line. Consider the case of $\dot{\theta}$ reversed in direction.

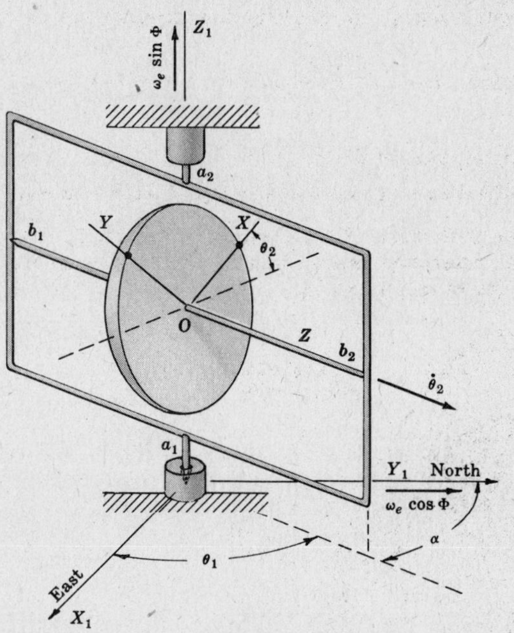

Fig. 8-31

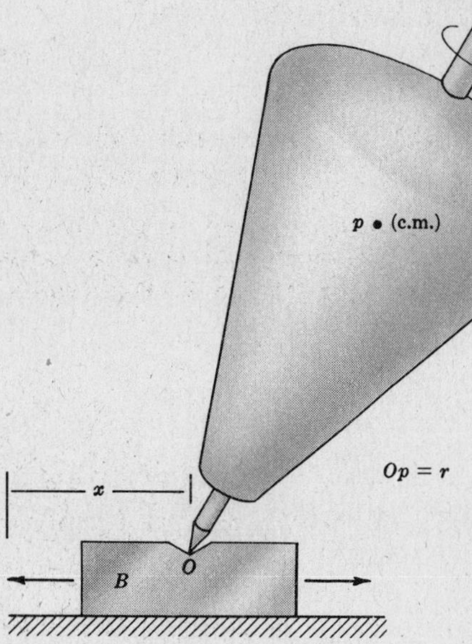

Fig. 8-32

8.23. The base B on which the top, Fig. 8-32, is spinning is made to oscillate horizontally according to $x = A\sin\omega t$. Taking body-fixed axes with origin at the tip and Z along the axis of the top, show that

$$T \;=\; \tfrac{1}{2}MA^2\omega^2\cos^2\omega t \;+\; \tfrac{1}{2}I_x(\dot{\theta}^2 + \dot{\psi}\sin^2\theta) \;+\; \tfrac{1}{2}I_z(\dot{\phi} + \dot{\psi}\cos\theta)^2$$
$$+\; MA\omega r\cos\omega t(\dot{\psi}\sin\theta\cos\psi + \dot{\theta}\cos\theta\sin\psi)$$

Show that the θ equation of motion is (note that first term in T may be dropped)

$$I_x\ddot{\theta} \;+\; (I_z - I_x)\dot{\psi}^2\sin\theta\cos\theta \;+\; I_z\dot{\phi}\dot{\psi}\sin\theta$$
$$-\; MA\omega^2 r\sin\omega t\cos\theta\sin\psi \;=\; Mgr\sin\theta$$

Write out the ψ and ϕ equations of motion.

8.24. The tip of the top, Fig. 8-33, remains at O on the horizontal rotating arm R. X_2, Y_2, Z_2 are fixed in space. X_1, Y_1, Z_1 are rigidly attached to the arm. X_1 is, for convenience, taken as an extension of R and X_1, Y_1 remain in the X_2Y_2 plane. Z_1 remains parallel to Z_2. X, Y, Z are body-fixed. Euler angles θ, ψ, ϕ are measured relative to X_1, Y_1, Z_1 as shown. This is a special case of the more general problem treated in Section 8.10, Page 162. Notation used is the same as in Fig. 8-21. Show that

$$v_0 \;=\; R\dot{\psi}_1 \quad \text{(always in the direction of } Y_1)$$
$$v_{0x} \;=\; R\dot{\psi}_1(\cos\phi\sin\psi + \sin\phi\cos\psi\cos\theta)$$
$$v_{0y} \;=\; R\dot{\psi}_1(\cos\phi\cos\psi\cos\theta - \sin\phi\sin\psi)$$
$$v_{0z} \;=\; -R\dot{\psi}_1\sin\theta\cos\psi$$
$$\omega_x \;=\; \dot{\psi}\sin\theta\sin\phi + \dot{\theta}\cos\phi + \dot{\psi}_1\sin\theta\sin\phi$$
$$\omega_y \;=\; \dot{\psi}\sin\theta\cos\phi - \dot{\theta}\sin\phi + \dot{\psi}_1\sin\theta\cos\phi$$
$$\omega_z \;=\; \dot{\phi} + \dot{\psi}\cos\theta + \dot{\psi}_1\cos\theta$$

Finally show that

$$T \;=\; \tfrac{1}{2}MR^2\dot{\psi}_1^2 \;+\; \tfrac{1}{2}[I_x^p(\omega_x^2 + \omega_y^2) + I_z^p\omega_z^2] \;+\; Mr(v_{0x}\omega_y - v_{0y}\omega_x)$$

Note that, assuming ψ_1, a known function of time (that is, the vertical shaft O_2b is forced to turn in a given manner), $T = T(\theta, \psi, \phi;\, \dot{\theta}, \dot{\psi}, \dot{\phi};\, t)$. Hence equations of motion give the motion of the top relative to the rotating X_1, Y_1, Z_1 frame.

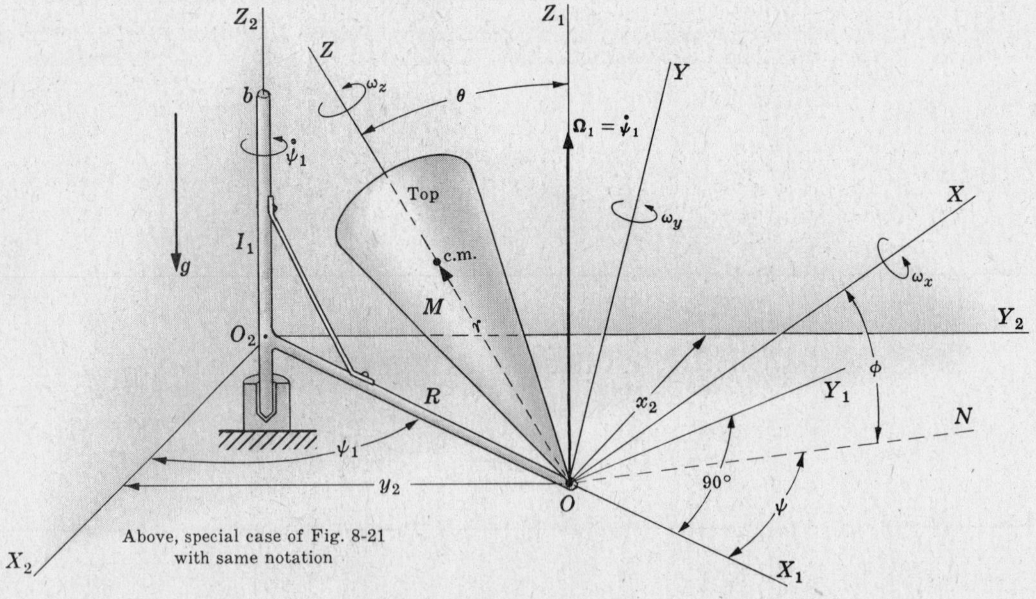

Fig. 8-33

8.25. Suppose the arm R, Fig. 8-33, and vertical shaft O_2b are free to rotate under the action of some known torque τ_{ψ_1}. How many degrees of freedom does the entire system now have? Write an expression for T of the entire system.

8.26. In Fig. 8-34 a rotating bearing B supports the shaft a_1b_1. On this shaft is mounted, in the manner shown, disk D. Angular displacements are measured relative to A, B, C respectively.

(a) Show that with axes attached to D as in Fig. 8-5, Page 146, (simple model suggested),

$$\omega_x = [\dot{\theta}_1 \cos\alpha \cos\theta_2 \cos\beta - (\dot{\theta}_2 + \dot{\theta}_1 \sin\alpha)\sin\beta]\sin\theta_3 + \dot{\theta}_1 \cos\alpha \sin\theta_2 \cos\theta_3$$

$$\omega_y = [\dot{\theta}_1 \cos\alpha \cos\theta_2 \cos\beta - (\dot{\theta}_2 + \dot{\theta}_1 \sin\alpha)\sin\beta]\cos\theta_3 - \dot{\theta}_1 \cos\alpha \sin\theta_2 \sin\theta_3$$

$$\omega_z = \dot{\theta}_3 + [\dot{\theta}_2 + \dot{\theta}_1 \sin\alpha]\cos\beta + \dot{\theta}_1 \cos\alpha \cos\theta_2 \sin\beta$$

(b) With the aid of principles outlined in Section 8.10, Page 162, write expressions for components of the inertial-space velocity of c.m. of D along X, Y, Z. (*Hint.* Take origin of X_1, Y_1, Z_1 axes at point p with Y_1 extending along r and Z_1 extending up along shaft a_1b_1.)

(c) Write out transformation equations relating the position of c.m. to inertial space. Differentiating these equations, find the velocity of c.m. Compare this value with the one found in (b).

(d) Without inserting the above explicit expressions for ω_x, v_{0x}, etc., write out T.

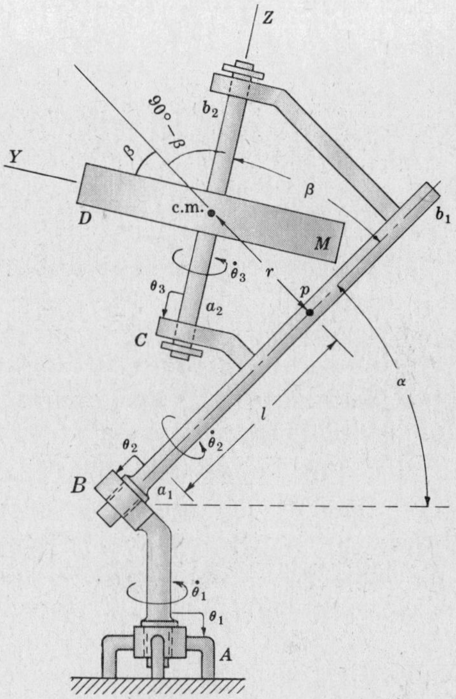

Fig. 8-34

8.27. Referring to Fig. 8-6, Page 147, a rigid body is free to move relative to the X, Y, Z axes shown, under the action of known forces. Taking body-fixed axes with origin at c.m., assuming $\dot{\theta}_1 = \text{constant}$, $\dot{\theta}_2 = \text{constant}$ and following the general procedure given in Section 8.10, Page 162, outline steps for finding T of the body.

8.28. In Example 8.20, Page 164, the supporting base is mounted at a point on the earth having latitude Φ. (See Fig. 14-2, Page 286.) Write expressions for $\omega_x, \omega_y, \omega_z, r_0$ and finally T for the rigid body taking account of the earth's rotation.

CHAPTER

9

The Euler Method of Rigid Body Dynamics

Rigid Body Dynamics: Part III

9.1 Preliminary Remarks.

The Lagrangian method just completed is, in most cases, more advantageous than the one about to be considered. Nevertheless, this chapter is included because (1) the Euler approach is quite helpful in making clear certain underlying physical and geometrical principles of rigid body dynamics, (2) the method has been and still is used extensively and (3) the examples and problems herein included furnish a means of making a direct comparison of the two methods.

The Euler treatment is based on the consideration of a "free rigid body", free in the sense that, if constrained, forces of constraint are included with those externally applied. Mathematically it leads to two fundamental vector equations (*9.3*) and (*9.15*), each of which in scalar form is equivalent to: (*a*) three *translational* equations of motion of the center of mass, equations (*9.2*); (*b*) three equations which determine the *rotational* motion of the body, equations (*9.10*). Hereafter the above six are referred to as "Euler's equations". For an understanding of their derivations and applications, close attention to detail is required. Considerable rereading may be necessary. However, no intrinsic difficulties will be encountered.

As shown in the following section, the first three are easily obtained from elementary considerations. The second set can be derived in several ways: from Lagrange's equations; by formal vector methods; or by a simple straightforward application of Newton's second law equations.

The latter is here employed because it leads to the general form of these equations in an easily understood manner and in such a way that sight is never lost of the basic physical principles involved. Moreover, the final equations of motion can be given a very simple physical interpretation.

The usual derivation of Euler's equations involves a consideration of the time rate of change of "angular momentum". But since it is felt that the method here presented offers certain pedagogic advantages, angular momentum is not discussed until near the end of the chapter.

9.2 Translational Equations of Motion of the Center of Mass.

Referring to Fig. 9-1 below and regarding the typical particle m' as "free", we write

$$m'\ddot{x}_1 = f_x, \quad m'\ddot{y}_1 = f_y, \quad m'\ddot{z}_1 = f_z \qquad (9.1)$$

where x_1, y_1, z_1 are coordinates of m' relative to the inertial X_1, Y_1, Z_1 frame and f_x, f_y, f_z are components of a net force $\mathbf{f}$ on m' giving it an acceleration $\mathbf{a}$ relative to inertial space. The vector sum of forces on m' due to attraction or repulsion of surrounding particles is assumed to be zero.

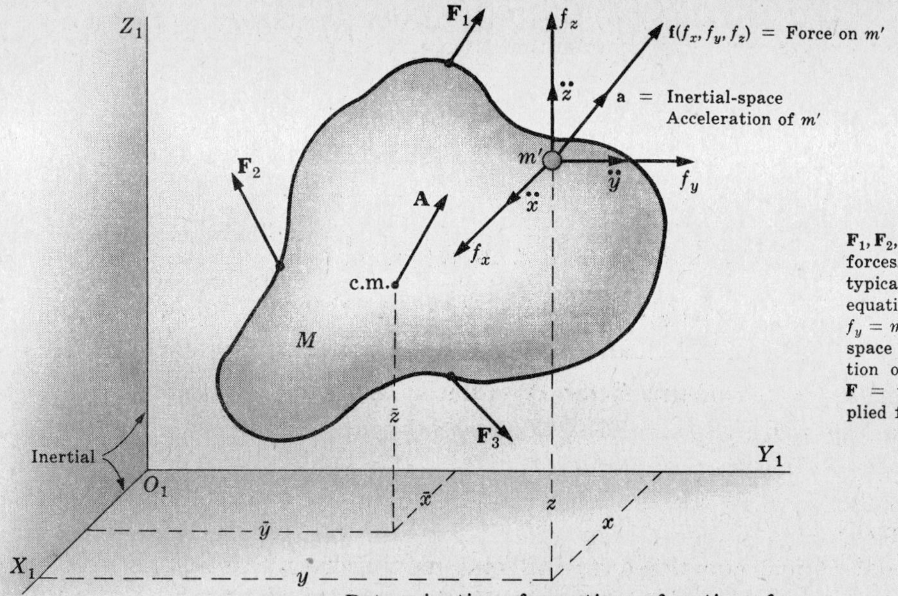

$\mathbf{F}_1, \mathbf{F}_2$, etc. = externally applied forces. $\mathbf{f}$ = force transmitted to typical particle m'. Free particle equations of motion: $f_x = m'\ddot{x}$, $f_y = m'\ddot{y}$, $f_z = m'\ddot{z}$. $\mathbf{A}$ = inertial-space acceleration of c.m. Equation of motion of c.m., $\mathbf{F} = M\mathbf{A}$. $\mathbf{F}$ = vector sum of externally applied forces.

Determination of equations of motion of c.m.

Fig. 9-1

Summing the first of (*9.1*) over all particles of the body, $\sum m_i'\ddot{x} = \sum f_x = F_x$ where F_x is the sum of the X_1 components of all *externally applied forces*. But from the definition of c.m., $\sum m'x_i = M\bar{x}$ where M is the total mass of the body and $\bar{x}$ is the X_1 coordinate of c.m. Hence $F_x = M\ddot{\bar{x}}$, $F_y = M\ddot{\bar{y}}$, $F_z = M\ddot{\bar{z}}$.

In order to avoid confusion in future notation we write $\ddot{\bar{x}} = A_x$, etc. Thus the three translational equations of motion of c.m. are written as

$$F_x = MA_x, \quad F_y = MA_y, \quad F_z = MA_z \tag{9.2}$$

It is clear that (*9.2*) may be regarded as component equations of the vector relation

$$M\mathbf{A} = \mathbf{F} \tag{9.3}$$

where **F** is the vector sum of all externally applied forces (regarded as acting at c.m.) and **A** represents, in vector notation, the acceleration of c.m. *relative to inertial space*.

Note the following important facts:

(*a*) The center of mass moves as if the entire mass of the body were concentrated at c.m. with all external forces transferred, without change in magnitude or direction, to this point.

(*b*) Applied forces $\mathbf{F}_1, \mathbf{F}_2$, etc., cause not only translation of c.m. but (as will soon be evident) rotational motion of the body as well. However, it should be noted that, *regardless of the rotation*, equation (*9.3*) is valid.

(*c*) Equation (*9.3*) obviously applies to a body constrained in any manner, provided forces of constraint (usually introduced as unknown quantities) are included in **F**.

9.3 Various Ways of Expressing the Scalar Equations Corresponding to (*9.3*).

In equations (*9.2*) the c.m. may be treated just as a single particle. Components of **A** and **F** (basically, of course **A** must be reckoned relative to inertial space) *can be taken along* *any axes, moving or stationary, and expressed in any convenient coordinates.* For example, assuming X, Y, Z as inertial, equations (*2.60*), Page 29, may be regarded as components of **A** along tangents to the coordinate lines corresponding to r, θ, ϕ. Or again, considering Fig. 9-8, Page 189, equations of motion of c.m. may be obtained by taking components of **A** and **F** either along *instantaneous directions* of the body-fixed axes or say X_1, Y_1, Z_1, etc.

Specific expressions for the components of **A** may be found (*a*) as indicated in Section 2.12(3), Page 29, (*b*) by the Lagrangian method outlined in Section 3.9, Page 48, or (*c*) in case components are to be taken along the axes of a rotating and translating frame, A_x, A_y, A_z may be obtained from relation (*9.6*).

9.4 Background Material For a Determination of Euler's Rotational Equations.

A. *General expressions for the components of the inertial-space acceleration of a free particle along the axes of a moving frame.*

Referring to Fig. 9-2, regard X_1, Y_1, Z_1 as inertial. Assume the X, Y, Z frame is translating and rotating in any manner. This frame could, for example, be one attached to the deck of a boat which is rolling, pitching, yawing and moving forward. X', Y', Z' axes, with origin attached to that of X, Y, Z, are assumed to remain parallel to X_1, Y_1, Z_1. Let $\mathbf{\Omega}$ represent the angular velocity of the X, Y, Z frame relative to X_1, Y_1, Z_1 (or to X', Y', Z'). Components of $\mathbf{\Omega}$ along instantaneous positions of X, Y, Z will be written as $\Omega_x, \Omega_y, \Omega_z$. Regard m as a free particle (not one forming part of a rigid body), acted on by a force **f** which gives it an acceleration **a** relative to inertial space.

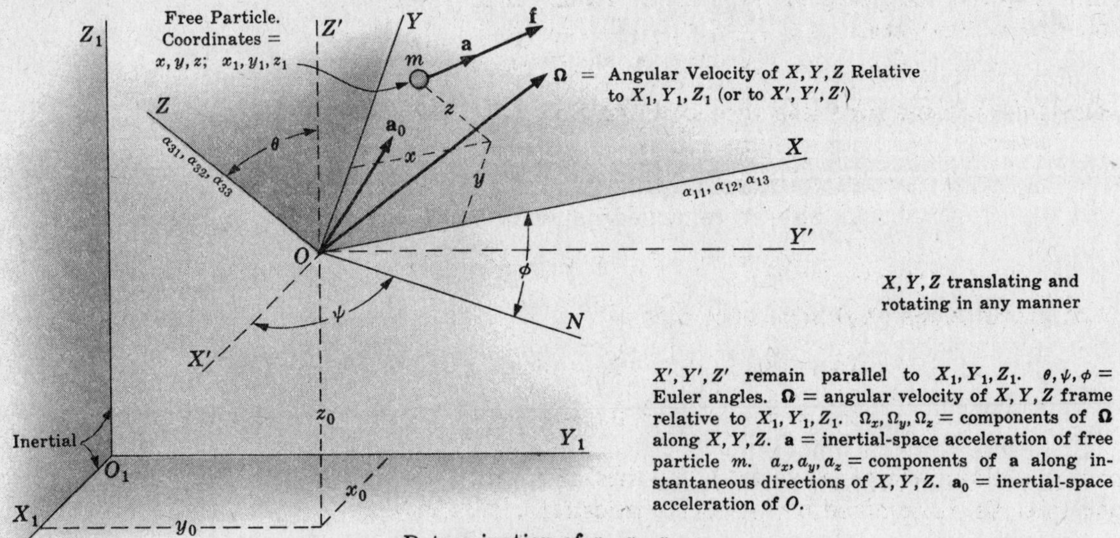

Determination of a_x, a_y, a_z.

Fig. 9-2

We shall now find expressions (relations (*9.6*) below) for a_x, a_y, a_z, the components of **a** *along the instantaneous directions of* X, Y, Z. As will be seen later these expressions play a vital part in the derivation of Euler's rotational equations of motion.

Perhaps the clearest and most direct way of obtaining the desired results is through the use of transformation equations. Let x_1, y_1, z_1 and x, y, z be coordinates of m relative to X_1, Y_1, Z_1 and X, Y, Z respectively. Denoting coordinates of O by x_0, y_0, z_0, we write the transformation equation

$$x_1 = x_0 + x\alpha_{11} + y\alpha_{21} + z\alpha_{31}$$

where, as indicated in the figure, $\alpha_{11}, \alpha_{12}, \alpha_{13}$ are direction cosines of X, etc. Differentiating the above twice with respect to time, we have

$$\ddot{x}_1 = \ddot{x}_0 + \ddot{x}\alpha_{11} + \ddot{y}\alpha_{21} + \ddot{z}\alpha_{31} + x\ddot{\alpha}_{11} + y\ddot{\alpha}_{21} + z\ddot{\alpha}_{31} + 2(\dot{x}\dot{\alpha}_{11} + \dot{y}\dot{\alpha}_{21} + \dot{z}\dot{\alpha}_{31}) \qquad (1)$$

Corresponding expressions follow for $\ddot{y}_1$ and $\ddot{z}_1$. Hence a_x, a_y, a_z, as defined above, are given by

$$a_x = \ddot{x}_1\alpha_{11} + \ddot{y}_1\alpha_{12} + \ddot{z}_1\alpha_{13}, \quad \text{etc.} \qquad (9.4)$$

These expressions can be put into final useful form, (*9.6*) below, as follows. Let Euler angles be measured relative to X', Y', Z' as shown in Fig. 9-2. Hence direction cosines $\alpha_{11}, \alpha_{12}, \alpha_{13}$ of X etc. can be written in terms of ψ, ϕ, θ by Table 8.2, Page 158, and expressions for $\dot{\alpha}_1, \ddot{\alpha}_1$, etc., may be obtained by differentiation.

Now eliminating $\ddot{x}_1, \ddot{y}_1, \ddot{z}_1$ from (*9.4*) by (*1*), etc.; eliminating the α's, $\dot{\alpha}$'s, $\ddot{\alpha}$'s from the resulting equations and making use of the following relations (see equations (*8.11*), Page 157)

$$\Omega_x = \dot{\psi}\sin\theta\sin\phi + \dot{\theta}\cos\phi, \quad \Omega_y = \dot{\psi}\sin\theta\cos\phi - \dot{\theta}\sin\phi, \quad \Omega_z = \dot{\phi} + \dot{\psi}\cos\theta \qquad (9.5)$$

equation (*9.4*) finally takes the form of (*9.6a*) below. In like manner (*9.6b*) and (*9.6c*) may be obtained.

However, in order to simplify the trigonometric manipulations, without the loss of generality, we shall proceed as follows. Let us assume (as a matter of convenience) that at any moment under consideration the inertial X_1, Y_1, Z_1 frame is chosen in a position such that $\theta = 90°$ and $\psi = \phi = 0$. Note that in this case X is parallel to X_1, Y to Z_1 and Z points in the negative direction of Y_1. From Table 8.2 it is seen that $\alpha_{11} = 1$, $\alpha_{12} = \alpha_{13} = 0$, etc. Hence from (*9.4*), etc.,

$$a_x = \ddot{x}_1, \quad a_y = \ddot{z}_1, \quad a_z = -\ddot{y}_1 \qquad (2)$$

It also follows that for these values of the Euler angles,

$$\begin{aligned} \alpha_{11} &= 1, & \dot{\alpha}_{11} &= 0, & \ddot{\alpha}_{11} &= -(\dot{\phi}^2 + \dot{\psi}^2) \\ \alpha_{21} &= 0, & \dot{\alpha}_{21} &= -\dot{\phi}, & \ddot{\alpha}_{21} &= (2\dot{\theta}\dot{\psi} - \ddot{\phi}) \\ \alpha_{31} &= 0, & \dot{\alpha}_{31} &= \dot{\psi}, & \ddot{\alpha}_{31} &= \ddot{\psi} \end{aligned} \qquad (3)$$

and from relations (*9.5*) it is seen that

$$\begin{aligned} \Omega_x &= \dot{\theta}, & \Omega_y &= \dot{\psi}, & \Omega_z &= \dot{\phi} \\ \dot{\Omega}_x &= \ddot{\theta} + \dot{\psi}\dot{\phi}, & \dot{\Omega}_y &= \ddot{\psi} - \dot{\phi}\dot{\theta}, & \dot{\Omega}_z &= \ddot{\phi} - \dot{\psi}\dot{\theta} \end{aligned} \qquad (4)$$

Finally, making use of (*3*) and (*4*), the first of (*2*) can be written as (*9.6a*) below. (*9.6b*) and (*9.6c*) may be determined by the same procedure.

$$\begin{aligned} a_x &= a_{0x} + \ddot{x} - x(\Omega_y^2 + \Omega_z^2) + y(\Omega_x\Omega_y - \dot{\Omega}_z) \\ &\quad + z(\Omega_x\Omega_z + \dot{\Omega}_y) + 2(\dot{z}\Omega_y - \dot{y}\Omega_z) & (a) \\ a_y &= a_{0y} + \ddot{y} + x(\Omega_x\Omega_y + \dot{\Omega}_z) - y(\Omega_x^2 + \Omega_z^2) \\ &\quad + z(\Omega_y\Omega_z - \dot{\Omega}_x) + 2(\dot{x}\Omega_z - \dot{z}\Omega_x) & (b) \\ a_z &= a_{0z} + \ddot{z} + x(\Omega_x\Omega_z - \dot{\Omega}_y) + y(\Omega_y\Omega_z + \dot{\Omega}_x) \\ &\quad - z(\Omega_x^2 + \Omega_y^2) + 2(\dot{y}\Omega_x - \dot{x}\Omega_y) & (c) \end{aligned} \qquad (9.6)$$

Components of **a**, the inertial space acceleration of m, Fig. 9-2, along instantaneous positions of the translating and rotating X, Y, Z axes.

The meaning of each symbol appearing in (*9.6*) must be kept in mind. $\mathbf{a}$ = acceleration of m, $\mathbf{a}_0$ = acceleration of O, $\boldsymbol{\Omega}$ = angular velocity of the X, Y, Z frame; *each measured relative to an inertial frame.* a_x, a_y, a_z = components of $\mathbf{a}$, a_{0x}, a_{0y}, a_{0z} = components of $\mathbf{a}_0$, $\omega_x, \omega_y, \omega_z$ = components of $\boldsymbol{\Omega}$; in each case taken *along instantaneous directions* of the translating and rotating X, Y, Z axes. $\dot{x}, \ddot{x}$, etc., are components of velocity and acceleration of m relative to X, Y, Z (as measured by an observer riding this frame).

In vector notation, equations (*9.6*) are equivalent to

$$\mathbf{a} = \ddot{\mathbf{r}}_0 + \mathbf{a}_1 + 2\boldsymbol{\omega}\times\mathbf{v} + \dot{\boldsymbol{\omega}}\times\mathbf{r} + \boldsymbol{\omega}\times(\boldsymbol{\omega}\times\mathbf{r})$$

where $\mathbf{a}$ is the inertial space acceleration of m, $\mathbf{r}_0$ = the position vector measured from O_1 to O, $\mathbf{a}_1 = \mathbf{i}\ddot{x} + \mathbf{j}\ddot{y} + \mathbf{k}\ddot{z}$ = acceleration of m relative to X, Y, Z, $\mathbf{r}$ = position vector measured from O to m, $\mathbf{v} = \mathbf{i}\dot{x} + \mathbf{j}\dot{y} + \mathbf{k}\dot{z}$ = velocity of m relative to X, Y, Z, $\mathbf{i}, \mathbf{j}, \mathbf{k}$ = unit vectors along X, Y, Z. See Chapter 18.

For another approach to the derivation of (*9.6*) see S. W. McCuskey, *Introduction to Advanced Dynamics*, Addison-Wesley, 1959, pp. 31, 32. Also see Problem 9.2, Page 197.

The basic nature and importance of (*9.6*) may be seen from the following example.

Example 9.1.

Referring to Fig. 2-21, Page 22, let us determine a_x, a_y the components of the inertial-space acceleration of m, along instantaneous directions of X_2, Y_2 respectively. Note that $\omega_{x_2} = \omega_{y_2} = 0$, $\omega_{z_2} = \dot{\theta}_1 + \dot{\theta}_2$. By elementary considerations a_{0x}, a_{0y}, the components of the inertial-space acceleration of the origin of the X_2, Y_2, Z_2 frame along X_2 and Y_2 respectively, are seen to be

$$a_{0x} = -s\dot{\theta}_1^2 \cos\theta_2 + s\ddot{\theta}_1 \sin\theta_2, \qquad a_{0y} = s\dot{\theta}_1^2 \sin\theta_2 + s\ddot{\theta}_1 \cos\theta_2$$

Applying (*9.6*), we obtain at once

$$a_x = -s\dot{\theta}_1^2 \cos\theta_2 + s\ddot{\theta}_1 \sin\theta_2 + \ddot{x}_2 - x_2(\dot{\theta}_1 + \dot{\theta}_2)^2 - y_2(\ddot{\theta}_1 + \ddot{\theta}_2) - 2\dot{y}_2(\dot{\theta}_1 + \dot{\theta}_2)$$

$$a_y = s\dot{\theta}_1^2 \sin\theta_2 + s\ddot{\theta}_1 \cos\theta_2 + \ddot{y}_2 - y_2(\dot{\theta}_1 + \dot{\theta}_2)^2 + x_2(\ddot{\theta}_1 + \ddot{\theta}_2) + 2\dot{x}_2(\dot{\theta}_1 + \dot{\theta}_2)$$

An observer riding D_2 and wishing to determine the motion of m relative to this moving disk would then write the equations of motion as $ma_x = f_x$, $ma_y = f_y$ where f_x and f_y are the X_2, Y_2 components of force on m.

Note the following: It easily follows that the kinetic energy of m is given by

$$T = \tfrac{1}{2}m[s\dot{\theta}_1^2 + (\dot{x}_2 - y_2\dot{\beta})^2 + (\dot{y}_2 + x_2\dot{\beta})^2 + 2s\dot{\theta}_1(\dot{x}_2 - y_2\dot{\beta}) \sin\theta_2 + 2s\dot{\theta}_1(\dot{y}_2 + x_2\dot{\beta}) \cos\theta_2]$$

where $\beta = \theta_1 + \theta_2$. See Problem 9.2, Page 197. Applying the method of Section 3.9, Page 48, the reader should check the above expressions for a_x and a_y.

B. *Form taken by equations (9.6) when m is a typical particle of a rigid body.*

Suppose that m, Fig. 9-2, is now the typical particle m', Fig. 9-3. Assume, for simplicity, that X, Y, Z are body-fixed as shown. In this case x, y, z are constants. Hence $\dot{x} = \dot{y} = \dot{z} = 0$, $\ddot{x} = \ddot{y} = \ddot{z} = 0$. The angular velocity $\boldsymbol{\Omega}$ of the frame is now the angular velocity $\boldsymbol{\omega}$ of the body relative to X_1, Y_1, Z_1 (or to X', Y', Z') and $\Omega_x = \omega_x$, etc., where $\omega_x, \omega_y, \omega_z$ represent components of the inertial space angular velocity of the body along instantaneous directions of X, Y, Z. Hence relations (*9.6*) immediately reduce to

$$\begin{aligned} a_x &= a_{0x} - x(\omega_y^2 + \omega_z^2) + y(\omega_y\omega_x - \dot{\omega}_z) + z(\omega_x\omega_z + \dot{\omega}_y) && (a) \\ a_y &= a_{0y} + x(\omega_x\omega_y + \dot{\omega}_z) - y(\omega_x^2 + \omega_z^2) + z(\omega_y\omega_z - \dot{\omega}_x) && (b) \qquad (9.7) \\ a_z &= a_{0z} + x(\omega_x\omega_z - \dot{\omega}_y) + y(\omega_y\omega_z + \dot{\omega}_x) - z(\omega_x^2 + \omega_y^2) && (c) \end{aligned}$$

The above relations are, of course, applicable to any body-fixed axes with origin at any point O.

It should be noted that since a_x, a_y, a_z are components of $\mathbf{a}$, the inertial space acceleration of m', the component a_{0a} of $\mathbf{a}$ along any line O_a through O and having direction cosines

l, m, n relative to X, Y, Z is given by

$$a_{Oa} = a_x l + a_y m + a_z n \tag{9.7a}$$

Indeed O_a may be rotating about O relative to the body, in which case l, m, n are variable and (9.7a) gives a_{Oa} along the instantaneous position of this line.

9.5 Euler's Three Rotational Equations of Motion for a Rigid Body. General Form.

We shall now derive the rotational equations of motion of the body, Fig. 9-3, to which external forces $\mathbf{F}_1, \mathbf{F}_2$, etc., are applied.

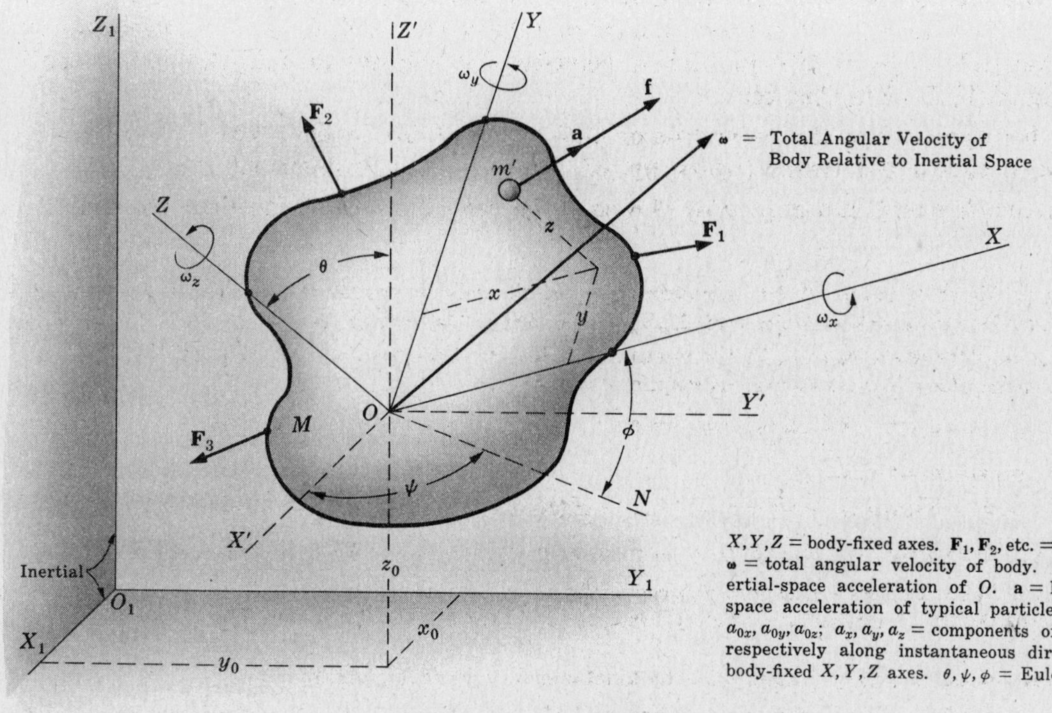

X, Y, Z = body-fixed axes. $\mathbf{F}_1, \mathbf{F}_2$, etc. = applied forces. $\boldsymbol{\omega}$ = total angular velocity of body. $\mathbf{a}_0$ = linear inertial-space acceleration of O. $\mathbf{a}$ = linear inertial-space acceleration of typical particle m'. $\omega_x, \omega_y, \omega_z$; a_{0x}, a_{0y}, a_{0z}; a_x, a_y, a_z = components of $\boldsymbol{\omega}$, $\mathbf{a}_0$ and $\mathbf{a}$ respectively along instantaneous directions of the body-fixed X, Y, Z axes. θ, ψ, ϕ = Euler angles.

Fig. 9-3

As the body rotates and translates, any typical particle m' will in general experience some acceleration $\mathbf{a}$ (exactly as in Section 9.2), here regarded as measured relative to inertial space. This is due to a force $\mathbf{f}$ which is the resultant of forces transmitted from F_1, F_2, etc., the direct pull of gravity for example, and forces of attraction or repulsion exerted by surrounding particles. In what follows the latter is assumed to cancel out in pairs. Letting a_x, a_y, a_z and f_x, f_y, f_z indicate components of $\mathbf{a}$ and $\mathbf{f}$ respectively *along instantaneous directions* of the body fixed X, Y, Z axes, we write "free particle" equations of motion as

$$m'a_x = f_x, \quad m'a_y = f_y, \quad m'a_z = f_z \tag{1}$$

Multiplying the last of (1) by y, the second by $-z$ and adding, we have

$$m'(a_z y - a_y z) = f_z y - f_y z \tag{2}$$

(Note that insofar as the validity of (2) is concerned, y and z could be replaced by any arbitrary quantities. Hence (2) is, in a sense, a type of d'Alembert's equation.) From Fig. 9-4 below it is seen that $f_z y - f_y z$ is the moment of $\mathbf{f}$ about x. Hence summing (2) over all particles of the body, we write

$$\sum m'(a_z y - a_y z) = \sum (f_z y - f_y z) = \tau_x \tag{9.8}$$

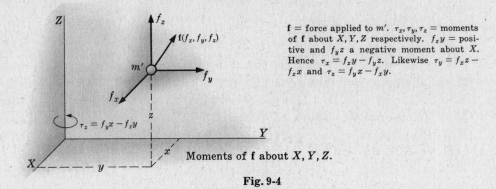

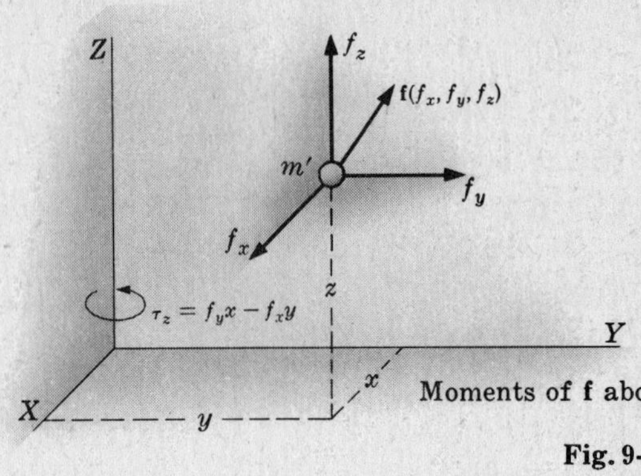

f = force applied to m'. τ_x, τ_y, τ_z = moments of f about X, Y, Z respectively. $f_z y$ = positive and $f_y z$ a negative moment about X. Hence $\tau_x = f_z y - f_y z$. Likewise $\tau_y = f_x z - f_z x$ and $\tau_z = f_y x - f_x y$.

Moments of f about X, Y, Z.

Fig. 9-4

Since the summation is over all particles of the body, τ_x represents merely the sum of the moments of all *externally applied forces* (including forces of constraint, if the body is in any way constrained) about X. Equation (*9.8*) and two similar expressions for τ_y and τ_z are the basic equations of rotation. They can be put into convenient useful form as follows.

a_x, a_y, a_z are given by (*9.7*). Eliminating a_y and a_z from (*9.8*) we obtain

$$M(a_{0z}\bar{y} - a_{0y}\bar{z}) + \dot{\omega}_x \sum m'(y^2+z^2) - \omega_y\omega_z \sum m'(z^2-y^2) + (\omega_x\omega_z - \dot{\omega}_y)\sum m'xy - (\omega_x\omega_y + \dot{\omega}_z)\sum m'xz - (\omega_y^2 - \omega_z^2)\sum m'yz = \tau_x \qquad (9.9)$$

= sum of moments of all external forces about X, Fig. 9-3.

But $\sum m'(y^2+z^2) = I_x, \quad \sum m'(xy) = I_{xy},$

$$\sum m'(z^2-y^2) = \sum m'[(z^2+x^2) - (x^2+y^2)] = I_y - I_z, \quad \text{etc.}$$

Hence (*9.9*) together with expressions for τ_y and τ_z, found in the same way, may be written as

$$\begin{aligned} &M(a_{0z}\bar{y} - a_{0y}\bar{z}) + I_x\dot{\omega}_x + (I_z - I_y)\omega_y\omega_z + I_{xy}(\omega_x\omega_z - \dot{\omega}_y) \\ &\quad - I_{xz}(\omega_x\omega_y + \dot{\omega}_z) + I_{yz}(\omega_z^2 - \omega_y^2) = \tau_x \qquad (a) \\[6pt] &M(a_{0x}\bar{z} - a_{0z}\bar{x}) + I_y\dot{\omega}_y + (I_x - I_z)\omega_x\omega_z + I_{yz}(\omega_y\omega_x - \dot{\omega}_z) \\ &\quad - I_{xy}(\omega_y\omega_z + \dot{\omega}_x) + I_{xz}(\omega_x^2 - \omega_z^2) = \tau_y \qquad (b) \qquad (9.10) \\[6pt] &M(a_{0y}\bar{x} - a_{0x}\bar{y}) + I_z\dot{\omega}_z + (I_y - I_x)\omega_x\omega_y + I_{xz}(\omega_y\omega_z - \dot{\omega}_x) \\ &\quad - I_{yz}(\omega_x\omega_z + \dot{\omega}_y) + I_{xy}(\omega_y^2 - \omega_x^2) = \tau_z \qquad (c) \end{aligned}$$

A General Form of Euler's Rotational Equations.

9.6 Important Points Regarding (*9.10*).

(*a*) Equations (*9.10*) constitute a very general and useful form of Euler's rotational equations of motion. *These together with* (*9.2*) *determine completely the motion of a rigid body.* In Fig. 9-3, X, Y, Z = any body fixed axes, O located at any point.

(*b*) A simple physical interpretation of (*9.10*) may be given as follows. Remembering that a_x, a_y, a_z in equation (*9.7*) are relative to inertial space, $m'a_x$, etc., are inertial forces, "inertial force" being defined merely as (mass) × (acceleration) relative to inertial space. Hence $\sum m'(a_z y - a_y z)$ is the sum of the moments of all inertial forces about X. And clearly the left side of (*9.10*) must have the same meaning. Therefore this equation is a statement of the following "principle of moments",

$$\left(\begin{matrix}\text{Summation of moments of}\\ \text{inertial forces about } X\end{matrix}\right) = \left(\begin{matrix}\text{Summation of moments of}\\ \text{applied forces about } X\end{matrix}\right) \qquad (9.11)$$

which is likewise true for moments about Y and Z or *indeed any line*.

(c) It is important to realize that in setting up the first three Euler equations, (9.2), Page 177, the frame of reference there referred to need not be the same as the one employed in setting up the rotational equations (9.10).

(d) As is evident from (9.7a), Euler equations of rotation can be written for axes which may be rotating about O relative to the body. See Problem 9.10, Page 199. See Examples 9.8 and 9.9, Page 190.

(e) Determination of τ_x, τ_y, τ_z. Let $\mathbf{F}_i$ indicate one of the forces applied at p_i, Fig. 9-3. X, Y, Z components of $\mathbf{F}_i$ are $f_{x_i}, f_{y_i}, f_{z_i}$. Coordinates of p_i relative to this frame are x_i, y_i, z_i. Hence

$$\tau_x = \sum (f_{z_i} y_i - f_{y_i} z_i) \tag{9.12}$$

If components $(f'_{x_i}, f'_{y_i}, f'_{z_i})$ of $\mathbf{F}_i$ are given along, say, X_1, Y_1, Z_1, then

$$f_{x_i} = f'_{x_i}\alpha_{11} + f'_{y_i}\alpha_{12} + f'_{z_i}\alpha_{13} \tag{9.13}$$

(f) *Simplified forms of* (9.10). Assume O located at any point in the body and X, Y, Z body-fixed. Take X, Y, Z along principal axes of inertia through O. Then, since $I_{xy} = I_{xz} = I_{yz} = 0$, all terms containing products of inertia drop out.

If O is taken at c.m., $\bar{x} = \bar{y} = \bar{z} = 0$. Hence the first term in each of (9.10) drops out, even though X, Y, Z may not be body-fixed.

If one point (any point) of the body is fixed in space (by means of a ball joint, for example) and O is taken at this point, the first term of each drops out since $a_{0x} = a_{0y} = a_{0z} = 0$.

Note that in the last two cases, *relations* (9.10) *have exactly the same form.*

If O is either fixed in space or located at c.m. and if, moreover, body-fixed axes are taken along principal axes of inertia, relations (9.10) reduce to the following important form.

$$I^p_x\dot{\omega}_x + (I^p_z - I^p_y)\omega_y\omega_z = \tau_x \qquad (a)$$
$$I^p_y\dot{\omega}_y + (I^p_x - I^p_z)\omega_x\omega_z = \tau_y \qquad (b) \tag{9.14}$$
$$I^p_z\dot{\omega}_z + (I^p_y - I^p_x)\omega_x\omega_y = \tau_z \qquad (c)$$

(g) Equations (9.10) can be derived from Lagrange's equations. See Problem 9.9, Page 198.

9.7 Vector Form of Euler's Rotational Equations.

As shown in Section 8.2F, Page 147, torque can be treated as a vector $\boldsymbol{\tau}$, rectangular components of which are $\tau_x = \sum f_z y - f_y z$, etc. See equation (9.8). In like manner $\sum m'(a_z y - a_y z)$ is the X component of a vector due to inertial forces.

For convenience let us write relations (9.10) as $B_x = \tau_x$, $B_y = \tau_y$, $B_z = \tau_z$ where B_x is merely shorthand for the left side of (9.10a), etc. Hence it is seen that (9.10) are component equations of

$$\mathbf{B} = \boldsymbol{\tau} \tag{9.15}$$

where components of $\mathbf{B}$ are B_x, B_y, B_z and those of $\boldsymbol{\tau}$ are τ_x, τ_y, τ_z.

Taking components of $\mathbf{B}$ and $\boldsymbol{\tau}$ along any line Oa through O (*which need not necessarily be fixed in space or to the body,* see Examples 9.8 and 9.9, Page 190) having direction cosines l, m, n, it is evident that

$$B_x l + B_y m + B_z n = \tau_x l + \tau_y m + \tau_z n = \tau_{Oa} \tag{9.16}$$

Euler's Equation: Applicable to any line Oa. (For a more direct derivation see Problem 9.10, Page 199.)

9.8 Specific Examples Illustrating the Use of Equations (*9.2*) and (*9.10*).

Note. Many of the examples in this chapter are taken from Chapter 8. Hence the reader may make a direct comparison of the Lagrange and Euler methods.

Example 9.2. *Consider Example 8.4(1), Fig. 8-8, Page 150.*

Taking body-fixed axes as indicated, $\omega_x = \omega_y = 0$, $\omega_z = \dot{\theta}$. Inspection shows that $F_x = -Mg\sin\theta + f_x$, $F_y = -Mg\cos\theta + f_y$, $F_z = 0$ where f_x and f_y are *components of the reactive force at p along the instantaneous directions of X and Y.* $\tau_x = \tau_y = 0$, $\tau_z = -Mgl\sin\theta$. $A_x = l\ddot{\theta}$, $A_y = l\dot{\theta}^2$, $A_z = a_{0x} = a_{0y} = a_{0z} = 0$. $I_{xz} = I_{yz} = 0$, $I_{xy} \neq 0$. Hence equations (*9.2*) become

$$Ml\ddot{\theta} = f_x - Mg\sin\theta, \qquad Ml\dot{\theta}^2 = f_y - Mg\cos\theta \tag{1}$$

and relations (*9.10*) finally reduce to

$$I_z\ddot{\theta} = -Mgl\sin\theta \tag{2}$$

For small motion, (*2*) may be integrated at once to give θ as a function of time. Thus f_x and f_y may be obtained from (*1*) as functions of time.

Note that (*2*) can be obtained directly by the Lagrangian method.

Example 9.3.

For the purpose of bringing out basic principles and illustrating important techniques (at the cost of making the solution more involved) let us again treat the above problem, taking body-fixed axes as shown in Fig. 9-5.

Again $\omega_x = \omega_y = 0$, $\omega_z = \dot{\theta}$ and it is seen that

$$F_x = f_x - Mg\sin(\theta + \beta), \qquad F_y = f_y - Mg\cos(\theta + \beta)$$

$$\tau_x = \tau_y = 0, \qquad \tau_z = f_y r\sin\beta - f_x r\cos\beta + Mg\bar{y}\sin(\theta+\beta) - Mg\bar{x}\cos(\theta+\beta)$$

$$a_{0x} = r\ddot{\theta}\cos\beta + r\dot{\theta}^2\sin\beta, \qquad a_{0y} = r\dot{\theta}^2\cos\beta - r\ddot{\theta}\sin\beta$$

$$A_x = l\ddot{\theta}\cos\alpha - l\dot{\theta}^2\sin\alpha, \qquad A_y = l\ddot{\theta}\sin\alpha + l\dot{\theta}^2\cos\alpha$$

Note that a_{0x}, a_{0y}, A_x, A_y are components of acceleration, *relative to an inertial frame*, of points O and c.m. respectively taken along *instantaneous positions of the body-fixed axes.* f_x and f_y are components of the reactive force on the body at the point of suspension. Note also that these reactive forces appear in τ_z. $\bar{x}, \bar{y}$ are known constants.

Thus equations (*9.2*) become

$$\begin{aligned} M(l\ddot{\theta}\cos\alpha - l\dot{\theta}^2\sin\alpha) &= f_x - Mg\sin(\theta+\beta) \\ M(l\ddot{\theta}\sin\alpha + l\dot{\theta}^2\cos\alpha) &= f_y - Mg\cos(\theta+\beta) \end{aligned} \tag{1}$$

and equation (*9.10c*) reduces to

$$M(a_{0y}\bar{x} - a_{0x}\bar{y}) + I_z\ddot{\theta} = \tau_z \tag{2}$$

Inserting expressions for a_{0x}, a_{0y} and τ_z into (*2*), the Euler equations are complete.

With some tedious work the reader can show that (*2*) reduces to (*2*) in the previous example. Note that I_z of this example is not equal to I_z of Example 9.2.

As an exercise the reader should determine the θ equation of motion by the Lagrangian method and compare with results above.

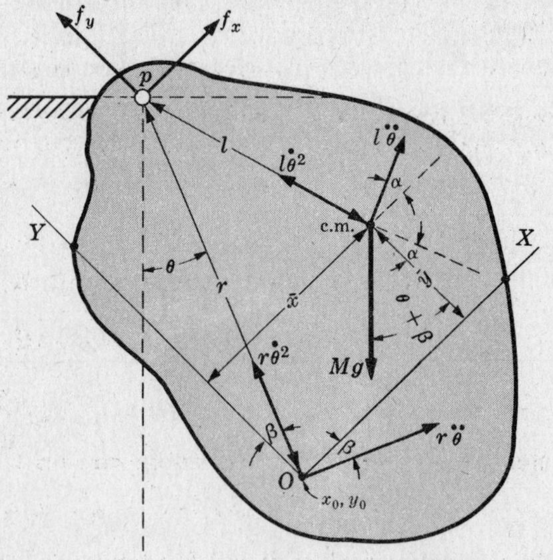

Fig. 9-5

Example 9.4. *Consider Example 8.7, Fig. 8-11, Page 152.*

Taking X, Y, Z as body-fixed and regarding the rod as a uniform slender one of length L, $\bar{y} = \frac{1}{2}L$, $\bar{x} = \bar{z} = 0$, $I_y = 0$, $I_x = I_z$, $I_{xy} = I_{xz} = I_{yz} = 0$. It is seen that $\omega_x = -\dot{\theta}_2$, $\omega_y = \dot{\theta}_1\cos\theta_2$, $\omega_z = \dot{\theta}_1\sin\theta_2$ about the body-fixed axes. Also, $a_{0x} = -R\ddot{\theta}_1$, $a_{0y} = -R\dot{\theta}_1^2\sin\theta_2$, $a_{0z} = R\dot{\theta}_1^2\cos\theta_2$ taken along the instantaneous directions of X, Y, Z respectively. Components of the acceleration of c.m. relative to inertial space and taken along the instantaneous positions of the body-fixed axes are found from (*9.7*) to be

$$A_x = -(R + \bar{y} \sin \theta_2)\ddot{\theta}_1 - 2\dot{\theta}_1\dot{\theta}_2\bar{y} \cos \theta_2$$

$$A_y = -(R + \bar{y} \sin \theta_2)\dot{\theta}_1^2 \sin \theta_2 - \dot{\theta}_2^2 \bar{y} \qquad (1)$$

$$A_z = (R + \bar{y} \sin \theta_2)\dot{\theta}_1^2 \cos \theta_2 - \ddot{\theta}_2\bar{y}$$

Hence equations (*9.2*) become

$$-M[(R + \bar{y} \sin \theta_2)\ddot{\theta}_1 + 2\dot{\theta}_1\dot{\theta}_2\bar{y} \cos \theta_2] = f_x$$

$$-M[(R + \bar{y} \sin \theta_2)\dot{\theta}_1^2 \sin \theta_2 + \dot{\theta}_2^2\bar{y}] = -Mg \cos \theta_2 + f_y \qquad (2)$$

$$M[(R + \bar{y} \sin \theta_2)\dot{\theta}_1^2 \cos \theta_2 - \ddot{\theta}_2\bar{y}] = -Mg \sin \theta_2 + f_z$$

where bearing forces f_x, f_y, f_z acting at O are assumed to be in the instantaneous directions of X, Y, Z.

Equations (*9.10*) reduce to

$$M\bar{y}R\dot{\theta}_1^2 \cos \theta_2 - I_x\ddot{\theta}_2 + I_z\dot{\theta}_1^2 \sin \theta_2 \cos \theta_2 = Mg\bar{y} \sin \theta_2$$

$$MR\bar{y}\ddot{\theta}_1 + I_x(\ddot{\theta}_1 \sin \theta_2 + 2\dot{\theta}_1\dot{\theta}_2 \cos \theta_2) = \tau_z, \quad \tau_y = 0 \qquad (3)$$

where τ_z is the torque about Z due to bearing forces.

The reader should set up the θ_2 equation of motion by the Lagrangian method (see expression for T given in Example 8.7, Page 152) and compare with the first of (*3*). Assuming θ_1 a known function of time, how can τ_z, f_x, f_y, f_z be found as functions of time?

Example 9.5. *Determination of equation of motion and forces of constraint acting on the disk, Fig. 8-12, Page 153.*

Considering body-fixed axes as shown, $\omega_x, \omega_y, \omega_z$ are as given on the diagram. Components of force on the disk are

$$F_x = -Mg \sin \theta \sin \phi + f_{x_1} + f_{x_2}, \quad F_y = -Mg \sin \theta \cos \phi + f_{y_1} + f_{y_2}, \quad F_z = -Mg \cos \theta + f_z$$

where f_{x_1}, f_{y_1} and f_{x_2}, f_{y_2} are bearing forces at a and b respectively, assumed to be in the instantaneous directions of X and Y.

$$\tau_x = f_{y_1}l_1 - f_{y_2}l_2, \quad \tau_y = f_{x_2}l_2 - f_{x_1}l_1, \quad \tau_z = 0$$

where l_1 and l_2 are distances Oa and Ob respectively. Assuming B fixed, $a_{0x} = a_{0y} = a_{0z} = 0$, $A_x = A_y = A_z = 0$, $\bar{x} = \bar{y} = \bar{z} = 0$. Hence equations (*9.2*) are

$$Mg \sin \theta \sin \phi = f_{x_1} + f_{x_2}, \quad Mg \sin \theta \cos \phi = f_{y_1} + f_{y_2}, \quad Mg \cos \theta = f_z \qquad (1)$$

and relations (*9.10*) become,

$$\bar{I}_x(\ddot{\psi} \sin \theta \sin \phi + \dot{\psi}\dot{\phi} \sin \theta \cos \phi) + (\bar{I}_z - \bar{I}_x)(\dot{\psi} \sin \theta \cos \phi)(\dot{\phi} + \dot{\psi} \cos \theta) = f_{y_1}l_1 - f_{y_2}l_2 \qquad (2)$$

$$\bar{I}_x(\ddot{\psi} \sin \theta \cos \phi - \dot{\psi}\dot{\phi} \sin \theta \sin \phi) - (\bar{I}_z - \bar{I}_x)(\dot{\psi} \sin \theta \sin \phi)(\dot{\phi} + \dot{\psi} \cos \theta) = f_{x_2}l_2 - f_{x_1}l_1 \qquad (3)$$

$$\bar{I}_z \frac{d}{dt}(\dot{\phi} + \dot{\psi} \cos \theta) = 0 \qquad (4)$$

Multiplying (*2*) by $\sin \theta \sin \phi$, (*3*) by $\sin \theta \cos \phi$, and adding, we obtain

$$\bar{I}_x\ddot{\psi} \sin^2 \theta = (f_{y_1}l_1 - f_{y_2}l_2) \sin \theta \sin \phi + (f_{x_2}l_2 - f_{x_1}l_1) \sin \theta \cos \phi \qquad (5)$$

the right side of which is just the torque τ_ψ tending to change ψ. Hence (*4*) and (*5*) are just the ϕ and ψ equations of motion respectively.

Neglecting the moment of inertia of the frame, τ_ψ is the torque applied to shaft cO by, say, a motor. Assuming τ_ψ known, integrating (*4*) and (*5*), $f_{x_1}, f_{y_1}, f_{x_2}, f_{y_2}$ can be found as functions of time.

To complete this example the reader should show that (*4*) and (*5*) may be obtained at once by an application of Lagrange's equations. See Example 8.8, Page 152.

Example 9.6. *Equation of motion and forces of constraint on disk D, Fig. 9-6 below.*

The edge of D rolls without slipping in contact with the inclined plane. A smooth ball joint at O holds the end of the shaft in place.

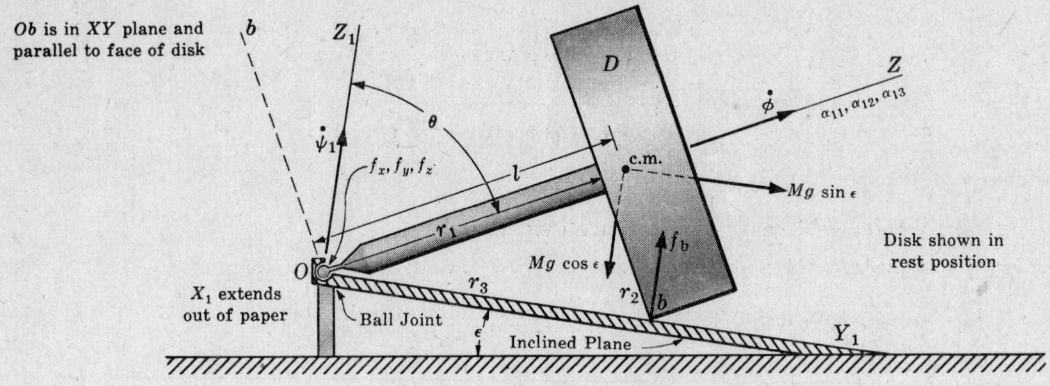

Oscillation of Disk on Inclined Plane

Fig. 9-6

Regard X_1, Y_1, Z_1 as inertial. Take X_1 horizontally (normal to paper) and Y_1 directly down the plane. X, Y, Z (X, Y not shown) with origin at center of the ball are body-fixed. θ and ϕ are Euler angles measured in the usual way. As a matter of convenience we shall introduce ψ_1, instead of ψ as defined in Fig. 8-16, Page 156, where ψ_1 is measured between Y_1 and the projection of OZ on the X_1Y_1 plane. Hence $\psi = \psi_1 + 180°$. Also note the following: $\theta =$ constant, $\sin\theta = r_1/r_3$, $\cos\theta = r_2/r_3$, $r_3\dot{\psi}_1 = -r_2\dot{\phi}$, $I_x = I_y$, $l =$ distance from O to c.m. of the system, $\epsilon =$ angle of the inclined plane, $a_{0x} = a_{0y} = a_{0z} = 0$, components of angular velocity along X, Y, Z are

$$\omega_x = \dot{\psi}_1\frac{r_1}{r_3}\sin\phi, \qquad \omega_y = \dot{\psi}_1\frac{r_1}{r_3}\cos\phi, \qquad \omega_z = -\dot{\psi}_1\frac{r_1^2}{r_2r_3} \tag{1}$$

From (9.7) or by elementary considerations it follows that

$$\begin{aligned} A_x &= (lr_1r_2/r_3^2)\dot{\psi}_1^2\sin\phi - (lr_1/r_3)\ddot{\psi}_1\cos\phi \\ A_y &= (lr_1r_2/r_3^2)\dot{\psi}_1^2\cos\phi - (lr_1/r_3)\ddot{\psi}_1\sin\phi \\ A_z &= -(lr_1^2/r_3^2)\dot{\psi}_1^2 \end{aligned} \tag{2}$$

Forces on the system are: Mg acting at c.m. and having components $Mg\sin\epsilon$ and $-Mg\cos\epsilon$ in the direction of Y_1 and Z_1 respectively; $f_b =$ a reactive force at b in the direction of Z_1; $f_b' =$ a reactive force at b tangent to the circular path described by b and assumed to be pointing in the positive direction of increasing ψ_1; a reactive force on the ball at O with components f_x, f_y, f_z along the body-fixed X, Y, Z axes. We assume that the total reactive force at b has no component in the direction of r_3.

Now writing F_{x_1} as the sum of X_1 components of the above forces, etc., and F_x the total X component of all forces, we have

$$F_{x_1} = F_x\alpha_{11} + F_y\alpha_{12} + F_z\alpha_{13} \tag{3}$$

where (not including the reactive force at O)

$$F_{x_1} = -f_b'\cos\psi_1, \qquad F_{y_1} = -f_b'\sin\psi_1 + Mg\sin\epsilon, \qquad F_{z_1} = f_b - Mg\cos\epsilon \tag{4}$$

Thus finally

$$\begin{aligned} F_x &= f_x + f_b\frac{r_1}{r_3}\sin\phi + f_b'\cos\phi - Mg\left[\sin\epsilon\left(\cos\phi\sin\psi_1 + \frac{r_2}{r_3}\sin\phi\cos\psi_1\right) + \frac{r_1}{r_3}\cos\epsilon\sin\phi\right] \\ F_y &= f_y + f_b\frac{r_1}{r_3}\cos\phi - f_b'\sin\phi + Mg\left[\sin\epsilon\left(\sin\phi\sin\psi_1 - \frac{r_2}{r_3}\cos\phi\cos\psi_1\right) - \frac{r_1}{r_3}\cos\epsilon\cos\phi\right] \\ F_z &= f_z + f_b\frac{r_2}{r_3} + Mg\left[\frac{r_1}{r_3}\sin\epsilon\cos\psi_1 - \frac{r_2}{r_3}\cos\epsilon\right] \end{aligned} \tag{5}$$

With a simple model and a little patience these expressions can be verified directly.

Equations corresponding to (9.2) can now be written at once from (2) and (5). No further details will be given. (Could equations of motion of c.m. be written employing components of acceleration and force along the X_1, Y_1, Z_1 axes?)

The rotational equations are found as follows. It is seen that the X, Y, Z coordinates of c.m. and b are $(0, 0, l)$ and $(-r_2\cos\phi, -r_2\sin\phi, r)$ respectively. Note that X, Y, Z components of the individual forces may be read directly from equations (5). Thus applying the general relations $\tau_x = \sum(f_zy - f_yz)$, etc., we finally obtain

$$\tau_x = f_b' r_1 \sin\phi - f_b r_3 \cos\phi - Mgl\left[\sin\epsilon\left(\sin\phi \sin\psi_1 - \frac{r_2}{r_3}\cos\phi\cos\psi_1\right) - \frac{r_1}{r_3}\cos\epsilon\cos\phi\right]$$

$$\tau_y = f_b' r_1 \cos\phi + f_b r_3 \sin\phi - Mgl\left[\sin\epsilon\left(\cos\phi \sin\psi_1 + \frac{r_2}{r_3}\sin\phi\cos\psi_1\right) + \frac{r_1}{r_3}\cos\epsilon\sin\phi\right] \qquad (6)$$

$$\tau_z = f_b' r_2$$

The reader may verify these relations by taking moments directly about X, Y, Z.

Equations (*9.10*), which for this problem reduce to (*9.14*), are easily shown to be

$$I_x \frac{r_1}{r_3}\left(\ddot{\psi}_1 \sin\phi - \dot{\psi}_1^2 \frac{r_3}{r_2}\cos\phi\right) - (I_z - I_x)\frac{r_1^3}{r_2 r_3^2}\dot{\psi}_1^2 \cos\phi = \tau_x \qquad (7)$$

$$I_x \frac{r_1}{r_3}\left(\ddot{\psi}_1 \cos\phi + \dot{\psi}_1^2 \frac{r_3}{r_2}\sin\phi\right) + (I_z - I_x)\frac{r_1^3}{r_2 r_3^2}\dot{\psi}_1^2 \sin\phi = \tau_y \qquad (8)$$

$$-I_z \frac{r_1^2}{r_2 r_3}\ddot{\psi}_1 = \tau_z = f_b' r_2 \qquad (9)$$

Multiplying (*7*) by $\sin\phi$, (*8*) by $\cos\phi$ and adding, we get, after eliminating f_b' by (*9*), the following equation of motion:

$$\frac{r_1}{r_3}\left(I_x + I_z \frac{r_1^2}{r_2^2}\right)\ddot{\psi}_1 = -Mgl \sin\epsilon \sin\psi_1 \qquad (10)$$

which is just the equation of motion obtained much more easily and quickly by the Lagrangian method in Example 8.11, Page 154.

The integral of (*10*), which for small motion is simple harmonic, gives ψ_1 (and also ϕ, since $r_3\psi_1 = -r_2\phi$) as a function of time. Hence f_b and f_b' can be found as functions of time from, say, (*8*) and (*9*). The (*9.2*) equations can be solved for f_x, f_y, f_z. Thus the motion as well as reactive forces have been determined.

The above treatment involves various tedious details. However, the procedure brings out clearly the principles and techniques of the Euler method. It also illustrates, by comparison with Example 8.11, the superiority of the Lagrangian method for obtaining equations of motion.

Example 9.7. *Bearing Forces.*

Regarding X_1, Y_1, Z_1, Fig. 9-7, as inertial we shall determine expressions for the forces exerted by bearings B_1 and B_2 on the shaft of the rotating body.

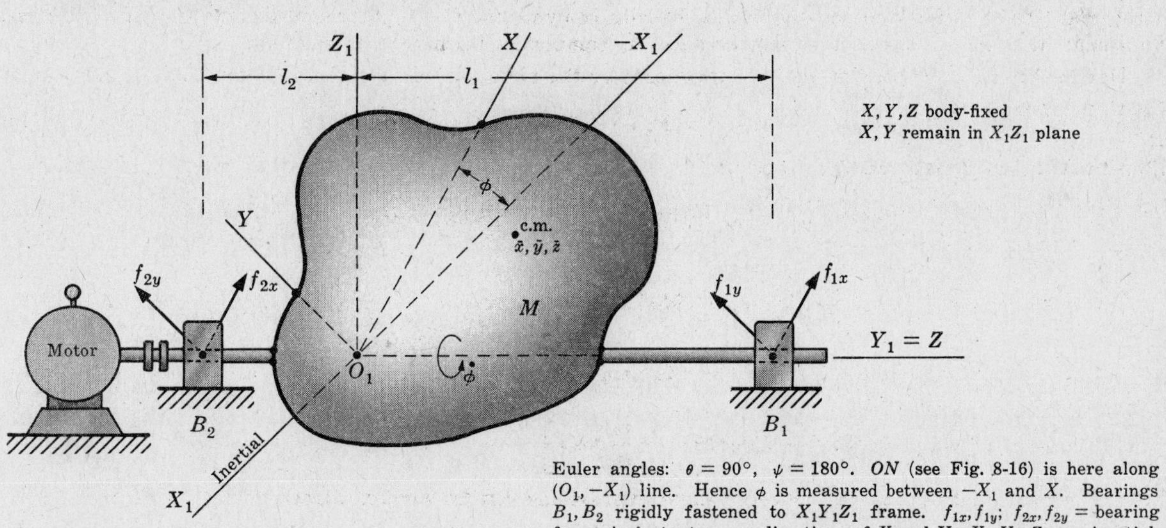

Euler angles: $\theta = 90°$, $\psi = 180°$. *ON* (see Fig. 8-16) is here along $(O_1, -X_1)$ line. Hence ϕ is measured between $-X_1$ and X. Bearings B_1, B_2 rigidly fastened to $X_1Y_1Z_1$ frame. f_{1x}, f_{1y}; f_{2x}, f_{2y} = bearing forces in instantaneous directions of X and Y. X_1, Y_1, Z_1 are inertial.

Fig. 9-7

Choosing body-fixed axes as shown and measuring Euler angles as indicated, it is seen that $\omega_x = \omega_y = 0$, $\omega_z = \dot{\phi}$; $a_{0x} = a_{0y} = a_{0z} = 0$. Also (by elementary principles or from equation (*9.7*)),

$$A_x = -(\ddot{\phi}\bar{y} + \dot{\phi}^2\bar{x}), \qquad A_y = \bar{x}\ddot{\phi} - \bar{y}\dot{\phi}^2, \qquad A_z = 0$$

Forces and torques are given by

$$F_x = f_{1x} + f_{2x} - Mg \sin\phi, \quad F_y = f_{1y} + f_{2y} - Mg\cos\phi, \quad F_z = 0$$

$$\tau_x = f_{2y}l_2 - f_{1y}l_1 + Mg\bar{z}\cos\phi, \quad \tau_y = f_{1x}l_1 - f_{2x}l_2 - Mg\bar{z}\sin\phi,$$

$$\tau_z = Mg\bar{y}\sin\phi - Mg\bar{x}\cos\phi + \tau_m$$

where τ_m is the torque exerted by the motor, and f_{1x}, f_{1y} and f_{2x}, f_{2y} are components of bearing forces at B_1 and B_2 respectively regarded as being in the instantaneous directions of X and Y. Thus equations (*9.2*) and (*9.10*) become

$$-M(\ddot{\phi}\bar{y} + \dot{\phi}^2\bar{x}) = f_{1x} + f_{2x} - Mg\sin\phi \tag{1}$$

$$M(\ddot{\phi}\bar{x} - \dot{\phi}^2\bar{y}) = f_{1y} + f_{2y} - Mg\cos\phi \tag{2}$$

$$-I_{xz}\ddot{\phi} + I_{yz}\dot{\phi}^2 = f_{2y}l_2 - f_{1y}l_1 + Mg\bar{z}\cos\phi \tag{3}$$

$$-I_{yz}\ddot{\phi} - I_{xz}\dot{\phi}^2 = f_{1x}l_1 - f_{2x}l_2 - Mg\bar{z}\sin\phi \tag{4}$$

$$I_z\ddot{\phi} = Mg(\bar{y}\sin\phi - \bar{x}\cos\phi) + \tau_m \tag{5}$$

Relations (*1*) and (*4*) may be solved for f_{1x} and f_{2x}, giving

$$f_{1x}(l_1 + l_2) = Mg(l_2 + \bar{z})\sin\phi - (Ml_2\bar{y} + I_{yz})\ddot{\phi} - (Ml_2\bar{x} + I_{xz})\dot{\phi}^2 \tag{6}$$

$$f_{2x}(l_1 + l_2) = Mg(l_1 - \bar{z})\sin\phi + (I_{yz} - Ml_1\bar{y})\ddot{\phi} + (I_{xz} - Ml_1\bar{x})\dot{\phi}^2 \tag{7}$$

In like manner (*2*) and (*3*) can be solved for f_{1y} and f_{2y}. For τ_m a known function of time, the integral of (*5*) gives ϕ as a function of t. Hence all bearing forces can be expressed in terms of time.

From the physics of the problem it is evident that bearing forces cannot depend on the location or orientation of the XYZ frame. The choice made above is merely for convenience.

Static and dynamic balancing: Consider the following two cases.

(*a*) If c.m. is on the axis of rotation there is no torque about this axis due to gravity and the body is said to be "statically" balanced.

(*b*) Suppose c.m. is on the axis of rotation and Z is a principal axis of inertia through some point O_1 on the rotational axis. Taking X and Y along the other two principal axes, (*6*) and (*7*) show that there are no bearing forces due to rotation. The body is now both statically and "dynamically" balanced.

For a derivation which shows much more clearly the physical meaning of (*6*) and (*7*), see Problem 9.17, Page 200.

9.9 Examples Illustrating the (*9.16*) Form of Euler's Equations [together with (*9.3*)].

First, consider the following important and somewhat more general techniques than heretofore discussed or illustrated. Since Euler angles will be used throughout, the reader should review Sections 8.7, Page 156, and 8.8, Page 157.

Regard the body, Fig. 9-8, as completely free to move under the action of forces $\mathbf{F}_1, \mathbf{F}_2$, etc. Consider X_1, Y_1, Z_1 as inertial and X, Y, Z as body-fixed. Dotted axes X_1', Y_1', Z_1', with origin attached to the body at O, are assumed to remain parallel to X_1, Y_1, Z_1. Euler angles θ, ψ, ϕ, indicated on the diagram and measured exactly as in Fig. 8-17, Page 157, determine the orientation of the body. Direction cosines of X, Y, Z relative to X_1', Y_1', Z_1' (or X_1, Y_1, Z_1) are indicated by $\alpha_{11}, \alpha_{12}, \alpha_{13}$, etc. Expressions for the α's in terms of Euler angles are given in Table 8.2, Page 158. Let F_{x_i} indicate one of the forces, applied at point p_i having coordinates (x_i, y_i, z_i), relative to the body-fixed frame.

If O were taken at c.m. and X, Y, Z along principal axes of inertia, (*9.3*), (*9.10*) and (*9.16*) would be greatly simplified. However, for pedagogic reasons, we shall assume O located at any arbitrary point in the body. Coordinates $\bar{x}, \bar{y}, \bar{z}$ of c.m. relative to X, Y, Z are assumed known.

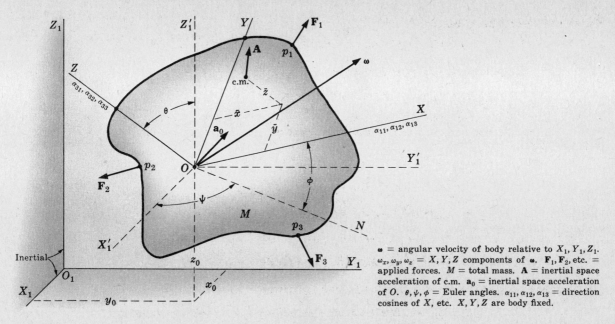

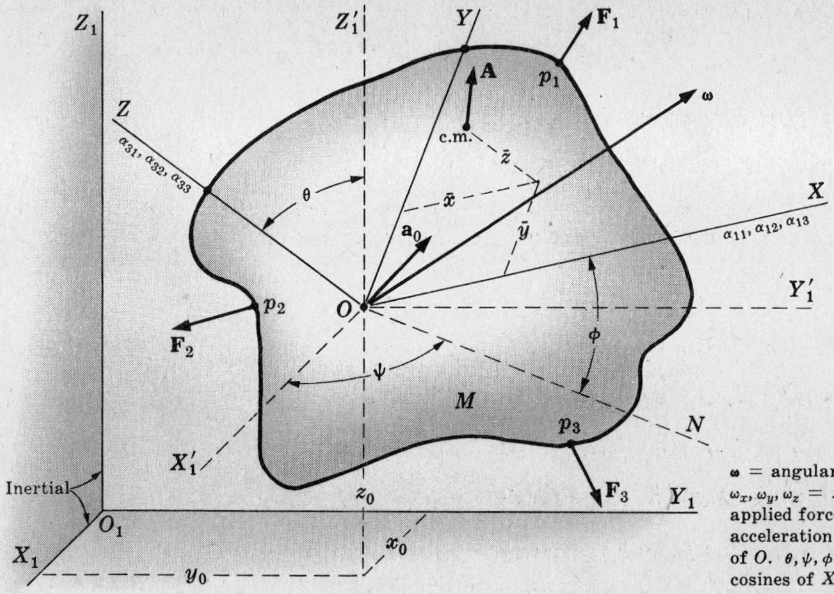

$\boldsymbol{\omega}$ = angular velocity of body relative to X_1, Y_1, Z_1. $\omega_x, \omega_y, \omega_z = X, Y, Z$ components of $\boldsymbol{\omega}$. $\mathbf{F}_1, \mathbf{F}_2$, etc. = applied forces. M = total mass. $\mathbf{A}$ = inertial space acceleration of c.m. $\mathbf{a}_0$ = inertial space acceleration of O. θ, ψ, ϕ = Euler angles. $\alpha_{11}, \alpha_{12}, \alpha_{13}$ = direction cosines of X, etc. X, Y, Z are body fixed.

Fig. 9-8

Scalar Equations corresponding to (*9.3*) may be found as outlined in Section 9.3. If components of $\mathbf{A}$ are taken along the body-fixed axes, A_x for example may easily be obtained from (*9.7a*) by setting $x = \bar{x}$ and $\omega_x = \dot{\psi}\sin\theta\sin\phi + \dot{\theta}\cos\phi$, etc. The quantities a_{0x}, a_{0y}, a_{0z} may be expressed in any convenient coordinates. Or we can write $a_{0x} = \ddot{x}_0\alpha_{11} + \ddot{y}_0\alpha_{12} + \ddot{z}_0\alpha_{13}$, etc. Writing $f_{x_i}, f_{y_i}, f_{z_i}$ as the X, Y, Z components of $\mathbf{F}_i, F_x$ for (*9.2*) is given by $F_x = \sum f_{x_i}$, etc.

Rotational Equations: Due to the vector nature of (*9.15*), three scalar equations of motion corresponding to (*9.16*) can be obtained by projecting $\mathbf{B}$ and τ along any three noncoplanar lines through O which are not necessarily fixed in direction relative to the body. Components of $\mathbf{B}$ and τ are usually taken along ON, Z_1' and Z. Note that ON and OZ_1' are not stationary with respect to the body except at O. Applying (*9.16*), it easily follows that (see Table 8.1, Page 157)

$$\begin{gathered} B_x \sin\theta\sin\phi + B_y \sin\theta\cos\phi + B_z\cos\theta = \tau_\psi, \\ B_x\cos\phi - B_y\sin\phi = \tau_\theta, \quad B_z = \tau_\phi \end{gathered} \tag{9.17}$$

where, of course, $\tau_\psi, \tau_\theta, \tau_\phi$ represent applied torques about Z_1', ON, Z respectively. Expressions for B_x, B_y, B_z are just the left sides of (*9.10a, b, c*). One way of writing $\tau_\psi, \tau_\theta, \tau_\phi$ is as follows. (In certain specific cases it may be possible to express them in a more direct manner.)

$$\begin{gathered} \tau_\psi = \tau_x\sin\theta\sin\phi + \tau_y\sin\theta\cos\phi + \tau_z\cos\theta, \\ \tau_\theta = \tau_x\cos\phi - \tau_y\sin\phi, \quad \tau_\phi = \tau_z \end{gathered} \tag{9.18}$$

where $\tau_x = \sum(f_{z_i}y_i - f_{y_i}z_i)$, etc.

Thus (*9.17*) are the three rotational equations of motion. As may be shown without difficulty (see Example 9.8 below) they are just the θ, ψ, ϕ equations so easily obtained by the Lagrangian method.

Again it should be emphasized that, with O located at c.m. (frequently, but not always convenient), both (*9.3*) and (*9.16*) simplify considerably. If X, Y, Z are taken along principal axes of inertia through c.m., then (*9.16*) greatly simplifies.

Example 9.8. *Spinning top with tip in fixed position.*

Imagine the body, Fig. 8-16, Page 156, replaced by a top with the tip located at O. For body-fixed axes located as shown, $\bar{x} = \bar{y} = 0$, $\bar{z} = r$. $I_x = I_y$, $I_{xy} = I_{xz} = I_{yz} = 0$.

Following the procedure outlined above, we will set up the six equations of motion.

Since O is fixed, $a_{0x} = a_{0y} = a_{0z} = 0$. Applying (*9.7*),

$$A_x = r(\dot{\psi}^2 \sin\theta\cos\theta\sin\phi + 2\dot{\theta}\dot{\psi}\cos\theta\cos\phi + \ddot{\psi}\sin\theta\cos\phi - \ddot{\theta}\sin\phi)$$

$$A_y = r(\dot{\psi}^2 \sin\theta\cos\theta\cos\phi - 2\dot{\theta}\dot{\psi}\cos\theta\sin\phi - \ddot{\psi}\sin\theta\sin\phi - \ddot{\theta}\cos\phi)$$

$$A_z = -r(\dot{\theta}^2 + \dot{\psi}^2\sin^2\theta)$$

and it may be seen that

$$F_x = -Mg\sin\theta\sin\phi + f_x, \qquad F_y = -Mg\sin\theta\cos\phi + f_y, \qquad F_z = -Mg\cos\theta + f_z$$

where f_x, f_y, f_z are components of the reactive force on the tip in the instantaneous directions of X, Y, Z. Hence the three equations for the motion of c.m.,

$$F_x = MA_x, \quad F_y = MA_y, \quad F_z = MA_z \tag{1}$$

can now be written out in full.

Taking moments about ON, Z and Z', equations (*9.17*) apply directly. For this problem B_x, etc., (see equations (*9.10*)) are

$$B_x = I_x(\ddot{\psi}\sin\theta\sin\phi + 2\dot{\psi}\dot{\theta}\cos\theta\sin\phi + \ddot{\theta}\cos\phi - \dot{\psi}^2\sin\theta\cos\theta\cos\phi) + \bar{I}_z(\dot{\psi}\sin\theta\cos\phi - \dot{\theta}\sin\phi)(\dot{\phi} + \dot{\psi}\cos\theta) \tag{2}$$

$$B_y = I_x(\ddot{\psi}\sin\theta\cos\phi + 2\dot{\psi}\dot{\theta}\cos\theta\cos\phi - \ddot{\theta}\sin\phi + \dot{\psi}^2\sin\theta\cos\theta\sin\phi) - \bar{I}_z(\dot{\psi}\sin\theta\sin\phi + \dot{\theta}\cos\phi)(\dot{\phi} + \dot{\psi}\cos\theta) \tag{3}$$

$$B_z = \bar{I}_z(\ddot{\phi} + \ddot{\psi}\cos\theta - \dot{\psi}\dot{\theta}\sin\theta) \tag{4}$$

From the diagram it is seen that $\tau_\theta = Mgr\sin\theta$, $\tau_\psi = 0$, $\tau_\phi = 0$. Hence the three rotational equations reduce to

$$I_x(\ddot{\theta} - \dot{\psi}^2\sin\theta\cos\theta) + \bar{I}_z(\dot{\psi}^2\sin\theta\cos\theta + \dot{\psi}\dot{\phi}\sin\theta) = Mgr\sin\theta \tag{5}$$

$$I_x(\ddot{\psi}\sin^2\theta + 2\dot{\psi}\dot{\theta}\sin\theta\cos\theta) + \bar{I}_z(\ddot{\psi}\cos^2\theta + \ddot{\phi}\cos\theta - 2\dot{\theta}\dot{\psi}\sin\theta\cos\theta - \dot{\theta}\dot{\phi}\sin\theta) = 0 \tag{6}$$

$$\bar{I}_z(\ddot{\phi} + \ddot{\psi}\cos\theta - \dot{\psi}\dot{\theta}\sin\theta) = 0 \tag{7}$$

Relations (*7*) and (*6*) can each be integrated once, giving

$$\bar{I}_z(\dot{\phi} + \dot{\psi}\cos\theta) = P_\phi = \text{constant}, \qquad I_x\dot{\psi}\sin^2\theta + P_\phi\cos\theta = P_\psi = \text{constant}$$

Thus (*5*), (*6*), (*7*) are just the θ, ψ and ϕ equations (*8.13*), Page 159, which were obtained at once and with much less effort by the Lagrangian method.

Note that, for θ, ψ, ϕ known functions of time, equations (*1*) give f_x, f_y, f_z as functions of time.

Example 9.9. *Euler equations of motion of the gyroscope.* (See Fig. 8-18, Example 8.16, Page 159.)

The following is a brief sketch of steps leading to the desired equations. Taking body-fixed axes as shown,

$$\bar{x} = \bar{y} = \bar{z} = 0, \quad \bar{I}_x = \bar{I}_y, \quad \bar{I}_{xy} = \bar{I}_{xz} = \bar{I}_{yz} = 0, \quad A_x = A_y = A_z = 0, \quad a_{0x} = a_{0y} = a_{0z} = 0$$

Let $f_{x_1}, f_{y_1}, f_{z_1}$ and $f_{x_2}, f_{y_2}, f_{z_2}$ be components (along instantaneous directions of X, Y, Z) of the reactive forces at c_1 and c_2 respectively. Write $Oc_1 = Oc_2 = l$. Then

$$F_x = f_{x_1} + f_{x_2} - Mg\sin\theta\sin\phi, \qquad F_y = f_{y_1} + f_{y_2} - Mg\sin\theta\cos\phi,$$

$$F_z = f_{z_1} + f_{z_2} - Mg\cos\theta, \qquad \tau_\theta = (f_{y_2} - f_{y_1})l\cos\phi - (f_{x_1} - f_{x_2})l\sin\phi,$$

$$\tau_\psi = (f_{y_2} - f_{y_1})l\sin\theta\sin\phi + (f_{x_1} - f_{x_2})l\sin\theta\cos\phi, \qquad \tau_\phi = 0$$

Expressions for B_x, B_y, B_z are just the left sides of relations (*9.10*), Page 182. Hence the translational and rotational equations can be written out in detail.

The reader should show that the rotational equations reduce to the form given as by the Lagrangian method.

9.10 Equations of Motion Relative to a Moving Frame of Reference.

The problem here treated by the Euler Method is exactly the one considered in Section 8.10, Page 162, by the Lagrangian method. Hence the reader should review that section, paying careful attention to the meaning of all symbols used. Neither a statement of the problem nor Fig. 8-21 will be repeated.

With proper care equations (*9.2*) are directly applicable. We must remember that A_x, A_y, A_z are components of the acceleration of c.m. *relative to inertial space.* Hence they must be expressed accordingly. Likewise, equations (*9.10*) or (*9.16*) are applicable provided $\omega_x, \omega_y, \omega_z$ express the components of $\boldsymbol{\omega}$ (the angular velocity of the body relative to inertial space) along the instantaneous directions of the body-fixed X, Y, Z axes.

Assuming for simplicity that O, Fig. 8-21, is located at c.m., expressions for $A_{x_1}, A_{y_1}, A_{z_1}$ (components of the inertial-space acceleration of c.m. along instantaneous directions of X_1, Y_1, Z_1) may be found from relations (*9.6*), Page 179. That is,

$$\begin{aligned} A_{x_1} &= a_{1x} + \ddot{x}_1 - x_1(\Omega_{1y}^2 + \Omega_{1z}^2) + y_1(\Omega_{1y}\Omega_{1x} - \dot{\Omega}_{1z}) \\ &\quad + z_1(\Omega_{1x}\Omega_{1z} - \dot{\Omega}_{1y}) + 2(\dot{z}_1\Omega_{1y} - \dot{y}_1\Omega_{1z}) \end{aligned} \qquad (9.19)$$

with similar expressions for A_{y_1} and A_{z_1}. Here $\Omega_{1x}, \Omega_{1y}, \Omega_{1z}$ are components of $\boldsymbol{\Omega}$ along the instantaneous directions of X_1, Y_1, Z_1. They are given by relations (*8.11*), Page 158; that is, $\Omega_{1x} = \dot{\psi}_1 \sin\theta_1 \sin\phi_1 + \dot{\theta}_1 \cos\phi_1$, etc. Writing $\mathbf{a}_1$ as the inertial space acceleration of O_1, a_{1x}, a_{1y}, a_{1z} = components of $\mathbf{a}_1$ *along instantaneous directions of* X_1, Y_1, Z_1. $a_{1x} = \ddot{x}_2\beta_{11} + \ddot{y}_2\beta_{12} + \ddot{z}_2\beta_{13}$, etc. (Of course a_{1x}, a_{1y}, a_{1z} may be expressed in terms of other coordinates. See Section 2.12, (*3*), Page 29.)

Hence the translational equations of motion of c.m. are just $MA_{x_1} = F_{x_1}$, etc., where A_{x_1} is given by (*9.19*) and F_{x_1} = sum of the X_1 components of all applied forces, including forces of constraint.

Proper expressions for $\omega_x, \omega_y, \omega_z$ may be found exactly as shown in Section 8.10. Thus rotational equations of motion have just the form of (*9.10*), without terms $M(a_{0z}\bar{y} - a_{0y}\bar{z})$, etc., since O is assumed located at c.m. If it is assumed that the motion (translation and rotation) of the $X_1Y_1Z_1$ frame relative to inertial space is known, then a_{1x}, Ω_{1x}, etc., are known functions of time. Thus solutions of the first three equations give the motion of c.m. relative to $X_1Y_1Z_1$, and the second three determine the rotational motion of the body relative to the same frame. Of course (*9.16*) can be applied in place of (*9.10*) if so desired.

9.11 Finding the Motions of a Space Ship and Object Inside, Each Acted Upon by Known Forces.

The Lagrangian treatment is given in Example 8.22, Page 165. A sketch of the Euler method is given below.

Referring to Fig. 8-23, Page 166, it is clear that six Euler equations for the space ship can be written in the usual manner. Then six equations for the rigid body can be set up exactly as outlined in Section 9.10.

The twelve equations of motion involve coordinates x_1, y_1, z_1; x_2, y_2, z_2; θ_1, ψ_1, ϕ_1; θ, ψ, ϕ. Thus solutions give the motion of the space ship relative to X_2, Y_2, Z_2 and that of the body relative to the space ship. In the treatment of this problem one must not forget that, for every force exerted on M by a light device attached to the space ship, there is an equal and opposite force on the ship.

Example 9.10(*a*).

Axes X_1, Y_1, Z_1, Fig. 9-9 below, with origin at O_1 are orientated as described on the diagram. Assuming O_1 moves northward along a great circle (X_1, Y_1, Z_1 attached to a train, for example) with constant velocity $R_1\dot{\Phi}$, Y_1 remaining tangent to the great circle through the poles, let us determine the equations of motion of the particle m acted upon by a known force $\mathbf{F}$.

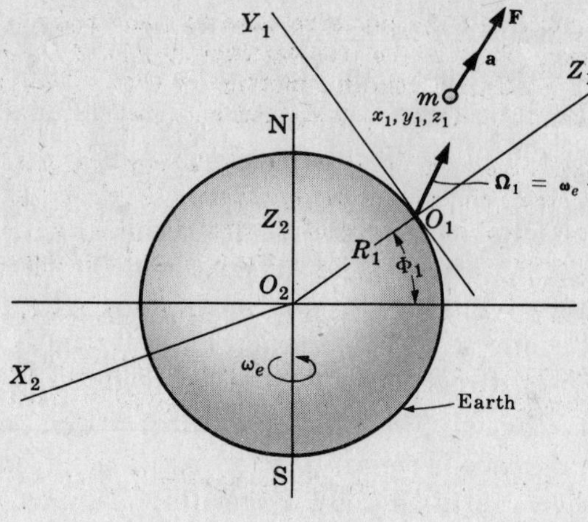

X_2, Y_2, Z_2 remain fixed in direction and are assumed inertial. O_2 is fastened to center of earth.

Earth here assumed spherical. Y_1 tangent to great circle. Z_1 = extension of R_1. X_1 points eastward (into paper). Φ_1 = latitude of O_1. ω_e = angular velocity of earth = 7.29211×10^{-5} radians/sec. Notation here same as in Fig. 8-21 with $\boldsymbol{\Omega}_1 = \boldsymbol{\omega}_e + \dot{\boldsymbol{\Phi}}_1$.

Fig. 9-9

Expressions for $a_{x_1}, a_{y_1}, a_{z_1}$, components of **a**, the inertial space acceleration of m, along instantaneous directions of X_1, Y_1, Z_1 respectively may be found by a proper application of relations (*9.6*), Page 179. To this end (see Fig. 8-21, Page 163) note that

$$\Omega_{1x} = -\dot{\Phi}_1, \quad \Omega_{1y} = \omega_e \cos\Phi_1, \quad \Omega_{1z} = \omega_e \sin\Phi_1$$

Also, $\quad a_{0x} = -2R_1\omega_e\dot{\Phi}_1 \sin\Phi_1, \quad a_{0y} = R_1\omega_e^2 \sin\Phi_1 \cos\Phi_1, \quad a_{0z} = -R_1\dot{\Phi}_1^2 - R_1\omega_e^2\cos^2\Phi_1$

[see equations (*2.60*), Page 29]. Thus applying (*9.6a*),

$$\begin{aligned} a_{x_1} = & -2R_1\omega_e\dot{\Phi}_1 \sin\Phi_1 + \ddot{x}_1 - x_1\omega_e^2 - 2\omega_e\dot{\Phi}_1(y_1\cos\Phi_1 + z_1 \sin\Phi_1) \\ & + 2\omega_e(\dot{z}_1\cos\Phi_1 - \dot{y}_1\sin\Phi_1) \end{aligned} \tag{9.20}$$

with similar expressions for a_{y_1}, a_{z_1}. Hence the desired equations of motion are

$$ma_{x_1} = F_x, \quad ma_{y_1} = F_y, \quad ma_{z_1} = F_z$$

Note that solutions give the motion of m relative to the moving $X_1Y_1Z_1$ frame. The same equations can more easily be obtained by the Lagrangian method. See Problem 9.7, Page 198.

Example 9.10(*b*).

Particle m, Fig. 9-9, is now replaced by a rigid body of mass M. We shall determine the equations of motion of the body relative to X_1, Y_1, Z_1. Let O, the origin of body-fixed axes X, Y, Z be located at c.m. X_1, Y_1, Z_1 coordinates of c.m. are indicated by $\bar{x}_1, \bar{y}_1, \bar{z}_1$.

Now note that, merely replacing m by M and x_1 by $\bar{x}_1$, etc., in (*9.20*) and corresponding expressions for a_{y_1}, a_{z_1}, we have the three translational equations of motion of c.m. (not repeated here).

The rotational equations follow at once from the procedure outlined in Section 9.10. From equations (*8.14*), Page 163, (see Fig. 8-21), it follows that components of $\boldsymbol{\omega}$ along the body-fixed X, Y, Z axes are given by

$$\omega_x = \dot{\psi}\sin\theta\sin\phi + \dot{\theta}\cos\phi - \dot{\Phi}_1\alpha_{11} + \omega_e\cos\Phi_1\alpha_{12} + \omega_e\sin\Phi_1\alpha_{13}$$

where Euler angles θ, ψ, ϕ determine, as in Fig. 8-17, Page 157, the orientation of the body relative to X_1, Y_1, Z_1. $\alpha_{11} = \cos\phi\cos\psi - \sin\phi\sin\psi\cos\theta$, etc., (see Table 8.2, Page 157.) Similar relations follow for ω_y and ω_z.

Finally, inserting $\omega_x, \omega_y, \omega_z$ in

$$\bar{I}_x\dot{\omega}_x + (\bar{I}_z - \bar{I}_y)\omega_y\omega_z + \bar{I}_{xy}(\omega_x\omega_z - \dot{\omega}_y) - \bar{I}_{xz}(\omega_x\omega_y + \dot{\omega}_z) + \bar{I}_{yz}(\omega_z^2 - \omega_y^2) = \tau_x$$

and in corresponding expressions for τ_y and τ_z, we have the desired rotational equations of motion.

Example 9.11. *Bearing Forces. Rotor mounted on Moving Frame.*

Suppose that the body, Fig. 9-7, is mounted in, say, a jet fighter plane which may be going through any type of maneuvers; to find the bearing forces. The $X_1Y_1Z_1$ frame and bearings are attached to the plane and hence move with it.

We shall assume that the motion of the plane relative to some $X_2Y_2Z_2$ frame (attached to the earth and regarded as inertial) is known. That is, the translational motion of O_1, Fig. 9-7, and rotational motion of X_1, Y_1, Z_1, each relative to X_2, Y_2, Z_2, are known functions of time. (The position of O_1 and the orientation of X_1, Y_1, Z_1 can be expressed in terms of x_2, y_2, z_2 and θ_1, ψ_1, ϕ_1, Fig. 8-21. See Section 8.10, Page 162.)

Let $\mathbf{a}_0$ be the inertial-space acceleration of O_1 with known components a_1, a_2, a_3 along X_1, Y_1, Z_1 respectively. Hence a_{0x}, a_{0y}, a_{0z}, the components of $\mathbf{a}_0$ along X, Y, Z, are given by $a_{0x} = a_1\alpha_{11} + a_2\alpha_{12} + a_3\alpha_{13}$, etc., where $\alpha_{11}, \alpha_{12}, \alpha_{13}$ are direction cosines of X relative to X_1, Y_1, Z_1, etc. But, since in Fig. 9-7, $\theta = 90°$ and $\psi = 180°$, $\alpha_{11} = -\cos\phi$, $\alpha_{12} = 0$, $\alpha_{13} = \sin\phi$, etc. (see Table 8.2, Page 158). Thus

$$a_{0x} = -a_1\cos\phi + a_3\sin\phi, \qquad a_{0y} = a_1\sin\phi + a_3\cos\phi, \qquad a_{0z} = a_2 \tag{8}$$

Let $\mathbf{\Omega}_1$ be the inertial-space angular velocity of the plane with known components $\Omega_{1x}, \Omega_{1y}, \Omega_{1z}$ about X_1, Y_1, Z_1 respectively. Then components of inertial-space angular velocity of the body along the body-fixed X, Y, Z axes are

$$\omega_x = -\Omega_{1x}\cos\phi + \Omega_{1z}\sin\phi, \qquad \omega_y = \Omega_{1x}\sin\phi + \Omega_{1z}\cos\phi, \qquad \omega_z = \Omega_{1y} + \dot{\phi} \tag{9}$$

Hence it follows from equations (*9.7*) that A_x, A_y, A_z, the components of the inertial-space acceleration of c.m. along X, Y, Z, are

$$A_x = -a_1\cos\phi + a_3\sin\phi - \bar{x}(\omega_y^2 + \omega_z^2) + \bar{y}(\omega_y\omega_x - \dot{\omega}_z) + \bar{z}(\omega_x\omega_z + \dot{\omega}_y) \tag{10}$$

with similar expressions for A_y and A_z.

Writing Mg_x, Mg_y, Mg_z as the X, Y, Z components of the weight (g_x, g_y, g_z, components of $\mathbf{g}$, may be expressed in terms of $\theta_1, \psi_1, \phi_1, \phi$), we have

$$F_x = f_{1x} + f_{2x} + Mg_x, \qquad F_y = f_{1y} + f_{2y} + Mg_y, \qquad F_z = f_z + Mg_z \tag{11}$$

and from $\tau_x = \sum(f_z y - f_y z)$, etc., it follows that,

$$\tau_x = f_{2y}l_2 - f_{1y}l_1 + Mg_z\bar{y} - Mg_y\bar{z}, \qquad \tau_y = f_{1x}l_1 - f_{2x}l_2 + Mg_x\bar{z} - Mg_z\bar{x}, \qquad \tau_z = Mg_y\bar{x} - Mg_x\bar{y} + \tau_m \tag{12}$$

We are now in a position to write equations (*9.2*) and (*9.10*). The first of (*9.2*) is

$$M[a_3\sin\phi - a_1\cos\phi - \bar{x}(\omega_y^2 + \omega_z^2) + \bar{y}(\omega_y\omega_x - \dot{\omega}_z) + \bar{z}(\omega_x\omega_z + \dot{\omega}_y)] = f_{1x} + f_{2x} + Mg_x \tag{13}$$

with similar expressions for the second and third. Equation (*9.10a*) becomes

$$\begin{aligned} M(a_{0z}\bar{y} - a_{0y}\bar{z}) + I_x\dot{\omega}_x + (I_z - I_y)\omega_y\omega_z + I_{xy}(\omega_x\omega_z - \dot{\omega}_y) \\ - I_{xz}(\omega_x\omega_y + \dot{\omega}_z) + I_{yz}(\omega_z^2 - \omega_y^2) = f_{2y}l_2 - f_{1y}l_1 + Mg_z\bar{y} - Mg_y\bar{z} \end{aligned} \tag{14}$$

with similar expressions for (*9.10b*) and (*9.10c*).

It is important to note that, for a given motion of the plane, ($x_2, y_2, z_2, \theta_1, \psi_1, \phi_1$, known functions of time) equations (*13*) and (*14*) can be expressed in terms of $t, \phi, \dot{\phi}, \ddot{\phi}$. Thus, as before, (*13*) and (*14*) can be solved for the bearing forces.

9.12 Non-Holonomic Constraints.

In all examples thus far given, equations of constraint have been written out in simple *algebraic form* as indicated by (*4.4*), Page 59. With these relations it has been possible to eliminate directly and without difficulty superfluous coordinates from T, V, etc. Constraints of this type are referred to as *holonomic*.

There is, however, a class of problems (sometimes having considerable importance) for which the constraints cannot be expressed as above. Instead, *they must be written out as differential relations of a type which cannot be integrated.* Such expressions may have the form

$$c_{i_1}\,\delta q_1 + c_{i_2}\,\delta q_2 + \cdots + c_{i_N}\,\delta q_N = 0, \qquad i = 1, 2, \ldots, s \tag{9.21}$$

where s = number of constraints and N = number of coordinates required, assuming no constraints of this form. The c's are usually functions of the coordinates. Relations (*9.21*) are called *non-holonomic* constraints.

For s such equations there are s coordinates which are not independently variable. But *since (9.21) cannot be integrated, they cannot be employed for the direct elimination of the s superfluous coordinates.* Degrees of freedom, $n = N - s$. A detailed treatment of non-holonomic systems would require a separate chapter. However, the following example illustrates the above general ideas and how the Euler method may be employed to find equations of motion and reactive forces.

Example 9.12.

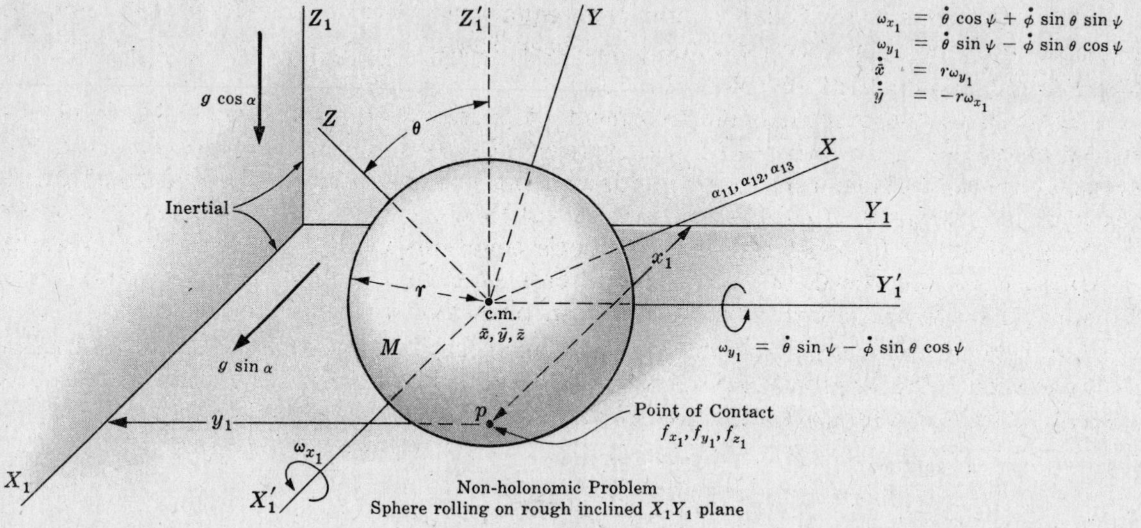

Fig. 9-10

The uniform sphere, Fig. 9-10, is allowed to roll, without slipping, in contact with the rough X_1Y_1 plane which is inclined at an angle ϵ with respect to the horizontal. The position of its center relative to X_1, Y_1, Z_1 is determined by $\bar x, \bar y, \bar z$ ($\bar z = r$ = radius of sphere) and its orientation by Euler angles θ, ψ, ϕ measured as shown. Since we assume no slipping, it may be shown (left to reader) that

$$\delta\bar x = r(\delta\theta\sin\psi - \delta\phi\sin\theta\cos\psi), \qquad \delta\bar y = -r(\delta\theta\cos\psi + \delta\phi\sin\theta\sin\psi) \tag{9.22}$$

which *cannot be integrated* to give relations between $\bar x, \bar y, \theta, \psi, \phi$. Relations (9.22) are typical non-holonomic constraints.

Euler's equations can, nevertheless, be applied to this problem as follows. Expressions (9.2) are

$$M\ddot{\bar x} = f_{x_1} + Mg\sin\alpha, \quad M\ddot{\bar y} = f_{y_1}, \quad M\ddot{\bar z} = f_{z_1} - Mg\cos\alpha \tag{1}$$

where $f_{x_1}, f_{y_1}, f_{z_1}$ are X_1, Y_1, Z_1 components of the reactive force at p.

Relations (9.10) reduce to

$$I\dot\omega_{x_1} = \tau_{x_1}, \quad I\dot\omega_{y_1} = \tau_{y_1}, \quad I\dot\omega_z = \tau_{z_1} \tag{2}$$

where I = moment of inertia of the sphere about any line through its center and $\omega_{x_1}, \omega_{y_1}, \omega_{z_1}$ are components of the angular velocity of the sphere about the direction-fixed X_1', Y_1', Z_1' axes. The above form is convenient because $I_x = I_y = I_z = I$ = constant, regardless of the orientation of the sphere. Hence (2) may be written as

$$\begin{aligned} I\frac{d}{dt}(\dot\theta\cos\psi + \dot\phi\sin\theta\sin\psi) &= f_{y_1}r \\ I\frac{d}{dt}(\dot\theta\sin\psi - \dot\phi\sin\theta\cos\psi) &= -f_{x_1}r \\ I\frac{d}{dt}(\dot\psi + \dot\phi\cos\theta) &= 0 \end{aligned} \tag{3}$$

By inspection of the figure (or regarding $\delta\bar x$, $\delta\bar y$, etc., in (9.22) as displacements in time dt), we have

$$\dot{\bar x} = r\omega_{y_1}, \quad \dot{\bar y} = -r\omega_{x_1}, \quad \dot{\bar z} = 0 \tag{4}$$

the first two of which can be written as

$$\dot{\bar{x}} = r(\dot{\theta}\sin\psi - \dot{\phi}\sin\theta\cos\psi), \qquad \dot{\bar{y}} = -r(\dot{\theta}\cos\psi + \dot{\phi}\sin\theta\sin\psi) \tag{5}$$

From (1), (3) and (5) it follows at once that

$$(I/r^2 + M)\ddot{\bar{x}} = Mg\sin\epsilon, \qquad (I/r^2 + M)\ddot{\bar{y}} = 0$$

Hence $\bar{x}, \bar{y}, \bar{z}$ as well as f_x, f_y, f_z can each be determined as functions of time.

9.13 Euler's Rotational Equations From the Point of View of Angular Momentum.

The development of Euler's rotational equations (Section 9.5, Page 181) and their physical interpretation [Section 9.6(*b*)] has been based on the "principle of moments" expressed by relations (*9.8*) and (*9.11*).

We shall now present a brief treatment of these equations in which the emphasis is placed on *angular momentum and time rate of change of angular momentum.* As far as classical dynamics is concerned, this adds nothing basically new to the results of previous sections. However, it is here given because (*a*) this approach represents another interesting point of view, (*b*) most texts treat Euler's equations in this way, (*c*) momentum is of importance in the development of Hamilton's equations, Chapter. 16, and (*d*) angular momentum plays an important role in certain phases of quantum mechanics.

Referring to Fig. 9-11, regard X_1, Y_1, Z_1 as inertial. Assume X, Y, Z remain parallel to these axes. The origin O may or may not be attached to the body. Coordinates of the typical particle m' are x, y, z and x_1, y_1, z_1 which are related by $x_1 = x_0 + x$, etc.

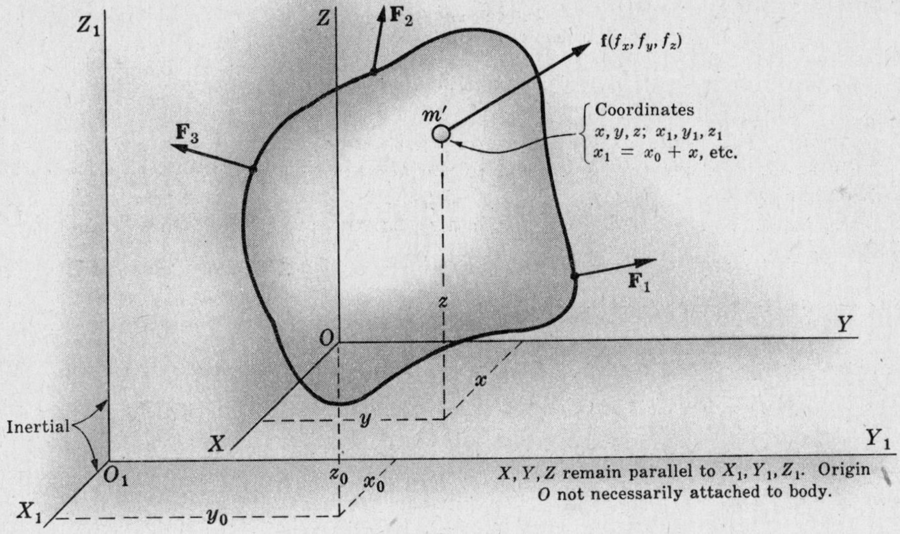

Fig. 9-11

Regarding $\mathbf{f}(f_x, f_y, f_z)$ as the net force on m', we write free particle equations as

$$f_x = m'\ddot{x}_1, \quad f_y = m'\ddot{y}_1, \quad f_z = m'\ddot{z}_1$$

Multiplying the third by y_1, the second by $-z_1$, adding and summing over all particles of the body, we have

$$\sum m'(\ddot{z}_1 y_1 - \ddot{y}_1 z_1) = \sum (f_z y_1 - f_y z_1) = \tau_{x_1} \tag{9.23}$$

where here τ_{x_1} is the torque exerted by the applied forces $\mathbf{F}_1, \mathbf{F}_2$ about the X_1 axis. But inspection shows that (*9.23*) can be written as

$$\frac{d}{dt}\sum m'(\dot{z}_1 y_1 - \dot{y}_1 z_1) = \tau_{x_1} \tag{9.24}$$

We now define angular momentum or moment of momentum, P_{x_1}, of the body about the inertial X_1 axis as

$$P_{x_1} = \sum m'(\dot{z}_1 y_1 - \dot{y}_1 z_1) \tag{9.25}$$

Likewise angular momentum P_{y_1}, P_{z_1} about Y_1 and Z_1 are defined. (As shown in Problem 9.22, P_x, P_y, P_z are components of an angular momentum vector $\mathbf{P}$. In vector notation (see Chapter 18), $\mathbf{P} = \sum m'(\mathbf{r}\times\dot{\mathbf{r}})$ where $\mathbf{r}$ is the position vector measured from O_1 to m'. For a final expression for P_x, see Problem 9.23.) Hence from (9.24) it is seen that the time rate of change of angular momentum about X_1 is equal to the torque of applied forces about this axis. That is,

$$\dot{P}_{x_1} = \tau_{x_1}, \quad \dot{P}_{y_1} = \tau_{y_1}, \quad \dot{P}_{z_1} = \tau_{z_1} \tag{9.26}$$

where in this case under consideration $P_{x_1}, P_{y_1}, P_{z_1}$ are determined relative to inertial space.

But $\tau_{x_1}, \tau_{y_1}, \tau_{z_1}$ are components of a vector τ (see Section 8.2F, Page 147). Likewise $\dot{P}_{x_1}, \dot{P}_{y_1}, \dot{P}_{z_1}$ are components of $\dot{\mathbf{P}}$ which is given in magnitude by $\dot{P}^2 = \dot{P}^2_{x_1} + \dot{P}^2_{y_1} + \dot{P}^2_{z_1}$ and in direction by $\dot{P}_{x_1}/\dot{P}$, etc.

The torque about any line O_1a having direction cosines l, m, n may be expressed as

$$\tau_{O_1a} = \dot{P}_{x_1} l + \dot{P}_{y_1} m + \dot{P}_{z_1} n \tag{9.27}$$

or in vector notation,

$$\tau = \dot{\mathbf{P}} \tag{9.28}$$

Consider now the moving (but non-rotating) X, Y, Z frame. Eliminating x_1, y_1, z_1 from (9.23) by $x_1 = x_0 + x$, etc., we have

$$\begin{aligned} \tau_{x_1} &= \sum m'[(\ddot{z}_0 + \ddot{z})(y_0 + y) - (\ddot{y}_0 + \ddot{y})(z_0 + z)] \\ &= \sum m'(\ddot{z}_1 y_0 - \ddot{y}_1 z_0) + \sum m'(\ddot{z}y - \ddot{y}z) + \sum m'(\ddot{z}_0 y - \ddot{y}_0 z) \end{aligned} \tag{9.29}$$

Making use of $\tau_{x_1} = \sum [f_z(y_0 + y) - f_y(z_0 + z)]$, $m'\ddot{z}_1 = f_z$, etc., $\sum m'\ddot{z}_0 y = M\ddot{z}_0\bar{y}$ (where M = total mass, $\bar{y} = Y$ coordinate of c.m.), (9.25) can be written as

$$\sum (f_z y - f_y z) = M(\ddot{z}_0\bar{y} - \ddot{y}_0\bar{z}) + \sum m'(\ddot{z}y - \ddot{y}z) \tag{9.30}$$

The term on the left is obviously τ_x, the moment of the applied forces about X (not X_1); and defining $P_x = \sum m'(\dot{z}y - \dot{y}z)$ as the angular momentum about X, (9.30) may be written as

$$\tau_x = M(\ddot{z}_0\bar{y} - \ddot{y}_0\bar{z}) + \dot{P}_x, \quad \tau_y = M(\ddot{x}_0\bar{z} - \ddot{z}_0\bar{x}) + \dot{P}_y, \quad \tau_z = M(\ddot{y}_0\bar{x} - \ddot{x}_0\bar{y}) + \dot{P}_z \tag{9.31}$$

These relations are equivalent to (9.10) and can be put in exactly the same form. (For the equivalent vector relation see Page 342.)

Note that if O is fixed or moves with constant velocity, $\ddot{x}_0 = \ddot{y}_0 = \ddot{z}_0 = 0$. If O is located at and moves with c.m., $\bar{x} = \bar{y} = \bar{z} = 0$. Hence, in either case, (9.31) reduce to $\tau_x = \dot{P}_x$, etc.

As to a physical interpretation of Euler's rotational equations from the point of view of angular momentum, (9.27) states that the projection of $\dot{\mathbf{P}}$ (a vector representing the time rate of change of the angular momentum of the body) on any line O_1a is equal to the sum of moments of applied forces about this line. To some this interpretation may present a rather vague "picture" or explanation of what takes place physically. On the other hand, equations (9.8), Page 181, and (9.16), Page 183, which express the simple fact that the sum of the moments of inertial forces about any line is equal to the sum of the moments of applied forces about the same line, make quite clear the meaning of Euler's equations in terms of elementary basic physical and geometrical principles. From the second point of view, (9.16) is no more involved than, for example, $f_x = m\ddot{x}$, etc.

9.14 Comparison of the Euler and Lagrangian Treatments.

The Euler method is one in which the body is regarded as "free" and forces of constraint must be included in equations (*9.2*) and (*9.16*). These relations lead to equations of motion as well as expressions for the reactive forces.

Summarizing the Lagrangian method: if the body is regarded as free and T is written, say, in terms of $\bar{x}, \bar{y}, \bar{z}$ and the Euler angles θ, ψ, ϕ, then $\frac{d}{dt}\left(\frac{\partial T}{\partial \dot{\bar{x}}}\right) - \frac{\partial T}{\partial \bar{x}} = F_x$, etc., are just equations (*9.2*). Also, $\frac{d}{dt}\left(\frac{\partial T}{\partial \dot{\theta}}\right) - \frac{\partial T}{\partial \theta} = F_\theta = \tau_{ON}$, etc., are equations (*9.16*) and of course reactive forces must appear in F_x, τ_{ON}, etc. (See Problem 9.9.) But if all superfluous coordinates are eliminated from T, $\frac{d}{dt}\left(\frac{\partial T}{\partial \dot{q}_r}\right) - \frac{\partial T}{\partial q_r} = F_{q_r}$ are the equations of motion free from reactive forces (assuming smooth constraints).

This is by far the quickest and easiest way of obtaining final equations of motion, especially when two or more rigid bodies are involved.

The following resource letter contains valuable comments on certain phases of rigid body dynamics as well as an excellent list of annotated references: *Resource Letter CM-1, on the Teaching of Angular Momentum and Rigid Body Motion,* by John I. Shonle, American Journal of Physics, Vol. 33, No. 11, November 1965, Pages 879-887. Remarks in the introduction are very pertinent.

Problems

9.1. Differentiating the following relation (see Fig. 9-2)

$$x_1 = x_0 + x\alpha_{11} + y\alpha_{21} + z\alpha_{31}$$

with respect to t and making use of relations (*3*), Section 9.4, Page 179, show that

$$v_x = v_{0x} + \dot{x} + \Omega_y z - \Omega_z y$$

for a free particle where v_x is the component of the inertial-space velocity of m along the instantaneous direction of X and v_{0x} is the component of the inertial-space velocity of O along X. Of course similar expressions follow for v_y and v_z. See equations (*8.3*), Page 142.

9.2. (*a*) Referring again to Fig. 9-2, write

$$T' = \tfrac{1}{2}[(v_{0x} + \dot{x} + \Omega_y z - \Omega_z y)^2 + (v_{0y} + \dot{y} + \Omega_z x - \Omega_x z)^2 + (v_{0z} + \dot{z} + \Omega_x y - \Omega_y x)^2]$$

where $v_{0x} = \dot{x}_0\alpha_{11} + \dot{y}_0\alpha_{12} + \dot{z}_0\alpha_{13}$, etc. Now show (see Section 3.9, Page 48) that $\frac{d}{dt}\left(\frac{\partial T'}{\partial \dot{x}}\right) - \frac{\partial T'}{\partial x} = a_x$, where a_x is the first expression in (*9.6*), Page 179. Note that in certain terms as $\dot{x}_0(\dot{\alpha}_{11} - \alpha_{21}\Omega_z + \alpha_{31}\Omega_y)$ the coefficient of $\dot{x}_0$ may be shown to be zero. The above is an easy way of obtaining relations (*9.6*).

(*b*) Write $T' = \tfrac{1}{2}(\dot{x}_1^2 + \dot{y}_1^2 + \dot{z}_1^2)$ where x, y, z are the X_1, Y_1, Z_1 coordinates of m, Fig. 9-2, and

$$\dot{x}_1 = \dot{x}_0 + \dot{x}\alpha_{11} + \dot{y}\alpha_{21} + \dot{z}\alpha_{31} + x\dot{\alpha}_{11} + y\dot{\alpha}_{21} + z\dot{\alpha}_{31}, \qquad \text{etc.}$$

Write out $\frac{d}{dt}\left(\frac{\partial T'}{\partial \dot{x}}\right) - \frac{\partial T}{\partial x}$ and introducing Euler angles, show that after considerable tedious work the same expression is obtained for a_x.

9.3. (*a*) Assuming, for example, that the motion of the rigid body, Fig. 9-3, is completely known, show that f_x, the X component of the force **f** acting on the typical particle m', can be obtained from

$$f_x = m'[\ddot{x}_0\alpha_{11} + \ddot{y}_0\alpha_{12} + \ddot{z}_0\alpha_{13} - x(\omega_y^2 + \omega_z^2) + y(\omega_y\omega_x - \dot{\omega}_z) + z(\omega_x\omega_z + \dot{\omega}_y)]$$

Similar expressions follow for f_y and f_z.

(*b*) A particle of mass m is glued to the periphery (and on the X axis) of disk D, Fig. 8-5, Page 146. Assuming ψ and ϕ are known functions of time, find the X, Y, Z components of force which the glue exerts on the particle. Express the results in terms of ψ, ϕ, and their time derivatives. See the following related problem.

9.4. Referring to Fig. 8-5, Page 146, a particle of mass m is acted upon by a known force having components f_x, f_y, f_z along the X, Y, Z disk-fixed axes. Motion of the particle is to be determined relative to the moving X, Y, Z frame, assuming ψ and ϕ are known functions of time. Show that equations of motion are

$$m[a_{0x} + \ddot{x} - x(\omega_y^2 + \omega_z^2) + y(\omega_y\omega_x - \dot{\omega}_z) + z(\omega_x\omega_z + \dot{\omega}_y) + 2(\dot{z}\omega_y - \dot{y}\omega_z)] = f_x, \quad \text{etc.}$$

where $\omega_x = \dot{\psi}\sin\theta\sin\phi, \quad \omega_y = \dot{\psi}\sin\theta\cos\phi, \quad \omega_z = \dot{\phi} + \dot{\psi}\cos\theta,$

$$a_{0x} = \ddot{\psi}s\sin\theta\cos\phi + \dot{\psi}^2 s\sin\theta\cos\theta\sin\phi,$$

$$a_{0y} = -\ddot{\psi}s\sin\theta\sin\phi + \dot{\psi}^2 s\sin\theta\cos\theta\cos\phi,$$

$$a_{0z} = -\dot{\psi}^2 s\sin^2\theta$$

Determine the above expressions for a_{0x}, a_{0y}, a_{0z} by a direct elementary method and also by an application of (*9.7*), Page 180.

9.5. Referring to equations (*14.15*), Page 287, note that the coefficients of m in these three equations are just the components a_x, a_y, a_z of the acceleration of m relative to inertial space, taken along the instantaneous directions of X_1, Y_1, Z_1 respectively. Show that exactly the same expressions can be found at once by applying equations (*9.7*), Page 180.

9.6. Referring to Example 8.7, Fig. 8-11, Page 152, determine expressions for A_x, A_y, A_z in a straightforward manner by the use of transformation equations. Compare results with (*1*), Example 9.4, Page 185.

9.7. Referring to Example 9.10(*a*), Fig. 9-9, Page 192, show that for the single particle,

$$T = \tfrac{1}{2}m[(R\omega_e\cos\Phi + z\omega_e\cos\Phi + \dot{x} - y\omega_e\sin\Phi)^2 + (R\dot{\Phi} + \dot{y} + x\omega_e\sin\Phi + z\dot{\Phi})^2 + (\dot{z} - y\dot{\Phi} - x\omega_e\cos\Phi)^2]$$

Applying Lagrange's equations show that (*9.20*), etc., Page 192, follow at once.

9.8. Imagine the body shown in Fig. 8-16, Page 156, replaced by a spinning top with its tip fixed at O. Axes X, Y, Z are fixed to the top. Find expressions for the X, Y, Z components of the inertial space acceleration of a particle in the top (*a*) using relations (*9.7*), (*b*) applying the Lagrangian method (see equation (*3.24*), Page 49). The particle is located at a normal distance r from the axis of spin and distance h, measured parallel to this axis, from the tip.

9.9. Derive the Euler equation (*9.10a*), Page 182, by means of Lagrange's equation.

Hints. With T in the form of (*8.10*), Page 148, write out the θ equation $\dfrac{d}{dt}\left(\dfrac{\partial T}{\partial\dot{\theta}}\right) - \dfrac{\partial T}{\partial\theta} = F_\theta$, regarding $\omega_x, \omega_y, \omega_z$ as functions of θ, ψ, ϕ; $\dot{\theta}, \dot{\psi}, \dot{\phi}$. (See relations (*8.11*), Page 157.) Since $v_{0x} = \dot{x}_0\alpha_{11} + \dot{y}_0\alpha_{12} + \dot{z}_0\alpha_{13}$, v_{0x} is a function of the Euler angles.

Now setting $\theta = 90°$, $\psi = \phi = 0$ and noting that for these values $F_\theta = \tau_x$, $\dot{\alpha}_{11} = 0$, $\dot{\alpha}_{12} = \dot{\psi} = \omega_y$, $\dot{\alpha}_{13} = \dot{\phi} = \omega_z$ etc., the above Lagrangian equation finally reduces to (*9.10a*). Of course (*9.10b*) and (*9.10c*) can be found in the same way. For the above values of θ, ψ, ϕ, $F_\psi = \tau_z$ and $F_\phi = -\tau_y$.

Considerable care is required in carrying through the steps of this problem.

9.10. Referring to Section 9.5, Fig. 9-3, Page 181, imagine axes X_2, Y_2, Z_2 with origin attached to the body at O. Assume that these axes may be rotating about O in any manner relative to the body. Coordinates of m' relative to X_2, Y_2, Z_2 are x_2, y_2, z_2. For this problem take $\alpha_{11}, \alpha_{12}, \alpha_{13}$ as direction cosines of the body-fixed X axis relative to X_2, Y_2, Z_2, etc. Let $a_{x_2}, a_{y_2}, a_{z_2}$ be components of the inertial space acceleration **a** of m' along instantaneous positions of X_2, Y_2, Z_2. That is, $a_{x_2} = a_x\alpha_{11} + a_y\alpha_{21} + a_z\alpha_{31}$ where a_x, a_y, a_z = components of **a** along the body-fixed X, Y, Z axes (a_x, a_y, a_z are given by (9.7), Page 180). Then

$$\sum m'(a_{z_2}y_2 - a_{y_2}z_2) \;=\; \tau_{x_2}, \quad \text{etc.} \tag{1}$$

where τ_{x_2} = moment of all external forces about the instantaneous position of X_2. Show that (1) can be written as

$$\alpha_{11}\sum m'(a_zy - a_yz) \;+\; \alpha_{21}\sum m'(a_xz - a_zx) \;+\; \alpha_{31}\sum m'(a_yx - a_xy) \tag{2}$$

This is just relation (9.16). Moreover it shows that (9.16) is applicable to any line through O, whether rigidly attached or rotating relative to the body.

9.11. Referring to Section 8.2F, Page 147, Fig. 8-7, consider a typical particle m' at point p. Suppose that **f** represents the net force on m'. Then $f_x = m'a_x$, etc., where a_x is the X component of the inertial-space acceleration of m'. Applying the method of this section to show the vector nature of torque, prove again relation (2), Problem 9.10.

9.12. (a) Referring to Example 8.5 and Fig. 8-9, Page 150, show that equations of motion of the lamina as determined by the Lagrangian method are

$$I_z\ddot{\theta} + M[(\ddot{y}\bar{x} - \ddot{x}\bar{y})\cos\theta - (\ddot{x}\bar{x} + \ddot{y}\bar{y})\sin\theta] \;=\; Mg[\bar{y}\sin\theta - \bar{x}\cos\theta] \;=\; \tau_\theta$$

$$M[\ddot{x} - \ddot{\theta}(\bar{y}\cos\theta + \bar{x}\sin\theta) + \dot{\theta}^2(\bar{y}\sin\theta - \bar{x}\cos\theta)] \;=\; F_x \;=\; -Mg\sin\theta$$

$$M[\ddot{y} + \ddot{\theta}(\bar{x}\cos\theta - \bar{y}\sin\theta) - \dot{\theta}^2(\bar{x}\sin\theta + \bar{y}\cos\theta)] \;=\; F_y \;=\; -Mg\cos\theta$$

where we have assumed gravity only acting in the negative direction of Y_1.

(b) Applying Euler's method, regarding X, Y, Z as body-fixed, show that

$$I_z\ddot{\theta} + M(a_{0y}\bar{x} - a_{0x}\bar{y}) \;=\; Mg(\bar{y}\sin\theta - \bar{x}\cos\theta)$$

$$Ma_{0x} - M(\ddot{\theta}\bar{y} + \dot{\theta}^2\bar{x}) \;=\; -Mg\sin\theta$$

$$Ma_{0y} + M(\ddot{\theta}\bar{x} - \dot{\theta}^2\bar{y}) \;=\; -Mg\cos\theta$$

Show that equations in (b) are equivalent to those in (a).

(c) Now employing non-rotating axes with origin attached to O, show that Euler's equations have just the same form as those given in (a). Notice how the equations simplify with O at c.m.

9.13. In Fig. 9-12 the rigid body pendulum is allowed to swing about the horizontal axis ab with no friction in bearings. Angle θ, measured from a vertical line through O, is positive in the direction shown. Using body-fixed axes X, Y, Z as indicated, show that

(1) $M(\ddot{\theta}\bar{z} - \dot{\theta}^2\bar{x}) \;=\; Mg\cos\theta + f_{ax} + f_{ay}$

(2) $f_{ay} + f_{by} \;=\; 0$

(3) $-M(\ddot{\theta}\bar{x} + \dot{\theta}^2\bar{z}) \;=\; Mg\sin\theta + f_{az} + f_{bz}$

(4) $-I_{xy}\ddot{\theta} - I_{yz}\dot{\theta}^2 \;=\; Mg\bar{y}\sin\theta + (f_{az} - f_{bz})s$

(5) $I_y\ddot{\theta} \;=\; Mg\bar{z}\cos\theta - Mg\bar{x}\sin\theta$

(6) $I_{xy}\dot{\theta}^2 - I_{yz}\ddot{\theta} \;=\; -Mg\bar{y}\cos\theta - (f_{ax} - f_{bx})s$

where f_{ax}, f_{bx}, etc., are X, Y, Z components of bearing forces at a and b.

Moments and products of inertia are for the entire system including rods ab and Op. c.m. indicates the center of mass of the system.

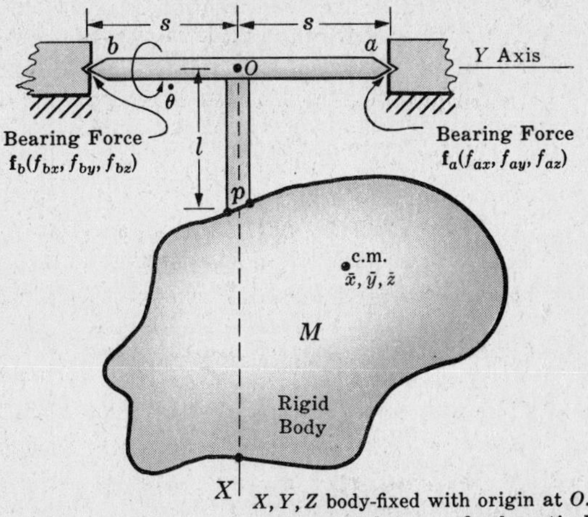

X, Y, Z body-fixed with origin at O. θ measured between fixed vertical line and the X axis. θ positive for body displaced into paper.

Fig. 9-12

Derive (*5*), the θ equation of motion, by the Lagrangian method. Show that θ_0, the rest angle, is given by $\tan\theta_0 = \bar{z}/\bar{x}$. Letting $\theta = \theta_0 + \beta$, (*5*) can be integrated at once for β small. Hence show how $f_{ax}, f_{bx}, f_{az}, f_{bz}$ can be determined as functions of time.

Write out the rotational equations taking body-fixed axes parallel to X, Y, Z with origin at c.m. Is this advantageous?

9.14. Imagine the rod Op, Fig. 9-12, hinged at O (door type of hinge) so that the body can now rotate about an axis through O perpendicular to the aOp plane; that is, Op can now swing through an angle α in the aOp plane as well as rotate about ab. Taking the body-fixed axes as in Problem 9.13 (Y no longer remains along Oa), show that components of angular velocity are given by

$$\omega_x = \dot{\theta}\sin\alpha, \qquad \omega_y = \dot{\theta}\cos\alpha, \qquad \omega_z = \dot{\alpha}$$

Show that X, Y, Z components of the inertial-space velocity of c.m. are (see equations (*8.1*), Page 140),

$$\bar{v}_x = \dot{\theta}\bar{z}\cos\alpha - \dot{\alpha}\bar{y}, \qquad \bar{v}_y = \dot{\alpha}\bar{x} - \dot{\theta}\bar{z}\sin\alpha, \qquad \bar{v}_z = \dot{\theta}\bar{y}\sin\alpha - \dot{\theta}\bar{x}\cos\alpha$$

Assuming $\bar{x}, \bar{y}, \bar{z}, I_x, I_{xy}$, etc. as known, write an expression for T. Applying Lagrange's equations, write the equations of motion corresponding to θ and α.

Find the same equations by the Euler method. Compare advantages of the two methods.

9.15. The double pendulum, Fig. 9-13, consists of two thin laminae supported from a smooth peg at p_1. The bearing at p_2 is smooth. Outline steps (do not give all details) for finding the θ, ϕ equations of motion. Compare this with the Lagrangian method.

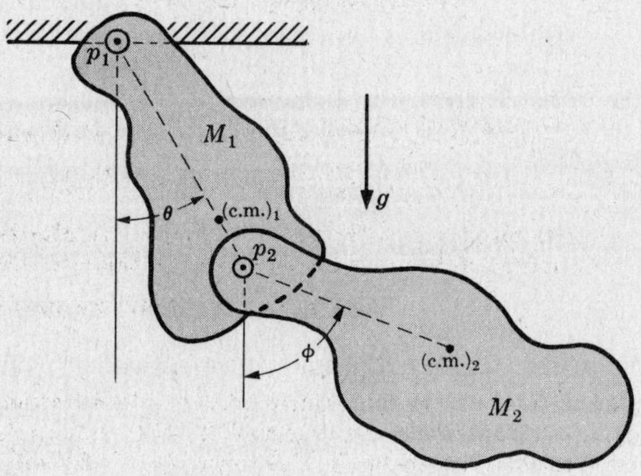

Fig. 9-13

9.16. Consider a system such as shown in Fig. 8-26, Page 169. Outline steps (no details) for finding equations of motion of the entire system by the Euler method. Compare this with the procedure required by the Lagrangian method. Assume, for example, that the uniform rod bd has appreciable mass and that the vertical shaft has a moment of inertia I_1 about Z_1.

9.17. Referring to Example 9.7, Fig. 9-7, Page 187, derive equations (*6*) and (*7*) from simple basic considerations.

Hint. Inertial forces on any typical particle are $-m'(\ddot{\phi}y + \dot{\phi}^2 x)$ in the direction of X and $m'(\ddot{\phi}x - \dot{\phi}^2 y)$ in the direction of Y. Sum moments of these forces for all particles of the body about an axis, say through B_2 and parallel to Y. Setting this equal to the applied torques about the same axis, (*6*) is obtained. This derivation lays bare the basic physical principles involved and also gives more meaning to products of inertia.

9.18. (*a*) Assume that the body, Fig. 9-7, is perfectly balanced statically and dynamically. A particle of mass m is now glued to it at a point x, y, z. Find expressions for the bearing forces.

(*b*) Imagine the particle replaced by a thin rod of known length and mass. The rod, one end at x, y, z and extending parallel to X, is rigidly glued to the body. Outline steps for finding bearing forces.

9.19. The rotating body, Fig. 9-14 below, is mounted on a rotating table. The body is driven by a light motor (not shown) at an angular velocity $\dot{\phi}$ with ϕ measured between the $-X_1$ axis and the body-fixed X axis (see notes on diagram; also see Example 9.7, Page 187). The table is driven at an angular velocity $\dot{\beta}$ about the vertical inertial Z_2 axis. Show that the bearing force f_{1x} is given by

$$\begin{aligned} f_{1x}(l_1 + l_2) = {} & Ms_1(\ddot{\beta}\bar{z} + \dot{\beta}^2\bar{x}) + I_y(\ddot{\beta}\cos\phi - \dot{\beta}\dot{\phi}\sin\phi) + (I_x - I_z)\dot{\beta}\dot{\phi}\sin\phi \\ & + I_{yz}(\dot{\beta}^2\sin\phi\cos\phi - \ddot{\phi}) - I_{xy}(2\dot{\beta}\dot{\phi}\cos\phi + \ddot{\beta}\sin\phi) \\ & + I_{xz}(\dot{\beta}^2\sin^2\phi - \dot{\phi}^2) + M[s_1\ddot{\beta}\cos\phi - \bar{x}(\dot{\beta}^2\cos\phi + \dot{\phi}^2) \\ & + \bar{y}(\ddot{\beta}\sin\phi\cos\phi - \ddot{\phi}) + \bar{z}\ddot{\beta}\cos\phi]l_2 + Mg(l_2 + \bar{z})\sin\phi \end{aligned}$$

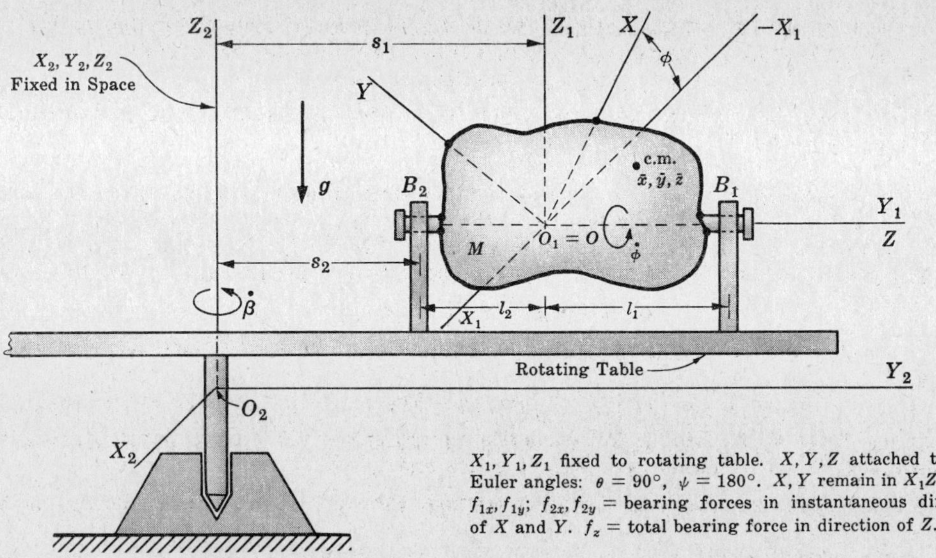

X_1, Y_1, Z_1 fixed to rotating table. X, Y, Z attached to body. Euler angles: $\theta = 90°$, $\psi = 180°$. X, Y remain in $X_1 Z_1$ plane. f_{1x}, f_{1y}; f_{2x}, f_{2y} = bearing forces in instantaneous directions of X and Y. f_z = total bearing force in direction of Z.

Fig. 9-14

Note that if X, Y, Z are principal axes of inertia and c.m. is located at O, the above reduces to

$$\bar{I}_y^p \ddot{\beta} \cos\phi + (\bar{I}_x - \bar{I}_y - \bar{I}_z)\dot{\beta}\dot{\phi} \sin\phi + M[s_1 l_2 \ddot{\beta} \cos\phi + g l_2 \sin\phi] = f_{1x}(l_1 + l_2)$$

which shows that even if the body is statically and dynamically balanced on a stationary table, there are bearing forces when the table is rotating.

Find expressions for the remaining bearing forces (see Example 14.11, Page 296).

9.20. Consider again Problem 9.19. Take body-fixed axes X^p, Y^p, Z^p along the principal axes of inertia with origin at the origin of X, Y, Z. Let l_{11}, l_{12}, l_{13} be direction cosines of X^p relative to X, Y, Z, etc. Note that since X, Y, Z and X^p, Y^p, Z^p are each body-fixed the direction cosines are constant. Numerical values of the l's as well as I_x^p, I_y^p, I_z^p can be found from values of I_x, I_{xy}, etc., relative to X, Y, Z (see Section 7.3, Page 119).

Show that components of inertial-space angular velocity of the body about X^p, Y^p, Z^p are given by

$$\omega_x = \dot{\beta} l_{11} \sin\phi + \dot{\beta} l_{12} \cos\phi + \dot{\phi} l_{13}$$
$$\omega_y = \dot{\beta} l_{21} \sin\phi + \dot{\beta} l_{22} \cos\phi + \dot{\phi} l_{23}$$
$$\omega_z = \dot{\beta} l_{31} \sin\phi + \dot{\beta} l_{32} \cos\phi + \dot{\phi} l_{33}$$

and that for these axes,

$$a_{0x} = s_1 \ddot{\beta} l_{11} \cos\phi - s_1 \ddot{\beta} l_{12} \sin\phi - \dot{\beta}^2 s_1 l_{13}, \quad \text{etc.}$$

Show that the first equation of (*9.2*) is

$$M[s_1 \ddot{\beta} l_{11} \cos\phi - s_1 \ddot{\beta} l_{12} \sin\phi - \dot{\beta}^2 s_1 l_{13} - \bar{x}(\omega_y^2 + \omega_z^2) + \bar{y}(\omega_y \omega_x - \dot{\omega}_z) + \bar{z}(\omega_x \omega_z + \dot{\omega}_y)] = F_x$$

and that the first of equation (*9.10*) becomes

$$M(a_{0z}\bar{y} - a_{0y}\bar{z}) + I_x^p \dot{\omega}_x + (I_z^p - I_y^p)\omega_y \omega_z = \tau_x$$

where in the above $\bar{x}, \bar{y}, \bar{z}$ are coordinates of c.m. relative to the X^p, Y^p, Z^p frame. The remaining Euler equations can be written at once.

9.21. The gyroscope, Fig. 8-18, Page 159, is placed at the origin O_1, Fig. 9-9, Page 192, with axis $a_1 a_2$ along Z_1. Let us assume that O_1 moves northward along the great circle with velocity $R\dot{\Phi}$, Y remaining tangent to the great circle. Applying the Euler method, set up the θ, ψ, ϕ equations of motion. See Problem 8.22, Page 173.

9.22. Referring to Fig. 9-15, let it be assumed that the body is free to move in space. The typical particle m' has a velocity $v(\dot{x}, \dot{y}, \dot{z})$ relative to the inertial frame X, Y, Z.

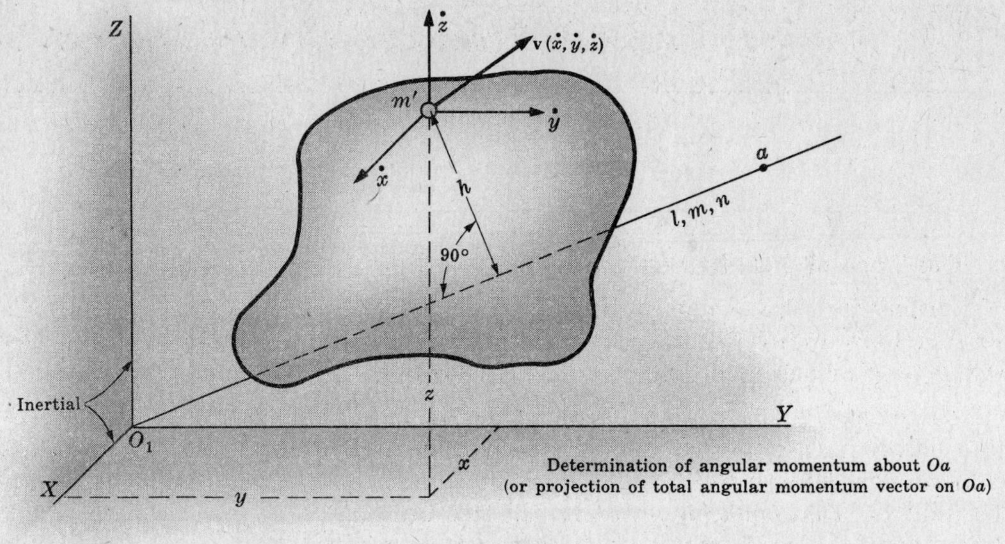

Fig. 9-15

The "angular momentum" of m' about line O_1a is defined as $m'hv'$ where v' is the component of v normal to the O_1am' plane. Following exactly the procedure outlined in Section 8.2F, Page 147, show that the total angular momentum, P_{O_1a}, of the body about line O_1a is given by

$$P_{O_1a} = l\sum m'(\dot{z}y - \dot{y}z) + m\sum m'(\dot{x}z - \dot{z}x) + n\sum m'(\dot{y}x - \dot{x}y)$$

where l, m, n are direction cosines of O_1a. Show from the diagram that $\sum m'(\dot{z}y - \dot{y}z) = P_x$ is the angular momentum about X, etc. Hence

$$P_{O_1a} = P_x l + P_y m + P_z n$$

Thus P_{O_1a} is the projection of a vector **P** (having magnitude $P = (P_x^2 + P_y^2 + P_z^2)^{1/2}$ and direction P_x/P, etc.) along O_1a.

Taking moments about O_1a, prove in a similar manner equation (*9.27*), Page 196.

9.23. Referring to Fig. 9-11 and assuming O located at c.m. of the body, show that P_{x_1}, the angular momentum of the body about X_1 (the component of the angular momentum vector along X_1) is given by

$$P_{x_1} = M(\dot{z}_0 y_0 - \dot{y}_0 z_0) + I_x\omega_x - I_{xy}\omega_y - I_{xz}\omega_z$$

where $\omega_x, \omega_y, \omega_z$ are components of the inertial space angular velocity of the body along X, Y, Z and I_x, I_{xy}, I_{xz} are determined relative to the X, Y, Z frame.

9.24. Taking O, Fig. 8-21, Page 163, at c.m. and regarding X, Y, Z as principal axes, show that

$$T = \tfrac{1}{2}Mv_0^2 + \tfrac{1}{2}(\bar{I}_x^p\omega_x^2 + \bar{I}_y^p\omega_y^2 + \bar{I}_z^p\omega_z^2)$$

where $\omega_x, \omega_y, \omega_z$ are given by (*8.14*), Page 163.

Now write the Lagrangian equation corresponding to θ, for example, and show that exactly the same relation is obtained by the second equation of (*9.17*), Page 189.

CHAPTER

10

Small Oscillations about Positions of Equilibrium

10.1 The Type of Problem Considered.

In order that the reader may commence the study of "small oscillations" with some general understanding of and feeling for the type of problem to be considered, let us examine the various mechanical systems shown in Fig. 10-1 and 10-2.

Considering Fig. 10-1(a), suppose either m_1 or m_2 (or both) slightly disturbed. ("Disturbed" here means: the masses are given some slight initial velocities and displacements from rest positions.) Subsequently each mass oscillates about its equilibrium position. Assuming vertical displacements only, the motion of each, as soon to be shown, is composed of *two* simple harmonic motions which can be expressed by

$$y_1 \;=\; A_1 \cos(\omega_1 t + \phi_1) + A_2 \cos(\omega_2 t + \phi_2), \qquad y_2 \;=\; B_1 \cos(\omega_1 t + \phi_1) + B_2 \cos(\omega_2 t + \phi_2)$$

where ω_1, ω_2 and the phase angles ϕ_1, ϕ_2 are the same in each relation, but corresponding amplitudes are not equal. Moreover, it will be seen that ω_1 and ω_2 depend only on values of m_1, m_2, k_1, k_2 and not on how the motion is started.

Now it is important to realize, as will be made clear in what follows, that the above remarks apply to every system shown in Fig. 10-1. Each has two degrees of freedom and two natural frequencies or "principal modes of motion".

The systems shown in Fig. 10-2 have from $n=3$ to $n=9$ degrees of freedom. When slightly disturbed each part (mass, disk, bar, etc.) of a given system will, in general, oscillate with n frequencies $f_1 = \omega_1/2\pi$, $f_2 = \omega_2/2\pi$, ..., $f_n = \omega_n/2\pi$; *each part has the same n frequencies,* values of which again depend only on constants of the system (masses, spring constants, dimensions, etc.).

Considering Fig. 10-2(b), for example, the oscillatory motion of the disks may be written as

$$\theta_1 \;=\; A_1 \cos(\omega_1 t + \phi_1) \;+\; A_2 \cos(\omega_2 t + \phi_2) \;+\; A_3 \cos(\omega_3 t + \phi_3)$$

with identical expressions for θ_2 and θ_3 except for values of the amplitudes.

Hence the purpose of this chapter is to give somewhat detailed treatment of the oscillatory motions of the parts of systems of the above general type *about their respective positions of static equilibrium.* The methods introduced are applicable to a wide variety of problems in classical dynamics and may be extended to atomic and molecular physics. However, the treatment here given is subject to the following limitations.

10.2 Restrictions on the General Problem.

Following usual practice, we shall only consider oscillations for the restricted case in which *velocities and displacements from rest positions do not exceed* (except in special cases) *very small values.* In Sections 10.5 through 10.15 only conservative forces are assumed acting. In Sections 10.16 through 10.19 both conservative and viscous are considered. *Dissipative forces other than viscous are not introduced.*

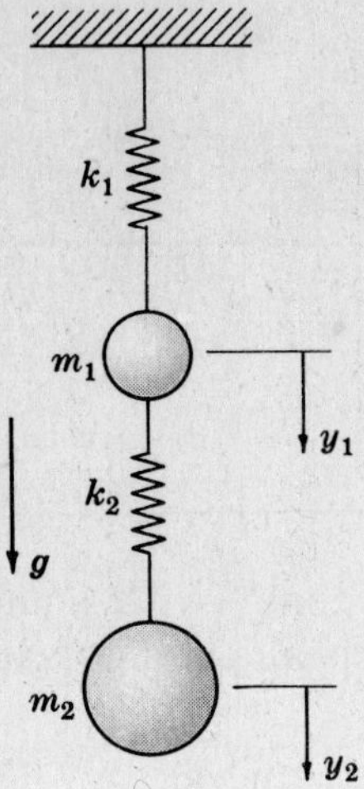

(*a*)

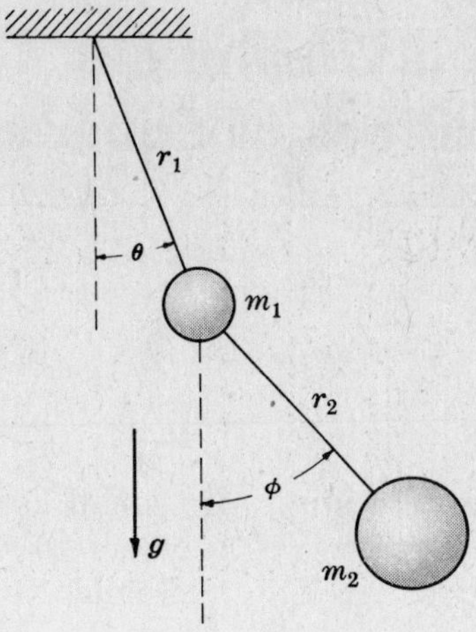

(*b*) Double pendulum
$r_1, r_2 =$ constants

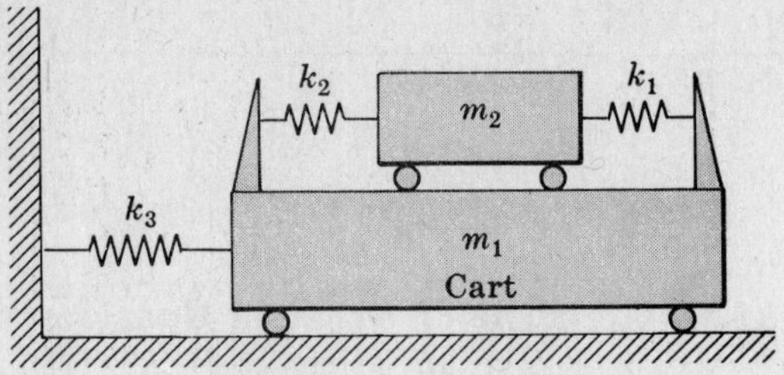

(*c*) Cart on horizontal track

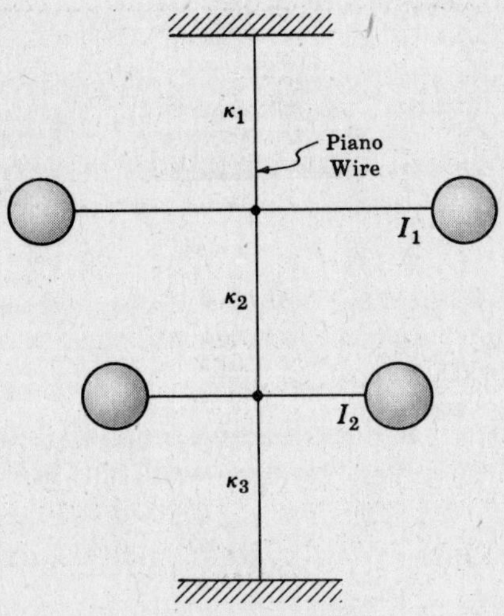

(*d*) Double torsion
pendulum

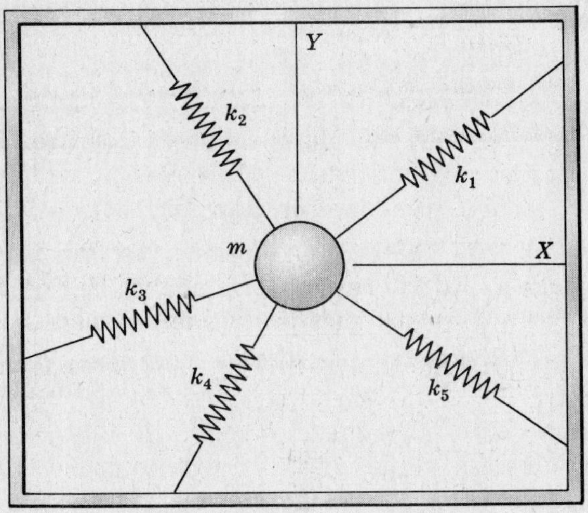

(*e*) Single "particle", motion in a plane

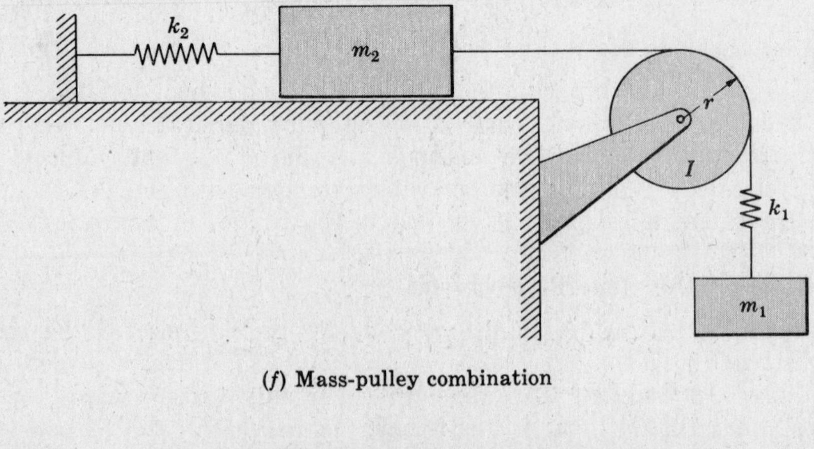

(*f*) Mass-pulley combination

Fig. 10-1. Systems Having Two Degrees of Freedom and Two Natural "Modes of Oscillation".

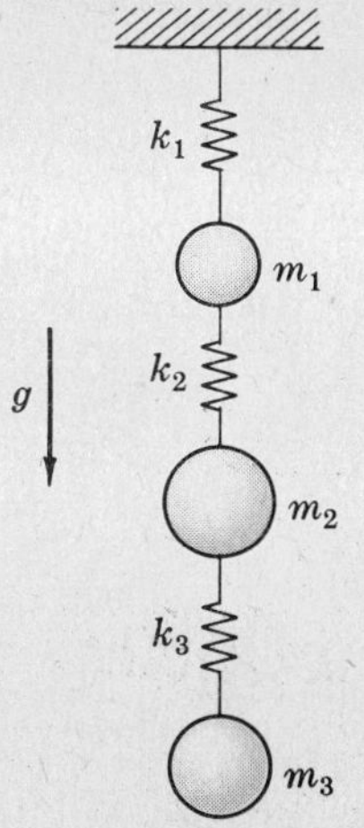

(*a*) Assuming vertical motion, d.f. = 3

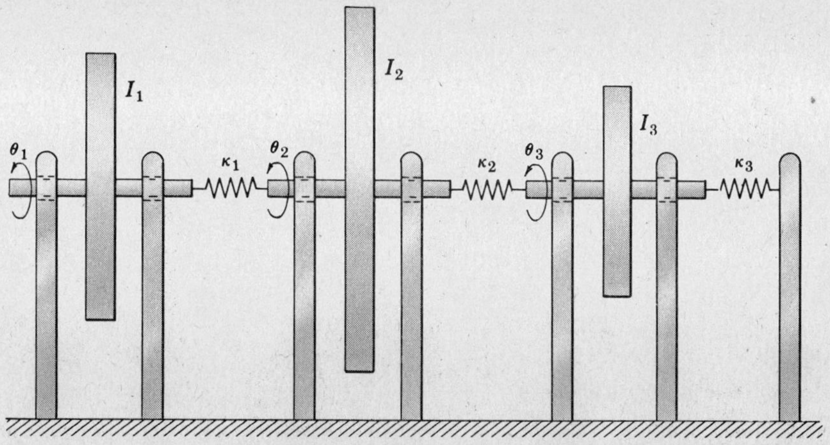

(*b*) Disks connected with flexible shafts
Torsional constants = $\kappa_1, \kappa_2, \kappa_3$; d.f. = 3

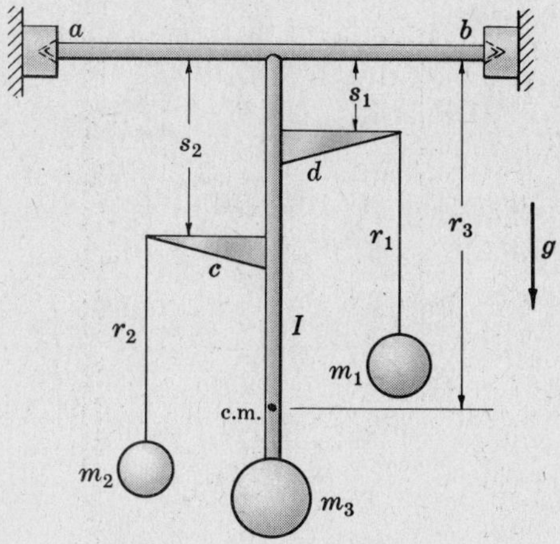

(*c*) For oscillations normal to paper, d.f. = 3

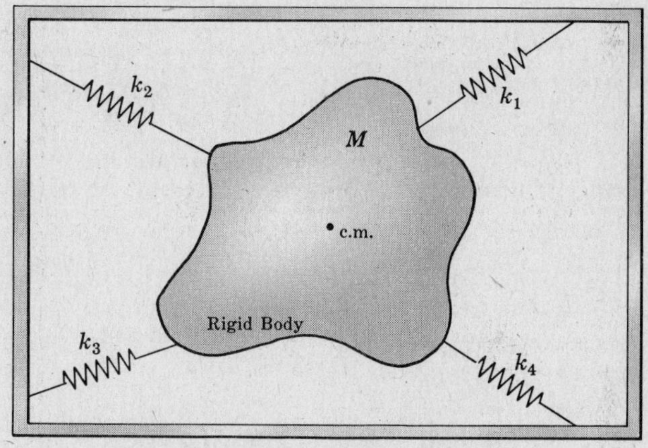

(*d*) For motion in three dimensions
d.f. = 6, six natural modes

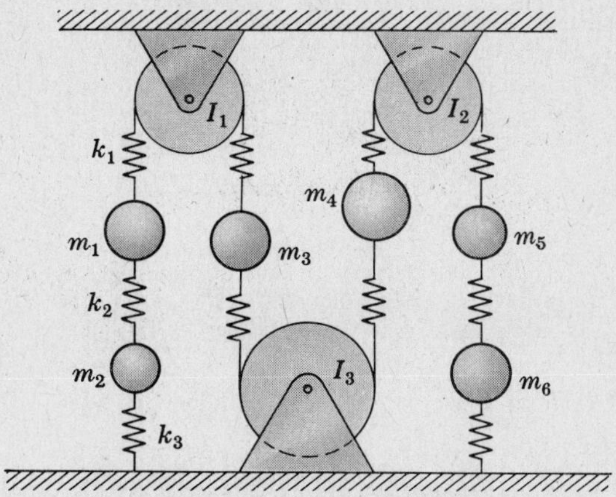

(*e*) Assuming vertical motion of masses, d.f. = 9

Fig. 10-2. Systems with Three or More Degrees of Freedom.

The reason for these drastic limitations, rather than considering the more general case in which oscillations may have large amplitudes and forces of any type may be acting, is quite simple. In the general case differential equations of motion are usually non-linear and so involved that general methods of integration are not available. Hence, except for solving specific problems with special techniques or with the aid of a computer, not very much can be done.

However, by making use of *"equilibrium coordinates"* and imposing the above restrictions, *approximate expressions for T, V, P can (with few exceptions) be written in a form such that resulting equations of motion are linear with constant coefficients* for which standard well-known methods of integration are available.

To illustrate the above statements we give, without proof at this point, the following example.

Example 10.1.

The equations of motion of a double pendulum (see Fig. 2-10, Page 14, and Example 4.6, Page 66) with gravity and viscous forces acting and *no restrictions on values of θ and ϕ*, are

$$\begin{aligned} &(m_1+m_2)r_1^2\ddot{\theta} + m_2r_1r_2\ddot{\phi}\cos(\phi-\theta) - m_2r_1r_2\dot{\phi}^2\sin(\phi-\theta) \\ &\quad + (m_1+m_2)gr_1\sin\theta + (b_1+b_2)r_1^2\dot{\theta} + b_2r_1r_2\dot{\phi}\cos(\phi-\theta) = 0 \\ &m_2r_2^2\ddot{\phi} + m_2r_1r_2\ddot{\theta}\cos(\phi-\theta) + m_2r_1r_2\dot{\theta}^2\sin(\phi-\theta) \\ &\quad + m_2gr_2\sin\phi + b_2r_2^2\dot{\phi} + b_2r_1r_2\dot{\theta}\cos(\phi-\theta) = 0 \end{aligned} \tag{10.1}$$

These non-linear relations are clearly quite complicated. However, if motion is limited to very small values of θ and ϕ, (*10.1*) may be replaced by the approximate equations

$$\begin{aligned} &(m_1+m_2)r_1^2\ddot{\theta} + (b_1+b_2)r_1^2\dot{\theta} + (m_1+m_2)gr_1\theta + m_2r_1r_2\ddot{\phi} + b_2r_1r_2\dot{\phi} = 0 \\ &m_2r_1r_2\ddot{\theta} + b_2r_1r_2\dot{\theta} + m_2r_2^2\ddot{\phi} + b_2r_2^2\dot{\phi} + m_2gr_2\phi = 0 \end{aligned} \tag{10.2}$$

which are linear with constant coefficients and can easily be integrated by methods soon to be presented.

10.3 Additional Background Material.

(*a*) "Equilibrium Coordinates" measure the displacements of the masses from their positions of static equilibrium. They are usually so chosen that when the system is in equilibrium the value of each is zero. Examples are y_1, y_2, Fig. 10-1(*a*), measured from rest positions of m_1 and m_2 respectively; θ and ϕ for the double pendulum of Fig. 10-1(*b*); $\theta_1, \theta_2, \theta_3$, Fig. 10-2(*b*), measured from rest positions of the disks.

(*b*) *Taylor's expansion for n variables.* A well-behaved function of n variables, $f(q_1, q_2, \ldots, q_n)$ may be represented to any degree of accuracy desired (depending on the number of terms retained) in the neighborhood of the "point" $q_1 = c_1$, $q_2 = c_2$, $q_n = c_n$ by the following relation:

$$\begin{aligned} f(q_1, q_2, \ldots, q_n) &= f(c_1, c_2, \ldots, c_n) + \sum_{r=1}^{n}\left(\frac{\partial f}{\partial q_r}\right)(q_r - c_r) \\ &\quad + \frac{1}{2!}\sum_{r}^{n}\sum_{s}^{n}\left(\frac{\partial^2 f}{\partial q_r\,\partial q_s}\right)(q_r - c_r)(q_s - c_s) \\ &\quad + \frac{1}{3!}\sum_{r}^{n}\sum_{s}^{n}\sum_{i}^{n}\left(\frac{\partial^3 f}{\partial q_r\,\partial q_s\,\partial q_i}\right)(q_r - c_r)(q_s - c_s)(q_i - c_i) + \cdots \end{aligned} \tag{10.3}$$

Partial derivatives must be evaluated for $q_1 = c_1$, $q_2 = c_2$, etc. Hence *the first term and all partial derivatives are constants.* If $q_1, q_2, \ldots, q_n$ are equilibrium coordinates and the expansion is about the equilibrium positions, then $c_1 = c_2 = \cdots = c_n = 0$.

(c) *An approximate expression for T in equilibrium coordinates.* In rectangular coordinates, $T = \frac{1}{2}\sum_{i=1}^{p} m_i(\dot{x}_i^2 + \dot{y}_i^2 + \dot{z}_i^2)$. Applying (*10.3*) to the transformation equations $x_i = x_i(q_1, q_2, \ldots, q_n)$, etc., (in which no moving coordinates or constraints are assumed and $q_1, q_2, \ldots, q_n$ are just the number of equilibrium coordinates required to represent the configuration of the system), we get

$$x_i = x_i(0) + \sum_{r=1}^{n}\left(\frac{\partial x_i}{\partial q_r}\right)_0 q_r + \frac{1}{2}\sum_r^n \sum_s^n \left(\frac{\partial^2 x_i}{\partial q_r\, \partial q_s}\right)_0 q_r q_s + \cdots$$

Now, if it is assumed that the displacements and velocities are so small that terms containing $q_r\dot{q}_s$, etc., may be neglected, it follows that

$$\dot{x}_i = \sum_{r=1}^{n}\left(\frac{\partial x_i}{\partial q_r}\right)_0 \dot{q}_r$$

which we shall write as $\dot{x}_i = \sum_{r=1}^{n} \alpha_{ir}\dot{q}_r$. The square of this is $\dot{x}_i^2 = \sum_{r=1}^{n}\sum_{l=1}^{n} \alpha_{ir}\alpha_{il}\dot{q}_r\dot{q}_l$. Similar expressions hold for $\dot{y}_i^2$ and $\dot{z}_i^2$. Hence the original expression for T becomes

$$T = \frac{1}{2}\sum_r^n \sum_l^n \left[\sum_i^p m_i(\alpha_{ir}\alpha_{il} + \beta_{ir}\beta_{il} + \epsilon_{ir}\epsilon_{il})\right]\dot{q}_r\dot{q}_l$$

or

$$T = \frac{1}{2}\sum_r^n \sum_l^n a_{rl}\dot{q}_r\dot{q}_l \qquad (10.4)$$

where $a_{rl} = \sum_{i=1}^{p} m_i(\alpha_{ir}\alpha_{il} + \beta_{ir}\beta_{il} + \epsilon_{ir}\epsilon_{il})$. It is important to note that since all values of a_{rl} are constant, T is a quadratic function of the velocities with constant coefficients.

(d) *An approximate expression for the power function for viscous forces.* As shown in Chapter 6, the power function for p particles, assuming viscous forces, may be written as $P = -\frac{1}{2}\sum_{i=1}^{p} k_i(\dot{x}_i^2 + \dot{y}_i^2 + \dot{z}_i^2)$, where k_i is the coefficient of viscous drag on the ith particle. Following the exact procedure outlined above, P may be written as

$$P = -\frac{1}{2}\sum_r^n \sum_l^n b_{rl}\dot{q}_r\dot{q}_l \qquad (10.5)$$

where the b_{rl} are exactly the same as the a_{rl} with the m_i replaced by k_i. Hence having found T by (*10.4*) for a particular system, we can immediately write down the corresponding P.

(e) *An approximate expression for V in equilibrium coordinates.* Since V is a function of coordinates only, it can be expanded directly. Thus

$$V = V_0 + \sum_{r=1}^{n}\left(\frac{\partial V}{\partial q_r}\right)_0 q_r + \frac{1}{2}\sum_r^n \sum_l^n \left(\frac{\partial^2 V}{\partial q_r\, \partial q_l}\right)_0 q_r q_l + \cdots$$

But since we assume that $q_1 = 0$, $q_2 = 0$, etc., are equilibrium positions, the generalized forces, $-\partial V/\partial q_r$, are zero at these points. Hence the second term above is zero. Moreover, V_0 is a constant. Hence as a first approximation we retain the third term and write

$$V = \frac{1}{2}\sum_r^n \sum_l^n c_{rl}q_r q_l \qquad (10.6)$$

where $c_{rl} = \left(\frac{\partial^2 V}{\partial q_r\, \partial q_l}\right)_0$ = constant. These partial derivatives, each evaluated at $q_1 = 0$, $q_2 = 0$, etc., *must be obtained from an exact expression for V written in terms of equilibrium coordinates.* (Note that $a_{rl} = a_{lr}$, $b_{rl} = b_{lr}$, $c_{rl} = c_{lr}$.)

Summarizing this section, we write

$$T = \frac{1}{2}\sum_{rl}^{n} a_{rl}\dot{q}_r\dot{q}_l \tag{10.4}$$

$$P = -\frac{1}{2}\sum_{rl}^{n} b_{rl}\dot{q}_r\dot{q}_l \tag{10.5}$$

$$V = \frac{1}{2}\sum_{rl}^{n} c_{rl}q_r q_l \tag{10.6}$$

Approximate expressions for T, P, V where a_{rl}, b_{rl}, c_{rl} are constants.

Example 10.2.

To illustrate the above results consider again the double pendulum, Fig. 2-10, Page 14. In rectangular coordinates,

$$T = \tfrac{1}{2}m_1(\dot{x}_1^2 + \dot{y}_1^2) + \tfrac{1}{2}m_2(\dot{x}_2^2 + \dot{y}_2^2) \tag{1}$$

Transformation equations relating rectangular and the equilibrium coordinates θ and ϕ are

$$\begin{aligned} x_1 &= x_0 + r_1 \sin\theta, \quad y_1 = y_0 - r_1\cos\theta \\ x_2 &= x_0 + r_1\sin\theta + r_2\sin\phi, \quad y_2 = y_0 - r_1\cos\theta - r_2\cos\phi \end{aligned} \tag{2}$$

But for any system having only two particles and two degrees of freedom,

$$a_{rl} = m_1\left(\frac{\partial x_1}{\partial q_r}\frac{\partial x_1}{\partial q_l} + \frac{\partial y_1}{\partial q_r}\frac{\partial y_1}{\partial q_l}\right) + m_2\left(\frac{\partial x_2}{\partial q_r}\frac{\partial x_2}{\partial q_l} + \frac{\partial y_2}{\partial q_r}\frac{\partial y_2}{\partial q_l}\right)$$

Thus (10.4) reduces to

$$\begin{aligned} 2T = &\left\{m_1\left[\left(\frac{\partial x_1}{\partial q_1}\right)^2 + \left(\frac{\partial y_1}{\partial q_1}\right)^2\right] + m_2\left[\left(\frac{\partial x_2}{\partial q_1}\right)^2 + \left(\frac{\partial y_2}{\partial q_1}\right)^2\right]\right\}\dot{q}_1^2 \\ &+ 2\left\{m_1\left(\frac{\partial x_1}{\partial q_1}\frac{\partial x_1}{\partial q_2} + \frac{\partial y_1}{\partial q_1}\frac{\partial y_1}{\partial q_2}\right) + m_2\left(\frac{\partial x_2}{\partial q_1}\frac{\partial x_2}{\partial q_2} + \frac{\partial y_2}{\partial q_1}\frac{\partial y_2}{\partial q_2}\right)\right\}\dot{q}_1\dot{q}_2 \\ &+ \left\{m_1\left[\left(\frac{\partial x_1}{\partial q_2}\right)^2 + \left(\frac{\partial y_1}{\partial q_2}\right)^2\right] + m_2\left[\left(\frac{\partial x_2}{\partial q_2}\right)^2 + \left(\frac{\partial y_2}{\partial q_2}\right)^2\right]\right\}\dot{q}_2^2 \end{aligned} \tag{3}$$

Let us regard q_1 as θ and q_2 as ϕ. From (2), $\left(\frac{\partial x_1}{\partial\theta}\right)_0 = r_1$, $\left(\frac{\partial y_1}{\partial\theta}\right)_0 = 0$, etc. Substituting these quantities in (3), we get

$$T_{\text{approx.}} = \tfrac{1}{2}[(m_1+m_2)r_1^2\dot{\theta}^2 + 2m_2r_1r_2\dot{\theta}\dot{\phi} + m_2r_2^2\dot{\phi}^2] \tag{4}$$

the terms of which are quadratic in the velocities with constant coefficients.

Let us assume that m_1 and m_2 are acted upon by viscous forces the magnitudes of which are b_1v_1 and b_2v_2 respectively. Replacing m_1 and m_2 in (4) by b_1 and b_2,

$$P = -\tfrac{1}{2}[(b_1+b_2)r_1^2\dot{\theta}^2 + 2b_2r_1r_2\dot{\theta}\dot{\phi} + b_2r_2^2\dot{\phi}^2] \tag{5}$$

The exact expression for V is

$$V = (m_1+m_2)gr_1(1-\cos\theta) + m_2gr_2(1-\cos\phi) \tag{6}$$

From (10.6), $\qquad V_{\text{approx.}} = \tfrac{1}{2}(c_{11}\theta^2 + 2c_{12}\theta\phi + c_{22}\phi^2)$

where $c_{11} = \left(\frac{\partial^2 V}{\partial\theta^2}\right)_0 = (m_1+m_2)gr_1$, $c_{12} = 0$, $c_{22} = m_2gr_2$. Thus

$$V_{\text{approx.}} = \tfrac{1}{2}[(m_1+m_2)r_1\theta^2 + m_2gr_2\phi^2] \tag{7}$$

Note that since $\cos\theta = 1 - \frac{1}{2}\theta^2 + \frac{1}{4}\theta^4 \cdots$, it is seen that, for small angles $1-\cos\theta = \frac{1}{2}\theta^2$. Hence, in this simple case, (7) follows at once from (6).

10.4 The Differential Equations of Motion.

Applying Lagrange's equations to the "prepared" expressions for T, P and V, equations of motion follow at once. Assuming for the sake of simplicity three degrees of freedom, the following equations are obtained.

$$
\begin{aligned}
a_{11}\ddot{q}_1 + b_{11}\dot{q}_1 + c_{11}q_1 + a_{12}\ddot{q}_2 + b_{12}\dot{q}_2 + c_{12}q_2 + a_{13}\ddot{q}_3 + b_{13}\dot{q}_3 + c_{13}q_3 &= 0 \\
a_{21}\ddot{q}_1 + b_{21}\dot{q}_1 + c_{21}q_1 + a_{22}\ddot{q}_2 + b_{22}\dot{q}_2 + c_{22}q_2 + a_{23}\ddot{q}_3 + b_{23}\dot{q}_3 + c_{23}q_3 &= 0 \\
a_{31}\ddot{q}_1 + b_{31}\dot{q}_1 + c_{31}q_1 + a_{32}\ddot{q}_2 + b_{32}\dot{q}_2 + c_{32}q_2 + a_{33}\ddot{q}_3 + b_{33}\dot{q}_3 + c_{33}q_3 &= 0
\end{aligned} \qquad (10.7)
$$

Conservative forces in these equations are represented by $c_{11}q_1$, $c_{12}q_2$, etc., and viscous forces by $b_{11}\dot{q}_1$, $b_{12}\dot{q}_2$, etc.

10.5 Solutions of the Equations of Motion; Conservative Forces Only.

In the following treatment it is assumed that conservative forces only are acting. Reasons: (*a*) pedagogic, (*b*) the assumption is justifiable in many branches of theoretical and applied physics. For this case equations (*10.7*) reduce to

$$
\begin{aligned}
a_{11}\ddot{q}_1 + c_{11}q_1 + a_{12}\ddot{q}_2 + c_{12}q_2 + a_{13}\ddot{q}_3 + c_{13}q_3 &= 0 \\
a_{21}\ddot{q}_1 + c_{21}q_1 + a_{22}\ddot{q}_2 + c_{22}q_2 + a_{23}\ddot{q}_3 + c_{23}q_3 &= 0 \\
a_{31}\ddot{q}_1 + c_{31}q_1 + a_{32}\ddot{q}_2 + c_{32}q_2 + a_{33}\ddot{q}_3 + c_{33}q_3 &= 0
\end{aligned} \qquad (10.8)
$$

We shall solve these equations and give a somewhat detailed treatment of the most important mathematical and physical considerations which they embody.

In the usual way let us assume the following solutions

$$q_1 = A\cos(\omega t + \phi), \quad q_2 = B\cos(\omega t + \phi), \quad q_3 = c\cos(\omega t + \phi)$$

where A, B, C, ω, ϕ are unknown constants. Substituting into (*10.8*), it follows at once that

$$
\begin{aligned}
(a_{11}\omega^2 - c_{11})A + (a_{12}\omega^2 - c_{12})B + (a_{13}\omega^2 - c_{13})c &= 0 \\
(a_{21}\omega^2 - c_{21})A + (a_{22}\omega^2 - c_{22})B + (a_{23}\omega^2 - c_{23})c &= 0 \\
(a_{31}\omega^2 - c_{31})A + (a_{32}\omega^2 - c_{32})B + (a_{33}\omega^2 - c_{33})c &= 0
\end{aligned} \qquad (10.9)
$$

It may be shown that values of A, B, C (other than zero) which satisfy (*10.9*) cannot be found unless the determinant of their coefficients is zero. Hence we write the determinant:

$$
D = \begin{vmatrix} a_{11}\omega^2 - c_{11} & a_{12}\omega^2 - c_{12} & a_{13}\omega^2 - c_{13} \\ a_{21}\omega^2 - c_{21} & a_{22}\omega^2 - c_{22} & a_{23}\omega^2 - c_{23} \\ a_{31}\omega^2 - c_{31} & a_{32}\omega^2 - c_{32} & a_{33}\omega^2 - c_{33} \end{vmatrix} = 0 \qquad (10.10)
$$

Fundamental Determinant D

(No dissipative forces acting)

Note. The above can be written down directly from T and V; (*10.4*) and (*10.6*).

The great importance of the above "fundamental determinant" will soon become strikingly evident. Indeed there is contained in this "small package" almost everything that can be known about the free oscillatory motions of systems of the type under consideration.

Relation (*10.10*) when expanded leads to a third degree algebraic equation in ω^2. For any specific problem in hand, numerical values of the a's and c's are known. Hence this equation can be written out with numerical coefficients.

At this point it is important to realize that several methods are available for finding approximate, yet quite accurate, values of the roots of any nth degree algebraic equation. For this purpose the "Graeffe root squaring method" is highly recommended. It is easy to apply, results are good and the time required is relatively short. For an excellent treatment of this see: R. E. Doherty and E. G. Keller, *Mathematics of Modern Engineering*, Vol. I, pp. 99-128, John Wiley, 1936.

Let us assume that the three roots ω_1, ω_2, ω_3 of (*10.10*) are each real and distinct. (It may be shown that if V is "positive definite", positive for all values which the q's may assume, all values of ω are real.)

Now inserting say ω_1 in (*10.9*), the reader can show that these relations determine *only relative values*, A_1, B_1, C_1, of the constants. That is if, for example, $A_1 = 3.5$, $B_1 = -9.2$, $C_1 = 7.6$ satisfy (*10.9*), they are also satisfied by $A_1 = 3.5c$, $B_1 = -9.2c$, $C_1 = 7.6c$ where c is any constant. Moreover, it is not difficult to show with a simple example that the relative values of A_1, B_1, C_1 are just the cofactors of the first, second and third elements respectively of *any row in* (*10.10*), each multiplied by an arbitrary constant. ("Cofactor" defined: Strike out row r and column c of a given element, leaving determinant M_{rc}, called a "Minor". Cofactor of this element $= D_{rc} = (-1)^{r+c} M_{rc}$.) That is, from row one we can write

$$A_1 = +c_1 \begin{vmatrix} a_{22}\omega_1^2 - c_{22} & a_{23}\omega_1^2 - c_{23} \\ a_{32}\omega_1^2 - c_{32} & a_{33}\omega_1^2 - c_{33} \end{vmatrix} \qquad B_1 = -c_1 \begin{vmatrix} a_{21}\omega_1^2 - c_{21} & a_{23}\omega_1^2 - c_{23} \\ a_{31}\omega_1^2 - c_{31} & a_{33}\omega_1^2 - c_{33} \end{vmatrix}$$

$$C_1 = +c_1 \begin{vmatrix} a_{21}\omega_1^2 - c_{21} & a_{22}\omega_1^2 - c_{22} \\ a_{31}\omega_1^2 - c_{31} & a_{32}\omega_1^2 - c_{32} \end{vmatrix} \tag{10.11}$$

For brevity we write the above as

$$A_1 = c_1 d_{11}, \quad B_1 = c_1 d_{21}, \quad C_1 = c_1 d_{31}$$

where, for example, d_{21} is the cofactor of the second element of *any selected row*, with ω_1 inserted. That is $d_{21} = D_{r2}$ (containing ω_1), where r may be either 1, 2, or 3. (The above notation is convenient because it shows the element number in a row and the ω number. The row number is immaterial.)

Finally, it is clear that the following satisfy (*10.8*):

$$q_1 = c_1 d_{11} \cos(\omega_1 t + \phi_1), \quad q_2 = c_1 d_{21} \cos(\omega_1 t + \phi_1), \quad q_3 = c_1 d_{31} \cos(\omega_1 t + \phi_1)$$

In exactly the same manner, two other sets of solutions are obtained corresponding to ω_2 and ω_3. Adding these to obtain the general solution, we have

$$\begin{aligned} q_1 &= c_1 d_{11} \cos(\omega_1 t + \phi_1) + c_2 d_{12} \cos(\omega_2 t + \phi_2) + c_3 d_{13} \cos(\omega_3 t + \phi_3) \\ q_2 &= c_1 d_{21} \cos(\omega_1 t + \phi_1) + c_2 d_{22} \cos(\omega_2 t + \phi_2) + c_3 d_{23} \cos(\omega_3 t + \phi_3) \\ q_3 &= c_1 d_{31} \cos(\omega_1 t + \phi_1) + c_2 d_{32} \cos(\omega_2 t + \phi_2) + c_3 d_{33} \cos(\omega_3 t + \phi_3) \end{aligned} \tag{10.12}$$

Integrated Equations of Motion.

in which the arbitrary constants $c_1, c_2, c_3, \phi_1, \phi_2, \phi_3$ can be determined from known initial conditions. Inserting initial displacements, (*10.12*) can be solved for $c_1 \cos\phi_1$, $c_2 \cos\phi_2$, $c_3 \cos\phi_3$. Differentiating (*10.12*) and inserting initial values of velocity, ${}_0\dot{q}_1, {}_0\dot{q}_2, {}_0\dot{q}_3$, the resulting equations can be solved for $c_1 \sin\phi_1$, $c_2 \sin\phi_2$, $c_3 \sin\phi_3$. Hence values of c and ϕ follow at once. A simpler method of evaluating these constants is given in Section 10.15, Page 224.

10.6 Summary of Important Facts Regarding the Above Type of Oscillatory Motion.

(a) When slightly disturbed, every component of the system, in general, oscillates with n natural frequencies or principal modes of motion. For example, in Fig. 10-2(e), $n=9$, there are nine values of ω and each mass or pulley oscillates with nine corresponding frequencies.

(b) Frequencies are given by $f_1 = \omega_1/2\pi$, etc., where $\omega_1, \omega_2, \ldots, \omega_n$ are roots of a fundamental determinant having the form of (*10.10*). Note that this determinant can be written down directly from T and V without writing out equations of motion.

As seen from (*10.10*), the ω's depend only on constants of the system.

(c) *Relative amplitudes* of a particular harmonic term appearing in expressions for $q_1, q_2, \ldots, q_n$ are determined *entirely by cofactors and not by initial conditions.*

Considering the oscillation corresponding to say ω_1 in solutions (*10.12*), relative amplitudes of $\cos(\omega_1 t + \phi_1)$ in q_1, q_2, q_3 are clearly just d_{11}, d_{21}, d_{31}, since c_1 is the same in each.

(d) Since constants c_1, c_2, c_3 are determined by initial conditions, it is evident that actual amplitudes of motion such as $c_1 d_{11}$, $c_1 d_{21}$, $c_1 d_{31}$ depend on how the system is started.

Note that, if the motion is properly started, any one or more of the arbitrary constants $c_1, c_2, \ldots, c_n$ may be zero. Hence *the system can oscillate with any one frequency alone or with any combination of the n.*

An experimental method of exciting any one mode alone is given in Section 10.20, Page 228.

(e) Assuming say ω_1 only excited, (*10.12*) gives

$$q_1 = c_1 d_{11} \cos(\omega_1 t + \phi_1), \quad q_2 = c_1 d_{21} \cos(\omega_1 t + \phi_1), \quad q_3 = c_1 d_{31} \cos(\omega_1 t + \phi_1)$$

The algebraic signs of d_{11}, d_{21}, d_{31} may be either positive or negative. Hence the above motions may be exactly in phase or exactly out of phase.

Consider Fig. 10-10, Page 230. For vertical motion only, there are three frequencies. The table to the left indicates how the masses move when either ω_1, ω_2 or ω_3 alone is excited. Such phase relations are determined entirely by the algebraic signs of the d's. However, it is seen that for a given ω excited, each of m_1, m_2, m_3 passes through its equilibrium position at the same instant. Likewise, maximum values are reached simultaneously.

(f) One final word. If one is concerned with values of the natural frequencies only, as is often the case, no work other than finding roots of the fundamental determinant is required.

10.7 Examples Illustrating Results of Past Sections.

Example 10.3.

Consider the system shown in Fig. 10-1(a), Page 204. Assuming vertical motion only and letting y_1 and y_2 represent the displacements of m_1 and m_2 respectively from equilibrium positions,

$$T = \tfrac{1}{2}(m_1 \dot{y}_1^2 + m_2 \dot{y}_2^2)$$

$$V_{\text{exact}} = \tfrac{1}{2}k_1(y_1 + s_1)^2 + \tfrac{1}{2}k_2(y_2 - y_1 + s_2) - m_1 g y_1 - m_2 g y_2$$

where s_1 is the difference between the equilibrium and unstretched lengths of the first spring and s_2 has the same meaning for the second spring. But since y_1 and y_2 are measured from rest points, $\partial V/\partial y_1 = \partial V/\partial y_2 = 0$ for $y_1 = y_2 = 0$. Hence the reader may show that V_{exact} above may be replaced by $V = \tfrac{1}{2}k_1 y_1^2 + \tfrac{1}{2}k_2(y_2 - y_1)^2$. Hence equations of motion are

$$m_1 \ddot{y}_1 + (k_1 + k_2)y_1 - k_2 y_2 = 0, \quad -k_2 y_1 + m_2 \ddot{y}_2 + k_2 y_2 = 0 \qquad (1)$$

Comparing with *(10.8)* and *(10.10)*, we write

$$\begin{vmatrix} m_1\omega^2 - (k_1+k_2) & k_2 \\ k_2 & m_2\omega^2 - k_2 \end{vmatrix} = 0 \tag{2}$$

from which $$m_1 m_2 \omega^4 - [k_2 m_1 + (k_1+k_2)m_2]\omega^2 + k_1 k_2 = 0 \tag{3}$$

For $m_1 = 400$ grams, $m_2 = 300$ grams, $k_1 = 6\times 10^4$ dynes/cm and $k_2 = 5\times 10^4$ dynes/cm, it follows from *(3)* that $\omega_1 = 8.16$, $\omega_2 = 19.37$. That is, $f_1 = 1.30$ and $f_2 = 3.08$ oscillations per sec.

Hence, following *(10.12)* we write (after inserting proper cofactors and dividing out a factor of 10^4) the general solutions as

$$\begin{aligned} y_1 &= 6.25c_1 \sin(19.37t+\phi_1) - 3c_2 \sin(8.16t+\phi_2) \\ y_2 &= -5c_1 \sin(19.37t+\phi_1) - 5c_2 \sin(8.16t+\phi_2) \end{aligned} \tag{4}$$

Note the following. (*a*) For this simple case T and V already have the forms of *(10.4)* and *(10.6)*. (*b*) For ω_1 only excited, m_1 and m_2 oscillate in phase with relative amplitudes of 3 to 5. With ω_2 excited the motion is exactly out of phase with relative amplitudes of 6.25 to 5. (*c*) For any given initial conditions, c_1, c_2, ϕ_1, ϕ_2 can be evaluated at once.

Example 10.4.

The mass m, Fig. 10-3, is free to move in a plane under the action of the springs and gravity. (In an actual experiment m consisted of two rather heavy disks fastened together with a short thin rod through the center of each over which wires from the springs were hooked. This effectively eliminates rotation of the disks, and hence m is treated as a particle.)

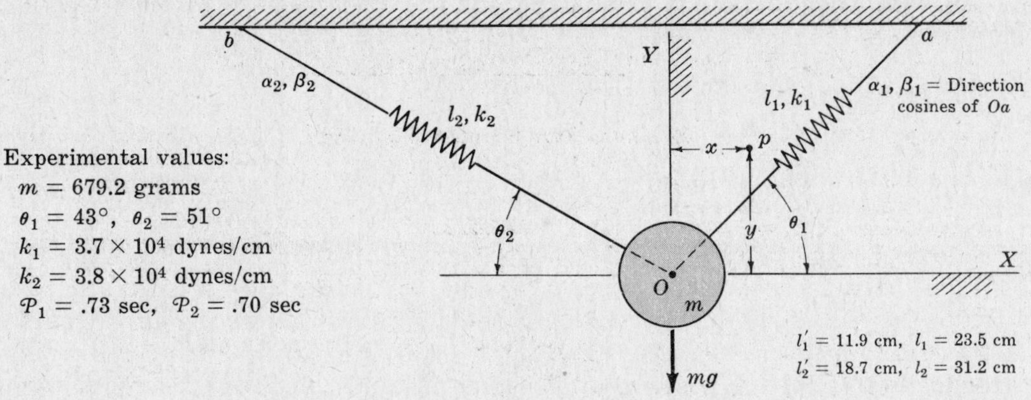

Fig. 10-3

For this arrangement T is merely $\frac{1}{2}m(\dot{x}^2+\dot{y}^2)$. Assuming small motion from the equilibrium position, an approximate expression for V is given by (see equation *(5.11)*, Page 89),

$$V_{\text{approx.}} = \frac{1}{2}\left[\left(k_1+k_2-\frac{k_1 l_1'}{l_1}\beta_1^2 - \frac{k_2 l_2'}{l_2}\beta_2^2\right)x^2 + \left(k_1+k_2-\frac{k_1 l_1'}{l_1}\alpha_1^2 - \frac{k_2 l_2'}{l_2}\right)y^2 + 2\left(\frac{k_1 l_1'}{l_1}\alpha_1\beta_1 + \frac{k_2 l_2'}{l_2}\alpha_2\beta_2\right)xy\right]$$

which has the form $$V = \tfrac{1}{2}(c_{11}x^2 + 2c_{12}xy + c_{22}y^2)$$

Hence, following exactly the steps outlined in the preceding example, equations of motion can be set up and integrated at once.

It is suggested that the reader, making use of values of m_1, k_1, etc., given on the figure, compute the two periods $\mathcal{P}_1, \mathcal{P}_2$ and compare with the given experimental values. It will be seen that the agreement is very close.

Note that for $(c_{11}+c_{22})^2 = 4(c_{11}c_{22}-c_{12}^2)$, $\omega_1 = \omega_2$. Is this physically possible? Why is gravity not considered in this example?

Example 10.5.

Consider the double pendulum, Fig. 10-1(*b*). See (*4*) and (*7*), Example 10.2. It is left to the reader to show that the basic determinant (which, of course, can be written out without writing equations of motion) is

$$\begin{vmatrix} (m_1+m_2)r_1^2\omega^2 - (m_1+m_2)g & m_2r_1r_2\omega^2 \\ m_2r_1r_2\omega^2 & m_2r_2^2\omega^2 - m_2gr_2 \end{vmatrix} = 0$$

From this point on the solution follows exactly as in the previous example. (See Prob. 10.1, Page 229.)

Example 10.6. *Small oscillations of the three bars suspended from strings as shown in* Fig. 10-4.

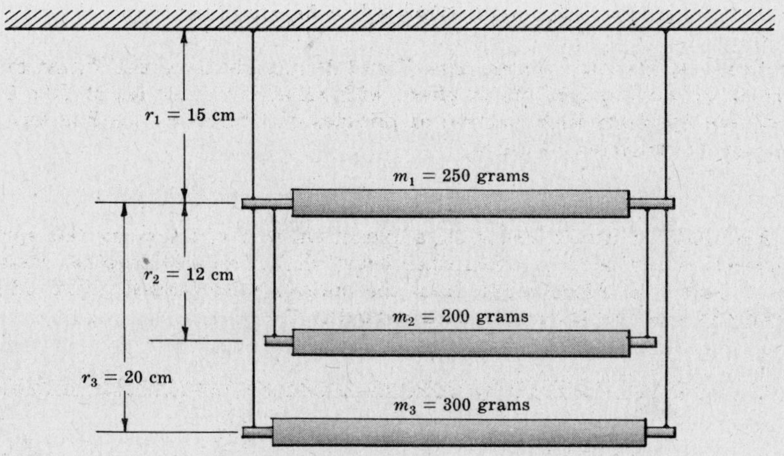

(*a*) Three Bars Suspended by Cords.

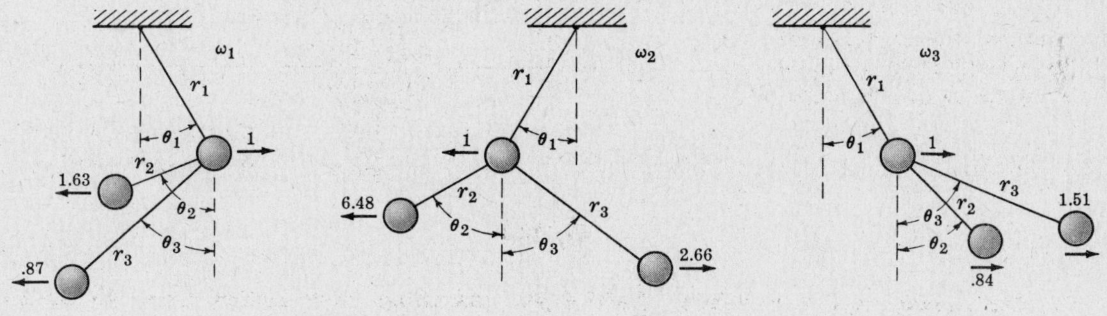

Fig. 10-4

The reader may show without much difficulty that $T_{\text{approx.}}$ is given by

$$T_{\text{approx.}} = \tfrac{1}{2}[(m_1+m_2+m_3)r_1^2\dot{\theta}_1^2 + m_2r_2^2\dot{\theta}_2^2 + m_3r_3^2\dot{\theta}_3^2 + 2m_2r_1r_2\dot{\theta}_1\dot{\theta}_2 + 2m_3r_1r_3\dot{\theta}_1\dot{\theta}_3] \qquad (1)$$

where $\theta_1, \theta_2, \theta_3$ are angular displacements of m_1, m_2, m_3 respectively.

$$V_{\text{exact}} = m_1gr_1(1-\cos\theta_1) + m_2g[r_1(1-\cos\theta_1) + r_2(1-\cos\theta_2)] + m_3g[r_1(1-\cos\theta_1) + r_3(1-\cos\theta_3)]$$

Writing $1 - \cos\theta_1 = \tfrac{1}{2}\theta_1^2$, etc.,

$$V_{\text{approx.}} = \tfrac{1}{2}[(m_1+m_2+m_3)gr_1\theta_1^2 + m_2gr_2\theta_2^2 + m_3gr_3\theta_3^2] \qquad (2)$$

From an inspection of (*1*) and (*2*), we write

$$\begin{vmatrix} (m_1+m_2+m_3)(r_1\omega^2-g)r_1 & m_2r_1r_2\omega^2 & m_3r_1r_3\omega^2 \\ m_2r_1r_2\omega^2 & m_2r_2(r_2\omega^2-g) & 0 \\ m_3r_1r_3\omega^2 & 0 & m_3r_3(r_3\omega^2-g) \end{vmatrix} = 0 \qquad (3)$$

Expanding and inserting numerical values given in the figure, we get

$$\omega^6 - 451\omega^4 + 37{,}616\omega^2 - 784{,}327 = 0 \qquad (4)$$

which is cubic in ω^2. Applying Graeffe's method, $\omega_1 = 18.71$, $\omega_2 = 8.21$, $\omega_3 = 5.72$. After evaluating cofactors, the general solutions become

$$\begin{aligned} \theta_1 &= 2.78c_1 \cos(18.71t+\phi_1) - 0.88c_2 \cos(8.21t+\phi_2) + 2.75c_3 \cos(5.72t+\phi_3) \\ \theta_2 &= -4.54c_1 \cos(18.71t+\phi_1) - 5.70c_2 \cos(8.21t+\phi_2) + 2.30c_3 \cos(5.72t+\phi_3) \\ \theta_3 &= -2.43c_1 \cos(18.71t+\phi_1) + 2.34c_2 \cos(8.21t+\phi_2) + 4.16c_3 \cos(5.72t+\phi_3) \end{aligned} \qquad (5)$$

For given initial conditions, $c_1, c_2, c_3, \phi_1, \phi_2, \phi_3$ can be determined.

For ω_1 only excited, it follows from (5) that m_2 and m_3 oscillate in phase and out of phase with m_1. Their relative amplitudes (relative maximum angular displacements) are 2.78, 4.54, 2.43 for m_1, m_2, m_3 respectively. The three "modes of motion" and their relative amplitudes are shown in Fig. 10-4(*b*), (*c*), (*d*).

It should again be emphasized that, as clearly shown by the above example, (*a*) the natural frequencies of the system, (*b*) the phase relations between oscillations corresponding to any one frequency, and (*c*) the relative amplitude of motion are all found from the basic determinant and thus depend on constants of the system.

Example 10.7.

A consideration of the oscillatory motion of the three "particles" connected with springs as shown in Fig. 10-5, illustrates most of the basic points regarding small oscillations and gives the reader a good overall picture of the general subject.

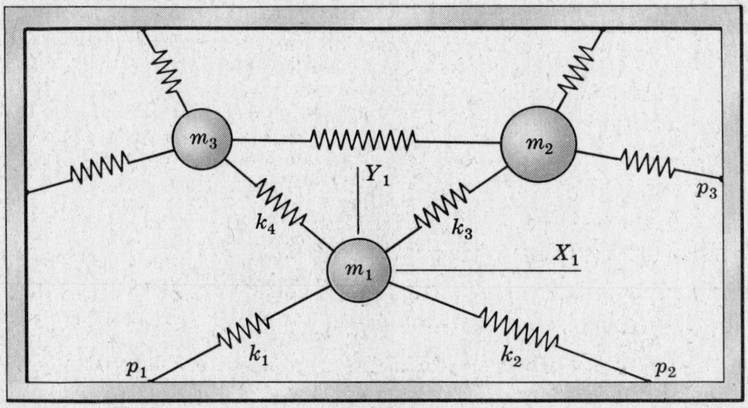

X_1, Y_1 = fixed axes, with origin at the rest position of m_1

Fig. 10-5

Considering motion in a plane, the system has six degrees of freedom and hence six natural frequencies of motion. Let us assume that all values of the k's, unstretched lengths of the springs, equilibrium positions of m_1, m_2, m_3, positions of p_1, p_2, p_3, etc., and equilibrium lengths of springs are known.

Let x_1, y_1; x_2, y_2; x_3, y_3 represent rectangular equilibrium coordinates of m_1, m_2, m_3, regarded as particles. Hence

$$T = \tfrac{1}{2}m_1(\dot{x}_1^2+\dot{y}_1^2) + \tfrac{1}{2}m_2(\dot{x}_2^2+\dot{y}_2^2) + \tfrac{1}{2}m_3(\dot{x}_3^2+\dot{y}_3^2)$$

Extending the principles outlined in Section 5.10, Page 89, V may be put in the form

$$\begin{aligned} V_{\text{approx.}} \;=\; & \tfrac{1}{2}(c_{11}x_1^2 + c_{22}y_1^2 + c_{33}x_2^2 + c_{44}y_2^2 + c_{55}x_3^2 + c_{66}y_3^2) \\ & + c_{12}x_1y_1 + c_{13}x_1x_2 + c_{14}x_1y_2 + c_{15}x_1x_3 + c_{16}x_1y_3 \\ & + c_{23}y_1x_2 + c_{24}y_1y_2 + c_{25}y_1x_3 + c_{26}y_1y_3 + c_{34}x_2y_2 \\ & + c_{35}x_2x_3 + c_{36}x_2y_3 + c_{45}y_2x_3 + c_{46}y_2y_3 + c_{56}x_3y_3 \end{aligned}$$

Determination of the c's is straightforward but in an actual case requires considerable tedious work. This having been done we are in a position to set up the fundamental determinant of the system, roots of which give $\omega_1, \omega_2, \ldots, \omega_6$. Finally, solutions have the form

$$x_1 \;=\; c_1d_{11}\cos(\omega_1 t + \phi_1) + c_2d_{12}\cos(\omega_2 t + \phi_2) + \cdots + c_6d_{16}\cos(\omega_6 t + \phi_6),$$

etc., for y_1, x_2, y_2, x_3, y_3.

For a general disturbance of the system, each particle oscillates with the six frequencies given by $f_1 = \omega_1/2\pi$, etc. If any one frequency alone is excited, amplitudes of motion of m_1, m_2, m_3 are not in general the same; moreover, the particles do not oscillate along parallel lines. (See Section 10.14, Page 222.)

Note that if motion out of the plane of the frame is permitted, d.f. = 9. Hence the system has nine natural modes of oscillation. It can be treated exactly as outlined above.

10.8 Special Cases of the Roots of D.

(a) *Multiple Roots.*

Consider the arrangement shown in Fig. 10-6. Suppose the frame attached to a smooth horizontal table. Assume all springs identical and that, with m at rest, the springs have an angular spacing of 120°.

For this case (see equation (*5.11*), Page 89),

$$T \;=\; \tfrac{1}{2}m(\dot{x}^2 + \dot{y}^2) \qquad \text{and} \qquad V \;=\; \tfrac{1}{2}[k(3 - 1.5l'/l)(x^2 + y^2)]$$

Hence the fundamental determinant may be written at once. Expanding this it is immediately evident that the two roots of D are equal, that is, $\omega_1 = \omega_2$. The equations of motion show that the general motion of m may be regarded as compounded of two simple harmonic motions at right angles, each having the same period. But this is only true for the special arrangement considered above. If the k's are not quite equal and/or the angular spacing is slightly changed, ω_1 and ω_2 will be distinct.

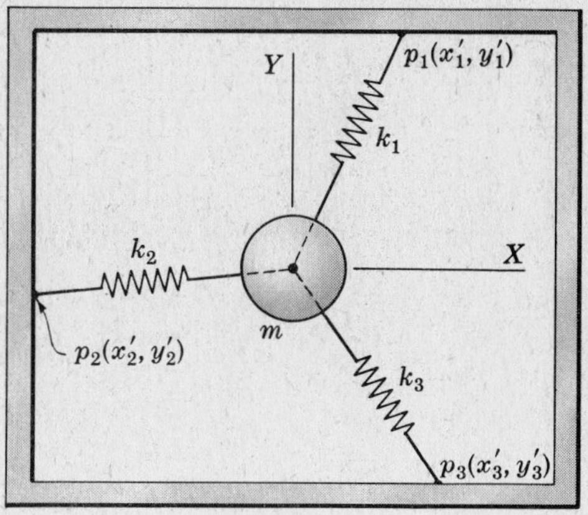

Fig. 10-6

Other systems can be found which, for special values of the constants, fall into the above class. However, *truly equal roots are rare.* When this is the case the "degeneracy" can usually be removed by a slight change in the constants of the system.

(b) *Zero Roots.*

The basic determinant for each system shown in Fig. 10-7 has one zero root. Consider Fig. 10-7(*a*), for example. A detailed treatment of the motion for θ small, is given in Example 4.4, Page 64, and as seen from the equations of motion

$$D \;=\; \begin{vmatrix} (m_1 + m_2)\omega^2 & m_2 r\omega^2 \\ m_2 r\omega^2 & m_2 r^2\omega^2 - m_2 g r \end{vmatrix} \;=\; 0$$

from which $(m_1 + m_2)(m_2 r^2 \omega^2 - m_2 g r)\omega^2 - m_2 r^2 \omega^4 = 0$. Hence one ω, say ω_1, is zero and $\omega_2 = [(m_1 + m_2)g/r]^{1/2}$. The zero root means an "infinite period" or more precisely a term vt, in the final solution, indicating motion with constant velocity. Note details of the solutions, Page 65.

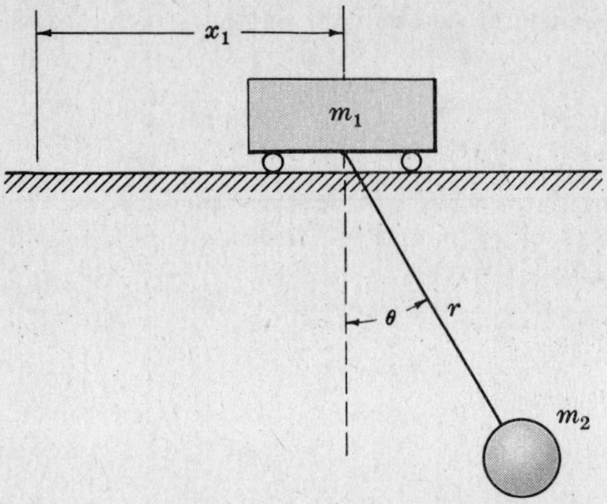

(a) Cart free to move along horizontal line

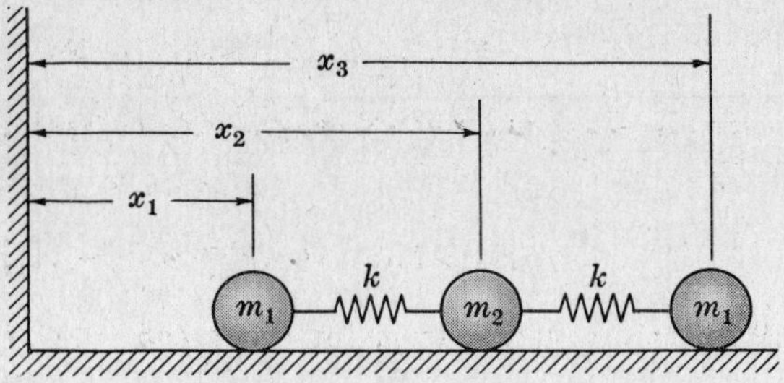

(b) CO_2 "molecule" free to move along a line

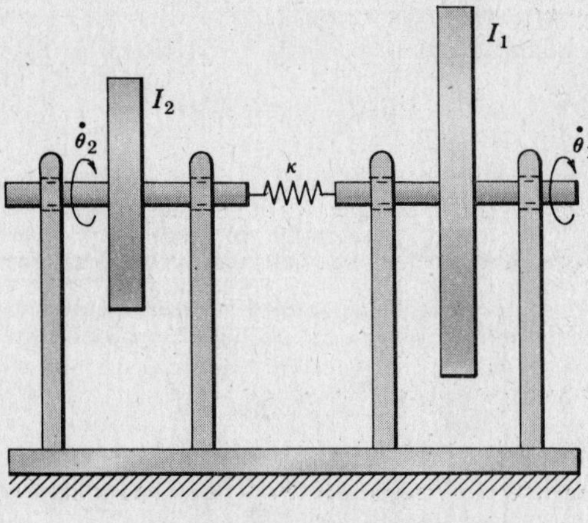

(c) Disks connected with flexible shaft. Torsional constant = κ.

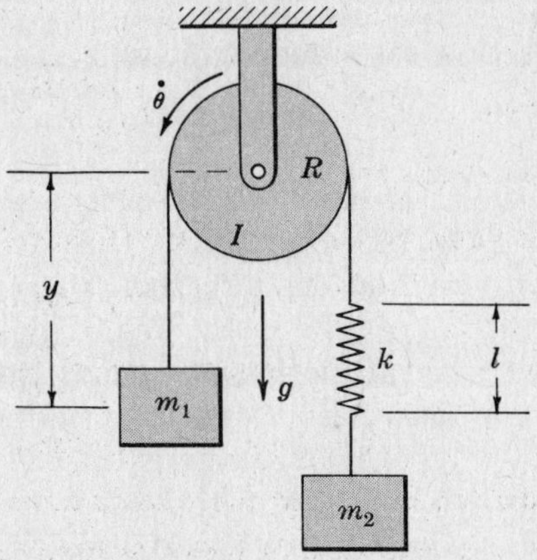

(d) Assume $m_1 = m_2$

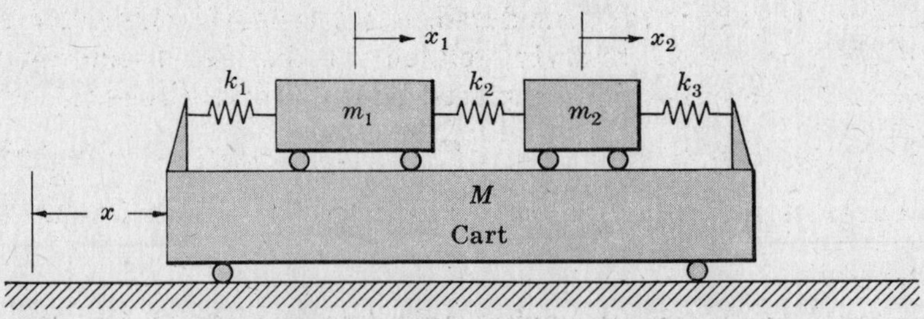

x_1, x_2 measured relative to cart. No friction assumed.

(e) Cart free to move along horizontal track

Fig. 10-7. Systems for which the Fundamental Determinant Has One Zero Root.

The reader may easily write T and V for the disks, Fig. 10-7(c), and show that D has one zero root and another which is not. Physically this means that the motion of each disk is compounded of an oscillatory term plus another representing constant angular velocity. (See Problem 10.9, Page 230.)

An example of a system, the determinant of which has two zero roots, is shown in Fig. 10-14, Page 232. For details see Problem 10.18.

Example 10.8. *The "CO_2 molecule"*, Fig. 10-7(*b*).

Assuming motion along the X axis,

$$T = \tfrac{1}{2}(m_1\dot{x}_1^2 + m_2\dot{x}_2^2 + m_1\dot{x}_3^2), \qquad V = \tfrac{1}{2}k[(x_2 - x_1 - l_0)^2 + (x_3 - x_2 - l_0)^2]$$

where l_0 is the unstretched length of each spring. Letting

$$q_1 = x_1 + l_0, \quad q_2 = x_2, \quad q_3 = x_3 - l_0 \tag{1}$$

$$T = \tfrac{1}{2}(m_1\dot{q}_1^2 + m_2\dot{q}_2^2 + m_1\dot{q}_3^2), \qquad V = \tfrac{1}{2}k[(q_2 - q_1)^2 + (q_3 - q_2)^2] \tag{2}$$

which now have the forms of (*10.4*) and (*10.6*) respectively. Hence

$$D = \begin{vmatrix} m_1\omega^2 - k & k & 0 \\ k & m_2\omega^2 - 2k & k \\ 0 & k & m_1\omega^2 - k \end{vmatrix} = 0 \tag{3}$$

Expanding D, we have

$$(m_1\omega^2 - k)[(m_2\omega^2 - 2k)(m_1\omega^2 - k) - k^2] - k^2(m_1\omega^2 - k) = 0$$

from which
$$\omega_1 = \left(\frac{k}{m_1}\right)^{1/2}, \quad \omega_2 = 0, \quad \omega_3 = \left[\frac{k(m_2 + 2m_1)}{m_1 m_2}\right]^{1/2}$$

Therefore D has one zero root.

The reader may show by direct substitution into the differential equations of motion that

$$\begin{aligned} q_1 &= -c_1k^2 \cos(\omega_1 t + \phi_1) + c_3k^2 \cos(\omega_3 t + \phi_3) + vt + b \\ q_2 &= -2c_3k^2\frac{m_1}{m_2}\cos(\omega_3 t + \phi_3) + vt + b \\ q_3 &= c_1k^2 \cos(\omega_1 t + \phi_1) + c_3k^2 \cos(\omega_3 t + \phi_3) + vt + b \end{aligned} \tag{4}$$

are solutions where constants c_1, c_3, v must be determined by initial conditions.

The term vt obviously indicates linear motion with constant velocity. It may be shown that v is just the velocity of the center of mass.

10.9 Normal Coordinates.

For systems of the type thus far considered, it is possible to determine a set of "normal coordinates" $g_1, g_2, \ldots, g_n$ (each linearly related to the usual equilibrium coordinates $q_1, q_2, \ldots, q_n$) such that when the q's are replaced by g's, T and V take the very simple forms

$$T = \tfrac{1}{2}(\dot{g}_1^2 + \dot{g}_2^2 + \cdots + \dot{g}_n^2), \qquad V = \tfrac{1}{2}(\omega_1 g_1^2 + \omega_2 g_2^2 + \cdots + \omega_n g_n^2)$$

(Advantages and uses of normal coordinates are listed in Section 10.12.)

(a) *Defining the g's.*

Consider, for example, a system having only two degrees of freedom and for which the integrated equations of motion are

$$\begin{aligned} q_1 &= c_1 d_{11} \cos(\omega_1 t + \phi_1) + c_2 d_{12} \cos(\omega_2 t + \phi_2) \\ q_2 &= c_1 d_{21} \cos(\omega_1 t + \phi_1) + c_2 d_{22} \cos(\omega_2 t + \phi_2) \end{aligned} \tag{10.13}$$

As a matter of convenience in what follows, let us replace c_1 by $c_1 A_1$ and c_2 by $c_2 A_2$ where A_1 and A_2 are now regarded as arbitrary constants and c_1, c_2 will later be determined to meet certain desired conditions. We must remember that c_1, c_2 are now *not regarded as arbitrary.*

Defining the quantities g_1, g_2 by $g_1 = A_1 \cos(\omega_1 t + \phi_1)$ and $g_2 = A_2 \cos(\omega_2 t + \phi_2)$, relations (*10.13*) become

$$q_1 = c_1 d_{11} g_1 + c_2 d_{12} g_2, \qquad q_2 = c_1 d_{21} g_1 + c_2 d_{22} g_2 \tag{10.14}$$

Note that *the quantities g_1, g_2 may be regarded as a new set of coordinates.* Thus (*10.14*) are transformation equations relating the q's and g's. As will be seen from what follows, g_1, g_2 are the desired normal coordinates.

(b) *Expressing T in normal coordinates and introducing "orthogonality conditions".*

Differentiating (*10.14*) and substituting in

$$T = \tfrac{1}{2}(a_{11}\dot{q}_1^2 + 2a_{12}\dot{q}_1\dot{q}_2 + a_{22}\dot{q}_2^2)$$

we get

$$\begin{aligned} T = \tfrac{1}{2}[c_1^2(a_{11}d_{11}^2 + 2a_{12}d_{11}d_{21} + a_{22}d_{21}^2)\dot{g}_1^2 + c_2^2(a_{11}d_{12}^2 + 2a_{12}d_{22} + a_{22}d_{22}^2)\dot{g}_2^2 \\ + 2c_1c_2(a_{11}d_{11}d_{12} + a_{12}d_{11}d_{22} + a_{21}d_{12}d_{21} + a_{22}d_{21}d_{22})\dot{g}_1\dot{g}_2] \end{aligned} \tag{10.15}$$

Writing coefficients of $\dot{g}_1^2, \dot{g}_2^2, \dot{g}_1\dot{g}_2$, as N_{11}, N_{22}, N_{12} respectively, it is seen that

$$N_{11} = c_1^2 \sum_{rl}^{2} a_{rl} d_{r1} d_{l1}, \quad N_{22} = c_2^2 \sum_{rl}^{2} a_{rl} d_{r2} d_{l2}, \quad N_{12} = c_1 c_2 \sum_{rl}^{2} a_{rl} d_{r1} d_{l2}$$

or in more compact form,

$$N_{sk} = c_s c_k \sum_{rl}^{2} a_{rl} d_{rs} d_{lk} \tag{10.16}$$

Relation (*10.16*) is of paramount importance because, as shown for a general case in Section 10.10, $N_{sk} = 0$ for $s \neq k$. But $N_{sk} \neq 0$ for $s = k$. Moreover (see paragraph (*a*) above) it is seen that by taking c_s as

$$c_s = \left[\sum_{rl}^{2} a_{rl} d_{rs} d_{ls}\right]^{-1/2} \tag{10.17}$$

$N_{ss} = 1$. Hence it follows (assuming for the moment the truth of the above statements) that $T = \tfrac{1}{2}(\dot{g}_1^2 + \dot{g}_2^2)$.

(c) *Expressing V in normal coordinates.*

A general expression for V for the case under consideration is

$$V = \tfrac{1}{2}(c_{11}q_1^2 + 2c_{12}q_1q_2 + c_{22}q_2^2)$$

Inserting (*10.14*),

$$\begin{aligned} V = \tfrac{1}{2}c_1^2[(c_{11}d_{11} + c_{12}d_{21})d_{11} + (c_{22}d_{21} + c_{12}d_{11})d_{21}]g_1^2 \\ + \tfrac{1}{2}c_2^2[(c_{11}d_{12} + c_{12}d_{22})d_{12} + (c_{22}d_{22} + c_{12}d_{12})d_{22}]g_2^2 \\ + \tfrac{1}{2}c_1c_2[2(c_{11}d_{12} + c_{12}d_{22})d_{11} + 2(c_{22}d_{22} + c_{12}d_{12})d_{21}]g_1g_2 \end{aligned} \tag{10.18}$$

If it is assumed that only one principal mode is excited, say ω_1,

$$q_1 = c_1 d_{11} A_1 \cos(\omega_1 t + \phi_1), \qquad q_2 = c_1 d_{21} A_1 \cos(\omega_1 t + \phi_1)$$

Putting these into the original differential equations of motion (which have the form of (*10.8*)), it follows that

$$c_{11}d_{11} + c_{12}d_{21} = \omega_1^2(a_{11}d_{11} + a_{12}d_{21})$$
$$c_{21}d_{11} + c_{22}d_{21} = \omega_1^2(a_{21}d_{11} + a_{22}d_{21})$$

Likewise two more similar relations are obtained assuming ω_2 excited. Substituting these four expressions in (*10.18*), we finally get

$$V = \tfrac{1}{2}(\omega_1^2 N_{11} g_1^2 + 2\omega_2^2 N_{12} g_1 g_2 + \omega_2^2 N_{22} g_2^2)$$

which, on applying (*10.16*) and (*10.17*), becomes $V = \tfrac{1}{2}(\omega_1^2 g_1^2 + \omega_2^2 g_2^2)$.

(d) ***The General Case.***

In like manner the above steps can be carried through for n degrees of freedom when T and V have the forms of (*10.4*) and (*10.6*) respectively. The solution corresponding to q_1 may be written as $q_1 = c_1 d_{11} g_1 + c_2 d_{12} g_2 + \cdots + c_n d_{1n} g_n$, etc. Or in general,

$$q_r = \sum_{k=1}^{n} c_k d_{rk} g_k \tag{10.19}$$

Expressions corresponding to (*10.16*) and (*10.17*) take the forms shown below.

$$(a) \qquad N_{sk} = c_s c_k \sum_{rl}^{n} a_{rl} d_{rs} d_{lk} = \begin{cases} 0 \text{ for } s \neq k \\ 1 \text{ for } s = k \end{cases} \tag{10.20}$$

$$(b) \qquad c_s = \left[\sum_{rl}^{n} a_{rl} d_{rs} d_{ls}\right]^{-1/2} \tag{10.21}$$

(*a*) = Orthogonality condition, (*b*) = Normalizing factor

N_{sk} is usually written as δ_{sk} and called the *Kronecker delta.*

In the general case T and V have the forms

$$\begin{aligned} T &= \tfrac{1}{2}(\dot{g}_1^2 + \dot{g}_2^2 + \cdots + \dot{g}_n^2) \\ V &= \tfrac{1}{2}(\omega_1^2 g_1^2 + \omega_2^2 g_2^2 + \cdots + \omega_n^2 g_n^2) \end{aligned} \tag{10.22}$$

T and V expressed in normal coordinates.

The above development has been carried through assuming solutions of the form (*10.12*). However, it is a theorem of algebra that when T and V have the forms (*10.4*) and (*10.6*), suitable linear relations between the q's and g's can be found which transform T and V to the form (*10.22*).

10.10 Proof of the Orthogonality Relation.

Before continuing further let us prove the important relation (*10.20*).

Consider a system having n degrees of freedom. Assuming only one oscillation ω_s excited, it is clear that

$$q_1 = c_s d_{1s} \cos(\omega_s t + \phi_s), \quad q_2 = c_s d_{2s} \cos(\omega_s t + \phi_s), \quad \text{etc.}$$

Putting these into any one of the original differential equations, say the rth, we get

$$c_{r1} d_{1s} + c_{r2} d_{2s} + \cdots + c_{rn} d_{ns} = (a_{r1} d_{1s} + a_{r2} d_{2s} + \cdots + a_{rn} d_{ns})\omega_s^2$$

which may be written as

$$\sum_{l=1}^{n} c_{rl} d_{ls} = \omega_s^2 \sum_{l=1}^{n} a_{rl} d_{ls} \tag{1}$$

Note that (*1*) represents n equations since $r = 1, 2, \ldots, n$.

Likewise assuming ω_k excited,

$$\sum_{l=1}^{n} c_{rl} d_{lk} = \omega_k^2 \sum_{l=1}^{n} a_{rl} d_{lk} \tag{2}$$

Now multiplying the first of (*1*) by d_{1k}, the second by d_{2k}, etc., and adding, we obtain

$$\sum_{l,r}^{n} c_{rl} d_{ls} d_{rk} \quad = \quad \omega_s^2 \sum_{l,r}^{n} a_{rl} d_{ls} d_{rk} \qquad (3)$$

In like manner we obtain from (*2*)

$$\sum_{l,r}^{n} c_{rl} d_{lk} d_{rs} \quad = \quad \omega_k^2 \sum_{r,l}^{n} a_{rl} d_{lk} d_{rs} \qquad (4)$$

But since $a_{rl} = a_{lr}$ and $c_{rl} = c_{lr}$, we may replace r by l and l by r in (*3*) without affecting the value of the sum. Hence the left sides of (*3*) and (*4*) are equal. Thus

$$(\omega_k^2 - \omega_s^2) \sum_{l,r}^{n} a_{rl} d_{rs} d_{lk} \quad = \quad 0 \qquad (5)$$

But for $k \neq s$, $\omega_k \neq \omega_s$. Hence $\displaystyle\sum_{r,l}^{n} a_{rl} d_{rs} d_{lk} \quad = \quad 0$ (*6*)

Furthermore it can be shown that for $k = s$ the summation in (*6*) is not zero. Hence the validity of (*10.20*) has been established.

10.11 Important Points Regarding Normal Coordinates.

(*a*) It follows from (*10.22*) that

$$\ddot{g}_1 + \omega_1^2 g_1 \;=\; 0, \quad \ddot{g}_2 + \omega_2^2 g_2 \;=\; 0, \quad \ddot{g}_n + \omega_n^2 g_n \;=\; 0 \qquad (10.23)$$

These greatly simplified equations of motion integrate at once to give $g_1 = A_1 \cos(\omega_1 t + \phi_1)$, etc., (which are indeed just the original expressions given in Section 10.9). Thus from (*10.23*) it is seen that:

(*b*) Principal modes of motion corresponding to $\omega_1, \omega_2, \ldots,$ are entirely independent. That is, one mode of oscillation in no way influences or is influenced by other oscillations. The system is reduced, mathematically speaking, to n completely unrelated harmonic oscillators. (But note (*c*) below.)

(*c*) If properly started, the system will oscillate with any one of the fundamental frequencies alone (as previously mentioned) or in any combination. However, one must not lose sight of the important fact that, if any one mode is excited, every component part of the entire system will, in general, oscillate with this particular frequency. For example, if ω_5, Fig. 10-2(*e*), Page 205, were excited, each of the six masses and three pulleys would oscillate with frequency $f_5 = \omega_5/2\pi$.

(*d*) Inspection of (*10.22*) shows that D in normal coordinates (assuming $n = 3$ for convenience) has the form

$$D \quad = \quad \begin{vmatrix} \omega^2 - \omega_1^2 & 0 & 0 \\ 0 & \omega^2 - \omega_2^2 & 0 \\ 0 & 0 & \omega - \omega_3^2 \end{vmatrix} \quad = \quad 0 \qquad (10.24)$$

D is said to be "diagonalized".

10.12 Advantages of Normal Coordinates.

(*a*) A consideration of normal coordinates leads to a better understanding of the physics as well as the mathematics of small oscillations. A more complete "picture" of what takes place is obtained.

(b) The treatment of systems of the above type to which external forces are applied is considerably facilitated by the use of normal coordinates. (See Section 10.18.)

(c) The determination of constants of integration in solutions having the form of (*10.12*) is considerably simplified by use of the orthogonality condition (*10.20*). See Section 10.15, Page 224.

(d) Normal coordinates can be employed to considerable advantage in various theoretical considerations without the necessity of first finding actual expressions for the g's.

(e) Normal coordinates are extensively used in the study of molecular vibrations, vibrations of atoms in crystals, etc.

However, it should be kept in mind that, except in very simple cases, actual expressions for the g's of a given system can only be found (see Section 10.13) after having determined $\omega_1, \omega_2, \ldots, \omega_n$ and the cofactors d_{rs} (frequently a laborious task) as outlined in Section 10.5. Moreover, it is clear that in applied problems where the ω's only may be required, normal coordinates offer no advantages.

10.13 Finding Expressions for Normal Coordinates.

Expressions for normal coordinates may be obtained by solving (*10.19*) directly for the g's in terms of the q's. However, the solution may be considerably simplified by employing the orthogonality condition (*10.20*).

Multiplying (*10.19*) through by $c_s a_{rl} d_{ls}$ and summing over r and l, we have

$$\sum_{rl}^{n} c_s q_r a_{rl} d_{ls} \;=\; \sum_{k}^{n} g_k \sum_{rl}^{n} c_s c_k a_{rl} d_{rk} d_{ls} \;=\; \sum_{k}^{n} g_k \delta_{ks} \;=\; g_s$$

Hence
$$g_s \;=\; c_s \sum_{rl}^{n} q_r a_{rl} d_{ls} \qquad (10.25)$$

where c_s is determined by (*10.21*).

For any particular problem in hand, numerical values of a_{rl} and d_{ls} are known. Hence specific expressions for $g_1, g_2, \ldots, g_n$ in terms of the q's can be written. (See Examples below.)

Example 10.9. *Normal coordinates for the system shown in* Fig. 10-1(*a*).

Referring to Example 10.3, Page 211, let us write the solutions there given as

$$\begin{aligned} y_1 &= 3c_1A_1\cos(8.16t+\phi_1) \;-\; 6.25c_2A_2\cos(19.37t+\phi_2) \\ y_2 &= 5c_1A_1\cos(8.16t+\phi_1) \;+\; 5c_2A_2\cos(19.37t+\phi_2) \end{aligned} \qquad (1)$$

where A_1 and A_2 are arbitrary and c_1, c_2 are to be determined by (*10.21*). Hence we write

$$y_1 \;=\; 3c_1g_1 - 6.25c_2g_2, \qquad y_2 \;=\; 5c_1g_1 + 5c_2g_2 \qquad (2)$$

Now expressions for g_1 and g_2 may be determined either by solving (*2*) or applying (*10.25*). Note that for this problem $a_{11} = m_1$, $a_{22} = m_2$, $a_{12} = 0$, $d_{11} = 3$, $d_{12} = -6.25$, etc., from (*1*). $c_1 = (9m_1 + 25m_2)^{-1/2}$, $c_2 = (6.25^2m_1 + 25m_2)^{-1/2}$. Hence finally,

$$g_1 \;=\; 11.39y_1 + 14.24y_2, \qquad g_2 \;=\; -16.44y_1 + 9.86y_2 \qquad (3)$$

As a check the reader may show that, differentiating (*2*) and substituting into $T = \frac{1}{2}(m_1\dot{y}_1^2 + m_2\dot{y}_2^2)$, we get, as would be expected, $T = \frac{1}{2}(\dot{g}_1^2 + \dot{g}_2^2)$. Likewise, putting (*2*) into the original expression for V, we get $V = \frac{1}{2}(\omega_1^2 g_1^2 + \omega_2^2 g_2^2)$. See Problem 10.5, Page 229.

Example 10.10. *Normal coordinates of the triple pendulum,* Fig. 10-4, Example 10.6, Page 213.

Equations (*10.19*), Page 219, may be written as

$$\begin{aligned}\theta_1 &= 2.78c_1g_1 - 0.88c_2g_2 + 2.75c_3g_3\\ \theta_2 &= -4.54c_1g_1 - 5.70c_2g_2 + 2.30c_3g_3\\ \theta_3 &= -2.43c_1g_1 + 2.34c_2g_2 + 4.16c_3g_3\end{aligned} \tag{1}$$

Applying relation (*10.21*), $c_1^{-1} = 694.03$, $c_2^{-1} = 1309.18$, $c_3^{-1} = 2478.69$. Solving (*1*) for g_1, g_2, g_3 or, more easily, applying (*10.25*), we finally get

$$\begin{aligned}g_1 &= 126.29\theta_1 - 43.82\theta_2 - 59.26\theta_3\\ g_2 &= -108.88\theta_1 - 149.41\theta_2 + 154.58\theta_3\\ g_3 &= 379.42\theta_1 + 67.70\theta_2 + 307.59\theta_3\end{aligned} \tag{2}$$

As a check the reader may show that, differentiating (*1*) and inserting into the original expression for T, we get $T = \frac{1}{2}(\dot{g}_1^2 + \dot{g}_2^2 + \dot{g}_3^2)$. Likewise, $V = \frac{1}{2}(\omega_1^2 g_1^2 + \omega_2^2 g_2^2 + \omega_3^2 g_3^2)$ may be obtained by inserting (*1*) in the original expression for V.

10.14 Amplitude and Direction of Motion of Any One Particle When a Particular Mode of Oscillation is Excited.

By way of introduction, suppose that any one (and only one) of the six natural frequencies of the system shown in Fig. 10-5, Page 214, is excited. In what direction (along what line) and with what amplitude would, say, m_1 be oscillating? The following is a treatment of this type of problem.

Consider the relatively simple system shown in Fig. 10-8. A dumbbell, consisting of particles m_1 and m_2 connected with a light rod, is supported by springs as shown. Its equilibrium position is O_1O_2. Assuming motion in a plane, displacements of m_1 and m_2 from rest positions are x_1, y_1 and x_2, y_2. Here $n = 3$ and we use as generalized coordinates q_1, q_2, q_3 where q_1, q_2 are rectangular coordinates of c.m. and $q_3 = \theta$. Thus $x_1 = x_1(q_1, q_2, q_3)$, etc., which could easily be written out in explicit form.

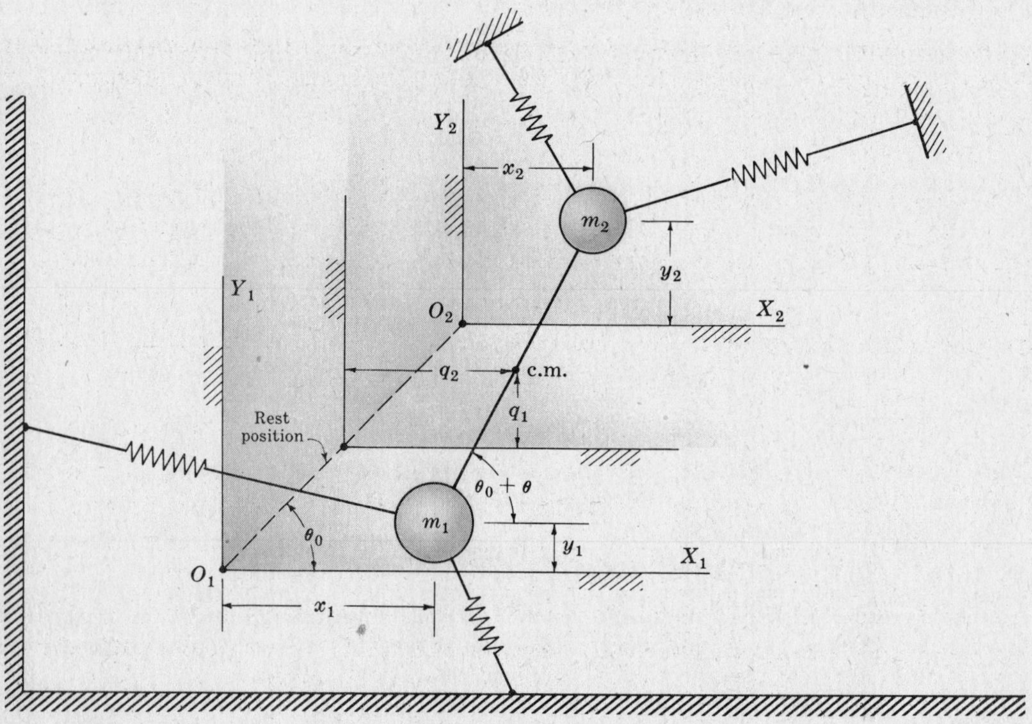

Fig. 10-8

Assuming small displacements, we write (see Section 10.3(*b*), (*c*)),

$$x_1 = \left(\frac{\partial x_1}{\partial q_1}\right)_0 q_1 + \left(\frac{\partial x_1}{\partial q_2}\right)_0 q_2 + \left(\frac{\partial x_1}{\partial q_3}\right)_0 q_3$$

or $$x_1 = \alpha_{11}q_1 + \alpha_{12}q_2 + \alpha_{13}q_3 \tag{1}$$

and likewise $$y_1 = \beta_{11}q_1 + \beta_{12}q_2 + \beta_{13}q_3$$

where all α's and β's are known constants determined by the geometry of the system.

Now considering solutions corresponding to (*10.12*) and supposing only one mode, say ω_1, excited,

$$q_1 = c_1 d_{11}\cos(\omega_1 t + \phi_1), \quad q_2 = c_1 d_{21}\cos(\omega_1 t + \phi_1), \quad q_3 = c_1 d_{31}\cos(\omega_1 t + \phi_1)$$

where c_1 is here determined by initial conditions, not by (*10.21*). Hence

$$x_1 = (\alpha_{11}d_{11} + \alpha_{12}d_{21} + \alpha_{13}d_{31})c_1\cos(\omega_1 t + \phi_1)$$

Likewise, $$y_1 = (\beta_{11}d_{11} + \beta_{12}d_{21} + \beta_{13}d_{31})c_1\cos(\omega_1 t + \phi_1) \tag{2}$$

or for brevity, $$x_1 = c_1 A_{11}\cos(\omega_1 t + \phi_1), \quad y_1 = c_1 B_{11}\cos(\omega_1 t + \phi_1)$$

Hence it is clear that, for ω_1 only excited, m_1 oscillates with amplitude $c_1(A_{11}^2 + B_{11}^2)^{1/2}$ along a straight line through O_1 having a slope of B_{11}/A_{11}. In like manner the amplitude and direction of motion of m_1 may be found assuming ω_2 or ω_3 excited.

Considering expressions for x_2, y_2, motions of m_2 corresponding to $\omega_1, \omega_2, \omega_3$ may be found in the same way.

Thus we have a detailed "picture" of the motion of each particle when any one mode is excited.

Obviously the above treatment can be extended to a general system of p particles having n degrees of freedom.

Note that the actual path traversed by, say, m_1 when all modes are simultaneously excited, may be drawn by inserting relations (*10.12*) in (*1*) above and plotting y_1, x_1 for equal values of time.

Example 10.11.

Let us determine the line along which point p, Fig. 10-16, Page 233, oscillates when ω_1 only is excited.

Taking x_p, y_p as coordinates of p, x, y those of c.m. and θ the angular rotation of the rod measured from its rest position (that is, x, y, θ are convenient equilibrium coordinates), it is seen that

$$x_p = x + l\cos(\theta + \theta_0), \quad y_p = y + l\sin(\theta + \theta_0)$$

where l is half the length of the rod. Thus for small motion (retaining zero and first order terms),

$$\begin{aligned} x_p &= x + l\cos\theta_0 - (l\sin\theta_0)\theta \\ y_p &= y + l\sin\theta_0 + (l\cos\theta_0)\theta \end{aligned} \tag{1}$$

Now for ω_1 only excited,

$$x = c_1 d_{11}\cos(\omega_1 t + \phi_1), \quad y = c_1 d_{21}\cos(\omega_1 t + \phi_1), \quad \theta = c_1 d_{31}\cos(\omega_1 t + \phi_1)$$

Hence $$\begin{aligned} x_p - l\cos\theta_0 &= c_1(d_{11} - ld_{31}\sin\theta_0)\cos(\omega_1 t + \phi_1) \\ y_p - l\sin\theta_0 &= c_1(d_{21} + ld_{31}\cos\theta_0)\cos(\omega_1 t + \phi_1) \end{aligned}$$

$x_p - l\cos\theta_0$ and $y_p - l\sin\theta_0$ are clearly displacements of p from its rest position. Hence p oscillates along a line making an angle α with X where $\tan\alpha = \dfrac{d_{21} + ld_{31}\cos\theta_0}{d_{11} - ld_{31}\sin\theta_0}$, and with an amplitude A determined by

$$A = c_1[(d_{11} - ld_{31}\sin\theta_0)^2 + (d_{21} + ld_{31}\sin\theta_0)^2]^{1/2}$$

Of course, c_1 must be found from given initial conditions.

For details of the motion of this system, for given values of the physical constants, see Problem 10.23, Page 233.

10.15 Determination of Arbitrary Constants With the Help of Orthogonality Conditions.

Values of the c's and ϕ's in (*10.12*), which, of course, depend on initial displacements and velocities, can be determined as outlined in the last part of Section 10.5. Or having replaced c_1 by c_1A_1, c_2 by c_2A_2, etc., as in Section 10.9 (where the c's are now not arbitrary but determined by relation (*10.21*)), the A's can be evaluated in the same way. However, the following method is more advantageous.

Putting known or assumed displacements for $t=0$, ${}_0q_1, {}_0q_2, \ldots, {}_0q_n$, into solutions having the form of (*10.12*), we have

$$\begin{aligned} {}_0q_1 &= c_1d_{11}A_1\cos\phi_1 + c_2d_{12}A_2\cos\phi_2 + \cdots + c_nd_{1n}A_n\cos\phi_n \\ {}_0q_n &= c_1d_{n1}A_1\cos\phi_1 + c_2d_{n2}A_2\cos\phi_2 + \cdots + c_nd_{nn}A_n\cos\phi_n \end{aligned} \qquad (10.26)$$

Now let us multiply the first of (*10.26*) through by $c_s\sum_{i=1}^{n} a_{i1}d_{is}$, the second by $c_s\sum_{i=1}^{n} a_{i2}d_{is}$, etc., where s can be any integer from 1 to n. Adding the resulting equations and making use of (*10.20*), it follows that

$$A_s\cos\phi_s = c_s\sum_{ir}^{n} {}_0q_r a_{ir} d_{is} \qquad (10.27)$$

In like manner, for given values of velocity ${}_0\dot{q}_1, {}_0\dot{q}_2, \ldots, {}_0\dot{q}_n$, at $t=0$, it can be shown that

$$A_s\sin\phi_s = -\frac{c_s}{\omega_s}\sum_{ir}^{n} {}_0\dot{q}_r a_{ir} d_{is} \qquad (10.28)$$

Thus all values of A_s and ϕ_s are determined by (*10.27*) and (*10.28*).

Note that if the system is displaced slightly and released from rest, all values of ${}_0\dot{q}_r = 0$. Hence all values of the phase angles are zero.

10.16 Small Oscillations With Viscous and Conservative Forces Acting.

As background for this section the student should review Sections 10.3(*d*) and 10.4.

(a) *Equations of motion and their solution.*

Assuming as before three degrees of freedom, the equations of motion, including viscous forces, are just (*10.7*), Page 209.

Solutions may be obtained by assuming

$$q_1 = A^{\lambda t}, \quad q_2 = B^{\lambda t}, \quad q_3 = C^{\lambda t}$$

where A, B, C, λ are, as yet, undetermined constants. Substitution into (*10.7*) gives

$$A(a_{11}\lambda^2 + b_{11}\lambda + c_{11}) + B(a_{12}\lambda^2 + b_{12}\lambda + c_{12}) + C(a_{13}\lambda^2 + b_{13}\lambda + c_{13}) = 0 \qquad (10.29)$$

and two more similar relations. Following the steps leading to (*10.10*), we write

$$D = \begin{vmatrix} a_{11}\lambda^2 + b_{11}\lambda + c_{11} & a_{12}\lambda^2 + b_{12}\lambda + c_{12} & a_{13}\lambda^2 + b_{13}\lambda + c_{13} \\ a_{21}\lambda^2 + b_{21}\lambda + c_{21} & a_{22}\lambda^2 + b_{22}\lambda + c_{22} & a_{23}\lambda^2 + b_{23}\lambda + c_{23} \\ a_{31}\lambda^2 + b_{31}\lambda + c_{31} & a_{32}\lambda^2 + b_{32}\lambda + c_{32} & a_{33}\lambda^2 + b_{33}\lambda + c_{33} \end{vmatrix} = 0 \qquad (10.30)$$

Expansion of this new form of the fundamental determinant leads to a sixth degree equation in λ. Roots of the equation again can be found by the Graeffe or other methods.

Let us assume that the six roots $\lambda_1, \lambda_2, \ldots, \lambda_6$ are distinct. Inserting values of, say, λ_1 into (*10.30*), relative values of A_1, B_1, C_1 are given (see Section 10.5) by cofactors of the elements of any row. That is,

$$q_1 = c_1 d_{11} e^{\lambda_1 t}, \quad q_2 = c_1 d_{21} e^{\lambda_1 t}, \quad q_3 = c_1 d_{31} e^{\lambda_1 t} \tag{10.31}$$

Similar solutions are obtained by introducing $\lambda_2, \lambda_3, \ldots, \lambda_6$.

Adding the six sets of solutions, the general solution takes the form

$$\begin{aligned} q_1 &= c_1 d_{11} e^{\lambda_1 t} + c_2 d_{12} e^{\lambda_2 t} + \cdots + c_6 d_{16} e^{\lambda_6 t} \\ q_2 &= c_1 d_{21} e^{\lambda_1 t} + c_2 d_{22} e^{\lambda_2 t} + \cdots + c_6 d_{26} e^{\lambda_6 t} \\ q_3 &= c_1 d_{31} e^{\lambda_1 t} + c_2 d_{32} e^{\lambda_2 t} + \cdots + c_6 d_{36} e^{\lambda_6 t} \end{aligned} \tag{10.32}$$

Values of the arbitrary constants $c_1, c_2, \ldots, c_6$ depend on initial conditions.

(b) ***Nature of the λ's.***

The roots of D may be real, complex or pure imaginary.

For the important case in which V is positive definite, it has been shown that under the following additional conditions:

(1) $P = 0$ (no viscous forces): All roots are pure imaginary. This is the case treated in previous sections.

(2) $P \neq 0$ but viscous forces small: Roots are complex, they occur in pairs as $\lambda = \mu \pm i\omega$, and μ is negative. That is, $\lambda_1 = \mu_1 + i\omega_1$, $\lambda_2 = \mu_1 - i\omega_1$, etc.

(3) Viscous forces large: Roots are real and negative.

If V is not positive definite, positive real roots may occur. In this case it is seen from solutions (*10.32*) that each coordinate increases indefinitely with time. Hence the assumption of "small motion" is quickly invalidated. The system is "unstable".

(c) ***Form taken by (10.32) when the roots are complex.***

This is the most important case.

Let $\lambda_1 = \mu_1 + i\omega_1$, $\lambda_2 = \mu_1 - i\omega_1$, $\lambda_3 = \mu_2 + i\omega_2$, $\lambda_4 = \mu_2 - i\omega_2$, etc. Considering, for the moment, only the first two terms of the first equation in (*10.32*), we write

$$c_1 d_{11} e^{\lambda_1 t} + c_2 d_{12} e^{\lambda_2 t} = e^{\mu_1 t}(c_1 d_{11} e^{i\omega_1 t} + c_2 d_{12} e^{-i\omega_1 t}) \tag{10.33}$$

But d_{11}, the cofactor of the first element of any row of (*10.30*), is complex. We write it as $d_{11} = k_{11} + ih_{11}$, where for any specific problem in hand k_{11} and h_{11} are known constants. Moreover, a little effort will show that $d_{12} = k_{11} - ih_{11}$. Since c_1 and c_2 are arbitrary, we write them as $c_1 = \frac{1}{2}(b_1 + ib_2)$, $c_2 = \frac{1}{2}(b_1 - ib_2)$. Hence, employing the relations

$$e^{i\omega t} = \cos\omega t + i\sin\omega t, \quad e^{-i\omega t} = \cos\omega t - i\sin\omega t$$

the right side of (*10.33*) takes the form

$$e^{\mu t}[b_1(k_{11}\cos\omega_1 t - h_{11}\sin\omega_1 t) - b_2(k_{11}\sin\omega_1 t + h_{11}\cos\omega_1 t)]$$

which, with some manipulation, may be reduced to

$$e^{\mu_1 t} R_1 (k_{11}^2 + h_{11}^2)^{1/2} \cos(\omega_1 t + \delta_{11} + \phi_1) \tag{10.34}$$

Here R_1 and ϕ_1 are arbitrary constants and $\tan\delta_{11} = h_{11}/k_{11}$.

Hence it is clear that if all roots of (*10.30*) are complex, the general solution for q_1 is

$$q_1 = R_1(k_{11}^2 + h_{11}^2)^{1/2} e^{\mu_1 t} \cos(\omega_1 t + \delta_{11} + \phi_1) + R_2(k_{12}^2 + h_{12}^2)^{1/2} e^{\mu_2 t} \cos(\omega_2 t + \delta_{12} + \phi_2) + R_3(k_{13}^2 + h_{13}^2)^{1/2} e^{\mu_3 t} \cos(\omega_3 t + \delta_{13} + \phi_3) \qquad (10.35)$$

with exactly similar expressions for q_2 and q_3. $R_1, R_2, R_3, \phi_1, \phi_2, \phi_3$ which appear in each of the solutions corresponding to q_1, q_2, q_3, are the six constants of integration to be determined by initial conditions.

The quantities μ_1, μ_2, μ_3 (which are a result of the viscous forces) are negative. Hence solutions having the form of (*10.35*) indicate damped harmonic oscillations.

Considering motion corresponding to ω_1 only,

$$q_1 = R_1(k_{11}^2 + h_{11}^2)^{1/2} e^{\mu_1 t} \cos(\omega_1 t + \delta_{11} + \phi_1), \quad q_2 = R_1(k_{21}^2 + h_{21}^2)^{1/2} e^{\mu_1 t} \cos(\omega_1 t + \delta_{21} + \phi_1),$$

$$q_3 = R_1(k_{31}^2 + h_{31}^2)^{1/2} e^{\mu_1 t} \cos(\omega_1 t + \delta_{31} + \phi_1)$$

Hence these motions are not in phase (for example q_1, q_2, q_3 do not reach their extreme values at the same instant) since $\delta_{11}, \delta_{21}, \delta_{31}$ are not equal.

10.17 Regarding Stability of Motion.

If after the masses of a system are given some small initial motions they never depart very far from their equilibrium positions, the motion is said to be stable. As can be seen from (*10.32*), positive real roots of (*10.30*), or complex roots with positive real parts, mean terms in the solutions which increase indefinitely with time, hence instability. For stability, *real roots or real parts of complex roots must be negative.* Pure imaginary roots mean stability in that they indicate oscillations with constant amplitudes.

To find whether or not a given system is stable, one of the two following procedures may be followed.

(*a*) Determine all roots of the fundamental determinant in the usual way. Examine the roots to see if all real parts are negative.

(*b*) Apply the Routh-Hurwitz test, which does not require finding the roots. The test is not reproduced here.

For details of the above as well as considerably more information on the subject of stability, the reader may consult the following references.

(1) A. Hurwitz, *Math. Ann.*, Volume 46, 1895, Pages 273-284.

(2) R. N. Arnold and L. Maunder, *Gyrodynamics and its Engineering Applications*, Page 453, Academic Press, 1961.

10.18 Use of Normal Coordinates When External Forces Are Acting. (No viscous forces.)

In the treatment of conservative systems on which externally applied forces are acting, normal coordinates (found as in Section 10.13) offer real advantages and although it is not our purpose to consider this long and detailed subject, we indicate below how equations of motion in the g's may be found.

Basically the method of setting up equations of motion is just the same as has been used throughout. It is only that here we propose to use coordinates $g_1, g_2, \ldots, g_n$.

Having expressed T and V in the form of (*10.22*), we apply $\dfrac{d}{dt}\left(\dfrac{\partial L}{\partial \dot{g}_r}\right) - \dfrac{\partial L}{\partial g_r} = F_{g_r}$ and obtain the following very simple equations of motion,

$$\ddot{g}_r + \omega_r g_r = F_{g_r} \qquad r = 1, 2, \ldots, n \qquad (10.36)$$

The generalized force F_{g_r}, which involves only externally applied forces, may easily be found as follows. Employing $q_1, q_2, \ldots, q_n$, δW_{total} is written in the usual way (see equation (*4.12*), Page 61). Now eliminating q's in favor of g's by (*10.19*), δW_{total} can be put in form

$$\delta W_{\text{total}} = [\cdots]_1 \delta g_1 + [\cdots]_2 \delta g_2 + \cdots + [\cdots]_n \delta g_n \tag{10.37}$$

Hence $F_{g_1} = [\cdots]_1$, etc. The advantage of this procedure is, of course, due to the simplicity of (*10.36*).

10.19 Use of Normal Coordinates When Viscous and External Forces Are Acting.

For this type of problem normal coordinates still offer advantages. Neglecting, for the moment, viscous and externally applied forces, normal coordinates can be found as usual and T and V expressed as in (*10.22*), Page 219. Note that the ω's found above are not the natural frequencies of the system when the viscous forces are acting.

Unfortunately the P function cannot, in general, be written as $P = b_1\dot{g}_1^2 + b_2\dot{g}_2^2 + \cdots + b_n\dot{g}_n^2$. However, making use of (*10.19*), (*10.5*) can easily be put in the form

$$P = -\frac{1}{2}\sum_{ri}^{n} p_{ri}\dot{g}_r\dot{g}_i \tag{10.38}$$

Hence, applying Lagrange's equation, the equations of motion become

$$\ddot{g}_r + \omega_r^2 g_r - p_{1r}\dot{g}_1 - p_{2r}\dot{g}_2 - p_{3r}\dot{g}_3 - \cdots - p_{nr}\dot{g}_n = F_{g_r} \tag{10.39}$$

The generalized force F_{g_r}, which involves external forces only, is determined exactly as explained in Section 10.18. "Viscous coupling" still exists but, even so, equations of motion in the g's are simpler than in the q's.

Example 10.12.

The following is a brief outline of the above method as applied to the triple pendulum of Fig. 10-4, Example 10.6, Page 213, assuming that it is suspended in a viscous fluid; no external forces. Here we write

$$T = \tfrac{1}{2}(\dot{g}_1^2 + \dot{g}_2^2 + \dot{g}_3^2), \quad V = \tfrac{1}{2}(\omega_1^2 g_1^2 + \omega_2^2 g_2^2 + \omega_3^2 g_3^2)$$

where $\omega_1 = 18.71$, $\omega_2 = 8.21$, $\omega_3 = 5.72$.

Referring to Section 10.3 and to equation (*1*) of Example 10.6, it follows that

$$P = -\tfrac{1}{2}[(b_1 + b_2 + b_3)r_1\dot{\theta}_1^2 + b_2 r_2^2\dot{\theta}_2^2 + b_3 r_3\dot{\theta}_3^2 + 2b_2 r_1 r_2\dot{\theta}_1\dot{\theta}_2 + 2b_3 r_1 r_3\dot{\theta}_1\dot{\theta}_3]$$

where b_1, b_2, b_3 are coefficients of viscous drag on the bars. Now making use of $\theta_1 = 2.78c_1g_1 - 0.88c_2g_2 + 2.75c_3g_3$, etc., (see Example 10.10), P can easily be expressed in terms of $\dot{g}_1, \dot{g}_2, \dot{g}_3$.

Hence $\ddot{g}_1 + \omega_1^2 g_1 = \partial P/\partial \dot{g}_r$, etc., are the equations of motion. Note that $p_1 = 2\pi/\omega_1$, etc., are no longer the periods of motion of the system. If viscous forces are not too great, oscillations are established and the periods of oscillation depend somewhat on the damping factors.

Example 10.13. *Viscous and external forces acting.*

Referring to Example 10.3, Page 211, and Fig. 10-1(*a*), imagine vertical forces $f_1 = A_1 \sin(\alpha_1 t + \delta_1)$ and $f_2 = A_2 \sin(\alpha_2 t + \delta_2)$ acting on m_1 and m_2 respectively. Also assume a viscous force $-b_1\dot{y}_1$ acting on m_1 and $-b_2\dot{y}_2$ on m_2 (b_1 and b_2 must be known from experiment). We shall set up equations of motion in normal coordinates. Here

$$T = \tfrac{1}{2}(\dot{g}_1^2 + \dot{g}_2^2), \quad V = \tfrac{1}{2}(\omega_1^2 g_1^2 + \omega_2^2 g_2^2) \tag{1}$$

where $\omega_1 = 8.16$, $\omega_2 = 19.37$ and (see Example 10.9, Page 221),

$$\begin{aligned} y_1 &= 3c_1g_1 - 6.25g_2, \quad & y_2 &= 5c_1g_1 + 5c_2g_2 \\ c_1 &= (9m_1 + 25m_2)^{-1/2}, \quad & c_2 &= (6.25^2 m_1 + 25m_2)^{-1/2} \end{aligned} \tag{2}$$

The P function is merely

$$P = -\tfrac{1}{2}(b_1\dot{y}_1^2 + b_2\dot{y}_2^2) \tag{3}$$

Making use of (2),

$$P = -\tfrac{1}{2}[b_1(3c_1\dot{g}_1 - 6.25c_2\dot{g}_2)^2 + b_2(5c_1\dot{g}_1 + 5c_2\dot{g}_2)^2] \tag{4}$$

Writing $\delta W_{\text{total}} = f_1\delta y_1 + f_2\delta y_2$ and applying (2),

$$\delta W_{\text{total}} = c_1(3f_1 + 5f_2)\delta g_1 + c_2(5f_2 - 6.25f_1)\delta g_2 \tag{5}$$

Hence $F_{g_1} = c_1(3f_1 + 5f_2)$ and the final equation of motion corresponding to g_1 is

$$\ddot{g}_1 + \omega_1^2 g_1 + c_1^2(9b_1 + 25b_2)\dot{g}_1 + c_1c_2(25b_2 - 18.75b_1)\dot{g}_2 = c_1(3f_1 + 5f_2) \tag{6}$$

with a similar relation corresponding to g_2. The applied forces $f_1 = A_1 \sin(\alpha_1 t + \delta_1)$, etc., (or those having any other desired form) can now be written into the equations of motion.

10.20 Suggested Experiments.

The field of "small oscillations" is replete with a wide variety of interesting and instructive experiments. In most cases the required apparatus is easily constructed. Nothing is very critical about values of masses, spring constants, etc., to be used. Many of the arrangements shown in this chapter can be set up in a short time from materials to be found in almost any laboratory.

Experimental work includes a determination of (a) the natural periods of motion, (b) the phase relations between various parts when a given mode is excited, and (c) relative amplitudes of motion for a given mode. Of course, constants of the system such as masses, spring constants, etc., must be determined by preliminary experiments. Finally (and this is, of course, the payoff) the above results are to be compared with computed values.

Experimental results are not difficult to obtain. Any one of the natural frequencies (if within certain limits) can easily be excited manually. Consider, for example, the arrangement shown in Fig. 10-1(a), Page 204. For vertical motion only, this has two natural frequencies $f_1 = \omega_1/2\pi$, $f_2 = \omega_2/2\pi$. Let us apply with the finger an oscillatory force to, say, the top of m_1, making it as nearly simple harmonic as possible. Now if the applied frequency is equal to or even close to either f_1 or f_2, the amplitude of that particular mode builds up rapidly. When the finger is removed, the oscillation continues. Of course, each mass oscillates with this one frequency. A rather accurate numerical value of the period can now be found by timing, say, 100 oscillations with a stop watch.

For either ω_1 or ω_2 excited, the phase relation between the motions of m_1 and m_2 (that is, whether at any instant they move in the same or opposite directions) can be observed directly. At the same time the amplitude of oscillation of m_1 compared with that of m_2 can be roughly estimated.

The above technique is applicable to a wide variety of systems having two, three or even four natural periods of oscillation. When the applied frequency is near one of the natural frequencies, this fact becomes evident at once since the force required to cause the oscillation to build up is noticeably small. After some practice, little difficulty is experienced in exciting any one of the natural modes *alone*. With reasonable care in the determination of the constants of the system and experimental values of the periods, excellent agreement between computed and experimental results may be expected.

Below are listed several systems, any one of which is quite suitable for a quantitative experiment or for classroom demonstration.

(a) Fig. 10-1(a), (b), or (d), Page 204. Easily constructed; results excellent.

(b) Fig. 10-4, Page 213. Easily duplicated as shown. Hence all results given in Example 10.6 can be checked.

(*c*) Fig. 10-10, Page 230. Easily constructed; results excellent. This makes a striking experiment.

(*d*) Fig. 10-7(*c*), Page 216. Must use good ball bearings to reduce friction.

(*e*) The following systems are especially recommended for classroom demonstrations: Fig. 10-1(*b*) and (*d*); Fig. 10-10; Fig. 10-13, Page 231; Fig. 10-16, Page 233.

Experiments of this type are very effective indeed as a means of arousing interest, giving physical meaning to the theory and greatly broadening the student's understanding of the subject.

Problems

A. ***Systems Having Two Degrees of Freedom.***

10.1. In Fig. 10-1(*a*), Page 204, a third spring (constant k_3 and unstretched length l_3') is attached to the bottom of m_2 and directly down to the floor. This spring is under tension when the masses are at rest. Find an expression for ω_1, ω_2 of the system. Compare results with those found in Example 10.3, Page 211.

10.2. Show that for the double pendulum, Fig. 10-1(*b*), ω_1 and ω_2 are given by

$$\omega_1, \omega_2 = \{g(m_1+m_2)(r_1+r_2) \pm g[(m_1+m_2)(m_2(r_1+r_2)^2 + m_1(r_2-r_1)^2)]^{1/2}\}^{1/2}(2m_1r_1r_2)^{-1/2}$$

Show that for $m_1 = m_2 = m$ and $r_1 = r_2 = r$, $\omega_1 = 1.85(g/r)^{1/2}$, $\omega_2 = .77(g/r)^{1/2}$ and that normal coordinates are

$$g_1 = \tfrac{1}{2}[(4-2\sqrt{2})^{1/2}\theta - (2-\sqrt{2})^{1/2}\phi](mr^2)^{1/2}$$

$$g_2 = -\tfrac{1}{2}[(4+2\sqrt{2})^{1/2}\theta + (2+\sqrt{2})^{1/2}\phi](mr^2)^{1/2}$$

10.3. Show that for the double torsion pendulum, Fig. 10-1(*d*), ω_1 and ω_2 are given by

$$\omega_1, \omega_2 = \left[\frac{I_1 b + I_2 a \pm \sqrt{(I_1 b + I_2 a)^2 - 4I_1 I_2 c}}{2I_1 I_2}\right]^{1/2}$$

where $a = k_1 + k_2$, $b = k_2 + k_3$, $c = k_1k_2 + k_1k_3 + k_2k_3$.

Show that for $I_1 = I_2 = I$ and $k_1 = k_2 = k_3 = k$, $\omega_1^2 = 3k/I$, $\omega_2^2 = k/I$ and normal coordinates are

$$g_1 = (\theta_1 + \theta_2)(I/2)^{1/2}, \quad g_2 = (\theta_2 - \theta_1)(I/2)^{1/2}$$

10.4. Find $\omega_1, \omega_2, g_1, g_2$ for the system shown in Fig. 10-1(*f*) for $m_1 = 300$ grams, $m_2 = 500$ grams, $k_1 = 3 \times 10^4$ dynes/cm, $k_2 = 4 \times 10^4$ dynes/cm, $R = 5$ cm and $I = 2000$ g-cm². Take x_1, x_2 as displacements of m_1, m_2 respectively from rest positions. $\omega_1 = 17.60$, $\omega_2 = 6.41$; $g_1 = 12.15x_1 - 18.3x_2$.

10.5. Prove in detail the statement made at the end of Example 10.9, Page 221.

10.6. Referring to Example 10.8, Page 217, show that normal coordinates for the "molecule" are

$$g_1 = (q_3 - q_1)\left(\frac{m_1}{2}\right)^{1/2}, \quad g_2 = \frac{m_1(q_1+q_3) + m_2 q_2}{(m_2 + 2m_1)^{1/2}},$$

$$g_3 = \frac{(q_1 - 2q_2 + q_3)}{(m_2 + 2m_1)^{1/2}}\left(\frac{m_1 m_2}{2}\right)^{1/2}$$

Check in T and V.

10.7. The frame A, Fig. 10-9, is supported by tightly stretched piano wires as shown. Disk D is likewise supported in the frame. Let κ_1 be the total torsional constant of wires supporting A, and κ_2 the corresponding constant for those supporting D. Show that

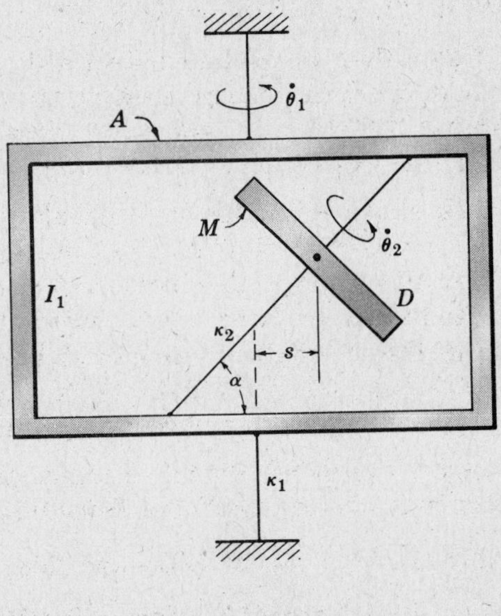

Fig. 10-9

$$T = \tfrac{1}{2}[(I_1 + Ms^2 + I_x \cos^2 \alpha + I_z \sin^2 \alpha)\dot{\theta}_1^2 + I_z\dot{\theta}_2^2 + 2I_z \sin \alpha \dot{\theta}_1\dot{\theta}_2]$$
$$V = \tfrac{1}{2}(\kappa_1\theta_1^2 + \kappa_2\theta_2^2)$$

Note that these are valid for any values of θ_1, θ_2 so long as the elastic limit of a wire is not exceeded.

Show that ω_1 and ω_2 are given by

$$\omega^2 = \frac{a_{11}\kappa_2 + I_z\kappa_1 \pm \sqrt{(a_{11}\kappa_2 + I_z\kappa_1)^2 - 4\kappa_1\kappa_2(I_1 + Ms^2 + I_x \cos^2 \alpha)I_z}}{2(I_1 + Ms^2 + I_x \cos^2 \alpha)I_z}$$

where $a_{11} = I_1 + Ms^2 + I_x \cos^2 \alpha + I_z \sin^2 \alpha$.

The above arrangement, which is not difficult to construct, works out well as a quantitative experiment and especially so since bearings and their unavoidable friction are eliminated.

10.8. In Fig. 10-7(*c*), Page 216, let $I_1 = 4000$ g-cm², $I_2 = 3000$ g-cm², $k = 10^5$ dyne-cm/radian. Show that $\omega_1 = 0$, $\omega_2 = 7.65$. What is the physical meaning of the zero root?

10.9. Show that for the system in Fig. 10-7(*d*), Page 216,

$$\omega_1 = 0, \quad \omega_2 = \left[\frac{k(m_1 + m_2 + I/R^2)}{m_2(m_1 + I/R^2)}\right]^{1/2}$$

Show that $y = A \cos(\omega_2 t + \phi) + (g/2M)(m_1 - m_2)t^2 + Bt + C$ where A, B, C are arbitrary and $M = m_1 + m_2 + I/R^2$.

B. *Systems Having Three or More Degrees of Freedom.*

10.10. Referring to Fig. 10-10, the masses and spring constants (taken from an actual experiment) have the values shown. Compute the periods and compare with the experimental values given.

The arrows in the chart to the left indicate experimentally observed directions of motion of m_1, m_2, m_3 corresponding to $\omega_1, \omega_2, \omega_3$. Verify these directions from the cofactors of the fundamental determinant.

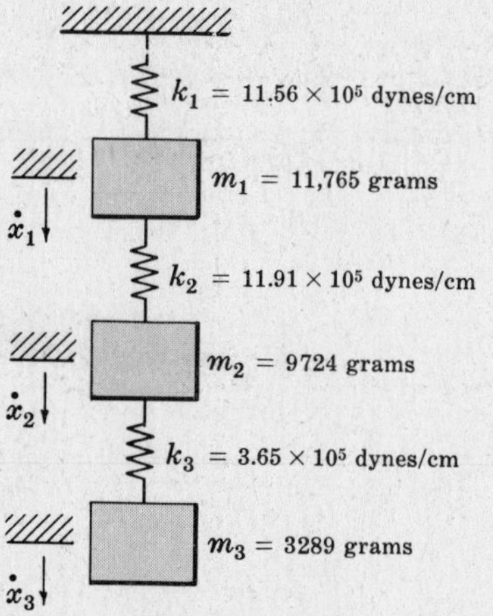

Directions of motion corresponding to:	ω_1	ω_2	ω_3
m_1	↓	↓	↓
m_2	↓	↓	↑
m_3	↓	↑	↓

Periods in seconds (experimental): $\mathcal{P}_1 = 1.09$, $\mathcal{P}_2 = 0.54$, $\mathcal{P}_3 = 0.36$.

Fig. 10-10

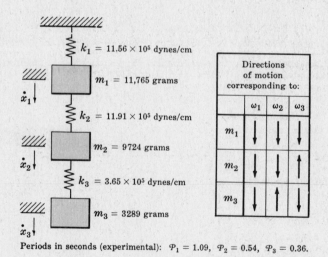

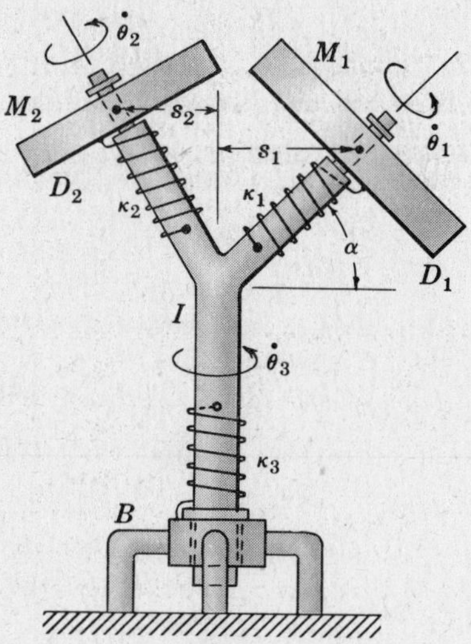

Fig. 10-11

10.11. Show that normal coordinates for the above system are

$$q_1 = 50.0x_1 + 68.3x_2 + 32.3x_3, \quad q_2 = -57.0x_1 - 30.0x_2 + 45.7x_3, \quad q_3 = 79.8x_1 - 65.4x_2 + 13.0x_3$$

where x_1, x_2, x_3 represent vertical displacements of m_1, m_2, m_3 from their rest positions.

Show that when the above are introduced into equations (*10.22*), Page 219, the original forms of T and V are obtained.

10.12. The disks D_1, D_2, Fig. 10-11, are coupled to their respective shafts by torsional springs as indicated. The vertical shaft is also connected to base B by a similar spring.

Torsional constants are $\kappa_1, \kappa_2, \kappa_3$. Angles θ_1, θ_2 are measured relative to the respective shafts, θ_3 relative to B. Write expressions for T and V. Note that exact expressions are, without approximations, in the form of (*10.4*) and (*10.6*), Page 208.

10.13. Referring to Problem 8.7, Page 168 and Fig. 8-26, suppose besides the springs shown, rod bd is coupled to D with a spring (torsional constant c_3) just as D_1 and D_2 are coupled to their supporting rods in Fig. 10-11, Page 230. (Neglect mass of bd.)

Show that T and V are given by

$$T_{\text{exact}} = \tfrac{1}{2}[((Ml^2+I_x)\cos^2\theta_2 + I_1 + I_z\sin^2\theta_2)\dot{\theta}_1^2 + (Ml^2+I_x)\dot{\theta}_2^2 + I_z\dot{\theta}_3^2 + 2I_z\dot{\theta}_1\dot{\theta}_2\sin\theta_2]$$

$$V_{\text{exact}} = \tfrac{1}{2}[c_1\theta_1^2 + c_2(\beta-\theta_2)^2 + c_3\theta_3^2] + Mgl\sin\theta_2$$

where β is the value of θ_2 for which the c_2 spring is undistorted.

Now assuming that when the system is at rest $\theta_2 = \theta_0$ and writing $\theta_2 = \theta_0 + \alpha$, show that for small motion,

$$T_{\text{approx.}} = \tfrac{1}{2}[((Ml^2+I_x)\cos^2\theta_0 + I_1 + I_z\sin^2\theta_0)\dot{\theta}_1^2 + (Ml^2+I_x)\dot{\alpha}^2 + I_z\dot{\theta}_3^2 + 2I_z\dot{\theta}_1\dot{\alpha}\sin\theta_0]$$

$$V_{\text{approx.}} = \tfrac{1}{2}(c_1\theta_1^2 + c_2\alpha^2 + c_3\theta_3^2)$$

Write out the fundamental determinant and find its roots.

10.14. Four equal masses, Fig. 10-12, connected to exactly equal springs, rest on a smooth horizontal table. The unstretched length of each spring $= l_0$; equilibrium length $= l$. Assuming motion along the line ab only, show that

$$V_{\text{exact}} = k(x_1^2 + x_2^2 + x_3^2 + x_4^2 - x_1x_2 - x_2x_3 - x_3x_4)$$

where x_1, x_2, x_3, x_4 are displacements of m_1, etc., from rest positions.

Taking $m = 300$ grams and $k = 2\times 10^4$ dynes/cm, compute $\omega_1, \omega_2, \omega_3, \omega_4$. Make a chart showing the directions of motion of each mass corresponding to each ω. (See Fig. 10-10.)

Making use of expression (*10.25*), Page 221, find the normal coordinates g_1, g_2, g_3, g_4. Show by direct substitution into original expressions for T and V that they take the form of (*10.22*), Page 219.

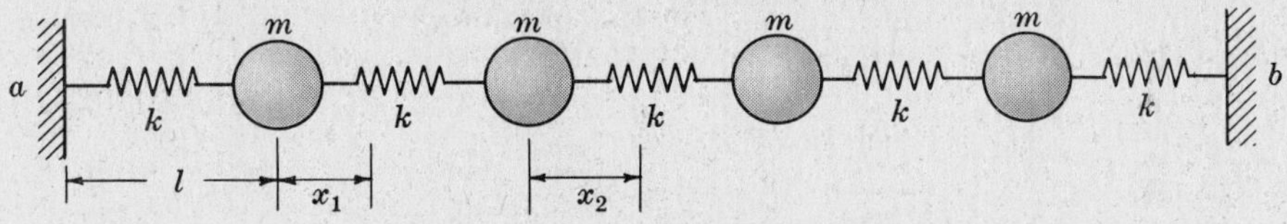

Fig. 10-12

10.15. (*a*) Write T, V for the triple torsion pendulum shown in Fig. 10-13. Here $\kappa_1, \kappa_2, \kappa_3, \kappa_4$ are torsional constants for the various sections of piano wire. Find g_1, g_2, g_3.

Now suppose that, due to a surrounding fluid, viscous torques $-b_1\dot{\theta}_1, -b_2\dot{\theta}_2, -b_3\dot{\theta}_3$ act on the dumbbells respectively. Show that $P = -\tfrac{1}{2}(b_1\dot{\theta}_1^2 + b_2\dot{\theta}_2^2 + b_3\dot{\theta}_3^2)$. Show how this can be expressed in the normal coordinates found above.

(*b*) Imagine the three dumbbells replaced by n exactly equal ones which are equally spaced along the wire. Show that

$$V = \kappa[\theta_1^2 + \theta_2^2 + \cdots + \theta_n^2 - (\theta_1\theta_2 + \theta_2\theta_3 + \theta_3\theta_4 + \cdots + \theta_{n-1}\theta_n)]$$

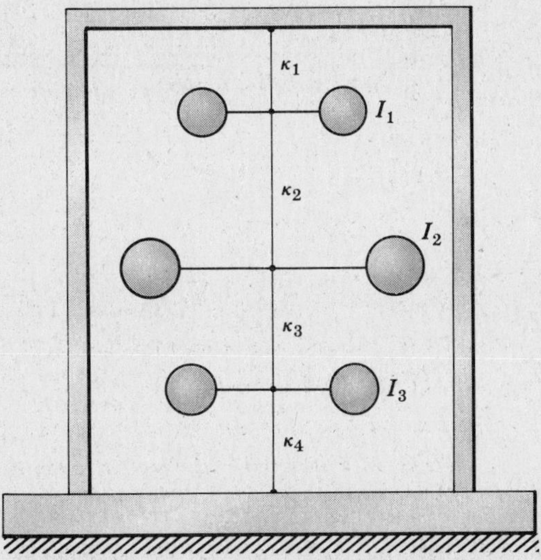

Fig. 10-13. Triple Torsion Pendulum.

10.16. Referring to the triple pendulum shown in Fig. 10-2(*c*), Page 205, r_1 and r_2 are strings supporting m_1, m_2. The rigid rod, the mass m_3 and arms c, d have a total moment of inertia I about axis ab. r_3 is the distance from the c.m. of the entire system (not including m_1, m_2) to ab.

Show that for small motion approximate expressions for T and V are

$$T_{\text{approx.}} = \tfrac{1}{2}[m_1 r_1^2 \dot{\theta}_1^2 + m_2 r_2^2 \dot{\theta}_2^2 + (m_1 s_1^2 + m_2 s_2^2 + I)\dot{\theta}_3^2 + 2m_1 s_1 r_1 \dot{\theta}_1 \dot{\theta}_3 + m_2 s_2 r_2 \dot{\theta}_2 \dot{\theta}_3]$$

$$V_{\text{approx.}} = \tfrac{1}{2}[m_1 g r_1 \theta_1^2 + m_2 g r_2 \theta_2^2 + g(Mr_3 + m_1 s_1 + m_2 s_2)\theta_3^2]$$

where $\theta_1, \theta_2, \theta_3$ determine the angular displacements of r_1, r_2, r_3 respectively, each measured from a vertical line. M is the mass of the entire system, not including m_1 and m_2. Write out D.

The above pendulum is easily constructed (use hardened point bearings at a, b) and works out well for demonstration or as a quantitative experiment.

10.17. Imagine viscous forces $-b_1 v_1, -b_2 v_2, -b_3 v_3$ acting on the spheres m_1, m_2, m_3, Fig. 10-2(c), Page 205. Making use of the results of the above problem, show that

$$P = -\tfrac{1}{2}[b_1 r_1^2 \dot{\theta}_1^2 + b_2 r_2^2 \dot{\theta}_2^2 + (b_1 s_1^2 + b_2 s_2^2)\dot{\theta}_3^2 + 2b_1 s_1 r_1 \dot{\theta}_1 \dot{\theta}_3 + b_2 s_2 r_2 \dot{\theta}_2 \dot{\theta}_3 + b_3 R^2 \dot{\theta}_3^2]$$

where R = distance from center of m_3 to axis ab.

Determine, for example, F_{θ_1} first by applying $F_{\theta_1} = \partial P / \partial \dot{\theta}_1$ and again from $\delta W_{\theta_1} = F_{\theta_1} \delta\theta_1$. Compare results.

10.18. Referring to Fig. 10-14, m_1 and m_2 move along smooth horizontal tracks. The two large wheels roll, without slipping, in contact with the upper surface of m_1. Show that

$$T = \tfrac{1}{2}[(m_1 + m_2)\dot{x}_1^2 + (m_2 + 2I/r^2)\dot{q}_2^2 + m_3 \dot{x}_3^2 - 2m_2 \dot{x}_1 \dot{q}_2]$$

$$V = \tfrac{1}{2}k[x_1^2 + q_2^2 + x_3^2 - 2x_1 x_3 + 2x_3 q_2 - 2x_1 q_2]$$

where q_2 = constant $- x_2$, m_2 is the total mass of the two wheels plus that of the rods on which they are mounted, I is the moment of inertia of each wheel about its axle.

Write D and show that it has two zero roots. Show that the one period of oscillation of the system follows from

$$m_3[m_1 m_2 + (m_1 + m_2)(2I/r^2)]\omega^2 = k[m_1 m_2 + m_1 m_3 + (m_1 + m_2 + m_3)(2I/r^2)]$$

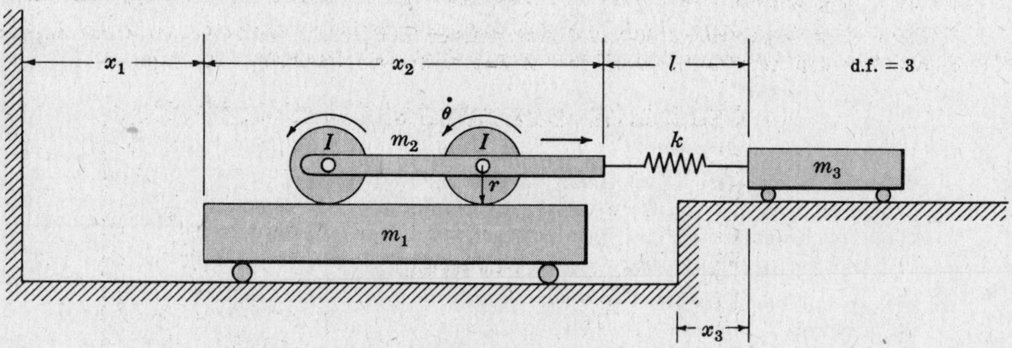

Fig. 10-14

10.19. Show that one root of the determinant for the system shown in Fig. 10-7(e), Page 216, is zero. Find a general expression for the two periods of oscillation.

10.20. The five disks, Fig. 10-15 below, are geared as shown. The springs represent flexible shafts having torsional constants $\kappa_1, \kappa_2, \kappa_3$. Show that

$$T = \tfrac{1}{2}[(I_1 + b_2^2 I_5)\dot{\theta}_1^2 + I_2 \dot{\theta}_2^2 + (I_3 + b_1^2 I_4)\dot{\theta}_3^2]$$

$$V = \tfrac{1}{2}[(\kappa_1 + b_2^2 \kappa_3)\theta_1^2 + (\kappa_1 + \kappa_2)\theta_2^2 + (\kappa_2 + b_1^2 \kappa_3)\theta_3^2 - 2\kappa_1 \theta_1 \theta_2 - 2\kappa_2 \theta_2 \theta_3 - 2\kappa_3 b_1 b_2 \theta_1 \theta_3]$$

where $\theta_4 = b_1 \theta_3$, $\theta_5 = b_2 \theta_1$.

Show that for $b_1 = b_2$, one root of the determinant is zero.

Pulleys geared at a and b and coupled by springs having torsional constants $\kappa_1, \kappa_2, \kappa_3$ (springs indicate flexible shafts).

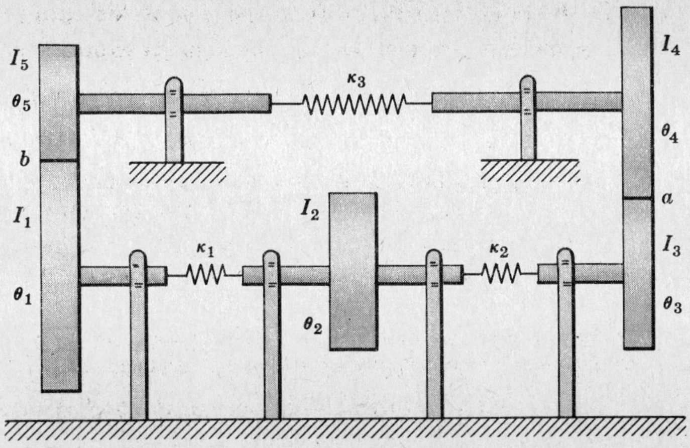

Fig. 10-15

10.21. Referring to Problem 5.14, Page 95 and Fig. 5-20 and assuming small motion, find $V_{\text{approx.}}$ for the entire system, including gravity. Note that gravity does not drop out of the final equations of motion. Determine ω_1, ω_2 and compare with same in Problem 10.2.

This arrangement is easily set up and constitutes a good experiment.

10.22. Assume the "particles", Fig. 10-12, Page 231, can move about in any manner on a horizontal plane (see Problem 10.14). Assuming small motion, write expressions for T and V. Assuming a viscous drag of $-bv$ on each mass, write P.

10.23. Data on the uniform bar and springs shown in Fig. 10-16 (taken from an actual experiment) are as follows: $k_1 = 2.01 \times 10^4$ dynes/cm; $k_2 = 1.77 \times 10^4$ dynes/cm; with springs unstretched, lengths $pd = 20.0$ cm and $ab = 19.0$ cm; with bar in its equilibrium position, $pd = 32.3$ cm and $ab = 44.4$ cm; mass of bar = 384.8 grams; I about a line normal to bp and through c.m. = 1.2×10^4 g-cm²; length $bp = 25.8$ cm. With rod in rest position, angles measured from horizontal lines are $\theta_0 = 15.4°$, $\theta_1 = 60.5°$, $\theta_2 = 52°$. Experimentally determined values of the three periods of the system (motion in a plane only) are $\mathcal{P}_1 = 1.0$, $\mathcal{P}_2 = .81$, $\mathcal{P}_3 = .33$ sec.

Using the above data, compute the periods and check with the experimentally determined values. Use coordinates $\bar{x}, \bar{y}, \theta$, shown in Fig. 5-21 (see Problem 5.15, Page 96).

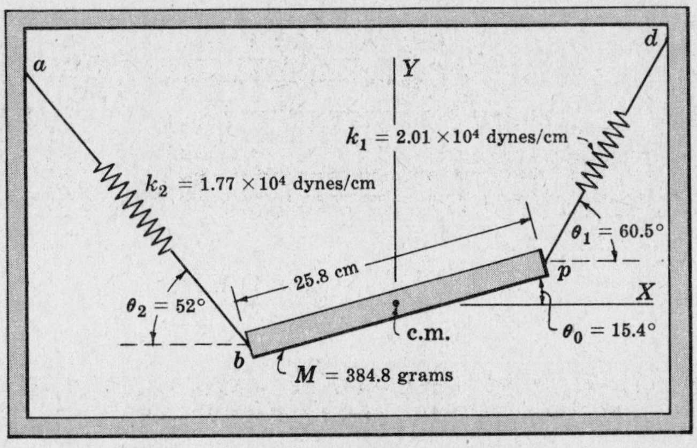

Fig. 10-16

10.24. For the system shown in Fig. 10-8, Page 222,

$$T = \tfrac{1}{2}(\dot{g}_1^2 + \dot{g}_2^2 + \dot{g}_3^2), \qquad V = \tfrac{1}{2}(\omega_1^2 g_1^2 + \omega_2^2 g_2^2 + \omega_3^2 g_3^2)$$

where the g's and ω's can be found in the usual way. Assuming viscous forces $-b_1 v_1, -b_2 v_2$ acting on m_1 and m_2 respectively, write an expression for P in normal coordinates.

Further assuming an external force $f = A \sin(\alpha t + \delta)$ applied vertically to m_1, write out equations of motion in normal coordinates.

CHAPTER 11

Small Oscillations about Steady Motion

11.1 Important Preliminary Considerations.

(a) *Physical meaning of steady motion.*

Consider the following three simple examples.

The pendulum bob, Fig. 11-1, properly started, will rotate in a horizontal circle with θ and $\dot{\psi}$ each constant. The top, Fig. 11-2, will under certain conditions move so that $\theta, \dot{\psi}, \dot{\phi}$ each remains constant. The arrangement shown in Fig. 11-3 may be started in such a way that $r, \theta, \dot{\psi}$ do not vary.

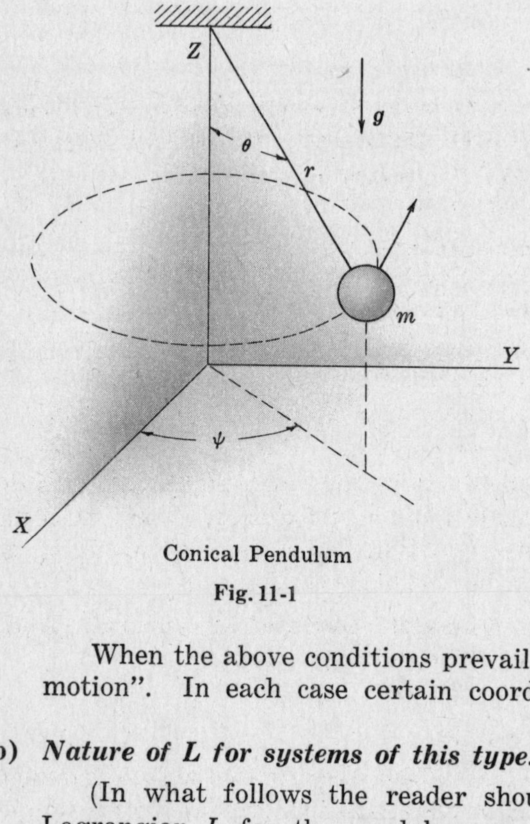

Conical Pendulum

Fig. 11-1

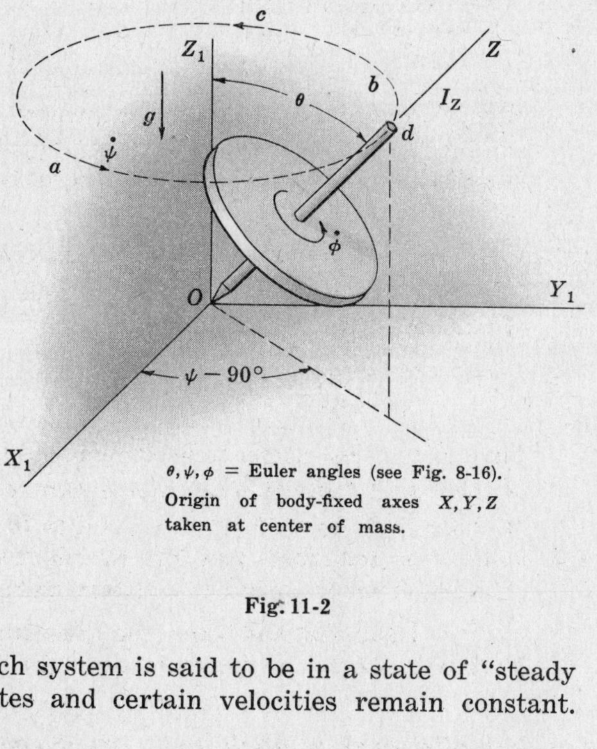

θ, ψ, ϕ = Euler angles (see Fig. 8-16). Origin of body-fixed axes X, Y, Z taken at center of mass.

Fig. 11-2

When the above conditions prevail, each system is said to be in a state of "steady motion". In each case certain coordinates and certain velocities remain constant.

(b) *Nature of L for systems of this type.*

(In what follows the reader should refer to Examples 11.1, 11.2, 11.3.) The Lagrangian L for the pendulum contains $\theta, \dot{\theta}, \dot{\psi}$ but ψ is absent. For the top, L contains $\theta, \dot{\theta}, \dot{\phi}, \dot{\psi}$ but ϕ and ψ are not present. For the system, Fig. 11-3, L contains $r, \dot{r}, \theta, \dot{\theta}, \dot{\psi}$ with ψ missing.

A common feature of the above Examples is that certain coordinates as well as their velocities appear in L while velocities only corresponding to others are present. Coordinates of the first type are referred to as "non-ignorable" and those of the second as "ignorable". (This terminology stems from the fact, shown in the following section, that ignorable coordinates can be completely eliminated from the equations

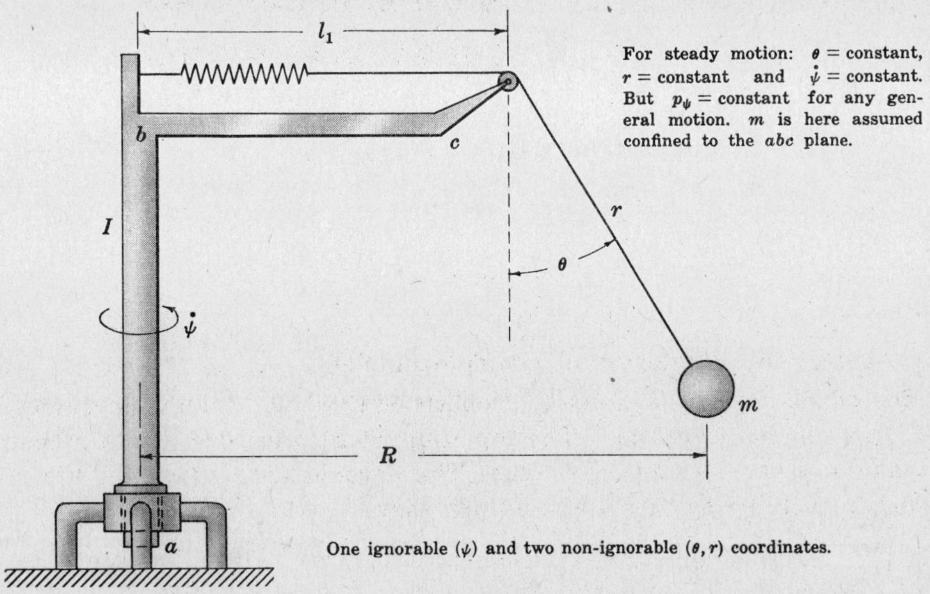

l_1
b
c
I
$\dot{\psi}$
r
θ
m
R
a
For steady motion: θ = constant, r = constant and $\dot{\psi}$ = constant. But p_ψ = constant for any general motion. m is here assumed confined to the abc plane.
One ignorable (ψ) and two non-ignorable (θ, r) coordinates.

Fig. 11-3

of motion.) Hence we define, in accord with the examples given, a state of "steady motion" as one in which *each non-ignorable coordinate remains constant and the velocity corresponding to each ignorable coordinate is constant.*

(c) *The momentum corresponding to an ignorable coordinate is constant.*

Consider again Fig. 11-3, Example 11.3. Clearly ψ is ignorable. Applying the Lagrange equation,

$$\frac{d}{dt}\left(\frac{\partial L}{\partial \dot{\psi}}\right) = 0 \quad \text{or} \quad \frac{\partial L}{\partial \dot{\psi}} = [m(l_1 + r\sin\theta)^2 + I]\dot{\psi} = p_\psi = \text{constant}$$

That is p_ψ, the momentum corresponding to ψ, is constant. (Note that $\partial L/\partial \dot{q}_r = p_r$ is the usual definition of momentum corresponding to q_r.) p_ψ is constant for any motion of the system whether or not it is steady motion. Moreover, if any existing motion is disturbed (certain forces momentarily applied and then removed) p_ψ is changed from its original constant value to a new value, also constant.

It is clear that the above remarks apply to ignorable coordinates in general. And, of course, $\partial L/\partial \dot{q}_r = p_r$ is not constant for the non-ignorable coordinates.

(d) *Establishment of oscillations about steady motion.*

Imagine the bob of the pendulum, Fig. 11-1, tapped very lightly with a hammer while rotating with steady motion. As soon to be shown, it now oscillates with simple harmonic motion about its steady motion path or about a new steady motion path close to the first one. Of course, $\dot{\psi}$ is no longer constant. It now varies with time in a manner which can be determined. After the blow p_ψ is constant but usually with a value slightly different from the original one.

As a second example, suppose the steady motion of Fig. 11-3 slightly disturbed. In this case both θ and r oscillate in magnitude about their steady motion values in a manner similar to the way any two-degree-of-freedom system (see Chapter 10) oscillates about equilibrium positions.

11.2 Eliminating Ignorable Coordinates from the General Equations of Motion. Method A. (Steady motion *not* assumed.)

Consider a system, having n degrees of freedom, the motion of which can be determined by k non-ignorable coordinates $q_1, q_2, \ldots, q_k$ and s ignorable coordinates $\mathcal{J}_{k+1}, \mathcal{J}_{k+2}, \ldots, \mathcal{J}_n$ $(n = k+s)$. Thus L contains the q's, $\dot{q}$'s and the $\dot{\mathcal{J}}$'s but the $\mathcal{J}$'s are absent.

A matter of basic importance in the treatment of this subject is that, for any system of the above type, *the s ignorable coordinates can be eliminated from the k equations of motion corresponding to the non-ignorable coordinates.*

In order to make clear the various steps involved let us carry through for $k=3$, $s=2$, $n=5$. Assuming no moving coordinates or moving constraints, the reader can show (see equation (*2.56*), Page 27) that a general expression for T takes the following form

$$\begin{aligned} T \;=\; & \tfrac{1}{2}(A_{11}\dot{q}_1\dot{q}_1 + A_{22}\dot{q}_2\dot{q}_2 + A_{33}\dot{q}_3\dot{q}_3 + 2A_{12}\dot{q}_1\dot{q}_2 + 2A_{13}\dot{q}_1\dot{q}_3 + 2A_{23}\dot{q}_2\dot{q}_3) \\ & + \dot{\mathcal{J}}_4(A_{14}\dot{q}_1 + A_{24}\dot{q}_2 + A_{34}\dot{q}_3) + \dot{\mathcal{J}}_5(A_{15}\dot{q}_1 + A_{25}\dot{q}_2 + A_{35}\dot{q}_3) \\ & + \tfrac{1}{2}(A_{44}\dot{\mathcal{J}}_4\dot{\mathcal{J}}_4 + 2A_{45}\dot{\mathcal{J}}_4\dot{\mathcal{J}}_5 + A_{55}\dot{\mathcal{J}}_5\dot{\mathcal{J}}_5) \end{aligned} \tag{11.1}$$

where the A's are functions of q_1, q_2, q_3 only. Likewise $V = V(q_1, q_2, q_3)$, *not containing* $\mathcal{J}_4, \mathcal{J}_5$.

Applying Lagrange's equations, the following relations, valid for any general type of motion, are obtained.

$$\begin{aligned} & (A_{r1}\ddot{q}_1 + A_{r2}\ddot{q}_2 + A_{r3}\ddot{q}_3 + A_{r4}\ddot{\mathcal{J}}_4 + A_{r5}\ddot{\mathcal{J}}_5) + \dot{q}_1\left(\frac{\partial A_{r1}}{\partial q_1}\dot{q}_1 + \frac{\partial A_{r1}}{\partial q_2}\dot{q}_2 + \frac{\partial A_{r1}}{\partial q_3}\dot{q}_3\right) \\ & + \dot{q}_2\left(\frac{\partial A_{r2}}{\partial q_1}\dot{q}_1 + \frac{\partial A_{r2}}{\partial q_2}\dot{q}_2 + \frac{\partial A_{r2}}{\partial q_3}\dot{q}_3\right) + \dot{q}_3\left(\frac{\partial A_{r3}}{\partial q_1}\dot{q}_1 + \frac{\partial A_{r3}}{\partial q_2}\dot{q}_2 + \frac{\partial A_{r3}}{\partial q_3}\dot{q}_3\right) \\ & + \dot{\mathcal{J}}_4\left(\frac{\partial A_{r4}}{\partial q_1}\dot{q}_1 + \frac{\partial A_{r4}}{\partial q_2}\dot{q}_2 + \frac{\partial A_{r4}}{\partial q_3}\dot{q}_3\right) + \dot{\mathcal{J}}_5\left(\frac{\partial A_{r5}}{\partial q_1}\dot{q}_1 + \frac{\partial A_{r5}}{\partial q_2}\dot{q}_2 + \frac{\partial A_{r5}}{\partial q_3}\dot{q}_3\right) - \frac{\partial L}{\partial q_r} = 0 \end{aligned} \tag{11.2}$$

where $r = 1, 2, 3$. Note that the above contains $\dot{\mathcal{J}}_4, \ddot{\mathcal{J}}_4, \dot{\mathcal{J}}_5, \ddot{\mathcal{J}}_5$.

Now since L contains no ignorable coordinates, $\dfrac{d}{dt}\left(\dfrac{\partial L}{\partial \dot{\mathcal{J}}}\right) = 0$. That is, $\partial L/\partial \dot{\mathcal{J}}_4 = p_4 =$ constant, $\partial L/\dot{\mathcal{J}}_5 = p_5 =$ constant. Writing these in full and rearranging, we have

$$\begin{aligned} A_{44}\dot{\mathcal{J}}_4 + A_{45}\dot{\mathcal{J}}_5 &= p_4 - A_{14}\dot{q}_1 - A_{24}\dot{q}_2 - A_{34}\dot{q}_3 \\ A_{54}\dot{\mathcal{J}}_4 + A_{55}\dot{\mathcal{J}}_5 &= p_5 - A_{15}\dot{q}_1 - A_{25}\dot{q}_2 - A_{35}\dot{q}_3 \end{aligned} \tag{11.3}$$

It is seen that (*11.3*) can be solved for $\dot{\mathcal{J}}_4$ and $\dot{\mathcal{J}}_5$ in terms of $p_4, p_5, \dot{q}_1, \dot{q}_2, \dot{q}_3$. Hence the $\dot{\mathcal{J}}$'s and $\ddot{\mathcal{J}}$'s can be eliminated from (*11.2*), *thus leaving three equations containing non-ignorable coordinates only.* It is as if the system were now reduced to one having only k degrees of freedom. ($\mathcal{J}_4$ and $\mathcal{J}_5$ have been "ignored.")

If the general motion of the system is desired, integrals of the above relations give q_1, q_2, q_3 as functions of time. Then returning to (*11.3*), $\mathcal{J}_4$ and $\mathcal{J}_5$ may also be found as functions of t.

11.3 Elimination of Ignorable Coordinates Employing the Routhian Function. Method B.

Regarding L as a function of $q_1, q_2, \ldots, q_k;\ \dot{q}_1, \dot{q}_2, \ldots, \dot{q}_k;\ \dot{\mathcal{J}}_{k+1}, \dot{\mathcal{J}}_{k+2}, \ldots, \dot{\mathcal{J}}_n$, a small variation in L is expressed by

$$\delta L = \sum_{r=1}^{k} \frac{\partial L}{\partial q_r}\delta q_r + \sum_{r=1}^{k} \frac{\partial L}{\partial \dot{q}_r}\delta \dot{q}_r + \sum_{i=k+1}^{n} \frac{\partial L}{\partial \dot{\mathcal{J}}_i}\delta \dot{\mathcal{J}}_i \tag{11.4}$$

But $\partial L/\partial \dot{\mathcal{J}}_i = p_i$ and $p_i\,\delta\dot{\mathcal{J}}_i = \delta(p_i\dot{\mathcal{J}}_i) - \dot{\mathcal{J}}_i\,\delta p_i$. Hence (*11.4*) may be written as

$$\delta\left(L - \sum_{i=k+1}^{n} p_i\dot{\mathcal{J}}_i\right) = \sum_{r=1}^{k} \frac{\partial L}{\partial q_r}\delta q_r + \sum_{r=1}^{k} \frac{\partial L}{\partial \dot{q}_r}\delta \dot{q}_r - \sum_{i=k+1}^{n} \dot{\mathcal{J}}_i\,\delta p_i \tag{11.5}$$

Let us now define a "Routhian" function by

$$R = L - \sum_{i=k+1}^{n} p_i\dot{\mathcal{J}}_i \tag{11.6}$$

Assuming that the $\dot{\mathcal{J}}$'s have been eliminated from R by relations having the form of (*11.3*), $R = R(q\text{'s}, \dot{q}\text{'s}, p\text{'s})$. Thus

$$\delta R = \sum_{r=1}^{k} \frac{\partial R}{\partial q_r}\delta q_r + \sum_{r=1}^{k} \frac{\partial R}{\partial \dot{q}_r}\delta \dot{q}_r + \sum_{i=k+1}^{n} \frac{\partial R}{\partial p_i}\delta p_i \tag{11.7}$$

Comparing (*11.5*) and (*11.7*), it is seen that

$$\frac{\partial R}{\partial \dot{q}_r} = \frac{\partial L}{\partial \dot{q}_r}, \quad \frac{\partial R}{\partial q_r} = \frac{\partial L}{\partial q_r}, \quad \frac{\partial R}{\partial p_i} = -\dot{\mathcal{J}}_i \tag{11.8}$$

Inserting the first two relations in the Lagrangian equation, we have

$$\frac{d}{dt}\left(\frac{\partial R}{\partial \dot{q}_r}\right) - \frac{\partial R}{\partial q_r} = 0 \qquad r = 1, 2, \ldots, k \tag{11.9}$$

which represents k equations of motion *free from ignorable coordinates*. Equations (*11.9*) are the same as (*11.2*) after having eliminated the $\dot{\mathcal{J}}$'s and $\ddot{\mathcal{J}}$'s.

Important points: (*a*) The above treatment applies to any motion the system may have. It is in no way restricted to steady motion. (*b*) In order to obtain k equations of motion free from ignorable coordinates, the first method requires eliminating the $\dot{\mathcal{J}}$'s and $\ddot{\mathcal{J}}$'s from each equation of (*11.2*), whereas by means of (*11.3*) the entire elimination is made in one step merely by removing the $\dot{\mathcal{J}}$'s from (*11.6*).

For simple problems, Method A is about as convenient as Method B. But for general considerations and for the solution of applied problems where k and s are large, the R method is superior.

11.4 Conditions Required for Steady Motion.

In a state of steady motion (continuing to assume $k=3$, $s=2$, $n=5$), $q_1 = \text{constant} = b_1$, $q_2 = b_2$, $q_3 = b_3$; $\dot{q}_1 = \dot{q}_2 = \dot{q}_3 = 0$; $\dot{\mathcal{J}}_4 = \text{constant}$, $\dot{\mathcal{J}}_5 = \text{constant}$; $\ddot{\mathcal{J}}_4 = \ddot{\mathcal{J}}_5 = 0$. Hence, as can be seen from (*11.2*) and the second relation of (*11.8*), conditions to be met for steady motion are

$$\left(\frac{\partial L}{\partial q_r}\right)_0 = 0 \quad \text{or} \quad \left(\frac{\partial R}{\partial q_r}\right)_0 = 0 \tag{11.10}$$

where the zero subscript indicates that steady motion values listed above are to be inserted.

11.5 Equations of Motion Assuming Steady Motion Slightly Disturbed.

To this end we set $q_1 = b_1 + s_1$, $q_2 = b_2 + s_2$, $q_3 = b_3 + s_3$ where b_1, b_2, b_3 are the steady motion values (determined by (*11.10*)) of the non-ignorable coordinates and s_1, s_2, s_3 represent variable displacements from these values. Thus $\dot{q}_1 = \dot{s}_1$, etc. Substituting in the Routhian, we have

$$R = R(b_1 + s_1,\; b_2 + s_2,\; b_3 + s_3,\; \dot{s}_1,\; \dot{s}_2,\; \dot{s}_3)$$

Now assuming the $\dot{s}$'s and s's small, expanding R and retaining zero, first and second order terms, we get

$$R_{\text{approx.}} = (R_0) + \sum_r^k \left(\frac{\partial R}{\partial q_r}\right)_0 s_r + \sum_r^k \left(\frac{\partial R}{\partial \dot{q}_r}\right)_0 \dot{s}_r + \frac{1}{2}\sum_{rl}^k \left(\frac{\partial^2 R}{\partial q_r \partial q_l}\right)_0 s_r s_l + \frac{1}{2}\sum_{rl}^k \left(\frac{\partial^2 R}{\partial \dot{q}_r \partial \dot{q}_l}\right)_0 \dot{s}_r \dot{s}_l + \sum_{rl}^k \left(\frac{\partial^2 R}{\partial q_l \partial \dot{q}_r}\right)_0 s_l \dot{s}_r$$

where zero subscripts indicate that steady motion values are inserted. Note that the coefficients of s_r, $\dot{s}_r$, $s_r\dot{s}_l$, etc., are all constants.

Equations of motion about steady motion are thus found by applying

$$\frac{d}{dt}\left(\frac{\partial R_{\text{approx.}}}{\partial \dot{s}_r}\right) - \frac{\partial R_{\text{approx.}}}{\partial s_r} = 0$$

which gives

$$\sum_{l=1}^k \left(\frac{\partial^2 R}{\partial \dot{q}_r \partial \dot{q}_l}\right)_0 \ddot{s}_l + \sum_{l=1}^k \left(\frac{\partial^2 R}{\partial q_l \partial \dot{q}_r}\right)_0 \dot{s}_l - \sum_{l=1}^k \left(\frac{\partial^2 R}{\partial q_r \partial \dot{q}_l}\right)_0 \dot{s}_l - \sum_{l=1}^k \left(\frac{\partial^2 R}{\partial q_r \partial q_l}\right)_0 s_l - \left(\frac{\partial R}{\partial q_r}\right)_0 = 0 \qquad (11.11)$$

But by (*11.10*), $\left(\frac{\partial R}{\partial q_r}\right)_0 = 0$. Hence the above general form of the equations of motion about steady motion may be written as

$$\sum_l^k (a_{rl}\ddot{s}_l + b_{rl}\dot{s}_l - c_{rl}s_l) = 0 \qquad (11.12)$$

where $a_{rl} = a_{lr}$, $c_{rl} = c_{lr}$ but $b_{rl} = -b_{lr}$ and $b_{rr} = 0$.

For the case we are carrying through, these equations are

$$\begin{aligned} a_{11}\ddot{s}_1 - c_{11}s_1 + a_{12}\ddot{s}_2 + b_{12}\dot{s}_2 - c_{12}s_2 + a_{13}\ddot{s}_3 + b_{13}\dot{s}_3 - c_{13}s_3 &= 0 \\ a_{21}\ddot{s}_1 + b_{21}\dot{s}_1 - c_{21}s_1 + a_{22}\ddot{s}_2 - c_{22}s_2 + a_{23}\ddot{s}_3 + b_{23}\dot{s}_3 - c_{23}s_3 &= 0 \\ a_{31}\ddot{s}_1 + b_{31}\dot{s}_1 - c_{31}s_1 + a_{32}\ddot{s}_2 + b_{32}\dot{s}_2 - c_{32}s_2 + a_{33}\ddot{s}_3 - c_{33}s_3 &= 0 \end{aligned} \qquad (11.13)$$

As will be seen from Examples to follow, it frequently happens that the b's are all zero. (The $b_{rl}\dot{s}_l$ are referred to as "gyroscopic terms".)

Note. (*a*) In the determination of a_{11}, c_{11}, etc., (see (*11.11*) above), R_{exact} is differentiated. Hence in the treatment of problems by this method we must first write out R_{exact}.

(*b*) If so desired equations (*11.13*) can be obtained by writing exact equations of motion, (*11.9*), inserting $q_1 = b_1 + s_1$, etc., expanding and retaining only first order terms. (See Examples.)

11.6 Solving the Equations of Motion.

It is seen that the above equations are very similar to (*10.7*), Page 209. Solutions may be found following the same procedure outlined in Section 10.16, Page 224. Hence only a few details will be given here.

Assuming as solutions $s_1 = Ae^{\lambda t}$, $s_2 = Be^{\lambda t}$, $s_3 = Ce^{\lambda t}$, substituting in (*11.13*) and following the steps referred to above, we write

$$D = \begin{vmatrix} a_{11}\lambda^2 - c_{11} & a_{12}\lambda^2 + b_{12}\lambda - c_{12} & a_{13}\lambda^2 + b_{13}\lambda - c_{13} \\ a_{21}\lambda^2 + b_{21}\lambda - c_{21} & a_{22}\lambda^2 - c_{22} & a_{23}\lambda^2 + b_{23}\lambda - c_{23} \\ a_{31}\lambda^2 + b_{31}\lambda - c_{31} & a_{32}\lambda^2 + b_{32}\lambda - c_{32} & a_{33}\lambda^2 - c_{33} \end{vmatrix} = 0 \qquad (11.14)$$

Important Notes:

(*a*) Since $a_{ir} = a_{ri}$, $c_{ir} = c_{ri}$ and $b_{ir} = -b_{ri}$, it may be shown (see E. J. Routh, *Advanced Rigid Dynamics*, vol. 2, 6th ed., Macmillan, 1930, page 78) that D contains only even powers of λ. The reader should expand D in (*11.14*) and show that terms containing $\lambda^5, \lambda^3, \lambda$ automatically drop out.

(*b*) When T and V are each positive definite, $\lambda_1 = i\omega_1$, $\lambda_2 = -i\omega_1$, $\lambda_3 = i\omega_2$, $\lambda_4 = -i\omega_2$, etc., where the ω's are real. As will be seen, this means that the motion is stable.

Now assuming that condition (*b*) is met, a general solution for s_1, for example, is

$$s_1 = A_1 e^{i\omega_1 t} + A_1' e^{-i\omega_1 t} + A_2 e^{i\omega_2 t} + A_2' e^{-i\omega_2 t} + A_3 e^{i\omega_3 t} + A_3' e^{-i\omega_3 t}$$

with similar expressions for s_2 and s_3. For the general case ($b_{rl} \neq 0$) solutions may be put in the form of relation (*10.35*), Page 226.

When gyroscopic terms ($b_{rl}\dot{s}_l$) are absent from equations (*11.13*), solutions take the form of relations (*10.12*), Page 210, and normal coordinates can be found. When gyroscopic terms are present normal coordinates cannot, in general, be found.

11.7 Ignorable Coordinates as Functions of Time After the Disturbance.

From the last relation of (*11.8*), or solving (*11.3*) for $\dot{\mathcal{J}}_i$, we have $\dot{\mathcal{J}}_i = -\partial R/\partial p_i = \phi_i(q\text{'s}, \dot{q}\text{'s})$. Replacing q_1 by $b_1 + s_1$, $\dot{q}_1$ by $\dot{s}_1$, etc., and using solutions of (*11.13*), we can write $\dot{\mathcal{J}}_i = \phi(t)$. Hence

$$\mathcal{J}_i(t) = \int \phi_i(t)\,dt + c_i \qquad (11.15)$$

For slight changes in $\dot{\mathcal{J}}_i$, $\mathcal{J}(t)$ can be found by expanding $\phi_i(s, \dot{s})$, retaining zero and first order terms.

11.8 Examples Illustrating the Above Treatment.

Example 11.1.

Properly started, the pendulum bob of Fig. 11-1 will rotate in a horizontal circle in which θ = constant and $\dot{\psi}$ = constant. For the pendulum,

$$L = \tfrac{1}{2}m(r^2\dot{\theta}^2 + r^2 \sin^2\theta\, \dot{\psi}^2) + mgr\cos\theta \qquad (1)$$

Quantities $\theta, \dot{\theta}, \dot{\psi}$, but not ψ, appear in L. Thus ψ is ignorable.

$$\frac{\partial L}{\partial \dot{\psi}} = mr^2 \sin^2\theta\, \dot{\psi} = p_\psi = \text{constant} \qquad (2)$$

Applying (*11.6*) and eliminating $\dot{\psi}$ by (*2*),

$$R = \frac{1}{2}mr^2\dot{\theta}^2 - \frac{1}{2}\frac{p_\psi^2}{mr^2\sin^2\theta} + mgr\cos\theta \qquad (3)$$

Applying (*11.9*), the general equation (not restricted to steady motion) corresponding to θ is

$$\ddot{\theta} - \frac{p_\psi^2 \cos\theta}{m^2r^4\sin^3\theta} + \frac{g}{r}\sin\theta = 0 \qquad (4)$$

(It is suggested that the reader obtain this same equation by Method A.) For steady motion, $\ddot{\theta} = \dot{\theta} = 0$, $\theta = \theta_0$, $p_\psi = c_0$, $\dot{\psi} = \dot{\psi}_0$ = constant. Thus from (*4*), or just as well applying (*11.10*), the condition for steady motion is

$$\frac{c_0^2 \cos\theta_0}{m^2r^4\sin^3\theta_0} = \frac{g}{r}\sin\theta_0$$

which may be put in the form

$$\cos\theta_0 = \frac{g}{r\dot{\psi}_0^2} \qquad (5)$$

Hence steady motion can exist at any angle θ for which $r\dot{\psi}_0^2 > g$. (Taking $r = 100$ cm, $g = 980$ cm/sec^2, (5) is satisfied for $\dot{\psi}_0 = \sqrt{9.8}$ rad/sec or greater and, for example, letting $\dot{\psi}_0 = 4$ rad/sec, $\cos\theta_0 = 9.8/16$.)

Now suppose that the bob (moving with steady motion) is very lightly tapped with a hammer. Assume, for the moment, that the impact is such that p_ψ is left unchanged. Writing $\theta = \theta_0 + \alpha$ and inserting in (4), we have

$$\ddot{\alpha} - \frac{\cos(\theta_0+\alpha)\,c_0^2}{m^2r^4\sin^3(\theta_0+\alpha)} + \frac{g}{r}\sin(\theta_0+\alpha) = 0 \tag{6}$$

Assuming that α remains very small, expanding and retaining only zero and first order terms, (6) becomes

$$\ddot{\alpha} + \left[\frac{c_0^2}{m^2r^4}\left(\frac{1+2\cos^2\theta}{\sin^4\theta_0}\right) + \frac{g}{r}\cos\theta_0\right]\alpha - \left(\frac{c_0^2\cos\theta_0}{m^2r^4\sin^3\theta_0} - \frac{g}{r}\sin\theta_0\right) = 0 \tag{7}$$

(This relation can be obtained by expanding R and retaining second order terms. See Problem 11.1.) But by (5) the last term is zero. Hence $\ddot{\alpha} + \omega^2\alpha = 0$ or $\alpha = A\sin(\omega t + \phi)$ where A and ϕ are arbitrary constants. Thus the bob oscillates about the steady motion path with a period

$$\mathcal{P} = 2\pi\left[\frac{c_0^2}{m^2r^4}\left(\frac{1+2\cos^2\theta_0}{\sin^4\theta_0}\right) + \frac{g}{r}\cos\theta_0\right]^{-1/2}$$

Making use of (2) and (5), the period may be written as

$$\mathcal{P} = 2\pi\left[\frac{r}{g}\left(\frac{\cos\theta_0}{1+3\cos^2\theta_0}\right)\right]^{1/2}$$

The manner in which ψ changes with time after the blow, is determined as follows (see Section 11.7):

$$\psi = \frac{c_0}{mr^2}\int\frac{dt}{\sin^2(\theta_0+\alpha)} + c \tag{8}$$

Expanding,
$$\frac{1}{\sin^2(\theta_0+\alpha)} = \frac{1}{\sin^2\theta_0} - \frac{2\cos\theta_0}{\sin^3\theta_0}\alpha + \cdots$$

Hence
$$\psi = \dot{\psi}_0 t - \frac{2c_0\cos\theta_0}{mr^2\sin^3\theta_0}\int\alpha\,dt + c \tag{9}$$

Since $\alpha = A\sin(\omega t+\phi)$, the integral can be evaluated at once and we have an approximate expression for ψ as a function of time.

It was assumed above that the disturbance did not change the steady motion value of p_ψ. Suppose now that it is changed from the constant value c_0 to a slightly different (but also constant) value c_1. Replacing c_0 by c_1 in equation (5) above, a new steady motion value $\theta = \theta_0'$ can be determined. Writing $\theta = \theta_0' + \alpha$ and continuing as before, it is clear that the bob oscillates with a period

$$\mathcal{P} = 2\pi\left[\frac{r}{g}\left(\frac{\cos\theta_0'}{1+3\cos^2\theta_0'}\right)\right]^{1/2}$$

about the new steady motion path. Hence it is usually assumed that the disturbance does not change the constant values of momenta.

Example 11.2.

Oscillations of the top (not vertical) about steady motion. (One non-ignorable, two ignorable coordinates.)

The top, Fig. 11-2, if set spinning above a certain speed and properly released, will move with steady motion in which $\theta, \dot{\phi}, \dot{\psi}$ each remains constant. (The top precesses with constant angular velocity $\dot{\psi}$, without nutation.)

(a) *General equations of motion and conditions for steady motion.* As previously shown (see Example 8.14, Page 159),

$$L = \tfrac{1}{2}[I_x(\dot{\theta}^2 + \dot{\psi}^2\sin^2\theta) + I_z(\dot{\phi} + \dot{\psi}\cos\theta)^2] - Mgr\cos\theta \tag{1}$$

It is seen that θ is non-ignorable and ψ, ϕ ignorable. Hence

$$p_\phi = I_z(\dot\phi + \dot\psi \cos\theta) = c_1, \quad p_\psi = I_x\dot\psi \sin^2\theta + c_1\cos\theta = c_2 \tag{2}$$

Here $R = L - p_\psi\dot\psi - p_\phi\dot\phi$, and eliminating $\dot\psi$ and $\dot\phi$ by (*2*) we get (no approximations)

$$R = \frac{1}{2}I_x\dot\theta^2 - \frac{1}{2}\frac{(c_2 - c_1\cos\theta)^2}{I_x\sin^2\theta} - Mgr\cos\theta - \frac{1}{2}\frac{c_1^2}{I_x} \tag{3}$$

Applying (*11.9*), the following equation of motion is obtained:

$$I_x\ddot\theta - \left(\frac{c_2 - c_1\cos\theta}{I_x\sin^2\theta}\right)^2 I_x\sin\theta\cos\theta + \left(\frac{c_2 - c_1\cos\theta}{I_x\sin^2\theta}\right)c_1\sin\theta - Mgr\sin\theta = 0 \tag{4}$$

Note that (*4*) is valid for any general motion the top may have. No approximations have been made.

For steady motion, (*11.10*) takes the form $I_x\dot\psi_0^2\cos\theta_0 - c_1\dot\psi_0 + Mgr = 0$, where the zero subscripts indicate steady motion values. Solving for $\dot\psi_0$,

$$\dot\psi_0 = \frac{c_1 \pm \sqrt{c_1^2 - 4I_xMgr\cos\theta_0}}{2I_x\cos\theta_0} \tag{5}$$

Hence for values of c_1 such that $c_1^2 > 4I_xMgr\cos\theta_0$ there are two distinct values of $\dot\psi_0$ for which θ remains constant.

(*b*) *Oscillations about steady motion assuming a slight disturbance such that c_1 and c_2 remain unchanged.* Writing $\theta = \theta_0 + \alpha$, inserting in (*4*), expanding and retaining first order terms, we finally get after some manipulations

$$\ddot\alpha + \alpha\left[\dot\psi_0^2 + \left(\frac{Mgr}{I_x\dot\psi_0}\right)^2 - \frac{2Mgr\cos\theta_0}{I_x}\right] = 0 \tag{6}$$

Hence as the top precesses, the point *d*, for example, oscillates with simple harmonic motion about the steady motion path *abc*, with a period given by

$$\mathcal{P} = 2\pi\left[\dot\psi_0^2 + \left(\frac{Mgr}{I_x\dot\psi_0}\right)^2 - \frac{2Mgr\cos\theta_0}{I_x}\right]^{-1/2} \tag{7}$$

The manner in which ϕ and ψ change with time can be determined as follows. Applying the third relation of (*11.8*) or merely solving equations (*2*), we get

$$\dot\phi = \frac{c_1}{I_z} - \frac{(c_2 - c_1\cos\theta)\cos\theta}{I_x\sin^2\theta}, \quad \dot\psi = \frac{c_2 - c_1\cos\theta}{I_z\sin^2\theta} \tag{8}$$

Inserting $\theta = \theta_0 + \alpha$, expanding and retaining the first two terms,

$$\dot\phi = \dot\phi_0 + \left(\frac{c_2 + c_2\cos^2\theta_0 - 2c_1\cos\theta_0}{I_x\sin^3\theta_0}\right)\alpha \tag{9}$$

and since α is a known function of t from (*6*), (*9*) can be integrated to give ϕ as a function of t. In like manner $\psi(t)$ can be found.

Additional facts regarding this example: (*a*) Relations (*2*) correspond to (*11.3*). (*b*) Equation (*4*) can be obtained by Method A. (*c*) Equation (*6*) can be obtained by first expanding R and then applying (*11.11*); see Problem 11.2. (*d*) No gyroscopic terms appear in (*6*).

Example 11.3. *One ignorable and two non-ignorable coordinates.*

Referring to Fig. 11-3,

$$L = \tfrac{1}{2}m(\dot r^2 + r^2\dot\theta^2) + \tfrac{1}{2}[m(l_1 + r\sin\theta)^2 + I]\dot\psi^2 + mgr\cos\theta - \tfrac{1}{2}k(r - r_1)^2 \tag{1}$$

where r_1 is the value of r when the spring is unstretched. It is seen that ψ is ignorable while θ and r are non-ignorable.

Applying (*11.10*), conditions for steady motion are

$$\begin{aligned} \dot{\psi}_0^2(l_1 + r_0 \sin\theta_0)\cos\theta_0 &= g\sin\theta_0 \\ \dot{\psi}_0^2(l_1 + r_0 \sin\theta_0)\sin\theta_0 &= \frac{k}{m}(r_0 - r_1) - g\cos\theta_0 \end{aligned} \tag{2}$$

from which it follows that
$$\dot{\psi}_0^2 = \frac{g\tan\theta_0}{l_1 + r_1\sin\theta_0 + \dfrac{mg}{k}\tan\theta_0} \tag{3}$$

which, for an assumed value of θ_0, (*3*) may be solved for $\dot{\psi}_0$, or for a given value of $\dot{\psi}_0$ can be solved graphically for θ_0. Thus r_0 may be found from (*2*).

Following the usual steps, R is

$$R = \tfrac{1}{2}m(\dot{r}^2 + r^2\dot{\theta}^2) - \tfrac{1}{2}c^2[m(l_1 + r\sin\theta)^2 + I]^{-1} + mgr\cos\theta - \tfrac{1}{2}k(r - r_1)^2 \tag{4}$$

where $p_\psi = c$. Equations of motion, with no approximations, corresponding to r and θ are

$$m\ddot{r} - mr\dot{\theta}^2 - mc^2[m(l_1 + r\sin\theta)^2 + I]^{-2}(l_1 + r\sin\theta)\sin\theta - mg\cos\theta + k(r - r_1) = 0 \tag{5}$$

$$mr^2\ddot{\theta} + 2mr\dot{r}\dot{\theta} - mc^2[m(l_1 + r\sin\theta)^2 + I]^{-2}(l_1 + r\sin\theta)r\cos\theta + mgr\sin\theta = 0 \tag{6}$$

Note that (*5*) and (*6*) can be obtained by Method A.

Writing $r = r_0 + s$, $\theta = \theta_0 + \alpha$, expanding and retaining first order terms, we finally get

$$\begin{aligned} a_{11}\ddot{s} + c_{11}s + c_{12}\alpha &= 0 \\ c_{21}s + a_{22}\ddot{\alpha} + c_{22}\alpha &= 0 \end{aligned} \tag{7}$$

where $a_{11} = m$, $c_{11} = m\dot{\psi}_0^2\sin^2\theta_0\left(\dfrac{3m(l_1 + r_0\sin\theta_0)^2 - I}{m(l_1 + r_0\sin\theta_0)^2 + I}\right) + k$, (see equation(*11.11*))

$$c_{12} = m\dot{\psi}_0^2\left[\frac{4m(l_1 + r_0\sin\theta_0)^2 r_0\sin\theta_0\cos\theta_0}{m(l_1 + r_0\sin\theta_0)^2 + I} - (l_1 + 2r_0\sin\theta_0)\cos\theta\right] + mg\sin\theta_0$$

Corresponding relations for c_{21}, a_{22}, c_{22} follow in a straightforward manner. (See Problem 11.3.) Since no gyroscopic terms appear in (*7*), solutions can be obtained by assuming $s = A\sin(\omega t + \phi)$, $\alpha = B\sin(\omega t + \phi)$.

For specific values (such as $m_1 = 400$ grams, $g = 980$ cm/sec², $k = 2\times 10^5$ dynes/cm, $l_1 = 20$ cm, $r_1 = 40 - 20 + 10 = 30$ cm, $\theta_0 = 30°$ (hence $r_0 = 32.26$ cm), $I = 2\times 10^5$ grams × cm²), $\dot{\psi}_0$ can be found from (*3*), the constants a_{11}, c_{11}, c_{12}, etc., evaluated and the periods of oscillation determined.

Example 11.4. *Selection of Proper Coordinates.*

It sometimes happens that chosen coordinates do not contain ignorable coordinates, yet from the physics of the system it may be evident that steady motion is possible. In this case a set containing ignorable coordinates can usually be found by inspection.

Consider the system shown in Fig. 11-4 below. The bar, spring and mass rest on the smooth horizontal XY plane. The bar is free to rotate about a smooth fixed vertical shaft at O.

Choosing θ, ϕ, r as coordinates,

$$L = \tfrac{1}{2}I\dot{\theta}^2 + \tfrac{1}{2}m[s^2\dot{\theta}^2 + \dot{r}^2 + r^2\dot{\phi}^2 + 2rs\dot{\theta}\dot{\phi}\cos(\phi - \theta) + 2s\dot{r}\dot{\theta}\sin(\phi - \theta)] - \tfrac{1}{2}k(r - r_1)^2 \tag{1}$$

Since $\theta, \dot{\theta}, r, \dot{r}, \phi, \dot{\phi}$ each appears in L, *neither coordinate is ignorable.*

But introducing $\beta = \phi - \theta$, $\dot{\phi} = \dot{\beta} + \dot{\theta}$, L may be written as

$$\begin{aligned} L = {} & \tfrac{1}{2}m\dot{r}^2 + \tfrac{1}{2}(I + ms^2 + mr^2 + 2mrs\cos\beta)\dot{\theta}^2 + \tfrac{1}{2}mr^2\dot{\beta}^2 \\ & + ms\dot{r}\dot{\theta}\sin\beta + m(r^2 + rs\cos\beta)\dot{\theta}\dot{\beta} - \tfrac{1}{2}k(r - r_1)^2 \end{aligned} \tag{2}$$

Hence it is seen that θ is non-ignorable.

$$\frac{\partial L}{\partial\dot{\theta}} = p_\theta = (I + ms^2 + mr^2 + 2mrs\cos\beta)\dot{\theta} + m(r^2\dot{\beta} + rs\dot{\beta}\cos\beta + s\dot{r}\sin\beta) = c \tag{3}$$

Thus $\dot{\theta}$ can be eliminated from the r and β equations of motion or, of course, an R function can be found. Therefore, proceeding in the usual way, small oscillations about steady motion can be determined.

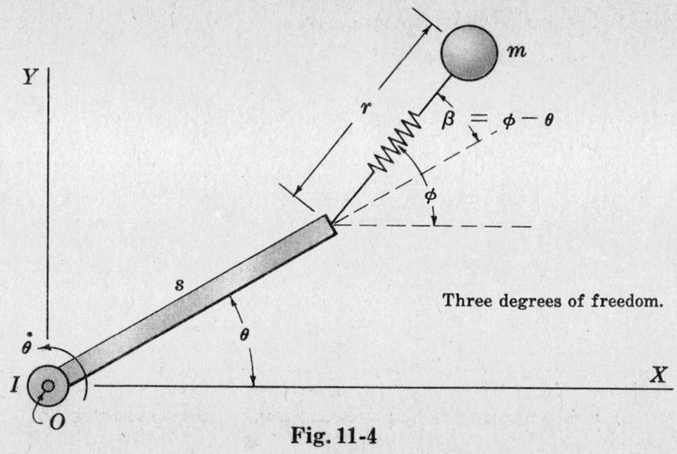

Fig. 11-4

Example 11.5. *Small oscillations of a top about its vertical position.*

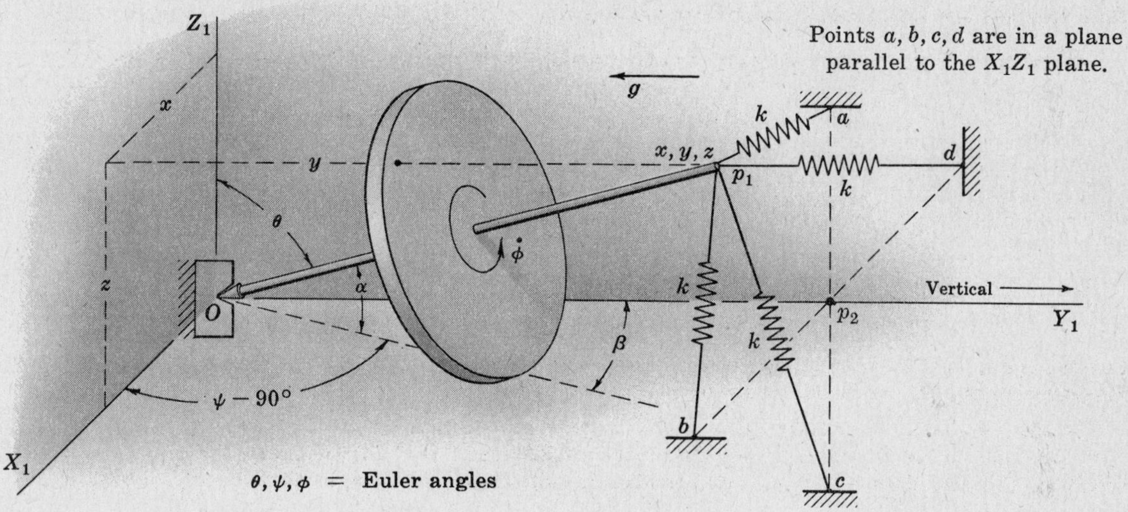

Fig. 11-5

Suppose the top (disk), Fig. 11-5, sleeping in a vertical position with axis Op_1 along Y_1, $\theta = 90°$ and $\beta = 0$. (The vertical is taken as shown because, if treated as in Fig. 11-2 with Z_1 vertical, ψ is indeterminate for $\theta = 0$.) Assuming this state of steady motion slightly disturbed, we shall find the subsequent motion of point p_1. Besides g acting in the negative direction of Y_1, let us assume that four equal springs are attached to a small smooth ring at p_1. With p_1 at p_2 the springs are unstretched and in the horizontal plane *abcd*, spaced at 90° intervals. As can be shown by equation (*5.11*), Page 89, $V_{\text{springs}} = \frac{2k}{2}(x^2 + z^2)$ for small displacements of p_1 away from p_2. x, y, z are coordinates of the end of the shaft Op_1.

Hence, referring to Example 8.14, Page 159, we write

$$L = \tfrac{1}{2}I_x(\dot{\theta}^2 + \dot{\psi}^2 \sin^2\theta) + \tfrac{1}{2}I_z(\dot{\phi} + \dot{\psi}\cos\theta)^2 - Mgr\cos\delta - k(x^2 + z^2) \qquad (1)$$

where r is the distance along Op_1 from O to c.m. of the disk, δ is the angle p_1Op_2 and other symbols have the usual meaning.

From the diagram it is seen that $\theta + \alpha = 90°$, $\psi + \beta = 180°$, $\cos\delta = \cos\alpha\cos\beta$, $x = l\cos\alpha\sin\beta$, $z = l\sin\alpha$, $y = l\cos\alpha\cos\beta$. Hence in the usual way we find

$$R = \tfrac{1}{2}I_x(\dot{\alpha}^2 + \dot{\beta}^2\cos^2\alpha) - c_1\dot{\beta}\sin\alpha - Mgr\cos\alpha\cos\beta + kl^2\cos^2\alpha\cos^2\beta \qquad (2)$$

where $c_1 = \partial L/\partial\dot{\phi} = p_\phi = \text{constant}$, l = length of shaft Op_1. The above expression is exact except for the approximation in V_{springs}. Certain constant terms have been dropped. Note that only one coordinate, ϕ, is ignorable.

Now assuming very small displacements of p_1 away from p_2 (α and β always small), the reader may show (see Problem 11.4) that the equations of motion are (see equations (*11.12*))

$$\begin{aligned} I_x\ddot{\alpha} + c_1\dot{\beta} - (Mgr - 2kl^2)\alpha &= 0 \\ I_x\ddot{\beta} - c_1\dot{\alpha} - (Mgr - 2kl^2)\beta &= 0 \end{aligned} \qquad (3)$$

Note that in this case gyroscopic terms are present.

Solutions may be obtained by assuming $\alpha = Ae^{i\omega t}$, $\beta = Be^{i\omega t}$. It follows in the usual way that

$$D = \begin{vmatrix} -(I_x\omega^2 + E) & -c_1 i\omega \\ c_1 i\omega & -(I_x\omega^2 + E) \end{vmatrix} = 0 \qquad (4)$$

where $E = Mgr - 2kl^2$; and from (*4*),

$$\omega^2 = \frac{1}{2I_x^2}\left(c_1^2 - 2I_xE \pm c_1\sqrt{c_1^2 - 4I_xE}\right) \qquad (5)$$

or

$$\pm\omega = \frac{1}{2I_x}\left(c_1 \pm \sqrt{c_1^2 - 4I_xE}\right)$$

It is seen that ω is real for $c_1^2 + 8I_xkl^2 > 4I_xMgr$. Also for $\dot{\psi}\cos\theta$ small compared with $\dot{\phi}$, $c_1 = I_x\dot{\phi}$ and thus

$$\pm\omega = \frac{1}{2I_x}\left(I_z\dot{\phi} \pm \sqrt{I_z^2\dot{\phi}^2 + 8I_xkl^2 - 4I_xMgr}\right) \qquad (6)$$

From (*5*) we write

$$\omega_1 = \pm\left[\frac{1}{2I_x}\left(c_1 + \sqrt{c_1^2 - 4I_xE}\right)\right] \quad \text{and} \quad \omega_2 = \pm\left[\frac{1}{2I_x}\left(c_1 - \sqrt{c_1^2 - 4I_xE}\right)\right]$$

Hence solutions can be put in the form

$$\begin{aligned} \alpha &= h_1d_{11}e^{i\omega_1 t} + h_2d_{12}e^{-i\omega_1 t} + h_3d_{13}e^{i\omega_2 t} + h_4d_{14}e^{-i\omega_2 t} \\ \beta &= h_1d_{21}e^{i\omega_1 t} + h_2d_{22}e^{-i\omega_1 t} + h_3d_{23}e^{i\omega_2 t} + h_4d_{24}e^{-i\omega_2 t} \end{aligned} \qquad (7)$$

which, making use of the fact that

$$d_{11} = d_{12}, \quad d_{13} = d_{14}, \quad d_{21} = -d_{22}, \quad d_{23} = -d_{24}$$

(*7*) can finally be written as

$$\begin{aligned} \alpha &= R_1(I_x\omega_1^2 + E)\cos(\omega_1 t + \epsilon_1) + R_2(I_x\omega_2^2 + E)\cos(\omega_2 t + \epsilon_2) \\ \beta &= R_1c_1\omega_1\sin(\omega_1 t + \epsilon_1) + R_2c_1\omega_2\sin(\omega_2 t + \epsilon_2) \end{aligned} \qquad (8)$$

where $R_1, R_2, \epsilon_1, \epsilon_2$ are arbitrary constants. The reader may show that, assuming $\alpha = A\cos(\omega t + \epsilon)$ and $\beta = B\sin(\omega t + \epsilon)$, solutions (*8*) may be obtained at once.

Note that for the disk hanging down (imagine a smooth ball joint at O) and g, Fig. 11-5, reversed in direction, values of ω are always real. For more details regarding this type of motion see A. G. Webster, *Dynamics*, 2nd ed., Dover, 1959, pages 288-296.

Example 11.6. *Two ignorable and two non-ignorable coordinates.*

In Fig. 11-6 below the frame AC is free to rotate about a vertical axis as shown. The light rod ab is hinged at a and can thus rotate about a horizontal axis through angle θ. Disk D rotates about a smooth collar s which can slide along ab. Angular velocity $\dot{\phi}$ of the disk is measured relative to ab.

Neglecting friction and assuming that the torque on ab due to the vertical springs is $k_2l^2\theta$, ($l = ab$), the Lagrangian is

$$\begin{aligned} L = {} & \tfrac{1}{2}M(\dot{r}^2 + r^2\dot{\theta}^2 + r^2\dot{\psi}^2\cos^2\theta) + \tfrac{1}{2}I_1\dot{\psi}^2 + \tfrac{1}{2}I_x(\dot{\psi}^2\cos^2\theta + \dot{\theta}^2) \\ & + \tfrac{1}{2}I_z(\dot{\phi} + \dot{\psi}\sin\theta)^2 - \tfrac{1}{2}k_1(r - l_0)^2 - \tfrac{1}{2}k_2l^2\theta^2 - Mgr\sin\theta \end{aligned} \qquad (1)$$

where I_1 is the moment of inertia of the frame about the vertical axis, I_x that of D about an axis through c.m. and parallel to a face, I_z that of D about ab, and l_0 the unstretched length of the k_1 spring.

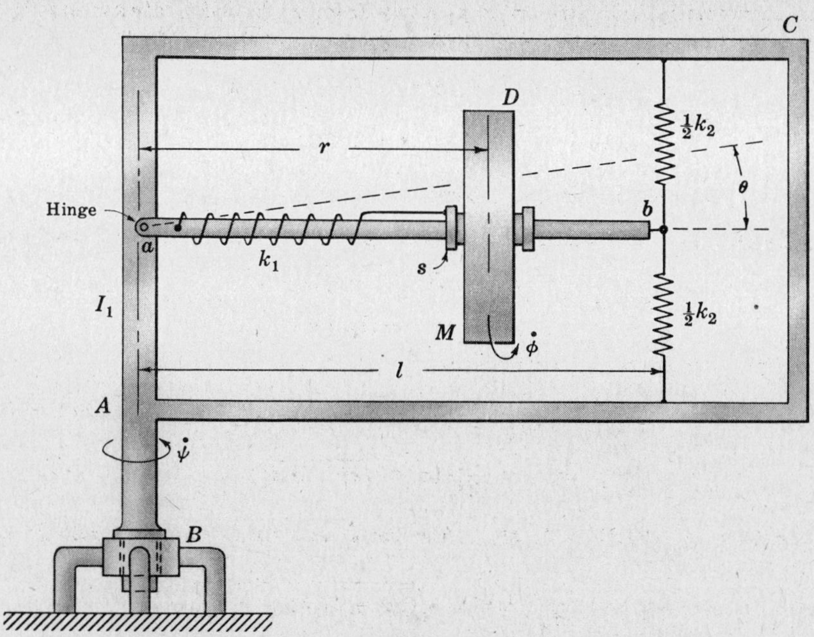

Fig. 11-6

From (*1*) it is seen that ϕ and ψ are ignorable while θ and r are non-ignorable.

$$\frac{\partial L}{\partial \dot\phi} = p_\phi = I_z(\dot\phi + \dot\psi \sin\theta) = c_1 \tag{2}$$

$$\frac{\partial L}{\partial \dot\psi} = p_\psi = (Mr^2\cos^2\theta + I_1 + I_x\cos^2\theta)\dot\psi + c_1\sin\theta = c_2 \tag{3}$$

Eliminating $\dot\phi$ and $\dot\psi$ from $L - c_1\dot\phi - c_2\dot\psi$, we have R_{exact}. Then, if so desired, exact equations of motion corresponding to r and θ are obtained at once by applying (*11.9*), Page 237.

Equations of motion for oscillations about steady motion follow from (*11.11*), Page 238. As usual, care must be taken in the differentiation of R_{exact} for the determination of a_{11}, c_{11}, etc.

Steady motion conditions for which $r, \theta, \dot\phi, \dot\psi$ each remains constant are

$$\left(\frac{\partial L}{\partial \theta}\right)_0 = (Mr_0^2 - I_z + I_x)\dot\psi_0^2 \sin\theta_0\cos\theta_0 - I_z\dot\psi_0\dot\phi_0\cos\theta_0 + k_2 l^2\theta_0 + Mgr_0\cos\theta_0 = 0 \tag{4}$$

$$\left(\frac{\partial L}{\partial r}\right)_0 = Mr_0\dot\psi_0^2\cos^2\theta_0 - k_1(r_0 - l_0) - Mg\sin\theta_0 = 0 \tag{5}$$

In an actual problem one could, for example, choose numerical values for the steady motion values of r and θ. Then, assuming all physical constants known, (*4*) and (*5*) can be solved for numerical values of $\dot\phi_0$ and $\dot\psi_0$. Hence numerical values of a_{11}, c_{11}, etc., are known and finally roots of D can be determined. (Regarding stability, see Section 11.11, Page 248.)

Example 11.7. *Three ignorable coordinates; one non-ignorable.*

In Fig. 11-7 below, a top pivoted at its c.m. is mounted on a rotating table. It can be shown that

$$L = \tfrac{1}{2}(I + MR_1^2)\dot\psi_1^2 + \tfrac{1}{2}[I_x(\dot\theta^2 + (\dot\psi_1 + \dot\psi)^2\sin^2\theta) + I_z(\dot\phi + (\dot\psi_1 + \dot\psi)\cos\theta)^2]$$

Since $\dot\psi_1, \dot\phi, \dot\psi$ appear and ψ_1, ϕ, ψ are absent, these three coordinates are ignorable. But since both θ and $\dot\theta$ are present, θ is non-ignorable. (Notation same as in Fig. 8-33, Page 174.)

For further details see Problem 11.13; also see Problem 11.5.

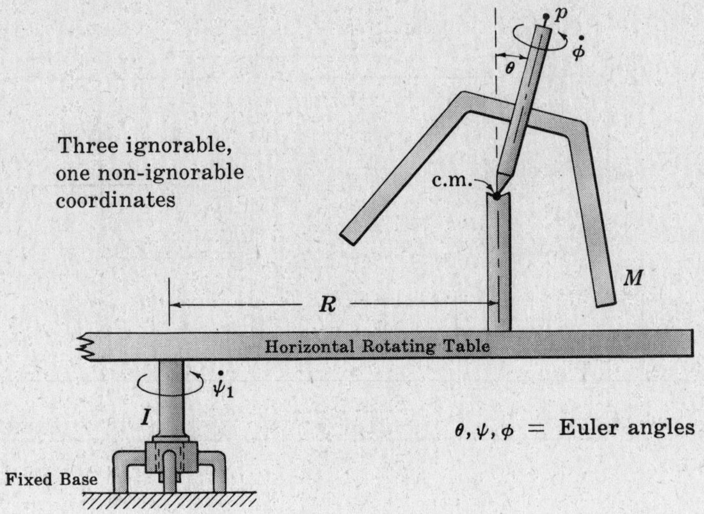

Fig. 11-7

11.9 Oscillation About Steady Motion when the System Contains Moving Constraints.

The small oscillations of a system involving a moving frame of reference or moving constraints may be quite important in certain applications. A few examples will make clear the nature and method of treating this type of problem.

Example 11.8.

In Fig. 11-8 the bead of mass m is free to slide along a smooth rigid circular wire which is forced to rotate with constant angular velocity ω about Z. Here

$$L \quad = \quad \tfrac{1}{2}m(r^2\dot{\theta}^2 + r^2\cos^2\theta\,\omega^2) \;-\; mgr\sin\theta$$

from which
$$\ddot{\theta} + \omega^2\sin\theta\cos\theta + \frac{g}{r}\cos\theta \quad = \quad 0$$

Hence for steady motion $\sin\theta_0 = -g/r\omega^2$. Assuming steady motion disturbed, writing $\theta = \theta_0 + \alpha$, expanding and retaining zero and first power terms, it easily follows (making use of the steady motion condition) that $\ddot{\alpha} + \alpha(\omega^2 - g^2/r^2) = 0$. Hence for $\omega^2 > g/r$ this represents simple harmonic motion.

Example 11.9.

Consider again the system shown in Fig. 11-3. Suppose the vertical shaft is driven at constant speed $\dot{\psi} = \omega$. The system now has two degrees of freedom and we write

$$L \quad = \quad \tfrac{1}{2}m(\dot{r}^2 + r^2\dot{\theta}^2) \;+\; \tfrac{1}{2}m(l_1 + r\sin\theta)^2\omega^2 \;+\; mgr\cos\theta \;-\; \tfrac{1}{2}k(r - r_1)^2 \tag{1}$$

from which the following two equations of motion are obtained:

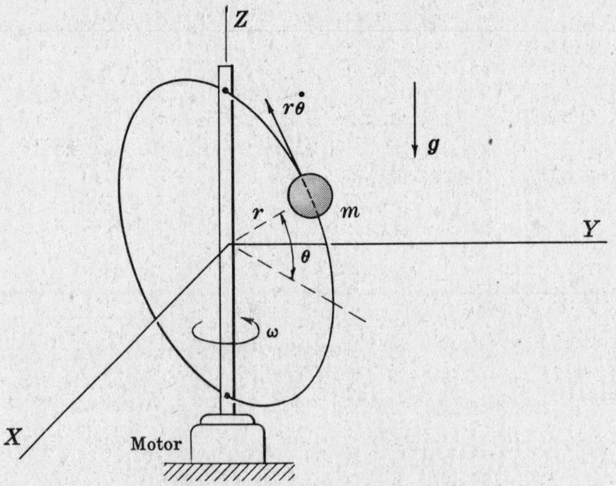

Fig. 11-8

$$\ddot{r} - r\dot{\theta}^2 - \omega^2(l_1 + r\sin\theta)\sin\theta - g\cos\theta + \frac{k}{m}(r - r_1) = 0 \tag{2}$$

$$r^2\ddot{\theta} + 2r\dot{r}\dot{\theta} - \omega^2(l_1 + r\sin\theta)r\cos\theta + rg\sin\theta = 0 \tag{3}$$

Steady motion conditions $(\ddot{\theta} = \dot{\theta} = 0,\ \ddot{r} = \dot{r} = 0,\ \theta = \theta_0,\ r = r_0)$ are

$$\omega^2(l_1 + r_0\sin\theta_0)\sin\theta_0 + g\cos\theta_0 - \frac{k}{m}(r_0 - r_1) = 0 \tag{4}$$

$$\omega^2(l_1 + r_0\sin\theta_0)r_0\cos\theta_0 - gr_0\sin\theta_0 = 0 \tag{5}$$

Assuming steady motion disturbed, putting $\theta = \theta_0 + \alpha$, $r = r_0 + s$ into (2) and (3) we get on expanding (retaining zero and first power terms and making use of (4), (5)) the following approximated equations of motion

$$\ddot{s} + s\left(\frac{k}{m} - \omega^2\sin^2\theta_0\right) + [g\sin\theta_0 - \omega^2(l_1\cos\theta_0 + 2r_0\sin\theta_0\cos\theta_0)]\alpha = 0 \tag{6}$$

$$\begin{aligned} r_0^2\ddot{\alpha} + \alpha\omega^2\left[(l_1 + r_0\sin\theta_0)r_0\sin\theta_0 - r_0^2\cos^2\theta_0 + \frac{gr_0}{\omega^2}\cos\theta_0\right] & \\ + s\omega^2\left[\frac{g}{\omega^2}\sin\theta_0 - l_1\cos\theta_0 - 2r_0\sin\theta_0\cos\theta_0\right] &= 0 \end{aligned} \tag{7}$$

which can be integrated without difficulty. Note that (6) and (7) do not contain gyroscopic terms.

Example 11.10.

In Fig. 11-9, AB represents a portion of a smooth horizontal rotating table. Axes X_1, Y_1 are fixed in space. X, Y are drawn on the table. Mass m is free to move about on the table under the action of the spring, one end of which is attached at p. Let us find the equations of small motion about the position of steady motion.

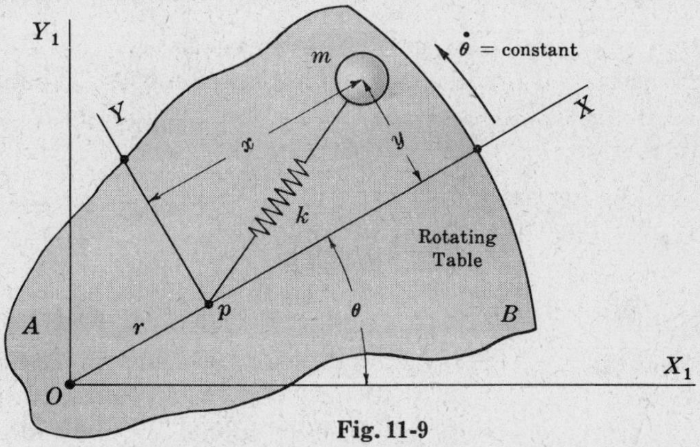

Fig. 11-9

It is easily shown that

$$T = \tfrac{1}{2}m\{\dot{x}^2 + \dot{y}^2 + [(x + r)^2 + y^2]\dot{\theta}^2 + 2\dot{\theta}[(x + r)\dot{y} - y\dot{x}]\} \tag{1}$$

$$V = \tfrac{1}{2}k(\sqrt{x^2 + y^2} - l_0)^2 \tag{2}$$

where l_0 is the length pm when the spring is unstretched. The following equations of motion are obtained from (1) and (2), assuming $\dot{\theta}$ constant:

$$\ddot{x} - 2\dot{\theta}\dot{y} - (x + r)\dot{\theta}^2 = -\frac{1}{m}\frac{\partial V}{\partial x} \qquad \ddot{y} + 2\dot{\theta}\dot{x} - y\dot{\theta}^2 = -\frac{1}{m}\frac{\partial V}{\partial y} \tag{3}$$

Writing $x = x_0$, $y = 0$ as steady motion values of x and y, we set $x = x_0 + s$, $y = y$. Inserting in V, regarding s and y as small quantities, expanding and retaining first and second order terms, we get

$$V_{\text{approx.}} = \frac{1}{2}k\left[s^2 + 2s(x_0 - l_0) + y^2\left(\frac{x_0 - l_0}{x_0}\right)\right] \tag{4}$$

Hence equations (3) may be written as

$$\ddot{s} - 2\dot{\theta}\dot{y} - (x_0 + r + s)\dot{\theta}^2 + \frac{k}{m}(s + x_0 - l_0) = 0 \qquad \ddot{y} + 2\dot{\theta}\dot{s} - y\dot{\theta}^2 + \frac{k}{m}y\left(\frac{x_0 - l_0}{x_0}\right) = 0 \tag{5}$$

But for steady motion, $\ddot{s} = \dot{s} = s = \ddot{y} = \dot{y} = 0$. Thus $m(x_0 + r)\dot{\theta}^2 = k(x_0 - l_0)$ and $y = 0$, which are obvious from elementary considerations.

Hence final desired equations are

$$\ddot{s} - 2\dot{\theta}\dot{y} + \left(\frac{k}{m} - \dot{\theta}^2\right)s = 0 \qquad \ddot{y} + 2\dot{\theta}\dot{s} + \left(\frac{k}{m}\left(\frac{x_0 - l_0}{x_0}\right) - \dot{\theta}^2\right)y = 0 \tag{6}$$

These equations have the same form as (3) in Example 11.5 and may be solved in the same way or merely by assuming solutions $s = A\cos(\omega t + \phi)$, $y = B\sin(\omega t + \phi)$. (See Problem 11.16.)

It is interesting to note that the left sides of equations (3) can be obtained at once from equations (9.6), Page 179.

11.10 When the System Is Acted Upon by Dissipative Forces.

Consider again the system shown in Fig. 11-6. Assuming forces due to the springs only, there are two non-ignorable coordinates (θ, r) and two ignorable (ψ, ϕ). But suppose there is a frictional and/or viscous drag at each of the four bearings. It is obvious that, regardless of what the initial motion of the system may be, all motion eventually stops. It is seen that p_ψ and p_ϕ are no longer constant, and hence steady motion as defined and treated above does not exist. (Of course, equations of motion corresponding to each of the four coordinates can easily be found, but they are not of the type previously considered.)

However, let us assume no damping at bearing B or between D and the collar s but that there is a viscous drag on the hinge a and a viscous force between collar s and the rod ab. This means that there are now generalized viscous forces $F_\theta = -b_1\dot{\theta}$, $F_r = -b_2\dot{r}$ corresponding to θ and r respectively, but no forces corresponding to ψ and ϕ.

Hence L for the system is still given by *(1)*, Example 11.6, Page 244. $p_\phi = c_1$ and $p_\psi = c_2$ as before. Thus R can be written as in *(4)*, and equations of motion are given by

$$\frac{d}{dt}\left(\frac{\partial R}{\partial \dot{\theta}}\right) - \frac{\partial R}{\partial \theta} = -b_1\dot{\theta}, \qquad \frac{d}{dt}\left(\frac{\partial R}{\partial \dot{r}}\right) - \frac{\partial R}{\partial r} = -b_2\dot{r}$$

Steady motion conditions are just those given by *(4)*, *(5)*. Hence the procedure from this point on is exactly as suggested in the above example. The final equations of motion may be integrated in the usual way and, for b_1 and b_2 not too large, lead to damped oscillations about steady motion.

Certain rather general conclusions may be drawn from the above example. If generalized forces are zero for each of the $\mathcal{J}_{k+1}, \mathcal{J}_{k+2}, \ldots, \mathcal{J}_n$ ignorable coordinates, then $\partial L/\partial \dot{\mathcal{J}}_i = p_i = c_i$ and R can be written as usual (see Section 11.5).

Now assuming viscous forces corresponding to the non-ignorable coordinates, we write a power function $P = P(\dot{s}_1, \dot{s}_2, \ldots, \dot{s}_k)$. Hence final equations of motion about steady motion may be obtained exactly as outlined in Section 11.5 where the right hand side of each is set equal to $\partial P/\partial \dot{s}_r$. They may be solved by usual methods.

11.11 Stability of Steady Motion.

If, when steady motion is slightly disturbed, the particles or parts of the system never depart widely from their steady motion paths but merely oscillate about them or, on account of damping, slowly return to them, the motion is said to be stable. On the other hand, if a slight disturbance causes a wide departure from steady motion, the system is said to be unstable.

A general solution of *(11.13)* may be written as $s_1 = A_1e^{\lambda_1 t} + A_2e^{\lambda_2 t} + \cdots + A_6e_6^{\lambda_6 t}$, etc. for s_2, s_3. As shown below stability depends on the nature of the λ's (the roots of D, equation *(11.14)*). In general the roots have the form $\lambda_1 = \mu_1 + i\omega_1$, $\lambda_2 = \mu_1 - i\omega_1$, etc., with the μ's and ω's real. However, the μ's may be positive, zero, or negative. Moreover, it may be that the ω's $= 0$ and thus the roots are real. Hence we note that:

(*a*) If the μ's are all negative and ω's $\neq 0$, the motion is damped simple harmonic. If the λ's are entirely real and negative, the disturbed system gradually settles back to steady motion. In either case it is stable.

(*b*) If the μ's are positive with ω's $\neq 0$, or if the λ's are entirely real and positive, the displacements increase exponentially with time, at least insofar as our approximate equations of motion are valid. Hence in this sense the motion is unstable.

Thus when roots of D have been determined (by the Graeffe or other methods) the condition of stability is immediately known.

For further details regarding this subject about which much has been written, see:

E. J. Routh, *Advanced Rigid Dynamics,* vol. 2, 6th ed., Macmillan, 1930, pages 78, 80.

Horace Lamb, *Higher Mechanics,* 2nd ed., Cambridge University Press, 1943, page 250.

E. H. Smart, *Advanced Dynamics,* vol. 2, Macmillan, 1951, pages 403, 404.

L. A. Pars, *Analytical Dynamics,* John Wiley and Sons, 1965, pages 143-145.

C. E. Easthope, *Three Dimensional Dynamics,* 2nd ed., Butterworth and Co., 1964, page 377.

Problems

11.1. Referring to Example 11.1, Page 239, show that on writing $\theta = \theta_0 + \alpha$, expanding in (*3*) and retaining second order terms, we obtain

$$R_{\text{approx.}} = \frac{1}{2}mr^2\dot{\alpha}^2 - \frac{1}{2}\left[\frac{c_0^2}{mr^2}\left(\frac{1+2\cos^2\theta_0}{\sin^4\theta_0}\right) + mgr\cos\theta_0\right]\alpha^2$$

from which (*7*) follows at once. Why not retain first order terms in the expansion?

11.2. Referring to Example 11.2, Page 240, show that on writing $\theta = \theta_0 + \alpha$, expanding in (*3*) and retaining second order terms, we get

$$R_{\text{approx.}} = \frac{1}{2}I_x\dot{\alpha}^2 - \frac{1}{2}I_x\alpha^2\left[\dot{\psi}_0^2\sin^2\theta_0 + \left(\dot{\psi}_0\cos\theta_0 - \frac{Mgr}{I_x\dot{\psi}_0}\right)^2\right]$$

from which (*6*) follows at once.

11.3. Referring to Example 11.3, Page 241, write $r = r_0 + s$, $\theta = \theta_0 + \alpha$, expand terms in (*4*), and obtain $R_{\text{approx.}}$ from which equations (*7*) can be obtained directly.

11.4. Referring to Example 11.5, Page 243, verify equations (*3*).

11.5. Consider that the arrangement shown in Fig. 11-7, Page 246, is so altered that θ remains constant (all other angles still variable). (*a*) Show how this can be accomplished. (*b*) Prove that in this case the system has three ignorable and no non-ignorable coordinates.

11.6. (*a*) Referring to Fig. 11-10 below, show that for steady motion,

$$(l + r\sin\theta_0)\dot{\psi}_0^2\cos\theta_0 = g\sin\theta_0$$

Assuming the motion of m confined to the *abd* plane, and writing $\theta = \theta_0 + \alpha$, show that

$$R_{\text{approx.}} = \frac{1}{2}mr^2\dot{\alpha}^2 - \frac{1}{2}mrc^2\left[\frac{4mr(l+r\sin\theta_0)^2\cos^2\theta_0}{(I+m(l+r\sin\theta_0)^2)^3} + \frac{l\sin\theta_0 + r(\sin^2\theta_0 - \cos^2\theta_0)}{(I+m(l+r\sin\theta_0)^2)^2}\right]\alpha^2 + [mgr\cos\theta_0]\alpha^2$$

where $c = \partial L/\partial\dot{\psi}$. Write out the equation of motion and find the period of oscillation for the following values: $r = 50$ cm, $m = 300$ grams, $l = 20$ cm, $I = 2\times10^4$ grams $\times$ cm^2, $\theta_0 = 45°$.

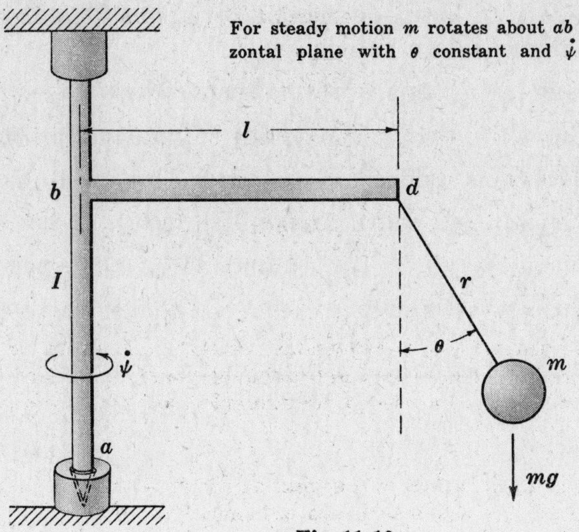

Fig. 11-10

(b) Show that the equation of motion obtained from $R_{\text{approx.}}$ above can also be found by approximating the exact equation of motion (found by either Method A or B) and retaining only first order terms.

(c) Assuming that ab is driven at a constant speed, $\dot{\psi} = \omega =$ constant, find the period of oscillation of the pendulum about its steady motion position.

11.7. The supporting string in Fig. 11-1, Page 234, is replaced by a coil spring of constant k and unstretched length l_0. Writing $\theta = \theta_0 + \alpha$, $r = r_0 + s$, determine $R_{\text{approx.}}$ and show that equations of motion about steady motion values are

$$mr_0^2\ddot{\alpha} + \left[\frac{c^2(3\cos^2\theta_0 + \sin^2\theta_0)}{r_0^2 m \sin^4\theta_0} + mgr_0\cos\theta_0\right]\alpha + \left[\frac{2c^2\cos\theta_0}{mr_0^3\sin^3\theta_0} + mg\sin\theta_0\right]s = 0$$

$$m\ddot{s} + \left[\frac{3c^2}{mr_0^4\sin^2\theta_0} + k\right]s + \left(\frac{2c^2\cos\theta_0}{mr_0^3\sin^3\theta_0} + mg\sin\theta_0\right)\alpha = 0$$

where $\partial L/\partial\dot{\psi} = p_\psi = c$ and where r_0 and θ_0 must satisfy the relations

$$r_0\dot{\psi}_0^2\cos\theta_0 = g, \qquad mr_0\dot{\psi}_0^2\sin^2\theta_0 + mg\cos\theta_0 = k(r_0 - l_0)$$

11.8. The mass m_1, Fig. 11-11, moves on a smooth horizontal plane. m_2 moves vertically under the force of gravity and the spring. Taking polar coordinates r, θ for m_1 and l for m_2, show that

$$L = \tfrac{1}{2}m_1(\dot{r}^2 + r^2\dot{\theta}^2) + \tfrac{1}{2}m_2\dot{l}^2 + m_2gl - \tfrac{1}{2}k(l + r - b)^2$$

where b is the total length of string plus the unstretched length of the spring. Show that for steady motion

$$m_1r_0\dot{\theta}_0^2 = m_2g \quad \text{and} \quad m_2g = k(l_0 + r_0 - b)$$

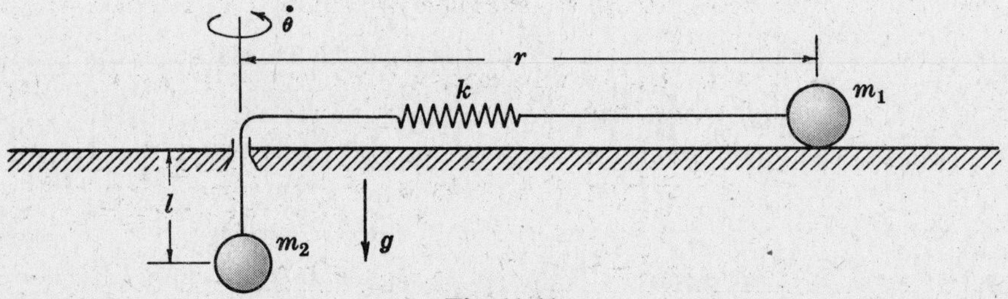

Fig. 11-11

Writing $r = r_0 + s_1$, $l = l_0 + s_2$, determine $R_{\text{approx.}}$ and show that

$$m_1\ddot{s}_1 + \left(\frac{3m_2 g}{r_0} + k\right)s_1 + ks_2 = 0$$

$$ks_1 + m_2\ddot{s}_2 + ks_2 = 0$$

and that ω_1, ω_2 are given by

$$\omega^2 = \frac{1}{2}\left(\frac{k}{\mu} + a \pm \sqrt{\left(\frac{k}{\mu} + a\right)^2 - \frac{4ka}{m_2}}\right)$$

where $\mu = \dfrac{m_1 m_2}{m_1 + m_2}$, $a = \dfrac{3m_2 g}{m_1 r_0}$.

Taking $m_1 = 300$ grams, $m_2 = 400$ grams, $k = 10^5$ dynes/cm, $b = 60$ cm, $g = 980$ cm/sec^2 and assuming $r_0 = 30$ cm, show that approximate values of ω are $\omega_1 = 25.9$, $\omega_2 = 7.1$. Note that the motion is stable and composed of two simple harmonic oscillations.

11.9. The two masses, Fig. 11-12, attached to a spring as shown are free to slide in the smooth horizontal tube. The shaft ab, with tube attached, has a moment of inertia I. r_1 = distance from c.m. of m_1 and m_2 to center of shaft. r_2 = distance between m_1 and m_2.

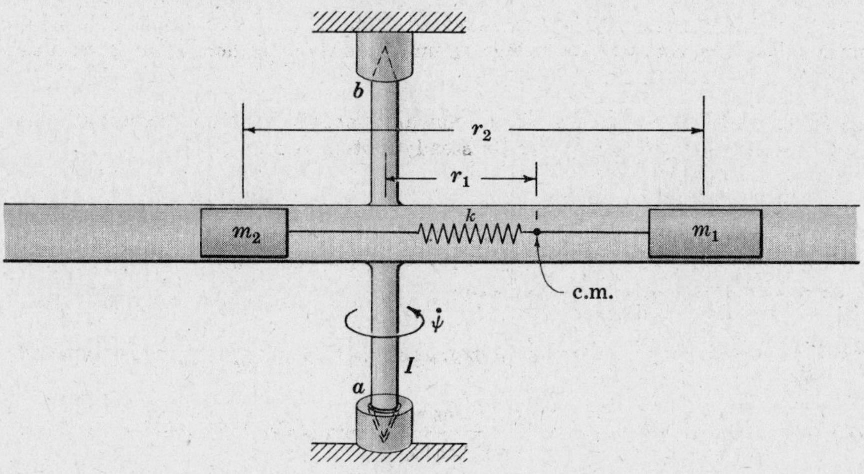

Fig. 11-12

Show that for steady motion, c.m. must be on the axis of rotation; that is, $r_1 = 0$.

Writing $r_1 = r' + s_1$, $r_2 = r_0 + s_2$, show that for slightly disturbed steady motion,

$$\ddot{s}_1 - \frac{k}{\mu r_0}(r_0 - l_0)s_1 = 0$$

$$\ddot{s}_2 + \frac{k(r_0 - l_0)}{\mu r_0}\left(\frac{3\mu r_0^2 - I}{\mu r_0^2 + I}\right)s_2 + \frac{k}{\mu}s_2 = 0$$

where $\mu = \dfrac{m_1 m_2}{m_1 + m_2}$. Is the motion stable? Discuss. ($l_0 = r_2$ for spring unstretched.)

11.10. Referring to Fig. 11-13 below, write R, determine the steady motion values of $r_1, r_2, \dot{\phi}$ and check results by elementary principles.

Assuming steady motion slightly disturbed, writing $r_1 = l_1 + s_1$, $r_2 = l_2 + s_2$, show that approximate equations of motion are

$$m_1\ddot{s}_1 + \left[\frac{m_1 c^2(3m_1 l_1^2 - m_2 l_2^2 - I)}{(I + m_1 l_1^2 + m_2 l_2^2)^3} + k_1 + k_2\right]s_1 + \left[\frac{4c^2 m_1 m_2 l_1 l_2}{(I + m_1 l_1^2 + m_2 l_2^2)^3} - k_2\right]s_2 = 0$$

$$m_2\ddot{s}_2 + \left[\frac{m_2 c^2(3m_2 l_2^2 - m_1 l_1^2 - I)}{(I + m_1 l_1^2 + m_2 l_2^2)^3} + k_2\right]s_2 + \left[\frac{4c^2 m_1 m_2 l_1 l_2}{(I + m_1 l_1^2 + m_2 l_2^2)^3} - k_2\right]s_1 = 0$$

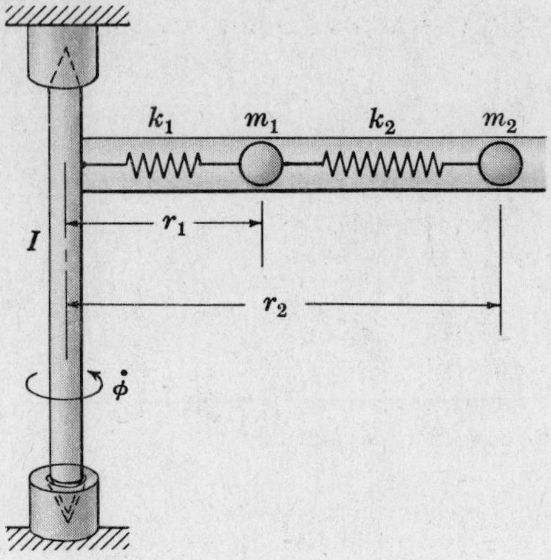

Particles m_1 and m_2 connected with springs in a smooth horizontal rotating tube.

Fig. 11-13

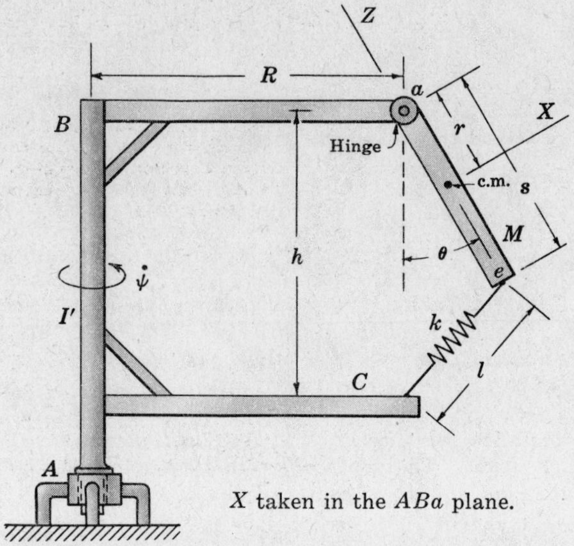

X taken in the ABa plane.

Fig. 11-14

11.11. The frame BC, Fig. 11-14, is free to rotate about the vertical axis AB. The bar ae, hinged at a can rotate through angle θ in the plane of the frame. Take body-fixed axes X, Y, Z with origin at c.m. of the bar. I_x, I_y, I_z are principal axes of inertia about X, Y, Z respectively and $I_x = I_y$. Writing $I_1 = Mr^2 + I_y$, $I_2 = I' + I_x$, show that

$$L = \tfrac{1}{2}I_1\dot{\theta}^2 + \tfrac{1}{2}[I_2 + M(R + r\sin\theta)^2]\dot{\psi}^2 + Mgr\cos\theta - \tfrac{1}{2}k(\sqrt{b - d\cos\theta} - l_0)^2$$

where $b = h^2 + s^2$, $d = 2sh$ and l_0 is the value of l when the spring is unstretched.

Now writing $\theta = \theta_0 + \alpha$, show that (retaining first and second order terms in the expansion)

$$\begin{aligned} R_{\text{approx.}} = \; & \tfrac{1}{2}I_1\dot{\alpha}^2 - \Big\{Mgr\sin\theta_0 + \tfrac{1}{2}kd\sin\theta_0\,[1 - l_0(b - d\sin\theta_0)^{-1/2}] \\ & \qquad - \left(\frac{Mrc^2(R + r\sin\theta_0)\cos\theta_0}{[I_2 + M(R + r\sin\theta_0)^2]^2}\right)\Big\}\,\alpha \\ & - \tfrac{1}{2}\Big\{Mgr\cos\theta_0 + \tfrac{1}{2}kd\cos\theta_0 - \tfrac{1}{2}kl_0d\cos\theta_0\,(b - d\cos\theta_0)^{-1/2} \\ & + \tfrac{1}{4}kl_0d^2\sin^2\theta_0\,(b - d\cos\theta_0)^{-3/2} \\ & + 2Mrc^2[2Mr(R + r\sin\theta_0)^2\cos^2\theta_0\,(I_2 + M(R + r\sin\theta_0)^2)^{-3}] \\ & - [r\cos^2\theta_0 - \sin\theta_0\,(R + r\sin\theta_0)][I_2 + M(R + r\sin\theta)^2]^{-2}\Big\}\,\alpha^2 \end{aligned}$$

Determine the condition for steady motion. Show that when steady motion is disturbed the bar oscillates with simple harmonic motion about the θ_0 position. Find an expression for the period.

The above is a good example of how "simple" problems may become surprisingly involved.

11.12. Employing θ, ϕ_1, ϕ_2 in Fig. 11-15, write L for the system and show that none of these coordinates is ignorable. However, using θ, β_1, β_2, where $\beta_1 = \phi_1 - \theta$, $\beta_2 = \phi_2 - \theta$, show that

$$\begin{aligned} L = \; & \tfrac{1}{2}I\dot{\theta}^2 + \tfrac{1}{2}m_1[s^2\dot{\theta}^2 + r_1^2(\dot{\beta}_1 + \dot{\theta})^2 + 2sr_1\dot{\theta}(\dot{\beta}_1 + \dot{\theta})\cos\beta_1] \\ & + \tfrac{1}{2}m_2[s^2\dot{\theta}^2 + r_1^2(\dot{\beta}_1 + \dot{\theta})^2 + r_2^2(\dot{\beta}_2 + \dot{\theta})^2 + 2sr_1\dot{\theta}(\dot{\beta}_1 + \dot{\theta})\cos\beta_1 \\ & + 2sr_2\dot{\theta}(\dot{\beta}_2 + \dot{\theta})\cos\beta_2 + 2r_1r_2(\dot{\beta}_1 + \dot{\theta})(\dot{\beta}_2 + \dot{\theta})\cos(\beta_2 - \beta_1)] \end{aligned}$$

and hence that θ is now ignorable, β_1, β_2 non-ignorable. (r_1 and r_2 are constants.)

Prove that for steady motion $\beta_1 = \beta_2 = 0$ and that this is possible for any value of $\dot{\theta}$.

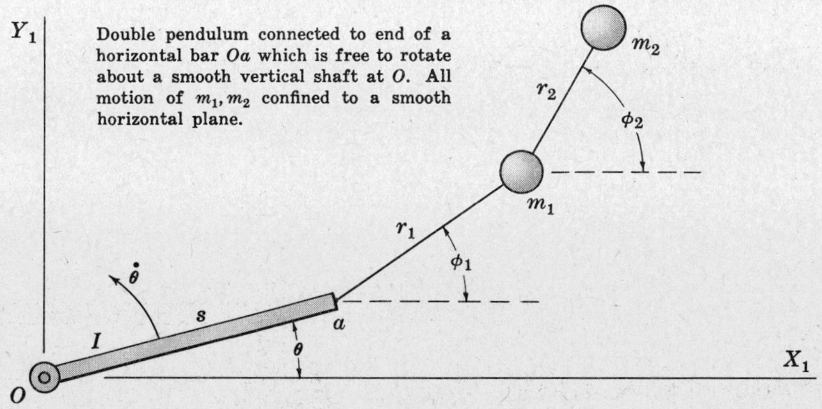

Fig. 11-15

11.13. Referring to Example 11.7 and Fig. 11-7, Page 246, derive the given expression for L. See Problem 8.24, Page 174.

Show that (dropping certain constant terms),

$$R = \frac{1}{2}I_x\dot{\theta}^2 - \frac{1}{2}\frac{(c_3 - c_2 \cos\theta)^2}{I_x \sin^2\theta} \qquad \text{where} \quad c_2 = \frac{\partial L}{\partial \dot{\phi}}, \; c_3 = \frac{\partial L}{\partial \dot{\psi}}$$

Writing $\theta = \theta_0 + \alpha$, show that the equation of motion is

$$I_x\ddot{\alpha} + \frac{1}{I_x}\left\{c_2^2 + \frac{(c_3 - c_2\cos\theta_0)}{\sin^4\theta_0}[c_3(1 + 2\cos^2\theta_0) - c_2(3 + \sin^2\theta_0)\cos\theta_0]\right\}\alpha = 0$$

11.14. The uniform disk, Fig. 11-16, is free to rotate on the smooth collar as a bearing. The collar, attached to the spring as shown, is free to slide along the light, smooth rod. Gravity is acting along Y_1 as indicated. r measures the distance from the ball joint O to c.m. of the disk. All angles are measured exactly as in Example 11.5, Page 243. Applying (*11.11*), Page 238, show that equa-

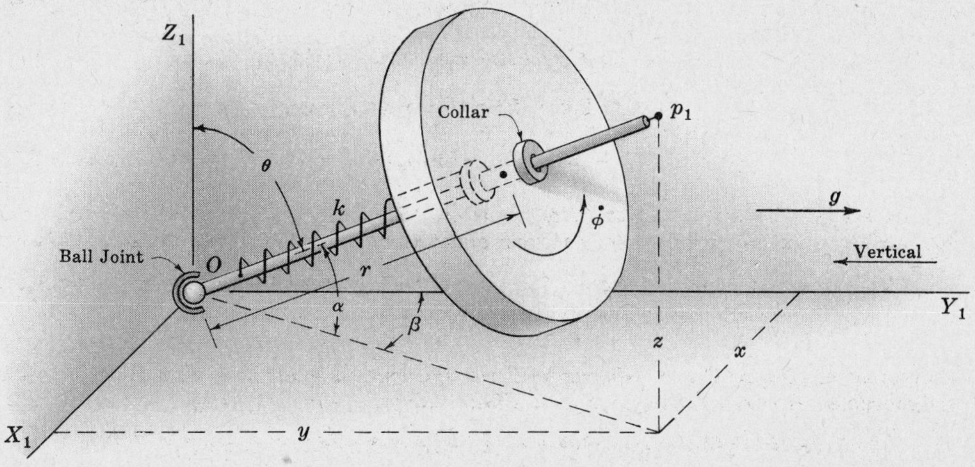

Fig. 11-16

tions of motion in α, β, s are $(I_x + mr_0^2)\ddot{\alpha} + c\dot{\beta} + mgr_0\alpha = 0$, $(I_x + mr_0^2)\ddot{\beta} - c\dot{\alpha} + mgr_0\beta = 0$, $m\ddot{s} + ks = 0$, where $r = r_0 + s$.

11.15. Referring to Fig. 11-17, write $r_1 = r_{10} + s_1$, etc., and show that the equations of motion about positions of steady motion are

$$m_1\ddot{s}_1 + (k_1 + m_1A\dot{\psi}_0^2)s_1 + m_1\ddot{s}_2 + m_1B\dot{\psi}_0^2 s_2 = 0, \qquad m_3\ddot{s}_3 + k_2 s_3 = 0,$$

$$(m_1 + m_2)\ddot{s}_2 + (k_2 + C\dot{\psi}_0^2)s_2 + m_1\ddot{s}_1 + m_1B\dot{\psi}_0^2 s_1 + k_2 s_3 = 0$$

where A, B, C = constants. Is the motion stable?

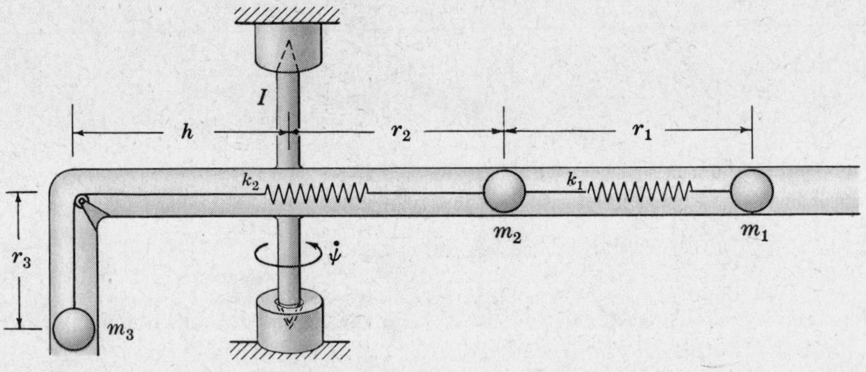

Fig. 11-17

11.16. Referring to Example 11.10, Page 247, take $m = 100$ grams, $l_0 = 25$ cm, $k = 4 \times 10^4$ dynes/cm, $r = 20$ cm, $\dot{\theta} = 10$ radians/sec. Show that $x_0 = 40$ cm, $\omega_1 = 27.0$, $\omega_2 = 4.58$. Write final integrated equations of motion.

11.17. Assuming that m, Fig. 11-9, Page 247, carries a concentrated charge Q (not affected by the table) and that there is a uniform magnetic field normal to the table, show that (for the table stationary) the equations of motion have the same form as *(6)* in Example 11.10.

11.18. The vertical shaft in Fig. 11-13, Page 252, is driven by a motor at a constant speed $\dot{\phi}$. Find equations of motion of m_1 and m_2 about steady motion positions. Compare results with equations of motion found in Problem 11.10.

11.19. The bead of mass m, Fig. 11-18 below, can slide along the smooth, rigid cylindrical helix of pitch p which is attached to the frame as shown. The frame can rotate about the vertical axis AB. Moment of inertia of the entire frame, including the helix, about AB is I. Taking θ and ϕ as coordinates, show that

$$L = \tfrac{1}{2}I\dot{\theta}^2 + \tfrac{1}{2}m[l^2\dot{\theta}^2 + r^2(\dot{\theta} + \dot{\phi})^2 + b^2\dot{\phi}^2 + 2lr\dot{\theta}(\dot{\theta} + \dot{\phi})\sin\phi] - mgb\phi$$

where r = constant and $b = p/2\pi$. Show that for steady motion, $\cos\phi_0 = \dfrac{gp}{2\pi r l\dot{\theta}_0^2}$.

Assuming that AB is driven at a constant speed, $\dot{\theta} = \omega$ = constant, and writing $\phi = \phi_0 + \alpha$, show that the equation of motion of the bead about its steady motion position is $\ddot{\alpha} + \left(\dfrac{rl\omega^2 \sin\phi_0}{r^2 + b^2}\right)\alpha = 0$. What is the period of oscillation?

Now assuming the frame is free to rotate, note that θ is ignorable. Show that

$$[I + m(l^2 + r^2 + 2lr\sin\phi)]\dot{\theta} + m(r^2 + lr\sin\phi)\dot{\phi} = p_\theta = c$$

and that the equation of motion corresponding to ϕ is

$$(r^2 + rl\sin\phi)\ddot{\theta} + (r^2 + b^2)\ddot{\phi} - rl\dot{\theta}^2\cos\phi + gb = 0$$

Complete the Routhian $R = L - c\dot{\theta}$.

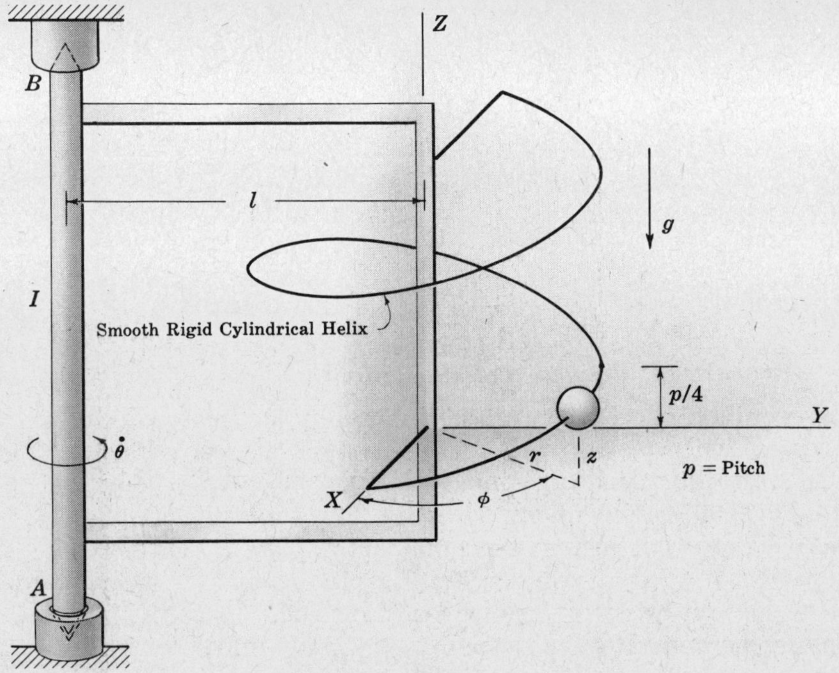

Fig. 11-18

11.20. In Fig. 11-19 the X, Y axes are attached to a horizontal table which rotates with constant angular velocity $\dot{\theta} = \omega$ about a vertical axis through 0. The particles, attached to equal springs as shown, can move about on the smooth table. With m_1 at p_1, etc., the springs are unstretched; that is, $Op_1 = p_1p_2 = p_2p_3 = p_3p_4 = l =$ unstretched length of each spring.

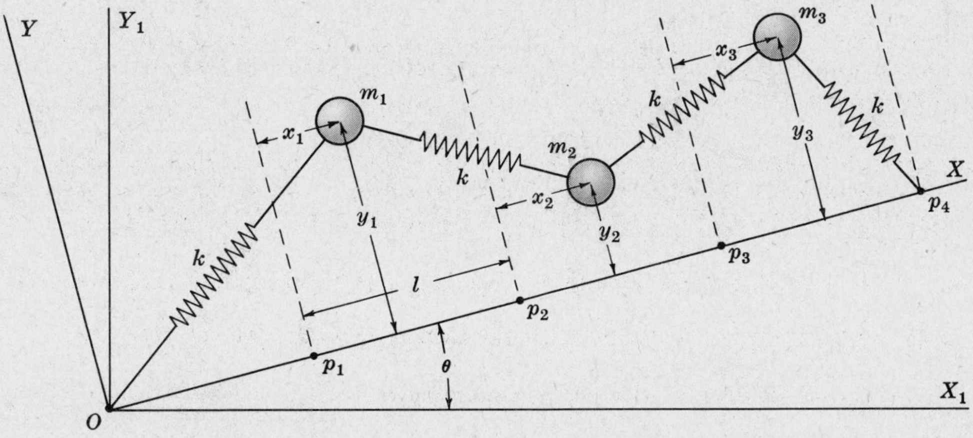

Fig. 11-19

Take x_1, y_1 as coordinates of m_1, etc. For steady motion $x_1 = x_{10}$, etc., and $y_1 = y_2 = y_3 = 0$. For small motion about steady motion positions, write $x_1 = x_{10} + s_1$, $x_2 = x_{20} + s_2$, $x_3 = x_{30} + s_3$, $y_1 = s_4$, $y_2 = s_5$, $y_3 = s_6$.

Assuming steady motion slightly disturbed, set up equations of motion for the system. *Hint.* Rather than write out T and apply Lagrange's equations, it is convenient to use equations *(9.6)*, Page 179, for a determination of the accelerations of m_1, m_2, m_3.

CHAPTER

12 Forces of Constraint

Newtonian, Lagrangian, and Euler Methods

12.1 Preliminary Considerations.

A. *Forces of constraint defined and illustrated.*

Forces which are exerted on the parts of a dynamical system by physical constraints and which do no work for arbitrary displacements $\delta q_1, \delta q_2, \ldots, \delta q_n$ $(\delta t = 0)$ are here referred to as "forces of constraint" or merely "reactive" forces. (See footnote on Page 30.) The following are a few typical examples: the normal reactive force exerted on a particle by a smooth surface over which it is moving; forces exerted on m_1 and m_2 by the rotating tubes, Fig. 4-12, Page 75; bearing forces on a smooth shaft; the tension or compression in a rigid rod connecting two masses of a system; tensions in the non-extensible ropes of any mass-pulley system.

It must be pointed out that frictional forces, although usually determined by a force of constraint and a coefficient of friction, are not to be regarded as forces of constraint. As a result of frictional forces, work is always done when sliding takes place. Hence they must be regarded as active applied forces.

B. *Regarding the Meaning and Use of Superfluous Coordinates.*

The meaning of "superfluous coordinates" (the term was introduced in Section 2.4, Page 18) may be made clear by the following simple example. Referring to Fig. 2-9, Page 13, it is clear that, neglecting masses of the pulleys, T may be written as

$$T = \tfrac{1}{2}m_1\dot{y}_1^2 + \tfrac{1}{2}m_2\dot{y}_2^2 + \tfrac{1}{2}m_3\dot{y}_3^2 + \tfrac{1}{2}m_4\dot{y}_4^2 \qquad (1)$$

However, the system has, for vertical motion only, but two degrees of freedom. Hence (*1*) is said to contain two superfluous coordinates.

Employing the equations of constraint,

$$(2)\quad y_1 + y_3 = C_1 \qquad\qquad (3)\quad 2y_3 - y_2 - y_4 = C_2$$

and regarding, say, y_3 as superfluous, we can eliminate $\dot{y}_3$ from T, leaving it expressed in terms of $\dot{y}_1, \dot{y}_2, \dot{y}_4$, hence containing only one superfluous coordinate. Of course, as has been done in previous chapters, all superfluous coordinates can be eliminated by equations of constraint (except the rather special case of "non-holonomic" systems). In the example both $\dot{y}_3$ and $\dot{y}_4$, or just as well $\dot{y}_1, \dot{y}_2$, can be eliminated from (*1*) by (*2*) and (*3*).

In the general case, where a system contains p particles and has n degrees of freedom, T may be written so as to contain any number of superfluous coordinates, s, from one to, and including, $3p - n$.

For a system of N rigid bodies having n degrees of freedom, s may range from one to, and including, $6N - n$.

Superfluous coordinates play an important part in the determination of forces of constraint, as will immediately be evident.

C. *An Introductory Example.*

As a means of making clear certain basic ideas on which this entire treatment is founded, consider the reactive force on the bead, Fig. 12-1, as it moves along the smooth rigid parabolic wire $y = bx^2$. Assume gravity and an external force F acting.

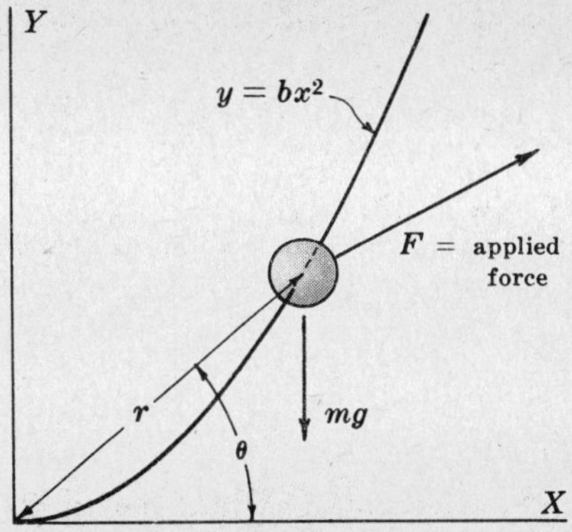

Fig. 12-1

Now regardless of the magnitude of F or its direction (both of which may vary with time), the motion takes place along the wire. In other words, the reactive force automatically and continuously adjusts itself in magnitude and direction as the bead moves so that the path is represented by $y = bx^2$. Thus in treating this problem we may take the point of view that the bead "knows" nothing about the existence of the wire and that it only "feels" the forces F, mg and the reactive force.

Hence *considering the force of constraint as an externally applied force, m may be regarded as a "free particle" having two degrees of freedom.* Therefore it is evident that either of the following two methods is applicable to finding the reactive force.

Newtonian: We write two "free particle" equations

$$(4)\quad m\ddot{x} = F_x + f_x \qquad\qquad (5)\quad m\ddot{y} = F_y + f_y - mg$$

where F_x, F_y are components of F, and f_x, f_y components of the unknown reactive force.

Now, if the motion of the bead is known either by experiment or from a solution of the following Lagrangian equation of motion (which contains no reactive force components; see Example 3.2, Page 44),

$$m\ddot{x}(1 + 4b^2x^2) + 4mb^2x\dot{x}^2 = -2mgbx + F_x + 2bxF_y \tag{6}$$

then f_x and f_y are determined as functions of time by (4) and (5).

Lagrangian: Suppose, for the sake of illustration, we represent the position of the "free particle" in polar coordinates. Thus, including one superfluous coordinate, $T = \frac{1}{2}m(\dot{r}^2 + r^2\dot{\theta}^2)$, and applying Lagrange's equations, regarding both r and θ as independent coordinates,

$$m\ddot{r} - mr\dot{\theta}^2 = f_r - mg\sin\theta + F_r \tag{7}$$

$$mr^2\ddot{\theta} + 2mr\dot{r}\dot{\theta} = rf_\theta - mgr\cos\theta + rF_\theta \tag{8}$$

where f_r, f_θ are the unknown components of the reactive force in the direction of r and increasing θ respectively. F_r, F_θ are corresponding known components of the applied force F.

Again for known motion, determined as mentioned above, f_r and f_θ are determined as functions of time by (7) and (8). From f_r and f_θ the magnitude and direction of the total reactive force can be found at once.

Note that, applying relation (4.10), Page 60, and making use of $x = r\cos\theta$, $y = r\sin\theta$ from which to determine $\frac{\partial x}{\partial r}, \frac{\partial y}{\partial r}, \frac{\partial x}{\partial \theta}, \frac{\partial y}{\partial \theta}$, equations (7) and (8), now containing f_x and f_y, may be written as

$$m\ddot{r} - mr\dot{\theta}^2 = (f_x + F_x)\cos\theta + (f_y + F_y - mg)\sin\theta \tag{9}$$

$$mr\ddot{\theta} + 2m\dot{r}\dot{\theta} = -(f_x + F_x)\sin\theta + (f_y + F_y - mg)\cos\theta \tag{10}$$

simultaneous solutions of which give expressions for f_x and f_y.

Important points regarding the above solutions:

(a) The system, in reality, has only one degree of freedom. But by introducing a superfluous coordinate and treating the reactive force as an additional applied force, it may be regarded as having two.

(b) On this basis two Newtonian equations (4), (5) or Lagrangian equations (7), (8) or (9), (10) have been written. In either set unknown components of the reactive force appear. *Either set can be solved for these components.*

(c) Expressions for the generalized forces in (7), (8) or (9), (10) were, in principle, determined exactly as outlined in Section 4.5, Page 61, where we *consider both r and θ as independently variable and the reactive force as a driving force.* For example, to find the generalized force corresponding to r, equation (7), θ is held constant and r increased to $r+\delta r$. This can only be accomplished by a slight "distortion" of the constraint. Moreover, as a result of the distortion, the reactive force does work to the extent of $f_r\,\delta r$. Hence it is seen that $\delta W_{q_r} = (F_r + f_r - mg\sin\theta)\delta r$, from which the right side of (7) is obtained.

(d) In order to find f_x, f_y or f_r, f_θ as functions of time, the motion (determined as previously mentioned) must be known.

12.2 General Procedure for Finding Forces of Constraint. (Constraints assumed smooth.)

A. *Newtonian method for a system of particles.*

Consider a system of p particles having n degrees of freedom. Regarding each particle as free, we write

$$m_i\ddot{x}_i = F_{x_i} + f_{x_i}, \qquad m_i\ddot{y}_i = F_{y_i} + f_{y_i}, \qquad m_i\ddot{z}_i = F_{z_i} + f_{z_i} \tag{12.1}$$

where $F_{x_i}, F_{y_i}, F_{z_i}$ are known components of the total applied force on m_i and $f_{x_i}, f_{y_i}, f_{z_i}$ are unknown components of the force of constraint on m_i.

Now suppose that Lagrange's equations in their usual form, containing no forces of constraint, have been solved. Or perhaps the motion of the system is known by experiment. Each of the $q_1, q_2, \ldots, q_n$ generalized coordinates is a known function of time, that is, $q_r = q_r(t)$. Hence by means of relations $x_i = x_i(q_1, q_2, \ldots, q_n; t)$, etc., and (12.1), the reactive components f_{x_i}, etc., can each be expressed as a function of time.

B. *Lagrangian Method.* (Particles and/or rigid bodies.)

Consider a system having n degrees of freedom and c constraints. (For p particles $c = 3p - n$; for N rigid bodies $c = 6N - n$.) Let us introduce s superfluous coordinates into T, where s may be any number from one to c. Thus

$$T = T(q_1, \ldots, q_{n+s};\ \dot{q}_1, \ldots, \dot{q}_{n+s};\ t) \tag{12.2}$$

Careful consideration of the derivation of equation (4.9) (at this point the reader should review Section 4.2, Page 58) will show that (as in the above example), for T containing s superfluous coordinates, $n+s$ Lagrangian equations may be written in the usual way *provided each of the n + s coordinates is treated as independently variable* and *forces of constraint, which enter wherever necessary to make a displacement δq not in conformity with constraints, are regarded as applied forces.*

For convenience we write these equations in the form

$$\frac{d}{dt}\left(\frac{\partial T}{\partial \dot{q}_r}\right) - \frac{\partial T}{\partial q_r} = F_{q_r} + \mathcal{F}_{q_r} \qquad r = 1, 2, \ldots, n+s \tag{12.3}$$

where F_{q_r} is the part of the total generalized force due to known applied forces and $\mathcal{F}_{q_r}$ that which involves only unknown forces of constraint.

Whether dealing with a system of particles or rigid bodies, expressions for F_{q_r} may be found by one of the methods outlined in Section 4.5, Page 61, introducing only applied forces and *considering each of the* $n+s$ *coordinates appearing in* T *as independently variable.* For certain coordinates this will require a "distortion of constraints", as illustrated in the example given above.

If equation (*4.10*), Page 60, is to be applied to a system of p particles, $\dfrac{\partial x_i}{\partial q_r}, \dfrac{\partial y_i}{\partial q_r}, \dfrac{\partial z_i}{\partial q_r}$ must be found from the following transformation equations

$$\begin{aligned} x_i &= x_i(q_1, q_2, \ldots, q_{n+s};\ t) \\ y_i &= y_i(q_1, q_2, \ldots, q_{n+s};\ t) \\ z_i &= z_i(q_1, q_2, \ldots, q_{n+s};\ t) \end{aligned} \tag{12.4}$$

which contain, not only $q_1, q_2, \ldots, q_n$, but also the s superfluous coordinates.

Expressions for $\mathcal{F}_{q_r}$ are found in just the same way as those for F_{q_r}, regarding each of the $n+s$ coordinates as independently variable and introducing proper components of the reactive forces as unknown quantities.

As previously mentioned, any number of superfluous coordinates up to a maximum of c may be retained in T. For example, considering a system of two particles for which $n=2$ we can, making use of equations of constraint, write T in any number of coordinates from two ($s=0$) to six ($s=4$). In the determination of $\mathcal{F}_{q_r}$ we always, in principle, find the work δW_{q_r} done by forces of constraint for a change of $+\delta q_r$ in q_r, all other coordinates and t held fixed. Hence it is clear that reactive forces will appear in δW_{q_r} (and hence in $\mathcal{F}_{q_r}$) *only when, on making the displacement* $+\delta q_r$, *one or more constraints are distorted.* Thus, for s less than c, in general, not all forces of constraint acting on the system will appear in the $n+s$ equations, (*12.3*). ("Distort" refers to an infinitesimal deformation.)

As a final step equations (*12.3*) are solved for the reactive forces which appear in the $\mathcal{F}_{q_r}$'s. Assuming the motion known, these forces may be expressed as functions of time.

As examples will show, the most suitable choice of superfluous coordinates and the number to be retained in T depends on the problem in hand. It may frequently happen that by the introduction of a single properly chosen superfluous coordinate, a desired force of constraint can be found with little effort.

12.3 Illustrative Examples.

Example 12.1.

Let us determine expressions for the components of reactive force exerted on the bead, Fig. 12-2, as it moves along the smooth spiral wire under the action of external forces F and mg. In order to illustrate basic ideas, various possible solutions will be given. Motion is assumed known.

(*a*) Regarding the particle as "free" and applying (*12.1*), we have

$$\begin{aligned} m\ddot{x} &= F_x + f_x \\ m\ddot{y} &= F_y + f_y \\ m\ddot{z} &= F_z + f_z - mg \end{aligned} \tag{1}$$

F_x, F_y, F_z are known components of F and f_x, f_y, f_z are unknown components of the force of constraint. Hence for known motion these components may be expressed as functions of time.

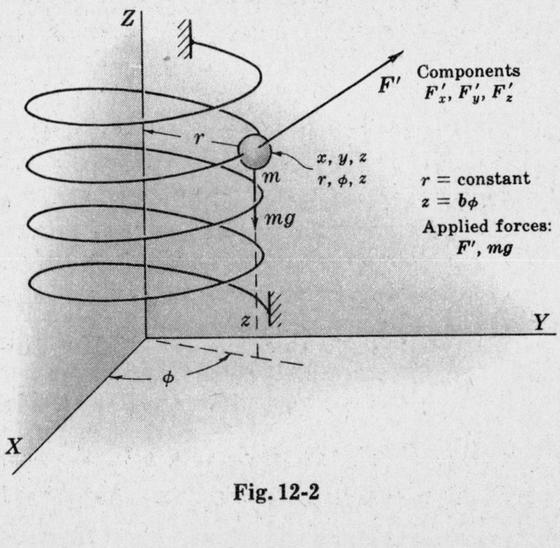

Fig. 12-2

(b) Using cylindrical coordinates, two of which are superfluous, $T = \frac{1}{2}m(\dot{r}^2 + r^2\dot{\phi}^2 + \dot{z}^2)$. Applying (12.3), we obtain

$$\begin{aligned} m\ddot{r} - mr\dot{\phi}^2 - F_x\frac{\partial x}{\partial r} - F_y\frac{\partial y}{\partial r} - F_z\frac{\partial z}{\partial r} &= f_x\frac{\partial x}{\partial r} + f_y\frac{\partial y}{\partial r} + f_z\frac{\partial z}{\partial r} \\ mr^2\ddot{\phi} + 2mr\dot{r}\dot{\phi} - F_x\frac{\partial x}{\partial \phi} - F_y\frac{\partial y}{\partial \phi} - F_z\frac{\partial z}{\partial \phi} &= f_x\frac{\partial x}{\partial \phi} + f_y\frac{\partial y}{\partial \phi} + f_z\frac{\partial z}{\partial \phi} \\ m\ddot{z} - F_x\frac{\partial x}{\partial z} - F_y\frac{\partial y}{\partial z} - (F_z - mg)\frac{\partial z}{\partial z} &= f_x\frac{\partial x}{\partial z} + f_y\frac{\partial y}{\partial z} + f_z\frac{\partial z}{\partial z} \end{aligned} \qquad (2)$$

Relations (12.4) are $x = r\cos\phi$, $y = r\sin\phi$; and equations of constraint are $r - \text{constant} = 0$, $z - b\phi = 0$. Applying the above to (2),

$$\begin{aligned} -mr\dot{\phi}^2 - F_x\cos\phi - F_y\sin\phi &= f_x\cos\phi + f_y\sin\phi \\ mr^2\ddot{\phi} + F_x r\sin\phi - F_y r\cos\phi - F_z b &= -f_x r\sin\phi + f_y r\cos\phi + f_z b \\ m\ddot{z} - F_z + mg &= f_z \end{aligned} \qquad (3)$$

which, of course, can be solved for f_x, f_y, f_z.

(c) Again using cylindrical coordinates but introducing F_r, F_ϕ, F_z, (the r, ϕ, z components of F) and f_r, f_ϕ, f_z (the corresponding components of the reactive force), equation (12.3) gives

$$m\ddot{r} - mr\dot{\phi}^2 - F_r = f_r, \qquad mr^2\ddot{\phi} + 2mr\dot{r}\dot{\phi} - rF_\phi = rf_\phi, \qquad m\ddot{z} - F_z + mg = f_z$$

Hence using $r = \text{constant}$, $z = b\phi$, the components f_r, f_ϕ, f_z are known at once.

Note that the above example illustrates well the meaning and necessity of "distorting constraints". In order to obtain the generalized force corresponding to r, for example, in either (b) or (c), basically we hold ϕ and z constant and imagine r increased to $r + \delta r$. But clearly this requires a slight distortion of the wire in the direction of r. Similar remarks may be made regarding generalized forces corresponding to ϕ and z.

(d) Eliminating z and writing T in terms of $r, \dot{r}, \dot{\phi}$ (that is, retaining only one superfluous coordinate), it easily follows that

$$\begin{aligned} -mr\dot{\phi}^2 &= F_r + f_r \\ m(r^2 + b^2)\ddot{\phi} &= (F_z + f_z - mg)b + (F_\phi + f_\phi)r \end{aligned}$$

from which f_r may be obtained, but not separate values of f_z and f_ϕ.

Example 12.2.

Refer to Fig. 2-10, Page 14 and equation (2.42), Page 24. Let us consider various approaches to determine the tensions in the strings of the double pendulum, assuming r_1 and r_2 are inextensible strings.

(a) The tension τ_1 in r_1: Regarding r_1 only as a superfluous coordinate, (2.42) reduces to

$$T = \tfrac{1}{2}m_1(\dot{r}_1^2 + r_1^2\dot{\theta}^2) + \tfrac{1}{2}m_2[\dot{r}_1^2 + r_1^2\dot{\theta}^2 + r_2^2\dot{\phi}^2 + 2r_1r_2\dot{\theta}\dot{\phi}\cos(\phi - \theta) - 2r_2\dot{r}_1\dot{\phi}\sin(\phi - \theta)] \qquad (1)$$

from which, after putting $\dot{r}_1 = \ddot{r}_2 = 0$, we get

$$m_2r_2\ddot{\phi}\sin(\phi - \theta) + m_2r_2\dot{\phi}^2\cos(\phi - \theta) + (m_1 + m_2)r_1\dot{\theta}^2 = \tau_1 - (m_1 + m_2)g\cos\theta \qquad (2)$$

which, for known motion, gives τ_1 as a function of time. The reader may show that equations corresponding to θ and ϕ will not contain τ_1.

(b) In like manner, introducing r_2 as a superfluous coordinate ($r_1 = \text{constant}$), τ_2, the tension in r_2, can be found at once.

Note. For "small motion", equations of motion of the double pendulum are easily integrated. Hence τ_1 and τ_2 can easily be expressed as functions of time.

(c) As a variation of the above method, one can introduce both r_1 and r_2 simultaneously as superfluous coordinates and write two equations in accord with (12.3) from which expressions for τ_1, τ_2 may be found. The reader should verify this statement.

(d) One can obviously find τ_1 and τ_2 by an application of (12.1):

$$m_1\ddot{x}_1 = f_{x_1}, \qquad m_1\ddot{y}_1 = f_{y_1} - m_1g, \qquad m_2\ddot{x}_2 = f_{x_2}, \qquad m_2\ddot{y}_2 = f_{y_2} - m_2g \qquad (3)$$

where $f_{x_1} = \tau_2\sin\phi - \tau_1\sin\theta$.

Example 12.3.

The rigid pendulum, Fig. 12-3, is free to swing in a vertical plane about a smooth bearing at p. We shall determine an expression for the torque F_β tending to change the angle β between r_1 and r_2.

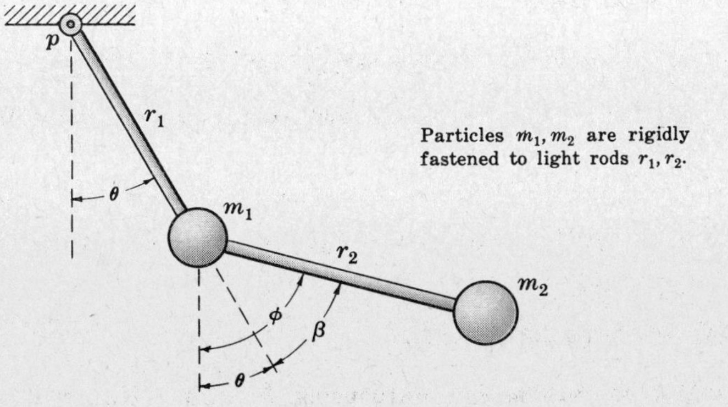

Fig. 12-3

Introducing β as a superfluous coordinate,

$$T \;=\; \tfrac{1}{2}(m_1+m_2)r_1^2\dot{\theta}^2 + \tfrac{1}{2}m_2[r_2^2(\dot{\theta}+\dot{\beta})^2 + 2r_1r_2\cos\beta(\dot{\theta}^2+\dot{\theta}\dot{\beta})]$$

from which $$F_\beta \;=\; m_2(r_2^2+r_1r_2\cos\beta)\ddot{\theta} + m_2r_1r_2\dot{\theta}^2\sin\beta + m_2gr_2\sin(\theta+\beta)$$

Although this expression appears complicated, it can be verified by elementary considerations.

Example 12.4.

Referring to Problem 2.20, Fig. 2-29, Page 36, we shall determine expressions for the components of the reactive force on m and the reactive torque exerted by the wire on the vertical shaft.

Introducing two superfluous coordinates, T may be written as

$$T \;=\; \tfrac{1}{2}I\dot{\alpha}^2 + \tfrac{1}{2}m(\dot{r}^2 + r^2\dot{\theta}^2 + \dot{z}^2)$$

where α is the angular position of the shaft and θ that of m. Regarding all coordinates as independent, we write

$$I\ddot{\alpha} = \tau+\tau', \qquad m\ddot{r} - mr\dot{\theta}^2 = f_r, \qquad mr^2\ddot{\theta} + 2mr\dot{r}\dot{\theta} = rf_\theta, \qquad m\ddot{z} = f_z - mg$$

where τ represents a known torque exerted on the shaft by, say, a motor, and τ' that exerted by the wire. f_r, f_θ, f_z are components of the reactive force on m. These relations together with $z = ar^2$, $\theta = \alpha$ give f_r, f_θ, f_z as functions of t for known motion of the system.

Example 12.5.

Consider Example 9.6, Page 185. Let us determine f_b and f_b', Fig. 9-6, by the Lagrangian method. We write L as

$$L \;=\; \tfrac{1}{2}[I_x(\dot{\theta}^2 + \dot{\psi}_1^2\sin^2\theta) + I_z(\dot{\phi}+\dot{\psi}_1\cos\theta)^2] + l\sin\epsilon\sin\theta\cos\psi_1$$

where θ and say ϕ are superfluous. Writing θ, ψ_1, ϕ equations of motion in the usual way and letting $r_3\psi_1 = -r_2\phi$, $\theta = \text{constant}$, etc., we finally have

(θ equation): $$\dot{\psi}_1^2\left(\frac{r_1}{r_2r_3^2}\right)(I_zr_1^2 + I_xr_2^2) \;=\; -F_\theta \;=\; -l\frac{r_2}{r_3}\sin\epsilon\cos\psi_1 + f_br_3$$

(ψ_1 equation): $$\ddot{\psi}_1\frac{r_1^2}{r_3^2}(I_x - I_z) \;=\; +F_{\psi_1} \;=\; -l\frac{r_1}{r_3}\sin\epsilon\sin\psi_1 + f_b'r_3$$

(ϕ equation): $$\ddot{\psi}_1\left(\frac{r_1^2}{r_2r_3}\right)I_z \;=\; -F_\phi \;=\; -f_b'r_2$$

where in finding $F_\theta, F_{\psi_1}, F_\phi$, θ, ψ_1, ϕ were regarded as independent variables.

The last two equations give the equation of motion (same as (*10*), Page 187). Assuming this integrated, we then have f_b' and f_b as functions of time.

Example 12.6.

In Fig. 12-4, the rigid body is free to rotate with angular velocity $\dot\theta_2$ about bc. At the same time the entire rigid rod abc can rotate with angular velocity $\dot\theta_1$ about a vertical axis. We shall determine the reactive moment τ_α about a horizontal axis through b (normal to the abc plane) which prevents α from changing.

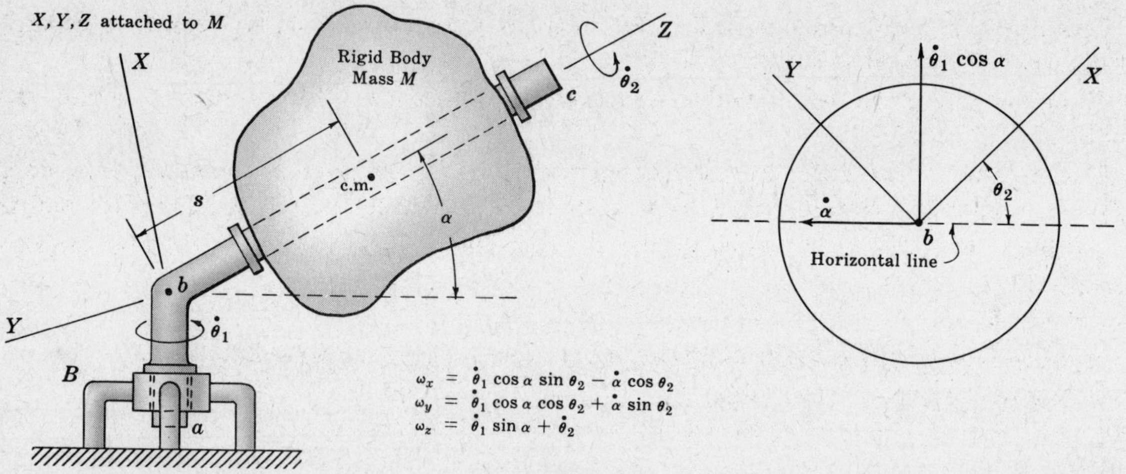

Fig. 12-4

In order to clarify the following treatment imagine ab and bc joined at b with a door-type hinge, axis of hinge normal to the abc plane. Thus, regarding α as variable, and taking body-fixed axes with origin at b, as indicated, it easily follows that

$$\omega_x = \dot\theta_1 \cos\alpha \sin\theta_2 - \dot\alpha \cos\theta_2, \qquad \omega_y = \dot\theta_1 \cos\alpha \cos\theta_2 + \dot\alpha \sin\theta_2, \qquad \omega_z = \dot\theta_1 \sin\alpha + \dot\theta_2$$

Hence, applying (*8.10*) and neglecting the mass of abc,

$$\begin{aligned} T = {} & \tfrac{1}{2}[I_x(\dot\theta_1 \cos\alpha \sin\theta_2 - \dot\alpha\cos\theta_2)^2 + I_y(\dot\theta_1\cos\alpha\cos\theta_2 + \dot\alpha\sin\theta_2)^2 + I_z(\dot\theta_1\sin\alpha + \dot\theta_2)^2 \\ & - 2I_{xy}(\dot\theta_1\cos\alpha\sin\theta_2 - \dot\alpha\cos\theta_2)(\dot\theta_1\cos\alpha\cos\theta_2 + \dot\alpha\sin\theta_2) \\ & - 2I_{xz}(\dot\theta_1\cos\alpha\sin\theta_2 - \dot\alpha\cos\theta_2)(\dot\theta_1\sin\alpha + \dot\theta_2) \\ & - 2I_{yz}(\dot\theta_1\cos\alpha\cos\theta_2 + \dot\alpha\sin\theta_2)(\dot\theta_1\sin\alpha + \dot\theta_2)] \end{aligned} \tag{1}$$

where I_x, I_{xy}, etc., are relative to the body-fixed axes. Note that we have introduced one superfluous coordinate.

Applying (*12.3*) we get for the α equation, after setting $\dot\alpha = \ddot\alpha = 0$,

$$\begin{aligned} & (I_y - I_x)\cos\alpha[\ddot\theta_1 \sin\theta_2\cos\theta_2 + \dot\theta_1\dot\theta_2(\cos^2\theta_2 - \sin^2\theta_2)] \\ & + I_x\dot\theta_1^2\sin\alpha\cos\alpha\sin^2\theta_2 + I_y\dot\theta_1^2\sin\alpha\cos\alpha\cos^2\theta_2 - I_z(\dot\theta_1\sin\alpha + \dot\theta_2)\dot\theta_1\cos\alpha \\ & + I_{xy}[\ddot\theta_1\cos\alpha(\cos^2\theta_2 - \sin^2\theta_2) - 4\dot\theta_1\dot\theta_2\cos\alpha\sin\theta_2\cos\theta_2 - 2\dot\theta_1^2\sin\alpha\cos\alpha\sin\theta_2\cos\theta_2] \\ & + I_{xz}[\ddot\theta_1\sin\alpha\cos\theta_2 + \ddot\theta_2\cos\theta_2 - 2\dot\theta_1\dot\theta_2\sin\alpha\sin\theta_2 - \dot\theta_2^2\sin\theta_2 + \dot\theta_1^2\sin\theta_2(\cos^2\alpha - \sin^2\alpha)] \\ & - I_{yz}[\ddot\theta_1\sin\alpha\sin\theta_2 + \ddot\theta_2\sin\theta_2 + 2\dot\theta_1\dot\theta_2\sin\alpha\cos\theta_2 + \dot\theta_2^2\cos\theta_2 + \dot\theta_1^2\cos\theta_2(\sin^2\alpha - \cos^2\alpha)] \\ & = \tau_\alpha - Mgs\cos\alpha \end{aligned} \tag{2}$$

which, for specified motion, gives τ_α.

If ab were driven by a motor mounted on B, and the rigid body by another light motor fastened, say, at c, would this change the right hand side of (*2*)?

Note that the above expression greatly simplifies if it is assumed that the rigid body is a uniform disk with bc normal to a face and through the center.

12.4 Forces of Constraint Using Euler's Equations.

As will be recalled from Chapter 9, Euler's equations (*9.2*), Page 177, and (*9.10*), Page 182, are essentially "free body" equations. F_x, F_y, F_z and τ_x, τ_y, τ_z in general contain all applied forces as well as forces of constraint. Hence these relations, as has already been shown in the examples of Chapter 9, may be solved for the reactive forces. Thus each is an illustration of the Euler method.

Below are listed a few examples which demonstrate well the basic principles and techniques. (The specified equations refer to those given in the pertinent examples.)

Example 9.2, Page 184. Assuming the solution of equation (*2*) to be known, equation (*1*) gives f_x and f_y each as a function of time.

Example 9.5, Page 185. For known motion, all bearing forces can be found from equations (*1*) through (*3*).

Example 9.6, Page 185. Forces of constraint f_x, f_y, f_z on the ball joint and f_b, f_b' at the point of contact *b*, are determined by equations (*9.2*) written in full and from (*6*) and (*8*).

Example 9.7, Page 187, also illustrates well the Euler method of finding forces of constraint.

Example 12.7.

Referring to Example 12.6 and Fig. 12-4, let us determine τ_α by the Euler method.

Referring to Section 9.7 and equation (*9.16*), Page 183, it is seen that

$$\tau_y \sin\theta_2 - \tau_x \cos\theta_2 = \tau_\alpha - Mgs\cos\alpha \qquad (1)$$

where

$$\tau_x = I_x\dot{\omega}_x + (I_z - I_y)\omega_y\omega_z + I_{xy}(\omega_x\omega_z - \dot{\omega}_y) - I_{xz}(\omega_x\omega_y + \dot{\omega}_z) + I_{yz}(\omega_z^2 - \omega_y^2) \qquad (2)$$

$$\tau_y = I_y\dot{\omega}_y + (I_x - I_z)\omega_x\omega_z - I_{xy}(\omega_y\omega_z + \dot{\omega}_x) + I_{xz}(\omega_x^2 - \omega_z^2) + I_{yz}(\omega_y\omega_x - \dot{\omega}_z) \qquad (3)$$

Putting in proper expressions for ω_x, $\dot{\omega}_x$, etc., (those given in Fig. 12-4), equation (*1*) finally, after considerable tedious work, becomes exactly the same as (*2*) in Example 12.6.

Example 12.8.

The rigid body, Fig. 12-5, is mounted in any manner in a rigid frame, here shown supported by, say, five points $p_1, p_2, \ldots, p_5$. Assume that outside forces F_1, F_2, F_3, etc., give the frame *any known motion.* Let us consider the reactive forces f_1, f_2, etc., exerted by the points on the body.

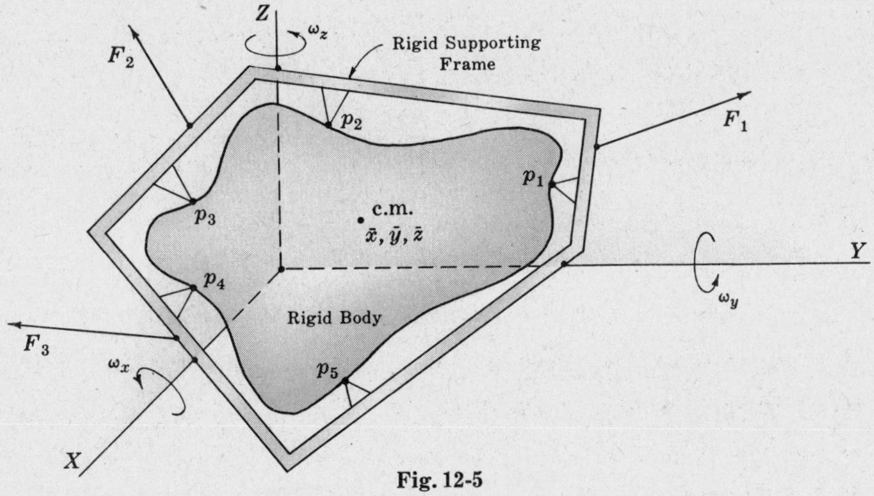

Fig. 12-5

So far as the body is concerned, these are just driving forces. From the known motion, expressions for $\omega_x, \omega_y, \omega_z$ and A_x, A_y, A_z can be determined. Hence equations (*9.2*), Page 177 and (*9.10*), Page 182, give at once $F_x, F_y, F_z, \tau_x, \tau_y, \tau_z$ where F_x, for example, is the sum of the X components of $f_1, f_2, \ldots, f_5$ and τ_x is the sum of the moments exerted by these same forces about X. For a given motion, F_x, τ_x, etc., will always have the same values regardless of how the body is attached to the frame. Note, however, that if it is fastened at several points as indicated, not enough information is given to find individual values of $f_1, f_2, \ldots, f_5$.

12.5 Forces of Constraint and Equations of Motion When Constraints are Rough.

Frictional forces are always present when one object moves in contact with and relative to another. The magnitude of a sliding frictional force F_f is given by $F_f = \mu f$ where μ is the coefficient of friction and f the reactive force normal to the surfaces in contact. The direction of F_f will be taken as opposite to that of the motion.

Frictional forces must be treated as externally applied driving forces since, when sliding takes place, work is always done. Their existence usually introduces considerable difficulties, and no general treatment of the above topic will be attempted here. However, the following two examples may help to point out the type of problem which can arise.

Example 12.9.

Referring to Fig. 12-6, let us determine the reactive force f and the equation of motion of the bead sliding *down* the rough parabolic wire.

Considering f as normal to the wire in the direction indicated and the frictional force μf tangent to the wire, we write

$$m\ddot{x} = \mu f \cos\theta - f \sin\theta + F_x, \qquad m\ddot{y} = \mu f \sin\theta + f\cos\theta - mg + F_y \tag{1}$$

But $\cos\theta = \dfrac{dx}{\sqrt{dx^2+dy^2}} = \dfrac{1}{\sqrt{1+4b^2x^2}}$ and $\sin\theta = \dfrac{2bx}{\sqrt{1+4b^2x^2}}$. Hence relations (*1*) become

$$m\ddot{x} = f\left(\frac{\mu - 2bx}{\sqrt{1+4b^2x^2}}\right) + F_x \tag{2}$$

$$m\ddot{y} = \frac{f(2\mu bx + 1)}{\sqrt{1+4b^2x^2}} - mg + F_y \tag{3}$$

Eliminating f between (*2*) and (*3*) and making use of the relation $y = bx^2$, the following equation of motion is obtained:

$$m\ddot{x}(1+4b^2x^2) + 4mb^2x\dot{x}^2 = 2\mu bm\dot{x}^2 + F_x + \mu(mg - F_y) + 2bx(\mu F_x - mg + F_y) \tag{4}$$

Note that a difficult non-linear equation is obtained for this apparently simple problem.

Either (*2*) or (*3*), of course, yields an expression for the reactive force f.

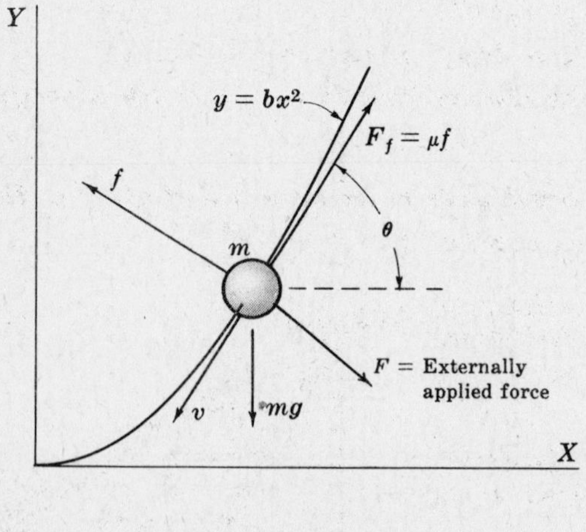

Fig. 12-6

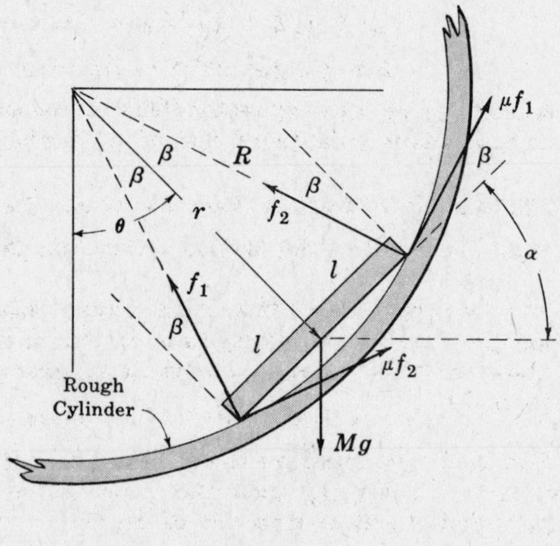

Fig. 12-7

Example 12.10.

A uniform rod of length $2l$ slides in a vertical plane *down* the inside of a rough cylinder of radius R as shown in Fig. 12-7. We shall find expressions for the reactive forces f_1, f_2 and the equation of motion.

Pretending that the rod is free to move in a vertical plane and using r, θ, α as coordinates,

$$T = \tfrac{1}{2}M(\dot{r}^2 + r^2\dot{\theta}^2) + \tfrac{1}{2}I\dot{\alpha}^2$$

where M is the total mass of the rod and I its moment of inertia about a transverse axis through c.m. Note that T contains two superfluous coordinates.

Applying (*12.3*), regarding the reactive forces f_1, f_2 and frictional forces $\mu f_1, \mu f_2$ as driving forces, the following equations are obtained:

$$Mr\dot{\theta}^2 + Mg\cos\theta = (f_1 + f_2)\cos\beta + \mu(f_1 - f_2)\sin\beta \qquad (1)$$

$$Mr^2\ddot{\theta} + Mgr\sin\theta = \mu r(f_1 + f_2)\cos\beta + r(f_1 - f_2)\sin\beta \qquad (2)$$

$$I\ddot{\alpha} = \mu l(f_1 + f_2)\sin\beta - l(f_1 - f_2)\cos\beta \qquad (3)$$

in which we have set $\dot{r} = \ddot{r} = 0$.

Now (*1*) and (*2*) can be solved for f_1 and f_2. Substituting these results, together with $\ddot{\alpha} = \ddot{\theta}$, into (*3*) gives the equation of motion.

Problems

12.1. A bead, acted upon by an applied force having components F_x, F_y is constrained to move along a smooth rigid wire, of any given shape, in a plane. Using polar coordinates show that regardless of the shape of the wire or the values F_x and F_y, general expressions for the components of the reactive force f_x and f_y are given by

$$f_x = -F_x + m(\ddot{r} - r\dot{\theta}^2)\cos\theta - m(r\ddot{\theta} + 2\dot{r}\dot{\theta})\sin\theta$$

$$f_y = -F_y + m(\ddot{r} - r\dot{\theta}^2)\sin\theta + m(r\ddot{\theta} + 2\dot{r}\dot{\theta})\cos\theta$$

12.2. In Fig. 3-9, Page 54, the vertical shaft is made to rotate in any manner. Angular displacement of this shaft is ϕ. Show that the reactive forces exerted by the rod on m are expressed by

$$f_\theta = -mr\dot{\phi}^2\sin\theta\cos\theta - mg\sin\theta, \qquad f_\phi = mr\sin\theta\,\ddot{\phi} + 2m\dot{r}\dot{\phi}\sin\theta$$

where these forces are in the direction of increasing θ and ϕ respectively. Hence for known motion, $\phi(t)$ and $r(t)$, each reactive force is a known function of time.

12.3. Show that the following equations are applicable to the above problem:

$$-mr\dot{\phi}^2\sin\theta\cos\theta - mg\sin\theta = f_x\cos\theta\cos\phi + f_y\cos\theta\sin\phi - f_z\sin\theta$$

$$mr\ddot{\phi}\sin\theta + 2m\dot{r}\dot{\phi}\sin\theta = -f_x\sin\phi + f_y\cos\phi$$

$$m\ddot{r} - mr\dot{\phi}^2\sin^2\theta + mg\cos\theta = f_x\sin\theta\cos\phi + f_y\sin\theta\sin\phi + f_z\cos\theta$$

where f_x, f_y, f_z are the rectangular components of the reactive force on m. Hence the rectangular components may be found instead of f_θ and f_ϕ.

12.4. The dumbbell, Fig. 4-3, Page 64, is moving in a vertical plane under the action of gravity. Show that the tension τ in the rod connecting m_1 and m_2 is given by $\tau = \dfrac{m_1 m_2}{m_1 + m_2} l\dot{\theta}^2$.

12.5. The two rods, Fig. 12-8, with upper ends rigidly fastened together are free to swing as a pendulum in a vertical plane. Show that the torque τ_α tending to change the angle α is given by

$$\tau_\alpha = I_2\ddot{\theta} + M_2 g r_2 \sin(\theta + \beta)$$

For small motion about the position of equilibrium, determine θ as a function of time and hence τ_α as a function of t. (r_2 = distance from p to c.m. of M_2.)

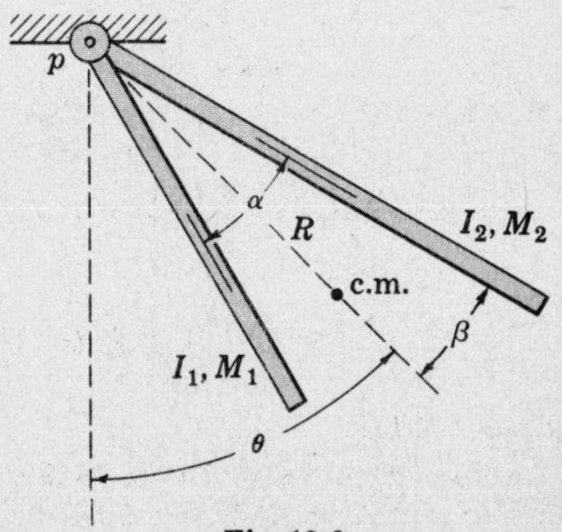

Fig. 12-8

12.6. A bead of mass m slides down the smooth conical spiral, Fig. 3-5, Problem 3.5, Page 52, under the action of gravity. Using spherical coordinates write out equations from which the rectangular components of the reactive force f_x, f_y, f_z may be obtained. Compare these with the equations given in Problem 12.3.

12.7. A particle of mass m slides down a great circle of a smooth sphere, radius r. Assuming that it starts from the highest point with a velocity $r\dot{\theta}_0$ (θ measured from a vertical diameter downward), show that the reactive force f_r exerted by the sphere on the particle is given by $f_r = 3mg\cos\theta - mr\dot{\theta}_0^2 - 2mg$ and that it leaves the sphere at an angle given by $\cos\theta = \dfrac{2g + r\dot{\theta}_0^2}{3g}$.

12.8. The upper end of the bar, Fig. 12-9 slides down the smooth wall. The disk rolls along the floor without slipping. Neglecting bearing and rolling friction, show that f_x, the force exerted by the wall on the end of the bar, is given by

$$f_x = (M_1 + 2M_2 + 2I_2/r^2)(l\ddot{\theta}\cos\theta - l\dot{\theta}^2\sin\theta)$$

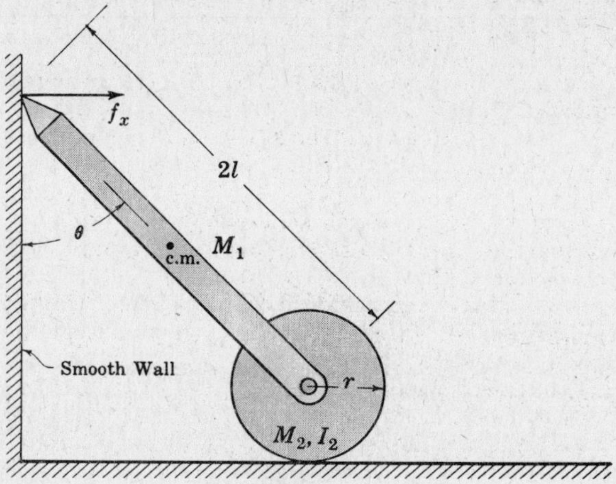

Fig. 12-9

12.9. Show that tension in r_1, Fig. 12-3, is $f = m_2r_2[\ddot{\phi}\sin(\phi-\theta) + \dot{\phi}^2\cos(\phi-\theta) + (m_1+m_2)(r_1\dot{\theta}^2 + g\cos\theta)]$.

12.10. Referring to Fig. 12-10, a particle moves in contact with the smooth surface given by $z = A\sin\dfrac{\pi x}{a}\sin\dfrac{2\pi y}{b}$, gravity acting in the negative direction of z. Using rectangular coordinates write out equations for the f_x, f_y, f_z components of the reactive force on m.

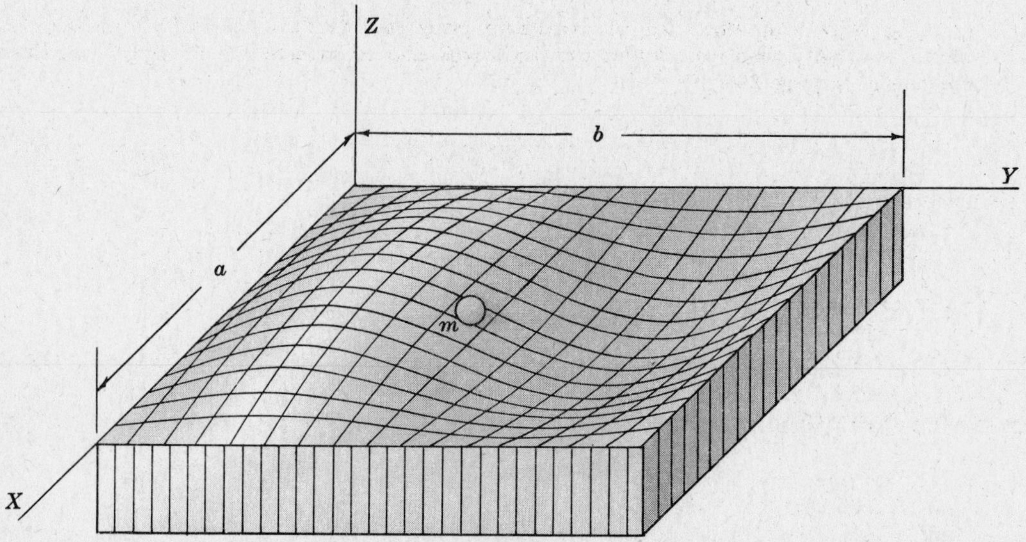

Fig. 12-10

12.11. The vertical shaft supporting the smooth wire, Fig. 2-29, Problem 2.20, Page 36, is made to rotate in any given manner $\theta = \theta(t)$. Show that the f_r, f_θ, f_z components of force exerted by the wire on the bead are given by

$$m\ddot{r} - mr\dot{\theta}^2 = f_r, \quad mr\ddot{\theta} + 2m\dot{r}\dot{\theta} = f_\theta, \quad m\ddot{z} = f_z - mg \tag{1}$$

Noting that
$$\delta W = f_r\,\delta r + f_\theta r\,\delta\theta + f_z\,\delta z = 0, \quad z = ar^2 \tag{2}$$

(principle of virtual work; see Section 2.13, Page 29) show that the usual r and θ equations of motion containing no forces of constraint can be obtained from (*1*) and (*2*).

12.12. A bead slides down a rough circular loop of wire, with the plane of the loop vertical. Show that, in rectangular coordinates with origin at the center of loop, the equation of motion (before eliminating, say, $\ddot{y}$ and y) is

$$m(\ddot{y} + g)(x - \mu y) = m\ddot{x}(\mu x - y)$$

and in polar coordinates,

$$mr\ddot{\theta} - mg\sin\theta = \mu(mr\dot{\theta}^2 - mg\sin\theta)$$

12.13. A particle of mass m moves over a rough spherical surface under the action of the frictional force and gravity. Show that the normal reactive force on the particle is

$$f_r = mg\cos\theta - m(r\dot{\theta}^2 + r\sin^2\theta\,\dot{\phi}^2)$$

and that the equations of motion corresponding to θ and ϕ are

$$mr^2\ddot{\theta} - mr^2\sin\theta\cos\theta\,\dot{\phi}^2 = mgr\sin\theta - \mu f_r\frac{r^2\dot{\theta}}{\dot{s}}$$

$$mr^2\sin^2\theta\,\ddot{\phi} + 2mr^2\sin\theta\cos\theta\,\dot{\theta}\dot{\phi} = \mu f_r\frac{r^2\sin^2\theta\,\dot{\phi}}{\dot{s}}$$

where $\dot{s}^2 = r^2\dot{\theta}^2 + r^2\sin^2\theta\,\dot{\phi}^2$. (Use spherical coordinates with origin at center of sphere.)

12.14. Referring to Fig. 8-5, Page 146, find expressions for the components of torque τ_x, τ_y, τ_z along X, Y, Z exerted by the bearing which supports D. Assume shaft ab driven by a motor at a known speed.

12.15. Referring to Fig. 8-18, Page 159, a particle of mass m is glued to the center of the rim of an otherwise perfectly balanced gyro. Find expressions for the forces on the fixed bearings a_1, a_2 as a result of this.

12.16. The base, Fig. 9-14, Page 201, is at latitude Φ on the earth. The shaft supporting the rotating table is vertical. Find expressions for the forces exerted by bearings B_1 and B_2 on the shaft. (See Problem 9.19, Page 200.)

CHAPTER 13

Driving Forces Required to Establish Known Motions

(Static Equilibrium as a Special Case)

13.1 Preliminary Considerations.

The usual dynamical problem is one in which forces are given to find consequent motions. In this chapter we treat the converse type in which motions are prescribed or known by experiment, to find driving forces necessary to produce such motions. (See Section 1.7, Page 5.) As will be seen, problems involving static equilibrium may be regarded as special cases of the above.

This branch of dynamics has many applications and, as will soon be evident, the Lagrangian method of treatment is especially suitable.

The developments of the chapter depend primarily on the contents of Chapter 4. But, in addition to this, special emphasis must be placed on the following facts.

(*a*) Each of the $q_1, q_2, \ldots, q_n$ independent coordinates *can be made to vary with time in any desired manner. The way in which one coordinate may be forced to change does not limit the manner in which any other can vary.* Consider Fig. 13-1. Assume vertical motion with ropes always under tension. The system has two degrees of freedom. Suitable pairs of coordinates are (s_1, y_1), (s_2, y_2), (y_1, y_2), etc. By a proper application of forces each of the two coordinates of any pair can be made to change with time in any (within limits) desired manner.

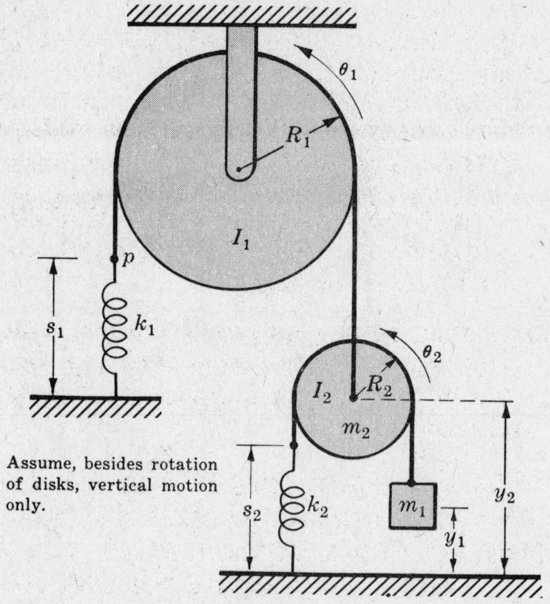

Fig. 13-1

(*b*) *Prescribed motions of a system can usually be attained by applying the driving forces in any one of several ways.* Again referring to Fig. 13-1, suppose a mechanism, *A*, attached to the ground exerts a vertical force on m_1 while another, *B*, also fastened to the ground exerts a vertical force on the left rope at point *p*. Clearly these two devices can give the system (within obvious limits) any desired motions. But suppose *A*, now attached to the shaft of the small pulley, exerts a force on m_1 while *B* continues to exert a force as before. These devices can again (for simplicity neglect the mass of *A*) give the system any desired motions. However, the force exerted by *A* in the first case will, in general, not equal the force it must exert in the second, even though the desired motions are the same. And, of course, this is likewise true of *B*. Hence, in general, there is a range of choices as to where forces are to be applied.

(*c*) There is the important question as to *how many* driving forces are required. In general, for a system of n degrees of freedom n forces, $f_1, f_2, \ldots, f_n$, must be applied in such a way that a change in the value of any one of the n coordinates can be produced by at least one (or perhaps several together) of the applied forces.

(*d*) As a result of (*b*), the first step in the solution of a problem of this type is to *decide on the exact manner in which driving forces are to be applied.* Moreover, since for every "action" there is an equal and opposite "reaction", it is important to specify the location of each driving mechanism.

13.2 General Method.

The following general results are based on a direct application of Lagrange's equations which for convenience and clarity we write as

$$\frac{d}{dt}\left(\frac{\partial T}{\partial \dot{q}_r}\right) - \frac{\partial T}{\partial q_r} = F_{q_r} + F'_{q_r} \qquad (13.1)$$

where F_{q_r} includes only the known forces already acting and F'_{q_r} contains just the unknowns $f_1, f_2, \ldots, f_n$.

Outline of General Procedure.

(*a*) Having expressed T in any n independent coordinates, n Lagrangian equations of motion are written out in the usual way.

(*b*) Expressions for F_{q_r} are found as usual, taking account of all known applied forces as well as those due to springs, gravity, etc.

(*c*) Having decided on exactly how $f_1, f_2, \ldots, f_n$ are to be applied, expressions for F'_{q_r} are written (also in the usual manner) in terms of the unknown f's.

(*d*) Since the motion is assumed known (that is, each coordinate is a given function of time, $q_1 = q_1(t)$, etc.), the left sides of the equations of motion may be expressed in terms of t and various constants.

(*e*) Simultaneous solutions of these n algebraic equations give each f in terms of t and the constants. Hence we have the final desired results. As will be seen from some examples below, it is sometimes easy to eliminate t and express the forces as functions of the coordinates.

Important Note. Consider the following two simple examples. (*a*) A ball thrown vertically upward moves, of course, along a vertical straight line. If pitched with initial velocity at some angle less than 90° with the horizontal, the path (neglecting air resistance and assuming g vertically downward and constant) is parabolic. Hence the actual path depends on initial conditions. (*b*) A satellite of mass m moves around a uniform spherical earth of mass M. The path is that of an ellipse if the total energy $\mathcal{E} = T + V$ is negative, a parabola if $\mathcal{E} = 0$, and a hyperbola for $\mathcal{E}$ positive. But in each case the force is the familiar gravitational pull GMm/r^2. $\mathcal{E}$ depends on initial values of position and velocity. Hence again the actual path depends on initial conditions.

Returning to the general problem, it is evident that in order to establish specific motions of a system (those originally specified by $q_1 = q_1(t)$, etc., in which definite initial conditions are included) we not only apply $f_1, f_2, \ldots, f_n$, determined as outlined above, but at the instant of application the system must have the specified initial conditions.

13.3 Illustrative Examples.

Example 13.1.

Certain basic principles are well illustrated by a consideration of the simple system shown in Fig. 13-2. For this reason we sketch here three solutions to the same problem. (*Note.* Throughout this example we assume that the rope is always under tension.)

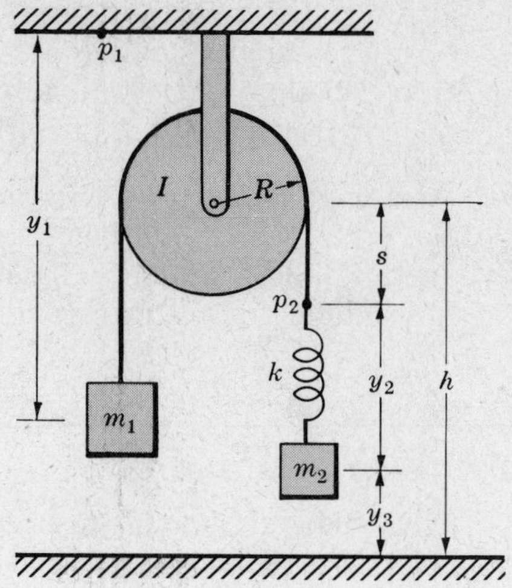

Fig. 13-2

(*a*) Using coordinates y_1 and y_2, it follows without difficulty that

$$(m_1 + m_2 + I/R^2)\ddot{y}_1 - m_2\ddot{y}_2 + (m_2 - m_1)g = F'_{y_1} \quad (1)$$

$$m_2(\ddot{y}_2 - \ddot{y}_1) - m_2 g + k(y_2 - l_0) = F'_{y_2} \quad (2)$$

where l_0 is the unstretched length of the spring. These relations must hold regardless of what motion may be assumed. Moreover, they are valid regardless of how driving forces are applied provided, of course, F'_{y_1} and F'_{y_2} are expressed properly in each case.

Let us now assume that a mechanism attached to p_1 exerts a vertical force f_1 of unknown magnitude on m_1 and likewise another (massless) attached to the rope at p_2 exerts a force f_2 on m_2. By inspection $F'_{y_1} = f_1$, $F'_{y_2} = f_2$. Hence (*1*) and (*2*) give directly the magnitudes of f_1 and f_2 in terms of $\ddot{y}_1$ and $\ddot{y}_2$ and constants.

When the desired motion is specified, as for example $y_1 = y_0 + vt$, $y_2 = l_0 + A\sin(\omega t + \delta)$ where $y_0, v, l_0, A, \omega, \delta$ are assumed to have known values, it follows at once that the required forces are

$$f_1 = m_2 A\omega^2 \sin(\omega t + \delta) + (m_2 - m_1)g, \qquad f_2 = A(k - m_2\omega^2)\sin(\omega t + \delta) - m_2 g$$

Note that in this case f_1 and f_2 can be expressed as functions of y_2.

(*b*) Let us again determine f_1 and f_2, making use of coordinates y_1 and y_3. Applying (*13.1*),

$$(m_1 + I/R^2)\ddot{y}_1 - m_1 g + k(y_1 - y_3 - c) = F'_{y_1} \quad (3)$$

$$m_2\ddot{y}_3 + m_2 g - k(y_1 - y_3 - c) = F'_{y_3} \quad (4)$$

where $y_1 - y_2 - y_3 = b =$ constant.

Assuming driving forces applied as in (*a*), $F'_{y_1} = f_1 + f_2$ and $F'_{y_3} = -f_2$ (note that F'_{y_1} is not the same as before). Putting these relations into (*3*) and (*4*) and solving simultaneously, we obtain the previously determined general expressions for f_1 and f_2.

(*c*) Finally let us determine f_1 and f_2, assuming f_1 applied as before but that f_2 is exerted by a mechanism attached to the ground.

For this purpose it is important to note that use may be made of either (*1*) and (*2*) or (*3*) and (*4*). Choosing (*3*) and (*4*), $F'_{y_1} = f_1$, $F'_{y_3} = f_2$ and finally, for the same motion assumed in (*a*),

$$f_1 = k(y_2 - l_0) - m_1 g, \qquad f_2 = (m_2\omega^2 - k)(y_2 - l_0) + m_2 g$$

The reader should show that the same expressions may be obtained employing (*1*) and (*2*).

The fact that these expressions for f_1 and f_2 are not the same as in (*a*), even though the assumed motions may be equal, is of course due to the change in the way of applying f_2.

Example 13-2. *Forces required to give the dumbbell, shown in Fig. 13-3 below, any motion in a vertical plane.*

Using coordinates x, y, θ, (*13.1*) gives

$$M\ddot{x} = F'_x, \qquad M\ddot{y} + Mg = F'_y, \qquad I\ddot{\theta} = F'_\theta \quad (1)$$

where $M = m_1 + m_2$.

Suppose forces f_{x_1}, f_{y_1} are applied to m_1 in the directions of x_1 and y_1 respectively, and f_{y_2} to m_2 in the direction of y_2. Thus

$$F'_x = f_{x_1}, \qquad F'_y = f_{y_1} + f_{y_2}, \qquad F'_\theta = f_{x_1} l_1 \sin\theta + (f_{y_2} l_2 - f_{y_1} l_1)\cos\theta \quad (2)$$

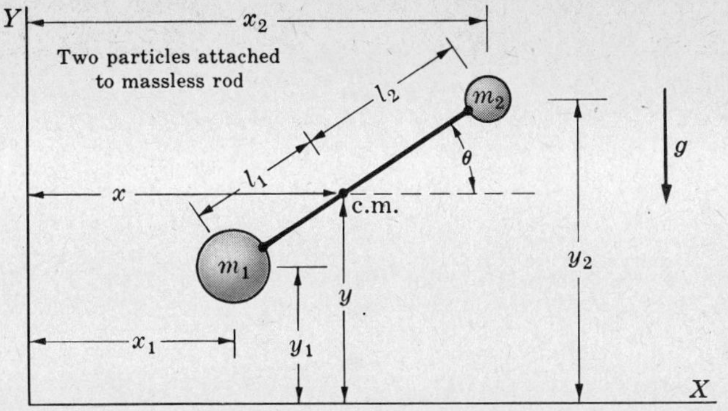

Dumbbell free to move in vertical plane under action of gravity and externally applied forces.

Fig. 13-3

From (1) and (2), $f_{x_1} = M\ddot{x}$,

$$f_{y_1} \quad = \quad \frac{M(\ddot{y}+g)l_2 \cos\theta \;-\; I\ddot{\theta} \;+\; M\ddot{x}l_1 \sin\theta}{(l_1+l_2)\cos\theta} \tag{3}$$

$$f_{y_2} \quad = \quad \frac{M(\ddot{y}+g)l_1 \cos\theta \;+\; I\ddot{\theta} \;-\; M\ddot{x}l_1 \sin\theta}{(l_1+l_2)\cos\theta} \tag{4}$$

Hence for any assumed motions the required forces are readily obtained as functions of time.

Consider another possibility as regards the application of forces. Suppose f_x and f_y are applied at the point c.m. and that two equal and oppositely directed forces f are applied normal to the rod at equal distances $s/2$ from c.m. Then

$$F'_x = f_x, \quad F'_y = f_y, \quad F_\theta = sf \tag{5}$$

Hence (1) and (5) give, at once, general expressions for the required driving forces for any desired motions.

Example 13.3.

The force f, Fig. 4-11, Page 74, is such that the cart oscillates according to the relation $x = x_0 + A\sin(\omega_1 t + \delta_1)$. A light mechanism attached to the lower portion of the incline exerts a force f_q in the direction of q, causing m to oscillate as $q = q_0 + B\sin(\omega_2 t + \delta_2)$. We shall find required expressions for f and f_q.

For this system,

$$T \quad = \quad \tfrac{1}{2}(M_1 + 4M + 4I/r^2 + m)\dot{x}^2 \;+\; \tfrac{1}{2}m(\dot{q}^2 - 2\dot{x}\dot{q}\cos\theta)$$

Hence

$$(M_1 + 4M + 4I/r^2 + m)\ddot{x} - m\ddot{q}\cos\theta \;=\; F'_x \;=\; f, \qquad m(\ddot{q} - \ddot{x}\cos\theta) + k(q - q_0) - mg\sin\theta \;=\; F'_q \;=\; f_q$$

For the assumed motions, $\ddot{x} = -\omega_1^2 x$, $\ddot{q} = -\omega_2^2 q$. Thus finally,

$$f \quad = \quad -\omega_1^2(M_1 + 4M + 4I/r^2 + m)x \;+\; m\omega_2^2 q\cos\theta$$

$$f_q \quad = \quad m(\omega_1^2 x\cos\theta - \omega_2^2 q) \;+\; k(q - q_0) \;-\; mg\sin\theta$$

Of course, f and f_q can be written as functions of time.

Example 13.4.

In Fig. 13-4 a mass is free to slide along a smooth inclined rod supported rigidly on a cart, the total mass of which is M. The cart is free to move along a straight horizontal track. By applying proper forces the cart can be given any desired horizontal motion at the same time that m is made to move in any manner along the rod. The system has two degrees of freedom and hence two independently controlled forces are required. Some of the possible ways of applying

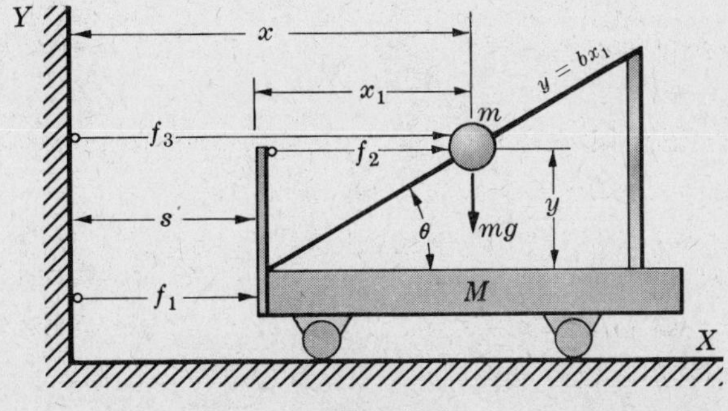

Fig. 13-4

driving forces are indicated by f_1, f_2, f_3. In the figure a circle attached to the tail of a force arrow indicates the location of the corresponding driving mechanism.

Note that any prescribed motion can be produced by proper values of any one of the pairs of forces (f_1, f_2), (f_1, f_3), (f_2, f_3); and in the process of finding expressions for the forces any one of the sets of coordinates (x_1, s), (x_1, x), (x, s) may be employed.

Choosing coordinates (x, s),

$$T = \tfrac{1}{2}(M + b^2m)\dot{s}^2 + \tfrac{1}{2}m(1+b^2)\dot{x}^2 - mb^2\dot{x}\dot{s}$$

where, as seen from the figure, $b = y/x_1 = \tan\theta$. Applying (*13.1*) we find

$$(M + b^2m)\ddot{s} - mb^2\ddot{x} - mgb = F'_s \qquad (1)$$

$$m(1+b^2)\ddot{x} - mb^2\ddot{s} + mgb = F'_x \qquad (2)$$

which are applicable regardless of the pair of forces we choose or what the assumed motion may be.

For f_1 and f_2 acting, $F'_s = f_1 - f_2$ (note that the mechanism exerting the force f_2 pushes forward on m and backwards on the cart) and $F'_x = f_2$. Hence from (*1*) and (*2*),

$$f_1 = M\ddot{s} + m\ddot{x} \qquad (3)$$

$$f_2 = m(1+b^2)\ddot{x} - mb^2\ddot{s} + mgb \qquad (4)$$

Up to this point no specific motions have been stated. But clearly (*3*) and (*4*) will give f_1 and f_2 as functions of time for any motion we may wish to assume. If it is assumed that f_1, f_2 and f_3 are all acting, there are insufficient equations for finding a separate value of each. However, the three will appear in F'_s and F'_x of (*1*) and (*2*). Thus if any one is specified, the other two can be found.

Example 13.5.

Consider the forces required to produce any desired motion of m, Fig. 2-21, Page 22, relative to the X_2, Y_2 frame for any assumed rotations of D_1 and D_2.

From equation (*2.31*) it follows that

$$T = \tfrac{1}{2}m\{\dot{r}^2 + r^2\dot{\alpha}^2 + [2s\dot{\theta}_1\sin(\theta_2+\alpha)]\dot{r} + [2r^2(\dot{\theta}_1+\dot{\theta}_2) + 2s\dot{\theta}_1 r\cos(\theta_2+\alpha)]\dot{\alpha}$$
$$+ [r^2(\dot{\theta}_1+\dot{\theta}_2)^2 + 2sr\dot{\theta}_1(\dot{\theta}_1+\dot{\theta}_2)\cos(\theta_2+\alpha) + s^2\dot{\theta}_1^2]\} \qquad (1)$$

Now for any specified rotations of D_1 and D_2, $\dot{\theta}_1$ and $\dot{\theta}_2$ can be replaced by functions of t. (For example, assuming $\theta_1 = \dot{\theta}_0 t + \tfrac{1}{2}at^2$, $\theta_2 = A\sin(\omega t + \delta)$, we have $\dot{\theta}_1 = \dot{\theta}_0 + at$, $\dot{\theta}_2 = A\omega\cos(\omega t+\delta)$.) Hence it is evident, without going into further detail, that an application of (*13.1*) leads at once to expressions for the forces (say f_r applied in the direction of r and f_α in the direction of increasing α) required to give m any desired motion relative to X_2, Y_2. See Problem 13.5, Page 278.

Notice how this method so easily takes full account of the rotations of D_1 and D_2 in expressions for required forces. It is clear that an extension of the procedure outlined above will lead to expressions for the forces required to cause the particles or rigid bodies of a very complex system to move in any manner relative to X_2, Y_2, Z_2 axes attached to D_2.

13.4 Equilibrium of a System.

(Special case of the general problem treated in Section 13.2.)

The subject of equilibrium deals with the forces required to maintain objects at rest, usually with respect to a stationary frame of reference but frequently relative to a moving frame or moving constraints. The subject is obviously a *special case* of the one just concluded in which all or certain motions are permanently zero. Two general types of problems may arise: (*a*) given the forces acting on a system, to determine whether they will hold it in equilibrium and, if so, to find values of the coordinates at which equilibrium occurs; (*b*) to find forces required to hold the masses of the system at given positions. Moreover, in either case, one may wish to determine forces of constraint.

Lagrange's equations when static conditions are imposed: Assuming moving coordinates and/or moving constraints, T has the form (see equation (*2.55*), Page 27)

$$T = \sum_{k,l}^{n} A_{kl}\dot{q}_k\dot{q}_l + \sum_{k=1}^{n} B_k\dot{q}_k + C$$

Thus $\dfrac{\partial T}{\partial \dot{q}_r} = 2\sum_{l=1}^{n} A_{rl}\dot{q}_l + B_r$ and

$$\frac{d}{dt}\left(\frac{\partial T}{\partial \dot{q}_r}\right) = 2\sum_{l=1}^{n}\frac{d}{dt}(A_{rl})\dot{q}_l + 2\sum_{l=1}^{n} A_{rl}\ddot{q}_l + \frac{d}{dt}(B_r) \qquad (1)$$

Since in general $B_r = B_r(q_1, q_2, \ldots, q_n; t)$,

$$\frac{d}{dt}(B_r) = \frac{\partial B_r}{\partial q_1}\dot{q}_1 + \frac{\partial B_r}{\partial q_2}\dot{q}_2 + \cdots + \frac{\partial B_r}{\partial q_n}\dot{q}_n + \frac{\partial B_r}{\partial t} \qquad (2)$$

Also,

$$\frac{\partial T}{\partial q_r} = \sum_{k=1}^{n}\sum_{l=1}^{n}\left(\frac{\partial A_{kl}}{\partial q_r}\right)\dot{q}_k\dot{q}_l + \sum_{k=1}^{n}\left(\frac{\partial B_k}{\partial q_r}\right)\dot{q}_k + \frac{\partial C}{\partial q_r} \qquad (3)$$

Now if it is assumed that all values of $\dot{q}$ and $\ddot{q}$ are zero, it follows from (*1*), (*2*), (*3*) that (*13.1*) reduces to

$$\frac{\partial B_r}{\partial t} - \frac{\partial C}{\partial q_r} = F_{q_r} + F'_{q_r} \qquad (13.2)$$

which, since $r = 1, 2, \ldots, n$, represents n equations.

Relation (*13.2*) is a very general and powerful tool. It wraps up almost the entire field of equilibrium ("Statics") in one tiny package. The equation is, of course, valid when the frame of reference and/or constraints are in motion. Coordinates of any type may be employed. Most of the usual "elementary" principles and methods of statics, frequently given considerable space in intermediate texts, are automatically accounted for by (*13.2*). Moreover, it is simple to apply.

Important points regarding the application of (*13.2*):

(*a*) In any expression for T, terms B_r and C are easily recognized. (They are zero if there are no moving coordinates or constraints; see expression (*1*), Example 13.5.)

(*b*) F_{q_r} and F'_{q_r} are just the generalized forces with which we are familiar and are treated in exactly the same way as in previous examples of this chapter.

(*c*) B_r and C (and thus $\partial B_r/\partial t$ and $\partial C/\partial q_r$) are, in general, functions of coordinates and t. (See derivation of relation (*2.55*), Page 27.) Hence it is clear that solutions of (*13.2*), regarded as algebraic equations, give the unknown forces $f_1, f_2, \ldots, f_n$ in terms of the q's and t.

(*d*) If neither the frame of reference nor constraints are in motion, $B_r = 0, C = 0$. Hence (*13.2*) becomes

$$F_{q_r} + F'_{q_r} = 0 \qquad (13.3)$$

In this case *no notice need be taken of T*.

(*e*) By introducing superfluous coordinates and following exactly the procedure outlined in Chapter 12, forces of constraint which now enter F_{q_r} can be solved for.

13.5 Examples Illustrating Problems in Static Equilibrium.

Example 13.6.

Just for the sake of easily demonstrating a basic idea, note that on setting $\ddot{x} = \ddot{y} = \ddot{\theta} = 0$ in Example 13.2, equations (*3*) and (*4*) give at once the forces

$$f_{x_1} = 0, \quad f_{y_1} = \frac{Mgl_2}{l_1 + l_2}, \quad f_{y_2} = \frac{Mgl_1}{l_1 + l_2}$$

required to hold the dumbbell in equilibrium.

Note that each of Examples 13.1 to 13.5 becomes a good example in statics by setting accelerations and velocities equal to zero.

Example 13.7.

A uniform rod of length $2l$ and total mass M is free to slide in contact with the fixed smooth semi-circular wire as shown in Fig. 13-5, under the action of gravity. Let us find the angle θ at which the rod would remain at rest. $F'_\theta = 0$ and as can be seen

$$V = -Mg\bar{y} = -Mg[(2R\cos\theta - l)\sin\theta]$$

Thus, applying *(13.2)*,

$$F_\theta = -\frac{\partial V}{\partial\theta} = Mg[2R(2\cos^2\theta - 1) - l\cos\theta] = 0 \qquad \text{from which} \qquad \cos\theta = \frac{l + \sqrt{l^2 + 32R^2}}{8R}$$

Is there a limitation on the value of l/R? ($l/R \leqq 2$)

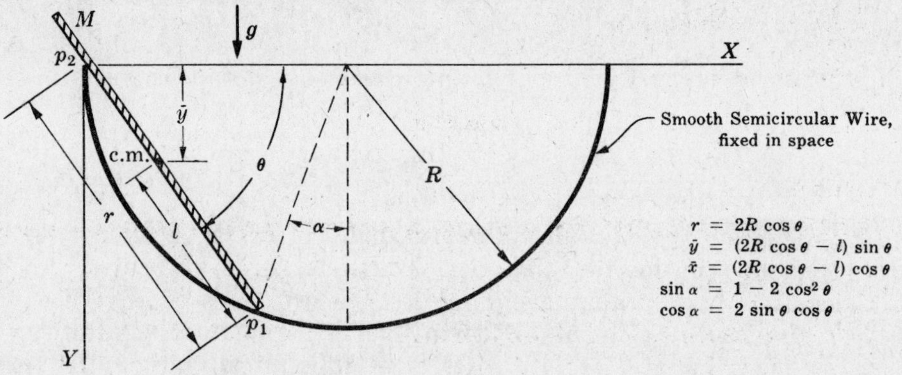

Fig. 13-5

As an extension of this suppose that the semicircular wire is moving with constant acceleration a_x in the positive direction of X; to find the equilibrium value of θ. For this case write

$$\bar{x} = x_0 + v_x t + \tfrac{1}{2}a_x t^2 + (2R\cos\theta - l)\cos\theta, \qquad \bar{y} = (2R\cos\theta - l)\sin\theta$$

Hence

$$T = \tfrac{1}{2}M[(v_x + a_x t - 4R\dot{\theta}\sin\theta\cos\theta + l\dot{\theta}\sin\theta)^2 + (2R\dot{\theta} - 4R\dot{\theta}\sin^2\theta - l\dot{\theta}\cos\theta)^2] + \tfrac{1}{2}I\dot{\theta}^2$$

from which it may be seen that

$$B_\theta = M[(v_x + a_x t)(l\sin\theta - 4R\sin\theta\cos\theta)], \qquad C_\theta = \tfrac{1}{2}M(v_x + a_x t)^2$$

Applying *(13.2)*, it follows that $(a_x\sin\theta + g\cos\theta)(4R\cos\theta - l) = 2gR$ from which θ can be determined graphically. Note that for $a_x = 0$ this gives the same expression for $\cos\theta$ as found above.

The reader may show that, if the rod is to be held at a given angle θ by a force f applied to its lower end in a clockwise direction tangent to the circle, f is given by

$$M(a_x\sin\theta + g\cos\theta)(l - 4R\cos\theta) + 2MgR = 2Rf$$

Note. Care must be used in writing δW_θ.

Example 13.8.

A particle is free to move under the action of gravity on the inside of a smooth hemispherical bowl of radius R, Fig. 13-6 below. The bowl, fastened to a rigid arm of length l, is made to rotate with angular velocity $\dot{\alpha}$ about a vertical axis ab. Let us find the equilibrium position of the particle assuming that $\dot{\alpha} = \omega =$ constant.

Axes X_1, Y_1, Z_1 are stationary. X_2, Y_2, Z_2 are attached to the arm. By inspection,

$$x_1 = l\cos\alpha + R\sin\theta\cos(\alpha+\phi), \qquad y_1 = l\sin\alpha + R\sin\theta\sin(\alpha+\phi), \qquad z_1 = R - R\cos\theta$$

from which

$$\begin{aligned} T = \tfrac{1}{2}m[&R^2\dot{\theta}^2 + (R^2\sin^2\theta)\dot{\phi}^2 + (2lR\dot{\alpha}\cos\theta\sin\phi)\dot{\theta} \\ &+ 2R\dot{\alpha}(R\sin^2\theta + l\sin\theta\cos\phi)\dot{\phi} + (l^2 + R^2\sin^2\theta + 2lR\sin\theta\cos\phi)\dot{\alpha}^2] \end{aligned} \qquad (1)$$

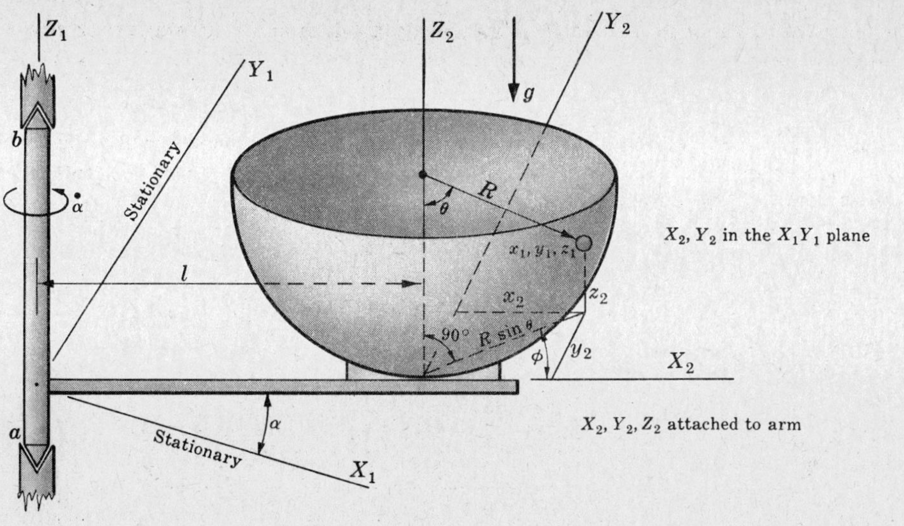

Fig. 13-6

From this it is seen that

$$B_\theta = mlR\dot{\alpha}\cos\theta\sin\phi, \quad B_\phi = mR\dot{\alpha}(R\sin^2\theta + l\sin\theta\cos\phi), \quad C = \tfrac{1}{2}m(l^2 + R^2\sin^2\theta + 2lR\sin\theta\cos\phi)\dot{\alpha}^2$$

For $\dot{\alpha}$ constant, $\partial B_\theta/\partial t = \partial B_\phi/\partial t = 0$. But

$$\frac{\partial C}{\partial \theta} = m(R^2\sin\theta\cos\theta + lR\cos\theta\cos\phi)\dot{\alpha}^2, \qquad \frac{\partial C}{\partial \phi} = (-mlR\sin\theta\sin\phi)\dot{\alpha}^2$$

Applying (*13.2*),

$$-m(R^2\sin\theta\cos\theta + lR\cos\theta\cos\phi)\dot{\alpha}^2 = -mgR\sin\theta \tag{2}$$

$$mlR\sin\theta\sin\phi\,\dot{\alpha}^2 = 0 \tag{3}$$

For $\sin\theta \neq 0$, $\sin\phi = 0$ by (*3*). Now putting $\cos\phi = 1$, (*2*) finally gives $g\tan\theta = \dot{\alpha}^2(R\sin\theta + l)$ which can readily be solved graphically for θ.

Example 13.9.

Referring to Fig. 2-21, Page 22, let us determine the forces necessary to hold a particle stationary with respect to D_2. From the general expression for T given in Example 13.5, it is seen that

$$B_r = ms\dot{\theta}_1\sin(\theta_2 + \alpha) \tag{1}$$

$$B_\alpha = mr^2(\dot{\theta}_1 + \dot{\theta}_2) + ms\dot{\theta}_1 r\cos(\theta_2 + \alpha) \tag{2}$$

$$C = \tfrac{1}{2}m[r^2(\dot{\theta}_1 + \dot{\theta}_2)^2 + 2s\dot{\theta}_1(\dot{\theta}_1 + \dot{\theta}_2)r\cos(\theta_2 + \alpha) + s^2\dot{\theta}_1^2] \tag{3}$$

For any specified rotations, $\dot{\theta}_1, \theta_2, \dot{\theta}_2$ can be replaced in (*1*), (*2*), (*3*) by specific functions of t. Now assuming, for example, that forces f_r and f_α are acting on m in the direction of r and increasing α respectively, it is clear that

$$\frac{\partial B_r}{\partial t} - \frac{\partial C}{\partial r} = f_r, \qquad \frac{\partial B_\alpha}{\partial t} - \frac{\partial C}{\partial \alpha} = rf_\alpha \tag{4}$$

give these forces in terms of r, α and t.

Assuming that $\theta_1 = a_1t + \tfrac{1}{2}b_1t^2$ and $\theta_2 = a_2t + \tfrac{1}{2}b_2t^2$, find expressions for f_r and f_α as functions of time for $\alpha = 30°$.

Example 13.10.

Reactive forces on the rod, Example 13.7, Fig. 13-5. We shall assume that a reactive force f_r acts on the rod at p_1 toward the center of the circle and that another f_1 acts normal to the rod at p_2. Regarding the rod as "free" to move in the XY plane,

$$T = \tfrac{1}{2}M(\dot{x}^2 + \dot{y}^2) + \tfrac{1}{2}I\dot{\theta}^2$$

which contains two superfluous coordinates. Equations of motion are merely

$$M\ddot{x} = F_x, \quad M\ddot{y} = F_y, \quad I\ddot{\theta} = F_\theta$$

By inspection generalized forces are seen to be

$$F_x = f_1 \sin\theta + f_r \sin\alpha, \quad F_y = Mg - f_1\cos\theta - f_r\cos\alpha, \quad F_\theta = f_1(2R\cos\theta - l) - f_r l \sin\theta$$

Thus assuming the bar at rest we get

$$f_r = Mg\tan\theta, \quad f_1 = Mg\left(\frac{2\cos^2\theta - 1}{\cos\theta}\right) \quad \text{and} \quad \cos\theta = \frac{l + \sqrt{l^2 + 32R^2}}{8R}$$

as previously found.

Problems

13.1. Motion is imparted to the system shown in Fig. 13-7 by a force f_x applied to the truck (resting on a smooth horizontal track) and a torque f_θ exerted by the armature of the motor. Show that for any assumed motions, f_x and f_θ are given by

$$f_x = M\ddot{x} - mr\ddot{\theta}\sin\theta - mr\dot{\theta}^2\cos\theta$$

$$f_\theta = I\ddot{\theta} - mr\ddot{x}\sin\theta + mgr\cos\theta - mr\dot{x}\dot{\theta}\cos\theta$$

where M is the mass of the entire system, I the total moment of inertia of the armature and arm about the axis of rotation, m is the mass of the arm and r is the distance from the axis of rotation to the center of mass of the arm.

Assuming constant speed ω of the motor and that the cart is moved with constant acceleration a in the direction of x, find expressions for f_x and f_θ. Repeat for $x = A\sin(\omega_1 t + \delta)$, $\dot{\theta} = \omega$.

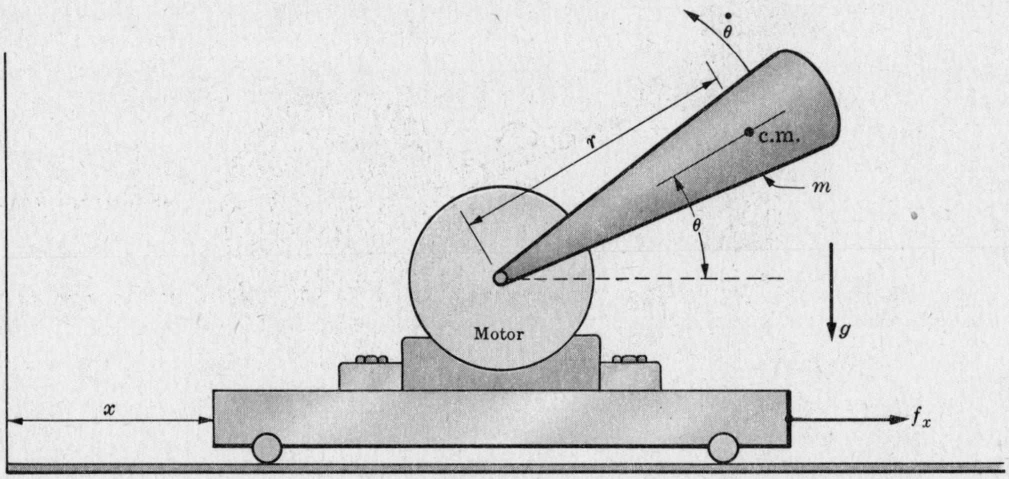

Fig. 13-7

13.2. (a) Assuming f_1 and f_3 only acting on the system discussed in Example 13.4, Page 271, find general expressions for these forces for any given motions. (*Answer.* Equations (*1*) and (*2*), Example 13.4, with $F'_s = f_1$ and $F'_x = f_3$.)

(b) Repeat (a) for f_2 and f_3 acting. (*Answer.* As above, with $F'_s = -f_2$, $F'_x = f_2 + f_3$.)

(c) Repeat (a) and (b) using coordinates (x_1, s). Show that results are the same as obtained above.

13.3. (a) A mechanism attached to m_1, Fig. 6-5, (see Example 6.14, Page 107) exerts a horizontal force f_3 on m_3. By means of devices attached to the fixed plane on which m_1 and m_2 rest, horizontal forces f_1 and f_2 are exerted on m_1 and m_2 respectively. Assuming that dissipative forces due to the dashpots and contacts of m_1 and m_2 with the plane are all viscous, show that for any assumed motion of the system, f_1, f_2, f_3 are determined by

$$(m_1+m_3)\ddot{x}_1 + m_3\ddot{q}_2 + b_1\dot{x}_1 + a_2(\dot{x}_1+\dot{q}_2-\dot{x}_2) = f_1$$
$$m_2\ddot{x}_2 + b_2\dot{x}_2 + a_2(\dot{x}_2-\dot{x}_1-\dot{q}_2) = f_2$$
$$m_3(\ddot{x}_1+\ddot{q}_2) + a_1\dot{q}_2 + a_2(\dot{x}_1+\dot{q}_2-\dot{x}_2) = f_3$$

where a_1, a_2 are the coefficients of viscous drag on the pistons and b_1, b_2 are corresponding coefficients for the bottoms of m_1 and m_2 respectively. Note that the springs shown have been neglected.

(b) Assuming that m_1 and m_2 move with equal uniform velocity to the right and that $q_2 = A + B\sin\omega t$, show that

$$f_1 = -m_3\omega^2 B\sin\omega t + a_2\omega B\cos\omega t + b_1\dot{x}_1$$
$$f_2 = -a_2\omega B\cos\omega t + b_2\dot{x}_2$$
$$f_3 = -m_3\omega^2 B\sin\omega t + (a_1+a_2)\omega B\cos\omega t$$

(c) Show that, if the mechanism producing f_2 is attached to m_1, f_1 on the right side of the first equation above must be replaced by $f_1 - f_2$ and that the other equations remain unchanged.

13.4. The uniform disk D, Fig. 13-8, with an unbalancing particle of mass m glued to its periphery as shown, can be made to rotate about the horizontal shaft cd by a motor (not shown). Torque applied by the motor $= \tau_\phi$. At the same time the vertical shaft can be rotated by a force F (torque τ_ψ) applied to the crank C.

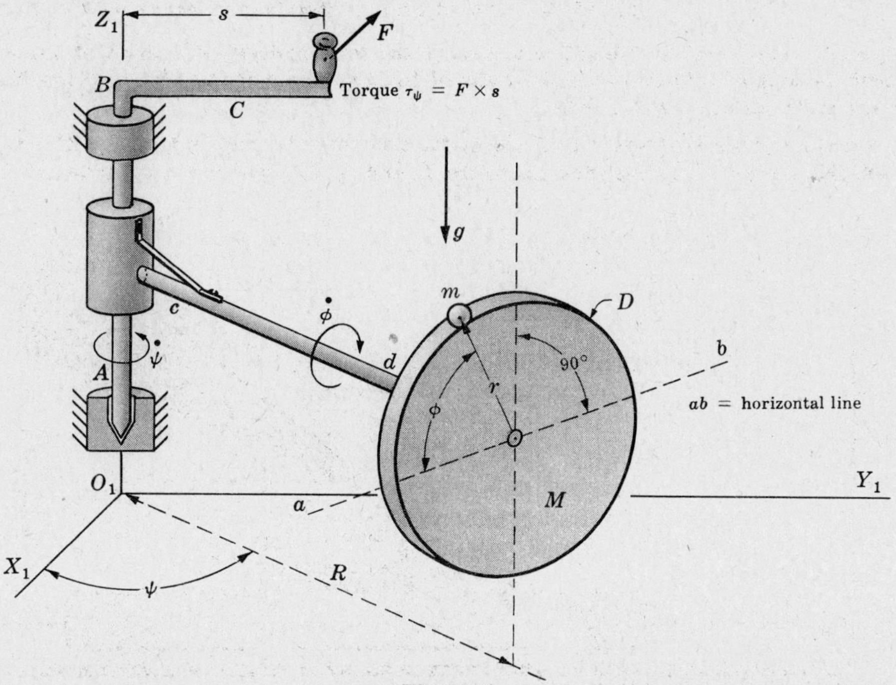

Fig. 13-8

Neglecting the motor, show that L for the system is given by

$$L = \tfrac{1}{2}[I_1\dot{\psi}^2 + m(R^2 + r^2\cos^2\phi)\dot{\psi}^2 + 2Rr\dot{\phi}\dot{\psi}\sin\phi + (I_2+mr^2)\dot{\phi}^2] - mgr\sin\phi$$

where I_1 is the moment of inertia of the entire system (not including m) about the vertical axis AB and I_2 is the moment of inertia of D about axis cd.

Write expressions for finding τ_ϕ and τ_ψ for any desired motions.

Assuming that $\phi = \omega_1 t + \phi_0$, $\psi = \psi_0\sin(\omega_2 t + \delta)$, where $\omega_1, \phi_0, \psi_0, \omega_2, \delta$ are constants, find expressions for τ_ϕ and τ_ψ.

13.5. The particle m, Fig. 2-21, Page 22, is made to move in a circle of radius r with constant angular velocity $\dot{\alpha} = \omega_3$. Assuming $\dot{\theta}_1 = \omega_1$ and $\dot{\theta}_2 = \omega_2$ are each constant, show that the required forces are (see Example 13.5)

$$f_r = -mr(\omega_1 + \omega_2 + \omega_3)^2 - ms\omega_1^2 \cos(\omega_2 + \omega_3)t, \qquad f_\alpha = msr\omega_1^2 \sin(\omega_2 + \omega_3)t$$

13.6. A flat board, total mass M and moment of inertia $\bar{I}$ about an axis normal to its surface and passing through c.m., is free to slide in contact with the X_2Y_2 plane, Fig. 2-21, Page 22. Show that its kinetic energy is given by $T = T_1 + \frac{1}{2}\bar{I}(\dot{\theta}_1 + \dot{\theta}_2 + \dot{\theta}_3)^2$ where T_1 is just the expression given in Example 13.5, Page 272, with m replaced by M. Here r, α locate c.m. and θ_3 is the angular displacement of the board relative to X_2.

Show that the force required to give c.m. any motion is just the same as required for a single particle of mass M. Show that for $\dot{\theta}_1$ and $\dot{\theta}_2$ each constant, the torque required to give the board any angular acceleration $\ddot{\theta}_3$ is merely $\bar{I}\ddot{\theta}_3$.

13.7. A dumbbell is to be given any motion relative to the X_1, Y_1, Z_1 frame, Fig. 14-2, Page 286. Outline briefly the steps required to find necessary forces, taking account of the earth's daily rotation. (See Section 14.8, Page 290.)

13.8. The base supporting disks D_1 and D_2, Fig. 2-21, Page 22, is located at the origin of coordinates, Fig. 14-2, Page 286. The particle is to be given any motion relative to the X_2, Y_2 axes shown on D_2. Outline briefly the steps required for finding the necessary forces f_r, f_α, taking account of the daily rotation of the earth as well as the rotations of D_1 and D_2.

13.9. Referring to Fig. 2-29, Page 36 (see Problem 2.20), show that for $\dot{\theta}$ having any constant value, a force $f_z = mg - m\dot{\theta}^2/2a$ applied to m in a direction parallel to Z will hold it at rest relative to the wire at any point on the wire. Note that for $\dot{\theta} = \sqrt{2ga}$, $f_z = 0$.

Show that if the force is applied in the direction of r, $f_r = 2mgar - mr\dot{\theta}^2$.

13.10. Referring to Example 13.8, Page 274 and Fig. 13-6, forces f_θ and f_ϕ are applied to m in the directions of increasing θ and ϕ respectively. Show that expressions for f_θ and f_ϕ required to hold m at rest relative to the bowl for any position (θ, ϕ) are

$$f_\theta = mg \sin\theta - m(R \sin\theta \cos\theta + l \cos\theta \cos\phi)\dot{\alpha}^2, \qquad f_\phi = ml\dot{\alpha}^2 \sin\phi$$

13.11. Show that for constant angular velocity ω of the vertical shaft, Fig. 3-9, Page 54 (see Problem 3.14), the equilibrium position of m is given by $r = \dfrac{k(l - l_0) - mg\cos\theta}{k - m\omega^2 \sin^2\theta}$.

13.12. Forces f_x, f_y, f_z are applied to the particle in Fig. 3-16, Page 56 (see Problem 3.27). Show for this system that C (the third term in the general expression for T) is given by (see equation *(14.15)*, Page 287)

$$C = \tfrac{1}{2}m\omega^2[x^2 + y^2 \sin^2\phi + (r + z)^2 \cos^2\phi - 2y(r + z)\sin\phi\cos\phi]$$

and hence that, in order to hold the particle at rest relative to the X_2, Y_2, Z_2 frame (gravity neglected),

$$f_x = -m\omega^2 x, \quad f_y = -m\omega^2[y\sin^2\phi - (r + z)\sin\phi\cos\phi], \quad f_z = -m\omega^2[(r + z)\cos^2\phi - y\sin\phi\cos\phi]$$

13.13. A board (total mass M, moment of inertia I about an axis through c.m.) is placed on a rough cylinder of radius R, Fig. 13-9. Show that $T = \frac{1}{2}MR^2(\theta - \theta_0)^2\dot{\theta}^2 + \frac{1}{2}I\dot{\theta}^2$ (where θ_0 is the value of θ when c.m. is in contact with the cylinder). Show that potential energy is given by

$$V = MgR[\sin\theta - (\theta - \theta_0)\cos\theta]$$

and finally, assuming no slipping, show that θ_0 is the equilibrium angular position.

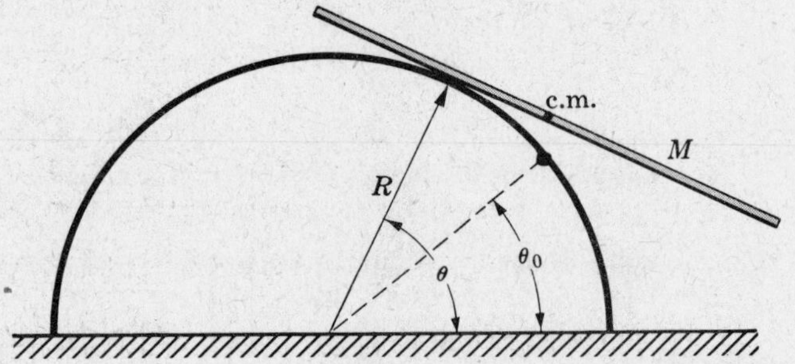

Fig. 13-9

13.14. Two uniform bars having masses and lengths $(M_1, 2l_1)$ and $(M_2, 2l_2)$ respectively are hinged at one end and free to slide in contact with a smooth semicircular rod as shown in Fig. 13-10. Show that

$$V = M_1 g l_1 \sin\theta + M_2 g l_2 \cos\theta - 2(M_1+M_2)gR\sin\theta\cos\theta$$

and that the angle θ at which equilibrium occurs is determined by

$$\tan\theta = \frac{2(M_1+M_2)R\cos\theta - M_1 l_1}{2(M_1+M_2)R\sin\theta - M_2 l_2}$$

How can θ be evaluated?

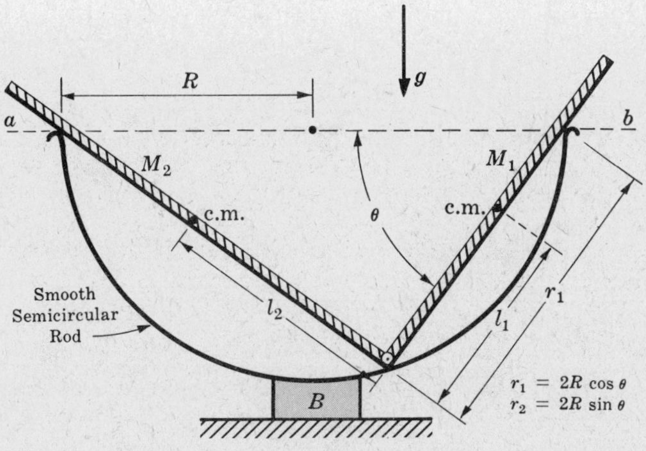

Fig. 13-10

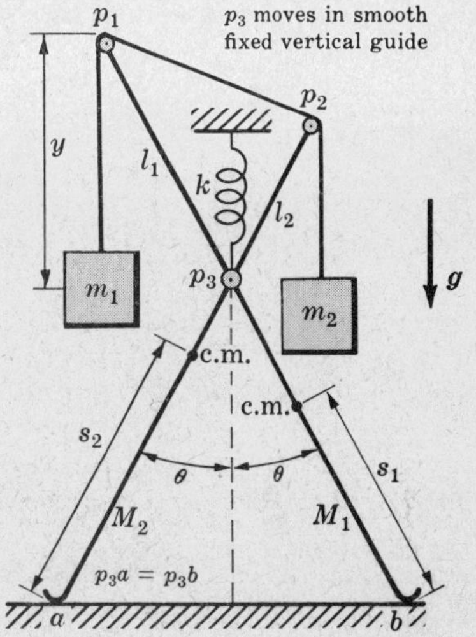

Fig. 13-11

13.15. Two rods having total lengths and masses (L_1, M_1) and (L_2, M_2) respectively are pivoted at p_3 as shown in Fig. 13-11. m_1 and m_2 are suspended from a cord which passes over the small pulleys p_1 and p_2. Length $l_1 = p_1p_3$, $l_2 = p_2p_3$ and $p_3a = p_3b$. The spring (unstretched length $= r_0$) and gravity act on the system. "Feet" a, b remain in contact with smooth floor. p_3 moves in a smooth vertical guide. Show that

$$V = (M_1s_1 + M_2s_2 + m_1L_1 + m_2L_2)g\cos\theta + (m_2 - m_1)gy$$
$$+\; m_2 g(l_1^2 + l_2^2 + 2l_1l_2 - 4l_1l_2\cos^2\theta)^{1/2} + \tfrac{1}{2}k[(L_1 - l_1)\cos\theta - c]^2$$

where $c =$ constant.

Write out the two equations which determine the equilibrium of the system. Is equilibrium possible for $m_1 \neq m_2$?

Given numerical values for all constants of the system, how can the equilibrium value of θ be found?

13.16. Regarding p, Fig. 4-13, Page 75, as a smooth ball joint, imagine the arrangement swinging in space around the vertical dotted line. Neglecting the mass of the rod and regarding m_1 and m_2 as particles, show that in spherical coordinates,

$$T = \tfrac{1}{2}m_1(r_1^2\dot\theta^2 + r_1^2\sin^2\theta\,\dot\phi^2) + \tfrac{1}{2}m_2(\dot r_2^2 + r_2^2\dot\theta^2 + r_2^2\sin^2\theta\,\dot\phi^2)$$

Now assuming a state of "steady motion" in which $\theta =$ constant, $r_2 =$ constant and $\dot\phi =$ constant, show that steady motion values of $r_2, \theta, \dot\phi$ are determined by the following relations

$$m_2 r_2 \sin^2\theta\,\dot\phi^2 = k(r_2 - r_0) - m_2 g\cos\theta \qquad (1)$$

$$(m_1r_1^2 + m_2r_2^2)\cos\theta\,\dot\phi^2 = (m_1r_1 + m_2r_2)g \qquad (2)$$

$$(m_1r_1^2 + m_2r_2^2)\sin^2\theta\,\dot\phi = P_\phi = \text{constant} \qquad (3)$$

where P_ϕ is the angular momentum corresponding to ϕ.

Note that for an assumed value of $\dot\phi$ (which by (2) must exceed a certain minimum value), (1) and (2) can be solved for the steady motion values of θ and r_2.

13.17. In Fig. 13-12 the "particle" of mass m is moving in the XY plane about the fixed mass M, under a "central force" f_r directed along r. f_r is some function of r (not necessarily an inverse square force) and it is assumed that no other force is acting. Equations of motion are

$$(1)\quad m\ddot{r} - mr\dot{\theta}^2 = f_r \qquad (2)\quad P_\theta = mr^2\dot{\theta} = \text{constant}$$

where P_θ is the angular momentum corresponding to θ.

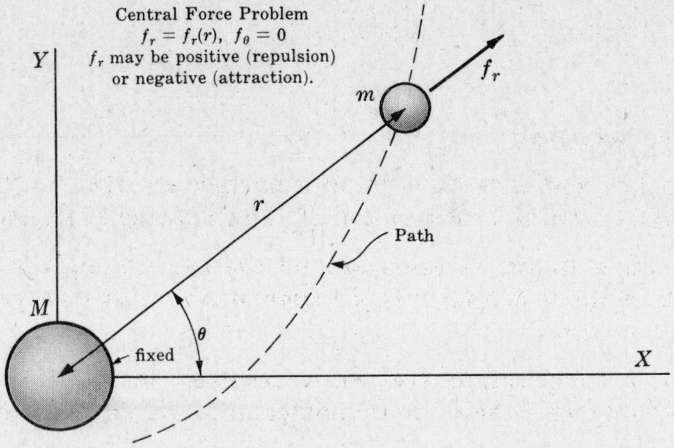

Fig. 13-12

(a) Eliminating $\dot{\theta}$ from (1) with (2), writing $\dfrac{d}{dt} = \dfrac{d\theta}{dt}\dfrac{d}{d\theta} = \dfrac{P_\theta}{mr^2}\dfrac{d}{d\theta}$ and finally substituting $u = 1/r$, show that the differential equation of the path is

$$\frac{d^2u}{d\theta^2} + u = -\frac{mf_r}{P_\theta^2 u^2} \qquad (3)$$

(b) Assuming that the path is a conic section $r = \dfrac{A}{1 - \epsilon\cos\theta}$, where ϵ = eccentricity, A = constant which depends on constants of the system and initial conditions, show that $f_r = -P_\theta^2/mAr^2$. (Whether the path is an ellipse, parabola or hyperbola depends on initial conditions; in each case f_r is proportional to $1/r^2$.)

(c) If the path is a rectangular hyperbola $xy = C$, show that $f_r = +\dfrac{P_\theta^2 r}{4mC^2}$.

(d) Given that the path described by m is a cardioid $r = a(1 + \cos\theta)$. Show that $f_r = -3P_\theta^2 a/mr^4$. Sketch the orbit.

(e) Show that for the circle $r = 2a\cos\theta$, $f_r = -8a^2P_\theta^2/mr^5$.

13.18. Referring to Example 13.8, Page 274 and assuming $\dot{\alpha} = bt$ (b = constant), find force components required to hold m in the bowl at a point for which $\theta = 45°$ and $\phi = 30°$.

CHAPTER 14

Effects of Earth's Figure and Daily Rotation on Dynamical Problems

14.1 Introductory Remarks.

An accurate treatment of the motion of a particle or rigid body relative to the surface of the earth requires careful consideration of the following matters.

(a) Due to the earth's annual rotation around the sun, its daily rotation about the polar axis and slight motions of this axis, *a frame of reference attached to the surface of the earth is not inertial.*

(b) The earth is not spherical, as frequently assumed, but slightly flattened at the poles. Its "sea-level" surface closely approximates an ellipsoid of revolution about the polar axis. See Fig. 14-1.

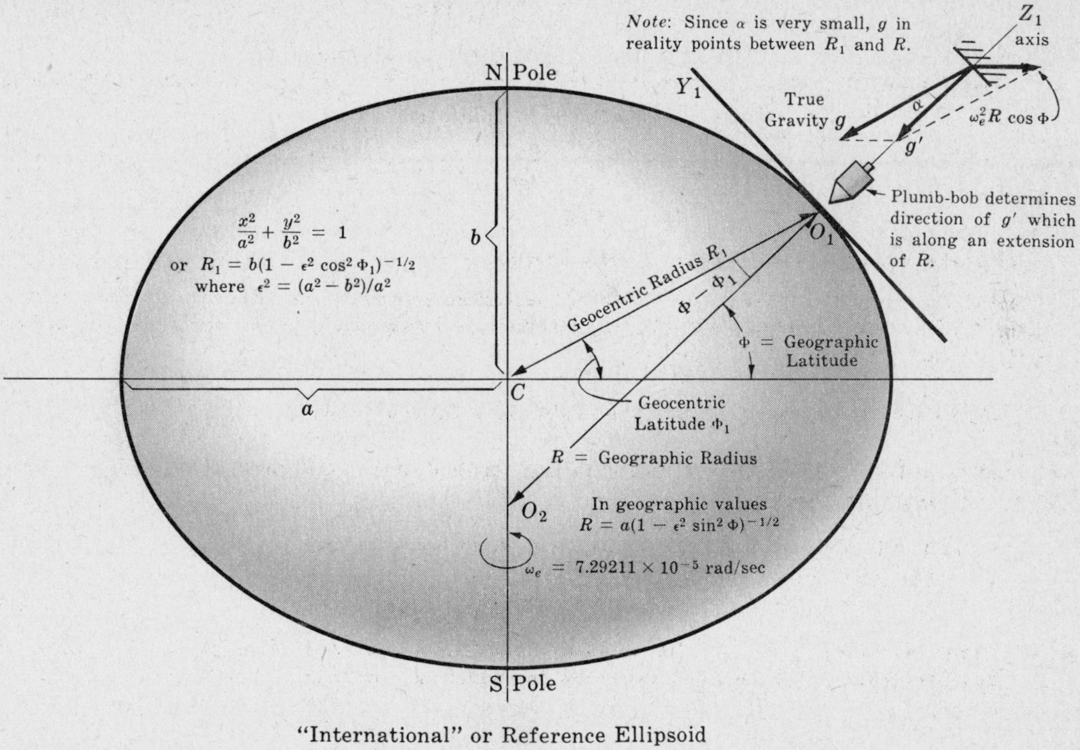

"International" or Reference Ellipsoid

Fig. 14-1

(c) As a result of this shape the true acceleration of gravity, g, (due only to the attraction of the earth) varies both in magnitude and direction with latitude. But since the earth is very nearly symmetrical about the polar axis, g is usually regarded as independent of longitude. In certain localities the value of g is affected by mountain ranges, non-uniformities in the density of the earth's crust, etc. These gravitational "anomalies" are in some cases important.

(*d*) Due to the earth's rotation and the consequent centrifugal force on all objects, the pendulum and plumb-line give a fictitious value of gravity, g', which except at the poles is slightly different in direction and less in magnitude than g.

(*e*) The ellipsoidal shape of the earth makes it desirable, though not necessary, to employ *geographic* values of latitude and radius rather than corresponding *geocentric* quantities. (These terms are defined and discussed in Section 14.2.)

(*f*) As will soon be evident, expressions for kinetic energy are in *no way affected by the shape of the earth or its gravitational field.* Assuming the frame of reference attached to the earth, the particular form taken by T depends on ω_e (the angular velocity of the earth) and on the orientation of the frame but not on the earth's shape.

(*g*) It is important to remember that in the determination of generalized forces which involve gravity *the true g and not g′ must be employed.* (See Section 4.5, Page 61.)

(*h*) The annual rotation of the earth around the sun is usually neglected except in the treatment of satellites. The motion of the polar axis is entirely negligible. Gravitational anomalies depend on local conditions and must be determined experimentally on the spot. Hence no further discussion of these matters is given. Moreover, no attempt is made to treat the effects of a "pear shaped" earth or other slight deviations from an ellipsoid of revolution. Such distortions may exist but if so they are very small. In Section 14.5, see Page 79 of reference (1) and Page 286 of reference (12).

14.2 Regarding the Earth's Figure. Geocentric and Geographic Latitude and Radius.

The combined action of gravity and centrifugal force have, throughout the ages, given the earth its very nearly ellipsoidal shape. Accurate measurements as well as theoretical considerations show that the mean sea level surface of the earth very closely approximates an ellipsoid of revolution (called the *reference ellipsoid* or *reference spheroid*) generated by rotating the ellipse $R_1 = b(1-\epsilon^2\cos^2\Phi_1)^{-1/2}$ (see Fig. 14-1) about the polar axis, where $\epsilon^2 = (a^2-b^2)/a^2$, a = equatorial radius, b = polar radius and R_1, Φ_1, measured as shown, are referred to as *geocentric* radius and latitude respectively.

For the treatment of many problems (but not all) the X_1, Y_1, Z_1 frame attached to the earth, as shown in Fig. 14-1 or Fig. 14-2, is quite convenient. Y_1 is tangent to a meridian line at O_1 and if extended would intersect the polar axis. Z_1 is normal to the surface (normal to a still pool of water) at O_1. Extended backward, Z_1 intersects the polar axis at O_2. X_1 is normal to the Y_1Z_1 plane and points eastward.

Now R, defined by the line O_2O_1 is called the *geographic radius* and Φ, measured as indicated, is the *geographic latitude.* (The term *geodetic* is sometimes used instead of geographic.) It is seen that at the equator $\Phi_1 = \Phi$ and $R_1 = R$, but in general there is a significant difference between geocentric and geographic values. Relations between them are given in Section 14.4. See Table 14.1.

14.3 Acceleration of Gravity on or Near the Earth's Surface.

As previously mentioned, it is convenient to treat two distinct values of gravity, each of which varies in magnitude and direction with latitude and is independent of longitude: (*a*) the "true" g due only to the gravitational pull of the earth (the value which would be determined by a pendulum and plumb-line if the earth were not rotating) and (*b*) a fictitious value g' which is the vector sum of g and the centrifugal force per unit mass ($\omega_e^2 R\cos\Phi$) due to the earth's rotation. It is g' which is measured in the laboratory with, say, a simple pendulum and plumb-line.

Now it is a fact of importance that, neglecting anomalies, g' is *normal to the surface of the reference ellipsoid* (normal to the surface of a still pool of water) and along the Z_1 axis, Fig. 14-1, while g tilts slightly northward in the northern hemisphere at an angle α with respect to Z_1. Assuming the earth symmetrical about the polar axis, both g and g' are in the Y_1Z_1 plane (the plane of a meridian). As will be seen, expressions (*14.11*) relating g and g' are easily derived.

14.4 Computational Formulas and Certain Constants.

For convenience in the treatment of specific problems the following constants and computational formulas are given. They are taken from references listed in Section 14.5, Page 285. Specific references and corresponding page numbers are indicated in each case. Notation used below is in accord with Fig. 14-1 and 14-2.

Equatorial radius, $a = 6{,}378{,}388$ meters. References: (2), page 334; (5), page 2.

Polar radius, $b = 6{,}356{,}912$ meters.

Flattening (or "ellipticity"), $f = (a-b)/a$. $f = 1/297.0 = .0033670$. References: (1), page 52; (5), page 25.

Angular velocity of earth relative to fixed stars, $\omega_e = 7.29211 \times 10^{-5}$ rad/sec. Reference: (11), page 132. $\omega_e^2 = 5.3175 \times 10^{-9}$, $\omega_e^2 a = 3.392$ cm/sec^2.

Reference ellipsoid may be written in terms of geocentric values as

$$R_1 = b(1 - \epsilon^2 \cos^2 \Phi_1)^{-1/2} \qquad (14.1)$$

where the square of eccentricity is $\epsilon^2 = (a^2 - b^2)/a^2 = 0.00672267$. Reference: (5), page 3. Note that $1 - \epsilon^2 = b^2/a^2 = 0.99327733$.

Geocentric radius R_1 in terms of *geographic* latitude Φ is

$$R_1 = 6{,}378{,}388(1 - 0.003367003 \sin^2 \Phi + 0.000007085 \sin^2 2\Phi) \text{ meters} \qquad (14.2)$$

Reference: (1), page 53, equation (*3.53a*). (*14.2*) is called the *International ellipsoid.*

Another expression for R_1 is

$$R_1 = 6{,}378{,}388(0.998320047 + 0.001683494 \cos 2\Phi - 0.000003549 \cos 4\Phi + \cdots) \text{ meters} \qquad (14.3)$$

Reference: (4), part II.

Geographic radius R in terms of geographic latitude Φ is

$$R = a(1 - \epsilon^2 \sin^2 \Phi)^{-1/2} \qquad (14.4)$$

Reference: (8), page 101, equation (*90*). In expanded form,

$$R = a(1 + \tfrac{1}{2}\epsilon^2 \sin^2 \Phi + \tfrac{3}{8}\epsilon^4 \sin^4 \Phi + \cdots)$$

Using the relation $\sin^4 \Phi = \sin^2 \Phi - \frac{1}{4} \sin^2 2\Phi$ and substituting numerical values,

$$R = 6{,}378{,}388(1 + 0.003378283 \sin^2 \Phi - 0.000004237 \sin^2 2\Phi) \text{ meters} \qquad (14.5)$$

Relation between Φ and Φ_1. Reference: (8), page 98, equation (*82*).

$$\tan \Phi = \frac{a^2}{b^2} \tan \Phi_1 \qquad (14.6)$$

The difference $\Phi - \Phi_1$, in seconds, in terms of Φ is

$$\Phi - \Phi_1 = 695.6635 \sin 2\Phi - 1.1731 \sin 4\Phi + 0.0026 \sin 6\Phi \qquad (14.7)$$

Reference: (5), page 26, formula (*20*). Or, in terms of Φ_1,

$$\Phi - \Phi_1 = 695.6635 \sin 2\Phi_1 + 1.1731 \sin 4\Phi_1 + 0.0026 \sin 6\Phi_1 \qquad (14.8)$$

Reference: (5), page 26, formula (*23*).

Gravity g' (as determined by a pendulum at the surface of the reference ellipsoid) in terms of geographic latitude Φ is

$$g' = 978.049(1 + 0.0052884 \sin^2 \Phi - 0.0000059 \sin^2 2\Phi) \tag{14.9}$$

Here 978.049 = sea level value of g' at the equator in cm/sec^2 or gals. (*14.9*) is the *International gravity formula.* Reference: (1), page 53, equation (*3.53b*); also (11), page 132, equation (*15*).

Gravity g'_h at some small height h above the reference ellipsoid is

$$g'_h = g' - (0.30855 + 0.00022 \cos 2\Phi - 0.000072h)h \tag{14.10}$$

where g', given by (*14.9*), is in gals and h in kilometers. Reference (4), part II; also (3), page 105, equation (*5.13*).

True gravity g in terms of g′ on the surface of the earth. Note that g' may be regarded as the vector sum of g and the centrifugal term $\omega_e^2 R \cos\Phi$. Hence from Fig. 14-1 it follows that

$$g \sin\alpha = \omega_e^2 R \sin\Phi \cos\Phi, \qquad g\cos\alpha = g' + \omega_e^2 R \cos^2\Phi \tag{14.11}$$

where α is the angle between g and g'. Thus (see Problem 14.33, Page 301)

$$\tan\alpha = \tfrac{1}{2}\omega_e^2 R\left(\frac{\sin 2\Phi}{g' + \omega_e^2 R\cos^2\Phi}\right) \tag{14.12}$$

Also, $g^2 = (g' + \omega_e^2 R \cos^2\Phi)^2 + (\omega_e^2 R \sin\Phi\cos\Phi)^2$ or

$$g^2 = g'^2 + \omega_e^2 R\cos^2\Phi(2g' + \omega_e^2 R) \tag{14.13}$$

Φ	At Equator, $\Phi = 0°$	30°	45°	60°	At Poles, $\Phi = 90°$
R_1 in meters	6,378,388 = a	6,373,053	6,367,695	6,362,315	6,356,912 = b
R in meters	6,378,388	6,383,755	6,389,135	6,394,529	6,399,936
g' in gals or cm/sec^2	978.049	979.338	980.629	981.924	983.221
g in gals	981.441	981.883	982.326	982.773	983.221
$g - g'$ in gals	3.392	2.545	1.697	0.849	0
α in minutes	0	5.15	5.95	5.15	0
$\Phi - \Phi_1$ in seconds	0	601.4463	695.6609	603.4782	0
$R - R_1$ in meters	0	10,702	21,430	32,214	43,024
$a - R_1$ in meters	0	5,335	10,693	16,073	21,476

Important Quantities for the Accurate Treatment of Motion Near the Surface of the Earth.

Table 14.1

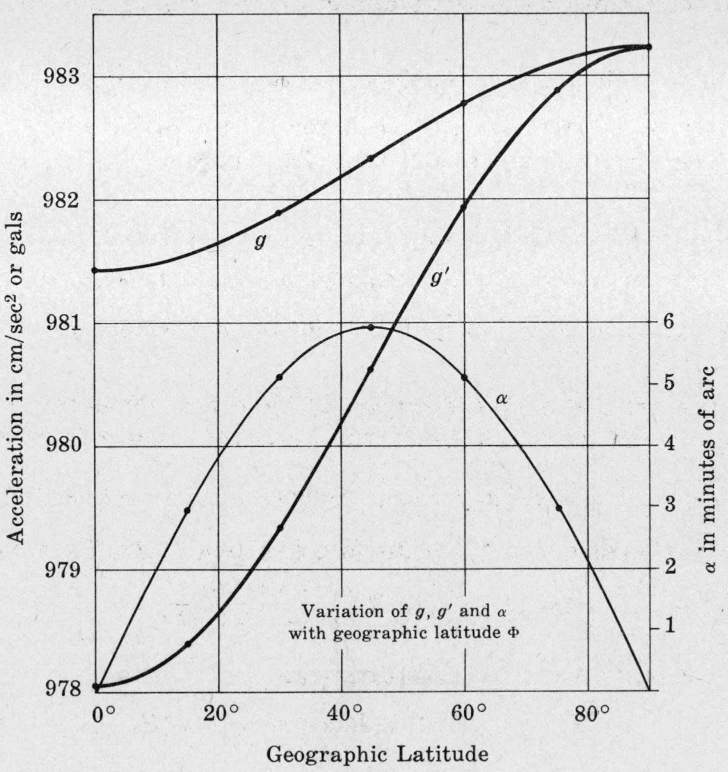

Graph 14.1

14.5 References on the Figure of the Earth and its Gravitational Field.

1. W. A. Heiskanen and F. A. Vening Meinesz, *The Earth and its Gravitational Field,* McGraw-Hill, 1958.
2. J. M. A. Danby, *Fundamentals of Celestial Mechanics,* Macmillan, 1962.
3. R. A. Hirvonen, *The Size and Shape of the Earth,* (*Advances in Geophysics,* Vol. 5, pages 93-113), Academic Press, 1958.
4. R. Parvin, *The Earth and Inertial Space,* Aero/Space Engineering; part I, April 1959; part II, May 1959.
5. W. D. Lambert and C. H. Swick, *Formulas and Tables for the Computation of Geodetic Positions on the International Ellipsoid,* Spl. Pub. No. 200, U. S. Coast and Geodetic Survey, 1935.
6. H. C. Mitchell, *Definition of Terms Used in Geodetic and Other Surveys,* Spl. Pub. No. 242, U. S. Coast and Geodetic Survey, 1948.
7. C. H. Swick, *Pendulum Gravity Measurements and Isostatic Reductions,* Spl. Pub. No. 232, U. S. Coast and Geodetic Survey, 1942.
8. W. Chauvenet, *A Manual of Spherical and Practical Astronomy,* Vol. I, Dover, 1960.
9. J. A. Duerksen, *Deflections of the Vertical in the United States,* Spl. Pub. No. 229, U. S. Coast and Geodetic Survey, 1941.
10. J. A. O'Keefe, *Geographical Positions,* Smithsonian Institution, 1956.
11. H. Jeffreys, *The Earth,* 3rd ed., Cambridge University Press, 1952.
12. G. P. Wollard, *Advances in Geophysics,* Vol. 1, Pages 281-300, Academic Press, 1952.

14.6 Kinetic Energy and Equations of Motion of a Particle in Various Coordinates. Frame of Reference Attached to Earth's Surface.

The following derivations illustrate well certain basic principles of dynamics, and the resulting expressions are convenient for the solution of a wide range of problems.

A. *Consider the $X_1Y_1Z_1$ frame, Fig. 14-2, rigidly fastened to the earth with origin at O_1.* Y_1 is tangent to a meridian, Z_1 is an extension of the geographic radius R (Z_1 is normal to the surface of the reference ellipsoid at O_1), X_1 is normal to the Y_1Z_1 plane and points eastward. Axes X_2, Y_2, Z_2, with origin attached to the axis of the earth at O_2, *do not rotate* but point always toward the same fixed stars. *We shall regard X_2, Y_2, Z_2 as inertial.* Note that $\omega_e t$ represents the angular rotation of the earth in time t. From the diagram it can be seen that $\beta_{11}, \beta_{12}, \beta_{13}$, the direction cosines of X_1 relative to X_2, Y_2, Z_2, etc., are given by

$$\begin{array}{lll} \beta_{11} = -\sin\omega_e t, & \beta_{12} = \cos\omega_e t, & \beta_{13} = 0 \\ \beta_{21} = -\sin\Phi\cos\omega_e t, & \beta_{22} = -\sin\Phi\sin\omega_e t, & \beta_{23} = \cos\Phi \\ \beta_{31} = \cos\Phi\cos\omega_e t, & \beta_{32} = \cos\Phi\sin\omega_e t, & \beta_{33} = \sin\Phi \end{array}$$

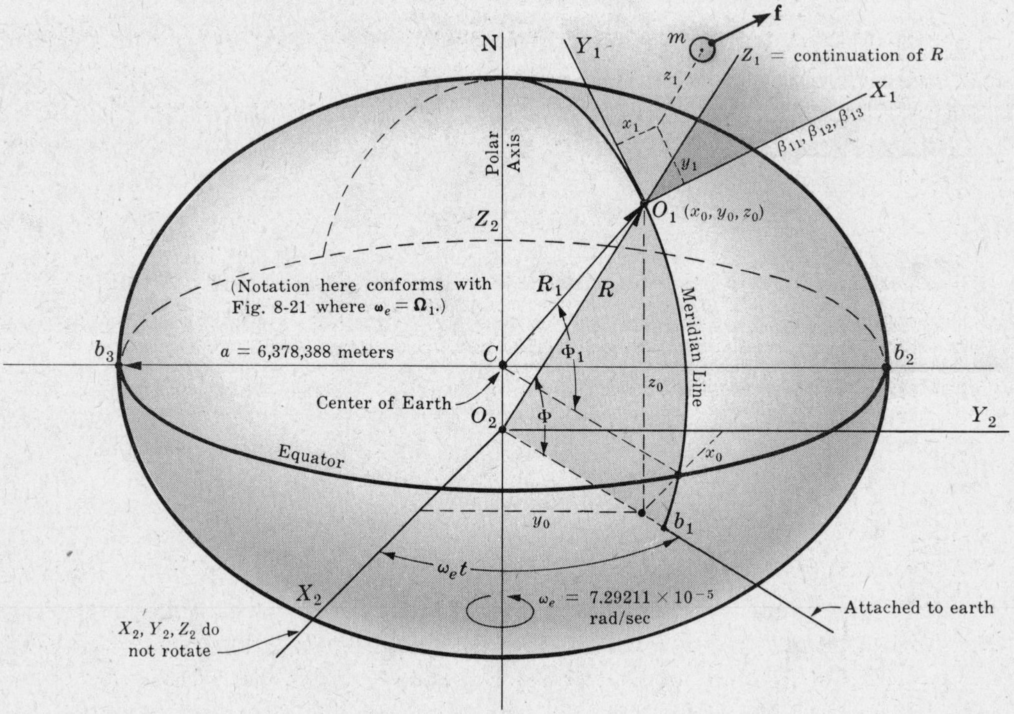

Fig. 14-2

Note that the orientation of X_1, Y_1, Z_1 relative to X_2, Y_2, Z_2 can be expressed in Euler angles (see Fig. 8-16, Page 156) where $\omega_e t = \psi - 90°$, $\theta = 90° - \Phi$ and $\phi = 0$. Hence expressions for the β's can be checked at once by Table 8.2, Page 158.

It is also seen that $x_0 = R\cos\Phi\cos\omega_e t$, $y_0 = R\cos\Phi\sin\omega_e t$, $z_0 = R\sin\Phi$. Hence transformation equations relating the x_2, y_2, z_2 and x_1, y_1, z_1 coordinates of particle m are

$$x_2 = R\cos\Phi\cos\omega_e t - x_1\sin\omega_e t - y_1\sin\Phi\cos\omega_e t + z_1\cos\Phi\cos\omega_e t$$

with similar expressions for y_2 and z_2. Since X_2, Y_2, Z_2 are regarded as inertial, $T = \frac{1}{2}m(\dot{x}_2^2 + \dot{y}_2^2 + \dot{z}_2^2)$.

Differentiating relations for x_2, y_2, z_2 and substituting in the above expression, we finally get

$$\begin{aligned} T \;=\; & \tfrac{1}{2}m(\dot{x}_1^2+\dot{y}_1^2+\dot{z}_1^2) + m\omega_e[(x_1\dot{y}_1 - y_1\dot{x}_1)\sin\Phi + (R\dot{x}_1 + z_1\dot{x}_1 - x_1\dot{z}_1)\cos\Phi] \\ & + \tfrac{1}{2}m\omega_e^2[x_1^2 + y_1^2\sin^2\Phi + (R+z_1)^2\cos^2\Phi - 2y_1(R+z_1)\sin\Phi\cos\Phi] \end{aligned} \qquad (14.14)$$

Applying Lagrange's equations, the following equations of motion are obtained.

$$\begin{aligned} m[\ddot{x}_1 + 2\omega_e(\dot{z}_1\cos\Phi - \dot{y}_1\sin\Phi) - \omega_e^2 x_1] &= F_{x_1} \\ m[\ddot{y}_1 + 2\omega_e\dot{x}_1\sin\Phi + \omega_e^2\sin\Phi((R+z_1)\cos\Phi - y_1\sin\Phi)] &= F_{y_1} \\ m[\ddot{z}_1 - 2\omega_e\dot{x}_1\cos\Phi - \omega_e^2\cos\Phi((R+z_1)\cos\Phi - y_1\sin\Phi)] &= F_{z_1} \end{aligned} \qquad (14.15)$$

Important points regarding ***(14.14)*** ***and*** ***(14.15).***

(*a*) Expression (*14.14*) in no way depends on the shape of the earth. The form of T depends only on ω_e and the location and orientation of X_1, Y_1, Z_1.

(*b*) Expressions (*14.15*) take complete account of the earth's rotation. Since $\omega_e = 7.29211 \times 10^{-5}$ rad/sec, terms containing ω_e^2 can frequently be neglected. However, R is about 6.4×10^8 cm and $R\omega_e^2$ is roughly 3.4 cm/sec². As will be seen, this term usually cancels out after introducing g'.

(*c*) Assuming, for example, that gravity is the only force on m, generalized forces in (*14.15*) are just $F_{x_1} = mg_{x_1}$, $F_{y_1} = mg_{y_1}$, $F_{z_1} = mg_{z_1}$ where $g_{x_1}, g_{y_1}, g_{z_1}$ are the X_1, Y_1, Z_1 components of true gravity g (not g'). Neglecting anomalies, g is in the Y_1Z_1 plane. Hence $F_{x_1} = 0$. Referring to Fig. 14-1 it is seen that $F_{y_1} = g\sin\alpha$ and $F_{z_1} = -g\cos\alpha$. Hence by (*14.11*),

$$F_{y_1} = \omega_e^2 R\sin\Phi\cos\Phi \quad \text{and} \quad F_{z_1} = -(g' + \omega_e^2 R\cos^2\Phi)$$

Note. We have tacitly assumed that g and g' are constant in magnitude and direction for any values of x_1, y_1, z_1. Strictly speaking they are functions of x_1, y_1, z_1 and could be so expressed if this degree of accuracy were required. See expression (*14.10*). Thus (*14.15*) reduce to

$$\begin{aligned} \ddot{x}_1 + 2\omega_e(\dot{z}_1\cos\Phi - \dot{y}_1\sin\Phi) - \omega_e^2 x_1 &= 0 \\ \ddot{y}_1 + 2\omega_e\dot{x}_1\sin\Phi + \omega_e^2\sin\Phi(z_1\cos\Phi - y_1\sin\Phi) &= 0 \\ \ddot{z}_1 - 2\omega_e\dot{x}_1\cos\Phi - \omega_e^2\cos\Phi(z_1\cos\Phi - y_1\sin\Phi) &= -g' \end{aligned} \qquad (14.16)$$

Terms containing $\omega_e^2 R$ automatically cancel and R no longer appears in the equations. For a stated value of Φ, g' is given by (*14.9*).

(*d*) Expression (*14.14*), found above by means of transformation equations, can more easily be obtained by an application of relations (*8.4*), Page 143. (See Problem 14.7.)

(*e*) Writing **a** as the total acceleration of m relative to inertial space, the quantities in the brackets of (*14.15*) are just the components a_x, a_y, a_z of **a** along the instantaneous directions of X_1, Y_1, Z_1 respectively. (See Section 3.9, Page 48.) Moreover, note that equations (*14.15*) can be written down at once from relations (*9.6*), Page 179. See Problem 14.8.

(*f*) Components of centripetal and Coriolis acceleration as $\omega_e^2 R$ and $2\omega_e\dot{x}_1$ respectively are automatically taken account of in equations (*14.15*).

(*g*) If the particle m is constrained in some known manner, T can easily be modified to take account of this. See Example 14.2, Page 292.

(*h*) Relation (*14.14*) expresses T for a single free unconstrained particle. T for several particles is obtained merely by summing this relation; and if the particles are constrained in some manner, superfluous coordinates can be eliminated from T in the usual way by means of equations of constraint (assuming holonomic constraints). Moreover, any convenient coordinates other than rectangular can be introduced by proper transformation equations as shown in B, C, D below.

B. *Consider cylindrical coordinates ρ, ϕ, z, with origin at O_1, Fig. 14-2.* Writing $x_1 = \rho\cos\phi$, $y_1 = \rho\sin\phi$ and $z_1 = z$, the reader can show that (*14.14*) may be put in the form,

$$\begin{aligned} T \;=\; & \tfrac{1}{2}m(\dot\rho^2 + \rho^2\dot\phi^2 + \dot z^2) \\ & + m\omega_e[\rho^2\dot\phi\sin\Phi + (R+z)(\dot\rho\cos\phi - \rho\dot\phi\sin\phi)\cos\Phi - \rho\dot z\cos\phi\cos\Phi] \\ & + \tfrac{1}{2}m\omega_e^2[\rho^2(\cos^2\phi + \sin^2\phi\sin^2\Phi) + (R+z)^2\cos^2\Phi - 2\rho(R+z)\sin\phi\sin\Phi\cos\Phi] \end{aligned} \tag{14.17}$$

Equations of motion in ρ, ϕ, z follow at once and basic expressions for generalized forces (assuming gravity only acting) are

$$F_\rho = mg\sin\alpha\sin\phi, \qquad F_\phi = mg\rho\sin\alpha\cos\phi, \qquad F_z = -mg\cos\alpha$$

which if desired can be written in terms of g', etc.

Following the same procedure it is easy to write T in spherical or other coordinates. See Problems 14.9 and 14.10.

C. *Consider an X', Y', Z' frame (not shown) with origin at O_1,* Fig. 14-2, where Z' is an upward extension of the geocentric radius R_1, Y' extended intersects the polar axis and X', normal to the $Y'Z'$ plane, points eastward. Note that the $X'Y'$ plane is not tangent to the earth at O_1 and g' is not along Z'.

Using *geocentric* values, T and the equations of motion have exactly the same form as (*14.14*) and (*14.15*) respectively where R_1, Φ_1 replace R, Φ and x', y', z' replace x_1, y_1, z_1. Again, for example, assuming gravity only acting on the particle,

$$F_{x'} = 0, \qquad F_{y'} = -mg\sin(\Phi - \Phi_1 - \alpha), \qquad F_{z'} = -mg\cos(\Phi - \Phi_1 - \alpha)$$

But

$$\begin{aligned} g\sin(\Phi - \Phi_1 - \alpha) &= g'\sin(\Phi - \Phi_1) - \omega_e^2 R_1\sin\Phi_1\cos\Phi_1, \\ g\cos(\Phi - \Phi_1 - \alpha) &= g'\cos(\Phi - \Phi_1) + \omega^2 R_1\cos^2\Phi_1 \end{aligned}$$

Thus the equations of motion finally take the form

$$\begin{aligned} \ddot x' + 2\omega_e(\dot z'\cos\Phi_1 - \dot y'\sin\Phi_1) - \omega_e^2 x' &= 0 \\ \ddot y' + 2\omega_e\dot x'\sin\Phi_1 + \omega_e^2\sin\Phi_1(z'\cos\Phi_1 - y'\sin\Phi_1) &= -g'\sin(\Phi - \Phi_1) \\ \ddot z' - 2\omega_e\dot x'\cos\Phi_1 - \omega_e^2\cos\Phi_1(z'\cos\Phi_1 - y'\sin\Phi_1) &= -g'\cos(\Phi - \Phi_1) \end{aligned} \tag{14.18}$$

Note that again terms containing $\omega_e^2 R_1$ automatically drop out.

It is important to remember that for any and all types of forces acting, generalized forces are determined in the usual way *disregarding the rotation of the earth.* See Section 4.5, Page 61.

D. *Consider the X_1, Y_1, Z_1 frame, Fig. 14-3 below.* Here Z_1 is taken parallel to Z_2 (the polar axis), X_1 in the plane of the meridian and Y_1 perpendicular to the X_1Z_1 plane as shown. In terms of x_1, y_1, z_1 relative to this frame, T for a single particle is given (dropping a constant term) by

$$T = \tfrac{1}{2}m[\dot x_1^2 + \dot y_1^2 + \dot z_1^2 + (x_1^2 + y_1^2)\omega_e^2 + 2\omega_e(x_1\dot y_1 - y_1\dot x_1) + 2R\omega_e(x_1\omega_e + \dot y_1)\cos\Phi] \tag{14.19}$$

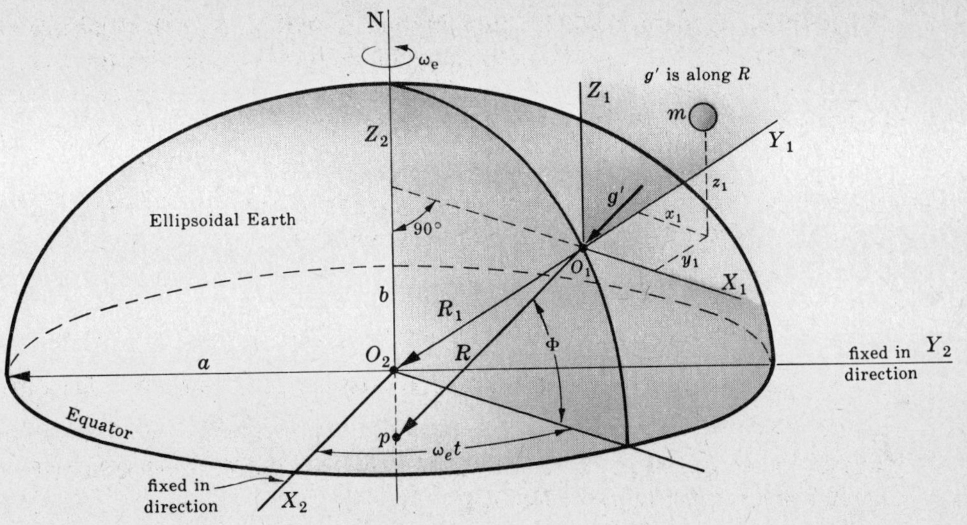

Fig. 14-3

The reader should show that (*14.19*) can be obtained by applying relations (*8.4*), Page 143.

Equations of motion of m are,

$$m(\ddot{x}_1 - x_1\omega_e^2 - 2\dot{y}_1\omega_e - R\omega_e^2 \cos\Phi) = F_{x_1}$$
$$m(\ddot{y}_1 - y_1\omega_e^2 + 2\omega_e\dot{x}_1) = F_{y_1} \qquad (14.20)$$
$$m\ddot{z}_1 = F_{z_1}$$

$F_{x_1}, F_{y_1}, F_{z_1}$ are determined by gravity and whatever other forces may be applied to m. But, as before, g (making an angle α with R) must be employed. (See Problem 14.25.) The reader should show that (*14.20*) follow directly from relations (*9.6*), Page 179.

E. *Spherical coordinates with origin at the center of the earth.* Axes X_1, Y_1, Z_1, Fig. 14-4, with origin at O_2, are fastened to the earth. Employing spherical coordinates r, θ, ϕ measured as shown and noting that $\theta + \Phi_1 = 90°$, it follows that

$$T = \tfrac{1}{2}m[\dot{r}^2 + r^2\dot{\Phi}_1^2 + r^2(\dot{\phi} + \omega_e)^2 \cos^2\Phi_1] \qquad (14.21)$$

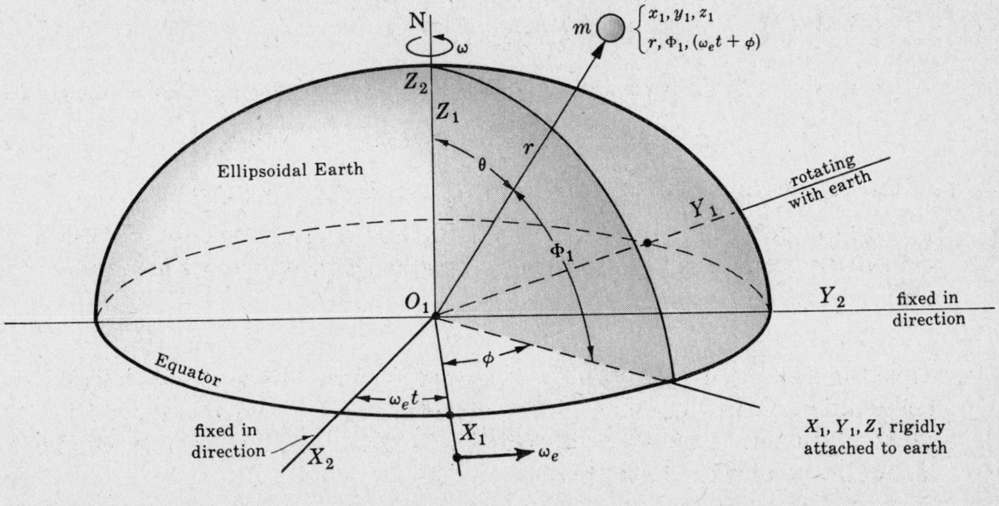

Fig. 14-4

which is applicable to motion near the surface of the earth, or to long range projectiles. Note that g is not parallel to r and decreases with height above the earth's surface. See equations (*14.9*), (*14.10*), (*14.11*).

Relation (*14.21*) is also applicable to the motion of satellites. However, in this case generalized forces F_r, F_{Φ_1}, F_ϕ must be determined from accurate expressions for the components of g at relatively great distances from the earth. (See Example 14.12, Page 297.)

14.7 *T* for a Particle, Frame of Reference in Motion Relative to Earth's Surface.

The following examples illustrate the general technique.

(*a*) A railroad car moves in the X_1Y_1 plane of Fig. 14-2, along a straight track which makes an angle β with respect to X_1. A rectangular frame X, Y, Z is attached to the car with X parallel to the track and Z parallel to Z_1. Letting S represent the distance from O_1 to the coach, relations between x_1, y_1, z_1 and x, y, z are

$$x_1 = S\cos\beta + x\cos\beta - y\sin\beta, \quad y_1 = S\sin\beta + x\sin\beta + y\cos\beta, \quad z_1 = z$$

Eliminating $x_1, \dot{x}_1$, etc., from (*14.14*) we obtain

$$\begin{aligned} T \;=\; & \tfrac{1}{2}m[(\dot{S}+\dot{x})^2 + \dot{y}^2 + \dot{z}^2] + m\omega_e[\dot{y}(S+x)\sin\Phi - y(\dot{S}+\dot{x})\sin\Phi \\ & + \cos\Phi((R+z)(\dot{S}\cos\beta + \dot{x}\cos\beta - \dot{y}\sin\beta) - (S\cos\beta + x\cos\beta - y\sin\beta)\dot{z})] \\ & + \tfrac{1}{2}m\omega_e^2[(S\cos\beta + x\cos\beta - y\sin\beta)^2 + (S\sin\beta + x\sin\beta + y\cos\beta)^2\sin^2\Phi \\ & - 2(S\sin\beta + x\sin\beta + y\cos\beta)(R+z)\sin\Phi\cos\Phi + (R+z)^2\cos^2\Phi] \end{aligned} \qquad (14.22)$$

S may be assumed to vary in any manner. Lagrangian equations of motion, of course, take complete account of the rotation of the earth as well as the motion of the coach. (Note that the assumed motion of the coach is in the X_1Y_1 plane and not along the earth's surface.)

(*b*) *Consider an expression for T in coordinates relative to a rotating table placed at* O_1, *Fig. 14-2, with axis of rotation along* Z_1. An X, Y, Z frame with Z along Z_1 is attached to the table. Its angular displacement β is measured between X_1 and X. Then

$$x_1 = x\cos\beta - y\sin\beta, \quad y_1 = x\sin\beta + y\cos\beta, \quad z_1 = z$$

Now eliminating $x_1, y_1, z_1; \dot{x}_1, \dot{y}_1, \dot{z}_1$ from (*14.14*), T expressed in terms of $\dot{x}, \dot{y}, \dot{z}$, etc., can be found.

However, employing relations (*8.2*), Page 140, we can write at once

$$T = \tfrac{1}{2}m[(v_{x_0} + \dot{x} + \omega_y z - \omega_z y)^2 + (v_{y_0} + \dot{y} + \omega_z x - \omega_x z)^2 + (v_{z_0} + \dot{z} + \omega_x y - \omega_y x)^2] \qquad (14.23)$$

where the reader may show that

$$v_{0x} = R\omega_e\cos\beta\cos\Phi, \quad v_{0y} = -R\omega_e\sin\beta\cos\Phi, \quad v_{0z} = 0$$

$$\omega_x = \omega_e\sin\beta\cos\Phi, \quad \omega_y = \omega_e\cos\beta\cos\Phi, \quad \omega_z = \dot{\beta} + \omega_e\sin\Phi$$

This method is considerably less tedious than the one suggested above.

14.8 Motion of a Rigid Body Near the Surface of the Earth.

In outlining this problem we shall follow the notation and method presented in Section 8.10, Page 162. The reader would do well to review this section. Indeed, the following treatment is merely a special case of the more general treatment referred to above.

Referring to Fig. 14-5, X_1, Y_1, Z_1 represent just the X_1, Y_1, Z_1 axes of Fig. 14-2. Here $\boldsymbol{\omega}_e$ corresponds to $\boldsymbol{\Omega}_1$ in Fig. 8-21, Page 163. Hence it can be seen that $\Omega_{1x} = 0$, $\Omega_{1y} = \omega_e \cos \Phi$, $\Omega_{1z} = \omega_e \sin \Phi$. Also $\Omega_x = \dot{\psi} \sin\theta \sin\phi + \dot{\theta}\cos\phi$, etc. (See relations (*8.11*), Page 157.) Hence components of the total inertial space angular velocity, $\boldsymbol{\Omega}_{\text{total}}$, of the body along the body-fixed X, Y, Z axes are given by (see (*8.14*), Page 163)

$$\begin{aligned} \omega_x &= \dot{\psi}\sin\theta\sin\phi + \dot{\theta}\cos\phi + \alpha_{12}\omega_e\cos\Phi + \alpha_{13}\omega_e\sin\Phi \\ \omega_y &= \dot{\psi}\sin\theta\cos\phi - \dot{\theta}\sin\phi + \alpha_{22}\omega_e\cos\Phi + \alpha_{23}\omega_e\sin\Phi \\ \omega_z &= \dot{\phi} + \dot{\psi}\cos\theta + \alpha_{32}\omega_e\cos\Phi + \alpha_{33}\omega_e\sin\Phi \end{aligned} \tag{14.24}$$

where $\alpha_{11}, \alpha_{12}, \alpha_{13}$ are direction cosines of the body-fixed X axis relative to X_1, Y_1, Z_1, etc. These may be written in terms of Euler angles θ, ψ, ϕ by Table 8.2, Page 158.

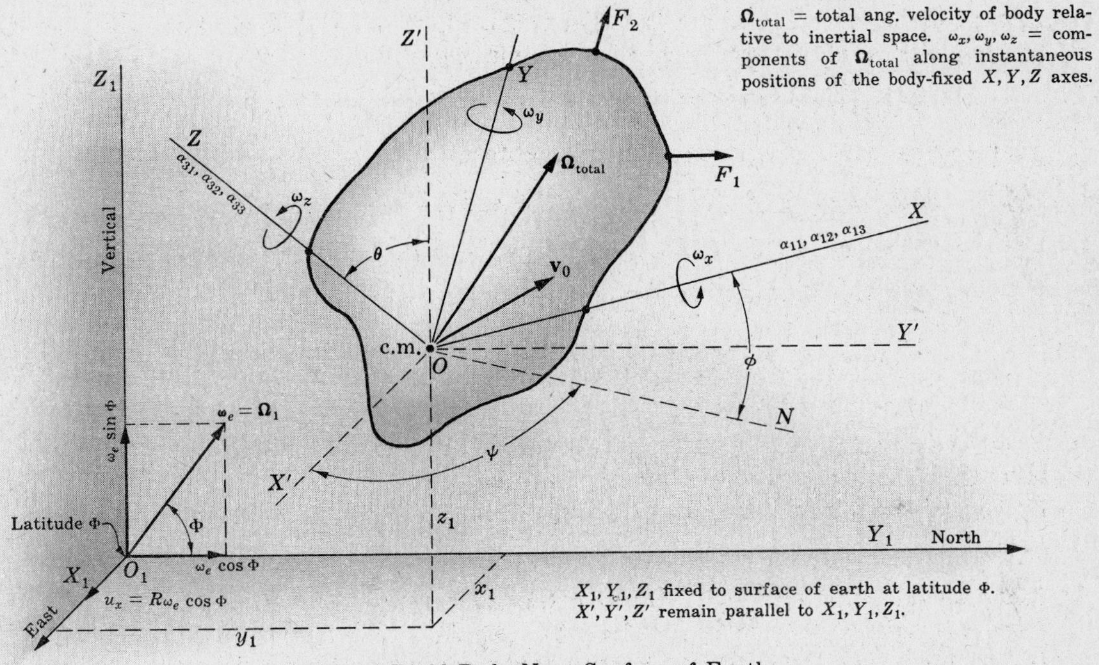

Motion of Rigid Body Near Surface of Earth

Fig. 14-5

Following equations (*8.4*), Page 143, we find (see equations (*8.15*), Page 163) that

$$\begin{aligned} v_1 &= R\omega_e\cos\Phi + \dot{x}_1 + \omega_e z_1\cos\Phi - \omega_e y_1 \sin\Phi, \\ v_2 &= \dot{y}_1 + \omega_e x_1 \sin\Phi, \qquad v_3 = \dot{z}_1 - \omega_e x_1\cos\Phi \end{aligned} \tag{14.25}$$

Now assuming for simplicity that O is at c.m. and inserting (*14.24*) and (*14.25*) into (*8.10*), Page 148, we have the proper expression for T, from which equations of motion follow at once. Generalized forces arising from gravity and any given applied forces are obtained in the usual way.

14.9 Specific Illustrative Examples.

In each of the following examples, unless otherwise stated, we shall assume that g and g' remain constant in magnitude and direction throughout the region traversed by the particle and equal to values computed at the origin of axes. Strictly speaking this is not quite true but if in any case accuracy requires it, corrections can be made. (See equations (*14.9*) and (*14.10*).)

Example 14.1. *Determination of the direction of a plumb-line.*

Assuming the bob at rest at O_1, Fig. 14-1, we set $x_1 = \dot{x}_1 = \ddot{x}_1 = 0$, etc., in (*14.15*) and find

$$F_{x_1} = 0, \quad F_{y_1} = m\omega_e^2 R \sin\Phi \cos\Phi, \quad F_{z_1} = -m\omega_e^2 R \cos^2\Phi \tag{1}$$

Regarding the bob as a free particle,

$$F_{x_1} = 0, \quad F_{y_1} = mg \sin\alpha, \quad F_{z_1} = \tau - mg\cos\alpha \tag{2}$$

where α is the unknown angle between g and the plumb-line and τ is the tension in the string. But $\tau = mg'$ defines g'. Hence from (*1*) and (*2*),

$$g\sin\alpha = \omega_e^2 R \sin\Phi\cos\Phi, \qquad g\cos\alpha = g' + \omega_e^2 R\cos^2\Phi$$

which are just relations (*14.11*). Hence α, determined by (*14.12*), is the angle through which the plumb-line is tilted as a result of the earth's rotation.

Example 14.2. *Motion of a bead on a smooth parabolic wire.*

A bead of mass m is free to slide along a smooth parabolic wire $z_1 = bx_1^2$ (wire in the X_1Z_1 plane, Fig. 14-2) under the action of gravity. Making use of the above relation and $y_1 = 0$, relation (*14.14*) for T can be put in proper form at once. The reader may show that the equation of motion finally takes the form

$$m(1+4b^2x_1^2)\ddot{x}_1 + 4mb^2x_1\dot{x}_1^2 - m\omega_e^2(2b^2x_1^3\cos^2\Phi + x_1) = -2mg'x_1b$$

Compare this with the equation of motion given in Example 3.2, Page 44.

Example 14.3. *Motion of a simple pendulum in the XZ plane.*

A pendulum of length l is suspended from a point on the Z_1 axis, Fig. 14-2, so that its rest position is at O_1. We shall assume that it is confined to swing without friction in the X_1Z_1 plane. Indicating the angular position of the pendulum by θ, relation (*14.14*) reduces to

$$T = \tfrac{1}{2}ml^2\dot{\theta}^2 + (m\omega_e lR\cos\Phi)\dot{\theta}\cos\theta - (m\omega_e l^2\cos\Phi)(1-\cos\theta)\dot{\theta}$$
$$+ \tfrac{1}{2}m\omega_e^2[l^2\sin^2\theta + (R+l-l\cos\theta)^2\cos^2\Phi]$$

The generalized force $F_\theta = -mgl\sin\theta\cos\alpha$. Applying Lagrange's equation and assuming θ small, we finally get $\ddot{\theta} = -(g'/l)\theta$, which shows that, of course, the pendulum measurements give g' rather than g.

If the pendulum is allowed to swing in the YZ plane,

$$T = \tfrac{1}{2}ml^2\dot{\theta}^2 + \tfrac{1}{2}m\omega_e^2[l^2\sin^2\theta\sin^2\Phi + (R+l(1-\cos\theta))^2\cos^2\Phi$$
$$- 2l\sin\theta(R+l(1-\cos\theta))\sin\Phi\cos\Phi]$$

$$F_\theta = -mgl\sin(\theta-\alpha) = -ml\sin\theta(g\cos\alpha) + ml\cos\theta(g\sin\alpha)$$

and, for θ small, the equation of motion, as the reader should show, again reduces to $\ddot{\theta} = -(g'/l)\theta$.

Example 14.4. *Rectangular components of force $f_{x_1}, f_{y_1}, f_{z_1}$ exerted by train tracks on a coach of mass M moving north along Y_1 with uniform velocity $\dot{y}_1$.*

Regarding the coach as a "free particle" and setting $x_1 = \dot{x}_1 = \ddot{x}_1 = 0$, etc., in (*14.15*) we get

$$f_{x_1} = -2M\omega_e\dot{y}_1\sin\Phi, \quad f_{y_1} = 0, \quad f_{z_1} = -Mg'$$

Thus the track exerts a force of $-2M\omega_e\dot{y}_1\sin\Phi$ in the negative direction of X_1. The vertical force f_{z_1} exerted by the track merely supports the weight Mg', (not Mg).

The reader may show that, for the train moving east along X with constant velocity $\dot{x}_1$,

$$f_{x_1} = 0, \quad f_{y_1} = 2M\omega_e\dot{x}_1\sin\Phi, \quad f_{z_1} = Mg' - 2M\omega_e\dot{x}_1\cos\Phi$$

Note that the coach "weighs" less to the extent of $2M\omega_e\dot{x}_1\cos\Phi$. If moving west it would weigh more. For $\dot{x}_1 = 60$ miles/hr., $M = 100$ tons and $\Phi = 45°$, the loss (or gain) in weight is about 56 pounds. (See Problem 14.14.)

Example 14.5. *Motion of a short-range projectile, neglecting atmospheric drag.*

Assuming no air resistance, no gravitational anomalies and that g' remains constant in magnitude and direction throughout the space traversed, equations *(14.16)* are directly applicable. Dropping terms containing ω_e^2, we write

$$\ddot{x}_1 + 2\omega_e(\dot{z}_1 \cos\Phi - \dot{y}_1 \sin\Phi) = 0 \qquad (1)$$

$$\ddot{y}_1 + 2\omega_e\dot{x}_1 \sin\Phi = 0 \qquad (2)$$

$$\ddot{z}_1 - 2\omega_e\dot{x}_1 \cos\Phi = -g' \qquad (3)$$

Integrating equation *(1)* once, substituting for $\dot{x}$ in *(2)* and *(3)*, dropping terms containing $\omega_e^2 y_1$ and $\omega_e^2 z_1$, the last two equations integrate at once. Putting these values back into *(1)* and again neglecting terms containing ω_e^2, this equation can be integrated. After evaluating the constants of integration, the final approximate solutions are

$$x_1 = x_0 + \dot{x}_0 t + \omega_e(\dot{y}_0 \sin\Phi - \dot{z}_0 \cos\Phi)t^2 + \tfrac{1}{3}\omega_e g' t^3 \cos\Phi \qquad (4)$$

$$y_1 = y_0 + \dot{y}_0 t - \omega_e \dot{x}_0 t^2 \sin\Phi \qquad (5)$$

$$z_1 = z_0 + \dot{z}_0 t + \tfrac{1}{2}(2\omega_e\dot{x}_0 \cos\Phi - g')t^2 \qquad (6)$$

where quantities with zero subscript indicate initial values. These equations have the usual simple form except for terms containing ω_e.

One should note that, aside from approximations made, *(4)*, *(5)* and *(6)* are based on the incorrect assumption that g' remains parallel to Z_1 for all values of the coordinates. Moreover, values of x_1, y_1, z_1 given by these equations are to be measured relative to the X_1, Y_1, Z_1 frame, whereas in actual practice the height of a projectile at any time and the final range are measured relative to the curved surface of the earth. Hence a more accurate and realistic treatment would involve several considerations not included above.

As a possible means of eliminating some of the above difficulties, the reader may consider the following. Take a reference point p on the surface of the ellipsoidal earth having a geographical latitude Φ_0. Indicate geographical latitude measured from this point by β; that is, $\Phi = \Phi_0 + \beta$. Let longitude, ϕ, be measured from a meridian passing through p. Let h, measured along an extension of the geographic R, be the vertical height of a particle above the ellipsoidal surface of the earth. It now follows without difficulty that

$$T = \tfrac{1}{2}m[(\dot{R}+\dot{h})^2 + (R+h)^2\dot{\beta}^2 + (R+h)^2(\dot{\phi}+\omega_e)^2 \cos^2(\Phi_0+\beta)]$$

Noting that R is a function of Φ (and thus of β) by relation *(14.4)* or *(14.5)*, equations of motion corresponding to β, h, ϕ can be written at once. The acceleration g_h' (for h not very great) is given by *(14.10)* and is always along h. Each of the quantities β, h, ϕ can be measured relative to the ellipsoidal surface of the earth.

Example 14.6. *Pendulum with sliding support.* (See Example 4.4, Page 64.)

Let m_1 be free to slide along X_1, Fig. 14-2. Assuming motion of pendulum confined to the X_1Z_1 plane, it follows, applying *(14.14)* to m_1 and m_2, that

$$\begin{aligned} T = {} & \tfrac{1}{2}m_1(\dot{x}_1^2 + 2\omega_e\dot{x}_1 R\cos\Phi + \omega_e^2 x_1^2) + \tfrac{1}{2}m_2(\dot{x}_1^2 + r^2\dot{\theta}^2 + 2\dot{x}_1\dot{\theta}r\cos\theta) \\ & + m_2\omega_e[(R - r\cos\theta)(\dot{x}_1 + r\dot{\theta}\cos\theta) - (x_1 + r\sin\theta)r\dot{\theta}\sin\theta]\cos\Phi \\ & + \tfrac{1}{2}m_2\omega_e^2[(x_1 + r\sin\theta)^2 + (R - r\cos\theta)^2\cos^2\Phi] \end{aligned} \qquad (14.26)$$

from which

$$\begin{aligned} (m_1+m_2)\ddot{x}_1 + m_2 r\ddot{\theta}\cos\theta - m_2 r\dot{\theta}^2\sin\theta - m_1\omega_e^2 x_1 & \\ + 2m_2\omega_e r\dot{\theta}\sin\theta\cos\Phi - m_2\omega_e^2(x_1 + r\sin\theta) &= F_{x_1} = 0 \end{aligned}$$

$$\begin{aligned} m_2\ddot{x}_1 r\cos\theta + m_2 r^2\ddot{\theta} - 2m_2\omega_e\dot{x}_1 r\sin\theta\cos\Phi & \\ - m_2\omega_e^2(x_1 + r\sin\theta)r\cos\theta - m_2\omega_e^2(R - r\cos\theta)r\sin\theta\cos^2\Phi & \\ = F_\theta = -m_2 g' r\sin\theta - m_2\omega_e^2 Rr\sin\theta\cos^2\Phi & \end{aligned} \qquad (1)$$

The reader should compare these with corresponding equations of motion, assuming no rotation of the earth. (See bottom of Page 64.)

Example 14.7. *The Foucault Pendulum.*

A mathematical analysis of the motion of a spherical pendulum, Fig. 14-6 below, the displacement of which from O_1 is always very small compared with the length l of the supporting string, shows that (*a*) relative to the earth (to the X_1Y_1 plane) the bob describes a rotating elliptical path (precessing ellipse) and (*b*) relative to a horizontal XY plane through O_1 rotating with angular velocity $-\omega_e \sin \Phi$ about $O_1 s$ the path described is a closed ellipse with its center at O_1.

Such an analysis will now be given. When justifiable assumptions are made the mathematics involved is quite simple.

Regarding m as "free", equations (*14.15*) apply directly and generalized forces are given by

$$F_{x_1} = -\tau x_1/l$$

$$F_{y_1} = mg \sin \alpha - \tau y_1/l \qquad (1)$$

$$F_{z_1} = -mg \cos \alpha + \tau(l - z_1)/l$$

where τ is the tension in the supporting string. Substituting in (*14.15*), eliminating $g \sin \alpha$ and $g \cos \alpha$ with (*14.11*) and neglecting terms containing ω_e^2 (terms containing $R\omega_e^2$ cancel), we get

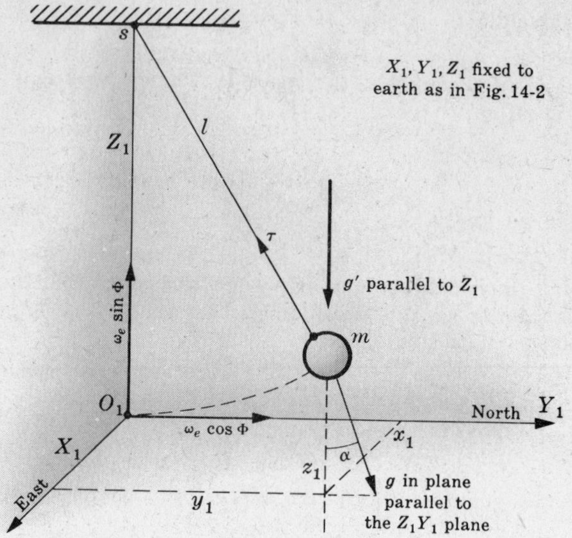

The Foucault Pendulum

Fig. 14-6

$$\ddot{x}_1 + 2\omega_e \dot{z}_1 \cos \Phi - 2\omega_e \dot{y}_1 \sin \Phi = -\tau x_1/ml \qquad (2)$$

$$\ddot{y}_1 + 2\omega_e \dot{x}_1 \sin \Phi = -\tau y_1/ml \qquad (3)$$

$$\ddot{z}_1 - 2\omega_e \dot{x}_1 \cos \Phi = -g' + \tau(l - z_1)/ml \qquad (4)$$

We now assume that l is so large compared with the amplitude of motion that, to a good approximation, the bob moves in the X_1Y_1 plane. Hence writing $z_1 = \dot{z}_1 = \ddot{z}_1 = 0$ and neglecting $2\omega_e \dot{x}_1 \cos \Phi$, (*4*) gives $\tau = mg'$. Thus (*2*) and (*3*) become

$$(5) \quad \ddot{x}_1 - 2\omega_1 \dot{y}_1 = -g' x_1/l \qquad\qquad (6) \quad \ddot{y}_1 + 2\omega_1 \dot{x}_1 = -g' y_1/l$$

where $\omega_1 = \omega_e \sin \Phi$. These equations may be simplified by referring the motion to axes X', Y' which are rotating in a clockwise direction (looking down) with angular velocity ω_1 relative to X_1, Y_1. Substituting equations

$$x_1 = x' \cos \omega_1 t + y' \sin \omega_1 t, \qquad y_1 = -x' \sin \omega_1 t + y' \cos \omega_1 t \qquad (7)$$

into (*5*) and (*6*), multiplying (*5*) through by $\sin \omega_1 t$ and (*6*) by $\cos \omega_1 t$ and adding, we get (*8*) below (after neglecting ω_1^2 as very small compared with g'/l). Likewise multiplying (*5*) by $\cos \omega_1 t$ and (*6*) by $\sin \omega_1 t$ and subtracting, we obtain (*9*).

$$(8) \quad \ddot{y}' + g' y'/l = 0 \qquad\qquad (9) \quad \ddot{x}' + g' x'/l = 0$$

These integrate at once to give

$$x' = A \sin(\sqrt{g'/l}\, t + \delta_1), \qquad y' = B \sin(\sqrt{g'/l}\, t + \delta_2) \qquad (10)$$

where A, B, δ_1, δ_2 are constants determined entirely by initial conditions. Hence the motion referred to the rotating axes is simple harmonic along each axis with a period $p = 2\pi\sqrt{l/g'}$ in each case. Thus the path is an ellipse with center at O_1.

An observer riding the rotating frame sees the above ellipse. But to an observer stationary with respect to the earth's surface the elliptic path rotates with period $2\pi/\omega_1$ or $2\pi/(\omega_e \sin \Phi) = 24/(\sin \Phi)$ hours. At either pole the period is 24 hours and at the equator there is no rotation. In the northern hemisphere the rotation is from N → E → S → W, and opposite to this in the southern.

For good experimental results, care must be given to the type of support, s, used. Various types are described in the literature. The supporting string should be long, and theory (not included here) shows that motion should be started in such a way that the area of the ellipse is as small as possible. See example below.

Example 14.8. *Starting the Foucault Pendulum.*

If the bob is pulled aside and released from rest *relative to the earth*, the motion referred to the rotating axes is very nearly along a line.

To show this, suppose that at $t = 0$, $x_1 = \dot{x}_1 = \dot{y}_1 = 0$ and $y_1 = y_0$ (bob displaced a distance y_0 directly north and released from rest *relative to the earth*). Putting these conditions into (*7*) in order to find initial conditions relative to the rotating axes and finally substituting the results into equations (*10*), it is found that

$$y' = y_0 \cos(\sqrt{g'/l}\,t), \qquad x' = -y_0(p/P_1)\sin(\sqrt{g'/l}\,t) \tag{11}$$

where $p = 2\pi\sqrt{l/g'}$ and P_1 = the period of the earth (24 hours). Since p is so small compared with P_1, x' is always very small. Hence the area of the ellipse is quite small, motion being very nearly along the Y_1 axis.

Example 14.9. *Motion of a rod in the X_1Y_1 plane, Fig. 14-3, Page 289.*

As a simple example involving the motion of a rigid body relative to the earth, consider the motion of a thin uniform rod of mass M and moment of inertia I about an axis normal to the rod through its center of mass.

We shall first determine its kinetic energy by a direct approach. Let x_1, y_1 locate c.m. and θ, measured relative to X_1, its angular position. Imagine the rod divided into a large number of small pieces each having coordinates x_i, y_i and mass m_i. Referring to expression (*14.19*), it is seen that

$$T = \tfrac{1}{2}\sum_i m_i[\dot{x}_i^2 + \dot{y}_i^2 + \omega_e^2(x_i^2 + y_i^2) + 2\omega_e(x_i\dot{y}_i - y_i\dot{x}_i) + 2R\omega_e(x_i\omega_e + \dot{y}_i)\cos\Phi]$$

But $x_i = x_1 + l_i\cos\theta$, $y_i = y_1 + l_i\sin\theta$, where l_i = distance measured along the rod from c.m. to m_i. Hence $\dot{x}_i = \dot{x}_1 - l_i\dot{\theta}\sin\theta$, $\dot{y}_i = \dot{y}_1 + l_i\dot{\theta}\cos\theta$. Eliminating $x_i, y_i, \dot{x}_i, \dot{y}_i$ from T, performing the summation and remembering that $\sum m_i l_i^2 = I$, we obtain

$$T = \tfrac{1}{2}M[(\dot{x}_1^2 + \dot{y}_1^2) + \omega_e^2(x_1^2 + y_1^2) + 2\omega_e(x_1\dot{y}_1 - y_1\dot{x}_1) + 2\omega_e R(x_1\omega_e + \dot{y}_1)\cos\Phi] + \tfrac{1}{2}I(\dot{\theta} + \omega_e)^2$$

The reader should show that this expression follows at once from (*8.10*), Page 148.

Assuming only gravity acting on the rod, it is seen, Fig. 14-3, that

$$F_{x_1} = -Mg\cos(\Phi - \alpha), \qquad F_{y_1} = 0, \qquad F_\theta = 0$$

Applying Lagrange's equations and relations (*14.11*) the equations of motion finally become, after dropping terms $x_1\omega_e^2$, $y_1\omega_e^2$,

$$\ddot{x}_1 - 2\dot{y}_1\omega_e + g'\cos\Phi = 0, \qquad \ddot{y}_1 + 2\omega_e\dot{x}_1 = 0, \qquad I\ddot{\theta} = 0$$

Example 14.10. *Equations of Motion of a top at a fixed point on the earth's surface.*

The following example merits careful consideration since it illustrates well the basic principles of a very general type of problem (see Problem 8.24, Fig. 8-33, Page 174).

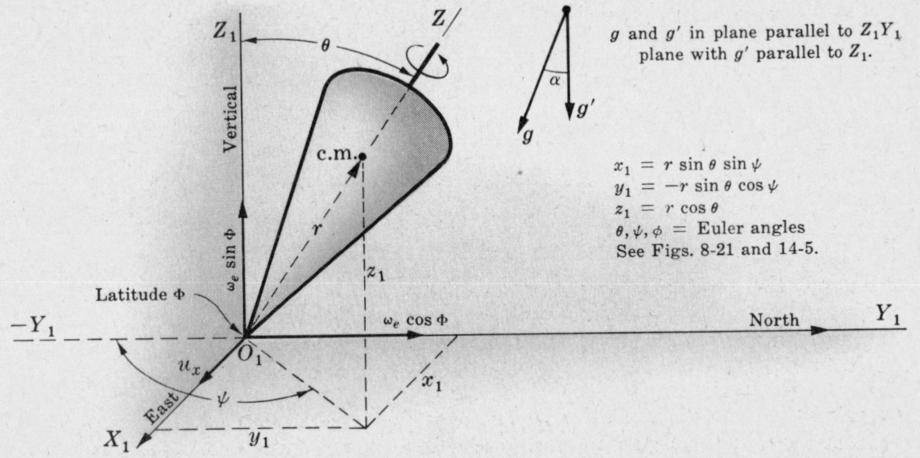

Spinning Top with Tip Fixed at O_1 on Surface of Earth

Fig. 14-7

Consider the top, Fig. 14-7 above, with tip fixed at O_1 on the earth. Following the notation employed in Section 8.10, Page 162, and in Section 14.8, Page 290, we shall outline steps for setting up equations of motion, first employing body-fixed axes with origin at O_1 and again using body-fixed axes with origin at c.m. (Note that X_1, Y_1, Z_1 of Fig. 14-7 correspond exactly to X_1, Y_1, Z_1 of Fig. 14-2.)

(*a*) Take body-fixed axes X, Y, Z with origin at O_1 (the tip) and Z along the axis of symmetry as shown. It is seen that $\bar{x} = \bar{y} = 0$, $\bar{z} = r$. Hence the last term in (*8.10*), Page 148, reduces to $M(v_{0x}\omega_y - v_{0y}\omega_x)r$, where $v_0 = R\omega_e \cos\Phi$ along X_1. Thus $v_{0x} = R\omega_e\alpha_{11}\cos\Phi$, $v_{0y} = R\omega_e\alpha_{21}\cos\Phi$. Also $I_{xy} = I_{xz} = I_{yz} = 0$, $I_x^P = I_y^P$. $\omega_x, \omega_y, \omega_z$ are given by relations (*14.24*) and α_{11}, etc., by Table 8.2, Page 158. Then by (*8.10*),

$$T = \tfrac{1}{2}MR^2\omega_e^2\cos^2\Phi + \tfrac{1}{2}I_x^P(\omega_x^2+\omega_y^2) + \tfrac{1}{2}I_z^P\omega_z^2 + M(v_{0x}\omega_y - v_{0y}\omega_x)r \qquad (14.27)$$

Note that the first term is constant.

The potential energy due to gravity is given by

$$\begin{aligned} V &= Mr\cos\theta(g\cos\alpha) + Mr\sin\theta(g\sin\alpha)\cos\psi \\ &= Mr[\cos\theta(g' + \omega_e^2R\cos^2\Phi) + \sin\theta(\omega_e^2R\sin\Phi\cos\Phi)\cos\psi] \end{aligned} \qquad (14.28)$$

Hence equations of motion follow at once.

(*b*) Now let us take body-fixed axes as above except with the origin at c.m. In this case $\bar{x} = \bar{y} = \bar{z} = 0$ and the last term in (*8.10*) drops out. $\omega_x, \omega_y, \omega_z$ are the same as above. $I_{xy} = I_{xz} = I_{yz} = 0$ and $\bar{I}_x^P = \bar{I}_y^P$. v_0 is now the inertial space velocity of c.m. and is considerably more difficult to express than in (*a*). Making use of $x_1 = r\sin\theta\sin\psi$, etc., and equations (*14.25*), Page 291, the reader may show that components of v_0 along X_1, Y_1, Z_1 (not along X, Y, Z) are given by

$$\begin{aligned} v_{x_1} &= R\omega_e\cos\Phi + r\dot{\theta}\cos\theta\sin\psi + r\dot{\psi}\sin\theta\cos\psi + \omega_e r\cos\theta\cos\Phi + \omega_e r\sin\theta\cos\psi\sin\Phi \\ v_{y_1} &= r\dot{\psi}\sin\theta\sin\psi - r\dot{\theta}\cos\theta\cos\psi + \omega_e r\sin\theta\sin\psi\sin\Phi \\ v_{z_1} &= -r\dot{\theta}\sin\theta - \omega_e r\sin\theta\sin\psi\cos\Phi \end{aligned} \qquad (14.29)$$

Thus $v_0^2 = v_{x_1}^2 + v_{y_1}^2 + v_{z_1}^2$ can be written in full.

$$T = \tfrac{1}{2}Mv_0^2 + \tfrac{1}{2}\bar{I}_x^P(\omega_x^2+\omega_y^2) + \tfrac{1}{2}\bar{I}_z^P\omega_z^2$$

The expression for V is the same as in (*a*). Hence equations of motion follow at once.

Example 14.11. *Bearing forces due to rotation of the Earth.* (See Fig. 9-7 and Section 9.12, Page 193.)

Consider a rotor mounted on the earth at latitude Φ as shown in Fig. 14-8. Note details given on this diagram. The rotor is statically and dynamically balanced for X_1, Y_1, Z_1 inertial. However, this is not the case and we will determine bearing forces taking account of the earth's rotation.

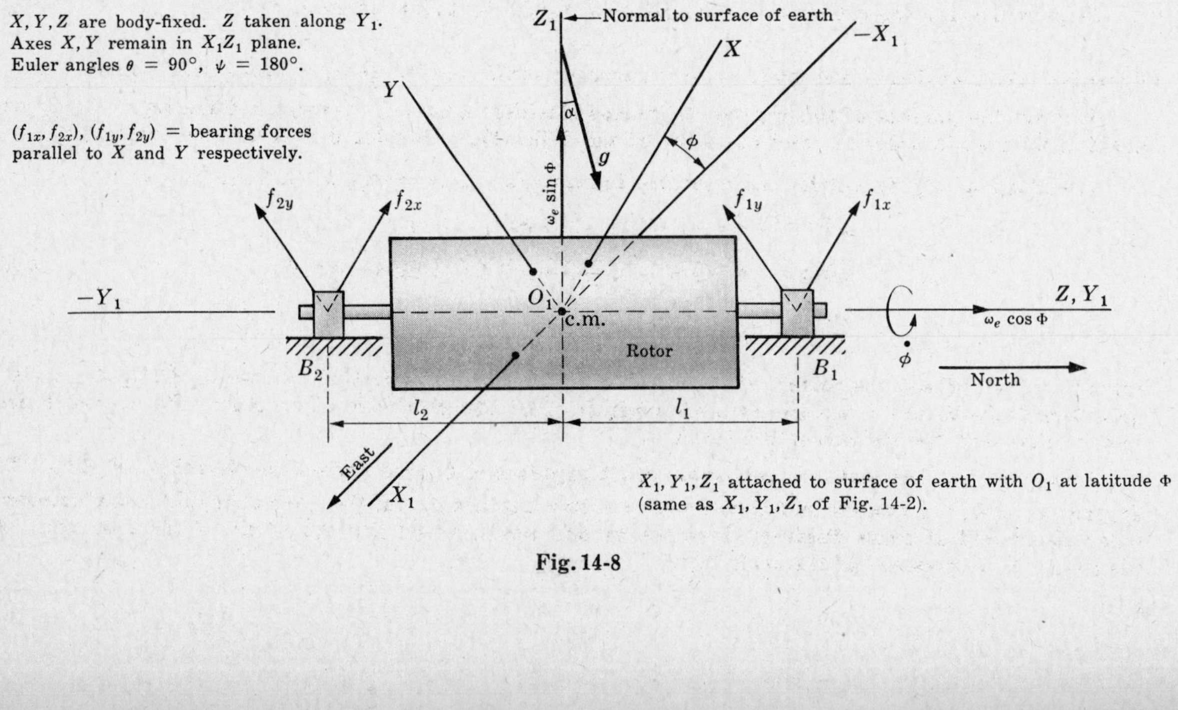

Fig. 14-8

Notation here used is exactly as in Fig. 9-7. Euler angles θ, ψ, ϕ locate the rotor relative to X_1, Y_1, Z_1 where $\theta = 90°$ and $\psi = 180°$. Note that X, Y, Z are principal axes of inertia through c.m. and $\bar{x} = \bar{y} = \bar{z} = 0$.

Inspection shows that components of the inertial-space angular velocity of the rotor along X, Y, Z are

$$\omega_x = \omega_e \sin\Phi \sin\phi, \qquad \omega_y = \omega_e \sin\Phi \cos\phi, \qquad \omega_z = \omega_e \cos\Phi + \dot{\phi} \tag{1}$$

Total X, Y, Z components of the forces are

$$F_x = f_{1x} + f_{2x} - Mg\cos\alpha\sin\phi, \quad F_y = f_{1y} + f_{2y} - Mg\cos\alpha\cos\phi, \quad F_z = f_z + Mg\sin\alpha \tag{2}$$

Components of the inertial-space acceleration of c.m. (the origin O_1) are

$$A_x = -\omega_e^2 R\cos^2\Phi\sin\phi, \qquad A_y = -\omega_e^2 R\cos^2\Phi\cos\phi, \qquad A_z = \omega_e^2 R\sin\Phi\cos\Phi \tag{3}$$

Equations (*9.2*), Page 177, are then $-M\omega_e^2 R\cos^2\Phi\sin\phi = f_{1x} + f_{2x} - Mg\cos\alpha\sin\phi$, etc., which after eliminating g in favor of g' (see equations (*14.11*), Page 284) become

$$f_{1x} + f_{2x} = Mg'\sin\phi \tag{4}$$

$$f_{1y} + f_{2y} = Mg'\cos\phi \tag{5}$$

$$f_z = 0 \tag{6}$$

Applying relations (*9.10*), Page 182, we have

$$I_x\omega_e\dot{\phi}\sin\Phi\cos\phi + (I_z - I_y)\omega_e\sin\Phi\cos\phi(\omega_e\cos\Phi + \dot{\phi}) = f_{2y}l_2 - f_{1y}l_1 \tag{7}$$

$$I_y\omega_e\dot{\phi}\sin\Phi\sin\phi + (I_z - I_x)\omega_e\sin\Phi\sin\phi(\omega_e\cos\Phi + \dot{\phi}) = f_{2x}l_2 - f_{1x}l_1 \tag{8}$$

$$I_z\ddot{\phi} + (I_y - I_x)\omega_e^2\sin^2\Phi\sin\phi\cos\phi = \tau_m \tag{9}$$

Solving (*4*) and (*8*) for f_{1x} we get

$$f_{1x} = \frac{\sin\phi}{l_1 + l_2}[Mg'l_2 + \omega_e\dot{\phi}(I_x - I_z - I_y)\sin\Phi + \omega_e^2(I_x - I_z)\sin\Phi\cos\Phi] \tag{10}$$

Note that the term $\dfrac{l_2}{l_1 + l_2}Mg'\sin\phi$ is due to the weight of the rotor while the remaining terms are a result of the earth's rotation. Neglecting the term containing ω_e^2 and assuming $I_x = I_y$, the above reduces to

$$f_{1x} = \frac{\sin\phi}{l_1 + l_2}(Mg'l_2 - \omega_e\dot{\phi}I_z\sin\Phi) \tag{11}$$

If $\dot{\phi}$ and I_z are each quite large, the second term can be appreciable. Hence even though the rotor is statically and dynamically balanced on a "stationary" earth it is somewhat unbalanced on the rotating earth.

Expressions for the remaining bearing forces f_{2x}, f_{1y}, f_{2y} follow at once.

Example 14.12. *Motion of a satellite or long range projectile relative to axes X_1, Y_1, Z_1, Fig. 14-4.*

It is not the purpose of this chapter to discuss satellite motion. However, the following rather general example is given in order to point out some of the difficulties encountered in a detailed treatment.

Assuming X_2, Y_2, Z_2 inertial and applying Lagrange's equations to (*14.21*), Page 289, we get

$$\begin{aligned} m\ddot{r} - mr\dot{\Phi}_1^2 - mr(\dot{\phi} + \omega_e)^2\cos^2\Phi_1 &= F_r \\ mr^2\ddot{\Phi}_1 + 2mr\dot{r}\dot{\Phi}_1 + mr^2(\dot{\phi} + \omega_e)^2\sin\Phi_1\cos\Phi_1 &= F_{\Phi_1} \\ \frac{d}{dt}[mr^2(\dot{\phi} + \omega_e)\cos^2\Phi_1] &= F_\phi \end{aligned} \tag{14.31}$$

solutions of which give the motion of the satellite (or long range projectile) relative to X_1, Y_1, Z_1. Φ_1 is the geocentric latitude and ϕ is a measure of longitude from any given meridian. Hence the motion is determined relative to the surface of the earth.

However, it is impossible to determine *exact* expressions for the generalized forces F_r, F_{Φ_1}, F_ϕ. They depend on (*a*) the magnitude and direction of g at any distance r from O_1, (*b*) a drag due to the atmosphere (very attenuated at some distance above the earth's surface), (*c*) the attraction of the sun, moon and planets, (*d*) the pressure of the sun's rays.

If the *exact* mass distribution of the earth were known, g could be accurately evaluated. However, this is not the case. The drag of the atmosphere must be determined largely from empirical results. The gravitational pull of the sun, moon, etc., can be evaluated. The pressure of sunlight on a satellite can be estimated with some accuracy.

Another important point to consider is the following. In the determination of *(14.31)* it was assumed that X_2, Y_2, Z_2 are inertial, which is not entirely true. For more accurate results T should be referred to non-rotating axes with origin attached to the center of the sun.

Problems

14.1. Verify values of R_1 and g' given in the 45° column of Table 14.1, Page 284.

14.2. Determine from Graph 14.1, Page 285, values of g and g' at Washington, Helsinki, Buenos Aires, Wellington. Determine the value of α at each point.

14.3. Find the difference between Φ and Φ_1 and the value of α at Cincinnati, Ohio; at El Paso, Texas.

14.4. Determine the difference between R and R_1 at Helsinki.

14.5. A simple pendulum has a length of 10 meters. Compute its period on the equator and at Seward, Alaska. Find the precessional period of a Foucault pendulum at each point.

14.6. Enclose the ellipsoidal earth in an imaginary sphere of radius a (the equatorial radius of the reference ellipsoid). At $\Phi_1 = 45°$ show that the distance, measured along an extension of R_1, between the surface of the ellipsoid and that of the sphere is 10,693 meters.

14.7. Obtain expression *(14.14)*, Page 287, for T making use of relations *(8.4)*, Page 143.

14.8. Write out equations *(14.15)*, Page 287, by a direct application of relations *(9.6)*, Page 179.

14.9. (*a*) Verify expression *(14.17)*, Page 288.
(*b*) Repeat the above making use of expressions *(8.4)*, Page 143.

14.10. Measuring cylindrical coordinates ρ, ϕ, z relative to X_1, Y_1, Z_1, Fig. 14-3, show that for a particle

$$T = \tfrac{1}{2}m[\dot{\rho}^2 + \rho^2\dot{\phi}^2 + \dot{z}^2 + 2\rho^2\omega_e\dot{\phi} + \rho^2\omega_e^2 + 2R\omega_e\dot{\rho}\sin\phi\cos\Phi + 2R\rho\omega_e(\omega_e + \dot{\phi})\cos\phi\cos\Phi]$$

Write out equations of motion. Obtain these same equations by an application of *(9.6)*, Page 179.

Assuming gravity only acting, show that generalized forces are given by

$$F_\rho = -mg\sin\phi\cos(\Phi - \alpha), \qquad F_\phi = -mg\rho\cos\phi\cos(\Phi - \alpha), \qquad F_z = -mg\sin(\Phi - \alpha)$$

Write out equations of motion. Introduce g' instead of g.

14.11. Referring the usual spherical coordinates r, θ, ϕ to X_1, Y_1, Z_1, Fig. 14-2, Page 286, verify the following expression for T applying equations *(8.4)*, Page 143.

$$\begin{aligned} T = {} & \tfrac{1}{2}m(\dot{r}^2 + r^2\dot{\theta}^2 + r^2\dot{\phi}^2\sin^2\theta) + m\omega_e[r^2\dot{\phi}\sin^2\theta\sin\Phi \\ & + (R + r\cos\theta)(\dot{r}\sin\theta\cos\phi + r\dot{\theta}\cos\theta\cos\phi - r\dot{\phi}\sin\theta\sin\phi)\cos\Phi \\ & - r\sin\theta\cos\phi(\dot{r}\cos\theta - r\dot{\theta}\sin\theta)\cos\Phi] + \tfrac{1}{2}m\omega_e^2[r^2\sin^2\theta(\cos^2\phi + \sin^2\phi\sin^2\Phi) \\ & + (R + r\cos\theta)^2\cos^2\Phi - 2r\sin\theta\sin\phi(R + r\cos\theta)\sin\Phi\cos\Phi] \end{aligned}$$

14.12. A small sphere is suspended in a viscous oil from a string having a length of 10 meters. It is held in the rest position it would occupy were the earth not rotating. When released, show that the sphere finally comes to rest at a point directly south a distance of about 1.7 cm where $\Phi = 45°$.

14.13. A ball is dropped from a point z_0 on the Z_1 axis, Fig. 14-2, Page 286. $z_0 = 100$ meters, $\Phi = 45°$. Show that it strikes the ground in $t = (2z_0/g')^{1/2}$ at a point $x_1 = 1.6$ cm approximately and $y_1 = 0$. (Ball dropped from rest, air resistance neglected.)

14.14. An elevator has an upward velocity along Z_1, Fig. 14-2, of 30 mi/hr., measured relative to the building. Mass of elevator = 3000 pounds, $\Phi = 45°$. Show that the X_1 and Y_1 components of side thrust on the elevator are $f_{x_1} = 13.6$ poundals, and at $z_1 = 0$, $f_{y_1} = 0$. (Why is it that $f_{y_1} \neq m\omega_e^2 R \sin\Phi\cos\Phi$?)

14.15. In Example 14.3, Page 292, verify expressions for T and the generalized forces in each case treated.

14.16. One edge of a smooth rectangular board remains in contact with the X_1 axis, Fig. 14-2. The opposite end is lifted up so that the board makes an angle θ with the X_1Y_1 plane. A particle is free to move in contact with this smooth inclined plane under the action of gravity. Verify the following equations of motion

$$m\ddot{x}_1 - 2m\omega_e\dot{s}\sin(\Phi-\theta) - m\omega_e^2 x_1 = 0$$

$$m\ddot{s} + m\omega_e\sin(\Phi-\theta)[2\dot{x}_1 - \omega_e s\sin(\Phi-\theta)] = -mg'\sin\theta$$

where s is measured up the incline. $z_1 = s\sin\theta$, $y_1 = s\cos\theta$. Care must be used in the determination of F_s.

14.17. When a mass m is placed on platform scales S (S located at some point on the equator) the dial reads a "weight" of mg'. S is now made to move eastward along the circular equator with uniform tangential velocity v relative to the earth's surface. Show that m loses weight to the extent of $m(v^2/R + 2\omega_e v)$; that is, the scales now read $mg' - m(v^2/R + 2\omega_e v)$.

Will a ship moving eastward displace the same amount of water as when at rest in the water? Consider the case for westward motion. (Repeat for motion north along great circle.)

14.18. Liquid is flowing due north in an open channel along the Y_1 axis, Fig. 14-2. Assuming that the entire liquid has a uniform velocity $\dot{y}_1$ and taking $x_1 = y_1 = z_1 = 0$, show that the surface of the liquid is tilted at an angle β from the horizontal, where $\tan\beta = 2\omega_e\dot{y}_1\sin\Phi/g'$. (Which way?)

14.19. Imagine the earth rotating at a speed such that an object at the equator has no weight. Prove that for a homogeneous spherical earth the plumb line at any point on the earth is parallel to the polar axis. Show that $g' = \omega_e^2 R\sin\Phi$.

14.20. A Foucault pendulum having a length of 20 meters is suspended on the earth at $\Phi = 30°$. Show that its period of oscillation is 8.98 seconds and that the precessional period is 48 hours.

14.21. Determine final expressions for T by each method suggested in Section 14.7, paragraph (b), Page 290, and compare results obtained.

14.22. Referring to Problem 3.5, Page 52, the conical spiral, Fig. 3-5, is placed so that X, Y, Z coincide with X_1, Y_1, Z_1 of Fig. 14-2. Taking full account of the earth's rotation, show that T is given by

$$\begin{aligned} T = {} & \tfrac{1}{2}m[a^2(1+b^2z^2)+1]\dot{z}^2 - m\omega_e a\dot{z}[abz^2\sin\Phi - (R+z)(\cos(bz) - bz\sin(bz))\cos\Phi \\ & + z\cos(bz)\cos\Phi] + \tfrac{1}{2}m\omega_e^2[a^2z^2(\cos^2(bz) + \sin^2(bz)\sin^2\Phi) + (R+z)^2\cos^2\Phi \\ & + 2az(R+z)\sin(bz)\sin\Phi\cos\Phi] \end{aligned}$$

Set up equations of motion and finally replace g by g'. (See equation (*14.17*), Page 288.)

14.23. Referring to Problem 3.14, Page 54, suppose the vertical shaft, Fig. 3-9, is mounted along Z_1, Fig. 14-2. Set up the equation of motion for m, taking account of the earth's rotation. Note that g is now not in the direction indicated in Fig. 3-9. (See Problem 14.11.)

$$\begin{aligned} & m\ddot{r} - mr\omega^2\sin^2\theta + 2\omega_e\omega rm\sin\theta(\cos\theta\sin\phi\cos\Phi - \sin\theta\sin\Phi) \\ & \quad - m\omega_e^2 r[(\cos\theta\cos\Phi - \sin\theta\sin\phi\sin\Phi)^2 + \sin^2\theta\cos^2\phi] = k(l - l_0 - r) - mg'\cos\theta \end{aligned}$$

14.24. Applying Lagrange's equations to *(14.17)*, Page 288. Show that the equations of motion corresponding to ρ, ϕ, z are

$$m\ddot{\rho} - m\rho\dot{\phi}^2 + m\omega_e(2\dot{z}\cos\phi\cos\Phi - 2\rho\dot{\phi}\sin\Phi) + m\omega_e^2[z\sin\phi\sin\Phi\cos\Phi - \rho(\cos^2\phi + \sin^2\phi\sin^2\Phi)] = 0$$

$$m\rho\ddot{\phi} + 2m\dot{\rho}\dot{\phi} + 2m\omega_e(\dot{\rho}\sin\Phi - \dot{z}\sin\phi\cos\Phi) + m\omega_e^2\cos\phi\cos\Phi(\rho\sin\phi\cos\Phi + z\sin\Phi) = 0$$

$$m\ddot{z} + 2m\omega_e\cos\Phi(\rho\dot{\phi}\sin\phi - \dot{\rho}\cos\phi) + m\omega_e^2\cos\Phi(\rho\sin\phi\sin\Phi - z\cos\Phi) = -mg'$$

14.25. Assuming gravity only acting, show that in equations *(14.20)*, Page 289,

$$F_{x_1} = -mg'\cos\Phi - m\omega_e^2R\cos\Phi, \qquad F_{y_1} = 0, \qquad F_{z_1} = -mg'\sin\Phi$$

Note that in the first of these equations $m\omega_e^2R\cos\Phi$ cancels out.

14.26. Equations of motion of m, Fig. 2-21, Page 22, are to be found relative to D_2, taking account of the earth's rotation. Assuming the bearing supporting D_1 is rigidly fastened to the earth at O_1, Fig. 14-2, Page 286, and that faces of D_1 and D_2 remain horizontal, show that T expressed in polar coordinates r, α is given by [Let X_1, Y_1 of Fig. 2-21 correspond to X_1, Y_1 of Fig. 14-2.]

$$\begin{aligned} T = {} & \tfrac{1}{2}m[s\dot{\theta}_1^2 + \dot{r}^2 + r^2(\dot{\theta}_1 + \dot{\theta}_2 + \dot{\alpha})^2 + 2s\dot{\theta}_1\dot{r}\sin(\theta_2 + \alpha) + 2s\dot{\theta}_1 r(\dot{\theta}_1 + \dot{\theta}_2 + \dot{\alpha})\cos(\theta_2 + \alpha)] \\ & + m\omega_e[s^2\dot{\theta}_1 + r^2(\dot{\theta}_1 + \dot{\theta}_2 + \alpha) + s\dot{r}\sin(\theta_2 + \alpha) + sr(2\dot{\theta}_1 + \dot{\theta}_2 + \dot{\alpha})]\sin\Phi \\ & + m\omega_e[\dot{r}\cos(\theta_1 + \theta_2 + \alpha) - s\dot{\theta}_1\sin\theta_1 - r(\dot{\theta}_1 + \dot{\theta}_2 + \dot{\alpha})\sin(\theta_1 + \theta_2 + \alpha)]R\cos\Phi \\ & - m\omega_e^2R[s\sin\theta_1 + r\sin(\theta_1 + \theta_2 + \alpha)]\sin\Phi\cos\Phi \\ & + \tfrac{1}{2}m\omega_e^2\{[s\cos\theta_1 + r\cos(\theta_1 + \theta_2 + \alpha)]^2 + [s\sin\theta_1 + r\sin(\theta_1 + \theta_2 + \alpha)]^2\sin^2\Phi\} \end{aligned}$$

θ_1, θ_2 are assumed to be any known functions of time. Note that for $\omega_e = 0$ this reduces to *(2.46)*, Page 25.

14.27. The base B, Fig. 13-10 (see Problem 13.14, Page 279) is placed on the surface of the earth at O_1, Fig. 14-2, Page 286. Assume that the plane of the semicircular rod is in the Y_1Z_1 plane and that the dotted line ab is horizontal. Note that g' and not g is now normal to ab. Write an expression for T and find the equilibrium value of θ.

14.28. The support B, Fig. 8-12, Page 153, is attached to the earth at O_1, Fig. 14-2. Regard X_1, Y_1, Z_1 of Fig. 8-12 as X_1, Y_1, Z_1 in Fig. 14-2, with c.m. at O. Assuming the disk is replaced by a body of any shape with c.m. at O, show that T is given by (See equations *(8.14)*, etc., Page 163.)

$$T = \tfrac{1}{2}M\omega_e^2R^2 + \tfrac{1}{2}(\bar{I}_x\omega_x^2 + \bar{I}_y\omega_y^2 + \bar{I}_z\omega_z^2 - 2\bar{I}_{xy}\omega_x\omega_y - 2\bar{I}_{xz}\omega_x\omega_z - 2\bar{I}_{yz}\omega_y\omega_z)$$

where

$$\omega_x = \dot{\psi}\sin\theta\sin\phi + \omega_e(\cos\phi\sin\psi + \sin\phi\cos\psi\cos\theta)\cos\Phi + \omega_e\sin\theta\sin\phi\sin\Phi$$

$$\omega_y = \dot{\psi}\sin\theta\cos\phi + \omega_e(\cos\phi\cos\psi\cos\theta - \sin\phi\sin\psi)\cos\Phi + \omega_e\sin\theta\cos\phi\sin\Phi$$

$$\omega_z = \dot{\phi} + \dot{\psi}\cos\theta - \omega_e\sin\theta\cos\psi\cos\Phi + \omega_e\cos\theta\sin\Phi$$

Note that the first term in T is constant and can thus be eliminated. Since Euler angles are here measured relative to the earth, equations of motion obtained from T above give the motion of the body relative to the earth.

14.29. Verify relations *(14.29)*, Page 296.

14.30. The disk D of Fig. 8-5, Page 146, is mounted on the earth with point b at the origin of the X_1, Y_1, Z_1 axes of Fig. 14-2. Axis ab is vertical along Z_1. Write an expression for T of the disk, taking account of the earth's rotation. Care must be used in getting the velocity of c.m. of D. (See Problem 14.28.) (See equations *(8.4)*, Page 143.)

14.31. The gyroscope, Fig. 8-18, Page 159, is mounted on the earth at O_1 with X_1, Y_1, Z_1 of Fig. 8-18 superimposed on X_1, Y_1, Z_1 of Fig. 14-2. Show that (see Example 8.16, Page 159),

$$\begin{aligned} T = {} & \tfrac{1}{2}MR^2\omega_e^2\cos^2\Phi + \tfrac{1}{2}\bar{I}_x^P[\omega_e^2\cos^2\Phi\sin^2\psi + \omega_e^2(\sin\Phi\sin\theta + \cos\Phi\cos\psi\cos\theta)^2 + \dot{\theta}^2 \\ & + (\dot{\psi} + 2\omega_e\sin\Phi)\dot{\psi}\sin^2\theta + 2\omega_e\cos\Phi(\dot{\theta}\sin\psi + \dot{\psi}\cos\psi\sin\theta\cos\theta)] \\ & + \tfrac{1}{2}\bar{I}_z^P[(\dot{\psi} + \omega_e\sin\Phi)\cos\theta + \dot{\phi} - \omega_e\cos\Phi\cos\psi\sin\theta]^2 \end{aligned}$$

Set up equations of motion (*a*) by the Lagrangian method, (*b*) by the Euler method.

14.32. A rotating table is located with its center at O_1, Fig. 14-2, and its axis of rotation along Z_1. The supporting base A, Fig. 8-5, Page 146, is mounted on the table at a distance r measured along a radial line from O_1 to the center of base A. The table is made to rotate with angular velocity $\dot{\alpha}$ (not necessarily constant) where α is measured from the X_1 axis of Fig. 14-2 to the radial line r. Angles θ and ϕ are measured as indicated on Fig. 8-5. Indicating the angle between an extension of r and the projection of bZ (Fig. 8-5) on the X_1Y_1 plane as β, we define ψ (in keeping with the definition of Euler angles) by $\psi = \beta + 90°$.

Show that components of the angular velocity of the disk (measured relative to inertial space) along the body-fixed X, Y, Z axes are given by

$$\omega_x = [(\omega_e \sin\Phi + \dot{\alpha} + \dot{\psi}) \sin\theta + \omega_e \cos\Phi \cos(\alpha + \psi) \cos\theta] \sin\phi + \omega_e \cos\Phi \sin(\alpha+\psi) \cos\phi$$

$$\omega_y = [(\omega_e \sin\Phi + \dot{\alpha} + \dot{\psi}) \sin\theta + \omega_e \cos\Phi \cos(\alpha + \psi) \cos\theta] \cos\phi - \omega_e \cos\Phi \sin(\alpha+\psi) \sin\phi$$

$$\omega_z = \dot{\phi} + (\omega_e \sin\Phi + \dot{\alpha} + \dot{\psi}) \cos\theta - \omega_e \cos\Phi \cos(\alpha+\psi) \sin\theta$$

Show that the X, Y, Z components of the inertial-space velocity of c.m. are given by

$$v_{0x} = v_1(\cos\phi \cos\psi - \sin\phi \sin\psi \cos\theta) + v_2(\cos\phi \sin\psi + \sin\phi \cos\psi \cos\theta)$$

etc. for v_{0y}, v_{0z}, where

$$v_1 = \omega_e R \cos\Phi \cos\alpha + l\dot{\psi} \sin\theta \cos\psi, \qquad v_2 = r\dot{\alpha} - \omega_e R \cos\Phi \sin\alpha + l\dot{\psi} \sin\theta \sin\psi, \qquad v_3 = 0$$

and l is the distance bO, Fig. 8-5. Note that T can now be written and equations of motion of the disk found at once.

14.33. Inserting the expanded form of R given directly below (*14.4*), Page 283, into the first relation of (*14.11*), Page 284, show that after introducing proper numerical values, α in minutes of arc is closely approximated by

$$\alpha = \frac{3437.75}{g}(3.392 + 1.14 \times 10^{-2} \sin^2\Phi) \sin\Phi \cos\Phi$$

This is a useful computational formula.

14.34. Taking account of the annual rotation of the earth about the sun, write T for the particle shown in Fig. 14-2 in terms of x_1, y_1, z_1. Regard non-rotating axes with origin attached to the center of the sun as inertial. Also, for simplicity, assume that the earth rotates with constant angular velocity in a circular path of radius $R_e = 93 \times 10^6$ miles. Set up equations of motion and compare with (*14.15*), Page 287. Note that the earth's polar axis makes a constant angle of about 23.5° with a normal to the plane of the earth's orbit.

CHAPTER 15

Application of Lagrange's Equations to Electrical and Electromechanical Systems

15.1 Preliminary Remarks.

Lagrange's equations are directly applicable to a wide variety of electrical and electromechanical systems. As will soon be evident, they are especially advantageous in treating the latter.

Generalized coordinates, velocities, kinetic energy, potential energy, the power function, equations of constraint, degrees of freedom and generalized forces, so familiar in mechanics, each has its counterpart in many types of electrical systems. Hence with suitably selected coordinates and T, V, etc., properly expressed, the Lagrangian equations for electrical or electromechanical systems have exactly the same form as equation (*4.9*), Page 60.

Since a detailed treatment of the many possibilities and ramifications into which this topic could lead would require several chapters, this discussion is limited to an outline of some of the more important phases of the subject.

15.2 Expressions for T, V, P, F_Q and Lagrange's Equations for Electrical Circuits.

A. *Suitable Coordinates.*

Referring to Fig. 15-1, the charges Q_1, Q_2, etc., which have flowed through the various branches of the network after a given instant of time, say $t = 0$, constitute suitable "coordinates". Thus the current $i = dQ/dt = \dot{Q}$ corresponds to a "velocity" and likewise $\ddot{Q}$ to an "acceleration". As in the usual treatment of circuits, a positive direction of flow (direction of the current) must arbitrarily be assigned to each charge, as indicated in the figure. This amounts to choosing a positive direction for the coordinate.

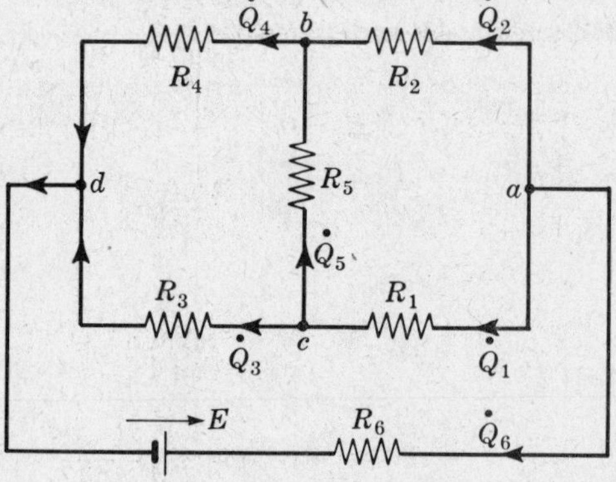

Fig. 15-1

B. *Equations of Constraint and Degrees of Freedom.*

Not all charges flowing through a network are independent. At any junction the algebraic sum of all charges flowing to the junction must be zero (Kirchhoff's law). Hence the number of independent junction equations represents just that many *equations of constraint*. For example, there are six charges flowing (six currents) in the six branches of the Wheatstone bridge, Fig. 15-1. At each of the junctions a, b, c, d, relations $\dot{Q}_6 = \dot{Q}_1 + \dot{Q}_2$ (or $Q_6 = Q_1 + Q_2$), etc., can be written. But only three of these are independent. That is, taking, say, $Q_6 = Q_1 + Q_2$, $Q_2 + Q_5 = Q_4$ and $Q_1 = Q_3 + Q_5$ as independent, the fourth equation can be obtained from these three. Thus since there are six coordinates (charges) and three equations of constraint, the bridge has only three degrees of freedom.

C. *Kinetic Energy.*

The magnetic energy $\mathcal{E}$ of a single coil of constant inductance M is $\mathcal{E} = \frac{1}{2}M\dot{Q}^2$. Comparing this with $T = \frac{1}{2}mv^2$, the kinetic energy of a particle, M corresponds to mass and $\dot{Q}$ to v.

The energy of two coils with self inductances M_{11}, M_{22} and mutual inductance M_{12} is

$$\mathcal{E} = \tfrac{1}{2}(M_{11}\dot{Q}_1^2 + 2M_{12}\dot{Q}_1\dot{Q}_2 + M_{22}\dot{Q}_2^2)$$

which again has the familiar form of kinetic energy. In the more general case of a network containing s coils, the *electrical kinetic energy* is given by

$$T_{El} = \tfrac{1}{2}\sum_{ir}^{s} M_{ir}\dot{Q}_i\dot{Q}_r \tag{15.1}$$

where it is seen that M_{ir} correspond to A_{ir} in equation (*2.56*), Page 27. Superfluous Q's should be eliminated from T_{El} by means of equations of constraint.

Important notes. (*a*) Consider, for example, two coaxial coils (1) and (2) in which fluxes ϕ_1 and ϕ_2 are established by currents i_1 and i_2. If there is mutual inductance between them, part of ϕ_1 threads (2) and part of ϕ_2 threads (1). Now if for positively chosen directions of i_1 and i_2, ϕ_1 threads (2) in the direction which ϕ_2 has in (2) (likewise ϕ_2 will thread (1) in the direction of ϕ_1), then M_{12} is positive; otherwise it must be taken negative. Hence M_{ir} can be either a positive or negative quantity.

(*b*) In the discussion leading to (*15.1*) we have tacitly assumed that all inductances are constant. But if, for example, the coils have iron cores, then M_{11}, M_{12}, etc., depend in a rather complicated manner on the currents. In this case Lagrange's equations, in the usual form, are not applicable. Moreover, iron cores introduce the complex phenomenon of hysteresis losses. Hence we shall assume in what follows that inductances do not depend on the currents. Mutual inductances may, however, depend on space coordinates.

D. *Potential Energy.*

The potential energy of a network may conveniently be regarded as composed of two parts: the energy of sources (batteries, generators, etc.) and the energy stored in condensers.

A source of constant terminal voltage E supplies energy EQ to the system, where Q is the charge "delivered by the source" in the direction of E. Hence referring potential energy to the "point" $Q = 0$, we write $V_{\text{source}} = -EQ$ where Q is assumed to flow in the positive direction of E. Note that this is entirely analogous to the simple relation $V = -mgy$ for the potential energy of mass m due to gravity, with y taken positive vertically upward. The above relation is still valid even though E may vary with time, as $E = E_0 \sin \omega t$, because in finding generalized forces t is held fixed.

The energy of an isolated charged condenser of capacity C may be written as $\mathcal{E} = \frac{1}{2}Q^2/C$ which corresponds exactly to the energy of a coil spring, ($1/C$ corresponds to k). Hence the potential energy of a network containing several sources and isolated condensers is given by

$$V_{El} = \tfrac{1}{2}\sum_{l} Q_l^2/C_l - \sum_{s} E_sQ_s \tag{15.2}$$

from which, as in the case of T_{El}, superfluous coordinates should be eliminated.

If at $t = 0$, condensers have initial charges Q_{01}, Q_{02}, etc., the corresponding energy is written as $\frac{1}{2}(Q_1 + Q_{01})^2/C_1$, etc. And if current $\dot{Q}_s$ flows opposite to the positive direction of E, then E_sQ_s must be taken *positive*.

E. *Generalized Forces, F_{Q_r}.*

The basic "forces" acting on an electrical network may be illustrated by reference to the simple circuit shown in Fig. 15-2. Applying here Kirchhoff's laws, we write

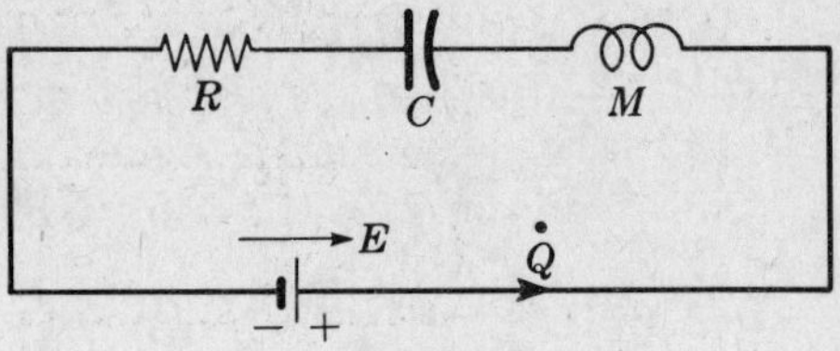

Fig. 15-2

$$M\ddot{Q} = E - Q/C - R\dot{Q}$$

from which it is seen that $M\ddot{Q}$ corresponds to an "inertial force" (as $m\ddot{x}$), Q/C corresponds to the force exerted by a spring (compare with kx), E is the "force" applied by the battery and $-R\dot{Q}$ corresponds exactly with a viscous force as $-a\dot{x}$. (Note that $R\dot{Q}$ is a dissipative force.)

F_{Q_r}, the total generalized force corresponding to Q_r, may conveniently be regarded as made up of $(F_{Q_r})_c$ due to conservative forces and $(F_{Q_r})_R$ due to resistances. Clearly $(F_{Q_r})_c = -\partial V/\partial Q_r$.

Expressions for $(F_{Q_r})_R$ may be obtained as follows. When charge δQ_i flows through R_i, the work involved (energy dissipated) is $\delta W_i = -R_i\dot{Q}_i\,\delta Q_i$. Hence for a system containing any number of resistances,

$$\delta W_{\text{total}} = -(R_1\dot{Q}_1\,\delta Q_1 + R_2\dot{Q}_2\,\delta Q_2 + \cdots) \tag{15.3}$$

After eliminating superfluous currents and charges and collecting terms, the $(F_{Q_r})_R$ can be read directly from (*15.3*). These forces may also be found from (*15.4a*) below.

The total generalized force is, of course, given by

$$F_{Q_r} = -\partial V/\partial Q_r + (F_{Q_r})_R$$

F. *Use of the Power Function.*

The following forms are useful in many problems:

$$(a)\quad P = -\tfrac{1}{2}\sum_i R_i\dot{Q}_i^2 \qquad \text{and} \qquad (b)\quad P = -\sum_i \frac{A_i}{b+1}\dot{Q}_i^{b+1} \tag{15.4}$$

The first (a special case of the second) is applicable in all cases where, for each resistance, $\delta W = -R\dot{Q}\,\delta Q$. The second applies when the "voltage drop" across a resistance is given by $E = A\dot{Q}^b$, that is, $\delta W = -A\dot{Q}^b\,\delta Q$. (See Example 15.2 below.) In either form superfluous currents must be eliminated.

G. *Lagrange's Equations for Electrical Circuits.*
(No moving parts considered at this point.)

The following form is applicable to electrical systems consisting of a finite number of "lumped" (not distributed) inductances, condensers, resistances and voltage supplies:

$$\frac{d}{dt}\left(\frac{\partial L_{El}}{\partial \dot{Q}_r}\right) - \frac{\partial L_{El}}{\partial Q_r} = F_{Q_r} \tag{15.5}$$

where the Lagrangian $L_{El} = T_{El} - V_{El}$, and $F_{Q_r} = (F_{Q_r})_R$, found from (*15.3*) or (*15.4*), is due to dissipative forces only. Conservative forces are of course automatically accounted for.

15.3 Illustrative Examples (purely electrical systems; no moving parts).
In what follows specific units are not introduced.

Example 15.1.

Consider the simple circuit shown in Fig. 15-3 below. The system has only two degrees of freedom, the one equation of constraint being

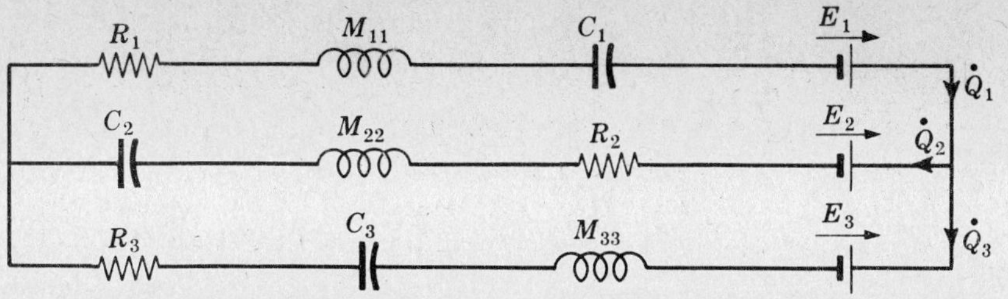

Assume mutual inductance between all coils.

Fig. 15-3

$$Q_1 = Q_2 + Q_3 \tag{1}$$

Assuming mutual inductance between all coils,

$$T = \tfrac{1}{2}[M_{11}\dot{Q}_1^2 + M_{22}\dot{Q}_2^2 + M_{33}\dot{Q}_3^2 + 2M_{12}\dot{Q}_1\dot{Q}_2 + 2M_{13}\dot{Q}_1\dot{Q}_3 + 2M_{23}\dot{Q}_2\dot{Q}_3] \tag{2}$$

Eliminating say $\dot{Q}_3$ from (2) by (1), the final form is

$$T = \tfrac{1}{2}[M_{11}\dot{Q}_1^2 + M_{22}\dot{Q}_2^2 + M_{33}(\dot{Q}_1 - \dot{Q}_2)^2 + 2M_{12}\dot{Q}_1\dot{Q}_2 + 2M_{13}\dot{Q}_1(\dot{Q}_1 - \dot{Q}_2) + 2M_{23}\dot{Q}_2(\dot{Q}_1 - \dot{Q}_2)] \tag{3}$$

It follows at once, after eliminating Q_3, that

$$V = \frac{1}{2}\left[\frac{Q_1^2}{C_1} + \frac{Q_2^2}{C_2} + \frac{(Q_1 - Q_2)^2}{C_3}\right] - E_1Q_1 + E_2Q_2 + E_3(Q_1 - Q_2) \tag{4}$$

Applying Lagrange's equations in the usual way, differential equations corresponding to Q_1 and Q_2 are

$$(M_{11} + M_{33} + 2M_{13})\ddot{Q}_1 + (M_{12} - M_{13} - M_{33} + M_{23})\ddot{Q}_2 + \left(\frac{1}{C_1} + \frac{1}{C_3}\right)Q_1 - \frac{Q_2}{C_3} - E_1 + E_3 = F_{Q_1}$$

$$(M_{22} + M_{33} - 2M_{23})\ddot{Q}_2 + (M_{12} - M_{33} - M_{13} + M_{23})\ddot{Q}_1 + \left(\frac{1}{C_2} + \frac{1}{C_3}\right)Q_2 - \frac{Q_1}{C_3} + E_2 - E_3 = F_{Q_2}$$

From the diagram it is seen that work $\delta W = -R_1\dot{Q}_1\,\delta Q_1 - R_2\dot{Q}_2\,\delta Q_2 - R_3\dot{Q}_3\,\delta Q_3$, and eliminating $\dot{Q}_3$ and δQ_3 by (1),

$$\delta W = [R_3\dot{Q}_2 - (R_1 + R_3)\dot{Q}_1]\delta Q_1 + [R_3\dot{Q}_1 - (R_2 + R_3)\dot{Q}_2]\delta Q_2$$

Hence $F_{Q_1} = R_3\dot{Q}_2 - (R_1 + R_3)\dot{Q}_1$, $F_{Q_2} = R_3\dot{Q}_1 - (R_2 + R_3)\dot{Q}_2$. Note that these generalized forces are also given by $F_{Q_1} = \partial P/\partial\dot{Q}_1$, $F_{Q_2} = \partial P/\partial\dot{Q}_2$ where (see equation (15.4a))

$$P = -\tfrac{1}{2}[R_1\dot{Q}_1^2 + R_2\dot{Q}_2^2 + R_3(\dot{Q}_1 - \dot{Q}_2)^2]$$

Example 15.2.

The circuit of Fig. 15-4 contains two identical two-element tubes connected as shown. We shall assume that E_3 is given by $A\dot{Q}_3^b$ where A and b are constants, or $E_3 = A\,|\dot{Q}_3^{b-1}|\,\dot{Q}_3$ where $|\dot{Q}_3^{b-1}|$ indicates absolute values. An external voltage $E_2 = E_0 \sin \omega t$ is applied as shown. The Lagrangian for the system, eliminating Q_3 and $\dot{Q}_3$, is

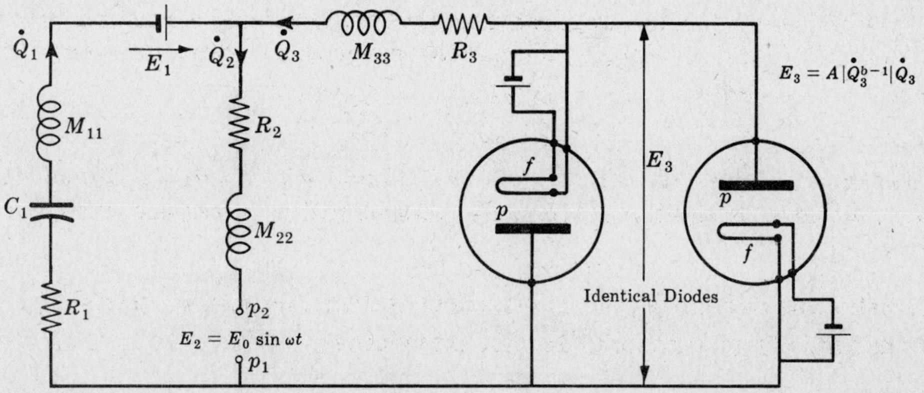

Fig. 15-4

$$L = \tfrac{1}{2}[M_{11}\dot{Q}_1^2 + M_{22}\dot{Q}_2^2 + M_{33}(\dot{Q}_2 - \dot{Q}_1)^2 + 2M_{12}\dot{Q}_1\dot{Q}_2 + 2M_{13}\dot{Q}_1(\dot{Q}_2 - \dot{Q}_1) + 2M_{23}\dot{Q}_2(\dot{Q}_2 - \dot{Q}_1)] - \tfrac{1}{2}Q_1^2/C + E_1Q_1 + Q_2E_0 \sin \omega t$$

from which equations of motion follow at once. Expressions for F_{Q_1} and F_{Q_2} may be found from

$$\delta W = -[R_1\dot{Q}_1\,\delta Q_1 + R_2\dot{Q}_2\,\delta Q_2 + R_3(\dot{Q}_2 - \dot{Q}_1)(\delta Q_2 - \delta Q_1) + A|(\dot{Q}_2 - \dot{Q}_1)^{b-1}|\,(\dot{Q}_2 - \dot{Q}_1)(\delta Q_2 - \delta Q_1)]$$

The reader should show that the same expressions for the generalized forces may be obtained from a P function obtained by taking the sum of *(15.4a)* and *(15.4b)*.

15.4 Electromechanical Systems: The Appropriate Lagrangian; Determination of Generalized Forces.

An electromechanical system is one in which the energy associated with it is in part electrical, magnetic and mechanical. An ordinary moving coil galvanometer is a simple example. The coil and its suspension have "mechanical" kinetic and potential energy. The coil and circuit to which it may be connected have "electrical" energy. As the coil moves, the torque acting on it and its angular velocity, displacement and acceleration are dependent on the electrical quantities of the system, and vice versa. Because of this interrelation, the mechanical motion and electrical performance cannot be treated separately. The system must be regarded as a whole.

The Lagrangian for an electromechanical system may be written as

$$L = T_{El} - V_{El} + T_{Me} - V_{Me} \tag{15.6}$$

where T_{El} and V_{El} are written out as illustrated above. T_{Me} and V_{Me} represent the mechanical kinetic and potential energies respectively, expressed as usual in any convenient generalized space coordinates $q_1, q_2, \ldots, q_{n_1}$. If, besides these n_1 space coordinates, n_2 independent charges are to be accounted for, the system may be said to have $n = n_1 + n_2$ degrees of freedom. An application of Lagrange's equations to *(15.6)* leads at once to $n_1 + n_2$ equations of motion.

In writing *(15.6)* for any specific problem, care must be used in the selection of units so that all terms in L are expressed in the same energy units. As previously mentioned, no specific units are introduced in this chapter. Generalized forces (not taken account of by potential energy terms in L) for both electrical and space coordinates are found in the usual way, as will be seen from examples which follow.

Example 15.3.

Consider the system shown in Fig. 15-5. The upper plate of condenser C, having mass m, is suspended from a coil spring of constant k. It is free to move vertically under the action of gravity, the spring and the electrical field between the plates. An unusual feature of the system is, of course, the variable capacitance C.

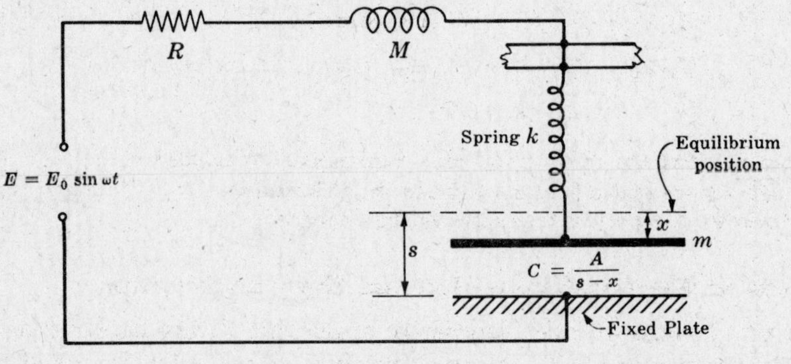

Fig. 15-5

Let the dotted line represent the rest position of the plate with condenser uncharged. Assuming air between plates we write, for convenience, $C = A/(s-x)$ where A is a constant the value of which depends on the area of the plate and the units employed, and s is the distance indicated. Hence the Lagrangian for the system is

$$L = \tfrac{1}{2}M\dot{Q}^2 + \tfrac{1}{2}m\dot{x}^2 + QE_0 \sin \omega t - \tfrac{1}{2}Q^2(s-x)/A - \tfrac{1}{2}kx^2$$

(A term containing mg cancels out.) The system has two degrees of freedom, the two coordinates being Q and x. Applying Lagrange's equations we get

$$M\ddot{Q} + Q(s-x)/A - E_0 \sin \omega t = -R\dot{Q}, \qquad m\ddot{x} + kx - \tfrac{1}{2}Q^2/A = 0$$

Note that the voltage of self inductance $M\ddot{Q}$, the voltage across the condenser $Q(s-x)/A$, and the force of attraction between plates $\tfrac{1}{2}Q^2/A$, have been automatically taken account of in the Lagrangian equations.

Example 15.4.

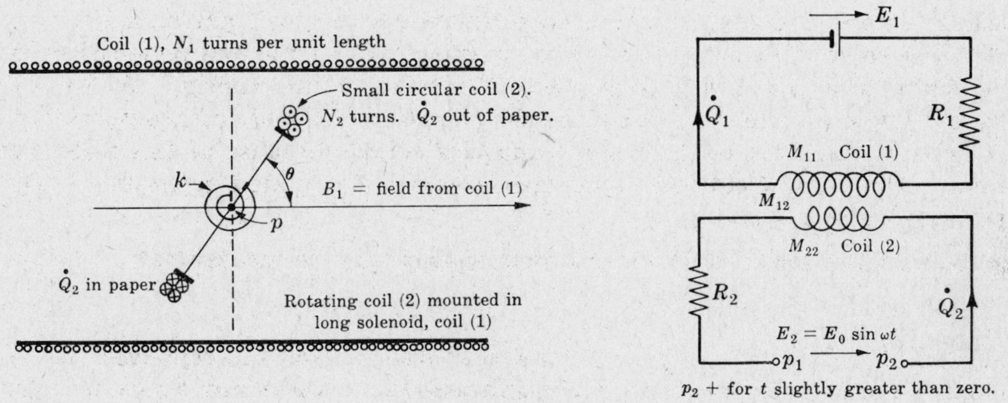

Fig. 15-6

A small shaft normal to the paper and passing through p, Fig. 15-6, is mounted on smooth bearings (not shown) and supports the small coil (2) inside a long stationary coil (1). Fastened to (2) is a spiral pancake spring, as shown, having a torsional constant k. The coils are connected to separate circuits as indicated to the right. Assuming (1) quite long, it may be shown without difficulty that the mutual inductance of (1) and (2) is given by

$$M_{12} = b(\pi r^2)N_1N_2 \sin \theta$$

where r = radius of coil (2), N_1 = turns per unit length on (1), N_2 = total turns on (2), and b is a constant depending on the specific units used. Hence replacing $b(\pi r^2)N_1N_2$ by A, we have

$$L = \tfrac{1}{2}M_{11}\dot{Q}_1^2 + \tfrac{1}{2}M_{22}\dot{Q}_2^2 + \tfrac{1}{2}I\dot{\theta}^2 + A\dot{Q}_1\dot{Q}_2 \sin \theta + E_1Q_1 + Q_2E_0 \sin \omega t - \tfrac{1}{2}k\theta^2$$

where M_{11}, M_{22} are self inductances (assumed known) of (1) and (2) respectively, and I is the moment of inertia of coil (2) about the axis on which it is mounted. It is assumed that for $\theta = 0$ the pancake coil is undistorted.

Applying Lagrange's equations the following differential equations corresponding to Q_1, Q_2, θ are obtained:

$$M_{11}\ddot{Q}_1 + A\ddot{Q}_2 \sin \theta + A\dot{\theta}\dot{Q}_2 \cos \theta - E_1 = -R_1\dot{Q}_1$$

$$M_{22}\ddot{Q}_2 + A\ddot{Q}_1 \sin \theta + A\dot{\theta}\dot{Q}_1 \cos \theta - E_0 \sin \omega t = -R_2\dot{Q}_2$$

$$I\ddot{\theta} - A\dot{Q}_1\dot{Q}_2 \cos \theta + k\theta = 0$$

Note, for example, that the term $A\dot{\theta}\dot{Q}_1 \cos \theta$ represents an induced voltage in coil (2) due to its rotational velocity $\dot{\theta}$ in the magnetic field established in (1) by current $\dot{Q}_1$. The term $B\dot{Q}_1\dot{Q}_2 \cos \theta$ is a torque on (2). The significance of all other terms should be examined.

15.5 Oscillations of Electrical and Electromechanical Systems.

The results of Chapter 10 are frequently applicable to the determination of the natural frequencies of oscillation of electrical or electromechanical systems, as shown by the following examples.

Example 15.5.

Consider again the circuit of Fig. 15-3. Equations corresponding to Q_1 and Q_2 may be written as

$$(M_{11}+M_{33}+2M_{13})\ddot{Q}_1 + (R_1+R_3)\dot{Q}_1 + \left(\frac{1}{C_1}+\frac{1}{C_3}\right)Q_1$$

$$+ (M_{12}+M_{23}-M_{33}-M_{13})\ddot{Q}_2 - R_3\dot{Q}_2 - \frac{Q_2}{C_3} = E_1 - E_3$$

$$(M_{12}+M_{23}-M_{33}-M_{13})\ddot{Q}_1 - R_3\dot{Q}_1 - \frac{Q_1}{C_3}$$

$$+ (M_{22}-2M_{23}+M_{33})\ddot{Q}_2 + (R_2+R_3)\dot{Q}_2 + \left(\frac{1}{C_2}+\frac{1}{C_3}\right)Q_2 = E_3 - E_2$$

Using "equilibrium coordinates" (see Problem 15.2, Page 312) these equations take exactly the form of equations *(10.7)*, Page 209. They can, of course, be solved by the same methods.

Example 15.6.

Consider again the system shown in Fig. 15-5 and treated in Example 15.3. For simplicity assume the variable voltage replaced by a constant voltage E. It is clear that at some time after switching on the battery, for even the slightest damping of the upper plate, x and Q reach constant values x_0, Q_0. Measuring displacements from these equilibrium values, that is, writing $x = x_0 + x_1$ and $Q = Q_0 + Q_1$,

$$V = -E(Q_0+Q_1) + \tfrac{1}{2}(Q_0+Q_1)^2(s-x_0-x_1)/A + \tfrac{1}{2}k(x_0+x_1)^2$$

From $(\partial V/\partial Q_1)_0 = 0$ and $(\partial V/\partial x_1)_0 = 0$ it follows that $x_0 = \frac{1}{2}Q_0^2/Ak$, $Q_0 = AE/(s-x_0)$.

Now assuming Q_1 and x_1 always small, we obtain after applying *(10.6)*, Page 207,

$$V_{\text{approx.}} = \frac{1}{2}\left[\left(\frac{s-x_0}{A}\right)Q_1^2 - \frac{2Q_0}{A}Q_1x_1 + kx_1^2\right]$$

Thus
$$L = \frac{1}{2}M\dot{Q}_1^2 + \frac{1}{2}m\dot{x}_1^2 - \frac{1}{2}\left[\left(\frac{s-x_0}{A}\right)Q_1^2 - \frac{2Q_0}{A}Q_1x_1 + kx_1^2\right]$$

from which
$$M\ddot{Q}_1 + \left(\frac{s-x_0}{A}\right)Q_1 - \frac{Q_0}{A}x_1 = -R\dot{Q}_1, \qquad m\ddot{x}_1 + kx_1 - \frac{Q_0}{A}Q_1 = 0$$

which have the same form as *(10.7)*, Page 209, and can be solved in the same way.

15.6 Forces and Voltages Required to Produce Given Motions and Currents in an Electromechanical System.

The results of Chapter 13 can be applied to electromechanical systems, as illustrated by the following examples.

Example 15.7.

Imagine a force f_x applied to the moving plate, Fig. 15-5, Page 306, and that $E_0 \sin \omega t$ is replaced by an unknown voltage, the nature of which is to be determined. The general equations of the system are now (see Example 15.3)

$$M\ddot{Q} + Q(s-x)/A + R\dot{Q} = E, \qquad m\ddot{x} + kx - Q^2/2A = f_x \qquad (1)$$

If the manner in which Q and x vary with time is given for each, corresponding expressions for E and f_x as functions of time can be found. Consider the following cases.

(*a*) Assume that $Q = Q_0 = \text{constant}$, $x = x_0 = \text{constant}$. Then from *(1)*,

$$E = Q_0(s-x_0)/A, \qquad f_x = kx_0 - Q_0^2/2A$$

(*b*) If it is assumed that $x = x_0 = \text{constant}$ and $Q = \dot{Q}_0 t$,

$$E = R\dot{Q}_0 + \dot{Q}_0 t(s-x_0)/A, \qquad f_x = kx_0 - \dot{Q}_0^2 t^2/2A$$

(*c*) Letting $\dot{Q} = \dot{Q}_0 \sin(\omega_1 t + \phi_1)$, $x = x_0 \sin(\omega_2 t + \phi_2)$, we obtain

$$E = M\dot{Q}_0\omega_1 \cos(\omega_1 t+\phi_1) - \frac{\dot{Q}_0}{A\omega_1}\cos(\omega_1 t+\phi_1)[s - x_0\sin(\omega_2 t+\phi_2)] + R\dot{Q}_0 \sin(\omega_1 t+\phi_1)$$

$$f_x = -mx_0\omega_2^2 \sin(\omega_2 t+\phi_2) + kx_0\sin(\omega_2 t+\phi_2) - \frac{\dot{Q}_0^2}{2A\omega_1^2}\cos^2(\omega_1 t+\phi_1)$$

Such a voltage and force might, of course, be difficult to apply. Moreover, if f_x and E are applied at random, certain transient effects may exist, which in any actual case would eventually be damped out by resistance and frictional drag on the plate. (See note at bottom of Page 269.)

Example 15.8.

In Fig. 15-3, Page 305, let us regard E_1 and E_2 as unknown applied voltages. Writing equations of motion in terms of Q_1, Q_3 and assuming that $Q_1 = Q_{01} = \text{constant}$, $Q_3 = Q_{03} = \text{constant}$, the reader may show that E_1 and E_2 must have the values

$$E_1 = E_3 + \frac{Q_{01}}{C_1} + \frac{Q_{03}}{C_3}, \qquad E_2 = E_3 + \frac{Q_{03} - Q_{01}}{C_2} + \frac{Q_{03}}{C_3}$$

Likewise for $Q_1 = A_1 \sin(\omega_1 t + \phi_1)$ and $Q_2 = A_2 \sin(\omega_2 t + \phi_2)$, E_1 and E_2 can be found at once as functions of time.

15.7 Analogous Electrical and Mechanical Systems.

It frequently happens that, for a given electrical system, there exists a mechanical one which is its exact counterpart in the sense that the differential equations for the two (by proper choice of coordinates) can be written in just the same form. This is illustrated by the following simple examples.

Example 15.9.

In Fig. 15-7(*a*) a sphere of mass m is suspended in a viscous liquid from a coil spring. l_0 = unstretched length of spring, y_0 = elongation of spring with m at rest, y = general displacement from rest position. We assume that the only effect of the liquid is to exert a viscous drag $-a\dot{y}$. Fig. 15-7(*b*) represents a simple series electrical circuit. Lagrangian functions for (*a*) and (*b*) respectively are

$$L_{Me} = \tfrac{1}{2}m\dot{y}^2 - \tfrac{1}{2}k(y + y_0)^2 + mgy, \qquad L_{El} = \tfrac{1}{2}M\dot{Q}^2 - \tfrac{1}{2}Q^2/C + EQ$$

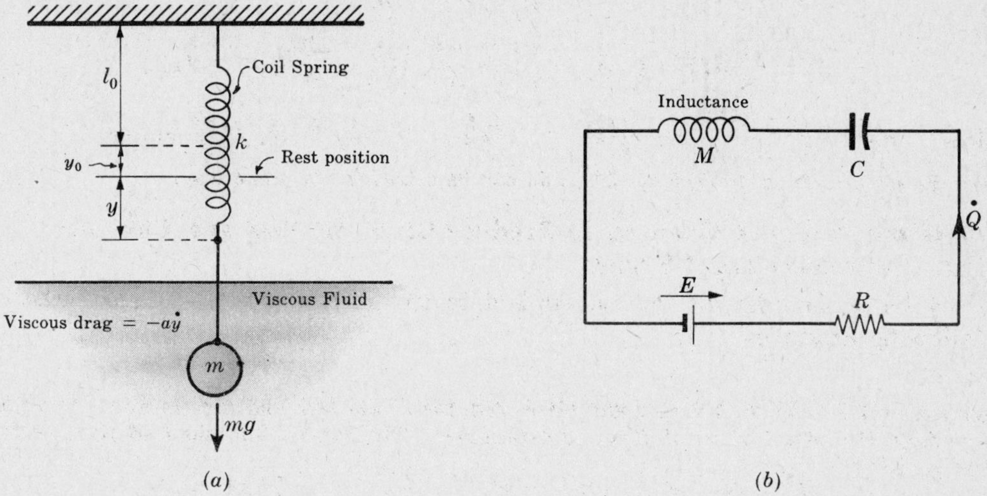

Fig. 15-7

Since $mg = ky_0$, the equations of motion are

$$m\ddot{y} + ky = -a\dot{y}, \qquad M\ddot{Q} + Q/C = -R\dot{Q}$$

Hence the two systems are "equivalent".

Example 15.10.

Consider the three systems shown in Fig. 15-8 below. In (*a*), E is a constant applied voltage and we assume no mutual inductance between the coils. In (*b*), F is a constant externally applied force and each block is acted upon by a viscous force $-a_1\dot{x}_1$, etc. In (*c*), τ is a constant externally applied torque and a brake exerts a viscous torque, $-b_1 r_1 \dot{\theta}_1$, etc., on each disk. Lagrangian functions for the three systems may be written as

$$\begin{aligned} L_a &= \tfrac{1}{2}(M_1\dot{Q}_1^2 + M_2\dot{Q}_2^2 + M_3\dot{Q}_3^2) - \frac{(Q_1 - Q_2)^2}{2C_1} - \frac{(Q_2 - Q_3)^2}{2C_2} + EQ_1 \\ L_b &= \tfrac{1}{2}(m_1\dot{x}_1^2 + m_2\dot{x}_2^2 + m_3\dot{x}_3^2) - \tfrac{1}{2}k_1(x_2 - x_1 - l_{10})^2 - \tfrac{1}{2}k_2(x_3 - x_2 - l_{20})^2 \qquad (1) \\ L_c &= \tfrac{1}{2}(I_1\dot{\theta}_1^2 + I_2\dot{\theta}_2^2 + I_3\dot{\theta}_3^2) - \tfrac{1}{2}k_1(\theta_1 - \theta_2)^2 - \tfrac{1}{2}k_2(\theta_2 - \theta_3)^2 \end{aligned}$$

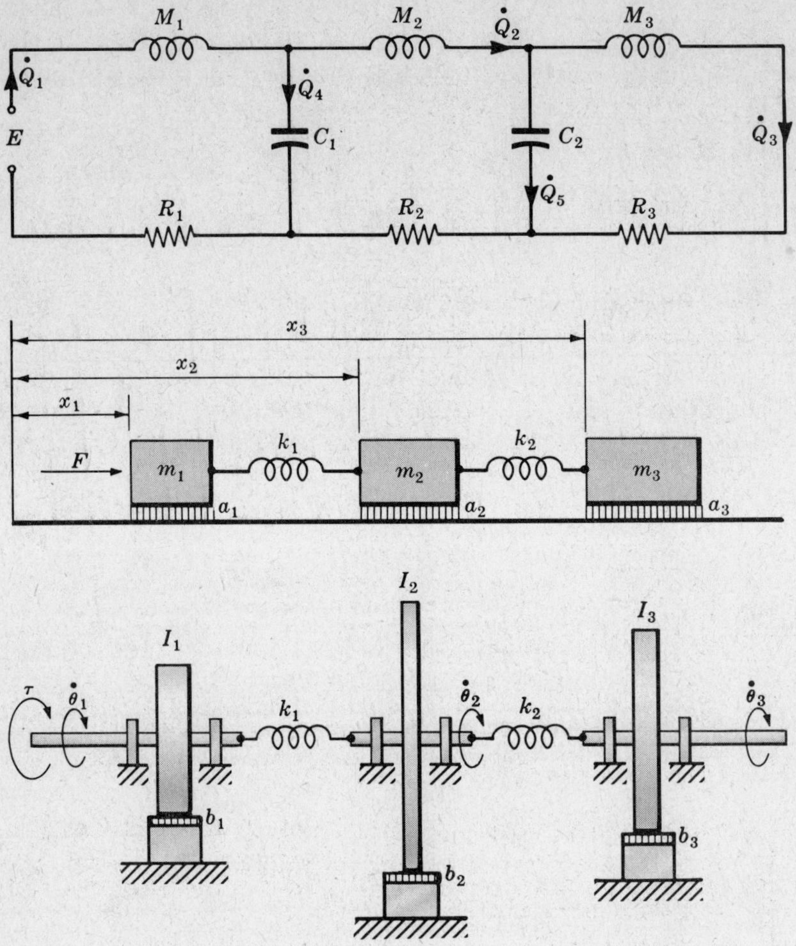

Fig. 15-8

Final equations of motion for (a) are

$$M_1\ddot{Q}_1 + \frac{Q_1}{C_1} - \frac{Q_2}{C_2} = E - R_1\dot{Q}_1$$

$$M_2\ddot{Q}_2 - \frac{Q_1}{C_1} + Q_2\left(\frac{1}{C_1} + \frac{1}{C_2}\right) - \frac{Q_3}{C_2} = -R_2\dot{Q}_2$$

$$M_3\ddot{Q}_3 - \frac{Q_2}{C_2} + \frac{Q_3}{C_2} = -R_3\dot{Q}_3$$

Equations having exactly the same form (except for constant terms) follow at once for (b) and (c). Here inductance corresponds to a mass in (b) and moment of inertia in (c). Electrical resistance R_1 corresponds to the coefficient of viscous drag a_1 in (b) and to br_1 in (c), etc. $1/C$ corresponds to a spring constant in each case. Note that in the above example coordinates were carefully chosen so that all three sets of equations have the same form. If, for example, equations of motion for (b) were written in coordinates x_1, q_1, q_2 where $q_1 = x_2 - x_1$ and $q_2 = x_3 - x_2$, it would not be immediately evident that (b) is equivalent to (a) and (c). *Note.* In L_b, $x_1 + l_{10}$ and $x_2 + l_{20}$ can be replaced by single variables.

For any given mechanical system, it is not always easy to find its exact electrical counterpart. Rather complex analog circuits may be required.

Example 15.11.

The mechanical and electrical systems shown in Fig. 15-9(*a*) and (*b*) below are strikingly similar in general appearance and, for (*a*) properly idealized, their physical characteristics are the same.

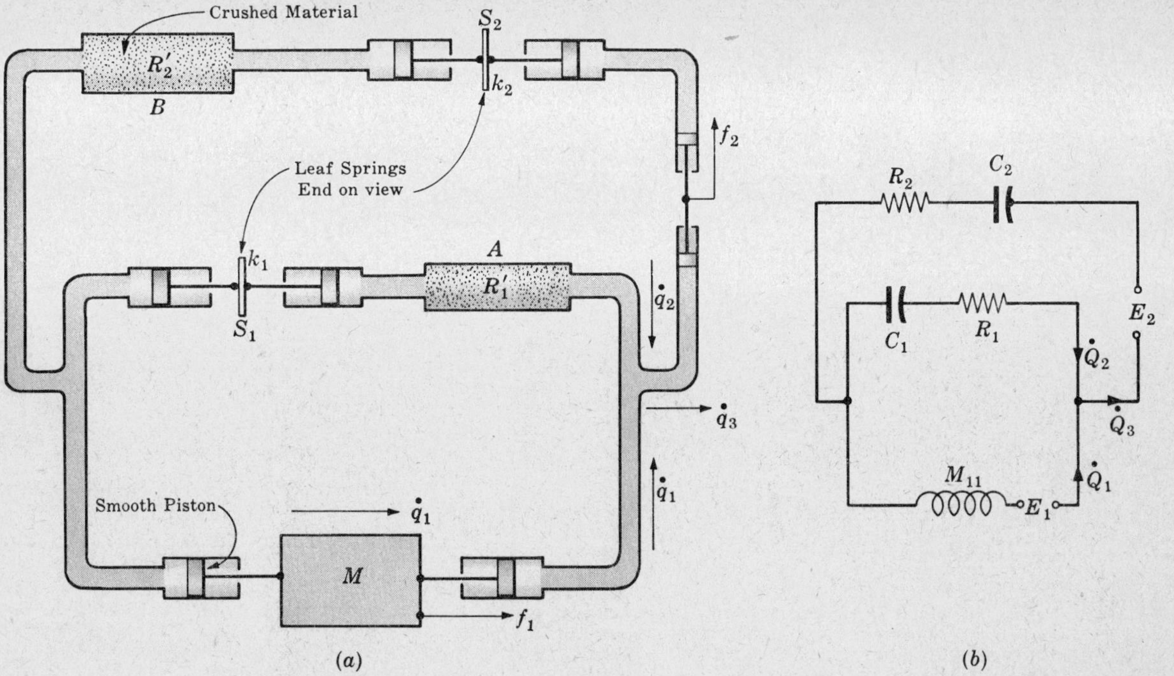

Fig. 15-9

In (*a*) the mass M and leaf springs S_1 and S_2 (end view shown) are coupled by a "massless" liquid in smooth tubes. Sections A and B are filled with some crushed material which offers a viscous drag to the flow of the liquid, $-R_1' \times$ (velocity of liquid); etc. An external force f_1 can be applied to M and another, f_2, directly to the liquid. The pistons shown are assumed smooth and massless.

Let q_1 represent the horizontal displacement of M from some fixed point and q_2, q_3 displacements of S_1 and S_2 respectively. The reader should write out equations of motion for the two systems and show that, mathematically, they are equivalent where M corresponds to M_{11}; k_1, k_2 to $1/C_1, 1/C_2$; R_1', R_2' to R_1, R_2; f_1, f_2 to E_1, E_2.

As seen from previous examples, analogous systems are usually not at all similar in general appearance.

15.8 References.

For more details regarding the application of Lagrange's equations to electromechanical systems and concerning the matter of electrical-mechanical analogs, the reader may consult the following references:

H. F. Olson, *Dynamical Analogies*, Van Nostrand, 1943

W. P. Mason, *Electromechanical Transducers and Wave Filters*, Van Nostrand, Second ed., 1948

R. M. Fano, L. J. Chu, R. B. Adler, *Electromagnetic Fields, Energy, and Forces*, John Wiley, 1960

D. C. White, and H. H. Woodson, *Electromechanical Energy Conversion*, John Wiley, 1959

J. R. Barker, *Mechanical and Electrical Vibrations*, John Wiley, 1964

G. W. Van Santen, *Mechanical Vibration*, N. V. Philips, Eindhoven, Holland, 1953

Problems

In the following problems specific units are not introduced.

15.1. Show that the Lagrangian and equations of motion for the circuit shown in Fig. 15-10, assuming no mutual inductance between M_{33} and remaining inductances, are

$$L = \tfrac{1}{2}[M_{11}\dot{Q}_1^2 + M_{12}\dot{Q}_1\dot{Q}_2 + (M_{22}+M_{33})\dot{Q}_2^2] + Q_1E_0 \sin \omega t - \tfrac{1}{2}Q_2^2/C$$

$$M_{11}\ddot{Q}_1 + M_{12}\ddot{Q}_2 - E_0 \sin \omega t = -R_1\dot{Q}_1$$

$$(M_{22}+M_{33})\ddot{Q}_2 + M_{12}\ddot{Q}_1 + Q_2/C = -R_2\dot{Q}_2$$

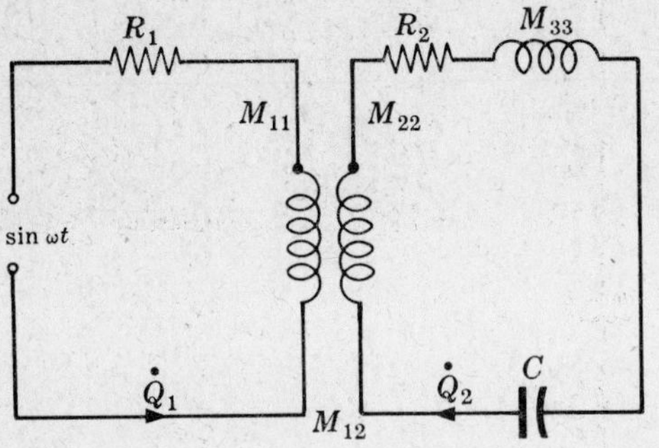

Fig. 15-10

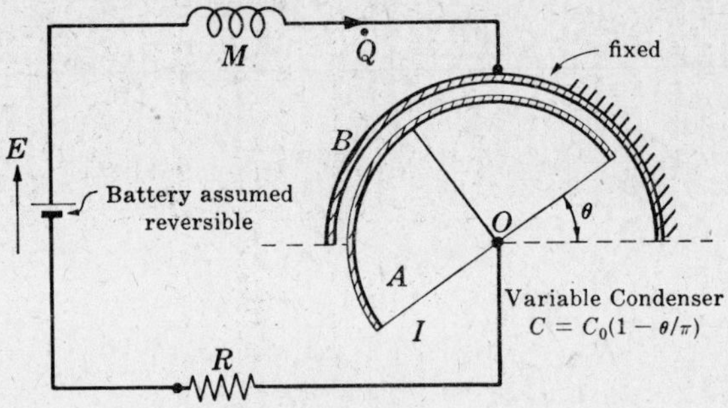

Fig. 15-11

15.2. Referring to Example 15.5 and Fig. 15-3, Page 305, it is seen that after some time $\dot{Q}_1 = \dot{Q}_2 = \dot{Q}_3 = 0$ and we write $Q_1 = Q_{01}$, $Q_2 = Q_{02}$, $Q_3 = Q_{03}$. Find expressions for these "equilibrium" charges. Now setting $Q_1 = Q_{01} + \alpha_1$, $Q_2 = Q_{02} + \alpha_2$, $Q_3 = Q_{03} + \alpha_3$, write L for the system and show that the equations of motion are

$$(M_{11}+M_{33}+2M_{13})\ddot{\alpha}_1 + (R_1+R_3)\dot{\alpha}_1 + (1/C_1 + 1/C_3)\alpha_1$$
$$+ (M_{12}+M_{23}-M_{13}-M_{33})\ddot{\alpha}_2 - R_3\dot{\alpha}_2 - \alpha_2/C_3 = 0$$

$$(M_{12}+M_{23}-M_{13}-M_{33})\ddot{\alpha}_1 - R_3\dot{\alpha}_1 - \alpha_1/C_3$$
$$+ (M_{22}-2M_{23}+M_{33})\ddot{\alpha}_2 + (R_2+R_3)\dot{\alpha}_2 + (1/C_2+1/C_3)\alpha_2 = 0$$

15.3. The inside half-cylinder A, Fig. 15-11, supported in a vertical position by a thin elastic rod (torsional constant k) fastened along its axis at O, can rotate within B. Assuming that the capacity of this variable condenser is given by $C = C_0(1-\theta/\pi)$ and that the rod is undistorted for $\theta = \theta_1$, show that the proper Lagrangian and equations of motion are

$$L = \tfrac{1}{2}m\dot{Q}^2 + \tfrac{1}{2}I\dot{\theta}^2 + EQ - \frac{Q^2}{2C_0(1-\theta/\pi)} - \tfrac{1}{2}k(\theta_1-\theta)^2$$

$$\ddot{\theta} + \frac{Q}{C_0(1-\theta/\pi)} - E = -R\dot{Q}$$

$$I\ddot{\theta} + \frac{Q^2}{2\pi C_0(1-\theta/\pi)^2} - k(\theta_1-\theta) = 0$$

15.4. The coils in Fig. 15-6, Page 307, are connected in series and to an external source of voltage $E_0 \sin \omega t$. (See Example 15.4.) Show that the equations of motion are

$$(M_{11}+M_{22})\ddot{Q} + 2B(\ddot{Q}\cos\theta - \dot{Q}\dot{\theta}\sin\theta) - E_0\sin\omega t = -R\dot{Q}$$

$$I\ddot{\theta} + B(\dot{Q}^2\sin\theta) + k\theta = 0$$

15.5. Coil (1), Fig. 15-6, is replaced by a permanent magnet. Assuming that the magnetic field is uniform and constant and that the moving coil is connected as indicated on the diagram, write out L and show that the equations of motion are

$$M_{22}\ddot{Q}_2 + N_2\Phi\dot{\theta}\cos\theta - E_0\sin\omega t = -R_2\dot{Q}_2, \qquad I\ddot{\theta} - N_2\Phi\dot{Q}_2\cos\theta + k\theta = 0$$

where Φ is the total flux threading the coil for $\theta = 90°$.

15.6. Two permanent-magnet wall type galvanometers are connected as shown in Fig. 15-12 below. Assuming radial magnetic fields, show that the proper Lagrangian for the system is given by

$$L = \tfrac{1}{2}(M_{11}\dot{Q}_1^2 + 2M_{12}\dot{Q}_1\dot{Q}_2 + M_{22}\dot{Q}_2^2) + \tfrac{1}{2}I_1\dot{\theta}_1^2 + \tfrac{1}{2}I_2\dot{\theta}_2^2 + N_1\Phi_1\dot{Q}_1\theta_1$$
$$+ N_2\Phi_2\dot{Q}_2\theta_2 + (Q_1+Q_2)E_1 - \tfrac{1}{2}(Q_1+Q_2)^2/C - \tfrac{1}{2}k_1\theta_1^2 - \tfrac{1}{2}k_2\theta_2^2$$

where it is assumed that M_{11} and M_{22} include the self inductance of galvanometer coils (1) and (2) respectively. Write out equations of motion.

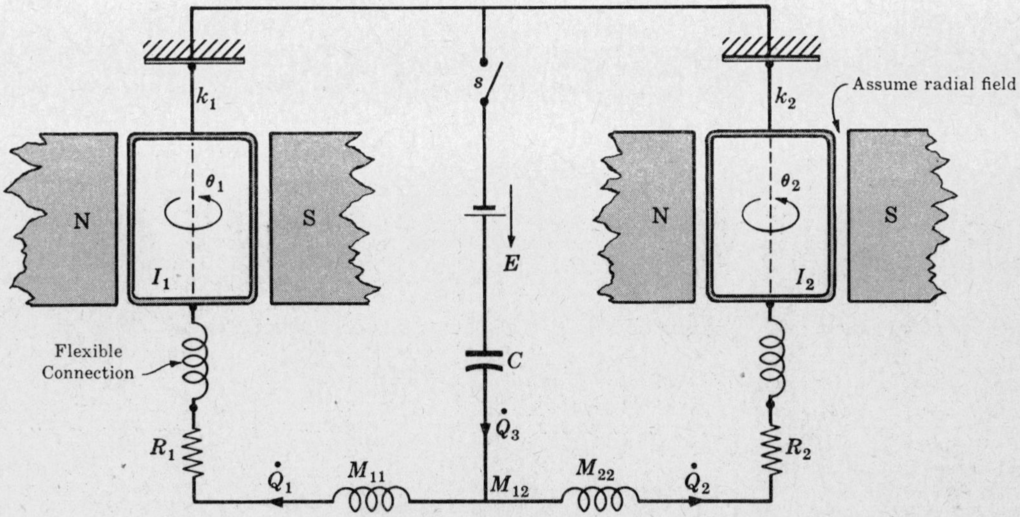

Permanent-magnet Wall Galvanometers

Fig. 15-12

15.7. Each plate of the variable condenser, Fig. 15-13, is free to move along a line ab without rotation, under the action of a spring and the electric field between them. Show that the Lagrangian for the system is

$$L = \tfrac{1}{2}(m_1\dot{x}_1^2 + m_2\dot{x}_2^2 + M\dot{Q}^2) - \tfrac{1}{2}(k_1x_1^2 + k_2x_2^2) + EQ - \tfrac{1}{2}Q^2(s - x_1 - x_2)/A$$

where A is a constant. Write out equations of motion.

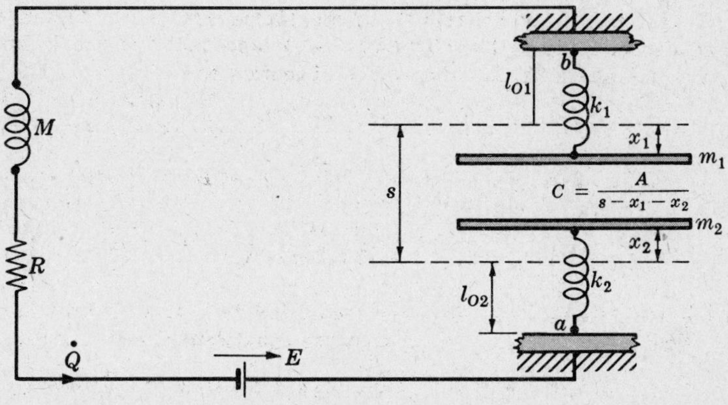

Fig. 15-13

15.8. The variable condenser and wall galvanometer are connected as in Fig. 15-14 below. Show that L for the system is

$$L = \tfrac{1}{2}(I\dot{\theta}^2 + m\dot{x}^2 + M_{11}\dot{Q}_1^2 + M_{22}\dot{Q}_2^2) + E_1Q_1 - E_2(Q_1 - Q_2)$$
$$+ N\Phi\dot{Q}_1\theta - \tfrac{1}{2}[kx^2 + (Q_1 - Q_2)^2(s-x)/A + k\theta^2] + mgx$$

Write out equations of motion and from them determine steady values of $\dot{Q}_1, \dot{Q}_2$ and equilibrium values of θ, x and Q_3. Check relations by elementary principles.

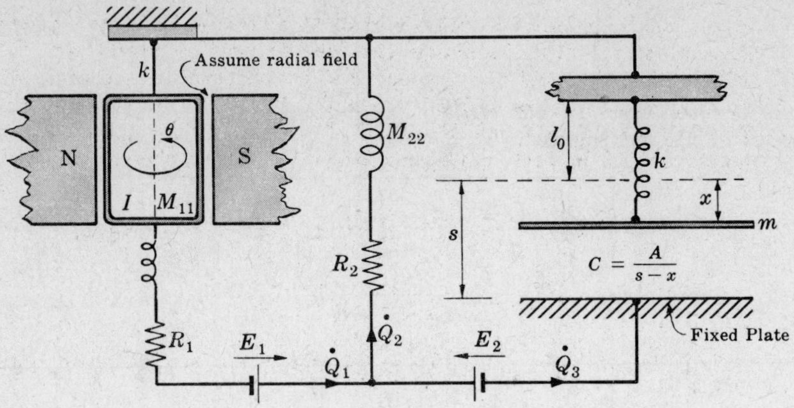

Fig. 15-14

15.9. Referring to Problem 15.3, Fig. 15-11, show that equilibrium values of θ and Q are given by $\theta_0 = \theta_1 - C_0E^2/2\pi k$, $Q_0 = C_0(1-\theta_0/\pi)E$. It can be seen from the physics involved that when the condenser is charged, $\theta_1 > \theta$.

Writing $\theta = \theta_0 + \alpha_1$ and $Q = Q_0 + \alpha_2$, find equations of motion which determine the oscillations of θ and Q about equilibrium values.

15.10. Set up equations for the determination of the oscillatory motions of the system shown in Fig. 15-12 about equilibrium values. See Problem 15.6.

15.11. Referring to Fig. 15-12, $\theta_1, \theta_2, Q_1, Q_3$ are each to be made to vary in a given manner with time. Torques $\tau_1(t), \tau_2(t)$ are applied to the moving coils respectively. Replace the battery with an unknown source of voltage $E_1 = E_1(t)$. Insert another voltage $E_2 = E_2(t)$ in the left leg of the circuit. Find expressions for τ_1, τ_2, E_1, E_2 which meet the stated conditions.

15.12. Set up equations of motion for systems (*a*) and (*b*), Fig. 15-15, and show that they are equivalent. Assume viscous forces acting on bases of m_1 and m_2. Also regard the dashpot as exerting a viscous force.

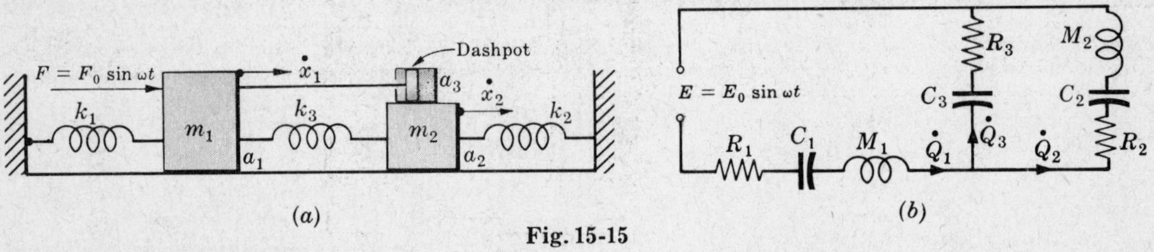

Fig. 15-15

15.13. The double pendulum, Fig. 15-16(*a*) (see equations (*10.2*), Page 206), consists of a heavy uniform bar (length r_1, mass M) and a slender light rod of length r_2 with the "particle" m attached. The upper bearing b_1 exerts a damping torque proportional to $\dot{\theta}$ and the lower bearing b_2 exerts another torque proportional to $\dot{\phi} - \dot{\theta}$. The spiral pancake spring (with one end attached to the bar, the other to the rod) is undistorted for $\theta = \phi$. In Fig. 15-16(*b*) the two coils have mutual inductance M_{12}.

Assuming θ and ϕ are small, show that equations of motion for these coordinates are exactly analogous to those corresponding to Q_1 and Q_2 (except for a constant term E).

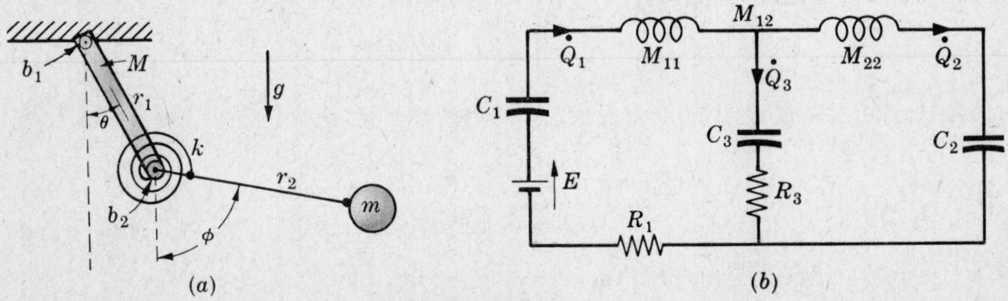

Fig. 15-16

15.14. In Fig. 15-17 the disk is mounted at the center of an elastic rod, the ends of which are rigidly fixed. Torsional constant of the rod and elastic constant of the coil spring are k_1 and k_2 respectively. Metal cylinders (masses m_1 and m_2), suspended from an insulating cord as shown, can move vertically in the fixed metal cylinders. Each rod and cylinder constitutes a variable condenser C_1 and C_2 respectively. M_{11}, R_1, E_1, C_1 and M_{22}, R_2, E_2, C_2 are independent electrical circuits except that they are coupled by the mutual inductance M_{12}. Show that T and V for this electromechanical system are given by

$$T = \tfrac{1}{2}(m_1\dot{y}_1^2 + m_2\dot{y}_2^2 + I\dot{y}_2^2/r^2) + \tfrac{1}{2}(M_{11}\dot{Q}_1^2 + 2M_{12}\dot{Q}_1\dot{Q}_2 + M_{22}\dot{Q}_2^2)$$

$$V = \frac{1}{2}\left[\frac{l_1Q_1^2}{C_{01}(l_1 - y_1)} + \frac{l_2Q_2^2}{C_{02}(l_2 - y_2)}\right] - Q_1E_0 \sin \omega t - E_2Q_2$$
$$+ \frac{1}{2}\left[k_1\left(\frac{y_2 - b_2}{r}\right)^2 + k_2(b_1 - y_1 - y_2)^2\right] + m_1gy_1 + m_2gy_2$$

where $C_1 = C_{01}(1 - y_1/l_1)$, $C_2 = C_{02}(1 - y_2/l_2)$, $y_1 + y_2 + l = b_1 =$ constant, $r\theta + b_2 = y_2$. Write out equations of motion corresponding to y_1, y_2, Q_1, Q_2.

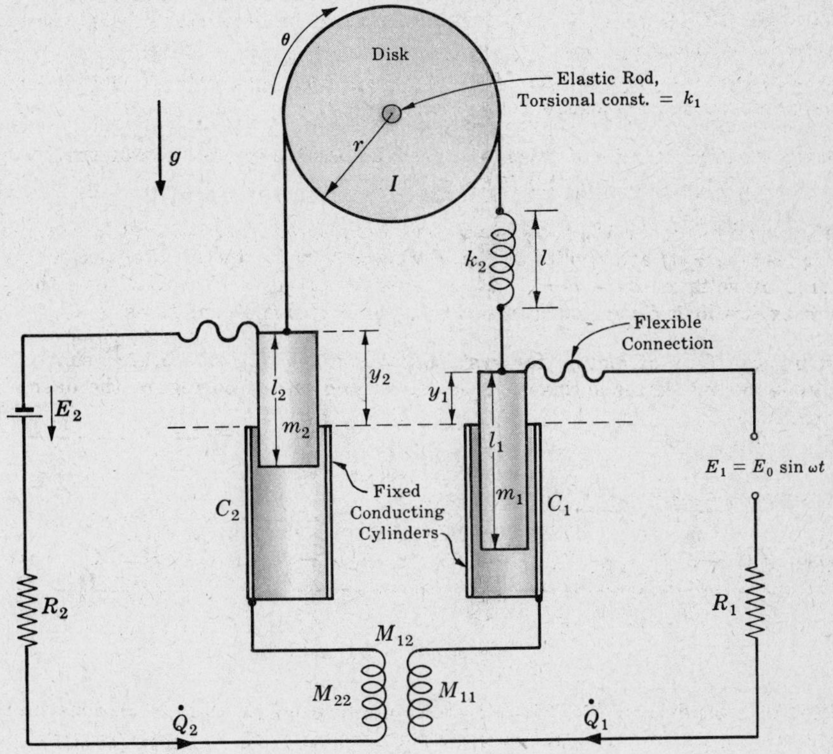

Fig. 15-17

15.15. Assuming $E_0 \sin \omega t$ in the above problem replaced by a constant voltage, determine equilibrium values of y_1, y_2, Q_1, Q_2. Expanding V, (see (*10.6*), Page 207) about these values, set up equations of motion for small oscillations of the system.

CHAPTER

16

Hamilton's Equations of Motion

16.1 General Remarks.

Hamilton's "canonical equations" constitute another way of expressing dynamical equations of motion and it will soon be seen that for a system having n degrees of freedom there are $2n$ first order Hamiltonian equations as compared with n second order Lagrangian equations.

As a means of treating most applied problems the Hamiltonian method is less convenient than the Lagrangian. However, in certain fields of physics (listed and discussed briefly at the end of this chapter) Hamilton's equations and the Hamiltonian point of view have been of great service.

16.2 A Word About "Generalized Momentum".

The quantity $\partial L/\partial \dot{q}_r$ is defined as the generalized momentum p_r corresponding to the generalized coordinate q_r, that is, $\partial L/\partial \dot{q}_r = p_r$. (Note that if $\dot{q}$'s occur only in T, $\partial L/\partial \dot{q}_r = \partial T/\partial \dot{q}_r = p_r$.) The following examples will show that for certain simple cases p_r, as defined above, is a momentum in the elementary and familiar sense of the word.

For a projectile, L may be written as $L = \frac{1}{2}m(\dot{x}^2 + \dot{y}^2 + \dot{z}^2) - mgz$ from which $\partial L/\partial \dot{x} = m\dot{x} = p_x$, $p_y = m\dot{y}$, $p_z = m\dot{z}$. Hence p_x, p_y, p_z are just the familiar components of linear momentum.

Referring to Example 5.7, Fig. 5-9, Page 88,

$$\partial L/\partial \dot{\bar{x}} = M\dot{\bar{x}} = p_{\bar{x}}, \quad \partial L/\partial \dot{r} = \mu\dot{r} = p_r, \quad \partial L/\partial \dot{\theta} = \mu r^2\dot{\theta} = p_\theta, \quad \partial L/\partial \dot{\phi} = \mu r^2 \sin^2\theta\,\dot{\phi} = p_\phi$$

where $p_{\bar{x}}$ and p_r are linear momenta while p_θ and p_ϕ are angular momenta.

16.3 Derivation of Hamilton's Equations.

The Lagrangian $L = T - V$ is in general a function of $q_1, q_2, \ldots, q_n; \dot{q}_1, \dot{q}_2, \ldots, \dot{q}_n; t$. Thus we can write

$$dL = \sum_{r=1}^{n}\left(\frac{\partial L}{\partial q_r}dq_r + \frac{\partial L}{\partial \dot{q}_r}d\dot{q}_r\right) + \frac{\partial L}{\partial t}dt \tag{16.1}$$

But $p_r = \dfrac{\partial L}{\partial \dot{q}_r}$, and from $\dfrac{d}{dt}\left(\dfrac{\partial L}{\partial \dot{q}_r}\right) - \dfrac{\partial L}{\partial q_r} = F_{q_r}$ (where F_{q_r} is determined in the usual way from all forces not taken account of by V) it is seen that $\partial L/\partial q_r = \dot{p}_r - F_{q_r}$. Hence (16.1) becomes

$$dL = \sum_{r=1}^{n}[(\dot{p}_r - F_{q_r})\,dq_r + p_r\,d\dot{q}_r] + \frac{\partial L}{\partial t}dt \tag{16.2}$$

Next, eliminating $p_r\,d\dot{q}_r$ from above by the relation $d(p_r\dot{q}_r) = p_r\,d\dot{q}_r + \dot{q}_r\,dp_r$ and rearranging terms, (*16.2*) may be written as

$$d\left[\sum_{r=1}^{n} p_r\dot{q}_r - L\right] = \sum_{r=1}^{n} [(F_{q_r} - \dot{p}_r)\,dq_r + \dot{q}_r\,dp_r] - \frac{\partial L}{\partial t}dt \tag{16.3}$$

At this point it is important to note that $p_r = \partial L/\partial\dot{q}_r$ is, in general, a function of the q's, $\dot{q}$'s and t. (For any particular case this takes the form of an algebraic equation. For example, as previously given, $\partial L/\partial\dot{\phi} = p_\phi = mr^2\sin^2\theta\,\dot{\phi}$). By means of these n relations all velocities $\dot{q}_1, \dot{q}_2, \ldots, \dot{q}_n$ can be eliminated from $\sum_{r=1}^{n} p_r\dot{q}_r - L$ in favor of the p's and q's. Assuming that this has been done, the *Hamiltonian Function*, H, is defined as

$$H = \sum_{r=1}^{n} p_r\dot{q}_r - L \tag{16.4}$$

Now since this is a function of the p's, q's and t,

$$dH = \sum_{r=1}^{n}\left(\frac{\partial H}{\partial q_r}dq_r + \frac{\partial H}{\partial p_r}dp_r\right) + \frac{\partial H}{\partial t}dt \tag{16.5}$$

Comparing terms on the right of (*16.3*) with those of (*16.5*) it is seen that

$$\frac{\partial H}{\partial p_r} = \dot{q}_r, \qquad \frac{\partial H}{\partial q_r} = F_{q_r} - \dot{p}_r, \qquad \frac{\partial H}{\partial t} = -\frac{\partial L}{\partial t} \tag{16.6}$$

The first two relations in (*16.6*) represent $2n$ first order differential equations. They are referred to as Hamilton's *canonical equations* of motion. Solutions of these, with properly evaluated constants of integration, give each coordinate and each momentum as a function of time; that is, they determine the complete dynamical behavior of the system. (For a good discussion of appropriate expressions for L and H when forces due to electric and magnetic fields exist, see: D. H. Menzel, *Mathematical Physics*, Dover, 1961, pages 359-360.)

It is well to note that H can usually be expressed in another and sometimes more convenient form. Let us write (*2.55*), Page 27, as

$$T = \sum_{r=1}^{n}\sum_{s=1}^{n} A_{rs}\dot{q}_r\dot{q}_s + \sum_{s=1}^{n} B_s\dot{q}_s + C \equiv T_1 + T_2 + T_3 \tag{16.7}$$

(As a specific example of this form of T note that expression (*2.50*), Page 27, can be written as

$$T = \tfrac{1}{2}m[\dot{q}_1^2 + \dot{q}_2^2 + 2\dot{q}_1\dot{q}_2\cos(\beta-\alpha)] + m\{[(v_x + a_xt)\cos\alpha + (v_y + a_yt)\sin\alpha]\dot{q}_1$$
$$+ [(v_x + a_xt)\cos\beta + (v_y + a_yt)\sin\beta]\dot{q}_2\}$$
$$+ \tfrac{1}{2}m[2(v_xa_x + v_ya_y)t + (a_x^2 + a_y^2)t^2 + v_x^2 + v_y^2]$$

Clearly the first, second and third terms are T_1, T_2, T_3 respectively. In any particular case, when T is written out in full, T_1, T_2, T_3 can be recognized by inspection.) Hence, assuming $\partial L/\partial\dot{q}_r = \partial T/\partial\dot{q}_r$, we have

$$p_r = \partial T/\partial\dot{q}_r = 2\sum_{s=1}^{n} A_{rs}\dot{q}_s + B_r$$

and so
$$\sum_{r=1}^{n} p_r\dot{q}_r = 2\sum_{r=1}^{n}\sum_{s=1}^{n} A_{rs}\dot{q}_r\dot{q}_s + \sum_{r=1}^{n} B_r\dot{q}_r = 2T_1 + T_2$$

Thus (*16.4*) may be written as $H = 2T_1 + T_2 - (T_1 + T_2 + T_3 - V)$ or

$$H = T_1 - T_3 + V \tag{16.8}$$

If t does not enter transformation equations, (see (*2.21*), Page 19), $T_2 = T_3 = 0$ and

$$H = T + V = \mathcal{E} = \text{energy of the system}$$

For convenience, the most important relations are summarized below.

$$(a) \quad H = \sum_{r=1}^{n} p_r\dot{q}_r - L \tag{16.4}$$

$$(b) \quad H = T_1 - T_3 + V \tag{16.8}$$

$$(c) \quad \frac{\partial H}{\partial p_r} = \dot{q}_r, \qquad \frac{\partial H}{\partial q_r} = F_{q_r} - \dot{p}_r \tag{16.6}$$

These relations are correct even though external and dissipative forces may be acting.

16.4 Procedure for Setting Up H and Writing Hamiltonian Equations.

(*a*) Write out $L = T - V$. Express T and V in the usual way just as if Lagrange's equations were to be applied.

(*b*) Obtain, by carrying out the differentiations $p_1 = \partial L/\partial\dot{q}_1$, $p_2 = \partial L/\partial\dot{q}_2$, etc., n algebraic equations. These relations express the p's as functions of the q's, $\dot{q}$'s, t.

(*c*) Solve these equations simultaneously for each $\dot{q}$ in terms of the p's, q's, t and eliminate the $\dot{q}$'s from (*16.4*) or (*16.8*). This gives H expressed as a function of the p's, q's, t only.

(*d*) To obtain the Hamiltonian equations of motion perform the differentiations $\partial H/\partial p_1$, $\partial H/\partial p_2, \ldots, \partial H/\partial p_n$ and in each case the result is set equal to $\dot{q}_1, \dot{q}_2, \ldots, \dot{q}_n$ respectively. Likewise perform the differentiation $\partial H/\partial q_1$, set the result equal to $F_{q_1} - \dot{p}_1$, etc. We thus have $2n$ first order equations. F_{q_1}, F_{q_2}, etc., are just the familiar generalized forces, found in the usual way except that conservative forces, as previously explained, are not included.

16.5 Special Cases of H.

(*a*) When conservative forces only, including those for which a potential energy function involving t can be written (see Section 5.11, Page 90), are acting, $F_{q_r} = 0$. Hence

$$\frac{\partial H}{\partial p_r} = \dot{q}_r, \qquad \frac{\partial H}{\partial q_r} = -\dot{p}_r \tag{16.9}$$

These are extensively used in many branches of dynamics.

(*b*) If the system is a "natural" one in which there are no moving coordinates or constraints (t does not enter transformation equations), $T_2 = T_3 = 0$ [see (*2.56*), Page 27]. Hence $T = T_1$ and by (*16.8*),

$$H = T + V = \mathcal{E}_{\text{total}} \tag{16.10}$$

That is, under these conditions, H is the total energy of the system. However, *in general, H is not total energy.*

16.6 Important Energy and Power Relations.

From (*16.5*), $\dfrac{dH}{dt} = \sum_{r=1}^{n}\left(\dfrac{\partial H}{\partial q_r}\dot{q}_r + \dfrac{\partial H}{\partial p_r}\dot{p}_r\right) + \dfrac{\partial H}{\partial t}$. Applying (*16.6*),

$$\frac{dH}{dt} = \sum F_{q_r}\dot{q}_r + \frac{\partial H}{\partial t} \tag{16.11}$$

from which the following important conclusions may be drawn.

(a) If the system is natural $\partial H/\partial t = 0$; and if no forces other than conservative are acting, $F_{q_r} = 0$. So, as shown above, $H = T + V = \mathcal{E}_{\text{total}}$. Thus

$$\frac{dH}{dt} = \frac{d\mathcal{E}_{\text{total}}}{dt} = 0 \quad \text{or} \quad \mathcal{E}_{\text{total}} = \text{constant} \tag{16.12}$$

That is, the total energy of the system, $T + V$, remains constant. (See Section 5.13, Page 91.) (*16.12*) expresses the law of conservation of energy for such systems.

(b) If the system is natural and forces other than conservative are acting, (*16.10*) and (*16.11*) give

$$\frac{dH}{dt} = \frac{d}{dt}(T+V) = \sum_{r=1}^{n} F_{q_r}\dot{q}_r \tag{16.13}$$

But $\sum_{r=1}^{n} F_{q_r}\dot{q}_r$ is just the rate at which all forces (not including those which are conservative) do work on the system. Hence the time rate of change of $\mathcal{E}_{\text{total}}$ is equal to the power delivered by these forces.

16.7 Examples. The Hamiltonian and Hamiltonian Equations of Motion.

No moving coordinates or moving constraints.

Example 16.1. *The projectile.*

Regarding a projectile as a particle and axes attached to the earth as inertial,

$$L = \tfrac{1}{2}m(\dot{x}^2 + \dot{y}^2 + \dot{z}^2) - mgz$$

from which $\partial L/\partial \dot{x} = m\dot{x} = p_x, \quad p_y = m\dot{y}, \quad p_z = m\dot{z}$ (*1*)

Hence, following Section 16.4, $H = \frac{1}{2m}(p_x^2 + p_y^2 + p_z^2) + mgz$ (*2*)

Applying (*16.6*) and neglecting air resistance,

$$\partial H/\partial p_x = p_x/m = \dot{x}, \quad \partial H/\partial p_y = p_y/m = \dot{y}, \quad \partial H/\partial p_z = p_z/m = \dot{z} \tag{3}$$

$$\partial H/\partial x = 0 = -\dot{p}_x, \quad \partial H/\partial y = 0 = -\dot{p}_y, \quad \partial H/\partial z = mg = -\dot{p}_z \tag{4}$$

(Note that in the above, $T = T_1$ ($T_2 = T_3 = 0$); hence $H = T + V = \mathcal{E}$.) Relations (*3*) and (*4*) are the $2n$ (six in this case) Hamiltonian equations.

Differentiating (*3*) with respect to time and eliminating $\dot{p}_x, \dot{p}_y, \dot{p}_z$ from (*4*), we have the usual equations of motion:

$$m\ddot{x} = 0, \quad m\ddot{y} = 0, \quad m\ddot{z} = -mg \tag{5}$$

Having integrated these we can, returning to (*3*), determine how the momenta vary with time.

Note that relations (*1*) and (*3*) are exactly the same. Moreover, (*5*) are just the relations found by a direct application of Newton's or Lagrange's equations. Hence it is evident that Hamilton's equations are of no advantage in this problem.

Example 16.2. *A pendulum bob suspended from a coil spring and allowed to swing in a vertical plane.*

In the usual r, θ coordinates;

$$L = \tfrac{1}{2}m(\dot{r}^2 + r^2\dot{\theta}^2) + mgr\cos\theta - \tfrac{1}{2}k(r - r_0)^2$$

Hence $\partial L/\partial \dot{r} = p_r = m\dot{r}, \quad \partial L/\partial \dot{\theta} = p_\theta = mr^2\dot{\theta}$ (*1*)

Thus by (*16.4*) or (*16.8*),

$$H = \frac{1}{2m}\left(p_r^2 + \frac{1}{r^2}p_\theta^2\right) - mgr\cos\theta + \tfrac{1}{2}k(r - r_0)^2 \tag{2}$$

Applying (*16.6*),
$$\partial H/\partial p_r = p_r/m = \dot{r}, \quad \partial H/\partial p_\theta = p_\theta/mr^2 = \dot{\theta} \tag{3}$$
$$\partial H/\partial r \;=\; -p_\theta^2/mr^3 - mg\cos\theta + k(r-r_0) \;=\; -\dot{p}_r \tag{4}$$
$$\partial H/\partial\theta \;=\; mgr\sin\theta \;=\; -\dot{p}_\theta \tag{5}$$

Equations (*3*) to (*5*) are the Hamiltonian equations. Eliminating $\dot{p}_r$ and p_θ from (*4*) by means of (*3*), and $\dot{p}_\theta$ from (*5*) by (*3*), we obtain
$$m\ddot{r} - mr\dot{\theta}^2 - mg\cos\theta + k(r-r_0) \;=\; 0 \tag{6}$$
$$mr^2\ddot{\theta} + 2mr\dot{r}\dot{\theta} + mgr\sin\theta \;=\; 0 \tag{7}$$
A simultaneous solution of (*6*) and (*7*) gives each coordinate as a function of time.

Note that (*6*) and (*7*) can be obtained with considerably less effort by a direct application of the Lagrangian equations.

Example 16.3. *The Hamiltonian for a central force problem.*

Two uniform spheres, Fig. 16-1, of masses m_1, m_2 are free to move in space under the action of their gravitational attraction; no external forces are applied. Treating the spheres as particles, the reader may show without difficulty that
$$L \;=\; \tfrac{1}{2}(m_1+m_2)(\dot{\bar{x}}^2+\dot{\bar{y}}^2+\dot{\bar{z}}^2) + \tfrac{1}{2}\mu(\dot{r}^2 + r^2\dot{\theta}^2 + r^2\dot{\phi}^2\sin^2\theta) + Gm_1m_2/r \tag{1}$$
where $\bar{x}, \bar{y}, \bar{z}$ are inertial coordinates of c.m., r, θ, ϕ are spherical coordinates measured relative to the non-rotating $X'Y'Z'$ frame, $r = r_1 + r_2$ is the distance between centers of the spheres, G is the gravitational constant, and the "reduced mass" $\mu = m_1m_2/(m_1+m_2)$.

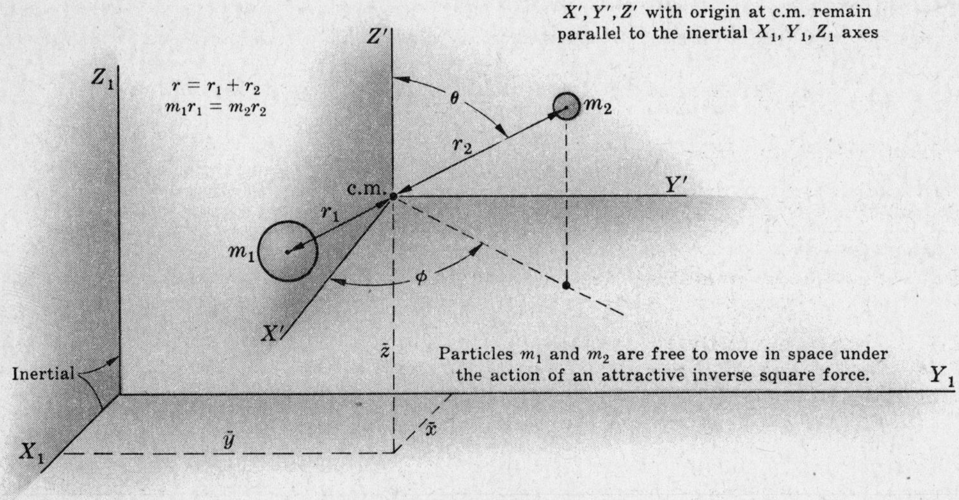

Fig. 16-1

Applying (*16.8*), the Hamiltonian is
$$H \;=\; \frac{1}{2(m_1+m_2)}(p_x^2+p_y^2+p_z^2) + \frac{1}{2\mu}\left(p_r^2 + \frac{p_\theta^2}{r^2} + \frac{p_\phi^2}{r^2\sin^2\theta}\right) - \frac{Gm_1m_2}{r} \tag{2}$$
and applying (*16.6*) the twelve Hamiltonian equations follow at once. It is suggested that from these twelve the reader eliminate the p's, determine the six equations of motion and compare with those obtained by a direct application of Lagrange's equations to L. (It is seen that for this example $T_2 = T_3 = 0$; thus $H = T + V = \mathcal{E}$.)

Example 16.4. *Hamiltonian for the double pendulum shown in Fig. 2-10, Page 14.*

The following example illustrates well the general form taken by the p's and the fact that finding an expression for H is not always as simple as previous examples might lead one to believe.

For the double pendulum with masses suspended from light coil springs having constants k_1, k_2 and motion confined to a plane (see equation (*2.42*), Page 24),

$$L = \tfrac{1}{2}(m_1+m_2)(\dot{r}_1^2 + r_1^2\dot{\theta}^2) + \tfrac{1}{2}m_2[\dot{r}_2^2 + r_2^2\dot{\phi}^2 + 2(\dot{r}_1\dot{r}_2 + r_1r_2\dot{\theta}\dot{\phi})\cos(\phi-\theta)$$
$$+ 2(r_1\dot{r}_2\dot{\theta} - r_2\dot{r}_1\dot{\phi})\sin(\phi-\theta)] + (m_1+m_2)gr_1\cos\theta \qquad (1)$$
$$+ m_2gr_2\cos\phi - \tfrac{1}{2}k_1(r_1-l_1)^2 - \tfrac{1}{2}k_2(r_2-l_2)^2$$

where l_1 and l_2 are unstretched lengths of the springs. Hence we have the following expressions for the momentum corresponding to r_1, r_2, θ, ϕ respectively.

$$\partial L/\partial\dot{r}_1 = (m_1+m_2)\dot{r}_1 + m_2\dot{r}_2\cos(\phi-\theta) - m_2r_2\dot{\phi}\sin(\phi-\theta) = p_{r_1} \qquad (2)$$

$$\partial L/\partial\dot{r}_2 = m_2\dot{r}_2 + m_2\dot{r}_1\cos(\phi-\theta) + m_2r_1\dot{\theta}\sin(\phi-\theta) = p_{r_2} \qquad (3)$$

$$\partial L/\partial\dot{\theta} = (m_1+m_2)r_1^2\dot{\theta} + m_2r_1r_2\dot{\phi}\cos(\phi-\theta) + m_2r_1\dot{r}_2\sin(\phi-\theta) = p_\theta \qquad (4)$$

$$\partial L/\partial\dot{\phi} = m_2r_2^2\dot{\phi} + m_2r_1r_2\dot{\theta}\cos(\phi-\theta) - m_2r_2\dot{r}_1\sin(\phi-\theta) = p_\phi \qquad (5)$$

Note that p_{r_1}, for example, contains $\dot{r}_1, \dot{r}_2, \dot{\phi}$; etc. Hence in order to find H we must solve the above four equations simultaneously for $\dot{r}_1, \dot{r}_2, \dot{\theta}, \dot{\phi}$, each in terms of the p's and coordinates. Having done this, these velocities can be eliminated from (*16.8*) giving, finally, the proper expression for H. Hence in certain cases the matter of finding H becomes a bit involved. No further details need be given.

Example 16.5. *The Hamiltonian for a Top.*

As shown in Example 8.14, Page 159, the Lagrangian for a top with tip stationary is

$$L = \tfrac{1}{2}[I_x(\dot{\theta}^2 + \dot{\psi}^2\sin^2\theta) + I_z(\dot{\phi} + \dot{\psi}\cos\theta)^2] - Mgr\cos\theta \qquad (1)$$

from which

$$p_\theta = I_x\dot{\theta}, \quad p_\phi = I_z(\dot{\phi} + \dot{\psi}\cos\theta), \quad p_\psi = I_x\dot{\psi}\sin^2\theta + I_z(\dot{\phi} + \dot{\psi}\cos\theta)\cos\theta \qquad (2)$$

Eliminating $\dot{\theta}, \dot{\phi}, \dot{\psi}$ from $T+V$ by (*2*), we have

$$H = \frac{1}{2}\left[\frac{p_\theta^2}{I_x} + \frac{(p_\psi - p_\phi\cos\theta)^2}{I_x\sin^2\theta} + \frac{p_\phi^2}{I_z}\right] + Mgr\cos\theta \qquad (3)$$

Applying relations (*16.6*), the Hamiltonian equations follow at once.

Note that in this case, $\dot{p}_\phi = 0$, $\dot{p}_\psi = 0$; hence $p_\phi = \text{constant}$, $p_\psi = \text{constant}$. (The same results follow at once by applying Lagrange's equations to L.)

Example 16.6. *Hamiltonian equations for the pendulum of Example 16.2, Page 319, assuming a viscous drag on the bob.*

For this problem H is exactly as given by (*2*), Example 16.2. The power function can be written at once (see Section 6.9, Page 105) as $P = -\tfrac{1}{2}a(\dot{r}^2 + r^2\dot{\theta}^2)$ where a is the coefficient of viscous drag on the bob. Hence applying (*16.6*),

$$\partial H/\partial p_r = p_r/m = \dot{r}, \quad \partial H/\partial p_\theta = p_\theta/mr^2 = \dot{\theta}$$

(as before) and

$$\partial H/\partial r = -p_\theta^2/mr^3 - mg\cos\theta + k(r-r_0) = a\dot{r} - \dot{p}_r, \quad \partial H/\partial\theta = mgr\sin\theta = ar^2\dot{\theta} - \dot{p}_\theta$$

16.8 Examples of H for System in which There Are Moving Coordinates and/or Moving Constraints.

Example 16.7.

Referring to Problem 2.20, Fig. 2-29, Page 36, let us assume that the vertical shaft has constant angular acceleration, so that $\theta = \theta_0 + \omega t + \tfrac{1}{2}\alpha t^2$. The kinetic energy of the bead is

$$T = \tfrac{1}{2}m[(1+4a^2r^2)\dot{r}^2 + r^2(\omega+\alpha t)^2], \quad \text{and} \quad V = mgar^2$$

(Note that $T = T_1 + T_3$, $T_2 = 0$.) From the above, $\partial T/\partial\dot{r} = p_r = m(1+4a^2r^2)\dot{r}$. Thus we can write

$$H = T_1 - T_3 + V = \frac{p_r^2}{2m(1+4a^2r^2)} - \tfrac{1}{2}mr^2(\omega+\alpha t)^2 + mgar^2$$

The same expression for H can, of course, be found from equation (*16.4*).

In all previous examples of this chapter, $H = T + V = \mathcal{E}$. However, here $H \neq \mathcal{E}$ since t enters explicitly into transformation equations of the form (*2.21*), Page 19.

Example 16.8.

Referring to the example given on Page 27, note that expression (*2.50*) can be grouped at once in the form $T = T_1 + T_2 + T_3$, from which

$$\partial T/\partial \dot{q}_1 = m[\dot{q}_1 + \dot{q}_2 \cos(\beta - \alpha)] + m[(v_x + a_x t)\cos\alpha + (v_y + a_y t)\sin\alpha] = p_{q_1}$$

with a similar expression for p_{q_2}. Eliminating $\dot{q}_1$ and $\dot{q}_2$ from $T_1 - T_3 + V$, we have the Hamiltonian H.

The form of H is not simple, but the above demonstrates well the general basic techniques. The reader can show that the same expression for H can be obtained from (*16.4*), and that $H \neq T + V$.

16.9 Fields in which the Hamiltonian Method is Employed.

As previously stated and as can now be seen from the various examples, this method of treating most applied problems is considerably less convenient than the Lagrangian. However, the Hamiltonian approach is used to great advantage in various other fields. As a matter of general information, the most important of these are listed below with brief comments and certain selected references.

(*a*) Transformation Theory.

The simplicity of equations of motion and ease with which they can be integrated depend to a large extent on the coordinates employed. It is sometimes possible to select by insight, intuition or trial and error a set of coordinates which render the integration less complex. General transformation theory, in which the Hamiltonian equations play the leading role, treats of a systematic method of making such transformations. See:

C. Lanczos, *The Variational Principles of Mechanics,* U. of Toronto Press, 1949, chapters 7 and 8.

H. Goldstein, *Classical Mechanics,* Addison-Wesley, 1950, chapters 8 and 9.

E. T. Whittaker, *A Treatise on Analytical Dynamics of Particles and Rigid Bodies,* Dover, 1944, chapter 11.

(*b*) Celestial Mechanics.

An exact determination of the motion of planets about the sun or of artificial satellites about the earth cannot be obtained because of difficulties in solving the equations of motion. Hence specialists in celestial mechanics are greatly concerned with perturbation methods of finding approximate, yet acceptable, solutions. Perturbation theory is closely related to the transformation theory mentioned under (*a*). See:

T. E. Sterne, *An Introduction to Celestial Mechanics,* Interscience, 1960, chapters 4 and 5.

H. C. Corben and P. Stehle, *Classical Mechanics,* John Wiley, 1950, pages 306-312.

O. Dziobek, *Mathematical Theories of Planetary Motion,* Dover.

D. Ter Haar, *Elements of Hamiltonian Mechanics,* North Holland, 1961, pages 146-166.

(*c*) Statistical Mechanics.

Since a general solution has not been found for even the *relatively simple* "problem of three bodies" (see above reference to E. T. Whittaker, chapter 13), it is clear that a determination of the exact motion of every individual molecule in a gas composed of say 10^{23} "elastic golf balls", is completely out of the question. Nevertheless, statistical methods in which Hamiltonian dynamics plays an important part have been used extensively for the determination of certain "average" properties. See:

R. C. Tolman, *The Principles of Statistical Mechanics,* Oxford U. Press, 1938.

(*d*) **Quantum Mechanics.**

Hamiltonian dynamics plays a very important role in the development of quantum mechanics. Indeed, it is a necessary prerequisite to a study of this subject. Excellent introductory treatments of the basic principles and methods of quantum mechanics are given in the following references:

C. W. Sherwin, *Introduction to Quantum Mechanics,* Henry Holt, 1959.

P. Fong, *Elementary Quantum Mechanics,* Addison-Wesley, 1962.

R. H. Dicke and J. P. Wittke, *Introduction to Quantum Mechanics,* Addison-Wesley, 1960.

Problems

A. Problems in which t does not enter the transformation equations.

16.1. Show that the Hamiltonian for the simple spring-mass arrangement, Fig. 16-2, is $H = \frac{1}{2}p_x^2/m + \frac{1}{2}kx^2$. Write out the Hamiltonian equations.

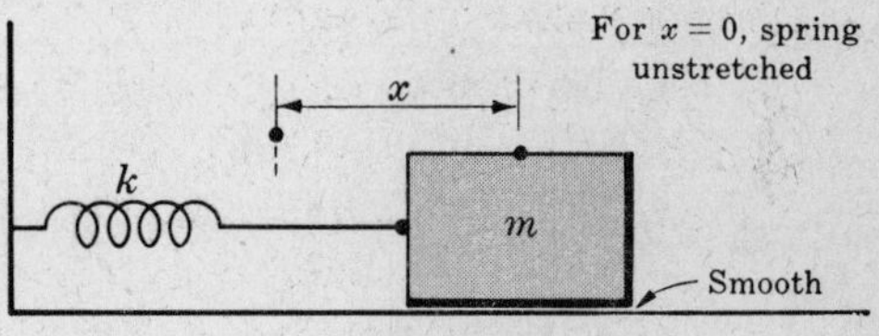

Fig. 16-2

16.2. Referring to Example 3.3, Page 45, show that H for the mass m, Fig. 3-1, is

$$H = \tfrac{1}{2}(p_r^2 + p_\theta^2/r^2)/m + \tfrac{1}{2}kr^2$$

16.3. Show that H for the bead, Problem 3.5, Fig. 3-5, Page 52, is given by

$$H = \frac{1}{2m}\left[\frac{p_z^2}{1 + a^2(1 + b^2z^2)}\right] + mgz$$

16.4. Show that the Hamiltonian for the two masses in Fig. 2-8, Page 13, employing coordinates y_1 and y_3, is

$$H = \frac{(p_{y_1} + p_{y_3})^2}{2m_1} + \frac{p_{y_3}^2}{2m_2} + m_1gy_1 + m_2g(y_1 - y_3) + \tfrac{1}{2}k(y_3 - l_0)^2$$

Write out the Hamiltonian equations.

16.5. Show that H for the pulley system, Example 5.3, Page 87, Fig. 5-6, is

$$H = \frac{Bp_{y_1}^2 + 2Cp_{y_1}p_{y_2} + Ap_{y_2}^2}{2(AB - C^2)} + m_1gy_1 + m_2gy_2 + \tfrac{1}{2}k_1(C_1 - y_2 - l_1)^2 + \tfrac{1}{2}k_2(2y_2 - y_1 - C_2 - l_2)^2$$

where $A = m_1 + I_2/R_2^2$, $B = m_2 + I_1/R_1^2 + I_2/R_2^2$, $C = I_2/R_2^2$; C_1 and C_2 are constants; l_1 and l_2 are unstretched spring lengths. Write out the Hamiltonian equations.

16.6. Referring to Example 5.5, Fig. 5-7, Page 88, show that H for the three masses, motion confined to a plane, is (V not approximated)

$$H = \frac{1}{2}\sum_{i=1}^{3}\frac{p_{y_i}}{m_i} + \frac{1}{2}\sum_{j=1}^{4} k_j\{[(y_j - y_{j-1})^2 + s_j^2]^{1/2} - s_j\}^2 \qquad (y_4 = y_0 = 0)$$

16.7. Show that H for the pendulum, Problem 4.10, Fig. 4-13, Page 75, is given by

$$H = \frac{p_\theta^2}{2(m_1r_1^2 + m_2r_2^2)} + \frac{p_r^2}{2m_2} + \tfrac{1}{2}k(r_2 - l_0)^2 - (m_1r_1 + m_2r_2)g\cos\theta$$

Show that the equations of motion given in Problem 4.10 can be obtained from the Hamiltonian equations.

16.8. The three masses (spheres), Example 4.5, Fig. 4-5, Page 65, are allowed to fall freely through a viscous liquid. Coefficients of drag on the spheres are a_1, a_2, a_3 respectively. Neglecting drag on the springs, buoyant effects and virtual mass due to liquid, show that H in coordinates y, q_1, q_2 is given by

$$H = \frac{p_y^2}{2M} + \frac{Cp_{q_1}^2 + 2Dp_{q_1}p_{q_2} + Bp_{q_2}^2}{2(BC - D^2)} + Mgy + \tfrac{1}{2}k_1(q_1 + q_2 - l_1)^2$$
$$+ \tfrac{1}{2}k_2\left[\frac{m_1}{m_3}q_1 - \left(\frac{m_2 + m_3}{m_3}\right)q_2 - l_2\right]^2$$

where $B = m_1(m_1 + m_2)/m_3$, $C = m_2(m_2 + m_3)/m_3$, $D = m_1m_2/m_3$. Write out the power function P power and the Hamiltonian equations of motion.

16.9. Set up H and write the Hamiltonian equations of motion for the system shown in Fig. 8-5, Page 146. Note that $\dot{p}_\psi = \dot{p}_\phi = 0$.

$$H = \frac{(p_\psi - p_\phi \cos\theta)^2}{2[I + (I_x + Ms^2)\sin^2\theta]} + \frac{p_\phi^2}{2I_z}$$

16.10. Assuming viscous drags $-b_1\dot{x}_1, -b_2\dot{x}_2$ on m_1 and m_2 respectively, Fig. 16-3, write the Lagrangian equations of motion. Determine H, write Hamiltonian equations and show that from them, equations can be found which are the same as those obtained by the Lagrangian method.

$$H = p_{x_1}^2/2m_1 + p_{x_2}^2/2m_2 + \tfrac{1}{2}k_1x_1^2 + \tfrac{1}{2}k_2(x_2 - x_1)^2, \qquad P = -\tfrac{1}{2}(b_1\dot{x}_1^2 + b_2\dot{x}_2^2)$$

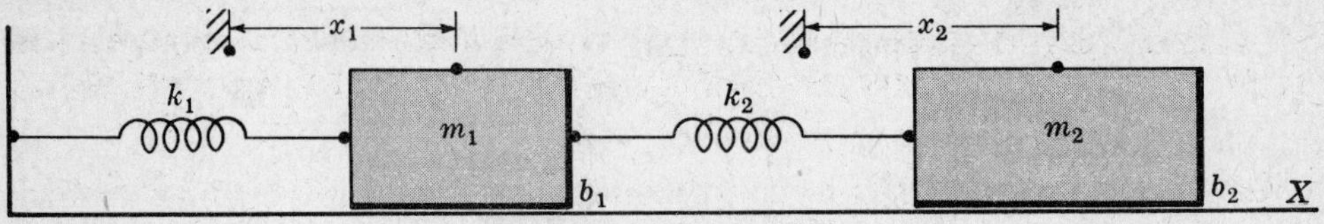

For $x_1 = x_2 = 0$, springs unstretched

Fig. 16-3

B. Problems in which moving coordinates and/or moving constraints are assumed.

16.11. Referring to Example 3.6, Page 48, Fig. 3-4, and assuming that the table and rod are moving as indicated in obtaining the second expression for T, show that the Hamiltonian for m is

$$H = p_r^2/2m - \tfrac{1}{2}mr^2\theta_0^2\omega_2^2\cos^2\omega_2 t - \tfrac{1}{2}m\omega_1^2[s + r\sin(\theta_0\sin\omega_2 t)]^2 + mgr\cos(\theta_0\sin\omega_2 t)$$

Show that $H \neq \mathcal{E}$.

16.12. Determine H for the pendulum, Problem 3.17, Page 54, Fig. 3-11. Write the Hamiltonian equations.

$$H = \frac{[p_\theta + m(l - A\sin\omega t)A\omega\cos\omega t\sin\theta]^2}{2m(l - A\sin\omega t)^2} - mA^2\omega^2\cos^2\omega t(1 - \cos\theta)$$
$$- mg[A\omega\cos\omega t + (l - A\sin\omega t)\cos\theta]$$

$$\dot{p}_\theta = mA^2\omega^2\cos^2\omega t\sin\theta(1 - \cos\theta) - \frac{p_\theta A\omega\cos\omega t\cos\theta}{(l - A\sin\omega t)} - mg(l - A\sin\omega t)\sin\theta$$

$$\dot{\theta} = \frac{p_\theta + m(l - A\sin\omega t)A\omega\cos\omega t\sin\theta}{m(l - A\sin\omega t)^2}$$

16.13. Write H for the pendulum shown in Fig. 4-19 (*1*), Page 79, in terms of coordinate θ. Show that $H \neq \mathcal{E}_{total}$.

$$H = \frac{p_\theta^2}{2m(r_0 - vt - \tfrac{1}{2}at^2)^2} - \tfrac{1}{2}m(v_0 + at)^2 - mgr\cos\theta$$

16.14. Determine H for the pendulum, Problem 3.23, Fig. 3-14, Page 55. Is it true that $H \neq \mathcal{E}_{\text{total}}$?

$$\begin{aligned} H = {} & \tfrac{1}{2}mr^2\left\{\frac{p_\theta}{mr^2} + s\cos\theta\sin\phi\left[\frac{(p_\alpha + p_\phi)r\sin\theta + (p_\phi\cos\phi + p_\theta\sin\theta\cos\theta\sin\phi)s}{mr^2\sin^3\theta(2r^2 + s^2\sin^2\phi)}\right]\right\}^2 \\ & + \tfrac{1}{2}mr^2\left\{\frac{p_\phi\sin^2\theta}{mr^2} + (s\cos\phi + r\sin\phi)\left[\frac{(p_\alpha + p_\phi)r\sin\theta + (p_\phi\cos\phi + p_\theta\sin\theta\cos\theta\sin\phi)s}{mr^2(2r^2 + s^2\sin^2\phi)}\right]\right\}^2 \\ & - \tfrac{1}{2}m(s^2 + r^2\sin^2\theta + 2sr\sin\theta\cos\phi)\left[\frac{(p_\alpha - p_\phi)r\sin\theta + (p_\phi\cos\phi + p_\theta\sin\theta\cos\theta\sin\phi)s}{mr\sin^3\theta(2r^2 + s^2\sin^2\phi)}\right]^2 \\ & - mgr\cos\theta \end{aligned}$$

16.15. Referring to Fig. 14-2 and expression (*14.4*), Page 283, show that, taking account of the earth's rotation, H is given by

$$\begin{aligned} H = {} & \tfrac{1}{2}m\{[p_x + m\omega_e(y\sin\Phi - z\cos\Phi) - m\omega_e R]^2 + (p_y - m\omega_e x\sin\Phi)^2 + (p_z + m\omega_e x\cos\Phi)^2\} \\ & + \tfrac{1}{2}m\omega_e^2[x^2 + y^2\sin^2\Phi + (R+z)^2\cos^2\Phi - 2y(R+z)\sin\Phi\cos\Phi] + V(x,y,z) \end{aligned}$$

$$\dot{x} = \frac{p_x + m\omega_e(y\sin\Phi - z\cos\Phi) - m\omega_e R}{m}, \qquad \text{etc.}$$

$$\dot{p}_x = (p_y\sin\Phi - p_z\cos\Phi)\omega_e - 2m\omega_e^2 x - \partial V/\partial x, \qquad \text{etc.}$$

16.16. Starting with the expression given for T in Example 4.8, Page 67, Fig. 4-6, show that $H = \sum p_r\dot{q}_r - L = T_1 - T_3 + V$ and that $H \neq \mathcal{E}_{\text{total}}$.

16.17. Assuming that the hydrogen atom, Fig. 16-4, is in field-free space, set up the classical Hamiltonian. Write out the Hamiltonian equations of motion. See Example 16.3, Page 320.

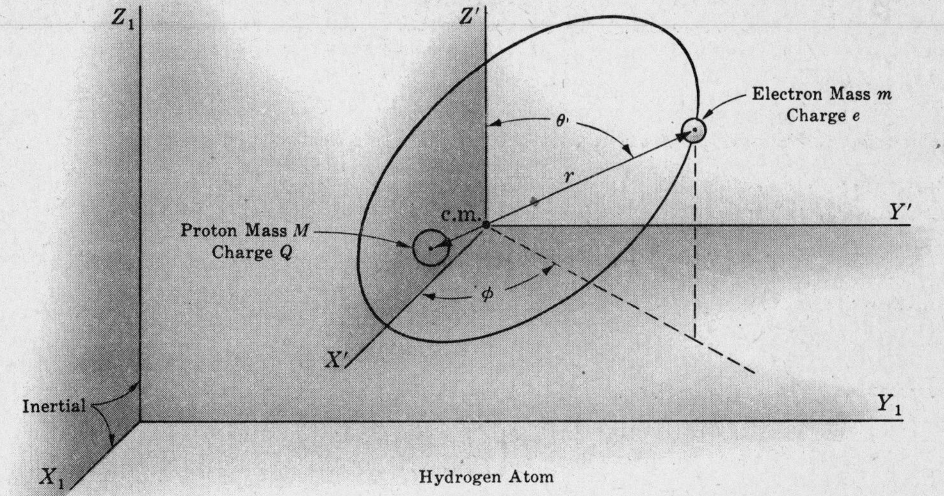

Fig. 16-4

16.18. Show that the Hamiltonian for the system of Problem 15.7, Page 313, is

$$H = \tfrac{1}{2}(p_{x_1}^2/m_1 + p_{x_2}^2/m_2 + p_Q^2/M) + \tfrac{1}{2}(k_1x_1^2 + k_2x_2^2) - EQ + \tfrac{1}{2}Q^2(s - x_1 - x_2)/A$$

16.19. Applying the relation $H = \sum p_r\dot{q}_r - L$, show that H for the electromechanical system of Problem 15.8, Page 313, is

$$H = \tfrac{1}{2}[p_\theta^2/I + p_x^2/m + (p_{Q_1} - N\Phi\theta)^2/M_{11} + p_{Q_2}^2/M_{22}] + V(x,\theta,Q_1,Q_2)$$

CHAPTER 17

Hamilton's Principle

17.1 Preliminary Statement.

With the hope of making clear the mathematical as well as physical basis on which Hamilton's principle rests, the following material is included: (*a*) A statement of certain illustrative problems; (*b*) a brief treatment of some necessary techniques in the calculus of variations; (*c*) solutions to problems proposed in (*a*); (*d*) derivation of Hamilton's principle by the calculus of variations method and again from D'Alembert's equation; (*e*) various specific examples illustrating principles of the calculus of variations and Hamilton's principle.

In order that the reader may have a broader view of the usefulness of Hamilton's principle, a brief discussion of this topic together with a list of suitable references are included.

17.2 Introductory Problems.

As a means of introducing important preliminary ideas let us first consider, in so far as we can at the moment, the following specific examples.

Example 17.1.

Referring to Fig. 17-1, suppose that coordinates x_1, y_1 and x_2, y_2 of points p_1 and p_2 respectively are given, to find the equation of the shortest line passing through these points. As indicated on the diagram, an element of length ds of any line, regardless of its shape, is given by $ds = (dx^2 + dy^2)^{1/2} = [1 + (dy/dx)^2]^{1/2}\,dx$. Hence l, the length of *any line* from p_1 to p_2, is given by

$$l \quad = \quad \int_{x_1}^{x_2} [1 + (dy/dx)^2]^{1/2}\,dx \qquad (1)$$

But what is the shortest line connecting these points? The problem reduces to one of finding a relation between y and x, $y = y(x)$, such that (*1*) is a minimum.

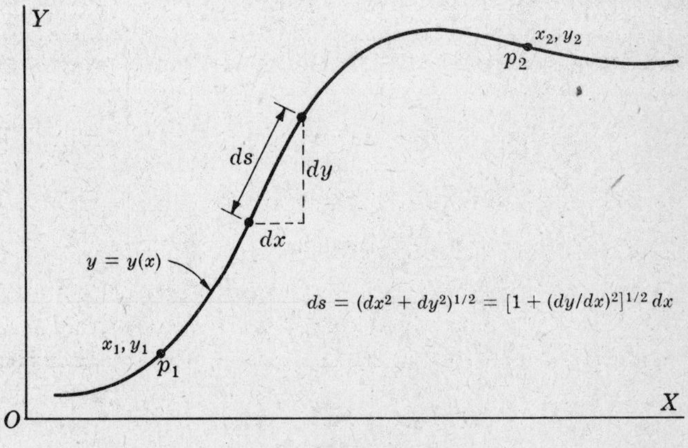

Fig. 17-1

Example 17.2.

In Fig. 17-2 below a bead of mass m is free to slide down a smooth rigid wire under the action of gravity. What shape must the wire have [what is the relation between y and x, $y = y(x)$] such that the time required to slide from a given point $p_1(x_1, y_1)$ to $p_2(x_2, y_2)$ is a minimum?

Note that for any path connecting these points, the time interval is given by $t = \int_{p_1}^{p_2} \frac{ds}{v}$, where $ds = (dx^2 + dy^2)^{1/2}$ and v is the instantaneous velocity of the bead. Since here energy $\mathcal{E}$ is conserved,

$$\mathcal{E} \quad = \quad \tfrac{1}{2}mv^2 + mgy \quad = \quad \tfrac{1}{2}mv_1^2 + mgy_1 \quad = \quad \text{constant}$$

Thus $v = [v_1^2 - 2g(y-y_1)]^{1/2}$ where v_1 and y_1 are known values at point p_1. Hence we may write

$$t \quad = \quad \int_{y_1}^{y_2} \left[\frac{1+(dx/dy)^2}{v_1^2 - 2g(y-y_1)}\right]^{1/2} dy \tag{2}$$

The problem now is, of course, to find a relation between y and x such that (2) is a minimum.

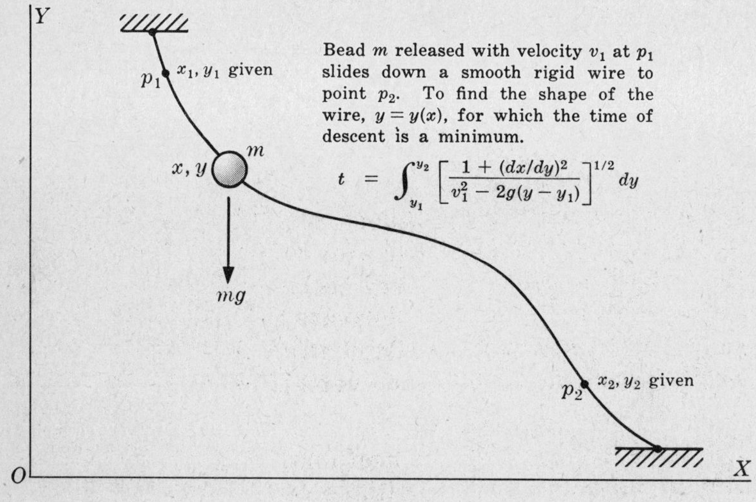

Fig. 17-2

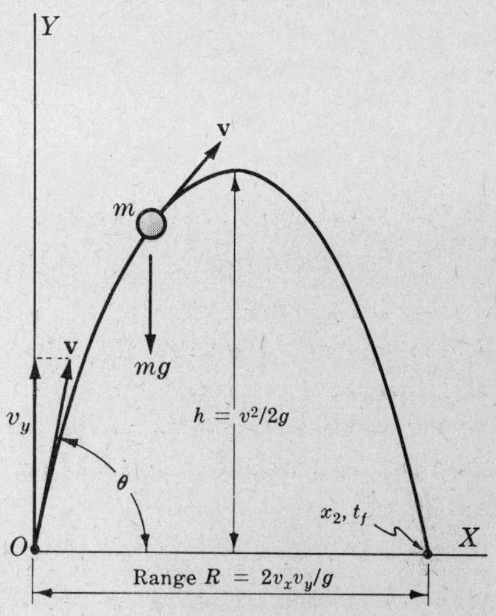

Fig. 17-3

Example 17.3.

Referring to Fig. 17-3, the ball is thrown upward with initial velocity **v** at an angle θ. As shown by elementary principles, it takes a path determined by

$$x \; = \; v_x t, \qquad y \; = \; v_y t - \tfrac{1}{2}gt^2 \tag{3}$$

where v_x and v_y are components of **v**.

Looking ahead at what is to follow, we ask ourselves: what are the relations $x = x(t)$, $y = y(t)$ such that the following integral

$$\mathcal{J} \quad = \quad \int_{t_1}^{t_2} L\,dt \quad = \quad \int_{t_1}^{t_2} [\tfrac{1}{2}m(\dot{x}^2 + \dot{y}^2) - mgy]\,dt \tag{4}$$

has a maximum or minimum value, where L is the usual Lagrangian?

As will soon be shown and as doubtless the reader has already guessed, relations (3) are just the required expressions.

Completion of the above three examples requires certain methods of the calculus of variations. We shall return to them at the end of the following section.

17.3 Certain Techniques in the Calculus of Variations.

Consider the more general type of problem in which some function $\phi(x, y, dy/dx)$ is given, to find a relation between y and x, $y = y(x)$, such that the following definite integral

$$\mathcal{J} \quad = \quad \int_{x_1}^{x_2} \phi(x, y, dy/dx)\,dx \tag{5}$$

has an extreme value (maximum or minimum).

Referring to Fig. 17-4 below, suppose that the solid line, $y = y(x)$, represents the desired relation. Let the dotted line represent a slightly "varied path" where for every point $p(x, y)$ on the solid line there is a "corresponding point" $p(x, y_v)$ on the varied path. Co-

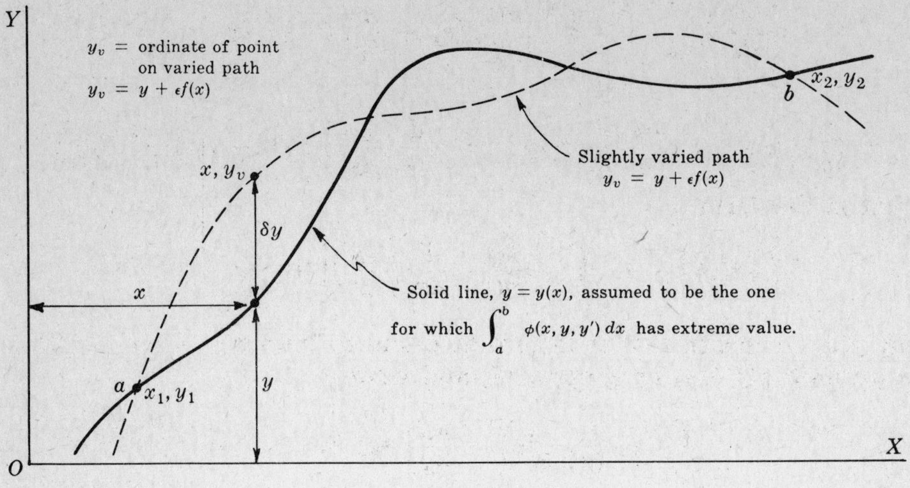
Y
y_v = ordinate of point on varied path
$y_v = y + \epsilon f(x)$
x_2, y_2
b
Slightly varied path
$y_v = y + \epsilon f(x)$
x, y_v
δy
x
Solid line, $y = y(x)$, assumed to be the one for which $\int_a^b \phi(x, y, y')\,dx$ has extreme value.
a
x_1, y_1
y
O
X

Fig. 17-4

ordinate x is *not varied* and $y_v = y + \delta y$ as shown. As a means of representing the varied path let

$$y_v \quad = \quad y(x) \ + \ \epsilon f(x) \tag{6}$$

where ϵ is an arbitrary small quantity (an "infinitesimal parameter") and $f(x)$ is an arbitrary differentiable function of x which, for reasons to follow, is assumed to vanish at points a and b. To illustrate the above important procedure suppose ϵ is a small number, say 10^{-6}, and that $f(x)$, meeting the above requirements, never reaches values large compared with $y(x)$. It is then clear that (6) represents a line very close to the solid line. Indeed if ϵ is taken sufficiently small, (6) is "close" to $y(x)$ regardless of what finite values $f(x)$ may assume.

It is here important to note that by assigning various values to ϵ, for a given $f(x)$, (6) represents a family of curves in the neighborhood of $y = y(x)$.

Now suppose an integral corresponding to (5) be taken along the varied path. That is,

$$\mathcal{I}_v \quad = \quad \int_{x_1}^{x_2} \phi(x, y_v, dy_v/dx)\,dx \tag{7}$$

where y_v is given by (6). For convenience in what follows, we write

$$\delta y \quad = \quad y_v - y(x) \quad = \quad \epsilon f(x) \tag{8}$$

and

$$dy_v/dx \quad = \quad y'_v \quad = \quad y'(x) \ + \ \epsilon f'(x) \tag{9}$$

where $y'(x) = dy/dx$ and $f'(x) = df'/dx$.

The definite integral (7) is a function of ϵ only; and the condition that (5) have an extreme value is that, regarding ϵ as variable,

$$d\mathcal{I}_v/d\epsilon = 0 \qquad \text{for } \epsilon = 0 \tag{10}$$

Differentiating (7) under the integral sign,

$$\frac{d\mathcal{I}_v}{d\epsilon} \quad = \quad \int_{x_1}^{x_2} \left[\frac{\partial \phi}{\partial y_v}\frac{\partial y_v}{\partial \epsilon} + \frac{\partial \phi}{\partial y'_v}\frac{\partial y'_v}{\partial \epsilon}\right] dx \tag{11}$$

But for $\epsilon = 0$, $\dfrac{\partial \phi}{\partial y_v} = \dfrac{\partial \phi}{\partial y}$, $\dfrac{\partial \phi}{\partial y'_v} = \dfrac{\partial \phi}{\partial y_v}$; and in any case, $\dfrac{\partial y_v}{\partial \epsilon} = f(x)$, $\dfrac{\partial y'_v}{\partial \epsilon} = f'(x)$. Hence (10) may be written as

$$\left(\frac{d\mathcal{J}_v}{d\epsilon}\right)_{\epsilon=0} = \int_{x_1}^{x_2}\left[\frac{\partial\phi}{\partial y}f(x) + \frac{\partial\phi}{\partial y'}f'(x)\right]dx = 0 \tag{12}$$

Noting that

$$\frac{\partial\phi}{\partial y'}f'(x) = \frac{\partial\phi}{\partial y'}\frac{d}{dx}[f(x)] = \frac{d}{dx}\left[\frac{\partial\phi}{\partial y'}f(x)\right] - f(x)\frac{d}{dx}\left(\frac{\partial\phi}{\partial y'}\right) \tag{13}$$

(12) can be put in the form

$$\left[\frac{\partial\phi}{\partial y'}f(x)\right]_{x_1}^{x_2} + \int_{x_1}^{x_2}\left[\frac{\partial\phi}{\partial y} - \frac{d}{dx}\left(\frac{\partial\phi}{\partial y'}\right)\right]f(x)\,dx = 0 \tag{14}$$

Assuming $f(x)$ so chosen that it is zero at a and b, the first of (14) is zero. Then for convenience we multiply (14) by ϵ, apply (8) and write

$$\int_{x_1}^{x_2}\left\{\left[\frac{d}{dx}\left(\frac{\partial\phi}{\partial y'}\right) - \frac{\partial\phi}{\partial y}\right]\delta y\right\}dx = 0 \tag{15}$$

Here δy is arbitrary for all values of x from x_1 to x_2. For example, δy may be chosen positive over any one or more regions and negative over the remainder. Hence (assuming for the moment that the expression in brackets in (15) is not zero), if we choose δy positive where the expression in brackets is positive and negative where it is negative, integral (15) is not zero. Therefore (15) can be zero for all possible choices of δy only under the condition that

$$\frac{d}{dx}\left(\frac{\partial\phi}{\partial y'}\right) - \frac{\partial\phi}{\partial y} = 0 \tag{16}$$

This then is a differential equation, the solution of which furnishes a relation between y and x, $y = y(x)$, such that when substituted in (5) gives this integral an extreme value. (Note the resemblance to Lagrange's equation.)

Integral (15) can be put into another useful form as follows. Multiplying (12) through by the infinitesimal quantity ϵ and writing

$$\epsilon\frac{\partial\mathcal{J}_v}{\partial\epsilon} = \delta\mathcal{J}, \qquad \delta y = \epsilon f(x), \qquad \delta y' = \epsilon f'(x)$$

we have

$$\delta\mathcal{J} = \int_{x_1}^{x_2}\left(\frac{\partial\phi}{\partial y}\delta y + \frac{\partial\phi}{\partial y'}\delta y'\right)dx = 0$$

which can be written as

$$\delta\mathcal{J} = \int_{x_1}^{x_2}\delta[\phi(x,y,y')]\,dx = 0 \tag{17}$$

Specific examples to follow will give more meaning to (15) and (17).

The above results may be extended to the case of n dependent variables $y_1, y_2, \ldots, y_n$ and an independent variable x. (Details are not given.) That is, considering the function

$$\phi_n = \phi_n(y_1, y_2, \ldots, y_n;\ y_1', y_2', \ldots, y_n';\ t) \tag{17.1}$$

the condition that $\int_{x_1}^{x_2}\phi_n\,dx$ have an extreme value is

$$\frac{d}{dx}\left(\frac{\partial\phi_n}{\partial y_r'}\right) - \frac{\partial\phi_n}{\partial y_r} = 0 \qquad r = 1, 2, \ldots, n \tag{17.2}$$

or what amounts to the same thing,

$$\delta\mathcal{J} = \int_{x_1}^{x_2}\delta(\phi_n)\,dx = 0 \tag{17.3}$$

17.4 Solutions to Previously Proposed Examples.

We are now in a position to complete Examples 17.1, 17.2 and 17.3.

Solution to Example 17.1.

Comparing equations (*1*) and (*5*) it is seen that $\phi = (1+y'^2)^{1/2}$ (a rather special case since it contains only y'). Applying relation (*12*) and noting that $\dfrac{\partial\phi}{\partial y} = 0$, $\dfrac{d}{dx}\left(\dfrac{\partial\phi}{\partial y'}\right) = 0$ or $\partial\phi/\partial y' = c_1 =$ constant. Thus $\partial\phi/\partial y' = (1+y'^2)^{-1/2}y' = c_1$ from which $y' = dy/dx = c_1/\sqrt{1-c_1^2} = c_2$. Integrating this we obtain $y = c_2x + c_3$, the equation of a straight line which, for properly chosen values of c_2 and c_3, will pass through the selected points a and b of Fig. 17-1. (For finding the shortest distance between two points on a cylinder see Example 17.4.)

Solution to Example 17.2.

As seen from (*2*), $\phi = \left[\dfrac{1+x'^2}{v_1^2 - 2g(y-y_1)}\right]^{1/2}$ where $x' = dx/dy$. We shall here regard y as the independent variable. Thus $\dfrac{d}{dy}\left(\dfrac{\partial\phi}{\partial x'}\right) - \dfrac{\partial\phi}{\partial x} = 0$. Now since $\dfrac{\partial\phi}{\partial x} = 0$, we have $\dfrac{d}{dy}\left(\dfrac{\partial\phi}{\partial x'}\right) = 0$ or $\dfrac{\partial\phi}{\partial x'} = c_1 =$ constant. But

$$\frac{\partial\phi}{\partial x'} \;=\; \frac{x'}{\{(1+x'^2)[v_1^2 + 2g(y_1 - y)]\}^{1/2}} \;=\; c_1$$

from which $x' = \left(\dfrac{v_1^2/2g + y_1 - y}{1/2gc_1^2 - v_1^2/2g - y_1 + y}\right)^{1/2}$. Now writing $c_2 = \dfrac{v_1^2}{2g} + y_1$, $c_3 = \dfrac{1}{2gc_1^2} - c_2$,

$$x' \;=\; \frac{dx}{dy} \;=\; \left(\frac{c_2 - y}{c_3 + y}\right)^{1/2} \tag{18}$$

which is the differential equation relating x and y. In order to integrate (*18*) we make the following change of variable:

$$c_2 - y \;=\; R(1-\cos\alpha) \tag{19}$$

where $R = (c_2 + c_3)/2$, from which $c_3 + y = R(1+\cos\alpha)$ and $dy = -R\sin\alpha\, d\alpha$. Putting these results into (*18*), we obtain

$$dx \;=\; -R\left(\frac{1-\cos\alpha}{1+\cos\alpha}\right)^{1/2}\sin\alpha\, d\alpha \;=\; +R(1-\cos\alpha)\,d\alpha \tag{20}$$

which integrates at once to give

$$x \;=\; x_0 + R(\alpha - \sin\alpha) \qquad \text{where } x_0 = \text{constant}$$

Hence the parametric equations of the path of most rapid descent are

$$x \;=\; x_0 + R(\alpha - \sin\alpha), \qquad y \;=\; y_0 - R(1-\cos\alpha) \tag{21}$$

where $y_0 = c_2 = v_1^2/2g + y_1$.

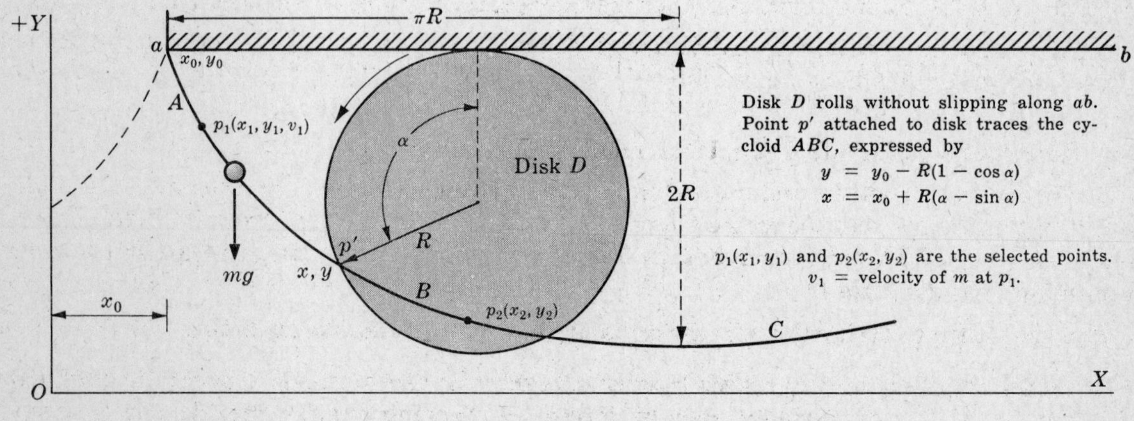
+Y
a
b
πR
x₀, y₀
A
p₁(x₁, y₁, v₁)
α
Disk D
2R
mg
x, y
p′
R
B
p₂(x₂, y₂)
C
x₀
O
X
Disk D rolls without slipping along ab. Point p′ attached to disk traces the cycloid ABC, expressed by
y = y₀ − R(1 − cos α)
x = x₀ + R(α − sin α)
p₁(x₁, y₁) and p₂(x₂, y₂) are the selected points.
v₁ = velocity of m at p₁.

Fig. 17-5

The reader may show that the curve ABC, Fig. 17-5 above, traced by point p' attached to the disk, as the disk rolls without slipping along line ab, is represented by equations (21). Hence the "brachistochrone" (path of shortest time) is here a cycloid.

For any specific problem (one for which values of v_1; x_1, y_1; x_2, y_2 are given), R and x_0 ($y_0 = c_2 = v_1^2/2g + y_1$ is not arbitrary) must be so chosen that the cycloid passes through $p_1(x_1, y_1)$ and $p_2(x_2, y_2)$. That this can be done and that the path is unique is shown by: W. D. Macmillan, *Statics and Dynamics of a Particle*, Dover, 1958, Page 328.

Solution to Example 17.3.

Comparing expressions (4) and (5), we write

$$\phi = L(x, y, \dot{x}, \dot{y}, t) = \tfrac{1}{2}m(\dot{x}^2 + \dot{y}^2) - mgy$$

where t is taken as the independent variable. Applying (17.2),

$$\frac{d}{dt}\left(\frac{\partial L}{\partial \dot{x}}\right) - \frac{\partial L}{\partial x} = 0, \qquad \frac{d}{dt}\left(\frac{\partial L}{\partial \dot{y}}\right) - \frac{\partial L}{\partial y} = 0 \tag{22}$$

(which are obviously Lagrange's equations). These give $m\ddot{x} = 0$, $m\ddot{y} + mg = 0$ and finally, by integration, $x = v_x t$, $y = v_y t - \frac{1}{2}gt^2$ which are just relations (3). That is, the relations between x and t and y and t which make $\int_{t_1}^{t_2} L\,dt$ an extreme value or $\int_{t_1}^{t_2} \delta L\,dt = 0$, are determined by Lagrange's equations.

17.5 Hamilton's Principle from the Calculus of Variations.

Notice that the general type of Lagrangian $L = L(q_1, \ldots, q_n; \dot{q}_1, \ldots, \dot{q}_n; t)$ has just the form of ϕ in equation (17.1) where q_1 corresponds to y_1, etc., $\dot{q}_1$ to y_1', etc., and t to the independent variable x. Hence it follows that

$$\mathcal{I} = \int_{t_1}^{t_2} L(q_1, \ldots, q_n; \dot{q}_1, \ldots, \dot{q}_n; t)\,dt = \int_{t_1}^{t_2} (T - V)\,dt \tag{17.4}$$

has an extreme value or

$$\int_{t_1}^{t_2} \delta[L(q_1, \ldots, q_n; \dot{q}_1, \ldots, \dot{q}_n; t)]\,dt = 0 \tag{17.5}$$

provided

$$\frac{d}{dt}\left(\frac{\partial L}{\partial \dot{q}_r}\right) - \frac{\partial L}{\partial q_r} = 0 \qquad r = 1, 2, \ldots, n \tag{17.6}$$

That is to say, when solutions of (17.6), $q_1 = q_1(t)$, $q_2 = q_2(t)$, etc., are substituted into (17.4) this integral has a maximum or minimum value. But (17.6) is just a familiar form of Lagrange's equations. Hence it can be said that the motion of a system, determined by Lagrange's equations, is such that the integral (17.4) has an extreme value or that (17.5) is zero.

Relation (17.5) is one form (not the most general) of *Hamilton's principle*.

In the following section we shall derive Hamilton's principle, in a more general form, making use of D'Alembert's equation.

17.6 Hamilton's Principle from D'Alembert's Equation.

A considerably better understanding of the physics involved in the steps leading to Hamilton's principle may be gained from the following derivation than from the one just completed. However, each approach makes a worthwhile contribution to a general understanding of the principle.

For the sake of clarity the derivation is divided into the following steps.

(a) Consider a system of p particles having n degrees of freedom and moving through space under the action of various types of forces. Following exactly the ideas expressed in Section 4.2, Page 58, (which should be reviewed) we copy below equation (4.2):

$$\sum_{i=1}^{p} m_i(\ddot{x}_i\,\delta x_i + \ddot{y}_i\,\delta y_i + \ddot{z}_i\,\delta z_i) \quad = \quad \sum_{i=1}^{p} (F_{x_i}\,\delta x_i + F_{y_i}\,\delta y_i + F_{z_i}\,\delta z_i) \quad = \quad \delta W_{\text{total}} \qquad (17.7)$$

where, insofar as the validity of (*17.7*) is concerned, the "virtual displacements" $\delta x_i, \delta y_i, \delta z_i$ are *completely arbitrary*. However, just as in the derivation of Lagrange's equations, we shall assume that $\delta x_i, \delta y_i, \delta z_i$ are displacements in which t does not vary. See Example 3.5, Fig. 3-3, Page 47.

(*b*) Suppose that at time t_0 one of the particles m_i is at point A, Fig. 17-6. At a later time, moving in accord with Newton's laws, it arrives at C along an "actual path" ABC. All other particles of the system follow their own paths during this interval, but attention need be given to m_i only.

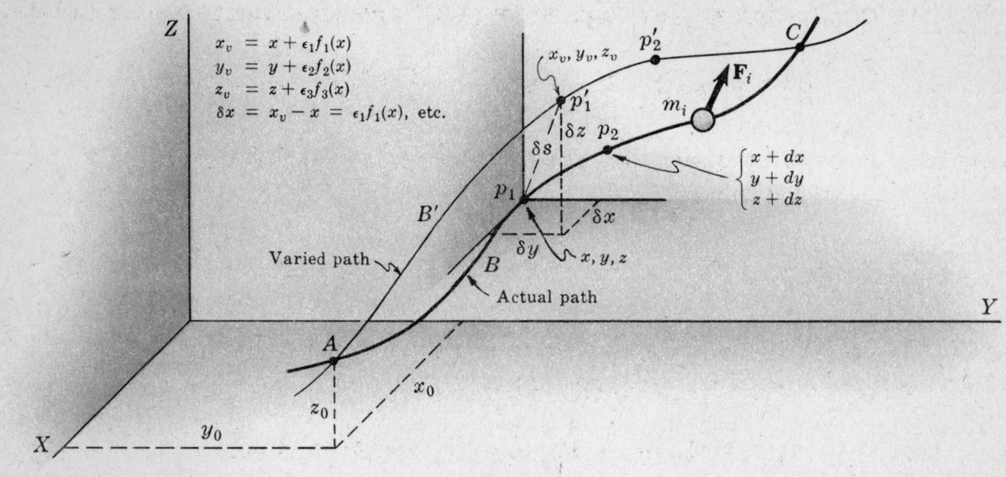

Fig. 17-6

Now regard ABC as divided into infinitesimal intervals by points $p_1, p_2, \ldots$. Assuming m_i at p_1 at time t_1, imagine it given an arbitrary infinitesimal displacement δs from p_1 to the "varied point" p_1'. Components of δs, as shown on the diagram are $\delta x, \delta y, \delta z$. For every point on ABC we locate in this manner a varied point. The path $AB'C$ determined by the varied points $p_1', p_2', \ldots$ is referred to as the "varied path". It should be remembered that $\delta x, \delta y, \delta z$ have exactly the same meaning as the virtual displacements used in the derivations of Lagrange's equations in Chapters 3 and 4.

(*c*) Just as in Section 17.3, [see equation (*6*)], we write

$$x_v = x + \epsilon_1 f_1(x), \qquad y_v = y + \epsilon_2 f_2(y), \qquad z_v = z + \epsilon_3 f_3(z) \qquad (23)$$

where x_v, y_v, z_v are coordinates of a point on the varied path and x, y, z those of a corresponding point on the actual path. $\epsilon_1, \epsilon_2, \epsilon_3$ are again infinitesimal quantities, here regarded as constants. $f_1(x), f_2(y), f_3(z)$ are arbitrary differentiable functions of x, y, z respectively but so chosen that at A and C, $\delta x = \delta y = \delta z = 0$.

We now define the following variations,

$$\delta x = x_v - x, \qquad \delta(dx) = dx_v - dx, \qquad \delta\dot{x} = \dot{x}_v - \dot{x} \qquad (24)$$

where $\dot{x} = dx/dt$, $\dot{x}_v = dx_v/dt$, $dx_v = dx + \epsilon_1\,d[f_1(x)]$. Hence from (*23*) and (*24*) it follows that

$$\delta x = \epsilon_1 f_1(x), \qquad \delta(dx) = \epsilon_1\,d[f_1(x)], \qquad \delta\dot{x} = \epsilon_1 \frac{d}{dt}[f_1(x)] = \frac{d}{dt}(\delta x) \qquad (25)$$

and corresponding relations are of course valid for $\delta y, \delta z$, etc. Note that the above are true for arbitrary differentiable functions $f_1(x)$ etc.

(*d*) Next let us consider the first term of (*17.7*). By the product rule of differentiation this can be written as

$$\delta x_i(m_i\ddot{x}_i) \quad = \quad \frac{d}{dt}(m_i\dot{x}_i\,\delta x_i) \;-\; m_i\dot{x}_i\frac{d}{dt}(\delta x_i) \tag{26}$$

But by (*25*), $\frac{d}{dt}(\delta x_i) = \delta\dot{x}$. Then $m_i\dot{x}_i\frac{d}{dt}(\delta x_i) = m_i\dot{x}_i\,\delta\dot{x}_i = \frac{1}{2}m_i\,\delta\dot{x}_i^2$ and

$$\delta x_i(m_i\ddot{x}_i) \quad = \quad \frac{d}{dt}(m_i\dot{x}_i\,\delta x_i) \;-\; \tfrac{1}{2}m_i\,\delta\dot{x}_i^2 \tag{27}$$

Similar expressions follow for $m_i\ddot{y}_i\,\delta y_i$ and $m_i\ddot{z}_i\,\delta z_i$.

Thus on eliminating $m_i\ddot{x}_i\,\delta x_i$, etc., from (*17.7*) and rearranging terms, we have

$$\delta\left[\frac{1}{2}\sum_{i=1}^{p} m_i(\dot{x}_i^2 + \dot{y}_i^2 + \dot{z}_i^2)\right] + \delta W_{\text{total}} \quad = \quad \frac{d}{dt}\left[\sum_{i=1}^{p} m_i(\dot{x}_i\,\delta x_i + \dot{y}_i\,\delta y_i + \dot{z}_i\,\delta z_i)\right] \tag{28}$$

Multiplying through by dt and integrating between the limits of t_0 and t_f (the time to go from A to C), (*28*) becomes

$$\int_{t_0}^{t_f} [\delta T + \delta W_{\text{total}}]\,dt \quad = \quad \sum_{i=1}^{p} m_i(\dot{x}_i\,\delta x_i + \dot{y}_i\,\delta y_i + \dot{z}_i\,\delta z_i)\Big|_A^C \tag{29}$$

(*e*) ***Hamilton's Principle.*** Assuming as above mentioned that at A and C, $\delta x_i = \delta y_i = \delta z_i = 0$, the term on the right of (*29*) is zero. Thus

$$\int_{t_0}^{t_f} (\delta T + F_{q_1}\,\delta q_1 + F_{q_2}\,\delta q_2 + \cdots + F_{q_n}\,\delta q_n)\,dt \quad = \quad 0 \tag{17.8}$$

which is a *very general form of Hamilton's principle.* F_{q_r} are the usual generalized forces due to any type of applied forces. They may, if superfluous coordinates are introduced into T as described in Chapter 12, include forces of constraint.

If all forces are conservative, $\delta W_{\text{total}} = -\,\delta V$ and

$$\int_{t_0}^{t_f} \delta(T - V)\,dt \quad = \quad \int_{t_0}^{t_f} \delta L\,dt \quad = \quad 0 \tag{17.9}$$

which is just the form (*17.5*) previously obtained.

17.7 Lagrange's Equations from Hamilton's Principle.

Note that, holding t constant,

$$\delta T \quad = \quad \sum_{r=1}^{n}\frac{\partial T}{\partial q_r}\delta q_r + \sum_{r=1}^{n}\frac{\partial T}{\partial \dot{q}_r}\delta\dot{q}_r \tag{30}$$

Eliminating $\delta\dot{q}_r$ from the second term by $\delta\dot{q}_r = \frac{d}{dt}(\delta q_r)$ and integrating the second term of (*30*) by parts, we get

$$\int_{t_0}^{t_f}\sum_{r=1}^{n}\frac{\partial T}{\partial \dot{q}_r}d(\delta q_r) \quad = \quad \sum_{r=1}^{n}\frac{\partial T}{\partial \dot{q}_r}\,\delta q_r\Big|_A^C - \int_{t_0}^{t_f}\left[\sum_{r=1}^{n}\frac{d}{dt}\left(\frac{\partial T}{\partial \dot{q}_r}\right)\delta q_r\right]dt \tag{31}$$

But $\sum_{i=1}^{n}\left(\frac{\partial T}{\partial \dot{q}_r}\right)\delta q_r\Big|_A^C = 0$ since all variations at A and C are assumed zero. Hence (*17.8*) can be written as

$$\int_{t_0}^{t_f}\left[\sum_{r=1}^{n}\left(\frac{d}{dt}\frac{\partial T}{\partial \dot{q}_r} - \frac{\partial T}{\partial q_r} - F_{q_r}\right)\delta q_r\right]dt \quad = \quad 0 \tag{17.10}$$

This integral must be zero for completely arbitrary values of $\delta q_1, \delta q_2, \ldots, \delta q_n$ along the paths. Hence suppose that all δq's except say δq_r are set equal to zero. Then, in accord with the argument given before equation (*16*), Page 329, it follows that the coefficient of δq_r must be zero. Hence in general,

$$\frac{d}{dt}\left(\frac{\partial T}{\partial \dot{q}_r}\right) - \frac{\partial T}{\partial q_r} - F_{q_r} \quad = \quad 0$$

Similarly, the form $\dfrac{d}{dt}\left(\dfrac{\partial L}{\partial \dot{q}_r}\right) - \dfrac{\partial L}{\partial q_r} = 0$ follows at once from (*17.9*).

From the above it is clear that, given Hamilton's principle, together with an understanding of T, V and F_{q_r}, Lagrange's equations, Newton's second law equation, etc., can be derived. Hence, if so desired, Hamilton's principle may in this sense be considered the basis of analytical dynamics. See references on Page 336.

17.8 Specific Examples Illustrating the Results of this Chapter.

Example 17.4.

Let us show that the shortest line between *any two points* p_1 and p_2 on a cylinder is a helix.

The length s of *any line* on the cylinder between p_1 and p_2 is given by

$$s \quad = \quad \int_{p_1}^{p_2} [1 + r^2(d\theta/dz)^2]^{1/2}\,dz$$

where r, θ, z are the usual cylindrical coordinates with $r = \text{constant}$. A relation between θ and z which will give this integral an extreme value is determined by

$$\frac{d}{dz}\left(\frac{\partial \phi}{\partial \theta'}\right) - \frac{\partial \phi}{\partial \theta} \quad = \quad 0$$

where $\phi = [1 + r^2\theta'^2]^{1/2}$ and $\theta' = d\theta/dz$. But since $\partial\phi/\partial\theta = 0$,

$$\partial\phi/\partial\theta' \;=\; (1 + r^2\theta'^2)^{-1/2}\,r^2\theta' \;=\; c_1 \;=\; \text{constant}$$

From this, $r\theta' = c_2$. Hence $r\theta = c_2 z + c_3$, which is the equation of a helix.

Suppose that at p_1 we have $\theta = 0$, $z = 0$; thus $c_3 = 0$. At p_2 let $\theta = \theta_2$ and $z = z_2$; hence $c_2 = r\theta_2/z_2$, and $r\theta = (r\theta_2/z_2)z$ is the final equation.

Example 17.5.

Referring to Fig. 17-3, Example 17.3, let us evaluate integral (*5*) along the actual path, determined by $x = v_x t$, $y = v_y t - \frac{1}{2}gt^2$ between the limits $t = 0$ and $t = t_f = 2v_y/g = \text{time of flight}$, and integral (*7*) along a varied path determined by $x = v_x t$, $y = h\sin(\pi v_x t/R)$ between the same limits, and compare the results.

Let $h = v_y^2/2g = \text{maximum height}$, and $R = 2v_x v_y/g = \text{range of projectile}$. Note that the real and varied paths intersect at $x = 0$ and $x = R$. Hence $\delta x = \delta y = 0$ at these points. (Show that at $t = t_f/4$, $y_v - y = 0.707 - 0.75$.) Integral (*5*) becomes

$$\mathcal{I} \quad = \quad \int_0^{t_f} \tfrac{1}{2}m[v_x^2 + v_y^2 - 4v_y gt + 2g^2t^2]\,dt \quad = \quad 2mh(v_x^2/v_y - \tfrac{1}{3}v_y)$$

Equation (*7*) may be written as

$$\mathcal{I}_v \quad = \quad \int_0^{t_f} \tfrac{1}{2}m[v_x^2 \;+\; (h^2\pi^2v_x^2/R^2)\cos^2(\pi v_x t/R) \;-\; 2gh\sin(\pi v_x t/R)]\,dt$$

and finally

$$\mathcal{I}_v \;=\; 2mh(v_x^2/v_y - cv_y)$$

where $c = (2/\pi - \pi^2/32) = 0.329$. Note that $\mathcal{I}$ is slightly less than $\mathcal{I}_v$, as expected.

Example 17.6.

For a pendulum bob suspended from a spring, find the equations of motion by a direct application of Hamilton's principle.

For the pendulum shown in Fig. 17-7 below,

$$L \quad = \quad \tfrac{1}{2}m(\dot{r}^2 + r^2\dot{\theta}^2) \;+\; mgr\cos\theta \;-\; \tfrac{1}{2}k(r - r_0)^2$$

Hence

$$\int_{t_1}^{t_2} \delta L\, dt \;=\; \int_{t_1}^{t_2} [m(\dot{r}\,\delta\dot{r} + r\dot{\theta}^2\,\delta r + r^2\dot{\theta}\,\delta\dot{\theta}) + mg\,\delta r\cos\theta - mgr\,\delta\theta\sin\theta - k(r-r_0)\,\delta r]\,dt$$

Following equation (*25*),

$$m\dot{r}\,\delta\dot{r}\,dt \;=\; m\dot{r}\,d(\delta r) \;=\; d(m\dot{r}\,\delta r) - m\,\delta r\,\ddot{r}\,dt$$

Likewise,

$$m r^2\dot{\theta}\,\delta\dot{\theta}\,dt \;=\; d(mr^2\dot{\theta}\,\delta\theta) - \delta\theta\,\frac{d(mr^2\dot{\theta})}{dt}\,dt$$

$$=\; d(mr^2\dot{\theta}\,\delta\theta) - \delta\theta(mr^2\ddot{\theta} + 2mr\dot{r}\dot{\theta})\,dt$$

Hence we write the above integral as

$$\int_{t_1}^{t_2} [\{m\ddot{r} - mr\dot{\theta}^2 - mg\cos\theta + k(r-r_0)\}\,\delta r \;+\; \{mr^2\ddot{\theta} + 2mr\dot{r}\dot{\theta} + mgr\sin\theta\}\,\delta\theta]\,dt$$

$$-\int_{t_1}^{t_2} [d(m\dot{r}\,\delta r) + d(mr^2\dot{\theta}\,\delta\theta)] \;=\; 0$$

Assuming δr and $\delta\theta$ are each zero at t_1 and t_2, the second integral is clearly zero. Since δr and $\delta\theta$ are (except as stated above) completely independent, the first integral can be zero only if

$$m\ddot{r} - mr\dot{\theta}^2 - mg\cos\theta + k(r-r_0) = 0 \qquad \text{and} \qquad mr^2\ddot{\theta} + 2mr\dot{r}\dot{\theta} + mgr\sin\theta = 0$$

But these are the equations of motion of the system. It is evident that they are just the relations that would be obtained by a direct application of D'Alembert's principle or Lagrange's equations.

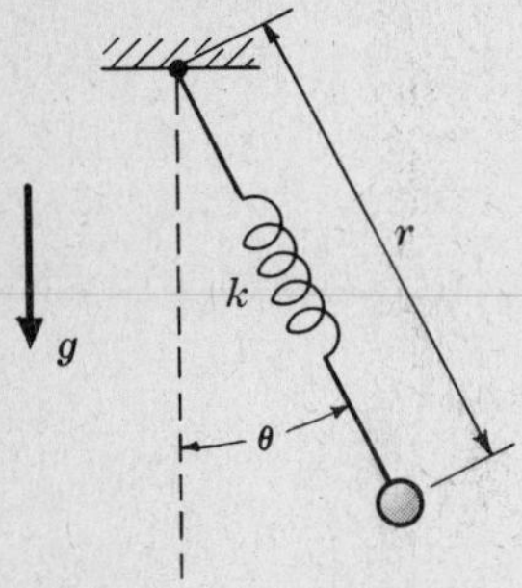

Fig. 17-7

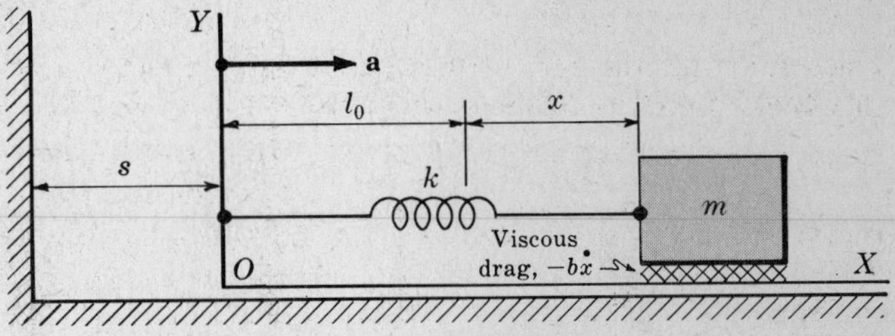

XY frame moves to right with constant acceleration **a**.

Fig. 17-8

Example 17.7.

Suppose that the entire *XY* frame, Fig. 17-8, is made to move in the positive direction of *X* so that the distance *s* of *O* from a fixed point is given by $s = vt + \frac{1}{2}at^2$. Let us also assume a viscous drag *f* on *m* given by $f = -b\dot{x}$. From (*17.8*) we have

$$\int_{t_1}^{t_2} [\delta L + f\,\delta x]\,dt \;=\; \int_{t_1}^{t_2} [\delta\{\tfrac{1}{2}m(v+at+\dot{x})^2 - \tfrac{1}{2}kx^2\} - b\dot{x}\,\delta x]\,dt$$

$$=\; \int_{t_1}^{t_2} [m(v+at+\dot{x})\,\delta\dot{x} - kx\,\delta x - b\dot{x}\,\delta x]\,dt$$

where t is not varied.

Writing

$$m(v+at+\dot{x})\,\delta\dot{x} \;=\; d[m(v+at+\dot{x})\,\delta x] - m(a+\ddot{x})\,\delta x\,dt$$

the above integral becomes

$$\int_{t_1}^{t_2} [\{m(a+\ddot{x}) + b\dot{x} + kx\}\,\delta x]\,dt - \int_{t_1}^{t_2} d[m(v+at+\dot{x})\,\delta x] \;=\; 0$$

The second integral is zero and from the first, $m(a+\ddot{x}) + b\dot{x} + kx = 0$, which is just the equation of motion obtained by applying Lagrange's equation in the usual way.

The above is another example of how equations of motion may be obtained by a direct application of Hamilton's principle.

17.9 Applications of Hamilton's Principle.

As illustrated by Examples 17.6 and 17.7, the equations of motion of a system may be obtained directly from Hamilton's principle. However, as is evident, the procedure is less convenient than the usual Lagrangian method.

Of course it may be said that, since Lagrange's equations are obtainable from Hamilton's principle, their use is equivalent to an application of the principle. However, it must be remembered that a derivation of Lagrange's equations, which in no way depends on Hamilton's principle, follows at once from D'Alembert's equation. Moreover, the route to Lagrange's equations via Hamilton's principle leaves much to be desired as regards clarification of basic physical principles. (Compare the derivation of Section 17.7 with that given on Pages 58-60.)

However, this principle represents a distinct and interesting point of view. Also, it has been the forerunner of the application of variational methods to many branches of theoretical physics. Within relatively recent years variational methods have proven quite useful in the development of the dynamics of continuous systems, relativity, quantum mechanics and quantum electrodynamics.

For further study of Hamilton's principle, general variational methods and other related topics the reader may consult the following references.

Cornelius Lanczos, *Variational Principles of Mechanics,* University of Toronto Press, 1949, 1966. This book is highly recommended not only as a reference on variational principles, but as a valuable source of information regarding the basic principles and ideas throughout the field of dynamics. No effort has been spared to lay bare the foundation stones and supporting framework around which the science of analytical dynamics is constructed. The language is clear and unencumbered with abstruse expressions. Seeking only to present basic truths in an understandable and unveiled manner, no attempt is made to present the material in its most "compact", "elegant" or fashionable form. Furthermore, the author makes quite clear certain very important points regarding the vectorial as compared with the analytical methods of dynamics. Finally, in referring to this book, do not fail to read both the preface and introduction.

Clive W. Kilmister, *Hamiltonian Dynamics,* John Wiley, 1964, Pages 34, 49, 50. Note the author's views regarding Hamilton's principle, Page 34.

Herbert Goldstein, *Classical Mechanics,* Addison-Wesley, 1950, Pages 30-37, 225-235. For a derivation of Hamilton's equations of motion from Hamilton's principle, see Pages 225-227. For an important statement regarding variational principles and their uses, see Page 235.

J. C. Coe, *Theoretical Mechanics,* Macmillan, 1938, Pages 412-417.

Robert Weinstock, *Calculus of Variations,* McGraw-Hill, 1952, Pages 16-48, 95-98, 261-294. This book includes many applications of variational methods.

Problems

17.1. Show that the shortest (or longest) line connecting two points on a sphere is a segment of a great circle.

17.2. A line $y = y(x)$ passing through two given points $p_1(x_1, y_1)$ and $p_2(x_2, y_2)$ is rotated about the X axis. Show that the surface area A generated by the line is given by

$$A = 2\pi \int_{p_1}^{p_2} y\, ds = 2\pi \int_{x_1}^{x_2} y[1 + (dy/dx)^2]^{1/2}\, dx$$

Show that the equation of the line which generates a minimum surface is given by

$$dy/dx = (y^2/c_1^2 - 1)^{1/2} \qquad \text{or} \qquad y = c_1 \cosh(x/c_1 + c_2)$$

where c_1 and c_2 are constants to be determined so that the line passes through the two given points p_1 and p_2. Details of how this may be accomplished are given in: R. Weinstock, *Calculus of Variations*, McGraw-Hill, 1952, Page 30. The above curve is referred to as a catenary.

17.3. A mass m attached to a coil spring having a constant k, oscillates along a smooth horizontal line with a motion given by $x = A \sin \omega t$ where $\omega = \sqrt{k/m}$. Assuming a varied path represented by $x = A \sin \omega t + \epsilon \sin 2\omega t$, where ϵ is a small constant quantity, show that for the actual path taken over the interval $t = 0$ to $t = \pi/2\omega$ (one fourth of a complete oscillation), $\int_{t=0}^{t=\pi/2\omega} \delta L\, dt = 0$; and that for the varied path this integral is equal to $\frac{3}{8} m\pi\omega\epsilon^2$.

17.4. Coefficients in a Fourier sine series development of the parabolic path, Example 17.5, Fig. 17-3, are given by

$$a_n = (16h/n^3\pi^3)(1 - \cos n\pi), \qquad n = 1, 2, 3, \ldots$$

(see any introductory treatment of Fourier series). Hence (retaining the first and third terms) the parabola is approximated by

$$y = \frac{32h}{\pi^3} \sin \frac{\pi x}{R} + \frac{32h}{27\pi^3} \sin \frac{3\pi x}{R}$$

(Note that $a_2 = 0$.) Taking the above as a varied path, show that the integral $\mathcal{J}_v$ for this path is

$$\mathcal{J}_v = \int_{t=0}^{t_f} L\, dt = 2mh(v_x^2/v_y + cv_y) \qquad \text{where} \quad c = (32 \times 82/81\pi^4) = .333$$

Show that $\int_{t=0}^{t_f} L\, dt$ over the actual path is slightly less than $\mathcal{J}_v$.

17.5. Referring to the above problem write $y_v = y + \epsilon \sin \omega t$ as a varied path, where $y = v_y t - \frac{1}{2} g t^2$, ϵ = some small number, $\omega = n\pi/t_f$, n = an integer. (Note that the varied path goes through the points $x = 0$, $x = x_2$, Fig. 17-3.)

Again show that the integral $\int_{t=0}^{t_f} L\, dt$ is greater for the varied than for the actual path.

17.6. The ball, Fig. 17-9, is thrown horizontally from p_1 with an initial velocity of v_x. Falling freely under gravity, its actual path is determined by $x = v_x t$, $y = \frac{1}{2} g t^2$.

Actual motion $x = v_x t$, $y = \frac{1}{2}gt^2$.
Assumed varied motion passing through p_1 and p_2,

$$x = v_x t, \quad y = \left(\frac{y_2}{e - 1}\right)(e^{x/x_2} - 1)$$

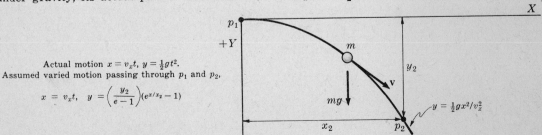

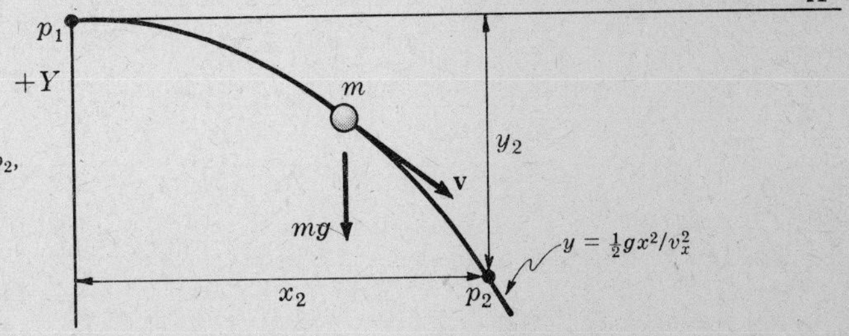

Fig. 17-9

Let us assume the following varied path $x = v_x t,\ y = \left(\frac{y_2}{e-1}\right)(e^{x/x_2} - 1)$ which passes through points p_1 and p_2. Show that for the actual path,

$$\int_{t_1=0}^{t_2=x_2/v_x} L\,dt = \frac{mv_x x_2}{2} + \frac{mg^2x_2^3}{3v_x^3} = \frac{mv_x x_2}{2} + \frac{2}{3}\frac{mgx_2y_2}{v_x}$$

and for the varied path,

$$\int_{t_1=0}^{t_2=x_2/v_x} L\,dt = \frac{mv_x x_2}{2} + 0.689\frac{mgx_2y_2}{v_x}$$

17.7. Referring to Fig. 2-8, Page 13, find equations of motion of the system by a direct application of Hamilton's principle as was done in Example 17.6. Use coordinates q_1, y; see (*2.44*), Page 25, for T. Check results by the Lagrange method.

17.8. Referring to Problem 3.21, Fig. 3-13, Page 55, set up the r equation of motion by a direct application of Hamilton's principle.

17.9. Referring to Example 4.6, Page 66, set up the equations of motion of the double pendulum by a direct application of Hamilton's principle.

17.10. The pendulum shown in Fig. 17-7 and discussed in Example 17.6 is now allowed to swing in space. In spherical coordinates,

$$L = \tfrac{1}{2}m(\dot{r}^2 + r^2\dot{\theta}^2 + r^2\sin^2\theta\,\dot{\phi}^2) + mgr\cos\theta - \tfrac{1}{2}k(r-r_0)^2$$

Assuming a viscous drag on the bob, the power function P is

$$P = \tfrac{1}{2}b(\dot{r}^2 + r^2\dot{\theta}^2 + r^2\sin^2\theta\,\dot{\phi}^2)$$

Show that $\int_{t_1}^{t_2} (\delta T + \delta W)\,dt$ reduces to

$$\begin{aligned}\int_{t_1}^{t_2} [(m\ddot{r} - mr\dot{\theta}^2 - mr\sin^2\theta\,\dot{\phi}^2 + k(r-r_0) - mgr\cos\theta + b\dot{r})\,\delta r \\ + (mr^2\ddot{\theta} + 2mr\dot{r}\dot{\theta} - mr^2\sin\theta\cos\theta\,\dot{\phi}^2 + br^2\dot{\theta} + mgr\sin\theta)\,\delta\theta \\ + (mr^2\sin^2\theta\,\ddot{\phi} + 2mr\dot{r}\dot{\phi}\sin^2\theta + 2mr^2\dot{\theta}\dot{\phi}\sin\theta\cos\theta + br^2\sin^2\theta\dot{\phi})\,\delta\phi]\,dt = 0\end{aligned}$$

from which the equations of motion may be read off at once.

17.11. Referring to Example 4.8, Fig. 4-6, Page 67, set up equations of motion of m_1 and m_2 by a direct application of Hamilton's principle. Is t allowed to vary? Compare results with those given.

17.12. Set up equations (*14.15*), Page 287, by a direct application of Hamilton's principle.

CHAPTER 18

Basic Equations of Dynamics in Vector and Tensor Notation

The Lagrangian method of dynamics is largely based on the scalar quantities $T, V, P, \delta W$ each of which can, for holonomic systems, easily be expressed in terms of any suitable generalized coordinates. Though the vector nature of force, velocity, acceleration, etc., is of basic importance, formal vector and tensor methods are usually of little or no use in obtaining proper expressions for the above quantities. On applying Lagrange's equations, equations of motion are obtained directly in just the desired coordinates. Moreover, complete account is automatically taken of vector quantities without the use of intervening formal vector relations, as shown in Section 3.10, Page 50. Hence the very general and easily applied Lagrangian procedure does not require or greatly benefit from formal vector and tensor methods. In all except relatively simple cases it is far easier and less time-consuming to write the Lagrangian equations of motion than to first determine appropriate vector relations and then translate into desired coordinates, to say nothing of the problem of eliminating forces of constraint.

However, vector and tensor notation and procedures have been introduced extensively in many branches of science and technology, and in various fields they offer decided advantages. Hence the following list of the most important relations of dynamics, expressed in the above notation, should be of interest and value to the reader (*a*) in developing a better understanding of this language and how it is related to Lagrangian methods, (*b*) as a background for reading many references. It will also serve to make more complete all points of view on this subject.

Following each relation given below is the number and page of the corresponding form in the text.

1. Position vector $\mathbf{r}$ and transformation equations.

$$\mathbf{r} = x\mathbf{i} + y\mathbf{j} + z\mathbf{k}$$

where $\mathbf{i}, \mathbf{j}, \mathbf{k}$ are unit vectors along rectangular orthogonal X, Y, Z axes. Or,

$$\mathbf{r} = x_1\mathbf{i}_1 + x_2\mathbf{i}_2 + x_3\mathbf{i}_3 = \sum_{k=1}^{3} x_k\mathbf{i}_k$$

where $\mathbf{i}_1, \mathbf{i}_2, \mathbf{i}_3$ correspond to the unit vectors above and X_1, X_2, X_3 replace X, Y, Z.

$x_i = x_i(q_1, q_2, \ldots, q_n, t)$, etc., = reduced transformation equations. See (*2.51*), Page 27.

2. Velocity $\dot{\mathbf{r}}$.

$$\text{velocity} = \dot{\mathbf{r}}_i = \dot{x}\mathbf{i} + \dot{y}\mathbf{j} + \dot{z}\mathbf{k}$$

$$\dot{\mathbf{r}}_i = \sum_{k=1}^{n} \frac{\partial \mathbf{r}_i}{\partial q_k}\dot{q}_k + \frac{\partial \mathbf{r}_i}{\partial t} \qquad (2.52), \text{ Page 27}$$

$\mathbf{v} = \mathbf{v}_0 + \dot{\mathbf{r}} + \boldsymbol{\omega} \times \mathbf{r}$ = inertial space velocity of a particle, where $\boldsymbol{\omega}$ = angular velocity of frame of reference, $\mathbf{v}_0$ = inertial space velocity of origin of frame, $\mathbf{r}$ = position vector of particle measured relative to moving frame. See (*8.4*), Page 143.

$\mathbf{v} = \mathbf{v}_0 + \boldsymbol{\omega} \times \mathbf{r}$ = velocity of typical particle in a rigid body. See (*8.3*), Page 142.

3. Acceleration **a**.

$$\mathbf{a} = \ddot{\mathbf{r}} = \ddot{x}\mathbf{i} + \ddot{y}\mathbf{j} + \ddot{z}\mathbf{k} \qquad (2.59), \text{ Page 29}$$

Components $a_{q_1}, a_{q_2}, a_{q_3}$ of **a** along coordinate lines of the generalized coordinates q_1, q_2, q_3:

$$a_{q_r} = \frac{1}{h_r}\left[\frac{d}{dt}\left(\frac{\partial T'}{\partial \dot{q}_r}\right) - \frac{\partial T'}{\partial q_r}\right] \qquad (3.24), \text{ Page 49}$$

$$\mathbf{a} = \ddot{\mathbf{r}}_0 + \dot{\boldsymbol{\omega}} \times \mathbf{r} + \boldsymbol{\omega} \times (\boldsymbol{\omega} \times \mathbf{r}) \qquad (9.7), \text{ Page 180}$$

where $\mathbf{a}$ = inertial space acceleration of a typical particle in a rigid body.

4. Force **F**, displacement $d\mathbf{r}$ and work W.

$$\mathbf{F} = F_x\mathbf{i} + F_y\mathbf{j} + F_z\mathbf{k}$$

$$d\mathbf{r}_i = dx_i\mathbf{i} + dy_i\mathbf{j} + dz_i\mathbf{k} = \sum_{k=1}^{n} \frac{\partial \mathbf{r}_i}{\partial q_k} dq_k$$

$$W = \int \mathbf{F} \cdot d\mathbf{r} \qquad (2.36), \text{ Page 23}$$

5. Kinetic energy T.

For a single particle, $T = \frac{1}{2}m\dot{\mathbf{r}} \cdot \dot{\mathbf{r}}$. For a system of p particles having n degrees of freedom,

$$T = \frac{1}{2}\sum_{i=1}^{p} m_i \dot{\mathbf{r}}_i \cdot \dot{\mathbf{r}}_i = \sum_{rs}^{n} A_{rs}\dot{q}_r\dot{q}_s + \sum_{r=1}^{n} B_r\dot{q}_r + C \qquad (2.55), \text{ Page 27}$$

where

$$A_{rs} = \frac{1}{2}\sum_{i=1}^{p} m_i\left(\frac{\partial \mathbf{r}_i}{\partial q_r} \cdot \frac{\partial \mathbf{r}_i}{\partial q_s}\right), \quad B_r = \sum_{i=1}^{p} m_i\left(\frac{\partial \mathbf{r}_i}{\partial t} \cdot \frac{\partial \mathbf{r}_i}{\partial q_r}\right), \quad C = \frac{1}{2}\sum_{i=1}^{p} m_i\left(\frac{\partial \mathbf{r}_i}{\partial t} \cdot \frac{\partial \mathbf{r}_i}{\partial t}\right)$$

See (*2.54*), Page 27.

6. D'Alembert's equation.

$$\sum_{i=1}^{p} [\mathbf{F}_i - m_i(\ddot{x}_i\mathbf{i} + \ddot{y}_i\mathbf{j} + \ddot{z}_i\mathbf{k})] \cdot (\delta x_i\mathbf{i} + \delta y_i\mathbf{j} + \delta z_i\mathbf{k}) = 0$$

or

$$\sum_{i=1}^{p} (\mathbf{F}_i - \dot{\mathbf{p}}_i) \cdot \delta\mathbf{r}_i = 0 \quad \text{where} \quad \dot{\mathbf{p}}_i = \frac{d}{dt}(m_i\dot{\mathbf{r}}_i) \qquad (4.6), \text{ Page 60}$$

To express in generalized coordinates, write $\delta\mathbf{r}_i = \sum_{k=1}^{n}\left(\frac{\partial \mathbf{r}_i}{\partial q_k}\right)\delta q_k$.

7. Lagrange's equations and generalized forces.

$$\frac{d}{dt}\frac{\partial}{\partial \dot{q}_r}\left[\frac{1}{2}\sum_{i=1}^{p} m_i(\dot{\mathbf{r}}_i \cdot \dot{\mathbf{r}}_i)\right] - \frac{\partial}{\partial q_r}\left[\frac{1}{2}\sum_{i=1}^{p} m_i(\dot{\mathbf{r}}_i \cdot \dot{\mathbf{r}}_i)\right] = F_{q_r} \qquad (4.8), (4.9), \text{ Page 60}$$

$$F_{q_r} = \sum_{i=1}^{p} \mathbf{F}_i \cdot \frac{\partial \mathbf{r}_i}{\partial q_r} = \frac{\delta W_{q_r}}{\delta q_r} \qquad (4.10), \text{ Page 60}$$

See Section 4.8, Page 69.

8. Potential energy V, power function P.

$$-V = \int \mathbf{F}_i \cdot d\mathbf{r}_i \quad \text{where } \mathbf{F}_i \text{ are conservative} \qquad (5.4), \text{ Page 82}$$

$$\mathbf{F}_i = -\operatorname{grad} V, \qquad F_{q_r} = -\frac{\partial V}{\partial q_r} \qquad (5.7), \text{ Page 85}$$

For viscous forces,

$$P = \frac{1}{2}\sum_{rs}^{n} b_{rs}\dot{q}_r\dot{q}_s \quad \text{where} \quad b_{rs} = \sum_{i=1}^{p} b_i\left(\frac{\partial \mathbf{r}_i}{\partial q_r}\cdot\frac{\partial \mathbf{r}_i}{\partial q_s}\right) \qquad (6.16), \text{ Page 105}$$

9. The inertia tensor $\mathbf{I}$, (momental dyadic).

$$\mathbf{I} = \sum m_i[r_i^2(\mathbf{ii}+\mathbf{jj}+\mathbf{kk}) - \mathbf{rr}]$$

$$\begin{aligned}\mathbf{I} &= \mathbf{ii}I_{xx} + \mathbf{jj}I_{yy} + \mathbf{kk}I_{zz} - I_{xy}(\mathbf{ij}+\mathbf{ji}) \\ &\quad - I_{xz}(\mathbf{ik}+\mathbf{ki}) - I_{yz}(\mathbf{jk}+\mathbf{kj})\end{aligned} \qquad (7.11), \text{ Page 119}$$

where $I_{xx} = \sum m_i(y^2+z^2)$, $I_{xy} = \sum m_i xy$, etc.

For X, Y, Z principal axes of inertia,

$$\mathbf{I} = \mathbf{ii}I_{xx}^p + \mathbf{jj}I_{yy}^p + \mathbf{kk}I_{zz}^p$$

10. Moment of inertia I_{Oa} about any line Oa having direction cosines l, m, n

$$I_{Oa} = \boldsymbol{\epsilon}\cdot\mathbf{I}\cdot\boldsymbol{\epsilon} \qquad (7.2), \text{ Page 118}$$

where $\boldsymbol{\epsilon} = \mathbf{i}l + \mathbf{j}m + \mathbf{k}n$.

11. Kinetic energy of a rigid body.

$$\begin{aligned} T &= \tfrac{1}{2}\sum m_i v_i^2 = \tfrac{1}{2}\sum m_i(\mathbf{v}_0 + \boldsymbol{\omega}\times\mathbf{r})\cdot(\mathbf{v}_0+\boldsymbol{\omega}\times\mathbf{r}) \\ &= \tfrac{1}{2}\sum m_i[v_0^2 + (\boldsymbol{\omega}\times\mathbf{r})\cdot(\boldsymbol{\omega}\times\mathbf{r}) + 2\mathbf{v}_0\cdot(\boldsymbol{\omega}\times\mathbf{r})]\end{aligned} \qquad (8.10), \text{ Page 148}$$

For one point of body fixed, origin at this point,

$$T = \tfrac{1}{2}\boldsymbol{\omega}\cdot\mathbf{I}\cdot\boldsymbol{\omega} = \tfrac{1}{2}(I_x\omega_x^2 + I_y\omega_y^2 + I_z\omega_z^2 - 2I_{xy}\omega_x\omega_y - 2I_{xz}\omega_x\omega_z - 2I_{yz}\omega_y\omega_z)$$

12. Angular momentum $\mathbf{P}$ about point O_1 fixed in space. Corresponding Euler equations, body moving in any manner, not fixed to O_1.

$$\mathbf{P} = \sum m_i(\mathbf{r}\times\dot{\mathbf{r}}) \qquad \text{Section 9.13, Page 195}$$

where $\mathbf{r}$ = position vector of m_i.

Torque about O_1, $$\boldsymbol{\tau} = \sum_s \mathbf{r}_s \times \mathbf{F}_s \qquad \text{Section 8.2F, Page 147}$$

where $\mathbf{F}_s$ = externally applied force, $\mathbf{r}_s$ = position vector of point of application of $\mathbf{F}_s$.

Euler's equation, $$\boldsymbol{\tau} = \frac{d}{dt}\mathbf{P} \qquad (9.28), \text{ Page 196}$$

13. Torque $\boldsymbol{\tau}_0$ and relative angular momentum $\mathbf{P}_0$ about point O moving with inertial-space velocity $\mathbf{v}_0$.

$$\tau_0 \;=\; \sum m_i \mathbf{r}_i \times \ddot{\mathbf{R}}_i \;=\; \sum m_i \mathbf{r}_i \times (\dot{\mathbf{v}}_0 + \ddot{\mathbf{r}})$$

where $\mathbf{R}_i$ = position vector of m_i measured from fixed point O_1.

$$\tau_0 \;=\; \sum m_i \mathbf{r}_i \times \ddot{\mathbf{r}}_i \;-\; \dot{\mathbf{v}}_0 \times \sum m_i \mathbf{r}_i$$

$$= \frac{d}{dt} \sum m_i \mathbf{r}_i \times \dot{\mathbf{r}}_i \;-\; M \dot{\mathbf{v}}_0 \times \mathbf{r}_c \qquad \textit{(9.30)}, \text{ Page 196}$$

where $\mathbf{r}_c$ = position vector of center of mass relative to O.

Defining $\mathbf{P}_0 = \sum m_i \mathbf{r}_i \times \dot{\mathbf{r}}_i$ as relative momentum, the Euler equation in vector form may be written as

$$\tau_0 \;=\; \dot{\mathbf{P}}_0 - M \dot{\mathbf{v}}_0 \times \mathbf{r}_c \qquad \textit{(9.31)}, \text{ Page 196}$$

14. The metric tensor.

Write transformation equations as

$$x_i \;=\; x_i(q^1, q^2, \ldots, q^n), \text{ etc.} \quad (t \text{ not entering})$$

$$dx_i \;=\; \frac{\partial x_i}{\partial q^1} dq^1 + \frac{\partial x_i}{\partial q^2} dq^2 + \cdots + \frac{\partial x_i}{\partial q^n} dq^n \;=\; \sum_{k=1}^{n} a_{ik}\, dq^k$$

Define the "element of length" ds in n-dimensional (Riemannian) space by

$$ds^2 \;=\; \sum_{i=1}^{p} (dx_i^2 + dy_i^2 + dz_i^2)$$

$$ds^2 \;=\; \sum_{k=1}^{n} \sum_{l=1}^{n} \left[\sum_{i=1}^{p} (a_{ik} a_{il} + b_{ik} b_{il} + c_{ik} c_{il}) \right] dq^k\, dq^l$$

or

$$ds^2 \;=\; \sum_{k=1}^{n} \sum_{l=1}^{n} g_{kl}\, dq^k\, dq^l$$

where g_{kl} are components of the "metric tensor." See, for example, *(2.54)*, Page 27.

Appendix Relations Between Direction Cosines

The relations given below are indispensable tools in the field of analytical dynamics as well as in many other branches of mathematical physics. This summary is intended as a convenient reference. Most of the relations have been used extensively throughout this text.

A.1 *Relations between* $\alpha_{11}, \alpha_{12}, \alpha_{13}$, *etc., Fig. A-1.*

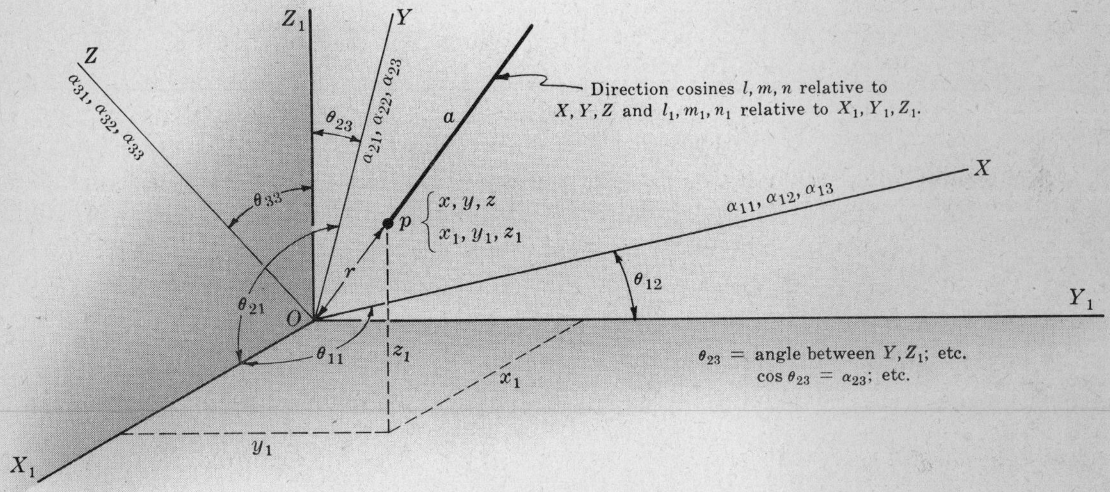

Fig. A-1

Here $\alpha_{11}, \alpha_{12}, \alpha_{13}$, for example, represent cosines of the angles $\theta_{11}, \theta_{12}, \theta_{13}$ between X and X_1, Y_1, Z_1, respectively. That is, $\alpha_{11} = \cos\theta_{11}$, etc.

$$\begin{aligned} \alpha_{11}^2 + \alpha_{12}^2 + \alpha_{13}^2 &= 1, \quad \alpha_{21}^2 + \alpha_{22}^2 + \alpha_{23}^2 = 1, \quad \alpha_{31}^2 + \alpha_{32}^2 + \alpha_{33}^2 = 1 \\ \alpha_{11}^2 + \alpha_{21}^2 + \alpha_{31}^2 &= 1, \quad \alpha_{12}^2 + \alpha_{22}^2 + \alpha_{32}^2 = 1, \quad \alpha_{13}^2 + \alpha_{23}^2 + \alpha_{33}^2 = 1 \end{aligned} \tag{1}$$

$$\begin{aligned} \alpha_{11}\alpha_{21} + \alpha_{12}\alpha_{22} + \alpha_{13}\alpha_{23} &= 0, \quad \alpha_{11}\alpha_{12} + \alpha_{21}\alpha_{22} + \alpha_{31}\alpha_{32} = 0 \\ \alpha_{11}\alpha_{31} + \alpha_{12}\alpha_{32} + \alpha_{13}\alpha_{33} &= 0, \quad \alpha_{11}\alpha_{13} + \alpha_{21}\alpha_{23} + \alpha_{31}\alpha_{33} = 0 \\ \alpha_{21}\alpha_{31} + \alpha_{22}\alpha_{32} + \alpha_{23}\alpha_{33} &= 0, \quad \alpha_{12}\alpha_{13} + \alpha_{22}\alpha_{23} + \alpha_{32}\alpha_{33} = 0 \end{aligned} \tag{2}$$

In compact form (*1*) and (*2*) are given by

$$\sum_{i=1}^{3} \alpha_{ir}\alpha_{is} = \begin{cases} 1 \text{ for } r = s \\ 0 \text{ for } r \neq s \end{cases} = \delta_{rs} = \text{Kronecker delta} \tag{3}$$

$$\begin{aligned} \alpha_{11} &= \alpha_{22}\alpha_{33} - \alpha_{23}\alpha_{32}, \quad \alpha_{21} = \alpha_{32}\alpha_{13} - \alpha_{12}\alpha_{33}, \quad \alpha_{31} = \alpha_{12}\alpha_{23} - \alpha_{22}\alpha_{13} \\ \alpha_{12} &= \alpha_{23}\alpha_{31} - \alpha_{33}\alpha_{21}, \quad \alpha_{22} = \alpha_{33}\alpha_{11} - \alpha_{13}\alpha_{31}, \quad \alpha_{32} = \alpha_{13}\alpha_{21} - \alpha_{23}\alpha_{11} \\ \alpha_{13} &= \alpha_{21}\alpha_{32} - \alpha_{31}\alpha_{22}, \quad \alpha_{23} = \alpha_{31}\alpha_{12} - \alpha_{11}\alpha_{32}, \quad \alpha_{33} = \alpha_{11}\alpha_{22} - \alpha_{12}\alpha_{21} \end{aligned} \tag{4}$$

A.2 *Relations between Direction Cosines l_1, m_1, n_1 and l, m, n of Line Oa, Fig. A-1.*

Note that l_1, m_1, n_1 are relative to X_1, Y_1, Z_1 and l, m, n are relative to X, Y, Z. Consider any point $p(x, y, z; x_1, y_1, z_1)$ on line Oa. Dividing the transformation equation $x_1 = x\alpha_{11} + y\alpha_{21} + z\alpha_{31}$ by $r = Op$ we have $x_1/r = (x/r)\alpha_{11} + (y/r)\alpha_{21} + (z/r)\alpha_{31}$. But $x_1/r = l_1$, $x/r = l$, etc. Hence

$$\begin{aligned} l_1 &= l\alpha_{11} + m\alpha_{21} + n\alpha_{31} \\ m_1 &= l\alpha_{12} + m\alpha_{22} + n\alpha_{32} \\ n_1 &= l\alpha_{13} + m\alpha_{23} + n\alpha_{33} \end{aligned} \tag{5}$$

Likewise it follows that

$$\begin{aligned} l &= l_1\alpha_{11} + m_1\alpha_{12} + n_1\alpha_{13} \\ m &= l_1\alpha_{21} + m_1\alpha_{22} + n_1\alpha_{23} \\ n &= l_1\alpha_{31} + m_1\alpha_{32} + n_1\alpha_{33} \end{aligned} \tag{6}$$

It is usually convenient to express the α's in terms of Euler angles as in Table 8.2, Page 158 or Table A.1 which follows.

A.3 *Direction Cosines Expressed in Specific Coordinates.*

In the solution of almost any actual problem, direction cosines must eventually be expressed in terms of specific coordinates. This is not difficult. The following examples are typical.

(a) ***Rectangular coordinates.***

Consider line Oa, Fig. A-2. Let x, y, z be the rectangular coordinates of any point p on Oa. Hence direction cosines l, m, n of Oa are

$$l = x/r, \quad m = y/r, \quad n = z/r \tag{7}$$

where $r = (x^2 + y^2 + z^2)^{1/2}$.

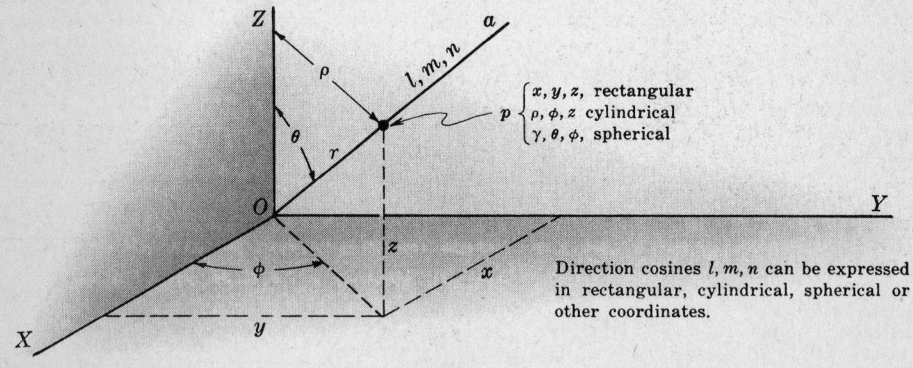

Fig. A-2

(b) ***Cylindrical coordinates.***

Letting ρ, ϕ, z be cylindrical coordinates of p, Fig. A-2,

$$l = \rho\cos\phi/r, \quad m = \rho\sin\phi/r, \quad n = z/r \tag{8}$$

where $r = (\rho^2 + z^2)^{1/2}$.

(c) ***Spherical coordinates.***

Letting r, θ, ϕ be spherical coordinates of p, Fig. A-2,

$$l = \sin\theta\cos\phi, \quad m = \sin\theta\sin\phi, \quad n = \cos\theta \tag{9}$$

(d) ***Direction cosines of the X, Y, Z coordinates, Fig. 8-16, Page 156, (or Fig. A-1) in terms of Euler angles.***

Euler angles are described in Section 8.7, Page 156, and illustrated in Fig. 8-16. Direction cosines $\alpha_{11}, \alpha_{12}, \alpha_{13}$ of X, etc., are given in Table 8.2, Page 158. For convenience the table is repeated below. These expressions are easily verified with the help of a simple model.

	X	Y	Z
X_1	$\alpha_{11} = \cos\phi\cos\psi - \sin\phi\sin\psi\cos\theta$	$\alpha_{21} = -\sin\phi\cos\psi - \cos\phi\sin\psi\cos\theta$	$\alpha_{31} = \sin\theta\sin\psi$
Y_1	$\alpha_{12} = \cos\phi\sin\psi + \sin\phi\cos\psi\cos\theta$	$\alpha_{22} = -\sin\phi\sin\psi + \cos\phi\cos\psi\cos\theta$	$\alpha_{32} = -\sin\theta\cos\psi$
Z_1	$\alpha_{13} = \sin\theta\sin\phi$	$\alpha_{23} = \sin\theta\cos\phi$	$\alpha_{33} = \cos\theta$

Table A.1

The above relations are very important in the treatment of rigid body dynamics as well as in other fields.

A.4 *Coordinates of Point p, Fig. A-3 (or m', Fig. 8-16) in Terms of Euler Angles ψ, ϕ, θ and Other Coordinates.*

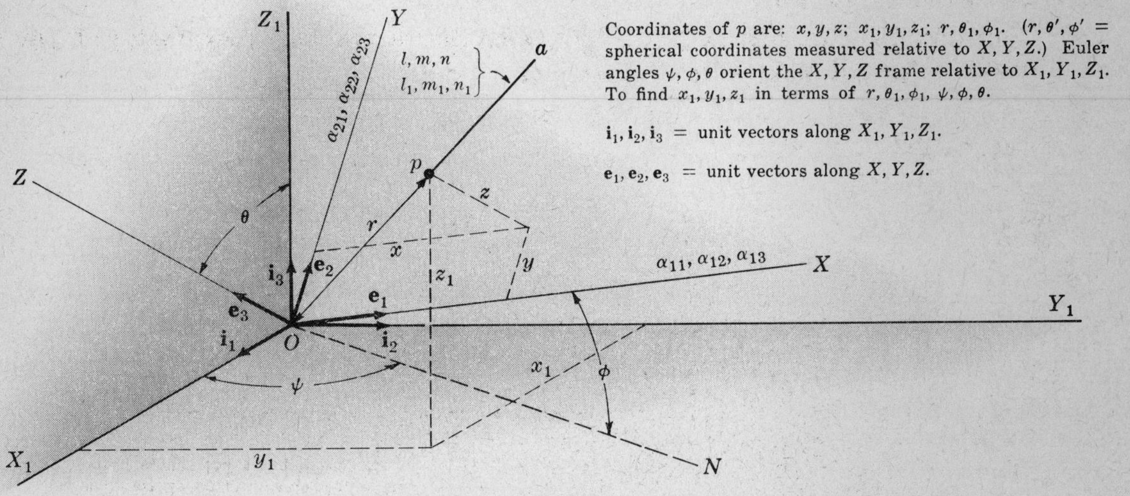

Fig. A-3

Rectangular coordinates of p are x_1, y_1, z_1 and x, y, z as indicated. Hence writing $x_1 = x\alpha_{11} + y\alpha_{21} + z\alpha_{31}$ and eliminating the α's by Table A.1, we have

$$x_1 = x(\cos\phi\cos\psi - \sin\phi\sin\psi\cos\theta) - y(\sin\phi\cos\psi + \cos\phi\sin\psi\cos\theta) + z\sin\theta\sin\psi \tag{10}$$

and similarly for y_1 and z_1. Or from $x = x_1\alpha_{11} + y_1\alpha_{12} + z_1\alpha_{13}$ we obtain

$$x = x_1(\cos\phi\cos\psi - \sin\phi\sin\psi\cos\theta) + y_1(\cos\phi\sin\psi + \sin\phi\cos\psi\cos\theta) + z_1\sin\theta\sin\phi \tag{11}$$

with similar expressions for y and z.

Now, for example, letting r, ϕ', θ' represent spherical coordinates of p measured relative to X, Y, Z, we have $x = r \sin\theta' \cos\phi'$, $y = r \sin\theta' \sin\phi'$ and $z = r\cos\theta'$. Eliminating x, y, z from (*10*), we obtain

$$\begin{aligned} x_1 &= r\sin\theta'\cos\phi'(\cos\phi\cos\psi - \sin\phi\sin\psi\cos\theta) \\ &\quad - r\sin\theta'\sin\phi'(\sin\phi\cos\psi + \cos\phi\sin\psi\cos\theta) + r\cos\theta'\sin\theta\sin\psi \end{aligned} \tag{12}$$

etc. Thus it is clear that relations of the above type can be written in terms of Euler angles and various other coordinates.

A.5 *Direction Cosines of Line Oa, Fig. A-3, in Terms of Euler Angles ψ, ϕ, θ and Rectangular Spherical or Other Coordinates.*

The direction cosines l, m, n of Oa, relative to X, Y, Z are just

$$l = x/r, \quad m = y/r, \quad n = z/r \tag{13}$$

where x, y, z are the X, Y, Z coordinates of p. Hence the first of equations (*5*) may be written as

$$\begin{aligned} l_1 &= (x/r)(\cos\phi\cos\psi - \sin\phi\sin\psi\cos\theta) \\ &\quad - (y/r)(\sin\phi\cos\psi + \cos\phi\sin\psi\cos\theta) + (z/r)\sin\theta\sin\psi \end{aligned} \tag{14}$$

with similar relations for m_1 and n_1, where $r = (x^2 + y^2 + z^2)^{1/2}$. Likewise, using (*6*) we have

$$\begin{aligned} l &= (x_1/r)(\cos\phi\cos\psi - \sin\phi\sin\psi\cos\theta) \\ &\quad + (y_1/r)(\cos\phi\sin\psi + \sin\phi\cos\psi\cos\theta) + (z_1/r)\sin\theta\sin\phi \end{aligned} \tag{15}$$

where x_1, y_1, z_1 are the X_1, Y_1, Z_1 coordinates of p.

Writing r, θ', ϕ' as spherical coordinates of p relative to the X, Y, Z frame,

$$\begin{aligned} l_1 &= \sin\theta'\cos\phi'(\cos\phi\cos\psi - \sin\phi\sin\psi\cos\theta) \\ &\quad - \sin\theta'\sin\phi'(\sin\phi\cos\psi + \cos\phi\sin\psi\cos\theta) + \cos\theta'\sin\theta\sin\psi \end{aligned} \tag{16}$$

etc. for m_1 and n_1. Likewise,

$$\begin{aligned} l &= \sin\theta_1\cos\phi_1(\cos\phi\cos\psi - \sin\phi\sin\psi\cos\theta) \\ &\quad + \sin\theta_1\sin\phi_1(\cos\phi\sin\psi + \sin\phi\cos\psi\cos\theta) + \cos\theta'\sin\theta\sin\phi \end{aligned} \tag{17}$$

where θ_1 and ϕ_1 are spherical coordinates of p measured relative to X_1, Y_1, Z_1.

Of course cylindrical or other coordinates could be introduced in the above relations instead of the rectangular or spherical.

A.6 *Components of Velocity and Acceleration.*

(*a*) Referring to Fig. 8-3, Page 143, let $\mathbf{v}(\dot{x}_1, \dot{y}_1, \dot{z}_1)$ indicate the velocity of m relative to X_1, Y_1, Z_1. Then components v_x, v_y, v_z of $\mathbf{v}$ along X, Y, Z are

$$v_x = \dot{x}_1\alpha_{11} + \dot{y}_1\alpha_{12} + \dot{z}_1\alpha_{13}, \quad \text{etc.} \tag{18}$$

Or (see equations (*8.4*), Page 143), these components can be expressed as

$$v_x = v_{0x} + \dot{x} + \Omega_y z - \Omega_z y, \quad \text{etc.} \tag{19}$$

where v_{0x}, the X component of the velocity of O, may, for example, be written as

$$v_{0x} = \dot{x}_0\alpha_{11} + \dot{y}_0\alpha_{12} + \dot{z}_0\alpha_{13}, \quad \text{etc.} \tag{20}$$

Components of $\mathbf{v}$ along X_1, Y_1, Z_1 can be written as

$$v_{x_1} = v_x\alpha_{11} + v_y\alpha_{21} + v_z\alpha_{31}, \quad \text{etc.} \tag{21}$$

where v_x, v_y, v_z can, for example, be expressed as in (*19*).

(b) Let **a** indicate the acceleration of m relative to X_1, Y_1, Z_1. Components a_x, a_y, a_z of **a** along X, Y, Z are given by

$$a_x = \ddot{x}_1\alpha_{11} + \ddot{y}_1\alpha_{12} + \ddot{z}_1\alpha_{13}, \qquad \text{etc.} \tag{22}$$

Of course $\ddot{x}_1, \ddot{y}_1, \ddot{z}_1$ can, if so desired, be expressed in terms of spherical or other coordinates.

But in terms of angular velocity components of the moving X, Y, Z frame (see Section 9.4A and equations (*9.6*), Page 179) we have

$$\begin{aligned} a_x = {} & a_{0x} + \ddot{x} - x(\Omega_y^2 + \Omega_z^2) + y(\Omega_y\Omega_x - \dot{\Omega}_z) \\ & + z(\Omega_x\Omega_z + \dot{\Omega}_y) + 2(\dot{z}\Omega_y - \dot{y}\Omega_z), \qquad \text{etc.} \end{aligned} \tag{23}$$

where a_{0x} can, for example, be written as

$$a_{0x} = \ddot{x}_0\alpha_{11} + \ddot{y}_0\alpha_{12} + \ddot{z}_0\alpha_{13} \tag{24}$$

It is also clear that components of **a** along X_1, Y_1, Z_1 can be written as

$$a_{x_1} = a_x\alpha_{11} + a_y\alpha_{21} + a_z\alpha_{31} \tag{25}$$

where a_x, a_y, a_z are given by (*23*), etc.

A.7 *Relations Between Direction Cosines and Unit Vectors.*

Let $\mathbf{i}_1, \mathbf{i}_2, \mathbf{i}_3$ be unit vectors along X_1, Y_1, Z_1 and $\mathbf{e}_1, \mathbf{e}_2, \mathbf{e}_3$ unit vectors along X, Y, Z as indicated in Fig. A-3. As before, $\alpha_{23} = \cos\theta_{23}$, etc.

Regarding Op as a vector $\mathbf{r}$, we write

$$\mathbf{r} = x\mathbf{e}_1 + y\mathbf{e}_2 + z\mathbf{e}_3 \tag{26}$$

$$\mathbf{r} = x_1\mathbf{i}_1 + y_1\mathbf{i}_2 + z_1\mathbf{i}_3 \tag{27}$$

Dividing (*26*) through by r (the magnitude of $\mathbf{r}$), $\dfrac{\mathbf{r}}{r} = \dfrac{x}{r}\mathbf{e}_1 + \dfrac{y}{r}\mathbf{e}_2 + \dfrac{z}{r}\mathbf{e}_3$. Now assuming, for example, that $\mathbf{r}$ is taken along X_1, we have $\mathbf{r}/r = \mathbf{i}_1$, $x/r = \alpha_{11}$, $y/r = \alpha_{21}$, $z/r = \alpha_{31}$. Hence

$$\mathbf{i}_1 = \alpha_{11}\mathbf{e}_1 + \alpha_{21}\mathbf{e}_2 + \alpha_{31}\mathbf{e}_3 \quad \text{or} \quad \mathbf{i}_s = \sum_{r=1}^{3} \alpha_{rs}\mathbf{e}_r \tag{28}$$

Likewise, from (*27*) it follows that

$$\mathbf{e}_1 = \alpha_{11}\mathbf{i}_1 + \alpha_{12}\mathbf{i}_2 + \alpha_{13}\mathbf{i}_3 \quad \text{or} \quad \mathbf{e}_r = \sum_{s=1}^{3} \alpha_{rs}\mathbf{i}_s \tag{29}$$

Since it is assumed that X_1, Y_1, Z_1 and X, Y, Z are orthogonal frames, $\mathbf{e}_1 \cdot \mathbf{e}_1 = 1$, $\mathbf{e}_1 \cdot \mathbf{e}_2 = 0$, etc.; $\mathbf{i}_1 \cdot \mathbf{i}_1 = 1$, $\mathbf{i}_1 \cdot \mathbf{i}_2 = 0$, etc.; or in general,

$$\mathbf{e}_r \cdot \mathbf{e}_l = \delta_{rl}, \quad \mathbf{i}_s \cdot \mathbf{i}_l = \delta_{sl} \tag{30}$$

From the dot product of $\mathbf{e}_1$ and the first equation of (*28*) we have

$$\mathbf{e}_1 \cdot \mathbf{i}_1 = \alpha_{11}\mathbf{e}_1 \cdot \mathbf{e}_1 + \alpha_{21}\mathbf{e}_1 \cdot \mathbf{e}_2 + \alpha_{31}\mathbf{e}_1 \cdot \mathbf{e}_3$$

which by (*30*) gives $\mathbf{e}_1 \cdot \mathbf{i}_1 = \alpha_{11}$. Thus from either (*28*) or (*29*) it can be shown that

$$\mathbf{e}_r \cdot \mathbf{i}_s = \alpha_{rs} \tag{31}$$

where the subscript of **e** is always written as the first subscript of α.

The dot product of $\mathbf{i}_1$ and the first equation of (*28*) is

$$\mathbf{i}_1 \cdot \mathbf{i}_1 = \alpha_{11}\mathbf{e}_1 \cdot \mathbf{i}_1 + \alpha_{21}\mathbf{e}_2 \cdot \mathbf{i}_1 + \alpha_{31}\mathbf{e}_3 \cdot \mathbf{i}_1$$

which by (*30*) and (*31*) reduces to $1 = \alpha_{11}^2 + \alpha_{21}^2 + \alpha_{31}^2$. Again, the dot product of $\mathbf{i}_2$ and the first equation of (*28*) gives $0 = \alpha_{11}\alpha_{12} + \alpha_{21}\alpha_{22} + \alpha_{31}\alpha_{32}$. In like manner all of relations (*1*) and (*2*) may be obtained.

In general it is seen from (*28*) that

$$\mathbf{i}_s \cdot \mathbf{i}_l = \sum_{r=1}^{3} \alpha_{rs} \mathbf{e}_r \cdot \mathbf{i}_l = \sum_{r=1}^{3} \alpha_{rs}\alpha_{rl} = \delta_{sl} \tag{32}$$

Likewise from (*29*),

$$\mathbf{e}_l \cdot \mathbf{e}_r = \sum_{s=1}^{3} \alpha_{rs} \mathbf{e}_l \cdot \mathbf{i}_s = \sum_{s=1}^{3} \alpha_{rs}\alpha_{ls} = \delta_{rl} \tag{33}$$

See equation (*3*).

A.8 *Illustrative Exercises and Problems.*

(*a*) *Proof of relations* (*1*) *and* (*2*). Referring to Section A.2, take line Oa along X_1, for example. In this case $l_1 = 1$, $m_1 = n_1 = 0$; $l = \alpha_{11}$, $m = \alpha_{21}$, $n = \alpha_{31}$. Hence relations (*5*) become

$$\alpha_{11}^2 + \alpha_{21}^2 + \alpha_{31}^2 = 1$$

$$\alpha_{11}\alpha_{12} + \alpha_{21}\alpha_{22} + \alpha_{31}\alpha_{32} = 0$$

$$\alpha_{11}\alpha_{13} + \alpha_{21}\alpha_{23} + \alpha_{31}\alpha_{33} = 0$$

In like manner the other relations of (*1*) and (*2*) may be verified. Note that proof of (*1*) and (*2*) constitutes a proof of (*3*).

(*b*) As an exercise the student may derive relations (*4*) from (*1*) and (*2*).

(*c*) Referring to Fig. A-1 suppose that the Euler angles, not shown on this figure, have the values $\psi = 60°$, $\phi = 30°$, $\theta = 45°$. What is the angle θ_{12}, for example? See Table A.1. Can each of the θ_{ir} angles be evaluated?

Given $\alpha_{12} = a$, $\alpha_{23} = b$, $\alpha_{33} = c$. Show that each of the remaining direction cosines can be evaluated.

(*d*) Making use of relations (*1*) and (*4*), show that the following determinant is equal to unity.

$$\begin{vmatrix} \alpha_{11} & \alpha_{12} & \alpha_{13} \\ \alpha_{21} & \alpha_{22} & \alpha_{23} \\ \alpha_{31} & \alpha_{32} & \alpha_{33} \end{vmatrix} = 1$$

(*e*) Referring to Section A.4, write expressions for x_1, y_1, z_1 in terms of cylindrical coordinates and Euler angles.

(*f*) Referring to Section A.4, Fig. A-3, let $r = 10$, $\phi' = 60°$, $\theta' = 30°$, $\psi = 25°$, $\phi = 45°$, $\theta = 20°$. Compute numerical values of x_1, y_1, z_1.

(*g*) Again referring to Fig. A-3, let $x = 4$, $y = 5$, $z = 6$, $\psi = 25°$, $\phi = 45°$, $\theta = 20°$. Compute x_1, y_1, z_1.

(*h*) Starting with equation (*10*) and regarding x, y, z as variables, derive the first of relations (*8.4*), Page 143.

(*i*) Using the data given in (*f*), compute l_1, m_1, n_1 of Fig. A-3.

(*j*) Referring to Fig. A-4 below, line Op has a length of 13. The triangle OBp has an area of 30, and the area of the rectangle $OABC$ is 12. Assuming x_1, y_1, z_1 are positive integers, show that $x_1 = 3$, $y_1 = 4$, $z_1 = 12$; $l_1 = 3/13$, $m_1 = 4/13$, $n_1 = 12/13$; $l = 5/13$, $m = 6/13$, $n = 6\sqrt{3}/13$.

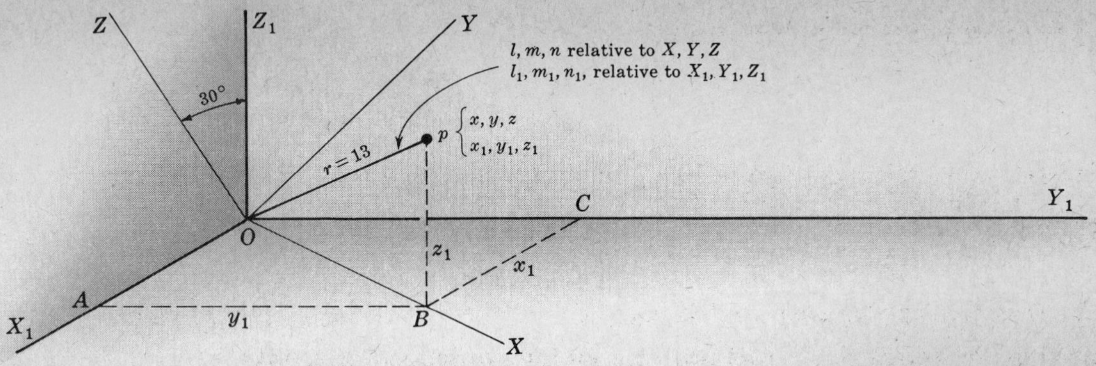

Fig. A-4

(*k*) Given $\mathbf{r} = x_1\mathbf{i}_1 + y_1\mathbf{i}_2 + z_1\mathbf{i}_3$ and using $x_1 = x\alpha_{11} + y\alpha_{21} + z\alpha_{31}$, etc. (see Fig. A-3), show that $\mathbf{r} = x\mathbf{e}_1 + y\mathbf{e}_2 + z\mathbf{e}_3$. Note relations (*1*), (*2*) and (*4*).

(*l*) An orthogonal X, Y, Z coordinate frame is determined by the following three vectors:

$$\mathbf{r}_1 = \mathbf{i}_1 + 2\mathbf{i}_2 + \mathbf{i}_3, \qquad \mathbf{r}_2 = 4\mathbf{i}_1 - \mathbf{i}_2 - 2\mathbf{i}_3, \qquad \mathbf{r}_3 = 2\mathbf{i}_1 + b\mathbf{i}_2 + c\mathbf{i}_3$$

Show that $b = -4$, $c = 6$; $l_1 = 3/13$, $m_1 = 4/13$, $n_1 = 12/13$; $l = 23/s$, $m = -16/s$, $n = 31/s$ where $s = 13\sqrt{14}$.

(*m*) Referring to Fig. A-5, writing $x = x_1\alpha_{11} + y_1\alpha_{12} + z_1\alpha_{13}$, $x_1 = x_2\beta_{11} + y_2\beta_{12} + z_2\beta_{13}$ and $x = x_2\gamma_{11} + y_2\gamma_{12} + z_2\gamma_{13}$, show that in general $\gamma_{ij} = \sum_{k=1}^{3} \alpha_{ik}\beta_{kj}$.

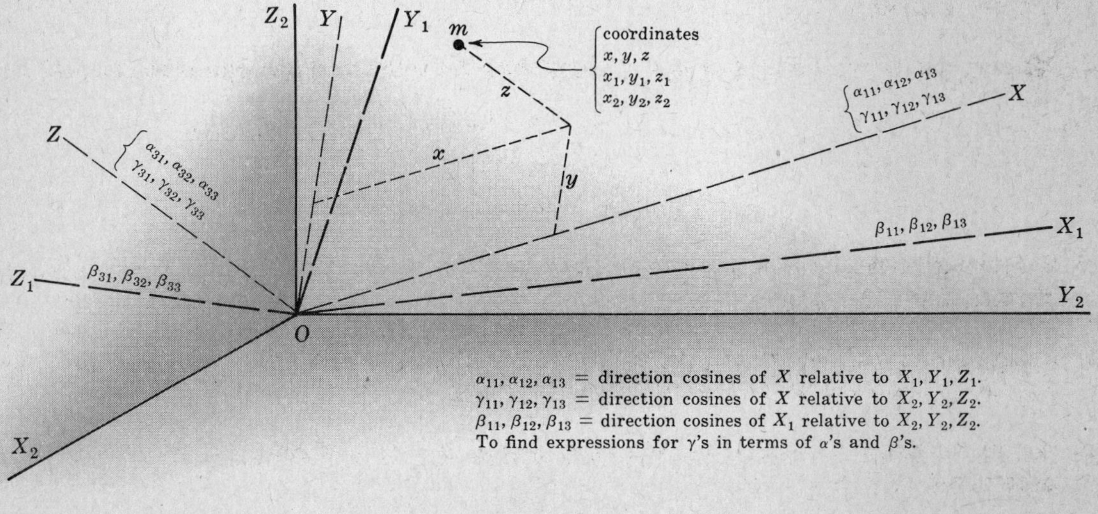

Fig. A-5

For a lucid discussion of matrix methods and a treatment of much of the above material in matrix form see: J. Heading, *Matrix Theory for Physicists*, Longmans, Green and Co., London, 1958.

Answers to Problems in Chapter 2

2.1. $2A = sr_2 \sin\alpha - r_2^2 \sin\alpha \cos\alpha, \qquad q(s - r_2\cos\alpha) = r_2 \sin\alpha\,(1-q^2)^{1/2}$

2.4. (*a*) $y_1 = y + q_1,\ \ y_2 = y - \dfrac{m_1}{m_2}q_1;$ (*b*) $y_1 = y + \left(\dfrac{m_2}{m_1+m_2}\right)y_3,\ \ y_2 = y - \left(\dfrac{m_1}{m_1+m_2}\right)y_3.$ No.

2.5.

$$x_1 = \tfrac{1}{2}a_x t^2 + s\cos\theta_1 + x_2\cos(\theta_1+\theta_2) - y_2\sin(\theta_1+\theta_2)$$
$$y_1 = s\sin\theta_1 + x_2\sin(\theta_1+\theta_2) + y_2\cos(\theta_1+\theta_2)$$

2.7. (*a*)

$$x_1 = (R+x_2)\cos\beta - y_2\sin\beta$$
$$y_1 = (R+x_2)\sin\beta + y_2\cos\beta, \quad z_1 = z_2 \qquad \text{where } \beta = \omega t + at^2/2R$$

(*b*)

$$m\ddot{x}_2 - 2m\dot{y}_2(\omega + at/R) - my_2a/R - m(R+x_2)(\omega+at/R)^2 = F_{x_2}$$
$$m\ddot{y}_2 + 2m\dot{x}_2(\omega + at/R) + m(R+x_2)a/R - m(R+x_2)(\omega+at/R)^2 = F_{y_2}, \qquad m\ddot{z}_2 = F_{z_2}$$

2.9. See bottom of Page 286.

2.10. (*a*) 1, (*b*) 7

2.11. (*a*) 9, (*b*) 6

2.12. (*a*) 5, (*b*) 10

2.13. Degrees of freedom = 1; $T = \frac{1}{6}Ml^2\dot{\theta}^2$, where θ is the angle made by the rod with the X axis.

2.16. (*a*) Degrees of freedom = 3

(*b*) Equation of constraint: $(x_2 - x_1)^2 + (y_2 - y_1)^2 = l^2$, where x_1, y_1 and x_2, y_2 are the coordinates of m_1 and m_2 respectively, l = length of rod.

(*c*)

$$T = \tfrac{1}{2}(m_1+m_2)(\dot{r}^2 + r^2\dot{\theta}^2) + \tfrac{1}{2}m_2[l^2\dot{\phi}^2 - 2l\dot{r}\dot{\phi}\sin(\phi-\theta) + 2lr\dot{\theta}\dot{\phi}\cos(\phi-\theta)]$$
$$T = \tfrac{1}{2}(m_1+m_2)(\dot{\bar{x}}^2 + \dot{\bar{y}}^2) + \tfrac{1}{2}I\dot{\phi}^2$$

2.17.

$$T = \tfrac{1}{2}M_1(\dot{x}_1^2 + \dot{y}_1^2) + \tfrac{1}{2}I_1\dot{\theta}_1^2 + \tfrac{1}{2}M_2(\dot{x}_2^2 + \dot{y}_2^2) + \tfrac{1}{2}I_2\dot{\theta}_2^2 + \tfrac{1}{2}M_3(\dot{x}_3^2 + \dot{y}_3^2) + \tfrac{1}{2}I_3\dot{\theta}_3^2$$
$$x_2 = x_1 + \tfrac{1}{2}l_1\cos\theta_1 + \tfrac{1}{2}l_2\cos\theta_2, \quad \text{etc.}$$

Four superfluous coordinates in T. No.

2.18. (*a*) $x_2 = x + (a-s)\cos\theta,\ \ y_2 = y + (a-s)\sin\theta,$ where $a = m_1 l/(m_1+m_3)$

(*b*)

$$T = \tfrac{1}{2}(m_1+m_2+m_3)(\dot{x}^2 + \dot{y}^2) + \tfrac{1}{2}I\dot{\theta}^2$$
$$+ \tfrac{1}{2}m_2[\dot{s}^2 + (a-s)^2\dot{\theta}^2 + 2\dot{\theta}(a-s)(\dot{y}\cos\theta - \dot{x}\sin\theta) - 2\dot{s}(\dot{y}\sin\theta + \dot{x}\cos\theta)]$$

2.19. Four degrees of freedom.

$$T = \tfrac{1}{2}m_1\dot{y}_1^2 + \tfrac{1}{2}m_2\dot{y}_2^2 + \tfrac{1}{2}(I_1/R_1^2 + m_3)\dot{s}_3^2 + \tfrac{1}{2}m_4(\dot{s}_3 + R_2\dot{\theta})^2 + \tfrac{1}{2}I_2\dot{\theta}^2$$

where I_1 and I_2 are moments of inertia of the upper and lower pulleys and $\dot{\theta}$ is the angular velocity of the lower pulley.

2.20. (*a*) $T = \frac{1}{2}m(\dot{r}^2 + r^2\dot{\theta}^2 + 4a^2r^2\dot{r}^2) + \frac{1}{2}I\dot{\theta}^2;$ (*b*) $T = \frac{1}{2}m(\dot{r}^2 + r^2\omega^2 + 4a^2r^2\dot{r}^2)$ + constant

2.21.

$$T = \tfrac{1}{2}M_2\dot{s}_1^2 + \tfrac{1}{2}I_2\dot{s}_3^2/R_2^2 + \tfrac{1}{2}m_3(\dot{s}_1+\dot{s}_3)^2 + \tfrac{1}{2}M_1(\dot{s}_1+\dot{s}_2)^2 + \tfrac{1}{2}I_1\dot{s}_4^2/R_1^2$$
$$+ \tfrac{1}{2}m_2(\dot{s}_1+\dot{s}_2+\dot{s}_4)^2 + \tfrac{1}{2}m_1(\dot{s}_1+\dot{s}_2-\dot{s}_4)^2$$

2.22.

$$T = \tfrac{1}{2}M\dot{y}_1^2 + \frac{m_1m_3}{2M}(\dot{y}_2+\dot{y}_3)^2 + \frac{m_2}{2M}(m_1\dot{y}_2^2 + m_3\dot{y}_3^2)$$

2.23.

$$T = \tfrac{1}{2}m_1[l^2\dot{\alpha}^2 + r_1^2\dot{\theta}_1^2 - 2r_1l\dot{\alpha}\dot{\theta}_1\sin(\theta_1-\alpha)] + \tfrac{1}{2}m_2[l^2\dot{\alpha}^2 + r_2^2\dot{\theta}_2^2 + 2r_1l\dot{\alpha}\dot{\theta}_2\sin(\theta_2-\alpha)] + \tfrac{1}{2}I\dot{\alpha}^2$$

2.27.

$$T = \tfrac{1}{2}m\left[\frac{R^2(1+\cos\theta_1)^4}{\sin^4\theta_1} - \frac{2Rl(1+\cos\theta_1)^2}{\sin\theta_1} + l^2\right]\dot{\theta}_1^2 + \tfrac{1}{2}(I_2 + MR^2)\left(\frac{\cos^2\theta_1 + \cos\theta_1}{\sin^2\theta_1}\right)^2\dot{\theta}_1^2 + \tfrac{1}{2}I_1\dot{\theta}_1^2$$

INDEX